MODERN STUDIES
IN ENGLISH

PRENTICE-HALL INTERNATIONAL, INC., London
PRENTICE-HALL OF AUSTRALIA, PTY. LTD., Sydney
PRENTICE-HALL OF CANADA, LTD., Toronto
PRENTICE-HALL OF INDIA PRIVATE LTD., New Delhi
PRENTICE-HALL OF JAPAN, INC., Tokyo

MODERN STUDIES
IN ENGLISH

Readings in Transformational Grammar

Edited by

DAVID A. REIBEL
University of York

SANFORD A. SCHANE
University of California at San Diego

PRENTICE-HALL, INC., Englewood Cliffs, New Jersey

13-598649-4

Library of Congress Catalog Card Number: 69–11383

Printed in the United States of America

Current printing (last number):
10 9 8 7 6 5 4

To
Pauline
&
Marjorie

PREFACE

Modern Studies in English is a collection of articles on the transformational syntax of English. These papers epitomize the approach that received its impetus in 1957 with the publication of Noam Chomsky's *Syntactic Structures*. Today, more than a decade later, transformational grammar is unquestionably one of the most vigorous and exciting movements in linguistics. The fruitfulness of the transformational approach is evidenced by the important contributions it has made to our understanding of language and the insights it has provided about individual languages.

Transformational grammar raises theoretical and descriptive questions fundamentally different from those asked previously by traditional or by structural grammarians. In particular, transformational grammar deals with the specification of a general linguistic theory from which the grammars of individual languages follow. The principal language of investigation has been and continues to be English. The linguist concerned with theory therefore must be familiar with the work done in English syntax. The English specialist, familiar with the long tradition of the study of English grammar, also needs an opportunity to see how transformational grammar provides a productive new way of looking at the facts of English. *Modern Studies in English* is therefore suitable both for courses in the structure of English and for courses in syntax or linguistic theory.

This anthology has been divided into six sections. The articles in the first section presuppose in the reader no specialized linguistic preparation. They present the fundamental questions that linguists are now asking, some of the problems faced in answering these questions, and the notational devices and conventions of transformational description. These articles provide the rationale for the research enterprise that the linguist commits himself to when he adopts the transformational point of view. They are likely to be of most interest to those introduced to transformational grammar for the first time.

Sections II–V treat specific aspects of English structure. Wherever possible we have grouped the articles around particular topics on which considerable work has been done, e.g. conjunction, pronominalization, relativization. Such a principle of organization serves a dual purpose. First, it provides a thorough understanding of some fundamental principles of English syntax. For example, after several articles on pronominalization, the reader will have more than a superficial understanding of the issues involved and an appreciation of the vastness of the pronominalization process. Second, a collection of articles on the same topic demonstrates that although the writers share a common theoretical viewpoint about how to investigate English syntax, there is by no means unanimity in the solutions proposed for specific problems. It should become clear that transformational grammar is far from being a *fait accompli* and that there are still many unresolved issues.

The selections of Section VI deal with application of the insights of transformational grammar to other areas of language study, such as historical change, child language, metrics, and language teaching. These problems, long of concern to the student of language, appear in a new light from the point of view of transformational grammar. Questions about language change, language acquisition, and language teaching cannot be answered meaningfully except in the context of some specific claims about the nature of language itself.

Several of the articles in this anthology represent the first transformational treatments of certain facts of English syntax. Subsequent researchers have often built on these pioneering studies. These important articles are included here since they are so frequently referred to in the modern linguistic literature. In organizing the sections on conjunction, pronominalization, and relativization, we have ordered the articles chronologically to show the reader how a particular topic has developed within the last few years and how later studies have expanded on, or sometimes even supplanted, the earlier investigation. Some of these later studies appear here for the first time.

The articles cover a time span of ten years. During this time significant changes have been made in the theory of generative grammar and in the format of language descriptions. In particular, the reader will want to keep in mind the following differences between earlier and later treatments; often a glance at the date of publication will indicate sufficiently the point of view.

First, the early studies contain transformational rules that change the meaning of the structures they are applied to. *Syntactic Structures*, for example, presented optional transformations that converted strings underlying affirmative sentences into the corresponding negatives, interrogatives, and so forth. A new development has been the introduction, via the phrase structure rules, of abstract markers such as *Neg* and *Q*, which trigger obligatory transformations for producing the appropriate surface forms of negative sentences, questions, and so forth. Thus, the later studies develop a dichotomy between deep and surface structures, where the deep structure of a sentence contains all the syntactic information relevant for its correct semantic interpretation. This means, in particular, that transformational rules, in converting one structure to another, do not affect the meaning of the original structure created by the phrase structure rules.

Second, in the early studies, complex sentences—subordinate and coordinate—

are formed by "generalized" transformations. Transformations of this type operate on a matrix (main) sentence and a constituent (subordinate) sentence, embedding elements or constituents from the latter into the former. The matrix and constituent sentences themselves result from independent applications of the phrase structure rules. Hence the recursive property of the syntactic component of the grammar is assigned to the transformational rules. A later development is the assignment of this recursive property to the phrase structure rules, by the reintroduction of the initial symbol *S* in the development of a deep structure; the set of rewrite (phrase structure) rules is then reapplied to the new *S*. Such structures are represented by branching tree diagrams as before, but they may now contain any number of embedded *S*'s. Transformations then apply cyclically from the most deeply embedded sentences to the topmost *S*, embedding constituents from an embedded sentence into its dominating sentence.

Third, in early versions of the theory, subcategorization of major lexical categories—such as the division of verbs into transitive-intransitive, and the classification of nouns into proper-common, animate-inanimate, or human-nonhuman—is accomplished by the same kinds of rewrite rules used for creating phrase structure. This method of treating subcategorization has proved inadequate, not only because it fails to distinguish between subcategorization and phrase structure but also because it cannot handle cross-classification within major lexical categories. A subsequent development has been to treat subcategorization phenomena as features of the individual lexical items. Since transformational rules need to refer to subcategories of lexical classes, they now do so by reference to these syntactic features.

In the early studies linguists attempted to state precisely, using various symbols and notational conventions, the exact environmental conditions under which a particular rule applied. Unfortunately the notations were frequently cumbersome and showed much individual variation from author to author, so that the rules were hard to read. Partly in reaction to this overconcern with formalism and partly because of the feeling that it is premature, or even not possible, to write formal rules, later studies often merely state in ordinary language what rules are supposed to do. Finally, in the early works there is a neat dichotomy between semantics and syntax. In later studies this division becomes more nebulous. Semantic evidence is used in order to determine sets of related sentences and to justify the deep structures posited for them. More recently some linguists have maintained that the semantic representation constitutes the level of deep structure. This view then obviates the necessity for a separate interpretive semantic component operating on "syntactic" deep structures.

BIBLIOGRAPHICAL NOTE

The papers in this anthology often cite articles that have been published in more than one place. Whenever the citation refers to the original place of publication, that reference has of course been retained. When a cited article has been reprinted in one of the anthologies listed below, a reference to that version is given in brackets since these collections are often more accessible than the journals in which the articles first appeared. If an author has cited only the anthology in which the article is reprinted, we have added no reference to the original place of publication. We have updated some references, added others where appropriate, and tried to adapt all references to a consistent format. For convenience the following abbreviations are used.

HMP   *Handbook of Mathematical Psychology*, Vol. II. R. Duncan Luce, Robert R. Bush, and Eugene Galanter, eds. New York: John Wiley & Sons, Inc., 1963.

MSE   *Modern Studies in English: Readings in Transformational Grammar.*

PAM   *Structure of Language and Its Mathematical Aspects*, Proceedings of Symposia in Applied Mathematics, Vol. XII. Roman Jakobson, ed. Providence, R. I.: American Mathematical Society, 1961.

RAEL   *Readings in Applied English Linguistics*. Harold B. Allen, ed. New York:
1958   Appleton-Century-Crofts, 1958.

RAEL   *Readings in Applied English Linguistics*, 2nd ed. Harold B. Allen, ed. New
1964   York: Appleton-Century-Crofts, 1964.

RIL   *Readings in Linguistics*. The development of descriptive linguistics in America since 1925. Martin Joos, ed. Washington, D.C.: American Council of Learned Societies, 1957; Chicago: University of Chicago Press, 1966.

RMP   *Readings in Mathematical Psychology*, Vol. II. R. Duncan Luce, Robert R. Bush, and Eugene Galanter, eds. New York: John Wiley & Sons, Inc., 1965.

RPL   *Readings in the Psychology of Language*. Leon A. Jakobovits and Murray S. Miron, eds. Englewood Cliffs, N.J.: Prentice-Hall, Inc., 1967.

SL   *The Structure of Language: Readings in the Philosophy of Language.* Jerry A. Fodor and Jerrold J. Katz, eds. Englewood Cliffs, N.J.: Prentice-Hall, Inc., 1964.

We should like to express our gratitude to all the contributors and publishers whose prompt and generous cooperation allowed us to carry out our original conception of this anthology. We are also grateful to the Department of Linguistics of the University of California at San Diego for providing us with secretarial assistance, and we thank Barbara Barnett for her help in the preparation of the manuscript.

D. A. R.
S. A. S.

CONTENTS

MODERN STUDIES
IN ENGLISH

Who climbs the Grammar-Tree, distinctly knows
Where Noun, and Verb, and Participle grows.

John Dryden, trans. (1693)
Juvenal's Satire VI, 583–584

I

BACKGROUND

This introductory section contains articles that touch on some questions concerning the nature and rationale of a generative transformational grammar. Because the literature on generative grammar is already fairly large, it is no longer possible to direct the reader to a small number of monographs, reviews, and articles. This section is composed therefore of items that are important for their summary function, their historical interest, and their clarification of the concerns of the transformational grammarian.

The first selection, Noam Chomsky's "The Current Scene in Linguistics," places the study of English grammar in an historical context, and suggests how the teacher as well as the linguist can make use of certain conceptualizations about the study of language to clarify the problems of studying and teaching grammar. Next, Chomsky's "Generative Grammars As Theories of Linguistic Competence," Section 1.1 of his *Aspects of the Theory of Syntax*, focuses on the notion "grammar of a language" and shows how a grammar can be viewed as essentially an idealization of the native speaker's knowledge of his language, that is, of his linguistic "competence." Such a grammar is quite neutral in regard to the speaker or hearer, specifying what *formal* knowledge each must have in order to produce and understand sentences.

"Underlying and Superficial Linguistic Structure," by Paul M. Postal, also emphasizes the abstract nature of linguistic descriptions. All sentences have an underlying deep structure, which is the basis of their semantic interpretation. Transformations then relate these deep structures to surface representations. In the following article, "Justification of Grammars," Section 1.4 of his *Aspects of the Theory of Syntax*, Chomsky discusses "justification" and "adequacy." There are two respects in which one can speak of "justifying" a generative grammar. On one level the grammar is justified if it correctly describes the native speaker's competence —that is, his intuitions about his language. On a deeper level a grammar is justified if there is a principled basis for selecting this grammar over all others, given that they are all compatible with observed data.

The introduction and first section of Morris Halle's "Questions of Linguistics" emphasize once again the abstract nature of linguistic representations. Of particular interest is the complex ordering of the different auxiliaries in English. The "hidden" simplicity of the system is revealed in an abstract order posited for auxiliaries and affixes. The surface complexity results from a single transformation, which "flips" affixes to the ends of words.

Finally, "Some Transformations in English," Chapter 7 of Chomsky's *Syntactic Structures*, exemplifies what a small segment of the grammar of English would look like, using certain of the notions outlined in the previous articles. This is perhaps the first account of how certain problems of English syntax might be treated explicitly in transformational terms. Although many features of the general and specific approach have since been modified, the clarity of presentation makes this largely self-contained section well worth careful study. Certainly many subsequent developments can be much better understood if one is well acquainted with this early treatment.

1

The Current Scene in Linguistics: Present Directions

NOAM CHOMSKY

The title of this paper may suggest something more than can be provided. It would be foolhardy to attempt to forecast the development of linguistics or any other field, even in general terms and in the short run. There is no way to anticipate ideas and insights that may, at any time, direct research in new directions or reopen traditional problems that had been too difficult or too unclear to provide a fruitful challenge. The most that one can hope to do is to arrive at a clear appraisal of the present situation in linguistic research, and an accurate understanding of historical tendencies. It would not be realistic to attempt to project such tendencies into the future.

Two major traditions can be distinguished in modern linguistic theory: one is the tradition of "universal" or "philosophical grammar," which flourished in the seventeenth and eighteenth centuries; the second is the tradition of structural or descriptive linguistics, which reached the high point of its development perhaps fifteen or twenty years ago. I think that a synthesis of these two major traditions is possible, and that it is, to some extent, being achieved in current work. Before approaching the problem of synthesis, I would like to sketch briefly—and, necessarily, with some oversimplification—what seem to me to be the most significant features in these two traditions.

As the name indicates, universal grammar was concerned with general features of language structure rather than with particular idiosyncrasies. Particularly in France, universal grammar developed in part in reaction to an earlier descriptivist

Reprinted from *College English*, 27.587–595 (1966), by permission of Noam Chomsky and the National Council of Teachers of English.

This paper was read at the National Council of Teachers of English convention in November 1965.

tradition which held that the only proper task for the grammarian was to present data, to give a kind of "natural history" of language (specifically, of the "cultivated usage" of the court and the best writers). In contrast, universal grammarians urged that the study of language should be elevated from the level of "natural history" to that of "natural philosophy"; hence the term "philosophical grammar," "philosophical" being used, of course, in essentially the sense of our term "scientific." Grammar should not be merely a record of the data of usage, but, rather, should offer an explanation for such data. It should establish general principles, applicable to all languages and based ultimately on intrinsic properties of the mind, which would explain how language is used and why it has the particular properties to which the descriptive grammarian chooses, irrationally, to restrict his attention.

Universal grammarians did not content themselves with merely stating this goal. In fact, many generations of scholars proceeded to develop a rich and far-reaching account of the general principles of language structure, supported by whatever detailed evidence they could find from the linguistic materials available to them. On the basis of these principles, they attempted to explain many particular facts, and to develop a psychological theory dealing with certain aspects of language use, with the production and comprehension of sentences.

The tradition of universal grammar came to an abrupt end in the nineteenth century, for reasons that I will discuss directly. Furthermore, its achievements were very rapidly forgotten, and an interesting mythology developed concerning its limitations and excesses. It has now become something of a cliché among linguists that universal grammar suffered from the following defects: (*a*) it was not concerned with the sounds of speech, but only with writing; (*b*) it was based primarily on a Latin model, and was, in some sense "prescriptive"; (*c*) its assumptions about language structure have been refuted by modern "anthropological linguistics." In addition, many linguists, though not all, would hold that universal grammar was misguided in principle in its attempt to provide explanations rather than mere description of usage, the latter being all that can be contemplated by the "sober scientist."

The first two criticisms are quite easy to refute; the third and fourth are more interesting. Even a cursory glance at the texts will show that phonetics was a major concern of universal grammarians, and that their phonetic theories were not very different from our own. Nor have I been able to discover any confusion of speech and writing. The belief that universal grammar was based on a Latin model is rather curious. In fact, the earliest studies of universal grammar, in France, were a part of the movement to raise the status of the vernacular, and are concerned with details of French that often do not even have any Latin analogue.

As to the belief that modern "anthropological linguistics" has refuted the assumptions of universal grammar, this is not only untrue, but, for a rather important reason, could not be true. The reason is that universal grammar made a sharp distinction between what we may call "deep structure" and "surface structure." The deep structure of a sentence is the abstract underlying form which determines the meaning of the sentence; it is present in the mind but not necessarily represented directly in the physical signal. The surface structure of a sentence is the actual organization of the physical signal into phrases of varying size, into words of various categories, with certain particles, inflections, arrangement, and so on. The fundamental assumption of the universal grammarians was that languages scarcely differ at the level of deep structure—which reflects the basic properties of thought and conception—but that they may vary widely at the much less interesting level of surface structure. But modern anthropological linguistics does not attempt to deal with deep structure and its relations to surface structure. Rather, its attention is limited to surface structure—to the phonetic form of an utterance and its organization into units of varying size. Consequently, the information that it provides has no direct bearing on the hypotheses concerning deep structure postulated by the universal grammarians. And, in fact, it seems to me that what information is now available to us suggests not that they went too far in assuming universality of underlying structure, but that they may have been much too cautious and restrained in what they proposed.

The fourth criticism of universal grammar—namely, that it was misguided in seeking explanations in the first place—I will not discuss. It seems to me that this criticism is based on a misunderstanding of the nature of all rational inquiry. There is particular irony in the fact that this criticism should be advanced with the avowed intention of making linguistics "scientific." It is hardly open to question that the natural sciences are concerned precisely with the problem of explaining phenomena, and have little use for accurate description that is unrelated to problems of explanation.

I think that we have much to learn from a careful study of what was achieved by the universal grammarians of the seventeenth and eighteenth centuries. It seems to me, in fact, that contemporary linguistics would do well to take their concept of language as a point of departure for current work. Not only do they make a fairly clear and well-founded distinction between deep and surface structure, but they also go on to study the nature of deep structure and to provide valuable hints and insights concerning the rules that relate the abstract underlying mental structures to surface form, the rules that we would now call "grammatical transformations." What is more, universal grammar developed as part of a general philosophical tradition that provided deep and important insights, also largely forgotten, into the use and acquisition of language, and, furthermore, into problems of perception and acquisition of knowledge in general. These insights can be exploited and developed. The idea that the study of language should proceed within the framework of what we might nowadays call "cognitive psychology" is sound. There is much truth in the traditional view that language provides the most effective means for studying the nature and mechanisms of the human mind, and that only within this context can we perceive the larger issues that determine the directions in which the study of language should develop.

The tradition of universal grammar came to an end more than a century ago. Several factors combined to lead to its decline. For one thing, the problems posed were beyond the scope of the technique and understanding then available. The problem of formulating the rules that determine deep structures and relate them to surface structures, and the deeper problem of determining the general abstract characteristics of these rules, could not be studied with any precision, and discussion therefore remained at the level of hints, examples, and vaguely formulated intentions. In particular, the problem of rule-governed creativity in language simply could not be formulated with sufficient precision to permit research to proceed very far. A second reason for the decline of traditional linguistic theory lies in the remarkable successes of Indo-European comparative linguistics in the nineteenth century. These achievements appeared to dwarf the accomplishments of universal grammar, and led many linguists to scoff at the "metaphysical" and "airy pronouncements" of those who were attempting to deal with a much wider range of problems—and at that particular stage of the development of linguistic theory, were discussing these topics in a highly inconclusive fashion. Looking back now, we can see quite clearly that the concept of language employed by the Indo-European comparativists was an extremely primitive one. It was, however, well-suited to the tasks at hand. It is, therefore, not too surprising that this concept of language, which was then extended and developed by the structural and descriptive linguists of the twentieth century, became almost completely dominant, and that the older tradition of linguistic theory was largely swept aside and forgotten. This is hardly a unique instance in intellectual history.

Structural linguistics is a direct outgrowth of the concepts that emerged in Indo-European comparative study, which was primarily concerned with language as a system of phonological units that undergo systematic modification in phonetically determined contexts. Structural linguistics reinterpreted this concept for a fixed state of a language, investigated the relations among such units and the patterns they form, and attempted, with varying success, to extend the same kind of analysis to "higher levels" of linguistic structure. Its fundamental assumption is that procedures of segmentation and classification, applied to data in a systematic way, can isolate and identify all types of elements that function in a particular language along with the constraints that they obey. A catalogue of these elements, their relations, and their restrictions of "distribution," would, in most structuralist views, constitute a full grammar of the language.

Structural linguistics has very real accomplishments to its credit. To me, it seems that its major achievement is to have provided a factual and a methodological basis that makes it possible to return to the problems that occupied the traditional universal grammarians with some hope of extending and deepening their theory of language structure and language use. Modern descriptive linguistics has enormously enriched the range of factual material available, and has provided entirely new standards of clarity and objectivity. Given this advance in precision and objectivity, it becomes possible to return, with new hope for success, to the problem of constructing the theory of a particular language—its grammar—and to the still more ambitious study of the general theory of language. On the other hand, it seems to me that the substantive contributions to the theory of language structure are few, and that, to a large extent, the concepts of modern linguistics constitute a retrogression as compared with universal grammar. One real advance has been in universal phonetics—I refer here particularly to the work of Jakobson. Other new and important insights might also be cited. But in general, the major contributions of structural linguistics seem to me to be methodological rather than substantive. These methodological contributions are not limited to a raising of the standards of precision. In a more subtle way, the idea that language can be studied as a formal system, a notion which is developed with force and effectiveness in the work of Harris and Hockett, is of particular significance. It is, in fact, this general insight and the techniques that emerged as it developed that have made it possible, in the last few years, to approach the traditional problems once again. Specifically, it is now possible to study the problem of rule-governed creativity in natural language, the problem of constructing grammars that explicitly generate deep and surface structures and express the relations between them, and the deeper problem of determining the universal conditions that limit the form and organization of rules in the grammar of a human language. When these problems are clearly formulated and studied, we are led to a conception of language not unlike that suggested in universal grammar. Furthermore, I think that we are led to conclusions regarding mental processes of very much the sort that were developed, with care and insight, in the rationalist philosophy of mind that provided the intellectual background for universal grammar. It is in this sense that I think we can look forward to a productive synthesis of the two major traditions of linguistic research.

If this point of view is correct in essentials, we can proceed to outline the problems facing the linguist in the following way. He is, first of all, concerned to report data accurately. What is less obvious, but nonetheless correct, is that the data will not be of particular interest to him in itself, but rather only insofar as it sheds light on the grammar of the language from which it is drawn, where by the "grammar of a language" I mean the theory that deals with the mechanisms of sentence construction, which establish a sound-meaning relation in this language. At the next level of study, the linguist is concerned to give a factually accurate formulation of this grammar, that is, a correct formulation of the rules that generate deep and surface structures and interrelate them, and the rules that give a phonetic interpretation of surface structures and a semantic interpretation of deep structures. But, once again, this correct statement of the grammatical principles of a language is not primarily of interest in itself, but only insofar as it sheds light on the more general question of the nature of language; that is, the nature of universal grammar. The primary interest of a correct grammar is that it provides the basis for substantiating or refuting a general theory of linguistic structure which establishes general principles concerning the form of grammar.

Continuing one step higher in level of abstraction, a universal grammar—a general theory of linguistic structure that determines the form of grammar—is primarily of interest for the information it provides concerning innate intellectual structure. Specifically, a general theory of this sort itself must provide a hypothesis concerning innate intellectual structure of sufficient richness to account for the fact that the child acquires a given grammar on the basis of the data available to him. More generally, both a grammar of a particular language and a general theory of language are of interest primarily because of the insight they provide concerning the nature of mental processes, the mechanisms of perception and production, and the mechanisms by which knowledge is acquired. There can be little doubt that both specific theories of particular languages and the general theory of linguistic structure provide very relevant evidence for anyone concerned with these matters; to me it seems quite obvious that it is within this general framework that linguistic research finds its intellectual justification.

At every level of abstraction, the linguist is concerned with explanation, not merely with stating facts in one form or another. He tries to construct a grammar which explains particular data on the basis of general principles that govern the language in question. He is interested in explaining these general principles themselves, by showing how they are derived from still more general and abstract postulates drawn from universal grammar. And he would ultimately have to find a way to account for universal grammar on the basis of still more general principles of human mental structure. Finally, although this goal is too remote to be seriously considered, he might envision the prospect that the kind of evidence he can provide may lead to a physiological explanation for this entire range of phenomena.

I should stress that what I have sketched is a logical, not a temporal order of tasks of increasing abstractness. For example, it is not necessary to delay the study of general linguistic theory until particular grammars are available for many languages. Quite the contrary. The study of particular grammars will be fruitful only insofar as it is based on a precisely articulated theory of linguistic structure, just as the study of particular facts is worth undertaking only when it is guided by some general assumptions about the grammar of the language from which these observations are drawn.

All of this is rather abstract. Let me try to bring the discussion down to earth by mentioning a few particular problems, in the grammar of English, that point to the need for explanatory hypotheses of the sort I have been discussing.

Consider the comparative construction in English; in particular, such sentences as

(1)   *I have never seen a man taller than John.*

(2)   *I have never seen a taller man than John.*

Sentences (1) and (2), along with innumerable others, suggest that there should be a rule of English that permits a sentence containing a noun followed by a comparative adjective to be transformed into the corresponding sentence containing the sequence: *Comparative Adjective–Noun*. This rule would then appear as a special case of the very general rule that forms such *Adjective–Noun* constructions as *the tall man* from the underlying form *the man who is tall*, and so on.

But now consider the sentence

(3)   *I have never seen a man taller than Mary.*

This is perfectly analogous to (1); but we cannot use the rule just mentioned to form

(4)   *I have never seen a taller man than Mary.*

In fact, the sentence (4) is certainly not synonymous with (3), although (2) appears to be synonymous with (1). Sentence (4) implies that Mary is a man, although (3) does not. Clearly either the proposed analysis is incorrect, despite the very considerable support one can find for it, or there is some specific condition in English grammar that explains why the rule in question can be used to form (2) but not (4). In either case, a serious explanation is lacking; there is some principle of English grammar, now unknown, for which we must search to explain these facts. The facts are quite clear. They are of no particular interest in themselves, but if they can bring to light some general principle of English grammar, they will be of real significance.

Furthermore, we must ask how every speaker of English comes to acquire this still unknown principle of English grammar. We must, in other words, try to determine what general concept of linguistic structure he employs that leads him to the conclusion that the grammar of English treats (1) and (2) as paraphrases but not the superficially similar pair (3) and (4). This still unknown principle of Englsih grammar may lead us to discover the relevant abstract principle of linguistic structure. It is this hope, of course, that motivates the search for the relevant principle of English grammar.

Innumerable examples can be given of this sort. I will mention just one more. Consider the synonymous sentences (5) and (6):

(5) *It would be difficult for him to understand **this**.*

(6) *For him to understand **this** would be difficult.*

Corresponding to (5), we can form relative clauses and questions such as (7):

(7)(i)   *something which it would be difficult for him to understand*
   (ii)   *What would it be difficult for him to understand?*

But there is some principle that prevents the formation of the corresponding constructions of (8), formed in the analogous way from (6):

(8)(i)   *something which for him to understand would be difficult*
   (ii)   *What would for him to understand be difficult?*

The nonsentences of (8) are formed from (6) by exactly the same process that forms the correct sentences of (7) from (5); namely, pronominalization in the position occupied by ***this***, and a reordering operation. But in the case of (6), something blocks the operation of the rules for forming relative clauses and interrogatives. Again, the facts are interesting because they indicate that some general principle of English grammar must be functioning, unconsciously; and, at the next level of abstraction, they raise the question of what general concept of linguistic structure is used by the person learning the language to enable him to acquire the particular principle that explains the difference between (7) and (8).

Notice that there is nothing particularly esoteric about these examples. The processes that form comparative, relative, and interrogative constructions are among the simplest and most obvious in English grammar. Every normal speaker has mastered these processes at an early age. But when we take a really careful look, we find much that is mysterious in these very elementary processes of grammar.

Whatever aspect of a language one studies, problems of this sort abound. There are very few well-supported answers, either at the level of particular or universal grammar. The linguist who is content merely to record and organize phenomena, and to devise appropriate terminologies, will never come face to face with these problems. They only arise when he attempts to construct a precise system of rules that generate deep structures and relate them to corresponding surface structures. But this is just another way of saying that "pure descriptivism" is not fruitful, that progress in linguistics, as in any other field of inquiry, requires that at every stage of our knowledge and understanding we pursue the search for a deeper explanatory theory.

I would like to conclude with just a few remarks about two problems that are of direct concern to teachers of English. The first is the problem of which grammar to teach, the second, the problem why grammar should be taught at all.

If one thinks of a grammar of English as a theory of English structure, then the question which grammar to teach is no different in principle from the problem facing the biologist who has to decide which of several competing theories to teach. The answer, in either case, is that he should teach the one which appears to be true, given the evidence presently available. Where the evidence does not justify a clear decision, this should be brought to the student's attention and he should be presented with the case for the various alternatives. But in the case of teaching grammar, the issue is often confused by a pseudo-problem, which I think deserves some further discussion.

To facilitate this discussion, let me introduce some terminology. I will use the term "generative grammar" to refer to a theory of language in the sense described above, that is, a system of rules that determine the deep and surface structures of the language in question, the relation between them, the semantic interpretation of the deep structures and the phonetic interpretation of the surface structures. The generative grammar of a language, then, is the system of rules which establishes the relation between sound and meaning in this language. Suppose that the teacher is faced with the question: which generative grammar of English shall I teach? The answer is straightforward in principle, however difficult the problem may be to settle in practice. The answer is, simply: teach the one that is correct.

But generally the problem is posed in rather different terms. There has been a great deal of discussion of the choice not between competing generative grammars, but between a generative grammar and a "descriptive grammar." A "descriptive grammar" is not a theory of the language in the sense described above; it is not, in other words, a system of rules that establishes the sound-meaning correspondence in the language, insofar as this can be precisely expressed. Rather, it is an inventory of elements of various kinds that play a role in the language. For example, a descriptive grammar of English might contain an inventory of phonetic units, of phonemes, of morphemes, of words, of lexical categories, and of phrases or phrase types. Of course the inventory of phrases or phrase types cannot be completed since it is infinite, but let us put aside this difficulty.

It is clear, however, that the choice between a generative grammar and a descriptive grammar is not a genuine one. Actually, a descriptive grammar can be immediately derived from a generative grammar, but not conversely. Given a generative grammar, we can derive the inventories of elements that appear at various levels. The descriptive grammar, in the sense just outlined, is simply one aspect of the full generative grammar. It is an epiphenomenon, derivable from the full system of rules and principles that constitutes the generative grammar. The choice, then, is not between two competing grammars, but between a grammar and one particular aspect of this grammar. To me it seems obvious how this choice should be resolved, since the particular aspect that is isolated in the descriptive grammar seems to be of little independent importance. Surely the principles that determine the inventory, and much else, are more important than the inventory itself. In any event, the nature of the choice is clear; it is not a choice between competing systems, but rather a choice between the whole and a part.

Although I think what I have just said is literally correct, it is still somewhat misleading. I have characterized a descriptive grammar as one particular aspect of a full generative grammar, but actually the concept "descriptive grammar" arose in modern linguistics in a rather different way. A descriptive grammar was itself regarded as a full account of the language. It was, in other words, assumed that the inventory of elements exhausts the grammatical description of the language. Once we have listed the phones, phonemes, etc., we have given a full description of grammatical structure. The grammar is, simply, the collection of these various inventories.

This observation suggests a way of formulating the difference between generative and descriptive grammars in terms of a factual assumption about the nature of language. Let us suppose that a theory of language will consist of a definition of the notion "grammar," as well as definitions of various kinds of units (e.g., phonological units, morphological units, etc.). When we apply such a general theory to data, we use the definitions to find a particular grammar and a particular collection of units. Consider now two theories of this sort that differ in the following way. In one, the units of various kinds are defined independently of the notion "grammar"; the grammar, then, is simply the collection of the various kinds of units. For example, we define "phoneme," "morpheme," etc., in terms of certain analytic procedures, and define the "grammar" to be the collection of units derived by applying these procedures. In the other theory, the situation is reversed. The notion "grammar" is defined independently of the various kinds of units; the grammar is a system of such-and-such a kind. The units of various kinds are defined in terms of the logically prior concept "grammar." They are whatever appears in the grammar at such-and-such a level of functioning.

The difference between these two kinds of theory is quite an important one. It is a difference of factual assumption. The intuition that lies behind descriptive grammar is that the units are logically prior to the grammar, which is merely a collection of units. The intuition that lies behind the development of generative grammar is the opposite; it is that the grammar is logically prior to the units, which are merely the elements that appear at a particular stage in the functioning of grammatical processes. We can interpret this controversy in terms of its implications as to the nature of language acquisition. One who accepts the point of view of descriptive grammar will expect language acquisition to be a process of accretion, marked by gradual growth in the size of inventories, the elements of the inventories being developed by some sort of analytic or inductive procedures. One who accepts the underlying point of view of generative grammar will expect, rather, that the process of language acquisition must be more like that of selecting a particular hypothesis from a restricted class of possible hypotheses, on the basis of limited data. The selected hypothesis is the grammar; once accepted, it determines a system of relations among elements and inventories of various sorts. There will, of course, be growth of inventory, but it will be a rather peripheral and "external" matter. Once the child has selected a certain grammar, he will "know" whatever is predicted by this selected hypothesis. He will, in other words, know a great deal about sentences to which he has never been exposed. This is, of course, the characteristic fact about human language.

I have outlined the difference between two theories of grammar in rather vague terms. It can be made quite precise, and the question of choice between them becomes a matter of fact, not decision. My own view is that no descriptivist theory can be reconciled with the known facts about the nature and use of language. This, however, is a matter that goes beyond the scope of this discussion.

To summarize, as the problem is usually put, the choice between generative and descriptive grammars is not a genuine one. It is a choice between a system of principles and one, rather marginal selection of consequences of these principles. But there is a deeper and ultimately factual question, to be resolved not by decision but by sharpening the assumptions and confronting them with facts.

Finally, I would like to say just a word about the matter of the teaching of grammar in the schools. My impression is that grammar is generally taught as an essentially closed and finished system, and in a rather mechanical way. What is taught is a system of terminology, a set of techniques for diagramming sentences, and so on. I do not doubt that this has its function, that the student must have a way of talking about language and its properties. But it seems to me that a great opportunity is lost when the teaching of grammar is limited in this way. I think it is important for students to realize how little we know about the rules that determine the relation of sound and meaning in English, about the general properties of human language, about the matter of how the incredibly complex system of rules that constitutes a grammar is acquired or put to use. Few students are aware of the fact that in their normal, everyday life they are constantly creating new linguistic structures that are immediately understood, despite their novelty, by those to whom they speak or write. They are never brought to the realization of how amazing an accomplishment this is, and of how limited is our comprehension of what makes it possible. Nor do they acquire any insight into the remarkable intricacy of the grammar that they use unconsciously, even insofar as this system is understood and can be explicitly presented. Consequently, they miss both the challenge and the accomplishments of the study of language. This seems to me a pity, because both are very real. Perhaps as the study of language returns gradually to the full scope and scale of its rich tradition, some way will be found to introduce students to the tantalizing problems that language has always posed for those who are puzzled and intrigued by the mysteries of human intelligence.

2

Generative Grammars
As Theories of Linguistic Competence

NOAM CHOMSKY

... Linguistic theory is concerned primarily with an ideal speaker-listener, in a completely homogeneous speech-community, who knows its language perfectly and is unaffected by such grammatically irrelevant conditions as memory limitations, distractions, shifts of attention and interest, and errors (random or characteristic) in applying his knowledge of the language in actual performance. This seems to me to have been the position of the founders of modern general linguistics, and no cogent reason for modifying it has been offered. To study actual linguistic performance, we must consider the interaction of a variety of factors, of which the underlying competence of the speaker-hearer is only one. In this respect, study of language is no different from empirical investigation of other complex phenomena.

We thus make a fundamental distinction between *competence* (the speaker-hearer's knowledge of his language) and *performance* (the actual use of language in concrete situations). Only under the idealization set forth in the preceding paragraph is performance a direct reflection of competence. In actual fact, it obviously could not directly reflect competence. A record of natural speech will show numerous false starts, deviations from rules, changes of plan in mid-course, and so on. The problem for the linguist, as well as for the child learning the language, is to determine from the data of performance the underlying system of rules that has been mastered by the speaker-hearer and that he puts to use in actual performance. Hence, in the technical sense, linguistic theory is mentalistic, since it is concerned with discovering a mental reality underlying actual behavior.[1] Observed use of language or hypothesized dispositions to respond, habits, and so on, may provide evidence as to the nature of this mental reality, but surely cannot constitute the actual subject matter of linguistics, if this is to be a serious discipline. The distinction I am noting here is related to the "langue-parole" distinction of Saussure; but it is necessary to reject his concept of "langue" as merely a systematic inventory of items and to return rather to the Humboldtian conception of underlying competence as a system of generative processes. For discussion see Chomsky (1964).

A grammar of a language purports to be a description of the ideal speaker-hearer's intrinsic competence. If the grammar is, furthermore, perfectly explicit—in other words, if it does not rely on the intelligence of the understanding reader but rather provides an explicit analysis of his contribution—we may (somewhat redundantly) call it a *generative grammar*.

A fully adequate grammar must assign to each of an infinite range of sentences a structural description indicating how this sentence is understood by the ideal speaker-hearer. This is the traditional problem of descriptive linguistics, and tradi-

---

[1]To accept traditional mentalism, in this way, is not to accept Bloomfield's dichotomy of "mentalism" versus "mechanism." Mentalistic linguistics is simply theoretical linguistics that uses performance as data (along with other data, for example, the data provided by introspection) for the determination of competence, the latter being taken as the primary object of its investigation. The mentalist, in this traditional sense, need make no assumptions about the possible physiological basis for the mental reality that he studies. In particular, he need not deny that there is such a basis. One would guess, rather, that it is the mentalistic studies that will ultimately be of greatest value for the investigation of neurophysiological mechanisms, since they alone are concerned with determining abstractly the properties that such mechanisms must exhibit and the functions they must perform.

In fact, the issue of mentalism versus antimentalism in linguistics apparently has to do only with goals and interests, and not with questions of truth or falsity, sense or nonsense. At least three issues are involved in this rather idle controversy: (*a*) dualism—are the rules that underlie performance represented in a nonmaterial medium?; (*b*) behaviorism—do the data of performance exhaust the domain of interest to the linguist, or is he also concerned with other facts, in particular those pertaining to the deeper systems that underlie behavior?; (*c*) introspectionism—should one make use of introspective data in the attempt to ascertain the properties of these underlying systems? It is the dualistic position against which Bloomfield irrelevantly inveighed. The behaviorist position is not an arguable matter. It is simply an expression of lack of interest in theory and explanation. This is clear, for example, in Twaddell's critique (1935) of Sapir's mentalistic phonology, which used informant responses and comments as evidence bearing on the psychological reality of some abstract system of phonological elements. For Twaddell, the enterprise has no point because all that interests him is the behavior itself, "which is already available for the student of language, though in less concentrated form." Characteristically, this lack of interest in linguistic theory expresses itself in the proposal to limit the term "theory" to "summary of data" (as in Twaddell's paper, or, to take a more recent example, in Dixon, 1963, although the discussion of "theories" in the latter is sufficiently vague as to allow other interpretations of what he may have in mind). Perhaps this loss of interest in theory, in the usual sense, was fostered by certain ideas (e.g. strict operationalism or strong verificationism) that were considered briefly in positivist philosophy of science, but rejected forthwith, in the early nineteen-thirties. In any event, question (*b*) poses no substantive issue. Question (*c*) arises only if one rejects the behaviorist limitations of (*b*). To maintain, on grounds of methodological purity, that introspective judgments of the informant (often, the linguist himself) should be disregarded is, for the present, to condemn the study of language to utter sterility. It is difficult to imagine what possible reason might be given for this. We return to this matter later. For further discussion see Katz (1964).

tional grammars give a wealth of information concerning structural descriptions of sentences. However, valuable as they obviously are, traditional grammars are deficient in that they leave unexpressed many of the basic regularities of the language with which they are concerned. This fact is particularly clear on the level of syntax, where no traditional or structuralist grammar goes beyond classification of particular examples to the stage of formulation of generative rules on any significant scale. An analysis of the best existing grammars will quickly reveal that this is a defect of principle, not just a matter of empirical detail or logical preciseness. Nevertheless, it seems obvious that the attempt to explore this largely uncharted territory can most profitably begin with a study of the kind of structural information presented by traditional grammars and the kind of linguistic processes that have been exhibited, however informally, in these grammars.[2]

The limitations of traditional and structuralist grammars should be clearly appreciated. Although such grammars may contain full and explicit lists of exceptions and irregularities, they provide only examples and hints concerning the regular and productive syntactic processes. Traditional linguistic theory was not unaware of this fact. For example, James Beattie (1788) remarks that

> Languages, therefore, resemble men in this respect, that, though each has peculiarities, whereby it is distinguished from every other, yet all have certain qualities in common. The peculiarities of individual tongues are explained in their respective grammars and dictionaries. Those things, that all languages have in common, or that are necessary to every language, are treated of in a science, which some have called *Universal* or *Philosophical* grammar.

Somewhat earlier, Du Marsais defines universal and particular grammar in the following way:

> Il y a dans la grammaire des observations qui conviènnent à toutes les langues; ces observations forment ce qu'on appelle la grammaire générale: telles sont les remarques que l'on a faites sur les sons articulés, sur les lettres qui sont les signes de ces sons; sur la nature des mots, et sur les différentes manières dont ils doivent être ou arrangés ou terminés pour faire un sens. Outre ces observations générales, il y en a qui ne sont propres qu'à une langue particulière; et c'est ce qui forme les grammaires particulières de chaque langue. (1729; quoted in Sahlin, 1928, pp. 29–30)

---

[2]This has been denied recently by several European linguists (e.g. Dixon, 1963; Uhlenbeck, 1963, 1964). They offer no reasons for their skepticism concerning traditional grammar, however. Whatever evidence is available today seems to me to show that by and large the traditional views are basically correct, so far as they go, and that the suggested innovations are totally unjustifiable. For example, consider Uhlenbeck's proposal that the constituent analysis of *the man saw the boy* is [*the man saw*] [*the boy*], a proposal which presumably also implies that in the sentences [*the man put*] [*it into the box*], [*the man aimed*] [*it at John*], [*the man persuaded*] [*Bill that it was unlikely*], etc., the constituents are as indicated. There are many considerations relevant to the determination of constituent structure; to my knowledge, they support the traditional analysis without exception against this proposal, for which the only argument offered is that it is the result of a "pure linguistic analysis." Cf. Uhlenbeck (1964) and the discussion there. As to Dixon's objections to traditional grammars, since he offers neither any alternative nor any argument (beyond the correct but irrelevant observation that they have been "long condemned by professional linguists"), there is nothing further to discuss, in this case.

Within traditional linguistic theory, furthermore, it was clearly understood that one of the qualities that all languages have in common is their "creative" aspect. Thus an essential property of language is that it provides the means for expressing indefinitely many thoughts and for reacting appropriately in an indefinite range of new situations (for references, cf. Chomsky, 1966). The grammar of a particular language, then, is to be supplemented by a universal grammar that accommodates the creative aspect of language use and expresses the deep-seated regularities which, being universal, are omitted from the grammar itself. Therefore it is quite proper for a grammar to discuss only exceptions and irregularities in any detail. It is only when supplemented by a universal grammar that the grammar of a language provides a full account of the speaker-hearer's competence.

Modern linguistics, however, has not explicitly recognized the necessity for supplementing a "particular grammar" of a language by a universal grammar if it is to achieve descriptive adequacy. It has, in fact, characteristically rejected the study of universal grammar as misguided; and, as noted before, it has not attempted to deal with the creative aspect of language use. It thus suggests no way to overcome the fundamental descriptive inadequacy of structuralist grammars.

Another reason for the failure of traditional grammars, particular or universal, to attempt a precise statement of regular processes of sentence formation and sentence interpretation lay in the widely held belief that there is a "natural order of thoughts" that is mirrored by the order of words. Hence the rules of sentence formation do not really belong to grammar but to some other subject in which the "order of thoughts" is studied. Thus in the *Grammaire générale et raisonnée* (Lancelot and others, 1660) it is asserted that, aside from figurative speech, the sequence of words follows an "ordre naturel," which conforms "à l'expression naturelle de nos pensées." Consequently, few grammatical rules need be formulated beyond the rules of ellipsis, inversion, and so on, which determine the figurative use of language. The same view appears in many forms and variants. To mention just one additional example, in an interesting essay devoted largely to the question of how the simultaneous and sequential array of ideas is reflected in the order of words, Diderot concludes that French is unique among languages in the degree to which the order of words corresponds to the natural order of thoughts and ideas (Diderot, 1751). Thus "quel que soit l'ordre des termes dans une langue ancienne ou moderne, l'esprit de l'écrivain a suivi l'ordre didactique de la syntaxe française" (p. 390); "Nous disons les choses en français, comme l'esprit est forcé de les considérer en quelque langue qu'on écrive" (p. 371). With admirable consistency he goes on to conclude that "notre langue *pédestre* a sur les autres l'avantage de l'utile sur l'agréable" (p. 372); thus French is appropriate for the sciences, whereas Greek, Latin, Italian, and English "sont plus avantageuses pour les lettres." Moreover,

le bons sens choisirait la langue française; mais . . . l'imagination et les passions donneront la préférence aux langues anciennes et à celles de nos voisins . . . il faut parler français dans la société et dans les écoles de philosophie; et grec, latin, anglais, dans les chaires et sur les théâtres; . . . notre langue sera celle de la vérité, si jamais elle revient sur la terre; et . . . la grecque, la latine et les autres seront les langues de la fable et du mensonge. Le français est fait pour instruire, éclairer et convaincre; le grec, le latin, l'italien, l'anglais, pour persuader, émouvoir et tromper: parlez grec, latin, italien au peuple; mais parlez français au sage. (Pp. 371–372)

In any event, insofar as the order of words is determined by factors independent of language, it is not necessary to describe it in a particular or universal grammar, and we therefore have principled grounds for excluding an explicit formulation of syntactic processes from grammar. It is worth noting that this naive view of language structure persists to modern times in various forms, for example, in Saussure's image of a sequence of expressions corresponding to an amorphous sequence of concepts or in the common characterization of language use as merely a matter of use of words and phrases (for example, Ryle, 1953).

But the fundamental reason for this inadequacy of traditional grammars is a more technical one. Although it was well understood that linguistic processes are in some sense "creative," the technical devices for expressing a system of recursive processes were simply not available until much more recently. In fact, a real understanding of how a language can (in Humboldt's words) "make infinite use of finite means" has developed only within the last thirty years, in the course of studies in the foundations of mathematics. Now that these insights are readily available it is possible to return to the problems that were raised, but not solved, in traditional linguistic theory, and to attempt an explicit formulation of the "creative" processes of language. There is, in short, no longer a technical barrier to the full-scale study of generative grammars.

Returning to the main theme, by a generative grammar I mean simply a system of rules that in some explicit and well-defined way assigns structural descriptions to sentences. Obviously, every speaker of a language has mastered and internalized a generative grammar that expresses his knowledge of his language. This is not to say that he is aware of the rules of the grammar or even that he can become aware of them, or that his statements about his intuitive knowledge of the language are necessarily accurate. Any interesting generative grammar will be dealing, for the most part, with mental processes that are far beyond the level of actual or even potential consciousness; furthermore, it is quite apparent that a speaker's reports and viewpoints about his behavior and his competence may be in error. Thus a generative grammar attempts to specify what the speaker actually knows, not what he may report about his knowledge. Similarly, a theory of visual perception would attempt to account for what a person actually sees and the mechanisms that determine this rather than his statements about what he sees and why, though these statements may provide useful, in fact, compelling evidence for such a theory.

To avoid what has been a continuing misunderstanding, it is perhaps worthwhile to reiterate that a generative grammar is not a model for a speaker or a hearer. It attempts to characterize in the most neutral possible terms the knowledge of the language that provides the basis for actual use of language by a speaker-hearer. When we speak of a grammar as generating a sentence with a certain structural description, we mean simply that the grammar assigns this structural description to the sentence. When we say that a sentence has a certain derivation with respect to a particular generative grammar, we say nothing about how the speaker or hearer might proceed, in some practical or efficient way, to construct such a derivation. These questions belong to the theory of language use—the theory of performance. No doubt, a reasonable model of language use will incorporate, as a basic component, the generative grammar that expresses the speaker-hearer's knowledge of the language; but this generative grammar does not, in itself, prescribe the character or functioning of a perceptual model or a model of speech production. For various attempts to clarify this point, see Chomsky (1957), Gleason (1961), Miller and Chomsky (1963), and many other publications.

Confusion over this matter has been sufficiently persistent to suggest that a terminological change might be in order. Nevertheless, I think that the term "generative grammar" is completely appropriate, and have therefore continued to use it. The term "generate" is familiar in the sense intended here in logic, particularly in Post's theory of combinatorial systems. Furthermore, "generate" seems to be the most appropriate translation for Humboldt's term "erzeugen," which he frequently uses, it seems, in essentially the sense here intended. Since this use of the term "generate" is well established both in logic and in the tradition of linguistic theory, I can see no reason for a revision of terminology.

REFERENCES

Beattie, J. (1788), *Theory of Language*. London.

Chomsky, N. (1957), *Syntactic Structures*. The Hague: Mouton & Co.

———— (1964), *Current Issues in Linguistic Theory*. The Hague: Mouton & Co. A slightly earlier version appears in *SL*. This is a revised and expanded version of a paper presented to the session "The Logical Basis of Linguistic Theory" at the Ninth International Congress of Linguists, Cambridge, Mass., 1962. It appears under the title of the session in H. Lunt, ed., *Proceedings of the Ninth International Congress of Linguists* (The Hague: Mouton & Co., 1964).

———— (1966), *Cartesian Linguistics*. New York: Harper & Row, Publishers.

Diderot, D. (1751), *Lettre sur les sourds et muets*. Page references are to J. Assezat, ed., *Oeuvres completes de Diderot*, Vol. I (Paris: Garnier Frères, 1875).

Dixon, R. W. (1963), *Linguistic Science and Logic*. The Hague: Mouton & Co.

Du Marsais, C. Ch. (1729), *Les véritables principes de la grammaire*. On the dating of this manuscript, see Sahlin, p. ix.

Gleason, H. A. (1961), *Introduction to Descriptive Linguistics*, 2nd ed. New York: Holt, Rinehart & Winston, Inc.

Katz, J. J. (1964), "Mentalism in Linguistics." *Language*, 40. 124–137 [*RPL*].

Lancelot, C., A. Arnauld, and others, (1660). *Grammaire générale et raisonnée*.

Miller, G. A., and N. Chomsky (1963), "Finitary Models of Language Users," in *HMP*.

Ryle, G. (1953), "Ordinary Language." *Philosophical Review*, 62. 167–186.

Sahlin, G. (1928), *César Chesneau du Marsais et son rôle dans l'évolution de la grammaire générale*. Paris: Presses Universitaires.

Twaddell, W. F. (1935), *On Defining the Phoneme*. Language Monograph No. 16. Reprinted in part in *RIL*.

Uhlenbeck, E. M. (1963), "An Appraisal of Transformation Theory." *Lingua*, 12. 1–18.

———— (1964), Discussion in the session "Logical Basis of Linguistic Theory," in H. Lunt, ed., *Proceedings of the Ninth International Congress of Linguists* (The Hague: Mouton & Co.), pp. 981–983.

3

Underlying and Superficial Linguistic Structure

PAUL M. POSTAL

The following remarks based on examples from English are a rather informal discussion of some of the kinds of results and implications of linguistic research being done in the conceptual framework which has come to be called "generative grammar."[1]

A linguistic description of some natural language is designed to provide a specification of the knowledge which speakers of that language have which differentiates them from nonspeakers. This knowledge is evidently enormous in extent and varied in nature. It includes, among other things, the ability to distinguish those noises which are sentences of the language (*well-formed* or *grammatical*) from those which are not; to recognize similarities between utterances and their parts; to recognize identities of various sorts from full rhyme on the phonological level to identity of meaning or paraphrase on the semantic level, etc. Since each speaker is a finite organism, this knowledge must be finite in character, i.e. learnable. Yet a moment's thought is sufficient to show that someone who has learned a natural language is in fact in possession of full information about an infinite set of linguistic objects, namely the sentences. This follows because there is no longest sentence. Given any sentence we can always find a longer one by replacing some

Reprinted from the *Harvard Educational Review*, 34. 246–266 (1964), by permission of Paul M. Postal and the *Harvard Educational Review*.

The present work was supported in part by the U.S. Army Signal Corps, the U.S. Air Force Office of Scientific Research, the U.S. Office of Naval Research; and in part by the National Science Foundation. I am indebted to Morris Halle for helpful comments and criticisms.

[1]For a partial bibliography of such work see the footnote references and other references listed at the end of this article. The following abbreviations are used throughout the article: *NP = Noun Phrase; S = Sentence; VP = Verb Phrase; * = nonsentence.*

noun with a noun and following modifier, or by replacing some verbal phrase with a conjunction of two verbal phrases, etc. Of course, the finite and in fact rather small bound on human memory will prevent actual speech behavior from making use of more than a small finite subclass of all possible sentences. But this in no way affects the psychologically and linguistically fundamental fact that knowledge of a natural language provides a speaker in principle with knowledge of an infinite set of linguistic objects. Only this assumption, for example, makes it possible to explain why, as the limits on memory are weakened, as with the use of pencil and paper, speaker's abilities to use and understand sentences are extended to those of greater length. It is no accident that traditionally, for example, written German involves lengthy and complex constructions not normally found in the spoken language. The analogy with arithmetic is appropriate here. One who has learned the rules of arithmetic is clearly capable in principle of determining the result of multiplying any two of the infinite set of whole numbers. Yet obviously no one ever has or ever could compute more than a small finite number of such multiples.

In principle knowledge by a finite organism of an infinite set of linguistic facts is neither paradox nor contradiction, but results from the fact that there are kinds of finite entities which specify infinite sets of objects. In mathematics these are often referred to by the term "recursive." For example, consider the set of rules

(1) $A \rightarrow X$

(2) $X \rightarrow X + X$

where the arrow is to be interpreted as the instruction to rewrite the left symbol as the right-hand string of symbols. It is evident that continued application of these rules will specify an endless, unbounded, i.e. strictly infinite set of strings of the form X, XX, XXX, XXXX, etc. And a person who learned these two rules plus the finite set of instructions for applying them would, in a precise sense, have learned the infinite set of possible outputs.

It is in exactly this sense that we must postulate that a speaker has learned the infinite set of sentences of his language, by learning some finite set of rules which can enumerate, list, specify, or, as it is usually said, *generate* these sentences. Such a set of rules can be called a *grammar* or *syntax*.

A *language* in these terms is then just the set of strings of symbols (the X's in the above trivial example) enumerated by the grammar. We shall see below that this conception of language must be greatly enriched. Having come to the point of seeing each sentence as a string of symbols of some type, it is natural to ask about the nature of these symbols in actual natural languages like English, Chinese, etc. It is traditional to think of these as *words*, i.e. roughly as minimum units of pronunciation, those elements which may be uttered independently. Modern linguistics has greatly emphasized, however, that words are themselves in fact composed of or analyzable into syntactically significant parts, usually referred to as *morphemes*. For example, it would be pointed out that the word

(3)   *uninterrupted*

is composed of at least three morphemes, *un + interrupt + ed*, the first of which is also found in (4), the second of which is also found in (5), and the third of which is also found in (6):

(4) *unhappy*

(5) *interruptable*

(6) *destroyed*

It thus follows that the syntactic structure of each sentence must be represented as a string of words with morpheme boundaries also indicated.

However, all linguists are in effect agreed that sentence structure is not exhausted by division into words and morphemes. Most crucially, the words and morphemes must be considered as grouped into significant sequences; in other words, to be *parsed*, or *hierarchically bracketed*. Thus in the sentence

(7)   *Harry liked the nice girl.*

most linguists would probably agree that the elements must be bracketed something like

Harry	*liked*		*the*	*nice*	*girl*
	liked		*the*	*nice*	*girl*
	like	*ed*	*the*	*nice*	*girl*
				nice	*girl*

Such a bracketing indicates that the sentence is first made up of two basic parts, *Harry* and everything else; that everything else is made up of two primary parts, *liked* and the remainder, etc. However, it would further be agreed that such bracketing representations are inadequate if not accompanied by an associated *labelling* of the segments obtained by the bracketing. It has become common to represent such labelled bracketings in the form of rooted trees like Figure 1, but such are perfectly equivalent to (labelled) box diagrams like that above or labelled parenthesizations, or any other suitable diagrammatic equivalent.

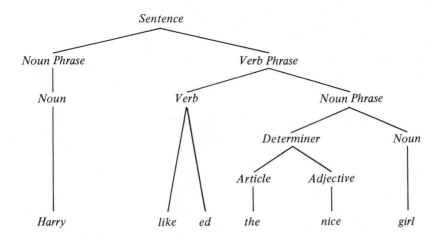

FIGURE 1

Such a labelled bracketing provides far more explanatory insight into the structure of a sentence than the mere bracketing alone. It accounts for similarities between various sequences, i.e., for example our knowledge that *Harry* and *the nice girl* are in some sense similar kinds of elements as against *liked*, or *the*. I shall refer to the kind of linguistic structure represented by labelled bracketings in any of their various forms as *phrase markers*. Such structures describe for each sentence (string of minimal syntactic symbols) what parts make it up, how these are grouped together into significant sequences, and what type of grouping each is.

Linguists are rather well agreed on the fact that each sentence of a natural language is correctly represented by at least one phrase marker of some kind. This agreement is, of course, accompanied by many disagreements of various types, both substantive and terminological, which need not concern us here. Since each speaker knows an unbounded set of sentences, and since it is agreed that each sentence has one phrase marker, it follows that each speaker must learn a finite set of rules which can enumerate not only strings of symbols (words or morphemes) but rather an infinite set of correct phrase markers. It follows then that a linguistic description of a language must contain just this finite set of rules. A crucial problem for linguistic theory is then the specification of the character or form of such rules, the way they associate phrase markers with an infinite output of strings of symbols, etc.[2]

UNDERLYING GRAMMATICAL STRUCTURE

However, in stopping at the point, in effect widely agreed upon, that the syntactic structure of a sentence is given by a *single* phrase marker, we will have seemed to embrace a position which we cannot in fact accept. There is overwhelming evidence showing that the syntactic structure of the sentences of natural languages is by no means adequately representable by single phrase markers, regardless of how elaborated. Although each sentence certainly has one phrase marker which provides a labelled bracketing of the actual string of morphemes and words which are directly related to its phonetic manifestation, this is only the most superficial aspect of syntactic structure. There is a whole other domain of required structure which is crucial for describing both the formal syntactic properties of sentences and the way they are understood, i.e. their semantic properties.[3] The superficial

---

[2]For a discussion of phrase markers, phrase marker assignment, rules which generate phrase markers, relation of phrase markers to generally held linguistic views, cf. Noam Chomsky, "On the Notion 'Rule of Grammar,' " in *PAM* [*SL*]; Noam Chomsky, "A Transformational Approach to Syntax," in A. A. Hill, ed., *Third Conference on Problems of Linguistic Analysis in English*, May 9–12, 1958 (Austin: University of Texas Press, 1962), pp. 124–158 [*SL*]; Noam Chomsky, "The Logical Basis of Linguistic Theory," in H. Lunt, ed., *Proceedings of IXth International Congress of Linguists* (The Hague: Mouton & Co., 1964) [reprinted as "Current Issues in Linguistic Theory" in *SL*]; and Paul Postal, *Constituent Structure*, Supplement to *International Journal of American Linguistics*, 30:1 (January 1964), Part III.

[3]This conclusion is in effect implied by the whole literature which argues that adequate grammatical description involves transformational rules.

phrase marker of each sentence is chiefly relevant only to the way sentences are pronounced. To determine what sentences mean, one must attend to the far more abstract underlying structure.

Consider the following English sentences:

(8)   *Drink the milk.*

(9)   *Go home.*

(10)   *Don't bother me.*

These are normally referred to as *imperative sentences*. And in terms of their superficial phrase markers it is evident that they consist of an uninflected verb plus other elements of the verb phrase but no preceding "subject" noun phrase of the kind found in declaratives like

(11)   *He drank the milk.*

(12)   *I went home.*

(13)   *John didn't bother me.*

English also contains so-called *reflexive pronouns* like the boldface "objects" in such sentences as

(14)   *The man cut **himself**.*

(15)   *John admired **himself** in the mirror.*

(16)   *You overestimate **yourself**.*

If one now inquires into the rules which govern the occurrence of this kind of reflexive form in English, one finds, among other things, that there are sentences of the form $NP_1 + Verb + reflexive\ pronoun + Y$ just in case one can also find sentences of the form $NP_2 + Verb + NP_1 + Y$. That is, those verbs which take reflexive pronoun "objects" are just those which can elsewhere occur with "objects" identical to the "subjects" of the reflexive sentences.[4] Hence one finds (14)–(16) and

(17)   *John cut the man.*

(18)   *I admired John in the mirror.*

(19)   *She overestimates you.*

but we do not find

(20)   **Harry demands himself.*

(21)   **You concede yourself.*

(22)   **Mary completes herself.*

and accordingly there are also no English sentences

(23)   **I demand Harry.*

(24)   **John concedes you.*

(25)   **You complete Mary.*

---

[4]The grammatical descriptions in this paper are highly oversimplified in a number of ways irrelevant to the points they are designed to illustrate. For more detailed and extensive description of reflexives, cf. Robert B. Lees and Edward S. Klima, "Rules for English Pronominalization," *Language*, 39.17–28 (1963) [*MSE*].

although one can find

(26)   *I demand the answer.*

(27)   *John concedes the game.*

(28)   *You complete the task.*

These facts show that the rule for forming reflexives of the type being considered is in effect based on *a possible equivalence* of "subject" and "object" noun phrase and suggests that reflexive sentences be described by rules which in some sense "derive" reflexive sentences from structures in which there are equivalent "subjects" and "objects." Hence (14)–(15) would be derived from abstract structures something like the following schematically indicated *phrase markers:*

(29)

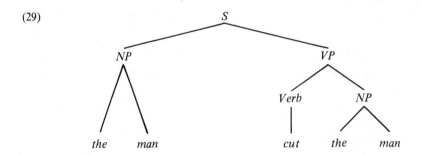

(30)

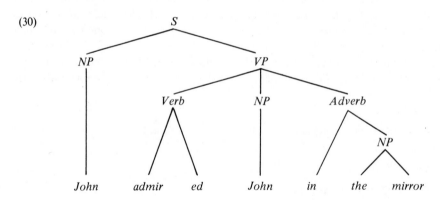

(31)

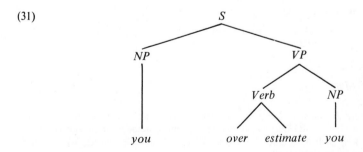

Notice that the rules which associate "subjects" and "objects" with verbs, these rules being part of the set which enumerate phrase markers like (29)–(31), will be *simpler* if they are allowed to produce such structures as (29)–(31) than if not, since, as we have seen, all the possible "subjects" and "objects" of (29)–(31) must be allowed with their respective verbs in any event. Hence to prevent derivation of structures like (29)–(31) and their analogues would require *adding* special restrictions to the grammar prohibiting identical "subjects" and "objects" with a single verb.

But now if structures like (29)–(31) are enumerated they provide a simple means for describing correctly reflexive sentences if one simply adds the rule that the second noun phrase in a structure $NP_1 + Verb + NP_2 + X$ is replaced by the appropriate reflexive pronoun when $NP_1 = NP_2$. This correctly derives just those reflexive strings which meet the equivalence condition stated before and permits retention of the noncomplicated verb–"object" and "subject"–verb selection rules by eliminating the need for special restrictions to prevent the enumeration of the analogues of (29)–(31). This follows because this new reflexive rule converts (29)–(31) and all similar phrase markers into the superficial phrase markers which must represent the occurring reflexive sentences like (14)–(16) and these must be described anyway.

But this analysis of reflexives provides an immediate explanation of why an English speaker *understands* reflexive sentences to refer to "objects" identical to their "subjects," *if* we insist that the understanding of a sentence refers to abstract structures like (29)–(31) rather than to the superficial phrase markers of actual sentences like (14)–(16) in which the "subject"–"object" equivalences cannot possibly be marked.[5]

This very natural and explanatorily powerful description of reflexive sentences requires, however, a radical shift in one's notion of grammatical structure. It requires that the grammatical structure of a sentence be taken to consist, not of a *single phrase marker*, but at least of a *set of phrase markers*, these being related by the kind of rules illustrated by our description of the reflexive. This leads to a picture of syntax in which there is a basic division into two components, one containing rules which derive very abstract *underlying phrase markers* like those represented by (29)–(31); the other containing rules like the reflexive above. These latter rules apply to whole phrase markers and derive new phrase markers. The last such phrase marker derived by the final rule of this second component is called a *final derived phrase marker* and represents the superficial labelled bracketing of the actual string of words of the sentence. Rules which derive phrase markers from phrase markers have been called *transformations*. The rules which enumerate underlying phrase markers are simpler in character. It was assumed at first that these were roughly variants of rules like (1) and (2) above, i.e. rules which operated

---

[5]The claim that the semantic interpretation or meaning of a sentence is determined by the *underlying* structure assigned it by the syntax is argued extensively in Jerrold Katz and P. M. Postal, *An Integrated Theory of Linguistic Descriptions* (Cambridge, Mass.: M.I.T. Press, 1964).

exclusively on strings of symbols by replacing single symbols by certain distinct strings of other symbols. These were called *phrase-structure* or *constituent-structure* rules. Such phrase-structure rules as the following have been proposed:

(32)   *Sentence* → *NP* + *VP*

(33)   *NP* → *Determiner* + *Noun*

It has become increasingly apparent, however, that underlying phrase markers cannot in fact be correctly described exclusively with rules of this type. It appears the such rules must be supplemented by more powerful devices to help account for so-called "selectional restrictions" such as the fact that certain verbs occur only with animate "subjects" and inanimate "objects," others with inanimate "subjects" and animate "objects," others with animate "subjects" and animate "objects," etc. It appears that the subcomponent of syntactic rules which enumerates underlying phrase markers is itself divided into two elements, one containing phrase structure rules and the other containing a *lexicon* or *dictionary* of highly structured morpheme entries which are inserted into the structures enumerated by the phrase-structure rules. Although quite new and too complicated to say more about here, research into this area of syntactic structure promises to yield great insights into many areas of traditional interest, including characterizations of such notions as *word, inflection, derivation, noun,* and *verb,* as well as resolving the original difficulties with selectional restrictions.[6]

We can provide more motivation for an extension of the notion of grammatical structure to include a whole set of phrase markers for each sentence, including most crucially abstract underlying phrase markers, by returning to imperative sentences which superficially have no "subjects." These may also contain reflexives:

(34)   *Wash yourself.*

(35)   *Don't kill yourself.*

However, there is a crucial restriction on the reflexive pronouns which can occur in imperative sentences, namely only *yourself* is permitted. Hence there are no sentences like

(36)   **Wash himself.*

(37)   **Wash themselves.*

(38)   **Don't kill myself.*

(39)   **Don't kill herself.*

But we recall the fact that reflexives are based on an equivalence of "subject" and "object." This means that if we are to embed imperative reflexives into the simple description of reflexives given earlier, imperatives must be derived from underlying phrase markers which contain *you* "subjects."

As support for this, consider so-called "tag" questions like

(40)   *Mary will come, won't she?*

(41)   *John can run, can't he?*

(42)   *I have won, haven't I?*

---

[6]For a discussion of the topics of this paragraph, cf. Noam Chomsky, *A Fragment of English Syntax* (to appear).

It is evident that the part of such questions which follows the intonation break (represented by the comma) involves a repetition of the auxiliary[7] and "subject" of the first pre-comma part, with the proviso that the order must be changed, the negative added, and the "subject" pronominalized.[8] But there are tag sentences in which the first part is *imperative* in form:

(43) *Eat the meat, will you.*

(44) *Go home, won't you.*

And there is a constraint here that the pronoun form after the commas can only be *you*. Hence we find no English sentences like

(45) **Eat the meat, will* $\begin{Bmatrix} she \\ he \\ they \end{Bmatrix}$

(46) **Go home, will* $\begin{Bmatrix} I \\ we \end{Bmatrix}$

But this can be readily explained in terms of the fact that the second noun phrase is a repeated pronominalized form of the "subject" noun phrase before the comma, if it is assumed that imperatives have in their underlying phrase markers a *you* "subject" noun phrase in front of the verb. We see then that the evidence of reflexives and tag sentences converges on the conclusion that the underlying structure of imperatives contains a second person "subject." But now this can immediately provide an explanation of the fact that every English speaker understands an imperative to refer to the second person if, as before, we assume that the structures relevant to understanding are the underlying phrase markers.

Here as before we must posit a transformational rule which will derive the superficial structure of imperatives from the underlying phrase markers. Notice that the auxiliary repetition of tag questions shows that the underlying phrase markers of imperatives must contain the modal *will* (*will + contracted not = won't*) since this is the form found in imperative tags and in fact is the only permitted auxiliary form:

(47) **Eat the meat, did he*

(48) **Eat the meat, can he*

But this provides an explanation of why we understand that imperative sentences refer to the future. The transformational rule which derives the superficial forms of imperative sentences will delete the *will* (and preceding tense morpheme) and optionally delete the "subject"—optionally only because we find imperatives with explicit *you*:

(49) *You eat your meat.*

(50) *You go home (or I'll tell your mother).*

These also have a *nonimperative* declarative semantic interpretation but this need not concern us here.

---

[7]That is, the constituent which in underlying phrase markers represents such elements as the tense morphemes, as well as *will, may, be, can, have*, etc.

[8]When the initial element is itself negative, then the part after the comma must be non-negative.

We have suggested that in order to provide an account of both the formal properties of sentences and the way in which they are understood it is necessary to extend the notion of grammatical structure in such a way that each sentence is represented by a whole set of phrase markers, including crucially quite abstract underlying ones. This conclusion is greatly strengthened if we consider so-called grammatical relations like *subject-verb*, or *verb-object*.[9] To understand a sentence it is obviously quite crucial to know which parts bear which relations to which other parts. For example, despite the fact that the following sentences contain identical elements we understand them differently:

(51)   *Mary loves John.*

(52)   *John loves Mary.*

In (51) we understand that it is Mary who does the loving and John who receives the affection; in (52) conversely. The fact that these differences are associated with a distinct order of elements might suggest that the various relations involved can be precisely characterized in terms of *order*. We can say that in a phrase marker the first noun phrase bears the *subject* relation to the verb, the noun phrase following the verb bears the *object* relation to this element, etc. However, attractive as this proposal is, it obviously fails for *superficial* phrase markers because of the enormous number of cases like

(53)   *John was loved by Mary.*

(54)   *Mary was loved by John.*

(55)   *John is anxious to please Mary.*

(56)   *John is easy for Mary to please.*

In (53) the relations between *John* and *Mary* and the verb are the same as in (51), while in (54) they are the same as in (52). Yet the order of constituents in (53) is like that in (52) and the order in (54) is like that in (51). Similarly in (55) we recognize that *John* is the "subject" of *please* while in (56) it is the "object" of this verb. Yet its relative order is the same. In short we see that in the actual superficial forms of sentences the crucial grammatical relations are not associated with any unique configurations of constituents.

It seems, however, that in underlying phrase markers this is the case. That is, in underlying phrase markers grammatical relations are uniquely and uniformly definable in terms of constituents and their order. Hence the underlying structures of (52) and (54) are quite similar to those of (51) and (52) respectively and the actual order to elements in (53) and (54) is derived by the so-called *passive transformation*[10] which, among other things, inverts "subject," and "object" noun phrases. This solution is formally motivated *inter alia* by the fact that for a fixed verb type

---

[9]For a fuller discussion of grammatical relations and their characterization in precise linguistic terms, cf. Chomsky, "Logical Basis of Linguistic Theory" and *Fragment of English Syntax*, and Katz and Postal, op. cit.

[10]For a description of this rule, cf. Noam Chomsky, *Syntactic Structures* (The Hague: Mouton and Co., 1957); and Chomsky, "Transformational Approach to Syntax." For a slightly revised and more up to date description, cf. Katz and Postal, op. cit., and Chomsky, *Fragment of English Syntax*.

those noun phrase elements which can occur in the initial position of passive sentences are just those which can occur in the "object" position of declaratives. Hence one finds

(57)   *John admires Harry.*

(58)   *John admires truth.*

but not

(59)   **Truth admires John.*

and similarly

(60)   *Harry is admired by John.*

(61)   *Truth is admired by John.*

but not

(62)   **John is admired by truth.*

and

(63)   *John demands a raise.*

(64)   *John believes Harry.*

but not

(65)   **John demands Harry.*

(66)   **John believes love.*

and similarly

(67)   *A raise is demanded by John.*

(68)   *Harry is believed by John.*

but not

(69)   **Harry is demanded by John.*

(70)   **Love is believed by John.*

If passive sentences are not derived from underlying structures in which the "subject" and "object" elements are in the same order as in active sentences, all these selectional facts must be stated twice. Thus again we find formal motivation for abstract underlying phrase markers which contain structures of just the type needed to explain the way the occurring sentences are understood.

Consider finally (55) and (56). These sentences are in a sense fundamentally different from any considered before because their underlying structure must be taken to include a *pair* of underlying phrase markers which are combined to produce the occurring sentences. The transformations which perform such combining operations have been called *generalized transformations.*[11] Sentences like (55) in which the initial noun phrase (*NP*) is understood as the "subject" of the verb in the infinitive phrase must be derived from a pair of structures of roughly the

---

[11]It now seems likely that combinations of phrase markers are in fact performed by a single generalized transformation which is part of the component which generates underlying phrase markers rather than the component which contains simple transformations like the reflexive, passive, etc. Cf. Katz and Postal, op. cit., and Chomsky, *Fragment of English Syntax.*

form $NP_1 + is + Adjective + Complement$, $NP_1 + Verb + NP_2$. That is, the two phrase markers which are combined must have identical "subject" noun phrases. This restriction is necessary to account for the fact that those verbs which can occur in the infinitives of sentences like (55) are just those which can take as "subject" the initial noun phrase. Hence one does not find

(71) *Truth is anxious to see Mary.*

(72) *Love is anxious to marry Mary.*

because there is no

(73) *Truth sees Mary.*

(74) *Love marries Mary.*

etc. But these formal reasons force us to derive sentences like (55) from underlying structures in which *John* is the "subject" of the verb *please* in terms of the uniform configurational account of grammatical relations roughly sketched earlier.

In (56) the situation is analogous although reversed. Here the sentences must be derived from a pair of underlying structures with the forms $NP_1 + is + Adjective + Complement$, $NP_2 + Verb + NP_1$. In this case the equivalence of noun phrases is between the "object" noun phrase of the second underlying phrase marker and the "subject" of the predicative type phrase marker. This is necessary because those verbs which can occur in the *for* phrases of sentences like (56) are just those which can occur with the sentence initial noun phrase as "object." Hence one does not find

(75) *Truth is easy for Mary to please.*

(76) *Meat is easy for Mary to prove.*

because one cannot find

(77) *Mary pleases truth.*

(78) *Mary proves meat.*

But this means that one is forced by these formal facts to derive sentences like (56) from underlying structures in which *John* is indeed the "object" (by the uniform characterization given above) of *please*. So that again the independently motivated underlying structures provide a correct account of the way sentences are understood with respect to grammatical relations.

LINGUISTIC SUMMARY

We have briefly considered a few of the enormous number of cases which support the view that the grammatical structure of sentences can only be adequately represented by structural descriptions which include highly abstract underlying phrase markers. We see then that a linguistic description must minimally include rules to generate the correct set of underlying phrase markers, rules to combine underlying phrase markers in the case of sentences which are complex (like (55) and (56)), and finally rules to derive the correct superficial phrase markers of sentences from their abstract structures. A full account of the nature of all such rules has yet to be given, although tremendous progress has been made in recent years and the outlines of correct solutions appear to be relatively clear. The crucial point is that any adequate theory of grammar must provide an account of such rules, for only in this way can such a theory provide the theoretical apparatus which individual linguistic descriptions must draw on in order to explain the finite mechanism a speaker has learned which yields his knowledge of the underlying and superficial structures of the endless class of well-formed utterances.

We have been speaking essentially only of syntactic structure. It is obvious that a full linguistic description must contain other aspects. First, it must contain a *phonological component* whose rules specify the phonetic character of each structure generated by the syntactic rules. It appears that the phonological component operates exclusively on the *final derived phrase markers* of the syntax and associates a phonetic representation with each. The phonetic rules must also, quite crucially, characterize the notion of "phonetically possible morpheme." That is, it is these rules which will state that in English, although neither *ftorts* or *geyk* is an actual morpheme, the latter but not the former is a possible morpheme, and might be introduced tomorrow as the name of a new soap, or a new concept. Much progress has also been made recently in our knowledge of the form and character of phonological rules but this will not concern us further.[12]

Most important, however, is the fact that a full linguistic description must contain a *semantic component* whose task is to assign each sentence a *meaning*. We have shown that the syntactic structure relevant to this task is present in underlying but not superficial grammatical structure. But nothing has been said precisely about how semantic interpretations are assigned to the structures which the syntactic rules generate. Obviously, however, a full linguistic description must specify this information, since it is evident that speakers know the meanings of the sentences of their language as well as their grammatical structure and pronunciation features.

Although fundamental insights into this question have recently been achieved, this topic is too complex and too new for extended treatment here.[13] The problem for a semantic description is to specify how the speaker who learns the meanings of a finite number of *lexical items,* morphemes, multimorpheme idioms, plus the rules which characterize the grammatical structure of the sentences which contain these lexical items, determines the meanings of sentences. This can be formulated as a purely formal problem of specifying rules which operate on the grammatical structure (the underlying phrase markers) and the meanings of lexical items, if the notion *meaning of a lexical item* can be formally characterized. This can be

---

[12]For descriptions of the phonological component, cf. Morris Halle, *The Sound Pattern of Russian* (The Hague: Mouton & Co., 1954); Morris Halle, "Phonology in Generative Grammar," *Word,* 18.54–73 (1962) [*SL*]; Noam Chomsky, "Explanatory Models in Linguistics," in E. Nagel, P. Suppes, A. Tarski, eds., *Logic, Methodology, and the Philosophy of Science* (Stanford, Calif.: Stanford University Press, 1961); Chomsky, "Logical Basis of Linguistic Theory"; and Noam Chomsky and G. A. Miller, "Introduction to the Formal Analysis of Natural Languages," in *HMP*.

[13]For descriptions of the semantic component, cf. Jerrold Katz and J. Fodor, "The Structure of a Semantic Theory," *Language,* 39.170–211 (1963) [*SL*]; Jerrold Katz, "Analyticity and Contradiction in Natural Languages," in *SL*; and Katz and Postal, op. cit.

done by postulating abstract atomic elements, *semantic markers*, which represent the conceptual content of lexical items. For example, we can postulate a semantic marker (male) which will be associated with the lexical items, *man, boy, father*, or *uncle*, to represent part of the conceptual similarity between these (as opposed for example, to *car, truth, mother, girl*). Besides a dictionary which associates sequences of such semantic markers (*readings*) with lexical items, the semantic component of a linguistic description will also contain a set of *projection rules* which will combine the readings of lexical items in order to obtain derived semantic characterizations for higher order constituents, on up to the constituent sentence itself. These rules will operate on the readings of lexical items plus the grammatical relations which hold between these items, these relations being indicated in the underlying phrase markers in the manner suggested earlier.

The output of the semantic component will be a formal semantic characterization of each constituent of each sentence. These characterizations will provide an explanation of such semantic properties as *ambiguity, paraphrase, synonymy*, or *anomaly*.[14] It should be emphasized that this kind of semantic theory leaves its primary descriptive objects, the semantic markers, uninterpreted. That is, it does not specify the relation of these elements to the nonlinguistic world. (This means that such notions as *reference*, and *truth*, are not characterized.) This task is left as a fundamental (and fantastically difficult) psychological problem independent of the problem of formulating linguistic descriptions and the theory underlying them. Interpretation of the system of markers is seen as part of the fundamental problems of concept formation, categorization of experience, etc.

It appears then that the linguistic knowledge whose possession characterizes a speaker of a language has the form of an abstract linguistic object containing three major components of rules. The basic element is a generative syntactic component whose rules generate highly complex structures including a set of phrase markers for each derived string of words. There are then two subsidiary *interpretive* components. The phonological component provides each sentence with a phonetic interpretation and accounts for the speaker's knowledge of the facts of pronunciation. The semantic component provides each sentence with a semantic interpretation in the form of a set of readings and accounts for the speaker's knowledge of the facts of meaning.

It seems that the two interpretive components are each based on a fixed, universal vocabulary of primitive conceptual elements with universally specified relations to the nonlinguistic world. In the case of the phonological component, this vocabulary consists of the set of phonetic features with which sentences are described (*voicing, stress*, and *nasality*). That is, there is a fixed universal phonetic alphabet which provides all the relevant phonetic information about each sentence. In the case of the semantic component, the vocabulary consists of the set of

---

[14]These properties are respectively illustrated by
(a)   *I observed the ball.*
(b)   *John is a farmer; John is someone who farms.*
(c)   *not living; dead*
(d)   *John married a potato pancake.*

semantic markers, about which, however, much less is known. The universality of the set of semantic markers is plausible but much work on a wide variety of languages will be needed before it can be verified to anything like the extent to which the universality of the phonetic features has been confirmed. In claiming that the atomic elements of both interpretive components are universal, one is saying that the child who learns a language based on them need not learn these elements or their relations to the nonlinguistic world. That is, for example, someone who learns English need not learn what the semantic marker (*male*) denotes or what properties of vocal utterances the phonetic feature (*nasal*) refers to. He only need determine *if* these elements play a role in English sentences, and if so, how, that is, what rules describe them, what other elements they are related to, etc.

It is unquestionable that the form of the rules in each of the components is a linguistic universal, to be characterized in general linguistic theory. It is also quite likely, I believe, that some of the content of the various components is universal. That is, there are very probably universal rules, and many of the elements which occur in linguistic rules may be universally specified. In particular, there is much hope that the goal of traditional universal grammar, namely, the cross-linguistic characterization of notions like *noun, verb, adjective*, and *modifier*, can be given in general linguistic theory by limiting the specification to highly abstract underlying phrase markers rather than by attempting to give it in terms of superficial phrase markers wherein all previous attempts have failed.[15]

IMPLICATIONS

In the above sections we have given a quite informal discussion of some of the properties which must be attributed to adequate linguistic descriptions and the theory of language which underlies them. Unfortunately, there has been much confusion about the nature of the subject matter or domain which a linguistic description describes, and the relation between the output of such generative devices and actual speech behavior. This then requires brief discussion.

It must be emphasized that in no sense is a linguistic description an account of actual "verbal behavior." Even the grosser aspects of the descriptions of sentences provided by a linguistic description, the phonetic outputs of the phonological component, cannot be identified with real utterances of speakers. Any real utterance will, for example, contain features which provide information about the speaker's age, sex, health, emotional state, etc. And these features have obviously nothing to do with the *language* which the linguistic description characterizes. It is just these "nonlinguistic" features which differentiate different speakers of the same language and different "verbal performances" by the same speaker. But it is of course impossible to observe any actual utterances which do not contain such features. It is thus necessary to posit a relation of *representation* which holds between real utterances and the output of linguistic descriptions. The output for any sentence S_1 must be assumed to specify a set of phonetic conditions which any utterance must meet if it is to be an *instance* of S_1.

---

[15]For discussion of these matters, cf. Chomsky, *Fragment of English Syntax*.

However, the relation between actual speech behavior and the output of linguistic descriptions is by no means exhaustively described in the above way. It is evident that actual verbal performances contain an enormous number of utterances which do not in the strict sense represent any sentences at all. These are nonetheless perfectly adequate for communication and often more appropriate to the occasion than utterances which do represent full sentences. For example, in answer to questions such as (79)–(81)

(79)   *Where is the car?*

(80)   *Is John inside?*

(81)   *Who did it?*

one can hear such answers as *Inside, Yes, Bill.* It is evident that these utterances are understandable because in the context of the previous question they are understood as *versions* of the full sentences

(82)   *The car is inside.*

(83)   *Yes, John is inside.*

(84)   *Bill did it.*

It is only the full sentences that should be generated by the linguistic description proper which must draw the line between full sentences and fragments which can represent full sentences in particular environments. Part of the differentia of these two classes of utterances, utterances which directly represent full sentences, and those which do not but are still understandable, is that the former have a *fixed* finite set of semantic interpretations independently of all context, and their interpretation in any one context is simply a selection from among this fixed set. For fragments, however, occurrence in isolation permits no interpretation at all. And their interpretation in context is directly determined by, and does not involve an elimination of fixed interpretations inappropriate to, the context. Thus the fragments given above can as well be answers to (85)–(87) as to (79)–(81):

(85)   *Where did you leave your coat?*

(86)   *Can Hitler really be dead?*

(87)   *Who was clawed by the tiger?*

And in these cases the fragments must be understood as versions of

(88)   *I left my coat inside.*

(89)   *Yes, Hitler really can be dead.*

(90)   *Bill was clawed by the tiger.*

In short we see that sentence fragments of the type being discussed have no finitely fixed number of interpretations at all and in this way are radically distinct from utterances which directly represent full sentences. The utterances *Inside, Yes, Bill* have an infinite number of possible interpretations and can hence not be described *as such* by a finite linguistic description. To account for the understanding of fragments and many other kinds of utterances, suitable for communication in various contexts but distinct from full sentences, it is then evident that linguistic theory must provide a means for extending the description of full sentences to a class of *semi-sentences*. We can say little about this here besides noting that (*a*) it would be surprising if the apparatus for extension to semi-sentences was not an inherent property of human beings, hence cross-linguistic, and (*b*) it is obviously impossible to carry out research on the topic of semi-sentences independently of extensive knowledge of the properties of full sentences. And it is just this knowledge which the study of linguistic descriptions in the narrow sense is designed to yield. We conclude then that a linguistic description does not describe actual speech behavior but rather an indefinite class of highly structured (in three distinct though interrelated ways, syntactic, semantic, phonological) abstract objects, *sentences*, which define the *language* which in various ways underlies all speech behavior. A linguistic description is, in other words, a partial account of linguistic *competence*. To extend the characterization of this to an account of linguistic *performance* then requires a number of studies of various types of the way in which this underlying knowledge of linguistic rules is put to use.

The distinction between *competence* and *performance* or *language* and *speech* is quite crucial for understanding at least three goals related to linguistic descriptions proper, goals whose pursuit is crucial if a full account of the domain of language study is to be given. First, there is the task of constructing a *model of speech recognition*, that is, a model of the way speakers use their linguistic knowledge (language) to understand noises that they hear.[16] In terms of the above outline of linguistic structure, this task is the task of determining what sentence the noise represents and then determining the underlying structure of that sentence in order to determine its possible range of semantic interpretations.

When the above tasks have been carried out successfully, the context of the utterance must be applied in some way to pick the interpretation which was "intended." Almost nothing can be seriously said at the moment about this problem of contextual *disambiguation* of utterances beyond the obvious point that the problem cannot be seriously posed without understanding of the nature of language or linguistic structure. It appears that every piece of possible human knowledge about the world is relevant to the disambiguation of some sentence and thus to its understanding in context.[17] This has rather obvious implications of two sorts. On the one hand it shows that theoretically there can be no *general* theory of the way contexts serve to permit choice of one of several possible interpretations for some sentence, and on the other it shows that practical attempts to utilize linguistic research for the mechanical replacement of human performers (as in so-called "machine translation") are doomed to failure.

A third goal which is involved in a full linguistic account is the problem of formulating a *model for the speaker*. This must involve specification of how a desired *message* is given as input to the linguistic description to yield as output a phonetic representation which is the input to the speaker's speech apparatus, the output of this being the actual utterances.[18] It appears that the inputs to the

---

[16]For a discussion of models of speech recognition and speech production, cf. Noam Chomsky and G. A. Miller, "Finitary Models of Language Users," in *HMP*, and Katz and Postal, op. cit.

[17]This is argued in Katz and Fodor, "The Structure of a Semantic Theory."

[18]It is because this output is determined by other factors besides the phonetic representations which are the most superficial aspects of linguistic structure generated by the linguistic description that the latter cannot be said to generate any actual utterances. That is, given a fixed phonetic

linguistic description must be taken to be *semantic objects*, i.e. *readings* in the sense of our earlier brief discussion. But just as linguistic theory as such does not specify the relation of semantic markers to the nonlinguistic world, so also it cannot deal with the relations between a speaker's experiences, verbal or otherwise, and the utterances he produces. That is, it cannot deal with the fantastically complicated question of the *causation* of verbal behavior, although this is a task which modern psychology has too prematurely tried to deal with. Too prematurely, because it is obviously impossible to even *formulate* the problem of causation prior to an understanding of the character of speech behavior. And this, as we have seen, requires prior knowledge of the abstract *language* which underlies such behavior. Hence study of the causation of verbal behavior is two steps removed from reasonable possibility if attempted independently of the kind of studies discussed earlier.[19]

It should be obvious at this point that a linguistic description as such which *generates* sentences, i.e. highly abstract triples of syntactic, semantic, and phonological properties, is neither a model of the speaker or of the hearer although it is often confused with these. *Generation* is not *production* or *recognition*. A linguistic description simply characterizes the objects which a model of recognition must recover from verbal noise and which a model of production must encode into such noise. The study of linguistic descriptions per se is hence logically prior to the study of questions of recognition, contextual determination, production, and causation since it defines the objects in terms of which the problems with which these latter studies deal must be formulated.

Finally, the kind of conclusions reached above have obvious and important implications for any study of the problem of language learning. If, as we have argued, the structure of the sentences of natural languages involves an extremely complex and highly abstract set of entities related to actual utterances only by an extensive set of highly structured rules, it follows that the problem of language learning must be phrased in quite specific terms. That is, it is necessary to study the question of how an organism, equipped with a quite complex and *highly specific* characterization of the possible nature of a natural language, determines from various kinds of linguistic data, heard sentences, contexts, corrections, the particular manifestation of this abstract theory used in the community into which he was born. Again the primary constraint on the study of language learning is the logically prior knowledge of the character of the linguistic system which must be learned. And the more specific and detailed this knowledge can be made, that is, the more closely one can describe the general theory of linguistic descriptions

---

or pronunciation code as input to the speech apparatus, the output is also determined by such factors as the presence or absence of food in the oral cavity, the speaker's age, sex, state of health (cleft palate or not, etc.), degree of wakefulness or intoxication, etc. Facts like these are sufficient in themselves to demonstrate the futility of any view of language which cannot go beyond the gross observations of utterances to the abstract structures which underlie them, i.e. the futility of any view of language which identifies the significant linguistic objects with what can be obtained from tape recorders.

[19]For a fuller discussion of these points, cf. Noam Chomsky, "Review of *Verbal Behavior* by B. F. Skinner," *Language*, 35.26–58 (1959) [*SL*].

which amounts to a hypothesis about the innate genetic knowledge which the human child brings to language learning, the greater is the possibility of being able to formulate the techniques or strategies which the child uses to apply this inherent knowledge of possible linguistic structure to induce the details of a particular language from his linguistic experience. From what was said earlier about the abstract character of linguistic structure, underlying phrase markers, and the like, it is clear that enough is already known about the nature of language to show that views of language learning which restrict attention to the gross phonetic properties of utterances, either by adherence to psychological theories which do not countenance concepts more abstract and specific than "stimulus," "generalization," "chaining," "response," etc., or linguistic theories which do not countenance more than the kind of linguistic structure representable by final derived phrase markers, cannot teach us very much about the fantastic feat by which a child with almost no direct instruction learns that enormously extensive and complicated system which is a natural language, a system which has thus far defied the efforts of the best students to describe it in anything like a complete or adequate way.

I hope that the too brief and inadequate remarks of this final section will nonetheless have shown that the study of any aspect of language or linguistic behavior cannot hope to progress beyond superficialities if it is not based on firm knowledge of the character of the highly complex, abstract, finitely specifiable though infinite linguistic system which underlies all observable linguistic performances. In short, I hope to have shown that the results of generative linguistics are not an obscure oddity, of interest only to the specialist in linguistics, but rather provide the kind of knowledge which is prerequisite to the understanding of the domains of the entire range of language studies.

ADDITIONAL REFERENCES

Klima, Edward S., "Negation in English," in *SL*.

Lees, Robert B. (1960), *The Grammar of English Nominalizations*. Supplement to *International Journal of American Linguistics*, 26:3, Part II.

———— (1957), "Review of *Syntactic Structures* by N. Chomsky." *Language*, 33.375–408.

Matthews, G. H. (1965), *Hidatsa Syntax*. The Hague: Mouton & Co.

4

Justification of Grammars

NOAM CHOMSKY

Before entering directly into an investigation of the syntactic component of a generative grammar, it is important to give some thought to several methodological questions of justification and adequacy.

There is, first of all, the question of how one is to obtain information about the speaker-hearer's competence, about his knowledge of the language. Like most facts of interest and importance, this is neither presented for direct observation nor extractable from data by inductive procedures of any known sort. Clearly, the actual data of linguistic performance will provide much evidence for determining the correctness of hypotheses about underlying linguistic structure, along with introspective reports (by the native speaker, or the linguist who has learned the language). This is the position that is universally adopted in practice, although there are methodological discussions that seem to imply a reluctance to use observed performance or introspective reports as evidence for some underlying reality.

In brief, it is unfortunately the case that no adequate formalizable techniques are known for obtaining reliable information concerning the facts of linguistic structure (nor is this particularly surprising). There are, in other words, very few reliable experimental or data-processing procedures for obtaining significant information concerning the linguistic intuition of the native speaker. It is important to bear in mind that when an operational procedure is proposed, it must be tested for adequacy (exactly as a theory of linguistic intuition—a grammar—must be tested for adequacy) by measuring it against the standard provided by the tacit knowledge that it attempts to specify and describe. Thus a proposed operational test for, say, segmentation into words, must meet the empirical condition of conforming, in a mass of crucial and clear cases, to the linguistic intuition of the native speaker concerning such elements. Otherwise, it is without value. The same, obviously, is true in the case of any proposed operational procedure or any proposed grammatical description. If operational procedures were available that met this test, we might be justified in relying on their results in unclear and difficult cases. This remains a hope for the future rather than a present reality, however. This is the objective situation of present-day linguistic work; allusions to presumably well-known "procedures of elicitation" or "objective methods" simply obscure the actual situation in which linguistic work must, for the present, proceed. Furthermore, there is no reason to expect that reliable operational criteria for the deeper and more important theoretical notions of linguistics (such as "grammaticalness" and "paraphrase") will ever be forthcoming.

Even though few reliable operational procedures have been developed, the theoretical (that is, grammatical) investigation of the knowledge of the native speaker can proceed perfectly well. The critical problem for grammatical theory today is not a paucity of evidence but rather the inadequacy of present theories of language to account for masses of evidence that are hardly open to serious question. The problem for the grammarian is to construct a description and, where possible, an explanation for the enormous mass of unquestionable data concerning the linguistic intuition of the native speaker (often, himself); the problem for one concerned with operational procedures is to develop tests that give the correct results and make relevant distinctions. Neither the study of grammar nor the attempt to develop useful tests is hampered by lack of evidence with which to check results, for the present. We may hope that these efforts will converge, but they must obviously converge on the tacit knowledge of the native speaker if they are to be of any significance.

One may ask whether the necessity for present-day linguistics to give such priority to introspective evidence and to the linguistic intuition of the native speaker excludes it from the domain of science. The answer to this essentially terminological question seems to have no bearing at all on any serious issue. At most, it determines how we shall denote the kind of research that can be effectively carried out in the present state of our technique and understanding. However, this terminological question actually does relate to a different issue of some interest, namely the question whether the important feature of the successful sciences has been their search for insight or their concern for objectivity. The social and behavioral sciences provide ample evidence that objectivity can be pursued with little consequent gain in insight and understanding. On the other hand, a good case can be made for the view that the natural sciences have, by and large, sought objectivity primarily insofar as it is a tool for gaining insight (for providing phenomena that can suggest or test deeper explanatory hypotheses).

In any event, at a given stage of investigation, one whose concern is for insight and understanding (rather than for objectivity as a goal in itself) must ask whether or to what extent a wider range and more exact description of phenomena is relevant to solving the problems that he faces. In linguistics, it seems to me that sharpening of the data by more objective tests is a matter of small importance for the problems at hand. One who disagrees with this estimate of the present situation in linguistics can justify his belief in the current importance of more objective operational tests by showing how they can lead to new and deeper understanding of linguistic structure. Perhaps the day will come when the kinds of data that we now can obtain in abundance will be insufficient to resolve deeper questions concerning the structure of language. However, many questions that can realistically and significantly be formulated today do not demand evidence of a kind that is unavailable or unattainable without significant improvements in objectivity of experimental technique.

Although there is no way to avoid the traditional assumption that the speaker-hearer's linguistic intuition is the ultimate standard that determines the accuracy of any proposed grammar, linguistic theory, or operational test, it must be emphasized, once again, that this tacit knowledge may very well not be immediately available to the user of the language. To eliminate what has seemed to some an air of paradox in this remark, let me illustrate with a few examples.

If a sentence such as *Flying planes can be dangerous* is presented in an appropriately constructed context, the listener will interpret it immediately in a unique way, and will fail to detect the ambiguity. In fact, he may reject the second interpretation, when this is pointed out to him, as forced or unnatural (independently of which interpretation he originally selected under contextual pressure). Nevertheless, his intuitive knowledge of the language is clearly such that both of the interpretations (corresponding to *Flying planes are dangerous* and *Flying planes is dangerous*) are assigned to the sentence by the grammar he has internalized in some form.

In the case just mentioned, the ambiguity may be fairly transparent. But consider such a sentence as

(5)   *I had a book stolen.*

Few hearers may be aware of the fact that their internalized grammar in fact provides at least three structural descriptions for this sentence. Nevertheless, this fact can be brought to consciousness by consideration of slight elaborations of sentence (5), for example: (i) *I had a book stolen from my car when I stupidly left the window open*, that is, *Someone stole a book from my car*; (ii) *I had a book stolen from his library by a professional thief who I hired to do the job*, that is, *I had someone steal a book*; (iii) *I almost had a book stolen, but they caught me leaving the library with it*, that is, *I had almost succeeded in stealing a book*. In bringing to consciousness the triple ambiguity of (5) in this way, we present no new information to the hearer and teach him nothing new about his language but simply arrange matters in such a way that his linguistic intuition, previously obscured, becomes evident to him.

As a final illustration, consider the sentences

(6)   *I persuaded John to leave.*

(7)   *I expected John to leave.*

The first impression of the hearer may be that these sentences receive the same structural analysis. Even fairly careful thought may fail to show him that his internalized grammar assigns very different syntactic descriptions to these sentences. In fact, so far as I have been able to discover, no English grammar has pointed out the fundamental distinction between these two constructions (in particular, my own sketches of English grammar in 1955, 1962, failed to note this).* However, it is clear that the sentences (6) and (7) are not parallel in structure. The difference can be brought out by consideration of the sentences

(8)(i) *I persuaded a specialist to examine John.*
(ii) *I persuaded John to be examined by a specialist.*
(9)(i) *I expected a specialist to examine John.*
(ii) *I expected John to be examined by a specialist.*

The sentences (9i) and (9ii) are "cognitively synonymous": one is true if and only if the other is true. But no variety of even weak paraphrase holds between (8i) and (8ii). Thus (8i) can be true or false quite independently of the truth or falsity of (8ii). Whatever difference of connotation or "topic" or emphasis one may find between (9i) and (9ii) is just the difference that exists between the active sentence *A specialist will examine John* and its passive counterpart *John will be examined by a specialist.* This is not at all the case with respect to (8), however. In fact, the underlying deep structure for (6) and (8ii) must show that *John* is the direct object of the verb phrase as well as the grammatical subject of the embedded sentence. Furthermore, in (8ii) *John* is the logical direct object of the embedded sentence, whereas in (8i) the phrase *a specialist* is the direct object of the verb phrase and the logical subject of the embedded sentence. In (7), (9i), and (9ii), however, the noun phrases *John, a specialist,* and *John,* respectively, have no grammatical functions other than those that are internal to the embedded sentence; in particular, *John* is the logical direct object and *a specialist* the logical subject in the embedded sentences of (9). Thus the underlying deep structures for (8i), (8ii), (9i), and (9ii) are, respectively, the following:[1]

(10)(i) *Noun Phrase – Verb – Noun Phrase – Sentence*
      (*I – persuaded – a specialist – a specialist will examine John*)
(ii) *Noun Phrase – Verb – Noun Phrase – Sentence*
      (*I – persuaded – John – a specialist will examine John*)
(11)(i) *Noun Phrase – Verb – Sentence*
      (*I – expected – a specialist will examine John*)
(ii) *Noun Phrase – Verb – Sentence*
      (*I – expected – a specialist will examine John*)

In the case of (10ii) and (11ii), the passive transformation will apply to the embedded sentence, and in all four cases other operations will give the final surface

---

*[Noam Chomsky, *The Logical Structure of Linguistic Theory*, mimeographed, M.I.T. Library, Cambridge, Mass., 1955; Noam Chomsky, "A Transformational Approach to Syntax," in A. A. Hill, ed., *Third Texas Conference on Problems of Linguistic Analysis in English*, May 9–12, 1958 (Austin: University of Texas Press, 1962), pp. 124–158, *SL*.]

[1]These descriptions are not fully accurate. In fact, the sentential complement in (10) should, more properly, be regarded as embedded in a prepositional phrase (cf. [*Aspects of the Theory of Syntax*] Chapter 3); and, as Peter Rosenbaum has pointed out, the sentential complement of (11) should be regarded as embedded in the noun phrase object of *expect*. Furthermore, the treatment of the verbal auxiliaries in (10) and (11) is incorrect, and there are other modifications relating to the marking of the passive transformation, to which we shall return in [*Aspects of the Theory of Syntax*, Chapter 2].

forms of (8) and (9). The important point in the present connection is that (8i) differs from (8ii) in underlying structure, although (9i) and (9ii) are essentially the same in underlying structure. This accounts for the difference in meaning. Notice, in support of this difference in analysis, that we can have *I persuaded John that* (*of the fact that*) *Sentence*, but not *I expected John that* (*of the fact that*) *Sentence*.

The example (6)–(7) serves to illustrate two important points. First, it shows how unrevealing surface structure may be as to underlying deep structure. Thus (6) and (7) are the same in surface structure, but very different in the deep structure that underlies them and determines their semantic interpretations. Second, it illustrates the elusiveness of the speaker's tacit knowledge. Until such examples as (8) and (9) are adduced, it may not be in the least clear to a speaker of English that the grammar that he has internalized in fact assigns very different syntactic analyses to the superficially analogous sentences (6) and (7).

In short, we must be careful not to overlook the fact that surface similarities may hide underlying distinctions of a fundamental nature, and that it may be necessary to guide and draw out the speaker's intuition in perhaps fairly subtle ways before we can determine what is the actual character of his knowledge of his language or of anything else. Neither point is new (the former is a commonplace of traditional linguistic theory and analytic philosophy; the latter is as old as Plato's *Meno*); both are too often overlooked.

A grammar can be regarded as a theory of a language; it is *descriptively adequate* to the extent that it correctly describes the intrinsic competence of the idealized native speaker. The structural descriptions assigned to sentences by the grammar, the distinctions that it makes between well-formed and deviant, and so on, must, for descriptive adequacy, correspond to the linguistic intuition of the native speaker (whether or not he may be immediately aware of this) in a substantial and significant class of crucial cases.

A linguistic theory must contain a definition of "grammar," that is, a specification of the class of potential grammars. We may, correspondingly, say that a *linguistic theory* is descriptively adequate if it makes a descriptively adequate grammar available for each natural language.

Although even descriptive adequacy on a large scale is by no means easy to approach, it is crucial for the productive development of linguistic theory that much higher goals than this be pursued. To facilitate the clear formulation of deeper questions, it is useful to consider the abstract problem of constructing an "acquisition model" for language, that is, a theory of language learning or grammar construction. Clearly, a child who has learned a language has developed an internal representation of a system of rules that determine how sentences are to be formed, used, and understood. Using the term "grammar" with a systematic ambiguity (to refer, first, to the native speaker's internally represented "theory of his language" and, second, to the linguist's account of this), we can say that the child has developed and internally represented a generative grammar, in the sense described. He has done this on the basis of observation of what we may call *primary linguistic data*. This must include examples of linguistic performance that are taken to be well-formed sentences, and may include also examples designated as nonsentences, and no doubt much other information of the sort that is required for language learning, whatever this may be (see [*Aspects of the Theory of Syntax*] pp. 31–32). On the basis of such data, the child constructs a grammar—that is, a theory of the language of which the well-formed sentences of the primary linguistic data constitute a small sample.[2] To learn a language, then, the child must have a method for devising an appropriate grammar, given primary linguistic data. As a precondition for language learning, he must possess, first, a linguistic theory that specifies the form of the grammar of a possible human language, and, second, a strategy for selecting a grammar of the appropriate form that is compatible with the primary linguistic data. As a long-range task for general linguistics, we might set the problem of developing an account of this innate linguistic theory that provides the basis for language learning. (Note that we are again using the term "theory"—in this case "theory of language" rather than "theory of a particular language"—with a systematic ambiguity, to refer both to the child's innate predisposition to learn a language of a certain type and to the linguist's account of this.)

To the extent that a linguistic theory succeeds in selecting a descriptively adequate grammar on the basis of primary linguistic data, we can say that it meets the condition of *explanatory adequacy*. That is, to this extent, it offers an explanation for the intuition of the native speaker on the basis of an empirical hypothesis concerning the innate predisposition of the child to develop a certain kind of theory to deal with the evidence presented to him. Any such hypothesis can be falsified (all too easily, in actual fact) by showing that it fails to provide a descriptively adequate grammar for primary linguistic data from some other language— evidently the child is not predisposed to learn one language rather than another. It is supported when it does provide an adequate explanation for some aspect of linguistic structure, an account of the way in which such knowledge might have been obtained.

Clearly, it would be utopian to expect to achieve explanatory adequacy on a large scale in the present state of linguistics. Nevertheless, considerations of explanatory adequacy are often critical for advancing linguistic theory. Gross coverage of a large mass of data can often be attained by conflicting theories; for precisely this reason it is not, in itself, an achievement of any particular theoretical interest or importance. As in any other field, the important problem in linguistics is to discover a complex of data that differentiates between conflicting conceptions of linguistic structure in that one of these conflicting theories can describe these

---

[2]It seems clear that many children acquire first or second languages quite successfully even though no special care is taken to teach them and no special attention is given to their progress. It also seems apparent that much of the actual speech observed consists of fragments and deviant expressions of a variety of sorts. Thus it seems that a child must have the ability to "invent" a generative grammar that defines well-formedness and assigns interpretations to sentences even though the primary linguistic data that he uses as a basis for this act of theory construction may, from the point of view of the theory he constructs, be deficient in various respects. In general, there is an important element of truth in the traditional view that "the pains which everyone finds in conversation . . . is not to comprehend what another thinketh, but to extricate his thought from the signs or words which often agree not with it" (Cordemoy [*A Philosophical Discourse Concerning Speech*] 1667 [The English translation is dated 1668.]), and the problem this poses for speech perception is magnified many times for the language learner.

data only by *ad hoc* means whereas the other can explain it on the basis of some empirical assumption about the form of language. Such small-scale studies of explanatory adequacy have, in fact, provided most of the evidence that has any serious bearing on the nature of linguistic structure. Thus whether we are comparing radically different theories of grammar or trying to determine the correctness of some particular aspect of one such theory, it is questions of explanatory adequacy that must, quite often, bear the burden of justification. This remark is in no way inconsistent with the fact that explanatory adequacy on a large scale is out of reach, for the present. It simply brings out the highly tentative character of any attempt to justify an empirical claim about linguistic structure.

To summarize briefly, there are two respects in which one can speak of "justifying a generative grammar." On one level (that of descriptive adequacy), the grammar is justified to the extent that it correctly describes its object, namely the linguistic intuition—the tacit competence—of the native speaker. In this sense, the grammar is justified on *external* grounds, on grounds of correspondence to linguistic fact. On a much deeper and hence much more rarely attainable level (that of explanatory adequacy), a grammar is justified to the extent that it is a *principled* descriptively adequate system, in that the linguistic theory with which it is associated selects this grammar over others, given primary linguistic data with which all are compatible. In this sense, the grammar is justified on *internal* grounds, on grounds of its relation to a linguistic theory that constitutes an explanatory hypothesis about the form of language as such. The problem of internal justification—of explanatory adequacy—is essentially the problem of constructing a theory of language acquisition, an account of the specific innate abilities that make this achievement possible.

5

Questions of Linguistics

MORRIS HALLE

We begin our consideration of the linguist's approach to the problem of speech communication by inquiring into the nature of the data that constitute the subject matter of linguistics. We want to know what kind of problems are of special interest to the linguist, for only if we understand this will we be in a position to appreciate the reasons for the ways of the linguist which frequently seem strange to the outsider.

As a first answer it might be proposed that linguistics is concerned with characterizing the class of acoustical signals which men make in speaking. The natural way of going about this would be by investigating in detail the anatomical structures in man that make it possible for him to emit this special set of signals. One would investigate the human vocal tract: the larynx, the pharynx, the nasal cavity, the mouth, the tongue, the lips, etc., and one would attempt to make statements about the motor capabilities of these organs. Once one had learned all there is to know about these physiological aspects of the problem, and, provided one knew a great deal of acoustics, one could give the desired description of the acoustical signals which such a mechanism was capable of emitting. One might further investigate the analogous mechanisms in other animals and might succeed in showing how the latter differ from those of man and how this difference accounts for the differences in the respective acoustical outputs. The results of this inquiry would explain why the acoustical signals emitted by men in speaking differ from those of other animals.

This is a very important area of study, and linguistics is vitally interested in these questions. Yet these questions do not exhaust the problems of concern

---

Reprinted from the supplement to *Il Nuovo Cimento*, Serie X, 13.494–503 (1959), by permission of Morris Halle and the Società Italiana di Fisica. This selection includes the Introduction and Part I of the original article; the remainder is reprinted in revised form as "On the Bases of Phonology" in *SL*.

to the linguist: they are but a small part of the puzzles that the linguist would like to solve. As a matter of fact, if linguistics were limited to a consideration of these problems, there would hardly be any need for a separate discipline, since all of the above problems are dealt with by physiology and acoustics.

What makes linguistics as a field of enquiry quite different from physiological acoustics is the fact that what is commonly referred to as "linguistic behavior" covers a much broader area than the acoustical properties of speech, though —as I have already said—it specifically includes the latter. Let me now describe a few of these additional problems.

We have all had the experience of hearing people speak with a foreign accent. Thus, for instance, we all know people who are physiologically normal, who yet find it difficult to distinguish sounds that we ourselves have no difficulty whatever in distinguishing. For instance, no English speaker would ever confuse the words *bitch* and *beach*—not even under conditions of high noise, as G.A. Miller has shown. Yet a speaker of Russian or Italian would find it extremely difficult to keep them consistently apart. Clearly the difference in the behavior of English and foreign speakers is not physiologically determined, because the foreigner can—when his attention is drawn to it—make the required distinction. The difference in behavior is, of course, due to the fact that English, Russian, and Italian are different languages, and that different languages use different sounds.

It may, therefore, be proposed that adult speakers have established a particular behavior pattern of their vocal organs and that this behavior pattern accounts for the observed difficulty. Differences in language may therefore be equated with different habitual movements of the tongue and lips and with different coordinations of these movements. In other words, one might conceivably explain linguistic differences on a physiological-acoustical basis, provided one allowed for some learning.

This, however, is not really an adequate explanation. Consider, for instance, the manner in which Latin is spoken by priests of different nationalities. An English-speaking priest may read mass with a sound repertory that is one hundred per cent English, and a French priest may read the same mass with a sound repertory that is one hundred per cent French. Yet there is no sense to the statement that the language of the mass is anything but Latin.

An attempt may still be made to save the view of language as a purely physiological-acoustical phenomenon by saying that, for example, the English priest uses the sounds of English with the statistics appropriate for Latin. This, however, is hardly a good solution since it raises a host of extremely difficult problems. For example, it raises the question of how it is possible to identify an utterance as English on the basis of a very short sample, which might be totally atypical. But even if this were possible, there are aspects of linguistic behavior which cannot be explained in terms of physiology and acoustics alone, regardless of the refinements introduced. I shall now give a few examples of this.

A joke quite popular among elementary school children in America is the following question and answer: *Why can't one starve in the desert? — Because of the sand which is there!* The pun is based on the fact that word boundaries are not always marked acoustically, and *sand which is* is frequently indistinguishable from *sandwiches*. Yet word boundaries are crucial in understanding the message correctly, and given enough context the speaker of English will know how to assign word boundaries even if they are not acoustically marked.

Word boundaries, moreover, are not the only boundaries which have no acoustical signal and which affect the behavior of the speaker. Consider the following ambiguities:

old | *men and women*   old men | *and women*
He rolled | *over the carpet.*   *He rolled over* | *the carpet.*

which are due to differences in phrase structure that are not marked acoustically.

I should like also to draw attention to another type of behavior. Every speaker of a language can perform rather elaborate transformations upon sentences. Thus, for instance, given a simple declarative sentence there is a standard way of converting it into a *yes/no* question; or given an active sentence there is a standard way for converting it into a passive. As an illustration of the latter take the sentence *A committee opposed the change in the bill*, which can be readily transformed into *The change in the bill was opposed by a committee*. In order to explain how to perform this operation we would normally use such terms as *noun phrase, verb phrase, transitive verb*, etc., in the obvious way. It is important to note, however, that here, too, there is no such thing as an acoustical signal for these categories, yet the categories are essential in order to explain the speaker's behavior.

Consider again the sentence *The change in the bill was opposed by a committee*. The choice of *was* as against *were* is governed by the number (singular or plural) of the head of the first noun phrase, i.e. *change*. But the head of the noun phrase, which itself is a noun phrase, does not have any acoustical marker to distinguish it from other noun phrases.

It must also be noted that the head of the noun phrase governs the choice of *was* as against *were* quite independently of the number of intervening words, e.g. *The change in the bill for the promotion of the study of the mating calls of rhinoceri. . . etc. . . **was** opposed by a committee.*

Engineers and other nonlinguists have usually neglected problems of the kind just surveyed, considering them either outside of their ken or relatively unimportant refinements. Linguists, on the other hand, have been keenly interested in such problems. The standard grammars of the different languages always try to do something towards solving such problems. Unfortunately the standard grammars fail to be consistent or to make clear the basis on which they operate. In what follows I shall try to present in outline a descriptive framework for language which I believe to be free of, at least, the most glaring of these failings. The exposition will begin with a review of some. . .work of N. Chomsky. . . .

According to Chomsky every language has three distinct sets of rules which operate on three different levels. On the highest level the rules are all of the type $X \to Y$ where $X \to Y$ stands for "replace X by Y," with the restriction that not more than a single symbol can be replaced in a single rule and that $X \neq Y$.

As an illustration of these rules we can take the following:[1]

---

[1] In applying a rule the symbols in parentheses may be omitted. The rules are only partially identical with those that would appear in an actual grammar of English.

(1)   *Sentence → Noun Phrase + Verb Phrase + (Adverbial Phrase)*

(2)   *Noun Phrase → (Article) + Noun + (Prepositional Phrase)*

(3)   *Verb Phrase → Verb + (Noun Phrase)*

(4)(a)   *Adverbial Phrase → Adverb*

  (b)   *Adverbial Phrase → Prepositional Phrase*

(5)   *Prepositional Phrase → Preposition + Noun Phrase*

(6)(a)   *Article → the*

  (b)   *Article → a*

(7)(a)   *Noun → committee*

  (b)   *Noun → change*

  (c)   *Noun → dog*

  (d)   *Noun → walk*

  (e)   *Noun → result*

  (f)   *Noun → bill*

(8)(a)   *Verb → opposed*

  (b)   *Verb → took*

  (c)   *Verb → barked*

(9)(a)   *Preposition → of*

  (b)   *Preposition → for*

  (c)   *Preposition → in*

The application of these rules yields a partially ordered set of symbol sequences. We shall call each symbol sequence a *string*, and the set of such strings generated by the rules a *derivation*. We may illustrate the process of applying the phrase structure rules by the following derivation:

Sentence	
Noun Phrase + Verb Phrase	(by rule (1))
Article + Noun + Verb Phrase	(by (2))
Article + Noun + Verb + Noun Phrase	(by (3))
Article + Noun + Verb + Article + Noun + Prepositional Phrase	(by (2))
Article + Noun + Verb + Article + Noun + Preposition + Noun Phrase	(by (5))
Article + Noun + Verb + Article + Noun + Preposition + Article + Noun	
	(by (2))

    A committee opposed the change in the bill.

            (By (6b), (7a), (8a), (6a), (7b), (9c), (6a), (7f))

Attention must be drawn to the following facets of the grammar just presented:

(*a*)   The order of application of the rules is partly fixed owing to the fact that a given rule can be applied only if the symbol to be replaced—i.e. the one appearing on the left-hand side of the rule—appears in the derivation. There must, therefore, be at least one *initial* symbol which must be supplied to the grammar from the outside and which starts things off. For the present set of rules the symbol *Sentence* will serve this function.

(*b*)   In order for the grammar to continue to operate it is necessary that instructions be provided for selecting the next rule to be applied. The instructions must be supplied from the outside. It is by exercising a choice, by selecting one rule from a set of possible alternatives that information is being transmitted. This choice must evidently be made by the user of the grammar, for only he can transmit information.

(*c*)   The grammar continues to operate as long as the string contains symbols which themselves appear on the left-hand side of one or more rules. The grammar stops operating when it has produced a string consisting of symbols which occur only on the right-hand side of the rules—e.g. *opposed* in rule (8a)—and hence are "irreplaceable." We shall call these irreplaceable symbols *terminal symbols;* strings consisting of terminal symbols only shall be called *terminal strings.*

It is always possible to convert a derivation into a tree like the one below.

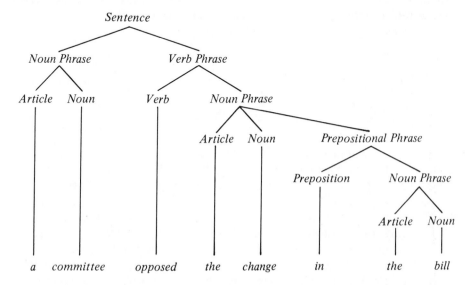

The tree may be familiar to some readers from their school days. It represents what is commonly known as "parsing" or "diagramming" or "immediate con-stituent analysis" of the sentence. It contains at least a partial answer to the question of whence come the boundaries which in spite of their possible lack of acoustical correlates are nevertheless important factors in the behavior of speakers.

The restriction on the number of symbols that can be rewritten in a single rule guarantees that given a terminal string—i.e. a string produced by the application of the phrase structure rules—it will be possible to discover the associated tree or trees. Since not more than one symbol can be rewritten in a single rule, every line in the derivation must have at least as many symbols as the one preceding it. Since repetitions of lines in the derivation are not admitted, there must be a finite number of lines between the first line and the terminal string. One can, therefore, try out all one-line derivations, two-line derivations, three-line derivations, etc., until one comes upon a derivation having the desired terminal string.

Since there may be more than one derivation yielding the same terminal string, there may be more than one tree associated with a single terminal string. The fact that some terminal strings have more than one phrase structure representation accounts for the ambiguity of phrases like *old men and women, He rolled over the carpet*, etc.

By repeated reapplication of rules (2) and (5) endless sequences of words may be generated. This is not an oversight but rather a reflection of the fact mentioned above that language places no upper bound on the length of sentences or of constituents, although all sentences are finite in length.

We have made much of the fact that terminal strings have phrase structure. It is now necessary to point out that terminal strings are abstract representations of certain features of sentences and that actual sentences are, in fact, not terminal strings. To see this, consider the English verb. Since verbs can be in the present tense as well as in the past we introduce a rule like the following:

(3a)   *Verb Phrase → Verb + (Past) + (Noun Phrase)*[2]

We would then also need rules like

(10)(a)   *oppose + Past → opposed*
   (b)   *write + Past → wrote*
   (c)   *have + Past → had*
   (d)   *think + Past → thought*
   (e)   *be + Past → was*

Rule (10a) is within the restrictions imposed on phrase structure rules, for it requires in effect that the symbol *Past* be replaced by *-d*. The other four rules, however, violate the phrase structure constraints. For example, in (10b) the two symbols *write* and *Past* are replaced by *wrote* in one step, and it is impossible to achieve the same result if only a single symbol were allowed to be replaced in a single rule. Consequently, rules (10b) to (10e) are beyond the power of the phrase structure level. Since all verbs violating the phrase structure constraints belong to the so-called "strong" or "irregular" verbs of English it may be proposed that these verbs be handled as exceptions; there would then be no need to utilize more powerful devices in the grammar. We shall see, however, that the phrase structure grammar is not powerful enough to handle other, perfectly regular verbal formations in a reasonably economical fashion. The proposal to consider the "strong" verbs as exceptions is therefore of little practical importance.

Consider now the verb phrases

had opposed	*was opposing*	*had been opposing*
had written	*was writing*	*had been writing*
had had	*was having*	*had been having*
had thought	*was thinking*	*had been thinking*
had been	*was being*	*had been being*

In order to generate the examples in the first column we should need the rule

(3b)   *Verb Phrase → have + (Past) + Verb + Perfect Participle + (Noun Phrase)*

as well as

(11)(a)   *oppose + Perfect Participle → opposed*
   (b)   *write + Perfect Participle → written*

---

[2]We are disregarding the problems raised by number and person.

(c)   *have + Perfect Participle → had*
(d)   *think + Perfect Participle → thought*
(e)   *be + Perfect Participle → been*

In order to generate the examples of the second column we should need the following rules:

(3c)   *Verb Phrase → be + (Past) + Verb + Present Participle + (Noun Phrase)*

and

(12)   *Verb + Present Participle → Verb + -ing*

Finally in order to generate the examples in the third column we need the following additional rule:

(3d)   *Verb Phrase → have + (Past) + be + Perfect Participle + Verb + Present
Participle + (Noun Phrase)*

This rule, however, is the sum of rules (3a–c). It is, therefore, natural to investigate whether the set of rules cannot be simplified. Examining rules (3a–d) we note the following regularities:

(*a*)   The symbol *Past* is always associated with the first element of the *Verb Phrase*.

(*b*)   If the *Verb Phrase* contains the auxiliary verb *have* the symbol *Perfect Participle* appears after the next element of the *Verb Phrase*.

(*c*)   If the *Verb Phrase* contains the auxiliary verb *be*, the symbol *Present Participle* appears after the next element of the *Verb Phrase*.

(*d*)   If both auxiliary verbs *have* and *be* occur in the same *Verb Phrase, have* precedes *be*.

(*e*)   The only element which must appear in the *Verb Phrase* is (the main) *Verb*.

(*f*)   The auxiliary verbs precede (the main) *Verb*.

The simplest way of handling these regularities is by positing the following two rules:

(3′)   *Verb Phrase → (Past) + (have + Perfect Participle) + (be + Present Participle)
+ Verb + (Noun Phrase)*

and

(Z) $G + V → V + G$

where *V* stands for any specific verb (lexical morpheme) like *oppose, have, be, think*, etc., and *G* stands for a grammatical operator like *Perfect Participle, Past*, etc.

Rule (Z) goes clearly beyond phrase structure, for it changes the order of the symbols, and once the order of the symbols in the strings is changed, there is no longer any possibility of associating a tree with a string. We are, therefore, faced with the alternative of either maintaining the phrase structure restriction and thereby greatly complicating our description—for example, we would be forced to have four separate rules in place of the single rule (3′)—or of admitting into the grammar new rules that are more powerful than those of the phrase structure level. There are various reasons why the latter alternative is to be preferred. Accordingly we establish a second grammatical level, which, following Chomsky, we call the *transformational level*.

It is not possible here to go into the details of the transformational level. These can be found in Chomsky's book *Syntactic Structures*. I should like, however, to draw attention to a few consequences of the decision to introduce the transformational rules.

Since rule (Z) must precede rules like (10) and (11), the latter together with (Z) are part of the transformational level. This makes it unnecesary to do anything special about the "strong" verbs (rules (10b–d), since on the transformational level the prohibition against replacing more than one symbol in a single rule does not hold.

The terminal strings, the final output of the phrase structure rules, will contain symbols of two types: lexical morphemes like *oppose, committee, of, the*, etc., and grammatical operators like *Past, Perfect Participle*, etc. This is due to the fact that at least some grammatical operators cannot be replaced by phrase structure rules; for example, *Past* is replaced in rules (10a–e), which are, however, transformational and not phrase structure rules.

The terminal string corresponding to our sample sentence is therefore represented, with some simplifications and omissions, as follows:

a + *committee* + *Past* + *oppose* + *the* + *change* + *in* + *the* + *bill*

The transformational rules operate on terminal strings *and* the trees associated with them. The notion "head of noun phrase" which we have had occasion to use in the above discussion has an obvious and simple meaning if reference is made to the tree associated with the particular noun phrase. It is a matter of considerable difficulty to give a clear meaning to this notion if one limits oneself only to the terminal string.

6

Some Transformations in English

NOAM CHOMSKY

7.1. . . . To specify a transformation explicitly we must describe the analysis of the strings to which it applies and the structural change that it effects on these strings.[1] Thus, the passive transformation applies to strings of the form $NP - Aux - V - NP$ and has the effect of interchanging the two noun phrases, adding *by* before the final noun phrase, and adding $be + en$ to *Aux* (Cf. (34)).* Consider now the introduction of *not* or *n't* into the auxiliary verb phrase.† The simplest way to

---

Reprinted from Noam Chomsky, *Syntactic Structures* (The Hague: Mouton & Co., 1957), Chap. 7, pp. 61–84, by permission of Noam Chomsky and Mouton & Co. The first paragraph of this chapter has been omitted, as well as a number of cross references.

[1]For a more detailed discussion of the specification of transformations in general and of specific transformations, see my "Three Models for the Description of Language," *I.R.E. Transactions on Information Theory*, Vol. IT-2, Proceedings of the Symposium on Information Theory, September 1956 [*RMP*]; *The Logical Structure of Linguistic Theory*, mimeographed, M.I.T. Library, Cambridge, Mass., 1955; *Transformational Analysis*, Ph.D. dissertation, University of Pennsylvania, 1955. See Zellig S. Harris, "Co-occurrence and Transformation in Linguistic Structure," *Language*, 33.283–340 (1957) [*SL*], for a somewhat different approach to transformational analysis.

*[*Syntactic Structures*, p. 43]

(34)   If S_1 is a grammatical sentence of the form

$NP_1 - Aux - V - NP_2$,

then the corresponding string of the form

$NP_2 - Aux + be + en - V - by + NP_1$

is also a grammatical sentence.

For example, if *John – C – admire – sincerity* is a sentence, then *sincerity – C + be + en – admire – by + John* (which [ultimately] becomes *Sincerity is admired by John*) is also a sentence.

†[The rules that develop the verb phrase are the following (*Syntactic Structures*, pp. 39–40). Note that, given rule (34), the element $be + en$ can be dropped from rule (28iii), since it is now introduced transformationally.]

(28) (i) $Verb \rightarrow Aux + V$

(ii) $V \rightarrow$ *hit, take, walk, read*, etc.

(iii) $Aux \rightarrow C(M)(have + en)(be + ing)(be + en)$

describe negation is by means of a transformation which applies before (29ii) and introduces *not* or *n't* after the second morpheme of the phrase given by (28iii) if this phrase contains at least two morphemes, or after the first morpheme of this phrase if it contains only one. Thus this transformation T_{not} operates on strings that are analyzed into three segments in one of the following ways:

(37)(i) $NP - C - V \ldots$
  (ii) $NP - C + M - \ldots$
 (iii) $NP - C + have - \ldots$
 (iv) $NP - C + be - \ldots$

where the symbols are as in (28), (29), and it is immaterial what stands in place of the dots. Given a string analyzed into three segments in one of these ways, T_{not} adds *not* (or *n't*) after the second segment of the string. For example, applied to the terminal string *they* $- \emptyset + can - come$ (an instance of (37ii)), T_{not} gives *they* $- \emptyset + can + n't - come$ (ultimately, *They can't come*); applied to *they* $- \emptyset + have - en + come$ (an instance of (37iii)), it gives *they* $- \emptyset + have + n't - en$

  (iv) $M \to$ *will, can, may, shall, must*

(29) (i) $C \to \begin{Bmatrix} S \text{ in the context } NP_{Sing}\underline{\quad} \\ \emptyset \text{ in the context } NP_{Pl}\underline{\quad} \\ Past \end{Bmatrix}$

  (ii)   Let *Af* stand for any of the affixes *Past, S*, $\emptyset$, *en, ing*. Let *v* stand for any *M* or *V*, or *have* or *be* (i.e. for any nonaffix in the phrase *Verb*). Then
$$Af + v \to v + Af \#$$
where $\#$ is interpreted as word boundary.[a]
 (iii)   Replace $+$ by $\#$ except in the context $v \underline{\quad} Af$. Insert $\#$ initially and finally.

The interpretation of the notations in (28iii) is as follows: we must choose the element C, and we may choose zero or more of the parenthesized elements in the given order. In (29i) we may develop C into any of three morphemes, observing the contextual restrictions given. As an example of the application of these rules, we construct a derivation . . . omitting the initial steps.

(30)   *the* $+$ *man* $+$ *Verb* $+$ *the* $+$ *book*
    the $+$ *man* $+$ *Aux* $+$ *V* $+$ *the* $+$ *book*   (by (28i))
    the $+$ *man* $+$ *Aux* $+$ *read* $+$ *the* $+$ *book*   (by (28ii))
    the $+$ *man* $+$ *C* $+$ *have* $+$ *en* $+$ *be* $+$ *ing* $+$ *read* $+$ *the* $+$ *book*
                           (by (28iii)—we select the elements *C, have* $+$ *en*, and *be* $+$ *ing*)
    the $+$ *man* $+$ *S* $+$ *have* $+$ *en* $+$ *be* $+$ *ing* $+$ *read* $+$ *the* $+$ *book*   (by (29i))
    the $+$ *man* $+$ *have* $+$ *S* $\#$ *be* $+$ *en* $\#$ *read* $+$ *ing* $\#$ *the* $+$ *book*   (by (29ii)—three times)
    $\#$ *the* $\#$ *man* $\#$ *have* $+$ *S* $\#$ *be* $+$ *en* $\#$ *read* $+$ *ing* $\#$ *the* $\#$ *book* $\#$ (by (29iii))

The morphophonemic rules will convert the last line of this derivation into

(31)   *The man has been reading the book.*

in phonemic transcription. Similarly, every other auxiliary verb phrase can be generated. We return later to the question of further restrictions that must be placed on these rules so that only grammatical sequences can be generated. Note, incidentally, that the morphophonemic rules will have to include such rules as: *will* $+ S \to$ *will, will* $+ Past \to$ *would*. These rules can be dropped if we rewrite (28iii) so that either C or M, but not both, can be selected. But now the forms *would, could, might, should* must be added to (28iv), and certain "sequence of tense" statements become more complex. It is immaterial to our further discussion which of these alternative analyses is adopted. Several other minor revisions are possible.

---

[a]If we were formulating the theory of grammar more carefully, we would interpret $\#$ as the concatenation operator on the level of words, while $+$ is the concatenation operator on the level of phrase structure. (29) would then be part of the definition of a mapping which carries certain objects on the level of phrase structure . . . into strings of words. See my *The Logical Structure of Linguistic Theory* for a more careful formulation.

+ *come* (ultimately, *They haven't come*); applied to *they* − ∅ + *be* − *ing* + *come* (an instance of (37iv)), it gives *they* − ∅ + *be* + *n't* − *ing* + *come* (ultimately, *They aren't coming*). The rule thus works properly when we select the last three cases of (37).

Suppose, now, that we select an instance of (37i), i.e. a terminal string such as

(38)   *John* − *S* − *come*

which would give the kernel sentence *John comes* by (29ii). Applied to (38), T_{not} yields

(39)   *John* − *S* + *n't* − *come*

But we specified that T_{not} applies before (29ii), which has the effect of rewriting *Af* + *v* as *v* + *Af* #. However, we see that (29ii) does not apply at all to (39) since (39) does not now contain a sequence *Af* + *v*. Let us now add to the grammar the following obligatory transformational rule which applies *after* (29):

(40)   # *Af* → # *do* + *Af*

where *do* is the same element as the main verb in *John does his homework*. (Cf. (29iii) for introduction of #.) What (40) states is that *do* is introduced as the "bearer" of an unaffixed affix. Applying (40) and morphological rules to (39) we derive *John doesn't come*. The rules (37) and (40) now enable us to derive all and only the grammatical forms of sentence negation.

As it stands, the transformational treatment of negation is somewhat simpler than any alternative treatment within phrase structure. The advantage of the transformational treatment (over inclusion of negatives in the kernel) would become much clearer if we could find other cases in which the same formulations (i.e., (37) and (40)) are required for independent reasons. But in fact there are such cases.

Consider the class of *yes*-or-*no* questions such as *Have they arrived?*, *Can they arrive?*, *Did they arrive?* We can generate all (and only) these sentences by means of a transformation T_q that operates on strings with the analysis (37), and has the effect of interchanging the first and second segments of these strings, as these segments are defined in (37). We require that T_q apply *after* (29i) and *before* (29ii). Applied to

(41)(i)   *they* − ∅ − *arrive*
  (ii)   *they* − ∅ + *can* − *arrive*
  (iii)   *they* − ∅ + *have* − *en* + *arrive*
  (iv)   *they* − ∅ + *be* − *ing* + *arrive*

which are of the forms (37i–iv), T_q yields the strings

(42)(i)   ∅ − *they* − *arrive*
  (ii)   ∅ + *can* − *they* − *arrive*
  (iii)   ∅ + *have* − *they* − *en* + *arrive*
  (iv)   ∅ + *be* − *they* − *ing* + *arrive*

Applying to these the obligatory rules (29ii, iii) and (40), and then the morphophonemic rules, we derive

(43)(i)   *Do they arrive?*

    (ii)   *Can they arrive?*
  (iii)   *Have they arrived?*
  (iv)   *Are they arriving?*

in phonemic transcription. Had we applied the obligatory rules directly to (41), with no intervening T_q ,we would have derived the sentences

(44)(i)   *They arrive.*
  (ii)   *They can arrive.*
 (iii)   *They have arrived.*
 (iv)   *They are arriving.*

Thus (43i–iv) are the interrogative counterparts to (44i–iv).

In the case of (42i), *do* is introduced by rule (40) as the bearer of the unaffixed element $\emptyset$. If *C* had been developed into *S* or *Past* by rule (29i), rule (40) would have introduced *do* as a bearer of these elements, and we would have such sentences as *Does he arrive?, Did he arrive?* Note that no new morphophonemic rules are needed to account for the fact that $do + \emptyset \longrightarrow /\text{duw}/$, $do + S \longrightarrow /\text{dəz}/$, $do + past \longrightarrow /\text{did}/$; we need these rules anyway to account for the forms of *do* as a main verb. Notice also that T_q must apply after (29i), or number will not be assigned correctly in questions.

In analyzing the auxiliary verb phrase in rules (28), (29), we considered *S* to be the morpheme of the third person singular and $\emptyset$ to be the morpheme affixed to the verb for all other forms of the subject. Thus the verb has *S* if the noun subject has $\emptyset$ (*The boy arrives*) and the verb has $\emptyset$ if the subject has *S* (*The boys arrive*). An alternative that we did not consider was to eliminate the zero morpheme and to state simply that *no* affix occurs if the subject is not third person singular. We see now that this alternative is not acceptable. We must have the $\emptyset$ morpheme or there will be no affix in (42i) for *do* to bear, and rule (40) will thus not apply to (42i). There are many other cases where transformational analysis provides compelling reasons for or against the establishment of zero morphemes. As a negative case, consider the suggestion that intransitive verbs be analyzed as verbs with zero object. But then the passive transformation (34) would convert, for example, *John – slept – $\emptyset$* into the nonsentence $\emptyset$ *– was slept – by John $\rightarrow$ Was slept by John*. Hence this analysis of intransitives must be rejected. We return to the more general problem of the role of transformations in determining constituent structure in §7.6.

The crucial fact about the question transformation T_q is that almost nothing must be added to the grammar in order to describe it. Since both the subdivision of the sentence that it imposes and the rule for appearance of *do* were required independently for negation, we need only describe the inversion effected by T_q in extending the grammar to account for *yes*-or-*no* questions. Putting it differently, transformational analysis brings out the fact that negatives and interrogatives have fundamentally the same "structure," and it can make use of this fact to simplify the description of English syntax.

In treating the auxiliary verb phrase we left out of consideration forms with the heavy stressed element ***do*** as in *John **does** come*, etc. Suppose we set up a morpheme *A* of contrastive stress to which the following morphophonemic rule applies.

(45) $.. V .. + A \rightarrow .. \overset{''}{V} ..$, where $''$ indicates extra heavy stress.

We now set up a transformation T_A that imposes the same structural analysis of strings as does T_{not} (i.e. (37)), and adds A to these strings in exactly the position where T_{not} adds *not* or *n't*. Then just as T_{not} yields such sentences as

(46)(i) *John doesn't arrive.*   (From *John $\#$ S $+$ n't $\#$ arrive*, by (40))
  (ii) *John can't arrive.*   (From *John $\#$ S $+$ can $+$ n't $\#$ arrive*)
  (iii) *John hasn't arrived.*   (From *John $\#$ S $+$ have $+$ n't $\#$ en $+$ arrive*)

T_A yields the corresponding sentences

(47)(i) *John **does** arrive.*   (From *John $\#$ S $+$ A $\#$ arrive*, by (40))
  (ii) *John **can** arrive.*   (From *John $\#$ S $+$ can $+$ A $\#$ arrive*)
  (iii) *John **has** arrived.*   (From *John $\#$ S $+$ have $+$ A $\#$ en $+$ arrive*)

Thus T_A is a transformation of "affirmation" which affirms the sentences *John arrives, John can arrive, John has arrived*, etc., in exactly the same way as T_{not} negates them. This is formally the simplest solution, and it seems intuitively correct as well.

There are still other instances of transformations that are determined by the same fundamental syntactic analysis of sentences, namely (37). Consider the transformation T_{so} that converts the pairs of strings of (48) into the corresponding strings of (49):

(48)(i) *John – S – arrive, I – $\emptyset$ – arrive*
  (ii) *John – S $+$ can – arrive, I – $\emptyset$ $+$ can – arrive*
  (iii) *John – S $+$ have – en $+$ arrive, I – $\emptyset$ $+$ have – en $+$ arrive*
(49)(i) *John – S – arrive – and – so – $\emptyset$ – I*
  (ii) *John – S $+$ can – arrive – and – so – $\emptyset$ $+$ can – I*
  (iii) *John – S $+$ have – en $+$ arrive – and – so – $\emptyset$ $+$ have – I*

Applying rules (29ii, iii), (40), and the morphophonemic rules, we ultimately derive

(50)(i) *John arrives and so do I.*
  (ii) *John can arrive and so can I.*
  (iii) *John has arrived and so have I.*

T_{so} operates on the second sentence in each pair in (48), first replacing the third segment of this sentence by *so*, and then interchanging the first and third segment. (The element *so* is thus a *pro-VP*, in much the same sense in which *he* is a pronoun.) The transformation T_{so} combines with the conjunction transformation to give (49). While we have not described this in anywhere near sufficient detail, it is clear that both the analysis (37) of sentences and the rule (40) again are fundamental. Thus almost nothing new is required in the grammar to incorporate such sentences as (50), which are formed on the same underlying transformational pattern as negatives, questions, and emphatic affirmatives.

There is another remarkable indication of the fundamental character of this analysis that deserves mention here. Consider the kernel sentences

(51)(i) *John has a chance to live.*
  (ii) *John is my friend.*

The terminal strings that underlie (51) are

(52)(i)   *John* + *C* + *have* + *a* + *chance* + *to* + *live*
  (ii)   *John* + *C* + *be* + *my* + *friend*

where *have* in (52i) and *be* in (52ii) are main verbs, not auxiliaries. Consider now how the transformations T_{not}, T_q, and T_{so} apply to these underlying strings. T_{not} applies to any string of the form (37), adding *not* or *n't* between the second and the third segments, as given in (37). But (52i) is, in fact, an instance of both (37i) and (37iii). Hence T_{not} applied to (52i) will give either (53i) or (53ii):

(53)(i)   *John* – *C* + *n't* – *have* + *a* + *chance* + *to* + *live*
       (→ *John doesn't have a chance to live.*)
  (ii)   *John* – *C* + *have* + *n't* – *a* + *chance* + *to* + *live*
       (→ *John hasn't a chance to live.*)

But in fact both forms of (53) are grammatical. Furthermore *have* is the only transitive verb for which this ambiguous negation is possible, just as it is the only transitive verb that can be ambiguously analyzed in terms of (37). That is, we have *John doesn't read books* but not *John readsn't books*.

Similarly, T_q applied to (52i) will give either form of (54), and T_{so} will give either form of (55), since these transformations are also based on the structural analysis (37).

(54)(i)   *Does John have a chance to live?*
  (ii)   *Has John a chance to live?*

(55)(i)   *Bill has a chance to live and so does John.*
  (ii)   *Bill has a chance to live and so has John.*

But in the case of all other transitive verbs such forms as (54ii), (55ii) are impossible. We do not have *Reads John books?* or *Bill reads books and so reads John.* We see, however, that the apparently irregular behavior of *have* is actually an automatic consequence of our rules. This solves the problem raised in §2.3* concerning the grammaticalness of (3) but not (5).

Now consider (52ii). We have not shown this, but it is in fact true that in the simplest phrase structure grammar of English there is never any reason for incorporating *be* into the class of verbs; i.e. it will not follow from this grammar that *be* is a *V*. Just as one of the forms of the verb phrase is *V* + *NP*, one of the forms is *be* + *Predicate*. Hence, even though *be* is not an auxiliary in (52ii), it is nevertheless the case that of the analyses permitted by (37), only (37iv) holds of (52ii). Therefore the transformations T_{not}, T_q, and T_{so}, applied to (52ii), yield, respectively (along with (29i)),

(56)(i)   *John* – *S* + *be* + *n't* – *my* + *friend*   (→ *John isn't my friend.*)
  (ii)   *S* + *be* – *John* – *my* + *friend*   (→ *Is John my friend?*)
  (iii)   *Bill* – *S* + *be* – *my* + *friend* – *and* – *so* – *S* + *be* – *John*
       (→ *Bill is my friend and so is John.*)

---

*[*Syntactic Structures*, p. 15]

(3)   *Have you a book on modern music?*
(4)   *The book seems interesting.*
(5)   *Read you a book on modern music?*
(6)   *The child seems sleeping.*

Again, the analogous forms (e.g. *John readsn't books*, etc.) are impossible with actual verbs. Similarly, T_A gives *John is here* instead of *John does be here*, as would be the case with actual verbs.

If we were to attempt to describe English syntax wholly in terms of phrase structure, the forms with *be* and *have* would appear as glaring and distinct exceptions. But we have just seen that exactly these apparently exceptional forms result automatically from the simplest grammar constructed to account for the regular cases. Hence, this behavior of *be* and *have* actually turns out to be an instance of a deeper underlying regularity when we consider English structure from the point of view of transformational analysis.

Notice that the occurrence of *have* as an auxiliary in such terminal strings as *John + C + have + en + arrive* (underlying the kernel sentence *John has arrived*) is not subject to the same ambiguous analysis. This terminal string is an instance of (37iii), but not of (37i). That is, it can be analyzed as in (57i), but not (57ii).

(57)(i)   *John – C + have – en + arrive*   (*NP – C + have – . . .* , i.e. (37iii))
(ii)   *John – C – have + en + arrive*   (*NP – C – V . . .* , i.e. (37i))

This string is not an instance of (37i) since *this occurrence* of *have* is not a *V*, even though certain other occurrences of *have* (e.g. in (52i)) are *V*'s. The phrase structure of a terminal string is determined from its derivation, by tracing segments back to node points in the manner described in §4.1 [*Syntactic Structures*, pp. 26–30]. But *have* in (57) is not traceable to any node point labelled *V* in the derivation of this string. (52i) is ambiguously analyzable, however, since the occurrence of *have* in (52i) is traceable back to a *V*, and of course, is traceable back to a *have* (namely, itself), in the diagram corresponding to the derivation of the string (52i). The fact that (57ii) is not a permissible analysis prevents us from deriving such nonsentences as *John doesn't have arrived, Does John have arrived*, etc.

In this section we have seen that a wide variety of apparently distinct phenomena all fall into place in a very simple and natural way when we adopt the viewpoint of transformational analysis and that, consequently, the grammar of English becomes much more simple and orderly. This is the basic requirement that any conception of linguistic structure (i.e. any model for the form of grammars) must meet. I think that these considerations give ample justification for our earlier contention that the conceptions of phrase structure are fundamentally inadequate and that the theory of linguistic structure must be elaborated along the lines suggested in this discussion of transformational analysis.

7.2.   We can easily extend the analysis of questions given above to include such interrogatives as

(58)(i)   *What did John eat ?*
(ii)   *Who ate an apple ?*

which do not receive *yes*-or-*no* answers. The simplest way to incorporate this class of sentences into the grammar is by setting up a new optional transformation T_w which operates on any string of the form

(59) $X – NP – Y$

where X and Y stand for any string (including, in particular, the "null" string— i.e. the first or third position may be empty). T_w then operates in two steps:

(60)(i) T_{w_1} converts the string of the form $X - NP - Y$ into the corresponding string of the form $NP - X - Y$; i.e. it inverts the first and second segments of (59). It thus has the same transformational effect as T_q(cf. (41)–(42)).

(ii) T_{w_2} converts the resulting string $NP - X - Y$ into $who - X - Y$ if NP is an animate NP or into $what - X - Y$ if NP is inanimate.[2]

We now require that T_w can apply only to strings to which T_q has already applied. We specified that T_q must apply after (29i) and before (29ii). T_w applies after T_q and before (29ii), and it is conditional upon T_q in the sense that it can only apply to forms given by T_q. This conditional dependence among transformations is a generalization of the distinction between obligatory and optional transformations which we can easily build into the grammar, and which proves essential. The terminal string underlying both (58i) and (58ii) (as well as (62), (64)) is

(61)   *John – C – eat + an + apple* $(NP - C - V \ldots)$

where the dashes indicate the analysis imposed by T_q. Thus (61) is a case of (37i), as indicated. If we were to apply only obligatory transformations to (61), choosing *Past* in developing C by (29i), we would derive

(62)   *# John # eat + Past # an # apple #*   *(→ John ate an apple.)*

If we apply (29i) and T_q to (61), we derive

(63)   *Past – John – eat + an + apple*

where C is taken as *Past*. If we were now to apply (40) to (63), introducing *do* as the bearer of *Past*, we would have the simple interrogative

(64)   *Did John eat an apple?*

If we apply T_w to (63), however, we derive first (65), by T_{w_1}, and then (66), by T_{w_2}.

(65)   *John – Past – eat + an + apple*

(66)   *who – Past – eat + an + apple*

Rule (29ii) and the morphophonemic rules then convert (66) into (58ii). To form (58ii), then, we apply first T_q and then T_w to the terminal string (61) that underlies the kernel sentence (62). Note that in this case T_{w_1} simply undoes the effect of T_q, which explains the absence of inversion in (58ii).

To apply T_w to a string, we first select a noun phrase and then invert this noun phrase with the string that precedes it. In forming (58ii), we applied T_w to (63), choosing the noun phrase *John*. Suppose now that we apply T_w to (63), choosing the noun phrase *an + apple*. Thus for the purposes of this transformation we now analyze (63) as

(67)   *Past + John + eat – an + apple*

a string of the form (59), where Y in this case is null. Applying T_w to (67) we derive first (68), by T_{w_1}, and then (69), by T_{w_2}.

---

[2]More simply, we can limit application of T_w to strings $X - NP - Y$ where NP is *he, him,* or *it,* and we can define T_{w_2} as the transformation that converts any string Z into $Wh + Z$, where *Wh* is a morpheme. In the morphophonemics of English we shall have rules: $Wh + he \rightarrow$ /huw/, $Wh + him \rightarrow$ /huwm/, $Wh + it \rightarrow$ /wat/.

(68)   *an + apple – Past + John + eat*

(69)   *what – Past + John + eat*

(29ii) does not now apply to (69), just as it did not apply to (39) or (42i), since (69) does not contain a substring of the form *Af + v*. Hence (40) applies to (69), introducing *do* as a bearer of the morpheme *Past*. Applying the remaining rules, we finally derive (58i).

T_w as formulated in (59)–(60) will also account for all such *Wh*-questions as *What will he eat?*, *What has he been eating?* It can easily be extended to cover interrogatives like *What book did he read?*, etc.

Notice that T_{w_1} as defined in (60i) carries out the same transformation as does T_q; that is, it inverts the first two segments of the string to which it applies. We have not discussed the effect of transformations on intonation. Suppose that we set up two fundamental sentence intonations: falling intonations, which we associate with kernel sentences, and rising intonations, which we associate with *yes-or-no* questions. Then the effect of T_q is in part to convert the intonation from one of these to the other; hence, in the case of (64), to convert a falling intonation into a rising one. But we have seen that T_{w_1} applies only after T_q, and that its transformational effect is the same as that of T_q. Hence T_{w_1} will convert the rising intonation back into a falling one. It seems reasonable to put this forth as an explanation for the fact that the interrogatives (58i–ii) normally have the falling intonation of declaratives. There are many problems in extending our discussion to intonational phenomena and this remark is too sketchy to carry much weight, but it does suggest that such an extension may be fruitful.

To summarize, we see that the four sentences

(70)(i)   *John ate an apple.*   (=(62))

  (ii)   *Did John eat an apple?*   (=(64))

  (iii)   *What did John eat?*   (=(58i))

  (iv)   *Who ate an apple?*   (=(58ii))

are all derived from the underlying terminal string (61). (70i) is a kernel sentence, since only obligatory transformations enter into its "transformational history." (70ii) is formed from (61) by applying T_q. (70iii) and (70iv) are even more remote from the kernel, since they are formed from (61) by applying first T_q and then T_w.

7.3.   In §5.3 we mentioned that there are certain noun phrases of the form *to + VP, ing + VP* (*to prove that theorem, proving that theorem*—cf. (32)–(33)).* Among these we will have such phrases as *to be cheated, being cheated*, which are

---

*[*Syntactic Structures*, pp. 40–41]

Thus the morphemes *to* and *ing* play a very similar role within the noun phrase in that they convert verb phrases into noun phrases, giving, for example,

(32) $\begin{Bmatrix} \textit{To prove that theorem} \\ \textit{Proving that theorem} \end{Bmatrix}$ *was difficult.*

etc. We can exploit this parallel by adding . . . the rule

(33) $NP \rightarrow \begin{Bmatrix} ing \\ to \end{Bmatrix} VP$

The rule (29ii) will then convert *ing + prove + that + theorem* into *proving # that + theorem*.

derived from passives. But passives have been deleted from the kernel. Hence noun phrases of the type *to* + *VP*, *ing* + *NP* can no longer be introduced within the kernel grammar by such rules as (33). They must therefore be introduced by a "nominalizing transformation" which converts a sentence of the form *NP* – *VP* into a noun phrase of the form *to* + *VP* or *ing* + *VP*.[3] We shall not go into the structure of this very interesting and ramified set of nominalizing transformations except to sketch briefly a transformational explanation for a problem raised in §2.3 [*Syntactic Structures*, p. 15].

One of the nominalizing transformations will be the transformation T_{Adj} which operates on any string of the form

(71)   *T* – *N* – *is* – *Adj*   (i.e. *Article* – *Noun* – *is* – *Adjective*)

and converts it into the corresponding noun phrase of the form $T + Adj + N$. Thus, it converts *The boy is tall* into *the tall boy*, etc. It is not difficult to show that this transformation simplifies the grammar considerably, and that it must go in this, not the opposite direction. When we formulate this transformation properly, we find that it enables us to drop all adjective-noun combinations from the kernel, reintroducing them by T_{Adj}.

In the phrase structure grammar we have a rule

(72)   *Adj* → *old, tall*, . . .

which lists all of the elements that can occur in the kernel sentences of the form (71). Words like *sleeping*, however, will not be given in this list, even though we have such sentences as

(73)   *The child is sleeping.*

The reason for this is that even when *sleeping* is not listed in (72), (73) is generated by the transformation (29ii) (that carries $Af + v$ into $v + Af \#$) from the underlying terminal string

(74)   *the* + *child* + *C* + *be* – *ing* – *sleep*

where $be + ing$ is part of the auxiliary verb (cf. (28iii)). Alongside of (73), we have such sentences as *The child will sleep, The child sleeps*, etc., with different choices for the auxiliary verb.

Such words as *interesting*, however, will have to be given in the list (72). In such sentences as

(75)   *The book is interesting.*

interesting is an *Adj*, not part of the *Verb*, as can be seen from the fact that we do not have *The book will interest, The book interests*, etc.

An independent support for this analysis of *interesting* and *sleeping* comes from the behavior of *very*, etc., which can occur with certain adjectives, but not others. The simplest way to account for *very* is to put into the phrase structure grammar the rule

---

[3]This nominalizing transformation will be given as a generalized transformation such as (26) [*MSE*, p. 74]. It will operate on a pair of sentences, one of which it converts from *NP* – *VP* into *to* + *VP* (or *ing* + *VP*), which it then substitutes for an *NP* of the other sentence. See my *The Logical Structure of Linguistic Theory* and *Transformational Analysis* for a detailed discussion.

(76)   *Adj → very + Adj*

very can appear in (75), and in general with *interesting;* but it cannot appear in (73) or with other occurrences of *sleeping*. Hence, if we wish to preserve the simplest analysis of *very*, we must list *interesting* but not *sleeping* in (72) as an *Adj*.

We have not discussed the manner in which transformations impose constituent structure, although we have indicated that this is necessary; in particular, so that transformations can be compounded. One of the general conditions on derived constituent structure will be the following:

(77)   If *X* is a *Z* in the phrase structure grammar, and a string *Y* formed by a transformation is of the same structural form as *X*, then *Y* is also a *Z*.

In particular, even when passives are deleted from the kernel we will want to say that the *by*-phrase (as in *the food was eaten – by the man*) is a prepositional phrase (*PP*) in the passive sentence. (77) permits this, since we know from the kernel grammar that *by + NP* is a *PP*. (77) is not stated with sufficient accuracy, but it can be elaborated as one of a set of conditions on derived constituent structure.

But now consider (73). The word *sleeping* is formed by transformation (i.e. (29ii)) and it is of the same form as *interesting* (i.e. it is a *V + ing*), which, as we know from the phrase structure grammar, is an *Adj*. Hence, by (77), *sleeping* is also an *Adj* in the transform (73). But this means that (73) can be analyzed as a string of the form (71) so that T_{Adj} applies to it, forming the noun phrase

(78)   *the sleeping child*

just as it forms *the interesting book* from (75). Thus even though *sleeping* is excluded from (72), it will appear as an adjective modifying nouns.

This analysis of adjectives (which is all that we are required to give to account for the actually occurring sentences) will not introduce the word *sleeping*, however, into all the adjective positions of such words as *interesting* which remained in the kernel. For example, it will never introduce *sleeping* into the context *very_____*. Since *very* never modifies verbs, *very* will not appear in (74) or (73), and all occurrences of *sleeping* as a modifier are derived from its occurrence as a verb in (74), etc. Similarly, there will be phrase structure rules that analyze the verb phrase into

(79)   *Aux + seem + Adj*

just as other rules analyze *VP* into *Aux + V + NP*, *Aux + be + Adj*, etc. But *sleeping* will never be introduced into the context *seems_____* by this grammar, which is apparently the simplest one constructible for the actually occurring sentences.

When we develop this sketchy argument more carefully, we reach the conclusion that the simplest transformational grammar for the occurring sentences will exclude (80) while generating (81).

(80)(i)   *The child seems sleeping.*
　(ii)   *the very sleeping child*

(81)(i)   *The book seems interesting.*
　(ii)   *the very interesting book*

We see, then, that the apparently arbitrary distinctions noted in §2.3 [*Syntactic*

Structures, p. 15] between (3) (= *Have you a book on modern music?*) and
(4) (= (81i)) on the one hand, and (5) (= *Read you a book on modern music?*)
and (6) (= (80i)) on the other, have a clear structural origin, and are really
instances of higher level regularity in the sense that they are consequences
of the simplest transformational grammar. In other words, certain linguistic
behavior that seems unmotivated and inexplicable in terms of phrase structure
appears simple and systematic when we adopt the transformational point of view.
To use the terminology of §2.2 [*Syntactic Structures*, pp. 14–15], if a speaker were
to project his finite linguistic experience by using phrase structure and transformations in the simplest possible way, consistent with his experience, he would include
(3) and (4) as grammatical while rejecting (5) and (6).

7.4. In (28), §5.3 [*MSE*, p. 53], we analyzed the element *Verb* into *Aux* + *V*,
and then simply listed the verbal roots of the class *V*. There are, however, a large
number of productive subconstructions of *V* that deserve some mention, since
they bring to light some basic points in a rather clear way. Consider first such
verb + particle (*V* + *Prt*) constructions as *bring in, call up, drive away*. We can
have such forms as (82) but not (83).

(82)(i)   *The police brought in the criminal.*
  (ii)   *The police brought the criminal in.*
  (iii)   *The police brought him in.*

(83)   *The police brought in him.*

We know that discontinuous elements cannot be handled readily within the phrase
structure grammar. Hence the most natural way of analyzing these constructions
is to add to (28ii) the following possibility

(84) $V \rightarrow V_1 + Prt$

along with a set of supplementary rules to indicate which V_1 can go with which
Prt. To allow for the possibility of (82ii) we set up an optional transformation
T_{sep}^{op} which operates on strings with the structural analysis

(85) $X - V_1 - Prt - NP$

and has the effect of interchanging the third and fourth segments of the string to
which it applies. It thus carries (82i) into (82ii). To provide for (82iii) while excluding (83), we must indicate that this transformation is obligatory when the *NP*
object is a pronoun (*Pron*). Equivalently, we can set up an obligatory transformation T_{sep}^{ob} which has the same structural effect as T_{sep}^{op} but which operates on strings
with the structural analysis

(86) $X - V_1 - Prt - Pron$

We know that the passive transformation operates on any string of the form
NP – *Verb* – *NP*. If we specify that the passive transformation applies before
T_{sep}^{op} or T_{sep}^{ob}, then it will form the passives

(87)(i)   *The criminal was brought in by the police.*
  (ii)   *He was brought in by the police.*

from (82), as it should.

Further investigation of the verb phrase shows that there is a general verb + complement ($V + Comp$) construction that behaves very much like the verb + particle construction just discussed. Consider the sentences

(88) *Everyone in the lab considers John incompetent.*

(89) *John is considered incompetent by everyone in the lab.*

If we wish to derive (89) from (88) by the passive transformation we must analyze (88) into the structure $NP_1 - Verb - NP_2$, where $NP_1 = everyone + in + the + lab$ and $NP_2 = John$. That is, we must apply the passive not to (88), but to a terminal string (90) that underlies (88):

(90) *everyone in the lab – considers incompetent – John*

We can now form (88) from (90) by a transformation analogous to T_{sep}^{ob}. Suppose that we add to the phrase structure grammar the rule (91), alongside (84).

(91) $V \rightarrow V_a + Comp$

We now extend T_{sep}^{ob}, permitting it to apply to strings of the form (92) as well as to strings of the form (86), as before.

(92) $X - V_a - Comp - NP$

This revised transformation T_{sep}^{ob} will convert (90) into (88). Thus, the treatment of the *Verb + Complement* and *Verb + Particle* constructions is quite similar. The former, in particular, is an extremely well-developed construction in English.[4]

7.5. We have barely sketched the justification for the particular form of each of the transformations that we have discussed, though it is very important to study the question of the uniqueness of this system. I think it can be shown that in each of the cases considered above, and in many other cases, there are very clear and easily generalizable considerations of simplicity that determine which set of sentences belong to the kernel and what sorts of transformations are required to account for the nonkernel sentences. As a paradigmatic instance, we shall briefly review the status of the passive transformation.

In §5.4 [*Syntactic Structures*, pp. 42ff.] we showed that the grammar is much more complex if it contains both actives and passives in the kernel than if the passives are deleted and reintroduced by a transformation that interchanges the subject and object of the active, and replaces the verb V by $is + V + en + by$. Two questions about uniqueness immediately suggest themselves. First, we ask

---

[4]Further study shows that most of the verb + complement forms introduced by rule (91) should themselves be excluded from the kernel and derived transformationally from *John is incompetent*, etc. But this is a complex matter that requires a much more detailed development of transformational theory than we can give here. Cf. my *The Logical Structure of Linguistic Theory*, *Transformational Analysis*, and "A Transformational Approach to Syntax" [*SL*].

There are several other features of these constructions that we have passed over far too briefly. It is not at all clear that this is an obligatory transformation. With long and complex objects we can have, e.g. *They consider incompetent anyone who is unable to* . . . Hence we might extend T_{sep}^{op}, rather than T_{sep}^{ob}, to take care of this case. It is interesting to study those features of the grammatical object that necessitate or preclude this transformation. Much more than length is involved. There are also other possibilities for the passive that we shall not consider here, for lack of space, though they make an interesting study.

whether it is necessary to interchange the noun phrases to form the passive. Second, we ask whether passives could have been chosen as the kernel, and actives derived from them by an "active" transformation.

Consider first the question of the interchange of subject and object. Is this interchange necessary, or could we describe the passive transformation as having the following effect:

(93) $NP_1 - Aux - V - NP_2$ is rewritten $NP_1 - Aux + be + en - V - by + NP_2$

In particular, the passive of *John loves Mary* would be *John is loved by Mary*.

In §5.4 we argued against (93) and in favor of inversion on the basis of the fact that we have such sentences as (94) but not (95).

(94)(i)   *John admires sincerity.*   —*Sincerity is admired by John.*
   (ii)   *John plays golf.*   —*Golf is played by John.*
   (iii)   *Sincerity frightens John.*   —*John is frightened by sincerity.*

(95)(i)   *Sincerity admires John.*   —*John is admired by sincerity.*
   (ii)   *Golf plays John.*   —*John is played by golf.*
   (iii)   *John frightens sincerity.*   —*Sincerity is frightened by John.*

We pointed out, however, that this approach requires that a notion of "degree of grammaticalness" be developed to support this distinction. I believe that this approach is correct, and that there is a clear sense in which the sentences of (94) are more grammatical than those of (95), which are themselves more grammatical than *Sincerity admires eat*, etc. Any grammar that distinguishes abstract from proper nouns would be subtle enough to characterize the difference between (94i, iii) and (95i, iii), for example, and surely linguistic theory must provide the means for this distinction. However, since we have not gone into the question of category analysis in this discussion, it is interesting to show that there is even a stronger argument against (93). In fact, any grammar that can distinguish singular from plural is sufficiently powerful to enable us to prove that the passive requires inversion of noun phrases.

To see this, consider the *Verb + Complement* construction discussed in §7.4. Alongside (88), (89) we have such sentences as

(96)   *All the people in the lab consider John a fool.*

(97)   *John is considered a fool by all the people in the lab.*

In §7.4. we saw that (96) is formed by the transformation T_{sep}^{ob} from the underlying string

(98)   *all the people in the lab – consider a fool – John*   (*NP – Verb – NP*)

with the *verb* "*consider a fool*" being an instance of (91). We also saw that the passive transformation applies directly to (98). If the passive interchanges subject and object, it will correctly form (97) from (98) as the passive of (96). If, however, we take (93) as the definition of the passive, we will derive the nonsense

(99)   *All the people in the lab are considered a fool by John.*

by application of this transformation to (98).

The point is that we have found a verb—namely, *consider a fool*—which must agree in number both with its subject and its object.⁵ Such verbs prove quite conclusively that the passive must be based on an inversion of subject and object.

Consider now the question of whether passives could be taken as the kernel sentences instead of actives. It is quite easy to see that this proposal leads to a much more complex grammar. With actives as kernel sentences, the phrase structure grammar will include (28) with *be + en* dropped from (28iii). But if passives are taken as kernel sentences, *be + en* will have to be listed in (28iii), along with all the other forms of the auxiliary, and we will have to add special rules indicating that if *V* is intransitive, it cannot have the auxiliary *be + en* (i.e. we cannot have *is occurred*), whereas if *V* is transitive it must have *be + en* (i.e. we cannot have *Lunch eats by John*). Comparing the two alternatives, there is no doubt as to relative complexity; and we are forced to take actives, not passives, as the kernel sentences.

Notice that if passives were chosen as kernel sentences instead of actives we would run into certain difficulties of quite a different sort. The active transformation would have to apply to strings of the form

(100) $NP_1 - Aux + be + en - V - by + NP_2$

converting them to $NP_2 - Aux - V - NP_1$. For example, it would convert

(101)   *The wine was drunk by the guests.*

into *The guests drank the wine*, where *drunk* in (101) originates from *en + drink*. But there is also an adjective *drunk* that must be listed in (72) along with *old*, *interesting*, etc., since we have *He is very drunk, He seems drunk*, etc. (cf. §7.3), and this adjective will also originate from *en + drink*. It thus appears that in the simplest system of phrase structure for English, the sentence

(102)   *John was drunk by midnight.*

is also based on an underlying terminal string that can be analyzed in accordance with (100). In other words, there is no structural way to differentiate properly between (101) and (102), if both are taken as kernel sentences. But application of the "active" transformation to (102) does not give a grammatical sentence.

When we actually try to set up, for English, the simplest grammar that contains a phrase structure and transformational part, we find that the kernel consists of simple, declarative, active sentences (in fact, probably a finite number of these), and that all other sentences can be described more simply as transforms. Each transformation that I have investigated can be shown to be irreversible in the sense that it is much easier to carry out the transformation in one direction than in the other, just as in the case of the passive transformation discussed above. This fact may account for the traditional practice of grammarians, who customarily begin the grammar of English, for example, with the study of simple "actor-action" sentences and simple grammatical relations such as subject-predicate or verb-object. No one would seriously begin the study of English constituent structure

---

⁵The agreement between *a fool* and *John* in (98) is of course one support for the further transformational analysis of the *Verb + Complement + Noun Phrase* constructions mentioned in footnote 4.

with such a sentence as *Whom have they nominated?*, attempting to analyze it into two parts, etc.; and while some very detailed considerations of English structure (e.g. [E. Nida, *A Synopsis of English Syntax* (South Pasadena, 1951)]) do not mention interrogatives, none fails to include simple declaratives. Transformational analysis provides a rather simple explanation for this asymmetry (which is otherwise formally unmotivated) on the assumption that grammarians have been acting on the basis of a correct intuition about the language.[6]

7.6. One other point deserves some mention before we leave the topic of English transformations. At the outset of §5 [*Syntactic Structures*, pp. 34ff.; *MSE*, pp. 73–74] we noted that the rule for conjunction provides a useful criterion for constituent analysis in the sense that this rule is greatly simplified if constituents are set up in a certain way. Now we are interpreting this rule as a transformation. There are many other cases in which the behavior of a sentence under transformations provides valuable, even compelling evidence as to its constituent structure.

Consider for example the pair of sentences

(103)(i) *John knew the boy studying in the library.*
  (ii) *John found the boy studying in the library.*

It is intuitively obvious that these sentences have different grammatical structure (this becomes clear, for example, when we attempt to add *not running around in the streets* to (103)), but I do not believe that within the level of phrase structure grounds can be found for analyzing them into different constituents. The simplest analysis in both cases is as $NP - Verb - NP - ing + VP$. But consider the behavior of these sentences under the passive transformation. We have the sentences (104) but not (105).[7]

(104)(i) *The boy studying in the library was known (by John).*
  (ii) *The boy studying in the library was found (by John).*
  (iii) *The boy was found studying in the library (by John).*

(105) *The boy was known studying in the library (by John).*

The passive transformation applies only to sentences of the form $NP - Verb - NP$. Hence, to yield (104ii), (103ii) must be analyzable as

(106) *John – found – the boy studying in the library*

with the noun phrase object *the boy studying in the library*, (103i) will have a corresponding analysis, since we have the passive (104i).

---

[6]In determining which of two related forms is more central, we are thus following the reasoning outlined by Bloomfield for morphology: "... when forms are partially similar, there may be a question as to which one we had better take as the underlying form ... the structure of the language may decide this question for us, since, taking it one way, we get an unduly complicated description, and taking it the other way, a relatively simple one" (*Language*, New York, 1933, p. 218). Bloomfield continues by pointing out that "this same consideration often leads us to *set up* an artificial underlying form." We have also found this insight useful in transformational analysis, as, for example, when we set up the terminal string $John - C - have + en - be + ing - read$ underlying the kernel sentence *John has been reading.*

[7]The sentences of (104) without the parenthesized expression are formed by a second "elliptical" transformation that converts, for example, *The boy was seen by John* into *The boy was seen.*

But (103ii) also has the passive (104iii). From this we learn that (103ii) is a case of the verb + complement construction studied in §7.4; i.e. that it is derived by the transformation T_{sep}^{ob} from the underlying string

(107)   *John – found studying in the library – the boy*

with the verb *found* and the complement *studying in the library*. The passive transformation will convert (107) into (104iii), just as it converts (90) into (89). (103i), however, is not a transform of the string *John – knew studying in the library – the boy* (the same form as (107)), since (105) is not a grammatical sentence.

By studying the grammatical passives, then, we determine that *John found the boy studying in the library* (= (103ii)) is analyzable ambiguously as either *NP – Verb – NP*, with the object *the boy studying in the library*, or as *NP – Aux + V – NP – Comp*, a transform of the string (107) which has the complex verb *found studying in the library*. *John knew the boy studying in the library* (=(103i)), however, has only the first of these analyses. The resulting description of (103) seems quite in accord with intuition.

As another example of a similar type, consider the sentence

(108)   *John came home.*

Although *John* and *home* are *NP*'s, and *came* is a *verb*, investigation of the effect of transformations on (108) shows that it cannot be analyzed as a case of *NP – Verb – NP*. We cannot have *Home was come by John* under the passive transformation, or *What did John come?* under the question transformation T_w. We must therefore analyze (108) in some other way (if we are not to complicate unduly the description of these transformations), perhaps as *NP – Verb – Adverb*. Apart from such considerations as these, there do not appear to be very strong reasons for denying to (108) the completely counterintuitive analysis *NP – Verb – NP*, with *home* the object of *came*.

I think it is fair to say that a significant number of the basic criteria for determining constituent structure are actually transformational. The general principle is this: if we have a transformation that simplifies the grammar and leads from sentences to sentences in a large number of cases (i.e. a transformation under which the set of grammatical sentences is very nearly closed), then we attempt to assign constituent structure to sentences in such a way that this transformation always leads to grammatical sentences, thus simplifying the grammar even further.

The reader will perhaps have noted a certain circularity or even apparent inconsistency in our approach. We define such transformations as the passive in terms of particular phrase structure analyses, and we then consider the behavior of sentences under these transformations in determining how to assign phrase structure to these sentences. In §7.5 we used the fact that *John was drunk by midnight* (=(102)) does not have a corresponding "active" as an argument against setting up a passive-to-active transformation. In §7.6 we have used the fact that *John came home* (=(108)) does not have a passive as an argument against assigning to it the constituent structure *NP – Verb – NP*. However, if the argument is traced carefully in each case it will be clear that there is no circularity or inconsistency. In each case our sole concern has been to decrease the complexity of the grammar, and we have tried to show that the proposed analysis is clearly simpler than the rejected alternatives. In some cases the grammar becomes simpler if we reject a certain transformation; in some cases reassignment of constituent structure is preferable. We have thus been following the course outlined in §6 [*Syntactic Structures*, pp. 49–60]. Making use of phrase structure and transformations, we are trying to construct a grammar of English that will be simpler than any proposed alternative; and we are giving no thought to the question of how one might actually arrive at this grammar in some mechanical way from an English corpus, no matter how extensive. Our weaker goal of evaluation instead of discovery eliminates any fear of vicious circularity in the cases discussed above. The intuitive correspondences and explanations of apparent irregularities seem to me to offer important evidence for the correctness of the approach we have been following.

II

CONJUNCTION

The four articles in this section share a number of areas of common interest, but in particular the source of various conjoined structures. Some conjoined expressions seem to result from the conjunction of separate *sentences* that are later reduced to a single sentence containing conjoined elements. On the other hand, the grammatical behavior of other conjoined expressions indicates that these cannot be derived from the conjunction of sentences but instead must result from conjoined elements introduced directly into the deep structure.

The first article is Noam Chomsky's discussion of conjunction in *Syntactic Structures*, from the point in his book where he is discussing the limitations of phrase structure grammars. He shows not only that conjunction cannot be expressed as a phrase structure rule but also that conjunction provides a test for the constituent structure of forms. He gives a rule for deriving conjoined constituents from a conjunction of sentences. Carlota S. Smith, in "Ambiguous Sentences with *And*," presents grammatical evidence that leads to the postulation of *two* kinds of conjunction, *phrasal* as well as *sentential*. Lila R. Gleitman, in "Coordinating Conjunctions in English," considerably extends the scope of the preceding two treatments and provides explicit rules for conjunction, at the same time showing what the derived constituent structure would be. She relates conjunction to pronominalization and discusses the deletions, substitutions, and stress changes that take place after conjunction reduction. George Lakoff and Stanley Peters, in "Phrasal Conjunction and Symmetric Predicates," then discuss phrasal conjunction, bringing forth cases of conjoined elements that could not have resulted from the conjunction of two separate sentences. They show the relationship between sentences containing conjoined subjects and sentences in which the second conjunct may appear as a postverbal prepositional phrase.

7

Conjunction

NOAM CHOMSKY

One of the most productive processes for forming new sentences is the process of conjunction. If we have two sentences $Z + X + W$ and $Z + Y + W$, and if X and Y are actually constituents of these sentences, we can generally form a new sentence $Z - X + and + Y - W$. For example, from the sentences (20a–b) we can form the new sentence (21).

(20)(a) *the scene – of the movie – was in Chicago*
(b) *the scene – of the play – was in Chicago*

(21) *the scene – of the movie and of the play – was in Chicago*

If X and Y are, however, not constituents, we generally cannot do this.[1] For example we cannot form (23) from (22a–b).

Reprinted from Noam Chomsky, *Syntactic Structures* (The Hague: Mouton & Co., 1957), Sec. 5.2, pp. 35–37, by permission of Noam Chomsky and Mouton & Co.

[1](21) and (23) are extreme cases in which there is no question about the possibility of conjunction. There are many less clear cases. For example, it is obvious that *John enjoyed the book and liked the play* (a string of the form $NP–VP + and + VP$) is a perfectly good sentence, but many would question the grammaticalness of, for example, *John enjoyed and my friend liked the play* (a string of the form $NP + Verb + and + NP + Verb–NP$). The latter sentence, in which conjunction crosses over constituent boundaries, is much less natural than the alternative *John enjoyed the play and my friend liked it*, but there is no preferable alternative to the former. Such sentences with conjunction crossing constituent boundaries are also, in general, marked by special phonemic features such as extra long pauses (in our example, between *liked* and *the*), contrastive stress and intonation, failure to reduce vowels and drop final consonants in rapid speech, etc. Such features normally mark the reading of nongrammatical strings. The most reasonable way to describe this situation would seem to be by a description of the following kind: to form fully grammatical sentences by conjunction, it is necessary to conjoin single constituents; if we conjoin pairs of constituents, and these are major constituents (i.e. "high up" in the [tree]), the resulting sentences are semi-grammatical; the more completely we violate constituent structure by conjunction, the less grammatical is the resulting sentence. This description requires that we generalize the grammatical-ungrammatical dichotomy, developing a notion of degree of grammaticalness.

(22)(a)   *the – liner sailed down the – river*

  (b)   *the – tugboat chugged up the – river*

(23)   *the – liner sailed down the and tugboat chugged up the – river*

Similarly, if X and Y are both constituents, but are constituents of different kinds (i.e. if in [a tree] they each have a single origin, but this origin is labelled differently), then we cannot in general form a new sentence by conjunction. For example, we cannot form (25) from (24a–b).

(24)(a)   *the scene – of the movie – was in Chicago*

  (b)   *the scene – that I wrote – was in Chicago*

(25)   *the scene – of the movie and that I wrote – was in Chicago.*

In fact, the possibility of conjunction offers one of the best criteria for the initial determination of phrase structure. We can simplify the description of conjunction if we try to set up constituents in such a way that the following rule will hold:

(26)   If S_1 and S_2 are grammatical sentences, and S_1 differs from S_2 only in that X appears in S_1 where Y appears in S_2 (i.e. $S_1 = .. X .. $ and $S_2 = .. Y ..$), and X and Y are constituents of the same type in S_1 and S_2, respectively, then S_3 is a sentence, where S_3 is the result of replacing X by $X + and + Y$ in S_1 (i.e. $S_3 = .. X + and + Y ..$).

Even though additional qualification is necessary here, the grammar is enormously simplified if we set up constituents in such a way that (26) holds even approximately. That is, it is easier to state the distribution of *and* by means of qualifications on this rule than to do so directly without such a rule. . . .The essential property of rule (26) is that in order to apply it to sentences S_1 and S_2 to form the new sentence S_3 we must know not only the actual form of S_1 and S_2 but also their constituent structure—we must know not only the final shape of these sentences, but also their "history of derivation.". . .

It is immaterial to our discussion, however, whether we decide to exclude such sentences as *John enjoyed and my friend liked the play* as ungrammatical, whether we include them as semi-grammatical, or whether we include them as fully grammatical but with special phonemic features. In any event they form a class of utterances distinct from *John enjoyed the play and liked the book*, etc., where constituent structure is preserved perfectly; and our conclusion that the rule for conjunction must make explicit reference to constituent structure therefore stands, since this distinction will have to be pointed out in the grammar.

8

Ambiguous Sentences with And

CARLOTA S. SMITH

1. The following sentences contain compound (*N and N*) subjects or objects. Each sentence is ambiguous: the compound may be interpreted either as a unit or as a conjunction of separate entities. Sentences with compound noun phrases are often analyzed simply as conjunctions, optimally reduced, of two sentences. But an analysis that treats *and* as a morpheme occurring only in complex sentences is deficient, since it gives no formal basis for the systematic ambiguity discussed below. I think that the problem of ambiguous sentences with *and*, and other related problems, can be solved if a generative grammar of English produces both simplex and complex sentences with *and*.

(1) *John and Mary bought the new book by John Steinbeck.*

(2) *Bricks and stones make strong walls.*

(3) *George and Marmaduke have dogs.*

(4) *The man and the woman waited for the train.*

(5) *Gerry likes ice cream and cake.*

(6) *She invited Gwendolyn and Amanda.*

(7) *He knows Latin and Greek.*

The two readings of these sentences follow. Reading (a) interprets the compound subject (or object) as a unit; (b) interprets it as a conjunction of separate entities. The stress patterns of the compounds differ according to which reading is adopted.

(1)(a) One copy of the book was bought.

  (b) Two copies were bought.

(2)(a) The combination of stones and bricks makes strong walls.

  (b) Stone walls are strong and brick walls are strong.

This work was supported in part by the U. S. Army (Signal Corps), the U. S. Navy (Office of Naval Research), and the U. S. Air Force (Office of Scientific Research, Air Research and Development Command), and in part by the National Science Foundation.

(3)(a)   As a unit, the two have dogs—they own a kennel.

   (b)   George has one or more dogs and Marmaduke has one or more dogs.

(4)(a)   They waited together, perhaps for the same person.

   (b)   They waited separately.

(5)(a)   Gerry likes the combination of goodies.

   (b)   Gerry likes ice cream and Gerry likes cake.

(6)(a)   She invited the two girls together—they are friends, sisters, etc.

   (b)   She invited Gwendolyn and she invited Amanda.

(7)(a)   He knows Latin and Greek—therefore can cope with classics.

   (b)   He knows Latin and he knows Greek.

If *and* were introduced in both simplex and complex sentences, the ambiguity of the examples above would be explained: each would have two derivations. *And* should, I think, occur in noun phrases at the phrase structure level of a generative grammar of English, and also in conjunctions at the transformational level. Reading (a) for each sentence interprets it as a simplex, and reading (b) interprets it as a conjunction.

Certain devices that can optionally occur in conjunctions all have the function of indicating that a given sentence is, in fact, a conjunction. The words *both*, *each* (in these constructions); *as well as, too;* commas after first *N;* less than optimal reduction of the second half of the conjunction; all produce sentences with *N and N* that are *not* ambiguous. (They make the unit interpretation impossible by indicating that the elements have been "artificially" combined.) Unless the second half of a conjunction is optimally reduced, of course, the sentence can be interpreted only as a conjunction.

> She invited Gwendolyn, and Amanda.
> She invited Gwendolyn, and Amanda too.
> She invited Gwendolyn and she invited Amanda.
> Gerry likes both ice cream and cake.
> John and Mary each bought the new book by John Steinbeck.
> He knows Latin as well as Greek.   (Not comparative *as*)

The systematic ambiguity of compound *NP*'s with *and* seems in some sense to "explain" why English has so many variants on conjunctions with *and*.

2.   Not all sentences with compound subjects or objects are ambiguous. The following examples have only one reading, in which the *N*'s are one unit: they cannot in other words, be construed as conjunctions.

(8)   *The company lawyer and the union lawyer hammered out the agreement.*

(9)   *John and Mike paid my check.*

(10)   *Red and green complement each other.*

(11)   *Ice cream and cake are a popular combination.*

(12)   *Jimmie and Timmie are a pair of fools.*

(13)   *The child tried to mix oil and water.*

If they were conjunctions they would each have been formed from underlying sentences differing only as to subject (8–12) or object (10 and 13). The possible underlying sentences follow. Not one of them is the "right" conjunction of its "corresponding" sentences.

(8)   *The company lawyer hammered out the agreement.*
      The union lawyer hammered out the agreement.
      (*Conjunction should have two agreements.*)

(9)   *John paid my check.*
      Mike paid my check.
      (*Two separate acts*)

(10) *Red complements green.*
      Green complements red.
      (*Not reflexive*)

The underlying sentences for the remaining examples do not exist, e.g.

(11) **Ice cream is a popular combination.*
      *Cake is a popular combination.

(12) **Jimmie is a pair of fools.*
      *Timmie is a pair of fools.

(13) *The child tried to mix oil.*
      The child tried to mix water.
      (*Two separate acts*)

If all sentences with compound *NP*'s are conjunctions, it is not clear how these sentences are formed. I think it is clear that they are *not* conjunctions, and should be produced as simplex sentences by a grammar of English.

3.   Sentences with unit plural *NP*'s would, therefore, be produced at the phrase structure level of the grammar, and sentences with separate-entity plural *NP*'s would be produced by a conjunction transformation. Conjunctions with *and* are formed by a transformation that conjoins sentences with *and* and allows deletion of elements that occur identically in both sentences.

(14) *The secretary went to Europe*   (16) *The secretary went to Europe and the*
(15) *The suburbanite went to Europe* →   *suburbanite went to Europe.*

In a series of steps an optional reduction rule will delete elements in the second half of the conjunction, producing (for the above example) sentences like these:

> *The secretary went to Europe and the suburbanite went too.*
> *The secretary went to Europe and the suburbanite did too.*
> *The secretary went to Europe and so did the suburbanite.*

If all identical elements are deleted from the second sentence, the final steps will move differing elements and the conjoining morpheme to form compound *NP*'s or *VP*'s, and then change dependent verbal affixes from singular to plural.

> *The secretary went to Europe and the suburbanite →*
> *The secretary and the suburbanite went to Europe.*

Note that the elements that occur identically in both sentences are not affected by the rule outlined roughly above (except for the verbal affixes).

Now consider the following pairs of sentences, Like sentences (14) and (15), they differ only as to subject. The only structural difference is that these sentences have determiner *a* in the object, where (14) and (15) have determiner *the* in the subject. But when they are conjoined according to the procedure outlined for (14) and (15), the "wrong sentences" result.

(17) *John is a philosopher.*

(18) *Mike is a philosopher.*

(19) *Gwendolyn wants a cat.*

(20) *Amanda wants a cat.*

Conjunctions:

John is a philosopher
Mike is a philosopher → (21) **John and Mike are a philosopher.*

Gwendolyn wants a cat
Amanda wants a cat → (22) *Gwendolyn and Amanda want a cat.*

Sentence (21) is ungrammatical; (22) has a unit object, but a separate-entity object is necessary for the sentence to be interpretable as a conjunction.

An additional operation will change (21) and (22) to sentences that are interpretable as conjunctions. The objects—determiner and affix—must be changed to plural. (For the conjunction of sentences (17) and (18) and sentences (19) and (20), only the verb was changed to plural.)

(23) *John and Mike are philosophers.*

(24) *Gwendolyn and Amanda want cats.*

The same addition to the conjunction transformation must be made to conjoin this pair of sentences:

(25) *George pays his (own) check.*

(26) *Erwin pays his (own) check.*

(25) and (26) are identical except for their subjects, like the other pairs of sentences that have been considered. Their objects have the identical genitive determiner (which I assume will be marked as identical) rather than *the* or *a*. The simple conjunction procedure, when applied to these sentences, gives the "wrong" result:

(27) *George and Erwin pay his check.*

The object must be changed to plural to produce the "right" conjunction of (25) and (26):

(28) *George and Erwin pay their checks.*

It is clear that the rule for conjunction with *and* must for certain sentences change the object as well as the verb to plural. The additional step will be necessary when the conjoined sentences have identical verbs and objects (or predicate nouns); when the objects or predicate nouns have determiner *a* or an identical genitive determiner; and when the second half of the conjunction is partly reduced. I think that with this addition the general conjunction rule, only roughly outlined here, will successfully produce sentences that are interpretable as conjunctions of separate entities.

It will be possible to make this addition to the rule only if compound noun phrases are produced at the phrase structure level of the grammar. Otherwise there would be no source for sentences such as the "'wrong" conjunctions above, which are English sentences. That is, sentences like

(27) *George and Erwin pay his check.*   (*His not identical*)

(22) *Gwendolyn and Amanda want a cat.*

will be produced as simplex sentences with compound subjects. The conjunction of (19) and (20) without a change in the object is ungrammatical (22); predicate sentences must always have plural predicates with plural subjects.

SOME AMBIGUOUS SENTENCES

(1) *Angus and George proved new theorems.*
Derivations:
Simplex: same as 1
Conjunction 1:   *Angus proved new theorems.*
                          George proved new theorems.
Conjunction 2:   *Angus proved a new theorem.*
                          George proved a new theorem.

(2) *Jim and Mike met friends of theirs.*
Derivations:
Simplex: same as 2 (genitive marked identical)
Conjunction 1:   *Jim met friends of theirs.*   (Genitive not identical)
                          Mike met friends of theirs.   (Genitive not identical)
Conjunction 2:   *Jim met a friend of his.*   (Genitive identical)
                          Mike met a friend of his.   (Genitive identical)

(3) *Stones and bricks make strong walls.*
Derivations:
Simplex: same as 3
Conjunction: *Stones make strong walls.*
                       Bricks make strong walls.

(4) *The lion and the unicorn went to sea.*
Derivations:
Simplex: same as 4 . . . *in a beautiful pea-green boat*
Conjunction: *The lion went to sea.*
                       The unicorn went to sea.

9

Coordinating Conjunctions in English

LILA R. GLEITMAN

The traditional definition of conjoining particles in English is this:

    (i)   Conjunction: A connective or connecting particle with the special function of joining together sentences, clauses, phrases or words.[1]

This definition leaves a good deal to the imagination. None of the following sentences is excluded, although all seem questionable:

    (1)   *Why are you leaving and shut the door.*

    (2)   *There were books on the table and so did Caesar.*

    (3)   *It is raining and snow.*

    (4)   *The and a person were never identified.*

Definitions like (i) are not intended as prescriptions for the specification of well-formed sentences, and cannot fairly be disputed on such grounds; nevertheless, the examples above violate the spirit of the definition, and would presumably lead one to restrict it. A more precise statement in transformational terms was given by Chomsky:

    (ii)   If S_1 and S_2 are grammatical sentences, and S_1 differs from S_2 only in that X appears in S_1 where Y appears in S_2 (i.e. $S_1 = \ldots X \ldots$ and $S_2 = \ldots Y \ldots$), and X and Y are constituents of the same type in S_1 and S_2 respectively, then S_3 is a sentence, where S_3 is the result of replacing X by $X + and + Y$ in S_1 (i.e. $S_3 = \ldots X + and + Y \ldots$)[2]

Reprinted from *Language*, 41. 260–293 (1965), by permission of Lila R. Gleitman and the Linguistic Society of America.

This work was supported in part by the Transformations and Discourse Analysis Projects (National Science Foundation) under the direction of Zellig S. Harris at the University of Pennsylvania, and in part by a grant from the National Institutes of Health.

I wish to thank Paul Ziff, Hans Herzberger, and Carlota Smith for their help with this work.

[1]*Webster's New International Dictionary*, 2nd ed. (Springfield, Mass., 1960).

[2]Noam Chomsky, *Syntactic Structures* (The Hague, 1957).

This paper is an attempt to provide rules for conjunction that distinguish well-formed sentences from others on the basis of their grammatical descriptions. The rules differ only in detail from (i) and (ii), although other matters of English syntax will be brought in to give a more complete description. I will deal only with the so-called coordinating conjunctions, which Webster defines

(iii) Coordinating conjunction: A conjunction that marks equal grammatical rank between the words or word groups that it connects.

I. THE FORM OF CONJOINED SENTENCES

It is a familiar method in constructing a grammar to collect a sample of sentences that are uniformly acceptable to informants, and a sample of sentences that are uniformly rejected, and to use these as the basis for description, including all the acceptable ones and none of the unacceptable ones. A third sample of sentences, to which informants respond less uniformly, is described only in so far as the inclusion of all or part of it simplifies the description of the acceptable sentences. The grammar is perhaps more interesting if it can distinguish these questionable sentences from both acceptable and unacceptable ones, i.e. if it can assign some degree of grammaticalness to questionable sentences.

It is not necessarily a simple matter to collect from informants these judgments about sentences. Many people are unable or unwilling to judge utterances for grammaticalness or to describe them as "good," "bad," or "awkward" without further comment. Questions of procedure for validating (or invalidating) the assertions of grammarians concerning judgments of grammaticalness have been raised in the literature[3] during the past few years. Not surprisingly, the results of outright questioning of informants are at best ambiguous, no matter how controlled the questioning procedure. Critics of transformational theory take these experimental results as disconfirmation; those sympathetic to this kind of grammar just as implausibly suggest that behavioral criteria should therefore be taken less seriously in judging the adequacy of a grammar. It is entirely possible that the question "Is this a grammatical sentence?" is vague and incomprehensible, but it seems obvious that asking this question is not the only way to determine whether there are behavioral correlates of a particular grammar. Psychologists have pointed out[4] that the elicitation of introspective reports from subjects in such a way that the reliability of the interpretation may be evaluated requires varied and sophisticated techniques, convergent procedures, and internal validation. What we need are techniques for submitting sentences to informants for comparison under con-

---

[3]See, for example, A. A. Hill, "Grammaticality," *Word*, 17.1–10 (1961) [*RAEL*, 1964]; and H. Maclay and M. Sleator, "Responses to Language: Judgments of Grammaticalness," *International Journal of American Linguistics*, 26.275–282 (1960).

[4]For studies by psychologists describing the elicitation and evaluation of introspective reports see J. E. Hochberg, "Perception: Toward the Recovery of a Definition," *Psychological Review*, 63.400–405 (1956); W. R. Garner, H. W. Hake, and C. W. Erikson, "Operationism and the Concept of Perception," *Psychological Review*, 63.149–159 (1956); and L. J. Postman, "Perception, Motivation, and Behavior," *Journal of Personality*, 22.17–31 (1953).

trolled conditions, as well as indirect measures of the response characteristics as a function of syntactic structure.[5]

In the absence of such systematic procedures, I have had to make some rather tenuous judgments and to ignore much detail. Nevertheless, I believe the general outlines of a description of conjunction can be set out relying on informal informant responses, particularly in view of the strong confirmatory evidence for transformational descriptions now being provided by the experimental work of Miller and others. Where a solution seems to hang on a more systematic body of data than I have available, that fact has been stated.

Example sentences judged "grammatical" are unmarked in the text. Marginal sentences, including those which are called "awkward" and those to which responses are not uniform, are preceded by a question mark. Unacceptable sentences are preceded by an asterisk.

The remainder of this section describes responses of informants to various kinds of conjoined sentences. Section II proposes rules to account for these responses.

A. Conjunctions of sentences.   Most informants will accept almost any sentence of English of the general description $S - C - S$.[6] Certain types raise special problems.

1. REPETITION OF CONJUNCTION. When one conjunct (component sentence) is itself of the form $S - C - S$, the result is likely to be judged "awkward." This is occasionally so if the conjoining particle is *and*, usually so if it is *or*, and almost invariably so if it is *but*, for example,

(5)   *He walked out to the porch and he looked carefully around the garden and he jumped.*

(6)   ?*He walked out to the porch or he looked carefully around the garden or he jumped.*

(7)   **He walked out to the porch but he looked carefully around the garden but he jumped.*

If, however, the repeated conjoining particles have different syntactic status in the sentence, the result is accepted:

(8)   *The miners will reject the proposal and the company will turn to Federal and State arbitrators.*

(9)   *The miners will accept the proposal or the company will turn to Federal or State arbitrators.*

---

[5]Recent experimental work within what has come to be called psycholinguistics is related to formal linguistic models in at least three ways: (1) evaluation of the theoretical work of linguistics, e.g. studies of recognition of transformed sentences by Miller and Mehler as reported by G. A. Miller, "Some Psychological Studies of Grammar," *American Psychologist*, 17.748–762 (1962) [*RPL*]; (2) the introduction of linguistic concepts into traditional problems and procedures of psychology, e.g. M. Glanzer, "Grammatical Category: A Rote Learning and Word Association Analysis," *Journal of Verbal Learning and Verbal Behavior*, 1.31–41 (1962); and (3) the study of children's state of language development in naturalistic settings, e.g. Martin Braine, "The Ontogeny of English Phrase Structure: The First Phase," *Language*, 39.1–13 (1963); and through the use of nonsense words embedded in a verbal and sometimes also pictorial context, e.g. J. Berko, "The Child's Learning of English Morphology," *Word*, 14.150–177 (1958); R. W. Brown, "Linguistic Determinism and the Part of Speech," in S. Saporta, ed., *Psycholinguistics* (New York, 1961).

[6]A list of abbreviations appears at the end of this paper.

(10) *The miners will accept the proposal, but the company will turn to Federal but not State arbitrators.*

2. PHRASE STRUCTURE AND TRANSFORMATIONAL DIFFERENCES BETWEEN THE CONJUNCTS. It is ordinarily assumed that all sentences described by a generative grammar share the initial symbol *S*; thus every two sentences of English have in common at least one phrase structure representation. Assuming further that identical common strings are the necessary condition for conjunction, we could suppose that all English sentences are conjoinable by virtue of the shared string *S*. These assumptions are, in general, borne out by informant responses, even to rather pointless conjoined sentences like this one:

(11) *I wrote my grandmother a letter yesterday and six men can fit in the back seat of a Ford.*

Differences in internal phrase structure and transformational history of the conjuncts do not ordinarily alter this picture, e.g.

(12) *He was offered the job and he accepted it.*

(13) *It was snowing and that made the climb difficult.*

But the conjunction of an interrogative and an imperative sentence is rejected:

(14) **What are you doing and shut the door*

One further restriction on the conjoinability of sentences is worth mentioning here. When morphemes repeated in the two conjuncts are associated with different phrase structure representations, informants respond oddly (they laugh; they groan):

(15) *He turned in his income tax and he turned in his cramped compartment.*

3. ELLIPSIS. Elided or "tag" sentences are common as the second conjunct, but are acceptable as the first conjunct only in case the second is also elided:

(16) **Honesty does and virtue reaps its own reward.*

(17) *Virtue does and honesty does too.*

If (17) is questionable, it at least is not so questionable as (16).

Restrictions on the form of the tag for a particular conjoining particle and for a particular first conjunct are very strong:

(18) *The glass broke and the bottle did too.*
The glass broke but the bottle did too.
*The glass broke or the bottle did too.

(19) *John will come and Mary will.*
*Both John will come and Mary will.
John will come or Mary will.
Either John will come or Mary will.
*John will come but Mary will.

4. THE INTERNAL SIMILARITY OF THE CONJUNCTS. Particularly perplexing for informants are conjoined sentences with identical sentential components, e.g.

(20) *?I could not decipher the rest of the message and I could not decipher the rest of the message.*

(21) *I could not decipher the rest of the message but I could not decipher the rest of the message.*

Most informants accept instances in which the conjoining particle is *and*. At the opposite extreme are sentences, such as (11), which have conjuncts with little syntactic or morphological similarity. Again, a majority of informants accepts these in case the conjoining particle is *and*. A small adamant minority calls both (11) and (20) "run-on" sentences.

B. Conjunction of clauses, phrases, and words.   Chomsky (op. cit.) suggests that "...the possibility of conjunction offers one of the best criteria for the initial determination of phrase structure. We can simplify the description of conjunction if we try to set up constituents in such a way that ... (ii) holds." By and large, the conjunction of single constituents (as defined in most generative grammars of English) produces representations of sentences uniformly accepted by speakers, with some minor restrictions. Some apparent exceptions are

1. COORDINATING CONJUNCTIONS.

(22) *He ate and he slept too.*
       He ate but he slept too.
       **He ate and or but he slept too.*

2. ARTICLES.

(23) *I saw a man.*
       I saw the man.
       **I saw a and the man.*

3. CERTAIN VERB PARTICLES.

(24) *I washed the floors up.*
       I washed the floors down.
       **I washed the floors up and down.*

4. CERTAIN MORPHOLOGICALLY IDENTICAL CONSTITUENTS.

(25) *I saw an old man.*
       I saw an old man.
       **I saw an old and old man.*

(26) *I ran faster.*
       I ran faster.
       I ran faster and faster.
       **I ran faster or faster.*

Whether or not this list exhausts the exceptions to the statement that single constituents are conjoinable depends on certain decisions about constituent structure that cannot be answered without reference to a larger context. Restrictions on the conjunction of certain nominalizations suggests that their node names should differ:

(27) **Running and to overeat may be unhealthy.*

Similarly, the restriction on conjunction raises doubts as to the convenience of considering *Adjective – Noun* in a noun phrase a constituent:

(28) **The tall man and short woman walked away.*

The possibility of exceptions of this kind to (ii) poses no particular descriptive problem. A more serious difficulty is that certain conjunctions of nonconstituent sequences of constituents are uniformly accepted by speakers:

(29) *I gave the boy a nickel and the girl a dime.*

(30) *The soviets rely on military and on political indications of our intentions.*

(31) *He took John home and Mary to the station.*

(32) *The conjunction of an interrogative and an imperative sentence is excluded.*

(33) *The man was haggard and the girl sick with exhaustion.*

Given the crude method of data collection, I find no indication that speakers balk at any of these sentences. It is interesting, however, that they appear to recall them inexactly; sentence (30), for example, is invariably judged to be acceptable, but if the informant is asked to repeat it after judging it he usually says:

(34) *The soviets rely on military and political indications of our intentions.*

Subjects seem convinced that (34) was the sentence submitted to them.[7] Notice that (34) is in fact described by (ii). Perhaps such indirect tests for atypical reception of certain sentences may illuminate notions like "maximally grammatical sentence," and obviate the necessity for seeking out informants with "a good ear," or training their intuitions.

Other conjunctions that cross constituent boundaries are judged awkward but acceptable. Still others are rejected:

(35) ?*The man saw and the woman heard the shot fired.*

(36) **I want to know why John and when Mary are coming.*

but even (36) seems to be distinguished by informants from totally unacceptable sentences such as

(37) **I ran and mud.*

While (ii) accounts for the acceptance of (34), it fails to account for the acceptance of (29)–(33), and fails to distinguish these from (36) and (37). When Chomsky proposed (ii) he made some suggestions for assigning a "degree of grammaticalness" to intermediate cases, although he did not carry out this analysis in detail. Lacking the appropriate data, little detail can be provided.

5. Conjunction of verbs and verb phrases.   Restrictions on the conjunction of verbs seem capricious. There is perhaps some confusion between the sense and the syntax when informants respond:

(38) *I saw and heard the opera.*

(39) **I saw but heard the opera.*

(40) **I hated and ate my dinner.*

(41) ?*I hated but ate my dinner.*

The problem of verb conjunction is related to the very many distinctions among verbs that must be made to account for their differing transformational capacities. Relatively few verbs in English undergo all and only the same transforma-

---

[7]*On* must be pronounced in both instances with low stress to get this result.

tions, and this fact complicates the phrase structure description of verbs and their objects. Notice that (ii) applies only in case X and Y have the same structural description.

Verb phrases are uniformly conjoinable, with one exception: if the verb of VP_1 and the verb of VP_2 are identical, the conjunction of verb phrases is awkward:

(42) ?*I saw the tall man and saw the short man.*

C. The relation of but to negation. Zellig Harris has proposed a description of coordinating conjunctions that makes the following distinction. Two differences between the conjuncts are required for the use of *but*, while only one difference is required for the use of *or* and no difference is required for the use of *and*. This description is designed to explain informant responses like these:

(43)   *John washed and dried his hands.*
        ?*John washed but dried his hands.*
        John washed his face but dried his hands.

(44)   *He had a green and yellow apple.*
        **He had a green but yellow apple.*
        ?*He had a green but not yellow apple.*

(45)   *John and Mary arrived.*
        **John but Mary arrived.*
        John but not Mary arrived.

The kind of "opposition" necessary for the natural use of *but* is quite easy to grasp intuitively, but this opposition is apparently not always syntactically marked. Certain conjunctions with *but* containing only one (known) syntactic difference are acceptable, e.g.

(46)   *He respected but feared the Hungarians.*
        **He liked but knew the Hungarians.*

(47)   *He had an old but serviceable revolver.*
        ?*He had an old but decrepit revolver.*

The use of *but* as a coordinating conjunction[8] is in many ways more restricted than the use of *and* and *or*. Sentences, and certain predicates, adjectives, verbs, and adverbs may be conjoined with *but*, but other constituents (e.g. prepositions) may not; furthermore, iteration of conjunction with *but* is almost totally excluded.

However, when one conjunct contains a negative element and the other does not, the range of use of *but* becomes wider; this is part of the intuition that Harris's description captures. We shall see that most transformations introducing any coordinating particle introduce *and* in particular. The only exceptions are uses of *but* with negation, e.g.

(48)   *Not the method but the timing is questionable.*
        **Not the method and the timing is questionable.*

D. Repetition, reference, and conjunction. In conjoined sentences that have conjuncts partially alike, there is often an ambiguity of referent; when a noun phrase

---

[8]The word *but* has further uses that are traditionally called prepositional, e.g. *Nobody but John is coming*. These are not described in this paper.

is repeated or when a pronoun occurs in the position of *NP*, informants express doubt as to whether a repetition was intended. Consider the following sentences:[9]

(49) *A tall man observed the criminal.*

(50) *A tall man called the police.*

(51) *A tall man observed the criminal and a tall man called the police.*

(52) *A tall man observed the criminal and a tall one called the police.*

(53) *A tall man observed the criminal and **he** called the police.*

(54) *A tall man observed the criminal and he called the police.*

(55) *A tall man observed the criminal and called the police.*

The conjoined sentences (51)–(55) are presumably derived from strings underlying (49) and (50). Informant guesses concerning the referent of the subject noun phrase of the second conjunct differ systematically.[10] Informants guess that the tall men of the first and second conjuncts of (51) are "most probably" different people. Thus repetition of an identical phrase (*a tall man*) in this instance leads to the supposition that no repetition of referent was intended. The same is true of the indefinite pronominal of (52). The stressed[11] definite pronominal phrase in (53) leads to conflicting judgments: some informants guess that one man is involved, some guess two, and some say there is no way of deciding. Fewer informants guess that two referents are intended when an unstressed pronominal, (54), is used. If the repeated noun phrase is deleted, as in (55), informants respond uniformly that there was a repetition of referent.

In short, repetition of *NP* leads to the view that there was no repetition of referent; substitution of pronouns leads to intermediate judgments; nonrepetition leads to the view that there was repetition.

E. Number and conjunction. A characteristic effect of conjunction with *and* is the introduction of an ambiguity of number, e.g.

(56) *John and Mary were carrying baskets.*

This sentence has as approximate paraphrases either of the following pairs:

(57) *John was carrying a basket.*
      Mary was carrying a basket.

(58) *John was carrying baskets.*
      Mary was carrying baskets.

This vagueness of number is the more evident when number adjectives modify the noun:

---

[9]The intonation contour of these sentences strongly affects informant judgments. This fact will be reflected in the rules of Section II. Assume here that there is a "colorless" (noncontrastive) pattern associated with these sentences, and that this pattern is intended in the examples.

[10]It is obvious that the choice of the indefinite article is crucial to informant choices in all these examples. A different outcome is achieved by substituting *the*, but the same general conclusions hold. See Section II.E for a discussion of the relationship between the articles and pronominal replacement.

[11]Contrastive stress is indicated by boldface italic. Although physically the stress falls on a single syllable, the entire word or phrase assumed to receive stress is in boldface italic. Section II.H gives a more complete description of the stress patterns.

(59) *John and Mary were carrying four baskets.*

This may be intended to mean that each was carrying four, or that each was carrying two, or that one was carrying one and the other three. Yet the apparent syntactic source for (59) is a pair of strings underlying:

(60) *John was carrying four baskets.*
      Mary was carrying four baskets.

Certain constructions in which the noun phrases must agree in number pose similar descriptive problems:

(61) **John are linguists.*
      *Mary are linguists.
      John and Mary are linguists.

(62) **John are a couple.*
      *John is a couple.
      John and Mary are a couple.
      *John, Mary, and Bill are a couple.

Somewhat different are instances in which the singular forms are senseless, or seem to have an irregular relationship to conjunction:

(63) **Two is four.*
      *Two is four.
      Two and two is four.
      Two and two are four.

(64) *The glass is red.*
      The glass is blue.
      The glass is red and blue.

(65) **John met.*
      *Mary met.
      John and Mary met.

II. A DESCRIPTION OF ENGLISH CONJUNCTION

A. The intuitive basis of the analysis.   One simple hypothesis motivates the form and organization of the rules for conjunction that will be given here: conjunction is one of many syntactic processes that serve the purpose of indicating contrast or reducing repetition; a conjoined sentence that does not indicate contrast or reduce repetition has not served any purpose. It is often called a "run-on" sentence.

Repeated and nonrepeated material in English sentences are treated quite differently. Repeated material may be left out (or *deleted*), while nonrepeated material may not. Repeated material may be replaced by shorter or simpler (*Pro-*) forms, while nonrepeated material may not. Repeated material may be deemphasized (or *unstressed*), while nonrepeated material may be emphasized (or *stressed*).

These differences in the treatment of repeated and nonrepeated material are evident in both simplexes (single-kernel sentences) and complexes (multikernel sentences). There is considerable difference in detail in the treatment of repetition in simplexes as opposed to complexes, but there is a striking overall similarity.

The central feature of this account of conjunction is an operation marking repeated versus unrepeated symbols appearing in strings and certain pairs of strings.

Once this is done, it becomes simpler to describe conjunction and the related processes of deletion, substitution, and unstressing of repeated material.

B. The phrase structure grammar. This grammar of conjunction presupposes a phrase structure description of English. While no complete description exists, outlines for a phrase structure component of a grammar have been given by Chomsky (op. cit.) and others.[12]

The description of conjunction requires certain minor revisions in previously proposed phrase structure rules. Those rules relating to the expansion of the symbol *VP* (verb phrase) are reproduced here, following Fillmore, in abbreviated form and with the changes that we require. The details of the expansion of *VP* are particularly relevant to the generation of conjoined sentences with tags.[13]

(iv) $VP \rightarrow Prev\ Aux\ MV$
(v) $MV \rightarrow Vb\ (Loc)\ (Tm)$
(vi) $Vb \rightarrow V; \ldots$
(vii) $V \rightarrow Vtr\ Nom\ (Man); \ldots$
(viii) $Prev \rightarrow \sigma\ (Pvb)$
(ix) $\sigma \rightarrow Pos; Neg$
(x) $Neg\ Pvb \rightarrow Neg\ \gamma_1$
(xi) $Pvb \rightarrow \gamma_1; \gamma_2$
(xii) $Aux \rightarrow Aux_1\ (Aux_2)$
(xiii) $Aux_1 \rightarrow Tense\ (M)$
(xiv) $Aux_2 \rightarrow (Have\ en)\ (Be\ ing)$
(xv) $Tense \rightarrow Present; Past$
(xvi) $M \rightarrow can; may; must; shall; will$
(xvii) $\gamma_1 \rightarrow always; often; \ldots$
(xviii) $\gamma_2 \rightarrow never; seldom; \ldots$

The differences from previous versions are these: In (iv) *Prev* is introduced as a necessary (not optional) part of the expansion. *Prev* is then expanded, (viii) and (ix), into an obligatory element (σ) and an optional element (*Pvb*). (viii) and (ix) replace Fillmore's rule:

(xix) $Prev \rightarrow (E)\ (not)\ (Pvb)$

In (xix), the morpheme of affirmation (*E*) and the morpheme of negation (*not*) are viewed as optional phrase structure elements. In this revision, a symbol (σ) representing sign is obligatory; the morphological properties of *Pos* and *Neg* will be described in due course.

C. Contrastive stress and conjunction. Associated with every sentence is a pattern of intonation that can be called colorless (normal, noncontrastive). Robert Stockwell[14] has described rules that indicate the colorless patterns for kernel sentences

---

[12]See, for example, the phrase structure description given by Charles Fillmore in *Indirect Object Constructions in English and the Ordering of Transformations*, Ohio State University Research Foundation, Project on Syntactic Analysis, Report No. 1 (Columbus, 1962) [The Hague: Mouton & Co., 1965].

[13]Semicolons in formulas indicate alternative rewritings; parentheses indicate optional elements; ellipsis (. . .) indicates that a list is not exhaustive.

[14]R. P. Stockwell, *The Place of Intonation in a Generative Grammar of English*, Language, 36.360–367 (1960) [*RAEL*, 1964].

and unary transformations. Further, he describes a transformation of "emphasis" that introduces contrastive stress onto strings previously marked with the colorless pattern. This transformation in effect allows any constituent (excluding affixes) to receive the main stress.

We have seen, however, that there are stress patterns associated with conjoined sentences that are not characteristic of (that would be contrastive for) the conjuncts of these sentences. For example, while (67) below is contrastive,[15] (68) is colorless; while (66) is colorless, the same sequence as a conjunct, (69), is not.

(66)   *I saw an old **house.***

(67)   *I saw an **old** house.*

(68)   *I saw an **old** house and I saw a **new** house.*

(69)   *I saw an old **house** and I saw a new **house.***

(70)   *I saw an old **house** and I saw an old **barn.***

In short, stress is related to repetition. The repetitions that affect stress patterns are repetitions of morphemes; thus two sentences with the same phrase structure descriptions do not in general have the same colorless pattern of stress (e.g. (68), (70)). Since there are repetitions in a conjoined sentence where there were no repetitions in its conjuncts, the patterns of stress are affected by the fact of conjunction.

The rules below describe repetition-conditioned stress patterns in English sentences. They state that repeated material may be stressed only by use of an optional transformation, and that nonrepeated material under certain conditions is obligatorily stressed.

1. Stress on *NP*. Repetition of *NP* in a simplex (an oddity) is accompanied by increase in stress:

(71)   *John saw **John.***

Repeated *NP* in a complex (not an oddity) is ordinarily unstressed, but on rare occasions stressed:

(72)   *The **man** saw the child and the **woman** saw the child.*

(73)   *The man saw the child and the woman saw the **child.***

Repetition with increase in stress in both simplexes, (71), and complexes, (73), results in judgments by informants that no repetition of referent was intended, while unstressed repetition indicates repetition of referent. Contrast (the instance of nonrepetition among repetitions) is ordinarily accompanied by increase in stress, e.g. ***man, woman*** in (72).

Intuitively, increase in stress is always an indication of contrast or nonrepetition. Syntactically, it sometimes appears to be also an indication of repetition: when, on the face of it, there *seems* to have been a repetition, but a different referent is intended, the second instance receives heavy stress:

(xx) $(X) - NP - (Y) - NP' - (Z) \rightarrow (X) - NP - (Y)' - NP'^\star - (Z)$ (optional)
where $NP = NP'$

The mark $\star$ is, for one thing, a direction for a morphophonemic (pronunciation)

---

rule that associates primary stress with some terminal element in a string. These stress effects are systematically related to the form of grammar rules for embedding a constituent string into a matrix string. Furthermore, elements marked ⋆are not liable to deletion or replacement by pro forms.[16] Eventual outputs of (xx) are (71) and (73). The effects of $T_{emphatic}$ and (xx) are here identical. It should be understood that subsequent operations on ⋆-marked strings are independent of whether ⋆ results from (xx), (xxi), or $T_{emphatic}$.

2. STRESS ON ARTICLES.   It has been mentioned that *the* and *a* are unconjoinable (with such obvious exceptions as this sentence). This fact can be written into a rule of conjunction as a special restriction. However, there are conjoinable determiners (e.g. *this, that*). Such words in otherwise identical *NP* produce very much the same kind of reaction from informants as do stressed repeated *NP*; they result in judgments of nonrepetition of referent:

(74)   *I saw **this** painting and **that** painting.*

(75)   *I saw **this** painting and **this** painting.*

(76)   **I saw **the** painting and **the** painting.*

(77)   **I saw **the** painting and **a** painting.*

The distribution of *the* and *this* seems to be complementary—(75),(76). Where their distribution seems to overlap, it can be shown that they differ in the stress feature, or that the overlap is conditioned by a primary stress on the *N* to which they are adjoined. We can therefore treat *this* and *that* as stressed morpheme alternates for the definite article; similarly, *one* and *another* are stressed forms of *a*.[17] The need to restrict the conjunction rule for articles is now obviated. The relation of referent to stress described for *NP* is described for articles by a rule closely analogous to (xx):

(xxi) $(X) - T - (Y) - N - (Z) - T' - (Y') - N' - (W) \rightarrow$
        $(X) - T\star - (Y) - N - (Z) - T'\star - (Y') - N' - (W)$ (optional)
        where $T - (Y) - N$ is a noun phrase, $N = N'$, $Y = Y'$

(xxii) $the\star \rightarrow this;\ that;\ T + other\star$

(xxiii) $a\star \rightarrow one_1;\ T + other\star$

It will be shown that only stressed constituents appear contiguous to a conjoining particle. Thus conjoined articles are possible only in case the option of (xxi) is taken.

3. STRESS ON NONREPEATED ELEMENTS IN A COMPLEX.   The following rule indicates the heavy stress with which nonrepeated elements in a complex are characteristically pronounced. The rule states that if two sentences have associated with them any identical string, those elements of the strings that are associated with different morphemic representations receive the mark ⋆. The rule is germane to stress and

---

[16]The symbol ⋆ is thus an element of description of the written language (where stress is unmarked) as well as the spoken language. For descriptions of written English (e.g. those of Zellig S. Harris), it would seem that equivalent marking of repeated and contrastive elements is necessary.

[17]*One* always is the first instance, *another* the second; the same order is (much more weakly) evident with *this* and *that*. The choice between *this* and *that* is further conditioned by features of the nonlinguistic environment. The point here is that *that* is as much a repetition of *this* as *this* is; both are members of a single morpheme (*the*).

apparent deletion in English relative clauses, coordinate and subordinate conjunctions, and sentences with sentential verb objects:

(xxiv) $S_1: (X) - Y - (Z)$ $(X) - Y\star - (Z)$
        $S_2: (X') - Y' - (Z')$ $(X') - Y'\star - (Z')$ (obligatory)

        .
        . $\rightarrow$.
        .

        $S_n: (X^n) - Y^n - (Z^n)$ $(X^n) - Y^n\star - (Z^n)$

where $X - Y - Z$, $X' - Y' - Z'$, ... $X^n - Y^n - Z^n$ are identical strings and, in the phrase structure trees associated with these strings, X, X', ... X^n, Y, Y', ... Y^n, Z, Z', ... Z^n have identical dominators. Y, Y', ... Y^n are non-terminal constituents dominating nonidentical nodes.

(xxiv) applies but once to a particular constituent, but may apply more than once to a particular pair of strings. A morphophonemic rule later assigns heavy stress to terminal elements immediately dominated by $\star$:

(xxv) *Morpheme* $\rightarrow$ *Morpheme* + *Stress*
     where *morpheme* is immediately dominated by a $\star$-marked node.

A more detailed account of (xxv) will be given later. Notice that (xxiv) itself does not mark terminal elements. Figure 1 shows the phrase-structure trees associated with the sentences

(78) *I saw a tall man.*
     I saw a short man.

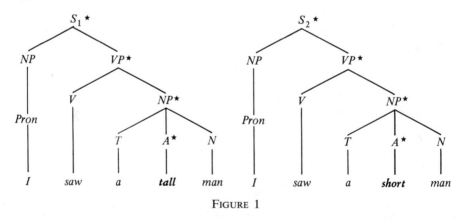

FIGURE 1

after (xxiv) and (xxv) have applied. These two sentences have in common (among others) the strings[18]

---

[18]In Figure 1, the expansions of *NP* are *T, A, N*. No intervening node is taken to dominate *TA* or *TN* or *AN*. In fact it would be convenient for the description of conjunction to assume a node (*PreN*) dominating *TA*. This would account for informant responses to *I saw a tall and a short man; *I saw a tall man and short woman.* Such decisions about constituent structure cannot be decided by reference to conjunction alone. Informant data for these marginal cases is in any case insufficient to describe the subtle choices here. For example, in the second instance above, one can generally get the informant to change his decision by asking him to imagine a monster who is at once a tall man and short woman.

$S; NP - VP; NP - V - NP; NP - V - T - A - N$ (before (xxiv))
$S\star; NP - VP\star; NP - V - NP\star; NP - V - T - A\star - N$ (after (xxiv))

In Section I, I discussed the fact that the conjunction of strings with like morphological structure and unlike phrase structure strikes informants as odd or amusing. An example was

(15)(a) *He turned in his income tax.*
  (b) *He turned in his cramped compartment.*
  (c) *He turned in his income tax and he turned in his cramped compartment.*
  (d) **He turned in his income tax and his cramped compartment.*

The conjuncts of (15c)—(a) and (b)—are conjoinable because they share the derivational string $S\star$. They share as well the string $NP - V - P - NP\star$. But (xxiv) does not in fact apply to this latter pair of strings; the dominators of P differ. The dominator of P is in one case V and in the other case *Adjunct*. Thus the contrasting NP's are not stressed by (xxiv), (xxv), despite the similarity in morphological shape. It is this incompatibility of phrase structure and morphological shape that makes (15c) seem odd; conjunctions that do not mark contrast are odd. Because NP is not marked by (xxiv), we will find further that the conjunction (15d) is excluded.

D. Rules for conjunction. The rule for conjunction[19] is no different from (ii) except for some restatement arising from the use of (xxiv). As stated earlier, (ii) has the virtue of specifying only fully grammatical sentences, although it requires some restriction.

1. CONJUNCTION.

(xxvi) $\left.\begin{array}{l} S_1: (X) - Y\star - (Z) \\ S_2: (X') - Y'\star - (Z') \\ \cdot \\ \cdot \\ \cdot \\ S_n: (X^n) - Y^n\star - (Z^n) \end{array}\right\} \rightarrow (X) - \bar{Y}\star - C - \bar{Y}'\star \ldots C - Y^n\star - (Z)$ (optional)

        where X and Z have no mark $\star$, and $Y, Y', \ldots Y^n$ are single constituents;
           $Y \neq C_c; Y \neq S_{\text{imperative}}$ if $Y' = S_{\text{interrogative}}$
(xxvii) $\bar{Y} \rightarrow Y +$ rising intonation
(xxviii) $NP \rightarrow NP + Plural$ (obligatory)
        where NP dominates $NP - and - NP$.
(xxix) $NP \rightarrow NP + Plural$ (optional)
        where NP dominates $N - and - N$
(xxx) $C \rightarrow but$ (optional)
        where $Y = S; A; VP; Adv$, and where $S_n = S_2$.[20]

---

[19]Noam Chomsky suggested to me the idea of conjoining strings *n* at a time, rather than two at a time (except, of course, for the case of *but*, which is noniterative). If conjunction is limited to two strings, a complex phrase structure must be built up to describe sentences with more than one conjoining particle. Not only is this picture of phrase structure counterintuitive, but it creates two problems of description: (*a*) the rule for deletion of the conjoining particle (comma intonation) becomes difficult, and (*b*) the distinction between coordinate and subordinate conjunction becomes obscure.

[20]Considerable subclassification is necessary here. For example, color adjectives and numerals are not conjoinable with *but*: **I have three but four decisions to make; *I have seven but green apples to sell.*

(xxxi) $C \rightarrow$ *and*; *or*   (obligatory)[21]

The output string of the conjunction rules has the phrase structure of the input string (S_1) except that (*a*) a node Y is introduced dominating $Y\star$, C, $Y'\star$,... C, $Y^n\star$, and (*b*) $\star$ is deleted from nodes not dominated by the derived node Y.[22]

(xxviii) and (xxix) will be required when we describe number agreement between subject and verb. Because the number of *NP* is affected by a variety of transformations, the rule for agreement is presumably a late one.

The conjunction of identical strings underlying the pair of sentences in (78) (see also Figure 1) generates

(79)   *I saw a **tall** man and I saw a **short** man.* $(S - C - S)$

(80)   ?*I saw a **tall** man and saw a **short** man.* $(VP - C - VP)$

(81)   *I saw a **tall** man and a **short** man.* $(NP - C - NP)$

(82)   ?*I saw a **tall** and **short** man.* $(A - C - A)$

Admission of the node *PreN* would result in the additional production:

(83)   *I saw a **tall** and a **short** man.* $(PreN - C - PreN)$

Sentences (80) and (82) are odd. It was mentioned that the conjunction of *VP*'s is odd where V_1 is identical to V_2. The problem in (82) is quite different. The deletion of *NP* leads to supposition that there was a repetition of referent. The same is true for deletion of *N*; a case was shown when what remains is a stressed article. The case for adjectives is the same. Thus we expect, in (82), that only one man is involved; that is what the syntactic feature (*N*-deletion) suggests. However, the sense of the adjectives makes this unlikely; no man is at once tall and short. In general, of course, the conjunction of adjectives is permissible. Only the conjunction of "polar" adjectives in contexts of this kind seems odd. The difficulty of the example may be compounded by substituting *the* for *a* in (82), since judgments of same referent are increased with the definite article.

Sentences that cannot be described as instances of the conjunction of single constituents have thus far been excluded. These may be described in part by relaxing the condition on (xxvi) that Y and Y' be single constituents. As Chomsky noted, the conjunction of pairs of constituents "high up" in the tree usually results in

---

[21]All the following discussion is limited to these three coordinating conjunctions, which are certainly the major ones in English. It is possible to exclude the whole host of subordinating conjunctions from this class on a single criterial basis: subordinating conjunctions allow the pronominalization (or "deletion") to precede their antecedent noun. For example:

After his retirement, Churchill maintained an active interest in public affairs.

Because he had been in Germany, Lenin was distrusted by the Cossacks.

While granting Churchill's point, the Tories continued the policy of disarmament.

(In order that the description of pronominalization remain simple, it is necessary to assume that permutation of the conjuncts is a feature of the structures exemplified above.) There are, nevertheless, conjoining morphemes not excluded by this criterion that are not to be discussed here. An example is *yet*.

[22]It may be argued that this deletion of $\star$ would be unnecessary had we assumed that (xxvi) preceded (xxiv). In that case it would be necessary to compare for morphological identity of the strings from which the conjoined sentence was generated in order to place the stress, i.e. to make reference to the transformational history of the conjoined string. In principle this is no difficulty, but it requires separate statement of the positions in which pronominal replacement is allowable, and seriously complicates the description of tag sentences.

passable constructions. It is difficult to carry this notion very much further without having available a more systematic body of informant data. It may be said, though, that a relaxation of the rule to include pairs of constituents will not entirely resolve the problem. Also, the notion "high up" in the tree is hard to define; substituents of object *NP*'s are "lower down" than substituents of subject *NP*'s by virtue of the node *VP*; yet the conjunction $P - A - C - P - A$ (see, for example, (30)) is as acceptable in one case as in the other. A rule of deletion something like this,

$$X - Y\star - Z - C - P - Q\star - R \rightarrow X - Y\star - C - Q\star - R$$

where $Y\star$ is the last $\star$-marked constituent of the first conjunct and $Q\star$ is the first $\star$-marked constituent of the second conjunct

will account for the productions of (xxvi) as well as all intermediate cases described in §I.5, but it will not distinguish between these two sets. For example, this rule generates

I want to know why John (is coming) and (I want to know) when Mary is coming
X $\quad Y\star \quad Z$ $\quad C \quad P \quad Q\star \quad R$

2. DELETION OF THE CONJOINING MORPHEME. When (xxvi) applies more than once in the derivation of a sentence, the way it is applied to the component strings affects the phrase structure representation of the output, but the sequence of segmental morphemes in the final output is always the same. Unless a difference in intonation contour can be shown, we would expect on theoretical grounds that ambiguity would be perceived by informants wherever nonequivalent trees with identical terminal strings are derived. For example, sentence (84) below can be derived from strings $(NP - V - NP)$ underlying (85) in more than one way. Some sample derivations—(86) and (87)—are given here. The derivation (86) is represented by the tree of Figure 2; the derivation (87) is represented by the tree of Figure 3.

A third and still different phrase structure tree results when we conjoin the strings underlying (85) in a single step, as shown in derivation (88) and Figure 4. It will be shown that this derivation is the source for "comma intonation," i.e. the deletion of the conjoining morpheme.

(84) *I saw John and Mary and Bill and Jim.*

(85) *I saw John.*
      I saw Mary.
      I saw Bill.
      I saw Jim.

(86) $\begin{matrix} NP - V - NP_1\star \\ NP - V - NP_2\star \end{matrix} \rightarrow NP - V - NP_1\star - C - NP_2\star = NP - V - NP_3$
      $\begin{matrix} NP - V - NP_4\star \\ NP - V - NP_3\star \end{matrix} \rightarrow NP - V - NP_4\star - C - NP_3\star = NP - V - NP_5$
      $\begin{matrix} NP - V - NP_6\star \\ NP - V - NP_5\star \end{matrix} \rightarrow NP - V - NP_6\star - C - NP_5\star = NP - V - NP_7$

(87) $\begin{matrix} NP - V - NP_1\star \\ NP - V - NP_2\star \end{matrix} \rightarrow NP - V - NP_1\star - C - NP_2\star = NP - V - NP_3$
      $\begin{matrix} NP - V - NP_4\star \\ NP - V - NP_5\star \end{matrix} \rightarrow NP - V - NP_4\star - C - NP_5\star = NP - V - NP_6$
      $\begin{matrix} NP - V - NP_3\star \\ NP - V - NP_6\star \end{matrix} \rightarrow NP - V - NP_3\star - C - NP_6\star = NP - V - NP_7$

(88) $NP - V - NP_1\star$
      $NP - V - NP_2\star$
      $NP - V - NP_3\star$ $\rightarrow NP - V - NP_1\star - C - NP_2\star - C - NP_3\star - C - NP_4\star$
      $NP - V - NP_4\star$

Figures 2 and 3 differ in the placement of rising intonation. In Figure 2, the morphemes *John, Mary,* and *Bill* are immediately dominated by bar-marked nodes; in Figure 3, *John* and *Bill* are dominated by bar-marked nodes. Similarly, there are two characteristic intonation patterns associated with sentences like (84), the one we would expect if a waitress said,

(89) *Today we have ham and tongue and tuna fish and pastrami.*

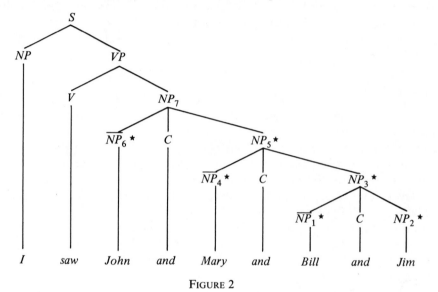

FIGURE 2

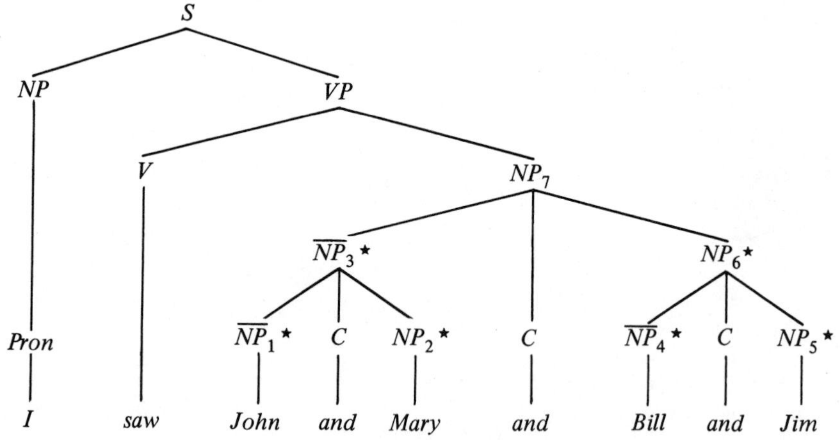

FIGURE 3

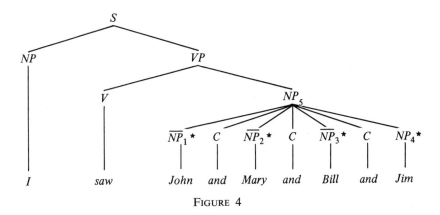

Figure 4

and the one we would expect if she said,

(90)   *Today we have ham and egg, and cream cheese and lox.*

Sentence (89) can be paraphrased: *Today we have ham, tongue, tuna fish, and pastrami,* but this rephrasing would alter the meaning of (90). That is to say, (90) has a "main" and two "subordinate" conjoining particles.[23]

While the placement of rising intonation in Figures 2 and 4 is identical, the configurations of the trees are quite different. That derivation (86) is allowable under the conjunction rule as we have given it is perhaps a misfortune, because on theoretical grounds we expect an ambiguity to be perceived by speakers when two nonequivalent trees terminate with the same string of morphemes. We can account for the lack of ambiguity by the simple stratagem of making the deletion of the conjoining morpheme obligatory where two *C*'s are dominated immediately by the same node, as in Figure 4. In that case the outputs of (86) and (88) are not ambiguous for the simple reason that (88) is never a terminal derivation:

(xxxii) $(Y) - \bar{X} - C - \bar{X}' - (Z) - C - X'' - (W) \rightarrow (Y) - \bar{X} - \bar{X}' - (Z) - C - X'' - (W)$
       (obligatory)
       where $C = C'$, $X = X' = X''$, and X, X', X'', Z are immediately dominated by a single node X

(xxxii) is of course applicable to its own outputs: the optional element in the formula (Z) can only be some multiple of $C-X$, since it is immediately dominated by the same node that dominates the other elements of the formula.

E. Pronominalization.   An effect of repetition (and thus of conjunction) is the substitution of pro forms. Rules for certain pro noun phrases have been proposed by Lees and Klima.[24] Some differences between that description and this one arise from the optional use of (xx) for increasing the stress on repeated *NP*, and from

---

[23]Stockwell [op. cit.] suggests that the lesser fade at the juncture between the two "main" conjuncts can be described as an environmentally conditioned allophone of terminal fade (i.e. a constituent string, which is always marked phrase structurally for terminal fade, has instead terminal sustain or lesser fade when it ends before the matrix sentence ends).

[24]R. B. Lees and E. S. Klima, "Rules for English Pronominalization," *Language,* 39.17–28 (1963) [*MSE*].

the rule for conjunction (xxvi). In addition to a description of pro noun phrases, we give in this section a description of pro nouns, and a description of the relationship between certain determiners and pronominals.

1. PRONOUNS.   The words ordinarily called pronouns (*I, you, he, she, it*) have a privilege of occurrence quite similar to that of *NP*; often (at least in the context of a grammar of independent sentences) they cannot be said to have "antecedent" *NP* to which they are in some sense identical, and for which they are replacements. Certain peculiarities in the distribution of third person pronouns can best be accounted for with transformational rules: there are stress features in some uses of these pronouns that differ from the stress on *NP* in identical positions. In just these cases, the antecedent *NP* of the pronoun is predictable and the problem of reference (same/other) that we have described is evident. In these same cases, we find agreement of number between the pronoun and its antecedent. We call pronouns that can be said to replace repeated *NP* "*Pro Noun Phrases.*" When the same phonemic entities cannot be said to replace repeated *NP* we call them "*Pronouns.*"

All first- and second-person pronouns, the "impersonal" pronoun *one* (*here* called *one₃*), and some instances of third-person pronouns are derived with phrase structure rules:

(xxxiii) $NP \rightarrow T - N$; N_{mass}; *Pronoun*
(xxxiv)   *Pronoun* $\rightarrow$ *Pronoun* + *case* ($+pl$)
 (xxxv)   *Case* $\rightarrow$ *Nom*; *Gen*; *Acc*
(xxxvi)   *Pronoun* $\rightarrow$ *I; you; he; she; it; one₃*

2. PRO NOUN PHRASES.   The transformational rule introducing pro noun phrases is parallel to (xx), which is repeated below for convenience. If the stress on a repeated *NP* is not increased (marked ⋆) by (xx), it may be decreased (marked *r*) by (xxxvii):

   (xx) $(X) - NP - (Y) - NP' - (Z) \rightarrow (X) - NP - (Y) - NP'\star - (Z)$ (optional)
       where $NP = NP'$, and $V \neq V_{reflex}$[25]
 (xxxvii) $(X) - NP - (Y) - NP' - (Z) \rightarrow (X) - NP - (Y) - NP'r - (Z)$ (optional for a complex; obligatory for a simplex)
       where $NP = NP' \neq NP\star$ in a simplex; $NP = NP'$ in a complex.
(xxxviii) $NP'r \rightarrow Pronoun'r$ (obligatory)
 (xxxix) $r \rightarrow$ reduced stress

Which pronominal replacement occurs depends on three features of strings containing the symbol *Pronoun'r*: (*a*) the transformational history of the symbol *Pronoun*; (*b*) the form of the string (simplex or complex); and (*c*) the determiner (definite or indefinite) of *NP* dominating the symbol *Pronoun*.

(*a*) *Transformational history of the symbol.*   The symbol *Pronoun* derived phrase structurally is expanded as indicated by (xxxiv)–(xxxvi). The morphemes of (xxxviii) are the same, but a low-stress feature accompanies the transformationally derived

---

[25]V_{reflex} is a class of verbs requiring a replica of the subject as their object. Such objects are obligatorily replaced by reflexive forms. A detailed description is given by Lees and Klima [ibid.].

symbol. The stress of phrase structure pronouns is not so prescribed. Thus there are ambiguities of pronouns versus pro noun phrases when the former happen to have low stress; in some cases we will not know whether or not the low stress word has an antecedent in the sentence, e.g.

(91) *John said he would come.*

(92) *When the queen arrived home she ate dinner.*

(*b*) *Pro noun phrases for simplex and complex.*   The symbol *Pronoun* in simplexes is either replaced by the reciprocal pronoun or marked by the affix *-self*:

(xl) $(X) - NP - (Y) - Pronoun'r + Pl - (Z) \rightarrow (X) - NP - (Y) - Recip - (Z)$ (optional)
    where the source string is a simplex

(xli)   *Recip* $\rightarrow$ *each other; one another*

(xlii) $(X) - NP - (Y) - Pronoun'r (+Pl) - (Z) \rightarrow$
    $(X) - NP - (Y) - Pronoun'r (+Pl) + self (+Pl) - (Z)$ (obligatory)
    where the source string is a simplex

(*c*) *Pronominal replacers.*   Rewritings of transformationally derived *Pronoun'r* differ according to the article of *NP* dominating *Pronoun'r*:

(xliii) $T_1 - (Y) - N - (Z) - r \rightarrow$ *he; she; it; one$_2$*

(xliv) $(T_2) - (Y) - N - (Z) - r \rightarrow$ *he; she; it*
    where $(T) - (Y) - N - (Z) - r$ is an *r*-marked *NP*
    $T_1 = a, some,$ and $T_2 = the$

(xlv) $(Y) - you + Acc + self - (Z) \rightarrow (Y) - you + Gen + self - (Z)$

(xlvi) $(Y) - I + Acc + self - (Z) \rightarrow (Y) - I + Gen + self - (Z)$

(xliii) and (xliv) account for the following restrictions on pronominal replacement:

(93) *The **queen** saw the man and the **king** saw him.*

(94) **The **queen** saw the man and the **king** saw one.*

These rules for pronominalization differ in several respects from those given by Lees and Klima. It should be pointed out that these writers were concerned only with a subset of pronouns (they exclude *one*) and with only a part of the distribution of pronouns (they do not discuss pronouns derived phrase structurally, i.e. the ambiguity of (91) and (92). Rules (xxxvii), (xl), and (xlii) are roughly similar to the Lees and Klima version. However, we assign the option not to the use of the reflexive morpheme (xlii), but to the assignment of stress (xx). If the option of increasing stress (i.e. intending two different referents) is not taken, pronominalization with the reflexive or reciprocal forms is obligatory in simplexes. Intuitively, pronominal replacement is obligatory in a simplex where a repetition of referent is intended.[26]

The pronominal replacers are marked for low stress (xxxviii). But we sometimes find stressed pronouns in complexes with statable antecedents:

(95) ***John** bowed to **Mary** and **she** bowed to **him**.*

This sentence contains the now familiar ambiguity of referent: *She* may or may not be *Mary*; *him* may or may not be *John*. The instance in which the *NP*'s are not the antecedents is a simple consequence of (xxiv) and the phrase structurally derived

---

[26]An anomaly is *Organisms reproduce themselves.*

pronouns: (xxiv) marks the nonidentical subject constituents (***John/she***) and the nonidentical object constituents (***Mary/him***). The instance in which *Mary* is antecedent of *she*, and *John* antecedent to *him* is more difficult; we must account for the heavy stress on the pronouns in the face of (xxxvii). In fact, the stressed pronouns follow from the rules as they have been stated. It sometimes, as here, happens in complexes that (xxxvii) prescribes pronominalization with low stress at the same time that (xxiv) prescribes heavy stress, e.g.

(96) $NP_1 - V - NP_2 \rightarrow NP_1{}^{\star} - V - NP_2{}^{\star}$
$NP_2 - V - NP_1 \rightarrow NP_2{}^{\star} - V - NP_1{}^{\star}$
(successive applications of (xxiv))

$NP_1{}^{\star} - V - NP_2{}^{\star}$
$NP_2{}^{\star} - V - NP_1{}^{\star}$ $\rightarrow NP_1{}^{\star} - V - NP_2{}^{\star} - C - NP_2{}^{\star} - V - NP_1{}^{\star}$ (xxvi)

$NP_1{}^{\star} - V - NP_2{}^{\star} - C - NP_2{}^{\star} - V - NP_1{}^{\star} \rightarrow NP_1{}^{\star} - V - NP_2{}^{\star} - C - NP_2{}^{\star}r - V - NP_1{}^{\star}r$
(successive applications of (xxxvii))

Since (xxxvii) is optional, we derive both (95) and

(97)   ***John*** *bowed to* ***Mary*** *and* ***Mary*** *bowed to* ***John.***

3. Conjunction with reflexive and reciprocal pronominalization. Sentences with conjoined nominal subjects may have reciprocal or reflexive objects, e.g.

(98)   *John and Mary saw themselves.*

(99)   *John and Mary saw each other.*

In describing these, differences in the grammar will depend on whether the rules for conjunction are taken to precede or follow the rules for pronominalization. We shall show that neither of these orderings allows us to describe (98) and (99), and that additional machinery is therefore required to describe reciprocal and reflexive conjunction.

If the rule for conjunction precedes the rule for pronominalization, we derive the string

(100) $NP + Pl - V - NP + Pl$

underlying (101) below. The string (100) in turn is derived from successive applications of the conjunction rule to strings (NP–V–NP) underlying (102), (103), (104), and (105):

(101) *?John and Mary saw John and Mary.*

(102)   *John saw John.*

(103)   *John saw Mary.*

(104)   *Mary saw Mary.*

(105)   *Mary saw John.*

Since (101), although awkward, is accepted by most speakers, and since (100) is a legitimate input to the reflexive and reciprocal rules, we might consider the problem solved. But there are two objections to this solution.

(*a*) Application of (xxvi) to strings underlying (103) and (104) generates the string (106) which is similarly available to the reflexive rule. The outcome here is an unacceptable reflexive sentence, (107):

(106) $NP_i - C - NP_j - V - NP_j \rightarrow NP_i - C - NP_j - V - NP_j r + self$

(107)   *John and Mary saw Mary* $\rightarrow$ **John and Mary saw herself*

(*b*)   For absolute reflexive verbs (V_{reflex}), there are no source kernels corresponding to (103) and (105); i.e. no derivation results in

(108)   **John behaved Mary.*

(109)   **Mary behaved John.*

Therefore the presumed source of the reflexive conjunction,

(110)   **John and Mary behaved John and Mary.*

(111)   *John and Mary behaved themselves.*

is never derived, and (111) cannot be described.

An alternative is to allow the rule for pronominalization to precede the rule for conjunction. But in this case the conjunction of the reflexive strings underlying (112) and (113) below is prohibited because there are two noncontiguous ★-marked elements. Because of the effect of (xxiv) on the strings (112) and (113), we derive (114)(S–C–S) as an instance of the restressed pronouns discussed earlier:

(112)   *John saw himself.*   ($NP\star - V - Pronoun\star r + self$)

(113)   *Mary saw herself.*   ($NP\star - V - Pronoun\star r + self$)

(114)   **John** saw **him***self* and **Mary** saw **her***self.*

The rule for pronominalization must be taken to precede conjunction to avoid deriving (107) and to succeed in deriving

(115)   *John and Mary took care of themselves and each other.*

But if this is the case, (98), (99), and (115) must be described without relying on the now impossible (101).

Intuitively, the reflexive conjunction (98) seems to have as conjuncts the sentences (102) and (104). The reciprocal conjunction (99) seems to have as conjuncts the sentences (103) and (105). If we accept these sources and extend (xxvi), the mechanical difficulties disappear:[27]

(xlvii) $(Y) - NP_i - (+Pl) - (X) - NP_i'r - (+Pl) + self - (+Pl) - (Z)$
        $(Y) - NP_j - (+Pl) - (X) - NP_j'r - (+Pl) + self - (+Pl) - (Z)$ $\rightarrow$
        $(Y) - NP_i - (+Pl) - and - NP_j - (+Pl) - (X) - NP'r + Pl + self + Pl - (Z)$

                                                                 (optional)

(xlviii) $(Y) - NP_i - (+Pl) - (X) - NP_j - (+Pl) - (Z)$
        $(Y) - NP_j - (+Pl) - (X) - NP_i - (+Pl) - (Z)$ $\rightarrow$
        $(Y) - NP_i - (+Pl) - and - NP_j - (+Pl) - (X) - Recip - (Z)$ (optional)

Notice that these rules differ from (xxvi) in specifying the conjoining particle *and*. The development of separate rules for reciprocal and reflexive conjunction is in part motivated by the entirely novel exclusion of *or* between *NP*'s, e.g.

---

[27] This point of view is described in more detail in my unpublished Master's thesis *Conjunction with 'Each Other'* (University of Pennsylvania, 1960).

(116) *John or Mary saw themselves in the mirror.*

(117) *John or Mary saw herself in the mirror.*

(118) *John or Mary saw each other in the mirror.*

(119) *The men or the women saw each other in the mirror.*

4. DELETION OF THE RECIPROCAL MORPHEME. The node dominating the reciprocal morpheme and everything that node dominates are deletable with certain
kinds of verb, e.g.

(120)   *The car and the bus collided with each other.*
        The car and the bus collided.

(121)   *He combined oxygen and hydrogen with each other.*
        He combined oxygen and hydrogen.

(122)   *Oxygen combines with hydrogen.*
        Oxygen and hydrogen combine with each other.
        Oxygen and hydrogen combine.
        **Oxygen combines.*

(123)   *John and Mary met each other.*
        John and Mary met.
        **John met.*

Because these verbs do not occur intransitively with singular subjects, there seems
no other explanation for the appearance of conjoined nominal subjects than the
reciprocal conjunction transformation (xlviii) applied to transitive forms (*John
met Mary; Mary met John*) and a rule of deletion.[28] There are similar constructions
with *be* and certain *A–P–NP*, e.g.

(124)   *These two lines are parallel to each other.*
        These two lines are parallel.
        **This line is parallel.*

(xlix) $X - Y - (Z) \rightarrow X - (Z)$ (optional)
        where $X - Y - Z$ is a simplex in which Y is a constituent immediately dominating
           Recip; the verb of the simplex is V_{cmb} or the adjective is A_{cmb}

   (l) $V_{cmb} \rightarrow$ *collide; meet; differ; separate; converge; . . .*

   (li) $A_{cmb} \rightarrow$ *similar; equivalent; opposite; akin; identical; . . .*

5. PRO NOUNS. Pronominalization occurs also on the head noun and contiguous
unstressed modifiers of noun phrases when they are repeated in a simplex or a
complex, e.g.

(125)   *I saw an **old** man and **you** saw a **young** one.*

(126)   *I asked the old man with a **moustache** and **he** asked the one with a **beard**.*

(127)   *The **green** brick house faced the **red** one.*

The rule describing these sentences is cumbersome, because it is necessary to
describe a noun phrase composed of optional stressed and unstressed prenominal
and postnominal modifiers with an unstressed head noun, and it is necessary
that this structure be repeated within the string. The rule is given in full (liiα),

---

[28]For a more complete description of this class of verbs and their relation to reciprocal conjunction, see my master's thesis, and also Lees and Klima, op. cit.

but a version simpler to read, (liiβ), shows only the relevant effect: the deletions and pronominalizations in the repeated noun phrase.[29]

(liiα) $(X)-(T)-(W_1)-\langle W_2\star\rangle-(W_3)-N-(W_4)-\langle W_5\star\rangle-(W_6)-Y-(T)-(W_1)-$
$\langle W_2\star\rangle-(W_3)-N-(W_4)-\langle W_5\star\rangle-(W_6) \rightarrow$
$(X)-(T)-(W_1)-\langle W_2\star\rangle-(W_3)-N-(W_4)-\langle W_5\star\rangle-(W_6)-Y-(T)-(W_1)-$
$\langle W_2\star\rangle-one_2-\langle W_5\star\rangle-(W_6)$ (optional)

(liiβ) $(T)-(W_1)-\langle W_2\star\rangle-(W_3)-N-(W_4)-\langle W_5\star\rangle-(W_6) \rightarrow$
$(T)-(W_1)-\langle W_2\star\rangle-one_2-\langle W_5\star\rangle-(W_6)$

where $T \ldots W_6$ is a noun phrase in which N is an unstressed head noun; W_2 and W_5 are constituents of NP; no marks $\star$ appear in W_3 or W_4 (Note that W_3, W_4, W_1, W_6 need not be single constituents)

(liii) $(X)-Y\star-one_2-(Z) \rightarrow (X)-Y\star-(Z)$ (obligatory when $Y = Gen, Pl, Numeral;$ optional when $Y = Ordinal, T, other$)

Rule (liii) describes instances in which one_2 may or must be deleted. Examples follow.

(128) *They crossed **Nobb**'s first defensive line but not **Merritt**'s first defensive line* →
*They crossed **Nobb**'s first defensive line but not **Merritt**'s one →
*They crossed **Nobb**'s first defensive line but not **Merritt**'s.*

(129) *I have a copy of his **second** novel but I **want** his **earlier** novel* →
*I have a copy of his **second** novel but I **want** his **earlier** one* →
I have a copy of his **second novel but I **want** his **earlier**.*

(130) *I have a copy of his **first** novel but I **want** his **second** novel* →
*I have a copy of his **first** novel but I **want** his **second** one* →
*I have a copy of his **first** novel but I **want** his **second**.*

F. Pro predicates; conjoined sentences with tags. VP partially alike may be replaced by pro forms, in the same way as like and partially like NP.

Fillmore (op.cit.) has proposed a simple description of elided (or "tag") sentences, independent of the structures to which they may be adjoined. But elided sentences may not uniformly serve as conjuncts, as was suggested in Section I. If the structures described by Fillmore are to be considered sentences (if the initial phrase structure symbol is S), then the rule of conjunction would have to be altered to account for

(131) **The Senate can and the House passed the bill.*
**It is snowing and so did the surrounding countryside.*

---

[29]Some notation has been added here. Parentheses indicate optional elements as usual, but $\langle \ \rangle$ indicate an element that is optional only in case some other $\langle$element$\rangle$ appears in the string. In (lii), W_5 is optional if W_5 occurs, and W_5 is optional if W_2 occurs. Alternatively, (lii) can be written as two rules.

The word *one* has been described previously as a stressed indefinite article (one_1), as a pronominal replacing indefinite noun phrases (one_2), and as an impersonal pronoun (one_3). The pronominal one_2 is never in contrast with the morpheme *one* introduced as a pronoun in (lii); therefore we do not distinguish between them. The numeral *one* is taken to be a case of one_1; thus by (liii):

$\ldots one_1\text{-}one_2 \ldots \rightarrow \ldots one_1 \ldots$

But $\ldots one_1\text{-}A\text{-}one_2$ remains unchanged, e.g.

He has **three books and **you** have **one** one* →
*He has **three** books and **you** have **one**.*
*He has **three** old books and **you** have **one** new one.*

As an alternative to (xxvi), the notion that all constituents are conjoinable may be abandoned in favor of a series of conjunction rules to specify the coordinate stress patterns and forms of tag sentences that would then be requisite to conjunction. For example, the rule

$$\frac{NP\star - Aux\star - Y}{NP\star - Aux\star} \rightarrow NP\star - Aux\star - Y - C - NP\star - Aux\star$$

would be a rule of conjunction.

This alternative to (xxvi) has certain disadvantages beyond the loss of generality. A specification of the forms of tags appropriate for given classes of sentences and morphemes of adjunction must be provided whether or not we substitute rules like that above for (xxvi). Whenever we examine a new type of binary transformation, we discover that the restrictions on the pairing of sentence with tag are different, both in the internal shape of the tag and in the similarities and differences that must exist between the sentence and the tag, e.g.

(132) *I'll come if you don't.*
    **I'll come and you don't.*

(133) *John saw Mary and Bill did.*
    **John saw Mary but Bill did.*

(134) *John can't eat what Bill can.*
    **John can't eat and Bill can.*

The form of the tag seems to be statable in the same adjunction rule that states the pairing restrictions and introduces the morpheme of adjunction; see, for example, the work of Carlota Smith on comparative and relative clauses.[30] All elided sentences of English may be derived by specifying the relationship of the conjunction of a sentence and a tag by use of the morpheme *and*. Since this is so, there seems to be no need to rederive them with a separate rule.

Independent occurrences of elided sentences can be described as instances in which the morpheme of adjunction is itself deleted, much as in (xxxii). This view has some force, because predictions can be made about the syntactic structure of sentences preceding elided sentences; to this extent they are not really independent. For example, the sequence

(135) **I hate rain. It is raining. So does John.*

is ungrammatical in the same sense that the corresponding conjunction is ungrammatical:

(136) **I hate rain, it is raining, and so does John.*

1. THE RULE FOR CONJOINED TAGS. The conjoined sentence with tag is derived from conjoined strings (marked by (xxiv)) of the following general form:

$$NP - \sigma - Tense - (M) - (Aux_2) - (Mod) - V - X - C - NP - \sigma - Tense - (M) - (Aux_2) - (Mod) - V - X$$

---

[30]Carlota Smith, "A Class of Complex Modifiers in English," *Language*, 37 (1961).

The rules positioning tense and σ have not yet been applied.[31] Effects of (xxiv) are not changed by the rules for pro predicates; if, for example, the second conjunct contains stressed M, the corresponding tag form also contains stressed M. The rules below optionally allow the deletion of repeated $V - X$ (liv), $Mod - V - X$ (lv), and $Aux_2 - (Mod) - V - X$ (lvi):[32]

(liv) $NP\star - \sigma - Tense - (M) - (Aux_2) - (Mod) - V - X - C - NP\star - \sigma' - Tense' - (M') -$
      $(Aux_2') - (Mod') - V' - X' \rightarrow$
      $NP\star - \sigma - Tense - (M) - (Aux_2) - (Mod) - V - X - C - NP\star - \sigma' - Tense' - (M') -$
      $(Aux_2') - (Mod')$ (optional)
      where $V = V'$; $X = X'$

(lv) $NP\star - \sigma - Tense - (M) - (Aux_2) - Mod - V - X - C - NP\star - \sigma' - Tense' - (M') -$
      $(Aux_2') - Mod' \rightarrow$
      $NP\star - \sigma - Tense - (M) - (Aux_2) - Mod - V - X - C - NP\star - \sigma' - Tense' - (M') -$
      (Aux_2') (optional)
      where $Mod = Mod'$

(lvi) $NP\star - \sigma - Tense - (M) - Aux_2 - (Mod) - V - X - C - NP\star - \sigma' - Tense' - (M') -$
      $Aux_2' \rightarrow$
      $NP\star - \sigma - Tense - (M) - Aux_2 - (Mod) - V - X - C - NP\star - \sigma' - Tense' - (M')$
      (optional)
      where $Aux_2 = Aux_2'$

Some outputs of these rules are

(137) *John may have wanted to come but Mary may have had to.* (liv)

(138) *John can come but Mary can't.* (liv)

(139) *John came but Mary didn't.* (liv)

(140) *John may have wanted to come but Mary may not have.* (lv)

(141) *John may have wanted to come but Mary may not.* (lvi)

Stress on the affirmative morpheme (which is zero, and thus cannot carry stress) is adjusted by morphophonemic rules preceding the rules positioning tense and σ. These rules apply to all $\star$-marked structures, not only to cases of ellipsis:

(lvii) $X - \sigma\star - Tense - Y \rightarrow X - \sigma - Tense\star - Y$ (optional if $\sigma = Neg$; obligatory if
      $\sigma = Pos$)

(lviii) $X - Pos - Y \rightarrow X - Y$

(lix) $Neg\star \rightarrow not\star$

(lx) $Neg \rightarrow not$; $+ nt$[33]

(lxi) $X - Tense\star - V - Y \rightarrow X - Tense - V\star - Y$ (optional)
      where $X \neq M$, and X does not dominate M

---

[31]For a description of the positioning of negatives, see Fillmore, op. cit. For a description of the positioning of verb affixes, see Chomsky, op. cit. A verb affix that cannot be affixed to its left neighbor (there is no M) is affixed to the verb, if the verb is its right neighbor. If something intervenes between the affix and the verb, this permutation cannot take place. In that case, the word *do* is introduced in the position of M to carry the affix.

[32]Some informants exclude outputs of (lv).

[33]$X+ =$ the prefix X; $+X =$ the suffix X.

Thus the stress on σ is moved onto tense (optionally in case $\sigma = Neg$, i.e. in case σ dominates a morpheme one syllable in length). The stressed tense affix will then be affixed to M, if there is one. This stress on tense (derived either from (lvii) or an original stressed tense (xxiv)) may now in the absence of M be shifted onto the verb (lxi), leaving an unstressed tense affix which eventually is shifted onto the stressed verb. If there is no M, and the stress on tense remains, the morpheme *do* (see footnote 31) is introduced to carry the stressed tense affix, i.e. the stress on tense is taken to intervene between tense and V.

This description of stressed *do* appearing as a consequence of moving stressed *Pos* back onto the tense morpheme is equivalent in effect to the transformation of affirmation proposed by Chomsky. This version is perhaps preferable because it gives a more symmetrical picture of the positive and negative forms (*I come; I do come* versus *I don't come; I do not come*), and at the same time describes the ambiguity between the stressed (*do*) form of negation and affirmation and cases of stressed tense (e.g. *He didn't come; He did come*).

The stressed tense morpheme affixed to M or *do* is less than a syllable; stress then falls on M or *do*. The stressed tense morpheme is the result either of a contrast in tense (xxiv) or a contrast in σ (lvii). Stress also falls on M in case there was an original M contrast (xxiv). Then there are three sources of stressed M:

(142)   *I could come but he couldn't.*   (Stressed σ)

(143)   *I could come but he should.*   (Stressed M)

(144)   *I could come but he can.*   (Stressed tense)

After (lxi) the stress on tense appears on V. The stressed tense morpheme again may be the result of either an original tense contrast or of (lvii). Thus there are three sources of stressed V, shown below in (145), (146), (147). Since (lxi) is optional, we also derive (148) and (149), and since (lvii) is optional with *Neg*, we derive (150). Some informants find (148) preferable to (145) and (149) preferable to (146). For this dialect, rule (lxi) is absent:

(145)   *I liked him and you didn't.*   (Stressed σ)

(146)   *I liked him and you like him.*   (Stressed tense)

(147)   *I liked him and you hated him.*   (Stressed V)

(148)   *I did like him and you didn't.*   (Stressed σ)

(149)   *I did like him and you do.*   (Stressed tense)

(150)   *I did like him and you did not.*   (Stressed σ)

2. PARTICLES OCCURRING WITH CONJOINED STRUCTURES.

(a) *Either/or; both/and.* Where σ is unstressed, the particles *either* and *both* may appear:

(lxii) $(X) - Y - and - Y - (Z) \rightarrow (X) - both - Y - and - Y - (Z)$ (optional)
where $Y \neq S$, and $\sigma = $ unstressed *Pos*

(lxiii) $(X) - Y - or - Y - (Z) \rightarrow (X) - either - Y - or - Y - (Z)$ (optional)
where $\sigma = $ unstressed *Pos* or *Neg*

(lxiv) $X - Neg - Y - either - Z - or - Z - W \rightarrow X - Y - Neg + -either - Z - Neg +$
$-or - Z - W$ (optional)

(lxv) $X - either - Y - or - Y - Z - Neg - W \rightarrow X - Neg + -either - Y - Neg +$
$-or - Y - Z - W$ (optional)

Examples:

(151) *I like both John and Mary.*

(152) **Both I like John and I like Mary.*

(153) *He both hates and fears the Hungarians.*

(154) *I like either John or Mary.*

(155) *I don't like either John or Mary.*

(156) *I like neither John nor Mary.*

(b) *Too/so/either/nor.* Stressed adverbials may be added to sentences identical to the right of the subject noun phrase, whether or not the second conjunct is an ellipsis. Some informants feel the addition of an adverbial is necessary in all cases; it is certainly necessary where the conjoining particle is *but*; for example,

(157) **John came but Mary came.*

(158) **John came but Mary did.*

(159) *John came and Mary came.*

(160) *?John came and Mary did.*

(161) *John came and Mary did too.*

(162) *John came but Mary did too.*

The following rules describe these stressed adverbials:

(lxvi) $S - C - NP\star - \sigma - Tense - (M) - (Y) \rightarrow S - C - NP\star - \sigma - Tense - (M) - (Y) - \beta\star$
(obligatory if $C = but$; optional if $C = and$; excluded if $C = or$)
where $\sigma - Tense - (M) - (Y)$ contains no mark $\star$.

(lxvii) $\beta \rightarrow too$, if $\sigma = Pos$

(lxviii) $\beta \rightarrow either$, if $\sigma = Neg$

(lxix) $S - C - NP\star - \sigma - Tense - (M) - \beta\star \rightarrow S - C - \sigma - \beta\star - Tense - (M) - NP\star$
(optional)

(lxx) $C - Neg - \beta\star \rightarrow C - neither\star$ (obligatory)

(lxxi) $C - Pos - \beta\star \rightarrow C - so\star$ (obligatory)

(lxxii) $C - neither\star \rightarrow nor$ (optional)

For example:

(163) *The **proposal** received support and the **candidate** did **too**.*
*The **proposal** received support and **so** did the **candidate**.*

(164) *The **proposal** wasn't explicit and the **report** wasn't **either**.*
*The **proposal** wasn't explicit and **neither** was the **report**.*
*The **proposal** wasn't explicit, nor was the **report**.*

3. TAGS WITH STRESSED NEG. Tags with stressed *Neg* are open to further reductions:

(lxxiii) $S - C - NP\star - Y - Neg\star \rightarrow S - C - Neg\star - NP\star$ (optional)
where Y contains no mark $\star$; $C = but$; *and*

(lxxiv) $S - C - Neg\star - NP\star \rightarrow S - Neg\star - NP\star$ (optional)

(lxxv) $NP\star - Y - (C) - Neg\star - NP'\star \rightarrow NP\star - (C) - Neg\star - NP'\star - Y$ (optional)

(lxxvi) $NP\star - Y - but - Neg\star - NP'\star \rightarrow Neg\star - NP'\star - but - NP\star - Y$ (optional)

Examples:

(165) *The **proposal** had merit, and **not** the **candidate**.*

*The **proposal** had merit, **not the candidate.***
*The **proposal** had merit, but **not the candidate.***
*The **proposal**, but **not the candidate**, had merit.*
*The **proposal**, and **not the candidate**, had merit.*
*The **proposal**, not the **candidate**, had merit.*
***Not** the **candidate** but the **proposal** had merit.*
**Not the candidate and the proposal had merit.*

The node dominating *NP–and–NP* introduced with conjunction is not introduced onto *NP–and–NP* derived from (lxxiii)–(lxxv). Therefore, the rule for subject-verb number agreement will not apply (e.g. *John and not Mary is coming; *John and not Mary are coming*).

A further reduction of the second conjunct occurs also with stressed *Neg* when the subject noun phrase and all verbal elements are identical, but what follows the verb differs. Unlike the previous group of rules, the reduction here is not dependent on a difference in *NP*, but applies as well to any right completions of the verb or right adjoined prepositional phrases. The only limitation is that this difference to the right of the verb must be a single constituent; furthermore, the source of this transformation is a pair of conjoined predicates, specifically not a tag:

(lxxvii) $NP - \sigma\star - X - V - Y\star - C - \sigma\star - X' - V' - Y'\star \rightarrow NP - \sigma\star - X - V - Y\star - C - \sigma\star - Y'\star$ (optional)
where $X = X'$, $V = V'$, $C = and; but$, Y is a single constituent

For example:

(166)   *You are **lost** but **not forgotten.***
         *You are **not lost** but **forgotten.***
          *They can move **down** but **not up.***
        **They ate their bread but not drank their milk.*
        **Cats eat fish in the morning but not onions at night.*

Outputs of (lxxvii) are not subject to permutations (lxxv) and (lxxvi). Outputs of (lxxvii) and (lxxiii) are sometimes (unless the context is clear) ambiguous in writing, but not in speech; the stress patterns are different. The following are ambiguous in ordinary English orthography:

(167)   **Cats** resemble lions but **elephants do not** $\rightarrow$
         Cats resemble lions but **not elephants.**   (lxxiii)

(168)   *Cats resemble **lions** but do **not** resemble **elephants** $\rightarrow$*
         *Cats resemble **lions** but **not elephants.**   (lxxvii)*

G. Number agreement and conjunction.   We now return to the problem of number and the particle *and*. It has been proposed[34] that conjoined nominals be introduced by a phrase structure rule, as well as by the rule for conjunction. Such a derivation would look something like this:

(lxxviii) $NP \rightarrow NP + Sg; NP + Pl$
 (lxxix) $NP + Sg \rightarrow N_{mass}; Pronoun; T - N; T - N_{cp}$
 (lxxx) $NP + Pl \rightarrow (T) - N + s; NP - and - NP; T - N_{cp}$
   ⋮
 (lxxxi) $N_{cp} \rightarrow couple; pair; committee; quartet; group; \ldots$

---

[34]C. S. Smith has discussed this notion in ["Ambiguous Sentences with *And*," *MSE*].

This proposal immediately solves certain difficulties. The source of both (169) and (170) below would be the phrase-structurally derived string (171):

(169) *John and Mary are linguists.*

(170) *The men are linguists.*

(171) $NP + Pl - V_{be} - NP + Pl$

The right completion of the verb *be* would have to be restricted, however, to disallow N_{cp} with singular subjects. Certain ambiguities in the use of *and* could be ascribed to the two sources of conjoined nominals, e.g.

(172) *John and Mary bought the new Faulkner novel.*

(173) *John and Mary were carrying baskets.*

This solution is not without difficulties.

　　1.　The conjunction of subject *NP* by (xxvi) still yields the string (174) below, which in turn yields the unacceptable sentence (175):

(174) $NP - C - NP - V_{be} - NP + Sg$

(175) **John and Mary are a linguist.*

An additional source of conjoined nominals thus does nothing to explain the agreement of nouns around V_{be}; in fact, by adding a new source it raises the question of why sentence (169) is not ambiguous.

　　2.　Plural noun phrases would also have to be developed in two ways to account for parallel ambiguities (e.g. *The men bought the new Faulkner novel, The men were carrying baskets*).

　　3.　The special character of words like *couple* is left partially unresolved by the simple distinction *Singular/Plural*. Any complete description verges on arithmetic, e.g.

(176) **The Smiths and the Browns are a happy couple.*

(177) **Brown, Smith, and Jones are a dubious pair.*

(178) **Smith and Brown make a marvelous trio.*

　　4.　Most conjoined nominals fail to be ambiguous, even in subject position:

(179) *John and Mary are dead.*

(180) *John and Mary bought the new Picasso painting.*

　　5.　Similar ambiguities occur when there is no question of conjoined nominals:

(181) *A copy of* Time *arrives on a million doorsteps every Wednesday morning.*

(182) *Every family has a bottle of milk.*

We must therefore reject this solution, even though an alternative of similar generality cannot now be proposed. Instead, we adopt a rule (lxxxii)–(lxxxiii) specifying the agreement of the verb with its subject *NP*, and a further rule (lxxxiv) describing the agreement of the second *NP* with *be*:

(lxxxii)　$NP + Pl - X - Present - Y \rightarrow NP + Pl - X - \emptyset - Y$　(obligatory)

(lxxxiii)　$NP + Sg - X - Present - Y \rightarrow NP + Sg - X - s - Y$　(obligatory)
　　　　　where *s* is the present-tense morpheme

(lxxxiv)　$NP + Pl - X - V_{be} - NP + Sg \rightarrow NP + Pl - X - V_{be} - NP + Pl$　(obligatory)

It is tempting to suppose that (lxxxiv), while obligatory with *be*, is optionally allowable for other verbs. This would immediately account for the ambiguity of (173). However, I can see no justification for this extension. At any rate, it would fail to shed light on the question of a satisfying derivation for

(183)   *John and Mary carried four baskets.*

A different case seems amenable to another description. Section I discussed difficulties in accounting for

(184)   *Two and two is (are) four.*

(185)   *Sugar and water make(s) syrup.*

(186)   *The flag is red, white, and blue.*

In treating reciprocal constructions, we defined a class of verbs (V_{cmb}) and adjectives (A_{cmb}) that have the special property of allowing deletion of the node dominating *Recip*, and everything that node dominates. Associated with such forms (see, for example, (187)) are the usual pronominalizations:

(187)   *He combined oxygen and hydrogen (with each other).*

(188)   *the combination of oxygen and hydrogen (with each other)*

We might suppose that the verbal components of the deleted nominalization are deletable when the verb is V_{cmb}; this solution would describe why the supposed conjoined nominal takes a singular verb (all nominalizations of this form take singular verbs), and why the deleted nominalization is always plural (V_{cmb} is intransitive only as the result of the reciprocal deletion transformation, and reciprocals are always plural). Thus sentences like *Two and two is four* are natural outputs of the rule

(lxxxv) $T - V_{cmb} + tion - of - NP - C - NP' \rightarrow NP - C - NP'$ (optional)

That the output of (lxxxv) serves as a subject *NP* only for a very restricted set of verbs (e.g. *give, yield, be, make*) is clear. We now assume that there is an optional rewriting of the phrase structure of *NP–and–NP* derived from (lxxxv) by analogy to the rewriting of phrase structure associated with conjunctions (xxvi): the node-name *Nominalization* is replaced by the node-name *NP*. The rule for agreement of subject and verb (lxxxii)–(lxxxiii) will then apply to this new tree; hence

(189)   *Two and two are four.*

In fact, when informants are asked whether *is* or *are* is "correct" for sentences like (189), they seem perplexed. They say they have always wondered which was correct. This fact seems to support (lxxxv). The deletion of verbal components of a nominalization is not an innovation in descriptions of English. Herzberger proposed a similar solution for

(190)   *(There being) too many cooks spoil(s) the broth.*
        (Doing) all work and no play make(s) Jack a dull boy.

Finally, it seems to me that the description of words like *pair* and *trio*, and sentences like (183), is not within the province of syntax.

H. Conjoinable constituents and stress.   We have assumed that all constituents (with a few named exceptions) could receive stress, and that all could be conjoined. Some more detailed distinctions are necessary.

Certain nonterminal constituents are marked by (xxiv); constituents so marked and immediately dominating terminal constituents are stressed by a morphophonemic rule (xxv). We have assumed in this that every morpheme is immediately dominated by a node that dominates no other morpheme; otherwise we would not know which morpheme to stress. For example, a node (*Adv**) must be assumed to dominate **pre-** and **post-** to account for

(191)   *This fact was true of **pre**revolutionary and **post**revolutionary France.*

(192)   *This fact was true of **pre** and **post**revolutionary France.*

(193)   **This fact was true of prerevolutionary and postrevolutionary France.*

On the other hand, we must assume that no separate node dominates the suffixes **-ful** and **-less** in

(194)   *?Can one be at once help**ful** and help**less**?*

(195)   **Can one be at once help**ful** and **less**?*

(196)   *Can one be at once **help**ful and **help**less?*

This distinction, in fact, dictates the form of the constituent description of adverbial prefixes as opposed to most other affixes. Bolinger[35] has provided a very thorough description of contrastive stress, in which he points out that there is considerable latitude in the placement of stress within a word under conditions where contrastive stress is required; no absolute rules can be stated. Very briefly, the general usage (described in careful detail by Bolinger) is this:

When a single morpheme has more than one syllable, stress introduced by (xxv) is generally placed where word stress is placed, e.g.

(197)   *She was a **hap**py and a**lert** child.*

This fails to hold true if pronunciation (i.e. the phonological and morphophonemic rules themselves) is the matter under discussion:

(198)   *I say both **a**ddress and a**ddress**.*

although, even here, if the basis of contrast is less than a syllable, or falls between syllables, or is greater than a syllable, the stress reverts to the place of word stress:

(199)   *I said **light**ning, not **light**ing.*

(200)   *I say a**p**surd and a**b**zurd.*

(201)   *I said ma**lig**nancy, not ma**lig**nity.*

Similarly, in a contrast between a word and its prefixed counterpart, while the stress in the first instance falls where word stress falls, in the second it falls on the prefix in contrast:

(202)   *They were at once **sim**ilar and **dis**similar.*

(203)   *That happened both in re**vol**utionary and **post**revolutionary France.*

I. Nonconjunctive uses of "and."   Instances of the use of *and* not described by the rules for conjunction and nominalization are given here in brief.

1. AND/TO.   Sometimes *and* is found where we might expect a preposition:

---

[35]Dwight L. Bolinger, "Contrastive Accent and Contrastive Stress," *Language*, 37.83–96 (1961).

(204) *Try and catch me.*

(205) *Do me a favor and sit down.*

The intonation contour for such sentences seems quite different from that associated with conjoined *X–C–X*. If that is so, such occurrences can be treated much like modal verbs, the *and* being classified as similar to infinitival *to*. Evidence for the oddity of this use, beyond the difference in intonation contour, is its unsystematic nature: (*a*) where affixes are required on the verb forms, this usage is avoided (e.g. *They try and get it;* but **He tries and get it; He tries to get it);* and (*b*) iteration is not uniformly allowable (e.g. *Do me a favor and run and get it;* but *?Run and do me a favor and get it.*)

2. "AND" AS AN INTENSIFIER.   (xxvi) disallows the conjunction of identical constituents, because (xxiv) does not mark them. However, we often find *and* between identical words and phrases without contrastive stress (e.g. *We went around and around, She hit him and hit him.*). Such repetitions have the effect of suggesting continuous or repeated or increasing action. They are not allowable on all constituents conjoinable by (xxvi) (e.g. **He had a green and green apple*). Therefore they must in any case be treated specially. The rule that describes them is presumed to be iterative, but deletion of the repeated *and* is excluded:

(lxxxvi) $(X) - Y - (Z) \rightarrow (X) - \bar{Y} - and - Y - (Z)$ (optional)
where $Y = A + comparative;$ some P; V; VP; some Adv

3. IDIOMATIC EXPRESSIONS.   Many pairs of nouns (or what appear to be nouns) are idiomatic with respect to this grammar, e.g.

(206) *We fought hammer and tongs.*

(207) *She kept the house spic and span.*

(208) *The horses ran neck and neck.*

SYMBOLS

S	Sentence	*V*	Verb
C	Conjunction	*P*	Preposition
C_c	Coordinating conjunction	*Adv*	Adverb
NP	Noun phrase	*Sg*	Singular
VP	Verb phrase	*Pl*	Plural
Pos	Positive	$+X$	The suffix X
Neg	Negative	$X+$	The prefix X
$\emptyset$	Zero	σ	Sign (*Pos/Neg*)
T	Article	*Aux*	Auxiliary
T_1	*a*	*M*	*can, will, shall, may, do*
T_2	*the*	*Gen*	Genitive
N	Noun	*Acc*	Accusative
PreN	Prenominal	*Nom*	Nominative
A	Adjective	*Mod*	Modal verb

10

Phrasal Conjunction and Symmetric Predicates

GEORGE LAKOFF and STANLEY PETERS

It has long been observed that there are at least two types of conjunction, sentence conjunction and phrasal conjunction:[1]

(1) *John and Mary are erudite.*
(2) *John and Mary are alike.*

Sentence (1) embodies a conjunction of two assertions:

(1′) *John is erudite and Mary is erudite.*

Sentence (2) cannot be interpreted in this way.

(2′) **John is alike and Mary is alike.*

Cases like (1) have been treated essentially correctly within the framework of transformational grammar since the inception of such studies; that is, (1) has been derived from the structure underlying (1′). Cases like (2) have only recently been dealt with in a transformational framework. Peters (1966) has pointed out that phrasal conjunction cannot be transformationally derived from sentence conjunction as some transformational grammarians had hoped it would turn out to be. The clearest suggestion that phrasal conjunction be derived from sentence conjunction can be found in Gleitman (1965). Many other transformational grammarians have hoped that some scheme of derivation such as that presented by

---

Reprinted from *Mathematical Linguistics and Automatic Translation*, Harvard Computation Laboratory, Report No. NSF-17, 1966, pp. VI-1 to VI-49, by permission of George Lakoff and Stanley Peters and the President and Fellows of Harvard College.

[1]For example Curme stated in his *Syntax* (p. 162) that "sentences containing coordinating conjunctions, however, are often not an abridgement of two or more sentences, but a simple sentence with elements of equal rank, connected by a conjunction: 'The King *and* Queen are an amiable pair.' 'She mixed wine *and* oil together.' "

Gleitman would solve the problem of phrasal conjunction. Later in this paper we give some of the evidence which shows why any such scheme is impossible. At least in the case of noun phrases, conjunction must occur in the base component. That is, there must be a rule schema of the form

(3) $NP \rightarrow and\ (NP)^n, n \geq 2$

We will refer to an *NP* which has been expanded this way as an *NP**.[2] The following are among the crucial examples which constitute evidence for this position:

(4)(a)   *John, Bill, and Harry met in Vienna.*
  (b)   **John met in Vienna, Bill met in Vienna, and Harry met in Vienna.*

(5)(a)   *The old man left all his money to Bill and Tom.*

is not a paraphrase of

(5)(b)   *The old man left all his money to Bill and the old man left all his money to Tom.*

(6)(a)   *John, Bill, and Harry wrote the book together.*

is not a paraphrase of

(6)(b)   *John wrote the book, Bill wrote the book, and Harry wrote the book.*

In each case, (a) may not be derived from the structure underlying (b).

---

[2]The reader should consult Peters (1966) for justification of this statement of the rule. Here we will merely describe the manner in which the rule is to be interpreted. Schema (3) represents an infinite collection of rules, namely all rules of the form $NP \rightarrow and\ NP\ NP \ldots NP\ NP$ where the number of occurrences of *NP* to the right of the arrow is finite and is greater than or equal to two. These rules generate base structures of the form

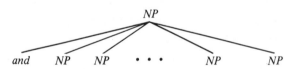

There is a universal principle which converts structures of this form to

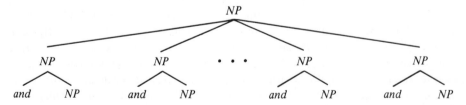

as the deep structure of a sentence enters the transformational component from the base component. English has two special transformational rules which apply to conjoined structures. There is an obligatory *and*-deletion rule which may be stated as follows:

$T_{and\text{-deletion}}$ (obligatory):
    SD: $X\ [[and\ A]_A\ Y\ ]_A\ Z$ for any category A
           1   2 3   4   5
    SC: delete 2

In addition, there is an optional transformation which deletes all but the last conjunction of a conjoined structure.

These two rules apply to *and* introduced by rule (3) as well as to *and* introduced by the schema that conjoins sentences, even though these two types of *and* are different. The two *and*'s must be marked with a difference in syntactic feature composition since they exhibit different syntactic behavior.

Since conjunction may arise either in the base component through rules like (3) or transformationally from sentence conjunction, one would expect there to be a large number of ambiguities of this sort. Indeed, there are. In cases like (7)

(7)(a)   *John and Mary left.*
  (b)   *Shakespeare and Marlowe wrote plays.*

we may either be asserting that the subjects left or wrote together, in which case we get paraphrases (8) and (9).

(8)(a)   *John and Mary left together.*
  (b)   *Shakespeare and Marlowe wrote plays together.*

(9)(a)   *John left with Mary.*
  (b)   *Shakespeare wrote plays with Marlowe.*

or we may be asserting two separate and not necessarily related facts, in which case we get the paraphrases (10) and (11).

(10)(a)   *Both John and Mary left.*
  (b)   *Both Shakespeare and Marlowe wrote plays.*

(11)(a)   *John left and Mary left.*
  (b)   *Shakespeare wrote plays and Marlowe wrote plays.*

The *together* and *with* paraphrases, (8) and (9), indicate underlying phrasal conjunction; the *both* and the full sentences paraphrases, (10) and (11), indicate underlying sentence conjunction (for details, see Peters, 1966). Note that the *both* paraphrase cannot co-occur with the *together* paraphrase:

(12)(a)   **Both John and Mary left together.*
  (b)   **Both Shakespeare and Marlowe wrote plays together.*

But the number of possible ambiguities of this sort is not as great as one might at first believe. Robin Lakoff has made the discovery (personal communication) that most stative verbs and adjectives may not have conjoined noun phrases in their underlying subjects*. Consider, for example,

---

*For the distinction between *stative* and *nonstative*, see George Lakoff, "Stative Adjectives and Verbs in English," Harvard Computation Laboratory, Report No. NSF-17, 1966. In this paper Lakoff postulates the syntactic property *stative* versus *nonstative* in order to account for the grammaticality of sentences such as *Slice the salami, Be careful,* and the ungrammaticality of sentences such as *Know the answer* and *Be tall. Slice* and *careful* are *nonstative,* while *know* and *tall* are *stative.* It is shown that this distinction is needed not only for command imperatives, but also for various other constructions in English:

Progressive forms:
    I am slicing the salami.
    *I am knowing the answer.
    I am being careful.
    *I am being tall.

Do-something pro-forms:
    What I did was slice the salami.
    *What I did was know the answer.

Do-so pro-forms:
    I sliced the salami, and George did so, too.
    *I knew the answer, and George did so, too.

Complement restrictions of *persuade, remind,* etc.:
    I persuaded John to slice the salami.
    *I persuaded John to know the answer.

(13)   *John and Mary know the answer.*

(13) is unambiguous with respect to conjunction; it can be paraphrased only by (14) and (15).

(14)   *Both John and Mary know the answer.*

(15)   *John knows the answer and Mary knows the answer.*

(13) may not be paraphrased by either (16) or (17).

(16)   **John and Mary know the answer together.*

(17)   **John knows the answer with Mary.*

Thus, *know* may not take an underlying conjoined subject.[3] The same is true of stative verbs in general.

Stative adjectives show the same property. Compare (18) and (19):

(18)   *John and Mary are careful.*   (Nonstative)

(19)   *John and Mary are erudite.*   (Stative)

(18) is ambiguous with respect to conjunction. In the sentence conjunction case, (18) represents the conjunction of two assertions which are not necessarily related to one another, as in (20).

(20)   *John is careful and Mary is careful.*

The phrasal conjunction sense of (18) shows up in (21).

(21)   *John and Mary are careful when making love together.*

In (21), *careful* clearly has a conjoined subject in its underlying structure. The same is true of (22).

(22)   *John and Mary are careful together.*

(19), on the other hand, is unambiguous, and may only come from sentence conjunction. (19) has the paraphrases

(23)   *Both John and Mary are erudite.*

(24)   *John is erudite and Mary is erudite.*

But (19) may not have the paraphrases of (25) and (26).

(25)   **John and Mary are erudite together.*

(26)   **John is erudite with Mary.*

The same is true of nearly all stative adjectives.

There are some nonobvious cases where this generalization about the subjects of statives holds true, in particular, those in which underlying subjects of stative verbs are superficial objects. Take, for example, verbs like *surprise, amuse, seem, appear,* etc., which on independent grounds have been analyzed as having superficial objects that are underlying subjects. (For discussion see Rosenbaum, 1965; Lakoff, 1965; and Lakoff, to appear.)

---

[3]This fact is reflected in the possibility of *John's and Mary's knowledge of the facts* ... as opposed to the impossibility of **John and Mary's knowledge of the facts* ... For a verb such as *arrive* which optionally takes *NP** subjects we get *John's and Mary's arrival* ... corresponding to *John arrived and Mary arrived,* and *John and Mary's arrival* ... corresponding to phrasal conjunction in the base component. We are indebted to Emily Norwood for this observation.

(27) *Sally's rude behavior amuses Mary and John.*

According to the claim made in the above mentioned studies, *Mary* and *John* are underlying subjects of *amuse* and *Sally's rude behavior* is the underlying object. Since *amuse* is stative in (27), one would expect (27) to be unambiguous with respect to conjunction. This is indeed the case. We get the paraphrases of (28) and (29), but not that of (30).

(28) *Sally's rude behavior amuses both Mary and John.*

(29) *Sally's rude behavior amuses Mary and Sally's rude behavior amuses John.*

(30) **Sally's rude behavior amuses Mary and John together.*

However, the underlying object (which is the superficial subject) of *amuse* does show ambiguity with respect to conjunction, as in (31).

(31) *Sally's rude behavior and Bill's polite reactions amuse John.*

If (31) is derived from sentence conjunction, then we get the paraphrase of (32).

(32) *Sally's rude behavior amuses John and Bill's polite reactions amuse John.*

In this sense, there is no necessary connection between Sally's behavior and Bill's reactions. However, if (31) is derived from underlying phrasal conjunction, such a connection is implied. In that case, we have paraphrases such as (33) and (34).

(33) *Sally's rude behavior and Bill's polite reactions together amuse John.*

(34) *Sally's rude behavior together with Bill's polite reactions amuses John.*

Thus, R. Lakoff's generalization holds for *amuse*, and it appears to hold for all similar cases.

Since there are exceptions to this generalization, it appears that the only way to state it is in terms of markedness. For stative verbs and adjectives, unmarked cases other than measure adjectives and possessive verbs may not take conjoined underlying subjects; unmarked possessive verbs and measure adjectives may or may not take them; marked cases must take conjoined subjects.[4] An example of a stative verb which must take conjoined subjects is *agree*.

(35) *John and Bill agree that Harry is an idiot.*

(36) *John agrees with Bill that Harry is an idiot.*

In sentences like (37) it appears that *agree* does not have a conjoined subject.

(37) *John agrees that Harry is an idiot.*

But in such sentences as (37) it is "understood" that John agrees with some un-

---

[4]The notion of markedness corresponds to the notion of "normal state." Most words in a class are normal (unmarked); some words in a class may be exceptional (marked). The theory of markedness claims that only marked cases contribute to the complexity of a grammar. Thus, generalizations in language may be of two kinds. Absolute generalizations state properties that are true for an entire class, with no exceptions. Markedness generalizations state properties that are true for most of a class (the normal or unmarked cases), but such generalizations may have exceptions (the marked cases). In addition, the theory of markedness claims that the exceptions themselves may not be random in their behavior, but rather form a subclass for which there is a subgeneralization. In this case, marked items *must* take NP* subjects. For further discussion, see Lakoff (1965) and Lakoff (to appear).

specified person, that is, the occurrence of *with someone* has been deleted. (37) would be derived from (38).

(38)   *John agrees (with some unspecified person) that Harry is an idiot.*

And (38) would be derived from (39).

(39)   *John (and some unspecified person) agree that Harry is an idiot.*

And in sentences like (40),

(40)   *Both John and Bill agree that Harry is an idiot.*

it is understood that John and Bill agree with a third party or parties. *Agree* is exceptional in this respect, since most verbs that take *NP** subjects cannot delete an unspecified *NP* following *with*. Thus *John conferred with Unspecified NP* does not reduce to **John conferred.*

An example of a stative measure adjective that may or may not take underlying conjoined subjects is *heavy*.

(41)   *John and Mary are heavy.*

(41) is ambiguous. It can mean that each is heavy, as in (42).

(42)   *Both John and Mary are heavy.*

Or (41) can mean that their combined weights are great, though their separate weights may not be, as in (43).

(43)   *John and Mary are heavy together.*

The ambiguity of (41) also appears in the question of (44).

(44)   *How heavy are John and Mary?*

In (44), one can either be asking for their separate weights or for their total weight. Note that the same ambiguity does not appear with the nonmeasure adjective *erudite*. When one asks,

(45)   *How erudite are John and Mary?*

one is never asking for the total amount of their erudition.

In nonstative verbs and adjectives the markedness situation is rather different. Unmarked nonstatives may take either nonconjoined subjects or conjoined subjects (*NP**). A typical example is the verb *leave* in examples (7) through (11) above. Marked nonstatives *must* take *NP** subjects. An example is the verb *confer*:

(46)   *John and Bill conferred.*
(47)   *John conferred with Bill.*
(48)   *John and Bill conferred together.*
(49)   **John conferred.*

So far, we have found no nonstative verb that may not take an *NP** underlying subject.

To sum up, nonmeasure stative adjectives and verbs normally do not take *NP** subjects; marked nonmeasure adjectives must take *NP** subjects. Measure adjectives normally may or may not take *NP** subjects. Exceptional measure adjectives may not take them. *Fast* is an example of the latter. In asking *How fast are Koufax's* *fast ball and curve?* we are not asking for the sum of their speeds. Nonstative adjectives and verbs normally may or may not take *NP** subjects. Exceptional cases of nonstatives (like *confer*) *must* take *NP** subjects.

We suggested above that sentences like

(50)   *John killed a man with Bill.*

were to be derived from structures underlying sentences like (51),

(51)   *John and Bill killed a man (together).*

where *John and Bill* forms a phrasally conjoined *NP* in the deep structure. That is, the underlying structure of (50) would be (52).

(52)

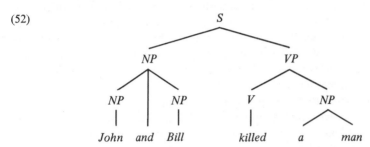

Sentence (50) would be formed from this structure by a rule (actually a sequence of rules) which

(i)   deletes *and* and adjoins *with* to the left of the *NP Bill*

and

(ii)   adjoins *with Bill* to the right of the *VP killed a man.*

We will call (i) PREPOSITION ADJUNCTION and (ii) CONJUNCT MOVEMENT. These rules must be constrained to apply (*a*) only in sentence-initial position,[5] (*b*) only in cases where there is a binary branching in the topmost *NP*, and (*c*) only when the con-

---

[5]If the rule could apply to an *NP** object we would derive *I hit John with Bill* from *I hit John and Bill.* But this is clearly incorrect in this case since the former is not a paraphrase of the latter. There are some apparent counterexamples to this claim:
(A)   *The prisoner stole the warden's wallet (together) with his keys.*
(B)   *I drink milk with meat.*
The *with*-phrase in these sentences cannot be derived by conjunct movement, since the derived structure is different than in the cases we have been discussing. We can see this in sentences that take a *do-so* in place of a verb phrase:
(C)   *I killed a man with Bill and Harry did so with Tom.*
(D)   **I stole the warden's wallet with his keys and John did so with his glasses.*
(E)   **I drink milk with meat and John does so with fish.*
In the conjunct movement cases, there is in the derived structure both an "inner" and an "outer" *VP* (see (109)), and *do-so* may substitute for the "inner" *VP*. In (A) and (B) there is no inner *VP*, and so (D) and (E) are impossible. Thus, the derived structures of (A) and (B) could not have been brought about by conjunct movement. We do not understand the process which forms these sentences.

joined *NP* is derived from phrasal conjunction in the base, not from sentence conjunction.[6]

So far, we have only asserted that sentences like (50) should be derived from structures underlying sentences like (51), and that the *with*-phrase of accompaniment (*with Bill* in (50)) is derived and not basic. Let us now consider some evidence for this assertion. Consider (53):

(53)   *John was killed with Bill.*

(53) is synonymous with (54).

(54)   *John and Bill were killed (together).*

Bill in (53) is understood as part of the superficial subject of *be killed*, which is to say, it is understood as part of the *underlying object* of *kill*. In (53) we know someone or something has killed Bill. Now compare the phrase *with Bill* in (53) to the same phrase in (50). In (50) *Bill* is understood again as part of the superficial subject of *kill*, but it is also understood as part of the *underlying subject* of *kill*. In (50), Bill does the killing, he doesn't get killed.

These examples show that the underlying grammatical relation that the object of *with* bears to the other elements in the sentence is not fixed, but depends at least on whether or not passivization has applied. But, by definition of underlying structure, grammatical relations are fixed in the base and cannot depend on transformations. Unless such a conception of grammar is incorrect, the *with*-phrases cannot be introduced in the base.

Moreover, the objects of *with* do not enter into any grammatical relations which are different from those already defined in the base component; in fact, they are limited exactly to grammatical subjects and grammatical objects. This fact lends credence to our claim that they are actually derived from real subjects and objects.

We can account for the way we understand (50) and (53) by hypothesizing that in each case the underlying structure contains the phrasally conjoined noun phrase *John and Bill* and by hypothesizing that rules such as (i) and (ii) above apply *after* the application of the passive transformation. This would account for the fact that in both cases the object of *with* is understood as part of the *superficial* subject of the sentence and that in passive constructions it is understood as part of the underlying object.

So far we have shown that it is not possible to derive phrasally conjoined noun phrases from underlying *with*-phrases since there can be no underlying *with*-phrases. We will now argue that if we derive *with*-phrases from underlying phrasally conjoined noun phrases, we can account automatically for a number of facts that

---

[6]*John and Bill are erudite* can only be derived from sentence conjunction, and we do not get **John is erudite with Bill.* Furthermore, the only reading of *John and Bill own houses* which is paraphrased by *John owns houses with Bill* is the reading which is derived from phrasal conjunction. In footnote 2 we stated that there will be a feature difference between the *and* which is introduced by sentence conjunction and the *and* which is introduced by phrasal conjunction. We can use this feature difference to allow this rule to apply only to structures containing *and* from phrasal conjunction. Or the restriction might be exercised in some other way.

would otherwise be inexplicable. For example, the object of a *with*-phrase of accompaniment may never be a reflexive pronoun:[7]

(55) **John left with himself.*

(56) **John killed a man with himself.*

(57) **John was killed with himself.*

This follows from the fact that we do not get reflexives in phrasally conjoined noun phrases:

(58) **John and himself left.*

(59) **John and himself killed a man.*

(60) **John and himself were killed.*

But this lack of reflexives follows from the fact that in any type of conjunction in the deep structure of a sentence, no two members of the conjunction may be identical. Thus in the sentence

(61)   *John and John left.*

we must be talking about two different people named *John*. If they are to be understood as the same person, then the sentence is ungrammatical. This is true not only of phrasal conjunction, but also of sentence conjunction. Thus the following sentences are ungrammatical:

(62) **I left and I left.*

(63) **I saw you and I saw you.*

(64) **You are tall and you are tall and you are tall.*

And this constraint on deep structure conjunctions appears to be universal.[8] Thus

---

[7]There are two apparent counterexamples to this statement. The first involves such metaphorical expressions as *John agreed with himself that Bill was an idiot* and *John struggled with himself over whether he should leave.* In such cases, one is thinking of John as two separate individuals, or possibly, as in the case of *agree*, as a single individual at two different points in time. We can see that such sentences are rather special by the nonoccurrence of **John struggled with himself in the back yard.* We can see here that the sense of "struggle" is rather different from that in *John struggled with Bill in the back yard.*

The second apparent counterexample has to do with sentences like *John left by himself.* It might be claimed that *by* in this sentence is derived from *with* whenever a reflexive appears, and that the source of this sentence has an *NP** subject containing two occurrences of *John*. If this were true, such an *NP** subject could occur with verbs such as *meet* which require *NP** subjects. But we never get sentences like *John met by himself.* Hence such a claim would be incorrect.

[8]Sentences like the following constitute apparent counterexamples to this claim:

 I hit him and I hit him and I hit him—until he died.

 John ran and ran and ran and ran.

But, as Wayles Browne has shown (Browne, 1964) such conjunctions do not appear in the deep structure and must be transformationally introduced. Consider the sentences

 John got taller and taller and taller.

 John got more and more and more confused.

Some adjectives may take either the *more* or *-er* form of the comparative:

 John got colder and colder and colder.

 John got more and more and more cold.

if we adopt our proposed analysis of *with*-phrases of accompaniment,[9] we can account for the lack of reflexives following *with* in terms of an independently motivated universal constraint on deep structure conjunctions.

Another fact that we can account for in terms of this analysis is the symmetric nature of sentences that have *with*-phrases.

(65)   *John left with Bill.*

is true if and only if

(66)   *Bill left with John.*

is true.

But the two types of conjunction may not be mixed:
   *John got more and more cold and colder and colder.
These examples show that such conjunctions must be introduced by a transformational rule that operates *after* the rule which reduces *more* to *-er* for certain adjectives (optionally for *cold*).

These conjunctions have other strange properties. They do not undergo normal conjunction reduction:
   I hit him and hit him and hit him—until he died.
   *I hit him and him and him—until he died.
Nor do they undergo optional *and* deletion:
   I ran and ran and ran and ran.
   *I ran, ran, ran, and ran.
Moreover, they are restricted to active verbs and to perceptual statives; they may not occur with nonperceptual statives. The above cases have active verbs. An example with a perceptual stative would be
   I saw his face and saw his face and saw his face—until it drove me crazy.
But such constructions are impossible with nonperceptual statives:
   *I knew that John left and knew that John left and knew that John left.
Note that such constructions indicate repetition or continuation and may be paraphrased with a verb like *keep:*
   I kept hitting him—until he died.
   I kept running.
   I kept seeing his face—until it drove me crazy.
Keep may also occur with actives and perceptual statives, but not with other statives:
   *I kept knowing that John left.
Negatives may not be conjoined in such constructions, nor may they appear in the complement following verbs like *keep:*
   *I didn't hit him and didn't hit him and didn't hit him.
   *I kept not hitting him.
Moreover, the range of adverbs that can co-occur with such constructions is exactly the range of adverbs that can occur with verbs of the *keep* class. Such facts lead us to the view that conjunctions of this sort do not occur in deep structures at all, but are derived by a late transformational rule. In the deep structure the conjoined sentence is probably a complement of a verb of the *keep, continue,* etc., class, perhaps just the bundle of features defining the class. In the transformation forming the conjunction, the bundle of features would be deleted. Such a solution would account both for the meaning of the conjoined structure and for the strange grammatical constraints on it. For a further discussion of this phenomenon, see Lakoff (to appear).

[9]Note that *I killed the man with Bill* is ambiguous. It can mean either *I killed the man who was with Bill* or *Bill and I killed the man.* We are considering only the latter interpretation. Observe that corresponding to the two interpretations we get two different derived structures. These are reflected in the relative clauses *the man with Bill who I killed . . .* and *the man who I killed with Bill . . .*

(67) *John drank a glass of beer with Harry.*

entails that

(68) *Harry drank a glass of beer with John.*

and vice versa.
Under our analysis of these constructions, these facts would also follow from a universal fact concerning deep structure conjunction, namely, that semantic interpretation is independent of the order of conjunction. Thus

(69) *John and Bill left together.*

is synonymous with

(70) *Bill and John left together.*

and

(71) *John and Harry drank a glass of beer together.*

is synonymous with

(72) *Harry and John drank a glass of beer together.*

This is true not only of phrasal conjunction but of sentence conjunction as well.

(73) *John is tall and Harry is fat.*

is synonymous with

(74) *Harry is fat and John is tall.*[10]

Thus we see that the symmetric nature of sentences containing *with*-phrases of accompaniment can be accounted for in terms of an independently motivated constraint on deep structure conjunction.

We can now account for the fact that verbs which must take *NP** subjects are necessarily symmetrical. Consider *confer. John conferred with Bill* entails *Bill conferred with John*, and vice versa, since those sentences are derived, respectively, from *John and Bill conferred* and *Bill and John conferred*. The same is true of certain adjectives that must take *NP** subjects—except that some items take *to* instead of *with*. Consider the adjective *similar*.

---

[10]An apparent counterexample to our claim that conjunctions are symmetrical is the *and then* type of conjunction. Consider
  Harry robbed the bank and drove off in a car.
This may be a paraphrase of
  Harry robbed the bank and then drove off in a car.
If it is, then it is not identical in meaning with
  Harry drove off in a car and robbed the bank.
We would claim that the type of *and* that means *and then* is actually derived from the ordinary symmetric *and* followed by a deep structure occurrence of *then*, which may be deleted under certain conditions. The lack of symmetry in the conjoined sentences derived in this manner would follow from the nature of *then* which is itself derived in these cases probably from *after it Sentence*, where the *Sentence* deletes under identity with the preceding sentence.
  This contention is supported by the fact that asymmetrical *and* constructions are possible only when a *then* can occur. The reason that we always get symmetry in cases like (73) and (74) is that *then* may not occur in these cases:
    *John was tall and then Harry was fat.
    *John knew that Bill left and then Harry doubted that the world was round.

(75)   *This problem is similar to that problem.*

entails that

(76)   *That problem is similar to this problem.*

and vice versa.
(75) would be derived from (77):

(77)   *This problem and that problem are similar.*

(76) would be derived from (78):

(78)   *That problem and this problem are similar.*

(77) and (78) are, of course, synonymous.
This accounts not only for the symmetric nature of *similar* but also for the fact that *similar* cannot take reflexives:

(79)   **This problem is similar to itself.*

Note that in mathematical parlance it would be possible to say something like

(80)   *This problem is similar to this problem.*

or

(81)   *A is similar to A.*

One of the many things that distinguish mathematical jargon from any natural language is that reflexivization does not take place. Another thing that distinguishes mathematical jargon from natural language is that phrasal conjunctions may contain identical elements and still be well-formed. Thus, sentences like

(82)   *A and A are similar.*
(83)   *This problem and this problem are similar.*
(84)   *Harry is tall and Harry is tall and Harry is tall.*

are quite normal in the artificial language of logic and mathematics. Thus, in mathematics, a predicate such as *similar* is both symmetric and reflexive (in the logical sense). In English, *similar* is symmetric and *logically reflexive*, but it is *grammatically irreflexive*. In English, the sentence **This problem is similar to itself* is ungrammatical, although, in semantic terms, it is perfectly meaningful and, in fact, true. This means that the general constraint on deep structures that forbids any two members of a conjoined structure from being identical is a *grammatical and not a semantic* constraint.[11]

We can explain still another fact on the basis of this analysis. We have already pointed out that in the *with-* and *to-*phrases under consideration, the object of the preposition is understood as part of the superficial subject of the sentence. The superficial subject, in turn, may come from either the underlying subject or object. It is a fact that the class of noun phrases that can occur as objects of such prepositions is identical to the class of noun phrases that can appear as superficial subject.

---

[11]Actually there does seem to be a semantic constraint of this sort for active verbs. *John left with himself* and *John met himself in Vienna* do not make sense at all. The possibility for semantic reflexivity seems to be limited only to certain stative verbs and adjectives.

Or more precisely, the selectional restrictions between the main verb and the noun phrase that appears as superficial subject are identical to the selectional restrictions on the object of these prepositions. But this is an automatic consequence of the analysis we have given. Since the objects of these prepositions are derived from the superficial subject, it follows that they would have exactly the selectional restrictions that superficial subjects would have.

Now consider the sentence

(85) *Kosygin met with Johnson and Rusk.*

We have not yet discussed the manner in which this sentence can be generated. Notice that (85) is ambiguous; one reading is derived from

(86) *Kosygin met with Johnson and Kosygin met with Rusk.*

by the ordinary conjunction transformation. The other reading must come from

(87) *Kosygin and Johnson and Rusk met.*

by CONJUNCT MOVEMENT. At first it might appear that the transformation must be modified to move two noun phrases contrary to our claim above. Notice, however, that (87) is itself ambiguous. The subject can have any one of the structures (88):

(88)(a)

(b)

(c)

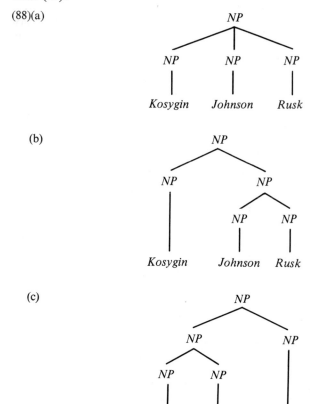

The version of CONJUNCT MOVEMENT discussed above will apply to (88b) to produce the desired structure for (85). In (88a) there is no internal grouping of the conjuncts—either syntactic or semantic. (88b) describes a grouping in which Johnson and Rusk are a unit on a par with Kosygin by himself. In (88c) the grouping classes Kosygin and Johnson together as opposed to Rusk. Structures (88b) and (88c) are generated by recursive application of schema (3). Note that these structures are semantically distinct and all three are possible. Note that in the reading of (85) under consideration, Johnson and Rusk form a unit. Therefore, the structure in (88b) is the correct underlying structure of (85). So here, as in the examples above, CONJUNCT MOVEMENT takes the second of two conjoined noun phrases and moves it to the end of the following verb phrase. The same transformation applies in both cases.

It is clear that structures like (88b and c) can exist for verbs like *meet*. For (88c) we would get

(89)   *Kosygin and Johnson met with Rusk.*

which, of course, is ambiguous in the same way that (85) is. That is, (89) could also be derived by ordinary conjunction rules from

(90)   *Kosygin met with Rusk and Johnson met with Rusk.*

So far, we have described the process of conjunct movement in informal terms. Let us now consider the details. We mentioned above that *with* is not the only preposition that may attach to conjuncts. *To* and *from* may do so as well.

(91)   *John, Bill, and Harry are similar to the Celtics in the way that they handle the basketball.*

(92)   *The earth is identical to the moon in its chemical composition.*

(93)   *Harvard and M.I.T. correspond to Berkeley in the quality and breadth of their combined course offerings.*

(94)   *China and Russia differ from England and America in their combined nuclear resources.*

(95)   *John, Bill, and Harry are distinct from the Celtics in their ability to handle a basketball.*

As is obvious, those verbs and adjectives that take *from* have a negative connotation, however that is to be described. We will distinguish them from the *to* cases by an arbitrarily chosen feature: *Positive*.

Note that in each of the above sentences, we have used a restrictive phrase to further specify the relationship signified by the verb or adjective. If we had not used such phrases the sentences would have been vague, bizarre, or meaningless:

(96)   *John, Bill, and Harry are similar to the Celtics.*

(97)   *The earth is identical to the moon.*

(98)   *Harvard and M.I.T. correspond to Berkeley.*

(99)   *China and Russia differ from England and America.*

(100)   *John, Bill, and Harry are distinct from the Celtics.*

This is not true of sentences containing verbs and adjectives that take *with*.

(101)   *John left with Bill and Mary.*

(102)   *John robbed a bank with Tom and Harry.*

We need a syntactic feature to distinguish the cases that take *with* from those that take *to* or *from*. Notice that there is a semantic correlation to this syntactic property. The verbs and adjectives that take *to* or *from* require special interpretation, which must be supplied from extralinguistic context or an additional restrictive phrase. This is not true of verbs and adjectives that take *with*. Since the requirement of a special interpretation correlates to the distinction between the *with* cases and the *to-from* cases, we will call the feature that distinguishes these cases *Special*.

We can now state precisely the rules for conjunct movement.

Rule 1:   PREPOSITION ADJUNCTION (optional)

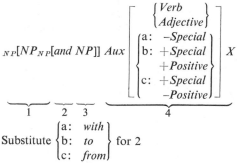

Rule 2:   CONJUNCT MOVEMENT (obligatory)

$$_{NP}[_{NP}[and\ NP]_{NP}[Prep\ NP]]\ Aux\ VP$$

$$\underbrace{\qquad}_{1}\ \underbrace{\qquad}_{2}\ \underset{3}{\ }\ \underset{4}{\ }$$

Adjoin 2 to the right of 4

Delete 2

These rules will yield derivations like the following:

(103)

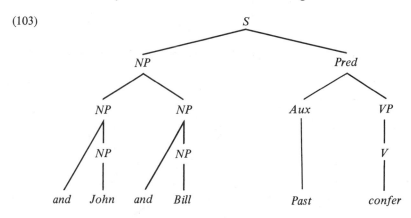

Recall that the reasons for assuming this structure in the subject noun phrase were discussed in footnote 2.

Applying Rule 1 we get:

(104)

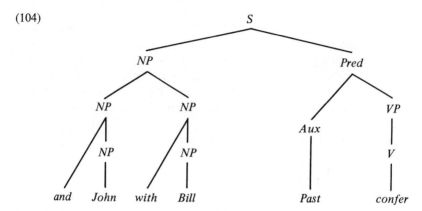

Applying Rule 2 we derive:

(105)

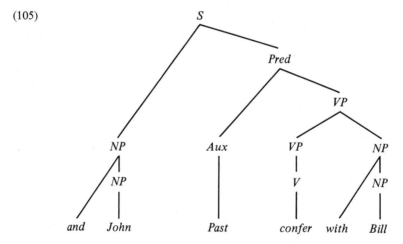

And after application of the obligatory *and*-deletion rule described in footnote 2 we get:

(106)

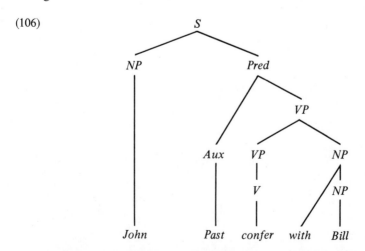

We will give two more sample derivations. First,
   John robbed a bank with Bill.

(107)

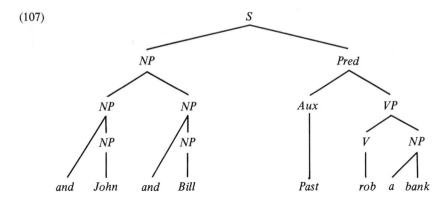

By Rule 1:

(108)

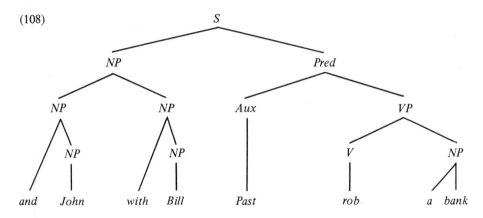

By Rule 2:

(109)

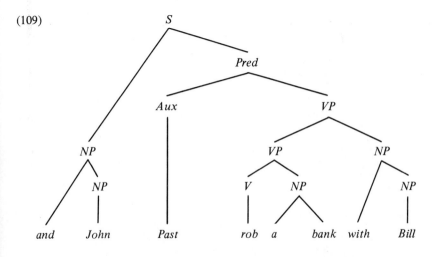

By obligatory *and*-deletion:

(110)

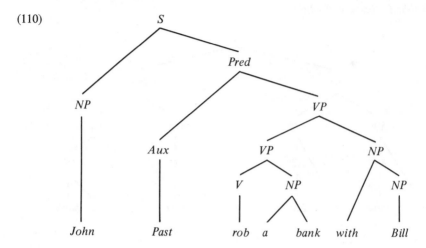

And in the following way we can get:
   John is similar to Bill.

(111)

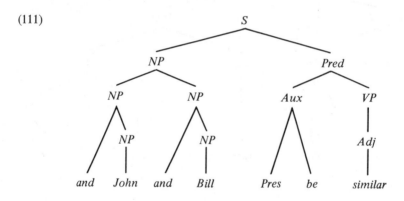

By Rule 1:

(112)

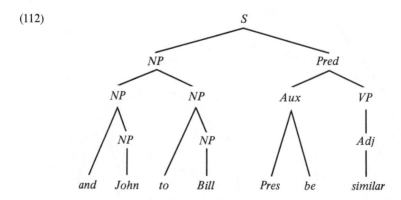

By Rule 2:

(113)

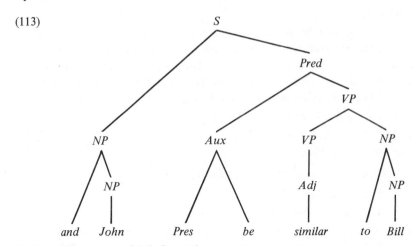

By the obligatory *and*-deletion rule:

(114)

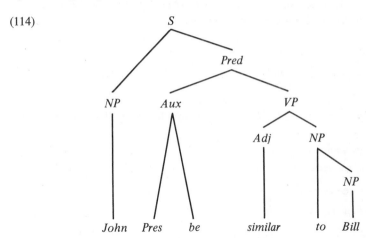

As we pointed out above, these rules must follow the passive transformation in order to account for the difference in grammatical relations between *John killed with Bill* and *John was killed with Bill*. These rules will account for an enormous number of cases. However, as is usual in natural language, there are exceptions to these rules. Consider the adjective *apart*. We get (115) but not (116) and (117).

(115) *New York and San Francisco are* 3000 *miles apart.*

(116) **New York is* 3000 *miles apart from San Francisco.*

(117) **New York from San Francisco is* 3000 *miles apart.*

Thus, *apart* is an exception to Rule 1; it may not undergo Rule 1. The adjective *far* on the other hand must meet the structural description of Rule 1 and must undergo it:[12]

---

[12]For a discussion of items that must meet the structural description of some rule, see Lakoff (1965) and Lakoff (to appear).

(118) **Washington and Hanoi are far.*

(119) *Washington is far from Hanoi.*

Note that by deriving (119) from a sentence with an *NP** subject, we can automatically explain the fact that *far* is symmetrical and irreflexive. *Near* works very much like *far* in that it too must meet the structural description of Rule 1 and undergo the rule. But *near* has an additional idiosyncrasy. In some dialects the *to* which follows it may optionally delete and in other dialects the *to* must delete:

(120) **Boston and New York are near.*

(121) *(*)Boston is near to New York.*

(122) *Boston is near New York.*

Note that *to* never deletes when *near* is nominalized to *nearness*:

(123) *Boston's nearness to New York*

(124) **Boston's nearness New York*

This is a consequence of a general fact about preposition deletion in English. At some point in their derivations, all object noun phrases take prepositions as a kind of case marking. When substantivization takes place, that is, when a verb is transformed into a noun, the preposition remains:

(125) *the killing **of** the men*

(126) **the killing the men*

(127) *the killer **of** the men*

(128) **the killer the men*

However, if the verb is not transformed into a noun, the preposition is deleted by a postcyclical rule:

(129) *John killed the man.*

(130) **John killed of the man.*

Observe the difference between

(131) *John's killing of the man*

and

(132) *John's killing the man*

In (131) *killing* is a noun. We know this, since adjectives may be preposed before it, as in (133).

(133) *John's merciless killing of the man*

In (132), however, *killing* is still a verb since adjectives may not be preposed before it.

(134) **John's merciless killing the man*

The preposition deletion rule has four cases:

Case 1:   Verbs that must take *NP** subjects.
Case 2:   All other verbs.
Case 3:   Adjectives that must take *NP** subjects.
Case 4:   All other adjectives.

In Case 1, the preposition *to* normally deletes (in the unmarked cases) but there are some exceptions, e.g. *correspond, relate*. The preposition *from* never deletes. *With*, on the other hand, normally does not delete, but there may be exceptions, e.g. *meet* (meaning *make the acquaintance of*). In Case 2, the preposition *of* usually deletes; exceptions are *conceive of, think of*, etc. Other prepositions also normally delete; an exception is *decide on*. In Case 3, *with* and *from* may never be deleted; there are no exceptions. *To* is usually kept, but there are exceptions, e.g. *near, like*. In Case 4, the preposition may never be deleted; there are no exceptions.

Near is an exception with respect to the preposition deletion rule, since it must take an *NP** subject (Case 3), but may undergo preposition deletion. Thus, *near* is an exception both to Rule 1, because it *must* undergo preposition adjunction, which is otherwise optional, and to the rule for preposition deletion, which normally does not apply to Case 3, but may with *near*. Note that deriving *near* in this fashion allows us to explain why it, like *far*, is symmetrical and irreflexive.

Resemble is another exception. Like *near* it must meet the structural description of Rule 1 and undergo the rule. It is normal in that it undergoes preposition deletion, since it has an *NP** subject and takes *to* (see Case 1).

(135) **John and Bill resemble.*

(136) **John resembles to Bill.*

(137) *John resembles Bill.*

Resemble is very close in meaning to *similar* and in a sentence like (138) a special interpretation or restrictive phrase is required, as in (139).

(138) *John, Bill, and Harry resemble the Celtics.*

(139) *John, Bill, and Harry resemble the Celtics in the way that they handle the basketball.*

Thus, *resemble* requires the feature [+ *Special*] and takes the preposition *to* when Rule 1 applies, even though the preposition is later deleted. However, the preposition *to* does show up as predicted in nominalizations:

(140) *John's resemblance **to** Bill*

(140) is parallel to (141):

(141) *John's similarity to Bill*

After Rule 2 has applied to *resemble*, the resulting structure meets the structural description of the passive transformation. But, as is well-known, we do not get sentences like

(142) **Bill is resembled by John.*

But this is precisely what we would predict, since as we pointed out above the passive transformation must precede conjunct movement. That is, at the time at which the passive transformation is reached in the sequence of rules, Rule 2 has not yet applied and *resemble* is still an intransitive verb. The same is true of *marry, equal*, and *meet* (in the sense of *make the acquaintance of*). Thus, we can explain not only why these verbs do not undergo the passive, but also why they are symmetric, irreflexive, and have the same selectional restrictions on their subjects and superficial objects.

Equal, by the way, turns out to be regular with respect to preposition deletion.

Equal would be unspecified in the lexicon for being either a verb or an adjective, and so could occur as both. If it occurred as an adjective we would get either *x and y are equal* or *x is equal to y*. The presence of *to* here is regular since *equal* is an adjective in this sentence. If *equal* occurs as a verb, we get *x equals y*, which again is regular since *to* normally deletes after verbs. The only thing irregular about *equal* would be the nonoccurrence of such sentences as *x and y equal* where *equal* is a verb. We could express this by entering *equal* in the lexicon with a Boolean condition stating that if it occurs as a verb, then it must undergo preposition adjunction (and consequently, conjunct movement and preposition deletion). Such Boolean conditions are discussed in Lakoff (1965) and Lakoff (to appear).

Note that our assumption that *with* and *to* are deleted by the ordinary post-cyclical preposition deletion rule can explain why *with* can never be deleted in the case of an underlying transitive verb (e.g. see (50)). The preposition deletion rule specifies that a preposition can be deleted only directly after a verb. In the case of transitive verbs, the *with* prepositional phrase can appear only following the entire verb phrase, and so it will always appear after the object noun phrase and never appear directly after the verb. The structural description of the deletion rule will never be met in such cases. Thus, we can explain an otherwise strange fact.

Let us now consider the words *married* and *engaged* as in the following examples:

(143)(a) *John and Mary are married.*
   (b) *John and Mary are engaged.*
(144)(a) *John is married to Mary.*
   (b) *John is engaged to Mary.*

Both *married* and *engaged* in the above sentences are adjectives that take *NP** subjects. They are regular in that they take *to* and do not undergo preposition deletion (Case 3). The fact that they are adjectives can be determined by their occurrence in certain diagnostic environments where adjectives, but not the passive participles of transitive verbs can occur. Note that *married* in the above sentences has the same phonological form as the passive participle of the transitive verb *to marry* as in (145).

(145)(a) *The preacher married John and Mary.*
   (b) *John and Mary were married by the preacher.*

If the agent in (145b) were not *the preacher* but some unspecified person, then the *by*-phrase would delete and we would get (146).

(146) *John and Mary were married.*

(146), however, is ambiguous while (145b) is not. (146) may either be derived from a passive sentence like (145b) with *by*-phrase deletion or it can be the past tense of the simple predicate adjective construction in (143a). The fact that (143a) is not ambiguous follows from the fact that the passive of the transitive verb *marry* cannot occur in the present tense (except the historical present, in which case (143a) is ambiguous).

(147) **John and Mary are married by the preacher.*

Note that the adjective *married* can occur directly after verbs like *seem* and *look*, while the passive participle cannot, regardless of tense.

(148)(a) *John and Mary seemed married.*
   (b) *John and Mary looked married.*
(149)(a) **John and Mary seemed married by the preacher.*
   (b) **John and Mary looked married by the preacher.*

(148) is unambiguous and only the adjective occurs. The sentences of (149) cannot occur at all, since the passive participle interpretation of *married* is forced by the presence of the *by*-phrase.

But the morphological variants of *marry* are certainly related in their occurrences in the following sentences:

(150)(a) *John and Mary are married.*
   (b) *John and Mary married.*
   (c) *The preacher married John and Mary.*
(151)(a) *John is married to Mary.*
   (b) *John married Mary.*
   (c) *The preacher married John to Mary.*

The (a), (b), and (c) sentences are related to one another in the same way as the following sentences:

(152)(a) *The room is dark.*
   (b) *The room darkened.*
   (c) *Harry darkened the room.*

It was claimed in Lakoff (1965) that the (b) and (c) sentences are transformationally derived from underlying structures which include the underlying structures of the (a) sentences. The (b) sentences are derived by embedding the structure underlying the (a) sentences in the subject of a verb semantically equivalent to the verb *come about*:

(153)

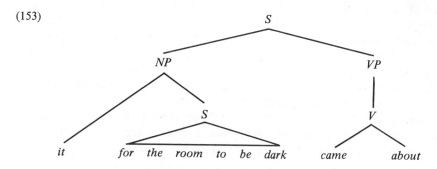

With the real verb *come about* we would derive sentences like

(154) *The room came to be dark.*

(155) *The room became dark.*

These are synonymous to (152b). If, instead of the real verb *come about*, there appeared in the underlying structure a pro-form with the same meaning, additional rules would apply which would substitute *dark* for the pro-form, yielding the verb *darkened* in sentence (152b). Thus, *darken* is a derived, not an underlying, verb. Precisely the same process yields (150b) and (151b). Thus, *marry* is a derived verb in these sentences. Note that the deletion of *to* in (151b) is perfectly regular since *marry* has become a verb by the time the postcyclical preposition deletion rule applies. (Recall that *marry* falls under Case 1 above.) Note that the *to* appears in the transformationally derived substantive *John's marriage to Mary*.

The sentence of (152c) would be derived by further embedding the structure underlying (152b) inside the object of a pro-form corresponding to a verb meaning *to cause, bring about, or effect.*

(156)

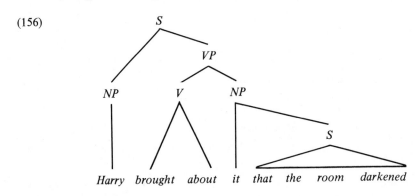

This would yield (157).

(157)   *Harry brought it about that the room darkened.*

(157) is synonymous with (152c). As before, if there appeared a pro-form in the deep structure instead of *bring about*, then an additional rule would substitute *darken* for the pro-form, yielding (152c). Here, as before, *darken* is a derived, not an underlying verb—in this case, a transitive verb in the superficial structure. Note that the underlying subject of *dark* turns out to be the superficial object of *darken*.

By the same process, we would derive (150c) and (151c). Thus, the transitive verb *to marry* in these sentences would be a derived verb, not an underlying one. Notice that in (151c) the *to* cannot be deleted postcyclically, since the above processes occur cyclically. By the time the rule is reached *to* is no longer immediately after the verb *marry* and so the rule cannot apply to it. Thus the sentences of (150) and (151) are all completely regular!

We have stated that these cases are completely regular. But one apparent irregularity which has long been noticed is that (151b), though superficially transitive, is not passivizable; but (150c) and (151c) are passivizable.

(158)   **Mary was married by John.*   (As the passive of (151b))

(159)   *John and Mary were married by the preacher.*   (The passive of (150c))

(160)   *John was married to Mary by the preacher.*   (The passive of (151c))

The occurrence of (159) and (160) shows that the rule which substitutes the intransitive *marry* for the *bring about* pro-form must precede the passive transformation.

Notice that the rules we have given allow two different ways of deriving the unique surface structure of

(161)   *John married Mary.*   (Equals (151b))

from a single deep structure. The two derivations are schematically represented below:

(162)(a)   *it for John and Mary to be married [came about Pro-form]*   Cycle 1
   (b)   *John and Mary [came about Pro-form] for to be married*   Cycle 2
   (c)   *John and Mary [came about Pro-form] married*
   (d)   *John and Mary married*
   (e)   *John to Mary married*
   (f)   *John married to Mary*
   (g)   *John married Mary.*   Postcycle

(163)(a)   *it for John and Mary to be married [came about Pro-form]*   Cycle 1
   (b)   *it for John to Mary to be married [came about Pro-form]*
   (c)   *it for John to be married to Mary [came about Pro-form]*
   (d)   *John [came about Pro-form] for to be married to Mary*   Cycle 2
   (e)   *John [came about Pro-form] married to Mary*
   (f)   *John married to Mary*
   (g)   *John married Mary.*   Postcycle

In (162) preposition adjunction and conjunct movement do not apply on the first cycle, but rather on the second. Recall that preposition adjunction is optional, and that conjunct movement depends on it. Since the process is optional, it can apply on either cycle, providing of course that the structural description is met. In (163), it has applied on the first cycle, not on the second. If it had not applied on either cycle, we would have derived (164).

(164)   *John and Mary married.*   (Equals (150b))

Since the passive transformation is a cyclical rule, we must explain in each case why it cannot apply. Let us consider (163) first. The only point at which the structural description of the passive transformation could be met is at line (f) of (163). Before that point is reached *married* must substitute for *[came about Pro-form]*, deriving line (f) from line (e). But before that can happen, the rule deleting *for to be* must apply. By ordering the passive before that rule, we can account in a natural way for the nonoccurrence of (158). We know from the study of English complementation that this can be done.[13]

This rule ordering would also account for the impossibility of passivization in the derivation of (162). But in (162) we have an independent explanation of the lack of passivization. As we pointed out in the case of *resemble* the passive transformation must precede preposition adjunction and conjunct movement. In this derivation, the verb *marry* would be intransitive at the point at which the passive transformation was reached in the cycle. So, passivization could not possibly apply.

If we derive the various forms of *marry* in this way, then we need not set up a transitive verb *marry* in the lexicon which would require an underlying *NP** object. Instead, we would have an intransitive adjective, which, like many other adjectives, requires an *NP** subject. But the other occurrences of verbs which apparently

---

[13]See Rosenbaum (1965), Ross (1966), and Lakoff (to appear).

require an underlying *NP** object can be treated in the same way. Consider the sentences

(165)(a)   *The sand and the loam are mixed.*
   (b)   *The sand and the loam mixed.*
   (c)   *John mixed the sand and the loam.*
(166)(a)   *The sand is mixed with the loam.*
   (b)   *The sand mixed with the loam.*
   (c)   *John mixed the sand with the loam.*

Mix in the (c) sentences is a case of an apparent transitive verb requiring an *NP** object. But it seems to work just like *marry* and we can handle it that way. We would like to claim that all transitive verbs which appear to require an *NP** object are derived in the same way from underlying intransitives. Most such verbs, like *mix*, have occurring underlying adjectives as in (165a). But there are a few exceptions such as *introduce*, *exchange*, and *switch* which have hypothetical underlying forms which must meet the structural description of the rule which derives the (c) sentences from the (b) sentences—the causative transformation. The underlying form of *introduce* would have the meaning and basic grammatical properties of *meet* in the sense of *make the acquaintance of*. The underlying forms of *exchange* and *switch* would resemble the adjective *reversed* as in (167).

(167)   *This pole and that pole seem reversed.*[14]

If we are correct in this assertion, then it follows that verbs need not be sub-categorized with respect to whether they are restricted to taking or not taking *NP** objects in the deep structure. In other words there is no need for a feature [———*NP**] which could distinguish between verbs that do and do not take *NP** objects in deep structure. Thus, all underlying transitive verbs may take *NP** or not freely in their underlying objects.

In terms of the features that we have already discussed there are certain generalizations that can be stated. Take the feature *Special*, for example, which correlates to the *to-from* versus *with* distinction. All of the verbs and adjectives which are [+*Special*] have the following grammatical properties: they *must* take *NP** subjects; they are intransitive; and they are stative. We might state these facts with the redundancy rule:

$$(168) \quad [+Special] \rightarrow \begin{bmatrix} +NP^* \underline{\quad\quad} \\ \underline{\quad\quad} NP \\ +Stative \end{bmatrix}$$

This is an absolute generalization. There is also a generalization that we can state in terms of markedness: It is normal for verbs and adjectives that *must* take *NP** subjects (those that are marked for that feature) to be intransitive. We know of

---

[14]There are certain transitive verbs with superficial *NP** objects which are clearly derived from intransitive adjectives with *NP** subjects, but are not causatives. Among them are *compare*, *equate*, *relate*, and *liken*. These are obviously derived from *comparable*, *equal*, *related*, and *like/alike* respectively. But they do not have the meaning of causatives. We have no idea as to the deep structure of such verbs, although we can be sure that they are not basic and are derived from their corresponding intransitive adjectives.

only a handful of verbs that are not intransitive that must take NP^* subjects (e.g. *agree, conspire . . .*). We might state his generalization by the redundancy rule:

(169) $\begin{bmatrix} m\ NP^* \underline{\hspace{1cm}} \\ u \underline{\hspace{1cm}} NP \end{bmatrix} \rightarrow [\text{–} \underline{\hspace{1cm}} NP]$

Let us now look at another property of verbs and adjectives that have NP^* subjects. Consider the difference between the sentences of (170) and those of (171):

(170)(a) *John and Bill are similar to Tom and Harry.*
   (b) *John and Bill are similar to that group.*
   (c) *[John and Bill]$_{NP}$ and that group are similar*
   (d) *[[John and Bill]$_{NP}$ and [Tom and Harry]$_{NP}$]$_{NP}$ are similar*
   (e) **That group is similar.*
   (f) *Those groups are similar.*

(171)(a) *John and Bill conferred with Tom and Harry.*
   (b) *John and Bill conferred with the committee.*
   (c) *[John and Bill]$_{NP}$ and the committee conferred*
   (d) *[[John and Bill]$_{NP}$ and [Tom and Harry]$_{NP}$]$_{NP}$ conferred*
   (e) *The committee conferred.*
   (f) *The committees conferred.*

In these sentences we are considering only the readings which are not derived from sentence conjunction. So, for example, the only underlying structure for (170a) that we are considering is (172).

(172)

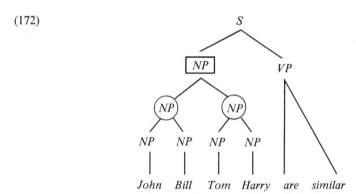

With this underlying structure, (170a) receives the interpretation that the group of John and Bill is similar in some unspecified respect to the group of Tom and Harry. But this structure does not assert that the four individuals, John, Bill, Tom, and Harry, are similar in any respect. The similarity is predicated only of the two groups. This is clearer in (170b) where *John and Bill* are considered as a unit on the one hand and *the group* is considered as a unit on the other.

But this "group interpretation" does not hold in the sentences of (171). In (171a), it is not only true that the groups conferred but that the individuals conferred as well. Thus, *confer* is predicated not only of the two groups, but also of the four individuals. This fact about group interpretation correlates with a syntactic fact, as can be seen in sentences (e) of (170) and (171). A singular collective noun (like *group* or *committee*) may not occur as the subject of a verb or adjective that takes a group interpretation (*similar* but not *confer*).

As we saw in (170b–c), a singular collective noun (*group*) functions like an *NP** embedded inside of an *NP**. That is, there is a significant grammatical distinction between a top-level *NP** (such as the *NP* enclosed in the square in (172)) and an embedded *NP** (such as the *NP*'s enclosed in circles in (172)). A singular collective noun always functions like an *NP**. But with verbs and adjectives that take a group interpretation, a singular collective noun functions always like an embedded *NP**, never like a top-level *NP**. That is why sentence (170e) is ungrammatical. *That group* there cannot play the role of a top-level *NP**, since *similar* takes a group interpretation. However, (171e) is grammatical since *confer* does not take a group interpretation. For verbs and adjectives of this class, any singular collective noun is equivalent to an *NP** subject.

Now we can state a further generalization: all [+*Special*] verbs and adjectives take a group interpretation. In addition, every verb and adjective that takes a group interpretation must obligatorily take an *NP** subject.

Let us now consider a subcategory of those verbs and adjectives that optionally take *NP** subjects. Consider the following sentences:

(173)(a) *John and Bill own the house together.*
　(b) *John and Bill robbed the bank together.*
　(c) *John and Bill opened the door together.*
　(d) *John and Bill killed Harry together.*

(174)(a) *John and Bill ran together.*
　(b) *John and Bill left the party together.*
　(c) *John and Bill hit Harry together.*
　(d) *John and Bill arrived late together.*

In the sentences of (174), it is entailed that each individual performed the indicated action. In other words, (174a) entails both *John ran* and *Bill ran*. That is, the phrasal conjunction entails the sentence conjunction (but not vice versa, of course). However, in the sentences of (173), this is not true. For example, if (173a) is true, then it is false that *John owns the house* and false that *Bill owns the house*. In these sentences the falsehood of each member of the corresponding sentence conjunction is entailed.

Before concluding, we would like to point out the impossibility of deriving sentences with *NP** subjects from *each other* constructions, a derivation which has been proposed in several places, e.g. Gleitman (1965). It might be claimed that sentences like (175) are derived from (176).

(175)(a) *John and Bill met.*
　(b) *John and Bill are similar.*
　(c) *John and Bill killed Harry (together).*

(176)(a) *John and Bill met each other.*
　(b) *John and Bill are similar to each other.*
　(c) **John and Bill killed Harry with each other.*

(175) would be derived from (176) by the deletion of *each other*—the deletion being obligatory in the case of (176c). (176) would be derived from sentence conjunction, as in (177).

(177)(a)   *John met Bill and Bill met John.*
   (b)   *John is similar to Bill and Bill is similar to John.*
   (c)   *John killed Harry with Bill and Bill killed Harry with John.*

This solution would presumably avoid the necessity of having *NP** subjects at all. It is the (c) cases that show that it is impossible to eliminate *NP** subjects in this manner. In the (c) cases, the *with* phrases would have to be considered as occurring in deep structures. But as we showed above, this is impossible since the grammatical relations they express depend upon whether or not the passive transformation has applied. To accept such an analysis would be to give up the concept of deep structure—a single level on which grammatical relations determine semantic interpretation. It would also mean that we would have to give up the natural explanations that we have given for the symmetry of the constructions, the lack of reflexives, the lack of passives, etc. All of these would then have to be given by *ad hoc* constraints, which would be difficult, if not impossible to state. This leads us to believe that such a solution is untenable.[15]

---

[15]It is fair to ask how we would get sentences like

   John and Bill are similar to each other.

One possible answer would be that such sentences are derived from deep structures like

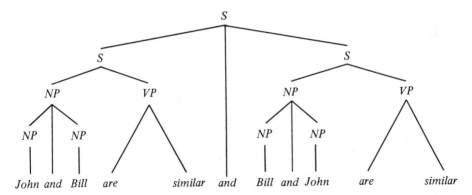

This would be transformed to

   John is similar to Bill and Bill is similar to John.

Then by the same rule that turns *John killed Bill and Bill killed John* into *John and Bill killed each other*, we would get

   John and Bill are similar to each other.

The deep structure of this sentence, under our analysis, would contain a conjunction of two sentences that are identical in meaning and differ syntactically only in the order of their *NP** subjects. Since the sentences do differ syntactically, such a deep structure would not violate the constraint that two identical sentences may not appear in a deep structure conjunction. However, since the two conjoined sentences would have the same meaning, we would predict that the derived sentence would be redundant. This is correct. English teachers commenting on style correctly tell us to avoid sentences like *John and Bill are similar to each other* since they are unnecessarily redundant and since *John and Bill are similar* will carry the meaning just as well with fewer words. With the proposed analysis we can *explain* the redundancy in such sentences and the lack of a similar redundancy in sentences like *John and Bill killed each other*, where the conjoined sentences in the deep structure are not semantically identical.

REFERENCES

Browne, W. (1964), "On Adjectival Comparison and Reduplication in English." Unpublished paper.

Curme, G. (1931), *A Grammar of English: Syntax*. Boston: D. C. Heath & Company.

Gleitman, L. (1965), "Coordinating Conjunctions in English." *Language*, 41.260–293 [*MSE*].

Lakoff, G. (1965), *On the Nature of Syntactic Irregularity* (Ph.D. dissertation, Indiana University), *Mathematical Linguistics and Automatic Translation*. Harvard Computation Laboratory, Report No. NSF-16, Cambridge, Mass.

—————— (to appear), *Deep and Surface Grammar*. Cambridge, Mass.: M.I.T. Press.

Lakoff, R., personal communication.

Peters, S. (1966), *Coordinate Conjunction in English*. Ph.D. dissertation, M.I.T.

Rosenbaum, P. (1965), *The Grammar of English Predicate Complement Constructions*. Ph.D. dissertation, M.I.T. [Cambridge, Mass.: M.I.T. Press, 1967].

Ross, J. R. (1967), *Constraints on Variables in Syntax*. Ph.D. dissertation, M.I.T.

III

PRONOMINALIZATION

Pronominalization is the process that replaces one or more co-referential noun phrases in the deep structure of a sentence with the corresponding personal pronouns in the surface structure. The first transformational treatment of pronominalization, R.B. Lees and Edward S. Klima's "Rules for English Pronominalization," shows how co-referential noun phrases on the right undergo pronominalization. Rules are presented for deriving simple, reflexive, and reciprocal pronouns.

The next two papers investigate the conditions on deep structure configurations necessary for pronominalization to take place—in particular, the constraints on forward and backward pronominalizations. Ronald W. Langacker, in "On Pronominalization and the Chain of Command," develops such a set of conditions, introducing the notion of "command"—a relation among nodes in the tree configuration. He then discusses the significance of this notion for other grammatical processes of English. John Robert Ross, in "On the Cyclic Nature of English Pronominalization," argues for the placement of pronominalization within the transformational cycle.

Whereas the first three articles are concerned with the nature of the pronominalization process, the fourth deals with the forms of the personal pronouns themselves. In "On So-Called 'Pronouns' in English," Paul M. Postal adduces syntactic evidence for considering pronouns as a variety of definite article. His treatment exemplifies the striking kinds of differences that can be found between the underlying and surface forms of sentences.

11

Rules for English Pronominalization

R. B. LEES and EDWARD S. KLIMA

Most contemporary handbooks of English recognize a class of so-called "function words" with special inflection, called pronouns, together sometimes with a wider class of words which are said to replace pronouns in certain environments and are called perhaps "pronominals"; all are often classified as a subset of nouns. More or less attention may be given to the peculiarities of English pronominal inflection,[1] but important regularities among obligatory choices of pronoun are usually avoided, no doubt because all previous discussions of this subject in older texts have had to resort heavily to semantic notions. In fact, the strong implication of most contemporary treatments is that the choice of pronominals is dictated, if at all, purely by the intended *meaning* of the sentence.

This view, as mentioned, overlooks several interesting formal contrasts of English grammar—contrasts which, in fact, impinge in their analysis upon one of the most fundamental features of natural language structure, namely the difference between simple and complex sentences. The very name "pronoun," taken directly from French and Latin in its original meaning, is still understood etymologically and, we believe, quite correctly, as "word used in place of a noun";

Reprinted from *Language*, 39.17–28 (1963), by permission of R. B. Lees and Edward S. Klima and the Linguistic Society of America.

[1]For example, A. A. Hill gives an elaborate "morphemic" analysis of English personal pronouns in his *Introduction to Linguistic Structures* (New York, 1958), pp. 145–152. He says of "pronominals" (p. 151): "No form class has been more confusingly defined, since the reliance is almost always on semantic characteristics. Thus, no less a scholar than George O. Curme was led to define *others* as a pronoun since it is a substitute. Yet since it shows all the formal characteristics of a noun, it must belong to that form class rather than to pronouns." By "formal characteristics" Hill presumably means characteristics based on (phonemic?) form, not characteristics which are abstract or mathematical as opposed to concrete, empirical, or contingent. Hill also describes a class of "pronominals" in initial /ð/ and /hw/ (pp. 370–389) and makes occasional references to pronouns as nominal elements in various constructions.

but what is not so widely appreciated is that this replacement is subject to very rigid grammatical rules. To illustrate this point and formulate certain of these rules we shall not attempt to discuss all of the various forms which have been called pronouns, but shall confine our attention to the major contrast between simple personal pronouns on the one hand and on the other the so-called reflexive pronouns in *-self* and the "reciprocal" *one another*.[2] We shall point to certain peculiarities in their use and ask how these might be accounted for by means of grammatical rules.

REFLEXIVE AND SIMPLE PRONOUN

It is all very well to explain to a child who already knows the rules of English how the following three sentences differ in meaning, say by using appropriate paraphrases:

(1)   *The boys looked at them.*

(2)   *The boys looked at themselves.*

(3)   *The boys looked at one another.*

For in these examples, as far as the individual sentences in isolation are concerned, the three pronominal expressions *are* independently selectable and in contrast. But one need not look far to find other simple examples in which certain of the pronominal forms are excluded and for which the most obvious rules of thumb begin to fail.

Thus, from the set

(4)   *I see him.*

(5)   *He sees me.*

(6)   *I see myself.*

(7)   *He sees himself.*

but not

(8)   **I see himself.*[3]

---

[2]We shall not attempt to study or analyze the so-called "emphatic" constructions in *-self*, as in *John did it himself.*

[3]We use the asterisk throughout to designate ungrammatical expressions. Naturally our judgments of grammaticalness are based directly and solely upon our own maximally formal speech style and usage, and the rules we formulate will, therefore, characterize sentences in our own dialect only. It is not likely that corresponding rules which could be formulated for other forms of English will diverge sharply from those which we use to construct sentences, but there will be readers who judge differently certain examples we quote.

It is also important to recognize in this connection that, except for utterly impeccable short sentences or for unintelligible gibberish, absolute judgments on grammatical acceptability cannot be given with assurance unless some independent knowledge has already been acquired about other formal features of English sentences and grammar relevant to the doubtful examples in question. Thus, we would reject the "queer sentence" **John astounded the dark green* with some conviction, since we know from independent analyses that the distinction between "animate" and "inanimate" nouns is relevant in English sentence structure. In any case, the point of such studies as this is, of course, not to legislate against the use of certain expressions nor to disparage certain styles or dialects of English, but rather to account for an indisputed widespread agreement among speakers of one dialect of English that certain types of expression are structurally deviant.

(9) *He sees myself.*

we might suppose that when the subject and the object of a sentence are identical the object must be the corresponding *-self* form (ignoring here the trivial question of which *-self* forms correspond to which subjects). Such a rule would then correctly explain why one understands that there are two people involved when one hears the sentence

(10) *He sees him.*

and why there is no sentence

(11) **I see me.*

However, there are many other examples in which the simple pronoun also appears in contrast with the reflexive pronoun in *-self*:

(12) *The men threw a smokescreen around themselves.*

(13) *The men found a smokescreen around them.*

and even cases in which the repeated nominal must be replaced by the simple pronoun, as in

(14) *I told John to protect himself.*

(15) *I told John to protect me.*

but not

(16) **I told John to protect myself.*

Having suggested already that a nominal which repeats the subject is to be replaced by a reflexive pronoun, we might attempt to preserve this rule by analyzing (13) as having roughly the same grammatical structure as

(17) *The men found a smokescreen to be around them.*

or ambiguously as

(18) *The men found a smokescreen which was around them.*

or even

(19) *The men found a smokescreen and it was around them.*

for in the latter three sentences we would expect the same pronominal replacements as in

(20) *The smokescreen was around them.*

This is to say, we might consider (13), (17), (18), and (19) all to contain *two* different component sentences each, i.e. to be "complex," and we might say further that the given pronominalization rule which yields reflexives must be applied first, before the components are joined; afterwards, some other rule applies which yields simple pronoun replacements.[4] Accordingly, we treat (14) and (15) in such a way that they are said to contain respectively

---

[4]Some classical grammarians also interpret the reflexive as the result of a change imposed on a more basic sentence, and thus in a sense transformationally. Cf., for example, H. Poutsma, *A Grammar of Late Modern English* (1916) Vol. 2, p. 836: "to denote that the person(s) or thing(s) referred to in any enlargement of the predicate are the same as that (those) indicated by the predicate." Or even more clearly O. Jespersen, *Essentials of English Grammar* (1937), p. 111: "When subject and object are identical, we use for the latter the so-called reflexive pronoun."

(21)   *John protects himself.*

and

(22)   *John protects me.*

There are several different ways in which a noun may be embedded twice in a sentence, and when the second occurrence is part of the same simplex (kernel) sentence the pronominal replacement is always reflexive; but when the two occurrences are from different component source sentences, the subordinate one is replaced by the simple pronoun.[5] We give here a brief indication of the grammatical analyses for several sentence types showing this contrast between simplex and complex.

(23)   *John has no control over himself.*

(24)   *John has no covering over him.*

Here the contrast is essentially between a composite transitive verb *have control* (*over*), generated in the kernel, and a complex sentence containing a discontinuous verb-plus-complement constituent *have . . . over him.* The latter complement-type sentence arises transformationally from two source sentences, thus:

(25)   *John has + Comp no covering* $\Big\}$ →
(26)   *No covering is over John*

(27)   *John has over John no covering* →

(28)   *John has no covering over John* →

(24)   *John has no covering over him.*

The shift of the object nominal into its correct position between the two parts of the verb phrase is an obligatory transformation required for many other sentence types also, and the replacement of the second occurrence of *John* by *him* is the obligatory pronominal transformation under discussion.

(29)   *John bought Mary a car to drive herself around in.*

(30)   *John bought Mary a car to drive him around in.*

The underlying source sentences which account for the contrast in pronominal replacements here are, for (29), *Mary drives herself around in the car*, and, for (30), *Mary drives John around in the car*. Both sentences are complex, containing "infinitival nominal" transforms of the second source sentence. As prototype derivation consider the following:

(31)   *John bought Mary a car for Nom* $\Big\}$ →
(32)   *Bill drives Jim around in the car*

(33)   *John bought Mary a car for for Bill to drive Jim around in* →

(34)   *John bought Mary a car for Bill to drive Jim around in.*

---

[5]Although the basic idea itself is ancient, the formal particularities in this analysis of certain sentences as transforms of underlying source sentences are taken directly from well-known works of N. A. Chomsky. The details of English syntactic structure lying behind our analyses, as well as a more general discussion of the theoretical basis for this view of grammar and of language, may be found in R. B. Lees, "The Grammar of English Nominalizations," *International Journal of American Linguistics*, 26.3, Part 2 (1960).

In (31) the symbol *Nom* represents a nominal, in this case an abstract noun which is to be replaced by an infinitival nominalization of the form *for N to V*.

Now, if in (32) we had had *Mary* in place of both *Bill* and *Jim*, we should have obtained the sentence

(35) *John bought Mary a car for for Mary to drive Mary around in*

Then the third occurrence of the noun *Mary* would be replaced by the reflexive *herself*, since it repeats a nominal (in *for Mary*) within the same simplex, or kernel, sentence. In the resulting sentence

(36) *John bought Mary a car for for Mary to drive herself around in*

the second occurrence of the noun *Mary* is then pronominalized, since it repeats the preceding noun *Mary* in the *other* source sentence (the so-called "matrix sentence" (31), the sentence into which the transformed infinitival is inserted in place of the unspecified abstract nominal *Nom*).

(37) *John bought Mary a car for for Mary + Pron to drive herself around in*

This pronominalized noun is next completely deleted by an obligatory transformation on all infinitival nominals appearing as subjects of *for*-phrase adverbials of "purpose" (rather than the usual pronoun substitution obligatory for other sentence types):[6]

(38) *John bought Mary a car for for to drive herself around in*

Finally, there is an obligatory ellipsis of prepositions before the *to* and *for* of infinitival nominals, yielding

(29) *John bought Mary a car to drive herself around in.*

If, on the other hand, we had had *John* in place of *Jim* in (32) and *Mary* in place of *Bill*, the derivation would have been

(31) *John bought Mary a car for Nom* $\Big\}\rightarrow$
(39) *Mary drives John around in the car*
(40) *John bought Mary a car for for Mary to drive John around in* →
(41) *John bought Mary a car for for Mary + Pron to drive John + Pron around in* →
(42) *John bought Mary a car for for to drive him around in*
(30) *John bought Mary a car to drive him around in.*

Here in (41) the noun *John*, since it repeats a noun *John* in the matrix sentence, is pronominalized instead of reflexivized, and becomes *him* under the appropriate morphophonemic rules.[7]

As a final example, consider the two contrasting sentences

(43) *John smeared the oil on himself.*

(44) *John ignored the oil on him.*

The first contains in the predicate an object *the oil* and an adverbial *on himself*; and it arises from the kernel sentence *John smeared the oil on John*. Since the second

---

[6]Ibid., rule (T68*).

[7]And the redundant preposition *for*, when it occurs before the *to* or *for* of an infinitival nominal, is also automatically deleted; ibid., rule (T69*).

occurrence of the noun *John* repeats a noun within the same simplex, it is pronominalized to the corresponding *-self* pronoun. But in (44) the object of the verb *ignored* is itself a transform of an underlying sentence of the form *The oil is on John*. The predicate of this copula-type sentence is introduced as a relative-clause modifier of *oil* in the matrix sentence *John ignored the oil*, yielding *John ignored the oil which was on John*, and the copula is then deleted to yield a postnominal modifier *on John*, thus:[8]

(45)   *John ignored the oil*⎫
(46)   *The oil is on John* ⎬ →
(47)   *John ignored the oil which is on John* →
(48)   *John ignored the oil on John* →
(49)   *John ignored the oil on John + Pron* →
(44)   *John ignored the oil on him.*

There are, of course, other restrictions on the various rules to which we have alluded here, which in some cases may affect the final outcome of pronominalizations. For example, when the pronominalized noun is a repetition of an indirect object in the matrix sentence in a sentence type like *You bought me a dog to amuse myself with*, the total deletion of an intermediate subject of the *for*-phrase is optional: *You bought me a dog for me to amuse myself with*. Furthermore, in this same sentence type, the rule which inserts the infinitival nominal into the matrix sentence *for*-phrase itself requires that the two source sentences share a certain noun, that this noun be the object of a verb or a preposition in the constituent sentence, and that it be totally deleted in the transform:[9]

(50)   *you bought John a dog for Nom*⎫
(51)   *John amuses John with the dog* ⎬ →
(52)   *you bought John a dog for for John to amuse John with the dog* →
(53)   *you bought John a dog for for John to amuse John + self with* →
(54)   *you bought John a dog for for John + Pron to amuse John + self with* →
(55)   *you bought John a dog for (for him) to amuse himself with* →
(56)   *You bought John a dog (for him) to amuse himself with.*

Another restriction is that the pronominalized verbal object may not become the subject of a passive sentence: *John shaves himself* → **Himself is shaved by John*. It is also best, no doubt, to reject such sentences as (*) *John is shaved by himself*. (If not, we can simply order the rules so that Passive precedes Reflexive.) Both restrictions might be incorporated into a constraint on the passive transformation itself, to the effect that the subject and object of the active verb may not be identical in the string to which the passive rule applies.[10]

---

[8]Ibid., rules (GT 19) and (T58).

[9]This rule would be an addition to rule (GT13) of Lees, op. cit., not discussed there. Also, in connection with these indirect-object examples, we shall consider sentences of the form *I bought me a hat*, confined to the first person, to be nonstandard colloquial variants of sentences of the form *I bought myself a hat*.

[10]This is an addition to rule (T2) of Lees, op. cit. Also cf. Jespersen, *A Modern English Grammar*, 3.§15.1₃.

Our simple rule based on repetition of nouns within the same simplex would seem to be violated by sentences like

(57)   *Protecting yourself is difficult here.*

where there does not appear to be any antecedent to govern the reflexive pronominalization in *yourself*. Noting parenthetically that it is probably best to consider *you* in such a sentence to be a variant of the impersonal noun *one*, we might say that (57) contains an action-type gerundive nominal[11] and that the impersonal subject is later deleted from such constructions, thus:

(58)   *Nom is difficult here* ⎱
(59)   *one protects one*   ⎰ →

(60)   *one's protecting one is difficult here* →
(61)   *one's protecting one + self is difficult here* →
(62)   *One's protecting oneself is difficult here* →
(63)   *Protecting oneself is difficult here* →
(64)   *Protecting yourself is difficult here.*

Another ostensible violation of our rule would seem to be the following imperative sentences:

(65)   *Protect yourself now.*

(66)   *Protect yourselves now.*

However, there are independent, compelling reasons to consider these sentences to be derived from sentences with *you*, singular or plural respectively, as the subject noun phrase (and perhaps with the modal *will* in the auxiliary).[12] The transformational rule which produces imperatives would then simply delete the auxiliary; the subject *you* would also be deleted optionally at a later point as a stylistic variant. This treatment would account for the fact that the rules which hold for the object nominal in the imperative sentence are the same as those which apply to the object nominal in a declarative sentence, viz., there is no **Protect you now*, but only *Protect yourself now*. Furthermore, we should account for the peculiar restriction that of the reflexives only those of the second person occur at all in imperative sentences, that only in the case of second person genitives can the intensive *own* be used:

> *Use my pencil, Use his pencil, Use your pencil.*
> *Use your own pencil.*
> **Use my own pencil, *Use his own pencil.*

and that there are no imperatives with the *have + Ppl* or *be + Ing* formatives:

> *Do it. *Have done it. *Be doing it.*

The derivation would be

---

[11]Lees, op. cit., rule (GT10) and the preceding discussion. By action-type gerundive nominal we mean that type which must have an indefinite human subject and no auxiliary accompanying the verb (i.e. we have no **John's protecting himself is hard* nor **Having protected oneself is hard.*)

[12]We ignore certain special expressions such as *Just look at you*, which might possibly go back to a hortatory *Let us just look at you* or the like.

(67)   *you + Sg Aux protect you + Sg →*

(68)   *you + Sg protect you + Sg →*

(69)   *you + Sg protect you + Sg + self →*

(70)   *you + Sg protect yourself →*

(71)   *You protect yourself →* (optional)

(72)   *Protect yourself.*

In still another, but opposite, type of counter example which might arise there is a repeated nominal but no reflexive pronominalization, as in

(73)   *Mary's father supported her.*

(74)   *Mary's father supported himself.*

but no

(75) **Mary's father supported herself.*

in which the underlying sentence must have been

(76)   *Mary's father supported Mary.*

However, there is a good deal of evidence supporting the view that all genitives in English are transformational in origin, so that the underlying sentence would then be rather *The father supported Mary*, with no repetition. (The second source sentence for the genitive itself would presumably have been *Mary has a father*, with intermediate stages: *The father that Mary has supported Mary* and *The father of Mary supported Mary*.)

Ignoring the various details of special deletions for "purpose" adverbials in *for* with the infinitival or gerundive nominals, the rules we propose for pronominalization are then these:

(A) Reflexive Rule:
$$X - Nom - Y - Nom' - Z \rightarrow X - Nom - Y - Nom' + Self - Z$$
where $Nom = Nom' = $ a nominal, and where Nom and Nom' are within the same simplex sentence

(B) Pronoun Rule:
$$X - Nom - Y - Nom' - Z \rightarrow X - Nom - Y - Nom' + Pron - Z$$
where $Nom = Nom'$, and where Nom is in a matrix sentence while Nom' is in a constituent sentence embedded within that matrix sentence

The two rules are to be applied in the order given.[13] Later morphophonemic rules will then yield the appropriate pronoun forms *me, myself, yourself, . . . , themselves*, etc.

The analysis which we have given for reflexive and simple pronominalization does not by any means give an immediate explanation for all known occurrences of the pronominals in question, but this may be due simply to our incomplete understanding of the structure of certain sentence types. For example, we may analyze

(75)   *John has many books about him.*

---

[13]Lees, op. cit., rules (T65*) and (T67*). Following a suggestion by L. R. Gleitman, we assume that the rules are optional for third person and obligatory for first and second.

as either a complement-type sentence from

(76) *John has + Comp many books* ⎱
(77) *Many books are about John*   ⎰ →

(78) *John has about John many books.*

or else we may analyze it as a postnominal-modifier-type sentence from

(79) *John has many books* ⎱
(80) *The books are about John* ⎰ →

(81) *John has many books which are about John.*

But one may also say

(82) *John has many books about himself.*

parallel to

(83) *John has written many books about himself.*

Sentence (82) is perhaps also parallel to

(84) *John found a picture of himself.*

Such constructions with *picture of, description of, book about, story of*, etc., are not at all like the prepositional periphrases of the genitive, despite the existence also of corresponding expressions *John's picture, John's story*, etc.[14] The genitive periphrasis is not possible with pronouns:

(85) *We showed him his picture.*

(86) *We showed him a picture of himself.*

(87) *We showed him his room.*

but not

(88) **We showed him a room of himself.*

nor

(89) **We showed him a room of him.*

The expression in

(90) *We showed him a room of his.*

is not parallel to the genitive in (87) but is more like the definite noun phrase in

(91) *We showed him this room.*

Notice further that there does not seem to be a transformational constituent-break in (86), for the subject itself also governs the reflexive:

(92) *We showed him a picture of ourselves.*

Thus, it would seem that such double-object-verb sentences with *give, show, buy, tell*, etc., are either kernel sentences or are simple transforms, but are not so-called generalized transforms (i.e. sentences arising transformationally from

---

[14]Also, incidentally, they are precisely those expressions of English which N. Goodman attempted to use in formulating a theory of synonymy as a part of the theory of reference: "On Likeness of Meaning," *Analysis*, 10 (1949), revised in L. Linsky's *Semantics and the Philosophy of Language* (1952), pp. 67–74.

two or more underlying source sentences).[15] Notice also that the prepositional-phrase form in some cases is quite unnatural:

(93)   *John gave Mary a picture of herself.*

but not

(94)   **John gave a picture of Mary to herself.*

not

(95)   **John gave a picture of herself to Mary.*

though

(96)   *John gave a picture of himself to Mary.*

It is just possible then that the prepositional-phrase periphrases of double-object-verb sentences are derived from the latter, and not vice versa, but with the restriction that the periphrasis transformation does not take place after reflexivization of the last noun when the latter repeats the *in*direct object. But, however we analyze double-object-verb sentences, the appearance of the reflexive pronoun in sentences like (82) still seems anomalous, for it appears to be natural to understand the sentence as exactly parallel to

(97)   *John has many books which are about John.*

The latter is a typical relative-clause-to-postnominal-modifier conversion. But in that case there would be no antecedent in the subordinate constituent sentence to govern the appearance of *himself.*

ABSOLUTE REFLEXIVE

Next we note that English also has reflexive verbs, i.e. verbs whose objects are, at least in part, restricted to reflexive pronouns. Thus, *express* is an absolute transitive verb (which means that it requires an object), but its object cannot be an animate noun:

(98)   **John expresses.*

(99)   **John expresses Mary.*

(100)   *John expresses emotions.*

yet it may be followed by a reflexive pronoun:

(101)   *John expresses himself.*

---

[15]In fact, C. J. Fillmore has given a reasonable analysis of the double-object construction in *Indirect Object Constructions in English and the Ordering of Transformations*, Ohio State Research Foundation Project on Syntactic Analysis, Report #1, Prof. 1303, Feb. 13, 1962 [The Hague: Mouton & Co., 1965]. Fillmore assumes an underlying construction of the form *John Tns give to Bill a bite* (exactly parallel to *John Tns shoot at Bill a gun*), which is later subject to the usual "separation" rule, yielding *John Tns give a bite to Bill*, i.e. the sentence *John gives a bite to Bill.* There is, however, an intervening optional rule which deletes the preposition *to*, yielding *John Tns give Bill a bite*, the sentence *John gives Bill a bite.* He is able to account also for the existence of two different passives for such indirect object sentences, and he gives an analysis of the contrasting indirect object construction in *for: John buys a car for Bill: John buys Bill a car*, for which there is no passive.

Indeed, the reflexive object *must* be animate:

(102) **John expresses itself.*

Furthermore, such verbs may not be separated from their reflexive objects under conjunction:

(103) **John excused and behaved himself.*

yet there is no general restriction of this sort on sentences containing reflexive pronouns:

(104) *John cut and scratched himself.*

Sentence (103) must be reworded as *John excused himself and behaved himself.* Finally there are among these special verbs some whose *only* objects are reflexives with the subject as antecedent:

(105) *John absents himself.*

(106) *John perjures himself.*

(107) *John bestirs himself.*

(108) *John behaves himself.*

(109) *John prides himself in that.*

but no

(110) **John absents Mary.*

nor

(111) **John absents it*, etc.

We shall say, then, that among the intransitive verbs V_{in} there are not only absolute intransitives V_i (*vanish, arrive*, etc.), which may yield prenominal gerundive modifiers as in *barking dogs, vanishing race*, etc., "locative" intransitives V_{loc} (*lie, stand*, etc.), which require locative adverbial (i.e. there is no **The baby lay*, but only *The baby lay in bed*, etc.), "motion" intransitives V_{mot} (*go, sneak*, etc.), which require adverbs of motion (i.e. there is no **John sneaked* (or *snuck*), but only *John sneaked into the house*, etc.), and perhaps many other subtypes, but there are also so-called "reflexive" intransitives V_{rf}, which may not be freely followed by an object nominal. Later all such reflexive verb phrases undergo an obligatory transformation which inserts a replica of the subject after the verb, and this obligatory "object" is then pronominalized in the usual way: being part of the same simplex as its subject, which it repeats, it yields the appropriate reflexive pronoun. This obligatory insertion of a reflexivizable object follows, in the grammar, the optional rules for *Wh*-questions, and hence these objects are not questionable like regular verbal objects:

(112) **Whom did John behave?*

As L. R. Gleitman has pointed out,* there are also certain constraints on ordinary conjunction for pronominalized sentences: the following pronominalizable noun may be conjoined with another noun, but not the antecedent noun:

**Lila R. Gleitman, "Coordinating Conjunctions in English," *Language*, 41.260–293 (1965); in *MSE*.

(113)   *John prefers John to them → John prefers himself to them.*

(114)   *I prefer John to them.*

(115)   *John prefers me to them.*

(116)   *John prefers John and me to them → John prefers himself and me to them.*

but not

(117)   **John and I prefer John to them.* (→ **John and I prefer himself to them.*)

It therefore seems probable that the pronominalization rule must precede the rule of conjunction.

RECIPROCAL PRONOMINALIZATION

We return now to example (3), in contrast to (1) and (2). We note that when the following pronominal is "reciprocal"—*one another or each other* (we shall ignore the difference, if any, between the two types)—the subject of the sentence must be plural:

(118)   **The boy looked at one another.*

Now, there are also several other important restrictions on the appearance of reciprocal objects. Note the following examples:

(119)   *Red and green complement one another.*

(120)   *John and Mary frighten one another.*

(121)   *Red and green frighten them.*

but not

(122)   **Red and green frighten one another.*

Thus, while *one another* can be the object of *frighten* (120), and while both animate and inanimate plural nouns may be the subject of *frighten* (120, 121), and while inanimate nouns may appear with the reciprocal (119) as well as animates (120), *one another* may not be the object of the verb *frighten* when the subject is inanimate. But this restriction applies precisely when the verb of the sentence belongs to that special class of verbs which require animate objects (*frighten, please, amaze*, etc.). Thus, we see that the object *one another* is a pronominalization of its subject, and it occurs only when the subject is plural and is repeated in the object.[16]

We shall say then that in addition to the reflexive pronominalization transformation there is an optional rule of the following form:

(C) Reciprocal Rule (optional):

$$X - N + Pl - Y - N' + Pl - Z \rightarrow X - N + Pl - Y - N' + Pl + Recip - Z$$

where $N = N'$ and they are within the same simplex, and where N is a noun, Pl is the plural morpheme, and $Recip$ is the reciprocal morpheme

---

[16]Cf. the very similar analysis of the reciprocal in Danish given by O. Jespersen, *Sprogets logik* (1931), pp. 79–80: "Når karen ligner maren, ligner maren også karen. I disse tilfelde er der intet i vejen for at gøre subjekt og objekt til to forbundne subjekten, og objektets plads udfylder vi da med ordet hinanden . . . As v Bo = Bs v Ao = (A + B)s v hinanden-o." This interpretation is again essentially transformational, as are many of Jespersen's grammatical analyses.

Later morphophonemic rules will then yield the appropriate forms *one another* and *each other* from $N + Pl + Recip$.

Again there may be some difficulties with conjoined expressions, as in

(123) *John and Mary frighten one another.*

for the source sentence would have to have been

(124) *John and Mary frighten John and Mary.*

a rather implausible sentence of English. On intuitive or semantic grounds one would suppose the correct source to be the pair of sentences

(125) *John frightens Mary | Mary frightens John.*

This implies that the process is conjunctional; but the expression *one another* appears in other ways to be pronominal, for it concatenates with other pronouns, as in

(126) *They preferred themselves and one another to the strangers.*

and it fails to separate from its verb

(127) *They set the men up in office.*
(128) *They set up the men in office.*
(129) *They set themselves up in office.*
(130) *They set one another up in office.*

but not

(131) **They set up themselves in office.*

nor

(132) **They set up one another in office.*

Therefore, it seems that the best course is to extend the conjunction rules to permit conjoining the members of reciprocal pairs in a special way and then have only one reciprocal pronominalization rule afterward:

(133) *John frightens Mary*⎫
(134) *Mary frightens John*⎬ →
(124) *John and Mary frighten John and Mary.*

This analysis now yields an explanation for a peculiar restriction on the subjects of certain apparently intransitive verbs, as in

(135) *They kissed.*
(136) *John and Mary met.*
(137) *Hydrogen and oxygen combine.*

The subject must be plural:

(138) **He kissed.*
(139) **Hydrogen combines.*

There is also another, even more restricted type of verb for which the subject may be only a plural noun or a mass noun (but not a conjoined nominal), as in

(140) *The soldiers scattered.*
(141) *The dew collected.*

but not

(142) *The soldier scattered.*

(143) *John and Mary scattered.*

(144) *The dewdrop collected.*

Furthermore, the conjoined subjects permitted in sentences like (136) would not seem to be ordinary conjunctions, for there is no

(145) *John met and Mary met.*

Thus, these verbs are not exactly like the larger class of apparent intransitives of the form

(146) *John ate.*

which may be analyzed as transitives with deleted object, in contrast to the absolute transitives:

(147) *John devoured the meal.*

but not

(148) *John devoured.*

and in contrast to the absolute intransitives V_i:

(149) *John arrived.*

The verbs in question here may also be regarded as deleted-object transitives, but with the restriction that the object must be *Nom + Recip*. Thus we should derive

(150) *John and Mary kissed John and Mary* →

(151) *John and Mary kissed each other* →

(152) *John and Mary kissed.*

In addition to this limited class of direct-object verbs with deletable reciprocal, there is also the freer case of verbs which require a preposition after them, somewhat like the case of locative and motion intransitives:

(153) *The sodium and chlorine combined **with** each other* →

(154) *The sodium and chlorine combined.*

but not

(155) *The sodium combined.*

nor do we have the derivation

(156) *They experimented with one another** →

(157) *They experimented.*

The antecedent noun for the reciprocal pronominal need not be the subject of the sentence, of course, and there are therefore some ambiguous expressions, such as

(158) *They pushed them toward one another.*

understood either as parallel to

(159) *The boys pushed the girl toward one another.*

or as parallel to

(160) *The boy pushed the girls toward one another.*

It might even be possible, for some speakers, to have the two pronominals contiguous as direct and indirect objects:

(161) *We showed each other ourselves.*

(162) *We showed ourselves each other.*

The reciprocal is not restricted in the same manner as the reflexive, viz. to simplexes (in contrast to generalized transforms or complexes). Thus we have

(163) *They placed their guns in front of them.*

(164) *They placed their guns in front of one another.*

but not

(165) **They placed their guns in front of themselves.*

though some speakers may have the latter sentence as a colloquial variant of (163). Similarly

(166) *They held firecrackers behind them.*

(167) *They held firecrackers behind one another.*

and not

(168) **They held firecrackers behind themselves.*

But, on the other hand, like the reflexive, the reciprocal may not occur in certain other subordinate clauses, as in

(169) *They forced the king to help them.*

but neither

(170) **They forced the king to help one another.*

nor

(171) **They forced the king to help themselves.*

Thus, for some dialects, it is not yet clear just how the reciprocal rule (C) needs to be constrained, though we have stated it with the condition imposed that the two relevant plural nouns must be within the same simplex.

12

On Pronominalization
and the Chain of Command

RONALD W. LANGACKER

SUMMARY

The purpose of this paper is to state the major restrictions on pronominalization in English. It is shown that the relation "commands," a binary relation between nodes that is defined in terms of tree structure, is crucial to the statement of these restrictions. The relations "commands" and "precedes" are grouped together as "primacy relations," allowing a considerable simplification in the formulation of the constraints. The command relation is then demonstrated to be of much more general significance for limiting the scope of transformational operations.

CONSTRAINTS ON PRONOMINALIZATION

Our goal is to answer the following question about English: Under what conditions can a definite noun phrase NP^a be used to pronominalize an identical noun phrase NP^p?[1] (NP^p will be used throughout to indicate a noun phrase that reduces to a pronoun; NP^a will indicate its antecedent.) The analysis to be pro-

---

[1] Cf. R. B. Lees and E. S. Klima, "Rules for English Pronominalization," *Language*, 39.17–28 (1963); in *MSE*. Lees and Klima give the following rule for pronominalization:

$X - Nom - Y - Nom' - Z \Rightarrow X - Nom - Y - Nom' + Pron - Z$

where $Nom = Nom'$, and where Nom is in a matrix sentence while Nom' is in a constituent sentence embedded within that matrix sentence.

This account of the scope of pronominalization fails in a number of ways. First, the two nominals may be constituents of conjoined sentences, where neither is embedded within the other:

That man can sing and *he* can dance.

Second, the pronoun may be in the matrix sentence with the antecedent being in the constituent sentence:

posed is essentially neutral with respect to various alternative ways of representing pronominalization in a generative grammar. For example, it makes no difference for our purposes whether pronominalization is effected by a single transformational rule or whether a series of operations is involved. Likewise, it makes no difference whether pronouns are derived by reducing fully specified underlying noun phrases or whether they are present in deep structure (although we will adopt the former alternative for purposes of exposition). The nature of the pronominalization process is outside the domain of this study, as is any detailed examination of pronominalization with respect to schemes of rule ordering.

Definite noun phrases are defined as proper names or noun phrases with the determiner *the, this, that, these,* or *those.* The facts of pronominalization involving indefinite *NP*'s (e.g. *each of those elephants, a mouse*) are far from clear and the problem will not be considered. It seems that pronominalization with indefinite *NP*'s observes the same restrictions that have to be imposed on the pronominalization of definites but that it may require further constraints which are not necessary for the expressions under investigation here.

We will begin by examining pronominalization in conjoined structures. The two instances of ***Peter*** in PM1, for example, are in separate conjoined structures (verb phrases in this case).

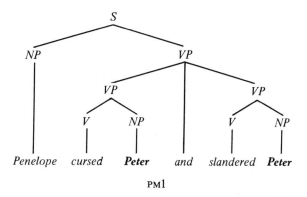

PM1

In discussing pronominalization, we will adopt the following convention: *Within a single sentence or tree structure, elements in bold face letters are always considered to have identical reference.*

In PM1, the first occurrence of ***Peter*** can be used to pronominalize the second,

---

*The woman who hated **Alexander** slandered **him**.*

Third, a pronoun may precede its antecedent:

*The woman who hated **him** slandered **Alexander**.*

Finally, both the pronoun and the antecedent may be elements of separate constituent sentences embedded within a third sentence:

*The girl who is going to marry **Peter** thinks that **he** is handsome.*

For another approach to the problem, see John Robert Ross, "On the Cyclic Nature of English Pronominalization," in *To Honor Roman Jakobson* (The Hague: Mouton & Co., 1967), reprinted in *MSE.* Ross proposes a constraint based on the notion "subordinate clause."

but not vice versa. In other words, (1) is permissible but not (2), where identity of reference is intended.

(1)   *Penelope cursed **Peter** and slandered **him**.*

(2)   **Penelope cursed **him** and slandered **Peter**.*

As (3) and (4) show, other conjoined structures may intervene between those containing NP^a and NP^p with pronominalization still being possible.

(3)   *Penelope cursed **Peter**, went to see her friends, and slandered **him** in front of them.*

(4)   *Penelope cursed **Peter**, went to see her friends, gathered them all together, and slandered **him** in front of them.*

We may thus formulate the following constraint on the pronominalization of definite NP's: *NP^a may not be used to pronominalize NP^p if NP^a and NP^p are elements of separate conjoined structures and NP^p precedes NP^a.* This constraint rules out (2) but permits (1), (3), and (4). Furthermore, it seems to be the only constraint that is necessary on pronominalization involving NP's in conjoined structures.[2] This is partially illustrated by the sets of sentences that follow:

Sentence Conjunction:

(5)   ***Peter** has a lot of talent and **he** should go far.*

(6)   ****He** has a lot of talent and **Peter** should go far.*

(7)   ***This woman** is almost blind and I won't feel safe on the road if you allow **her** to drive.*

(8)   ****She** is almost blind and I won't feel safe on the road if you allow **this woman** to drive.*

Verb Phrase Conjunction:

(1)–(4)

(9)   *Penelope cursed **the man** and thanked the woman who helped to subdue **him**.*

(10)   **Penelope cursed **him** and thanked the woman who helped to subdue **the man**.*

Noun Phrase Conjunction:

(11)   ***Peter's** wife and the woman **he** is living with just met.*

(12)   ****His** wife and the woman **Peter** is living with just met.*

(13)   *I met a woman who was dying to find out more about **that man** and another who had just been wronged by **him**.*

(14)   **I met a woman who was dying to find out more about **him** and another who had just been wronged by **that man**.*

Reflexivization may be regarded as a special form of pronominalization, the form that occurs when NP^a and NP^p are constituents of the same simple sentence. The most obvious constraint on reflexivization is that NP^p cannot precede NP^a.

(15)   ***Those men** outsmarted **themselves**.*

(16)   ****Themselves** outsmarted **those men**.*

(17)   *Penelope told **Peter** about **himself**.*

---

[2]There remains, however, an unexplored restriction concerning manner and time adverbials:

That was **the manner of disappearing John described to Mary and he actually disappeared in **it**.*

That was **the day John told Mary he would disappear and he actually disappeared on **it**.*

See S.-Y. Kuroda, "English Relativization and Certain Related Problems," in *MSE*.

(18) **Penelope told **himself** about **Peter**.*

The similarity of this constraint to the one adopted for pronominalization in conjoined structures is evident; we will see later that it follows as a special case from a more general principle governing pronominalization.[3]

By ordering the obligatory reflexivization rule before the regular pronominalization rule, we avoid having to restrict pronominalization so that it cannot apply when NP^a and NP^p are in the same simple sentence. For example, pronominalization must not apply to the underlying string (19) to yield (20).

(19)   ***Those women** admire **those women**.*

(20)   *****Those women** admire **them**.*

If reflexivization precedes pronominalization, (19) is obligatorily transformed to (21), and sentences like (20) can never result.[4]

(21)   ***Those women** admire **themselves**.*

On the other hand, it seems best to consider reflexivization and pronominalization as two variants of the same process; "pronominalization" will thus be used ambiguously in both the narrow and the broad sense. There are two reasons for this. First, the two operations are very similar, formally and intuitively. Second, the constraint we will formulate for pronominalization will serve without modification to rule out reflexive sentences such as (16) and (18).[5]

We have seen that the linear order of constituents is relevant for pronominalization when NP^a and NP^p are in separate conjoined structures and when they are in the same simple sentence structure. Now let us consider the constraints that must be imposed on pronominalization when NP^a and NP^p are in separate, nonconjoined structures. (22)–(26) are typical examples of sentences in which pronominalization has applied under these circumstances.

(22)   ***Ralph** is much more intelligent than **he** looks.*

---

[3]Further restrictions must be imposed on reflexivization, restrictions that will not concern us here. For instance, a reflexive pronoun cannot occur as the object of the agentive preposition *by* in passive sentences:

> **The woman sitting over there** *may kill* **herself**.
> ***The woman sitting over there** *may be killed by* **herself**.

Cf. Lees and Klima, op. cit., p. 21; in *MSE*, p. 150.

[4]Alternatively, reflexivization can be viewed as the result of regular pronominalization plus some other operation (such as *self* insertion).

[5]Some further points must be made. Sentences with verb phrase conjunction show pronominalization instead of reflexivization when the objects are identical:

> *Penelope cursed **Peter** and slandered **him**.*
> **Penelope cursed **Peter** and slandered **himself**.*

This indicates that reflexivization must occur before conjunction reduction, while the two verb phrases are constituents of separate simple sentences. In the case of noun phrase conjunction, the second *NP* cannot be either a pronominalized or a reflexivized form of the first:

> *****That man** and **he** robbed the bank.*
> *****That man** and **himself** robbed the bank.*

This does not reflect a constraint on pronominalization, but rather one on conjoining; the conjoined elements must differ. Underlying strings such as this one must be marked deviant:

(23) *This woman hates the man who wronged her.*

(24) *I will give these kittens to the girl who wants them.*

(25) *Tell that man that he can't go in there.*

(26) *The artist who painted these pictures must work while he is sleeping.*

In (22)–(26), NP^a uniformly precedes NP^p. Moreover, sentences (27)–(31), which are identical to (22)–(26) except that NP^p precedes NP^a, are all ungrammatical.

(27) **He is much more intelligent than Ralph looks.*

(28) **She hates the man who wronged this woman.*

(29) **I will give them to the girl who wants these kittens.*

(30) **Tell him that that man can't go in there.*

(31) **He must work while the artist who painted these pictures is sleeping.*

Thus it is clear that the linear order of constituents is relevant in some way in constraining pronominalization in those cases that do not involve reflexivization or conjoining. However, it is not sufficient to require that the antecedent precede the pronoun, since there are countless examples of well-formed sentences of English in which a pronoun precedes its antecedent, among them (32)–(34).

(32) *The woman who is to marry him will visit Ralph tomorrow.*

(33) *The man who wronged her is hated by this woman.*

(34) *The girl who wants them will receive these kittens as a present from me.*

Since NP^p precedes NP^a in these sentences, we must look for some more abstract constraint on pronominalization, one that excludes (27)–(31) while allowing (32)–(34).

One obvious difference between (27)–(31) and (32)–(34) is that the pronoun is in the main clause of (27)–(31), while in (32)–(34) the pronoun is in a subordinate clause. This suggests that we try to characterize the positional constraints on NP^a and NP^p in terms of relative depth of embedding. We might hypothesize, for example, that pronominalization is possible just in case NP^a is higher in the tree than NP^p, meaning that NP^a is dominated by fewer S-nodes than NP^p. Not only will this restriction account for (22)–(34), but it will also predict correctly that sentences like (35)–(38) are grammatical.

(35) *I think that Ralph is much more intelligent than he looks.*

(36) *I will give these kittens to the girl who said that she wants them.*

(37) *I will give these kittens to the girl who said that she knows a man who wants them.*

That man robbed the bank and that man robbed the bank.

Finally, notice that an infinitival clause may contain a reflexive pronoun which has the same reference as the subject (or object) of the matrix sentence:

Peter is reluctant to indulge himself with luxuries.

I told Carol to buy herself a new hat.

Such sentences are not counterexamples to the claim that reflexivization operates only within the bounds of a single simple sentence. In the underlying structures, the infinitival clauses must have subjects identical to some noun phrase in the matrix structure and hence identical to the noun phrase that is reflexivized. The subject of the embedded clause reflexivizes the object of the clause before the former is deleted as part of the process of infinitive embedding.

(38) *I will give **these kittens** to the girl who said that she knows a man who said that he wants **them**.*

(35) shows that NP^a does not have to be in the topmost simple sentence structure for pronominalization to occur, since the antecedent **Ralph** is in a subordinate clause. (36)–(38) show that the simple sentence structure containing NP^p does not have to be immediately subordinate to the one containing NP^a; the two may be indefinitely far away in the tree, separated by indefinitely many intermediate echelons of embedding. These observations are perfectly compatible with the hypothesis that it is relative depth of embedding that determines if NP^a can be used to pronominalize NP^p.

Although the constraints on pronominalization have something to do with the relative depth of embedding of the pronoun and its antecedent, it is apparent that this cannot be the whole story. Consider (39)–(41), for instance, which are perfectly acceptable.

(39) *The woman who is to marry **Ralph** will visit **him** tomorrow.*

(40) *The man who wronged **this woman** is hated by **her**.*

(41) *The girl who wants **these kittens** will receive **them** as a present from me.*

In (39)–(41), the pronoun is higher in the tree than its antecedent. Moreover, such sentences are grammatical regardless of whether or not the pronoun is in the topmost simple sentence and regardless of how many echelons of embedding separate NP^a from NP^p.

(42) *I think that the woman who is to marry **Ralph** will visit **him** tomorrow.*

(43) *The girl who said that she wants **these kittens** will receive **them** as a present from me.*

(44) *The girl who said that she knows a man who wants **these kittens** will receive **them** as a present from me.*

(45) *The girl who said that she knows a man who said that he wants **these kittens** will receive **them** as a present from me.*

Therefore, neither a constraint based on linear ordering nor a constraint based on relative depth of embedding is sufficient to handle pronominalization in non-conjoined structures. At the same time, however, both of these factors seem to be pertinent in some way, which suggests that the restrictions on pronominalization can be stated when they are considered simultaneously. The two factors of linear ordering and relative depth of embedding intersect to yield four possibilities, which are listed below with examples and schematic representations of tree structure.

(a) NP^a precedes NP^p and is higher in the tree than NP^p. Example:

(22) **Ralph** *is much more intelligent than **he** looks.*

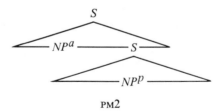

PM2

(b) NP^p precedes NP^a and is higher in the tree than NP^a. Example:

(27)   **He is much more intelligent than **Ralph** looks.*

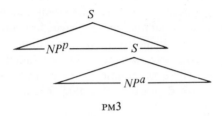

PM3

(c) NP^a precedes NP^p, but NP^p is higher in the tree than NP^a. Example:

(39)   *The woman who is to marry **Ralph** will visit **him** tomorrow.*

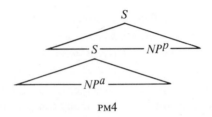

PM4

(d) NP^p precedes NP^a, but NP^a is higher in the tree than NP^p. Example:

(32)   *The woman who is to marry **him** will visit **Ralph** tomorrow.*

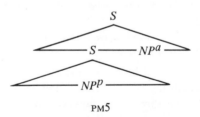

PM5

Only case (b) is not permitted. It would seem, then, than NP^a can be used to pronominalize NP^p unless NP^p both precedes NP^a and is in a higher echelon of embedding than NP^a. But although this constraint is very close to being correct, it is still not entirely adequate. The constraint is too strong, for it rules out sentences like (46)–(48), which are perfectly acceptable.

(46)   *The girl who loved **him** thinks that the woman who killed **Peter** is a fink.*

(47)   *After **she** left so hurriedly, it was discovered that Peter had insulted the man who was escorting **the pretty blond**.*

(48)   *The picture which **she** painted was snapped up by an art dealer who thought that **Penelope** had great talent.*

The tree structure of these sentences is represented in PM6.

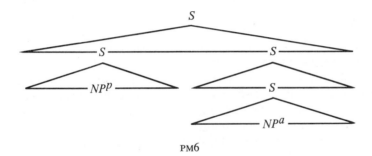

PM6

NP^p precedes NP^a in (46)–(48) as well as being in a higher echelon of embedding, and yet these sentences are perfectly well formed. There must be something about the configuration of PM6 that makes it crucially different from PM3, the representation of case (b).

In PM3, the *S*-node that most directly dominates NP^p also dominates NP^a. In PM6, however, the *S*-node most directly dominating NP^p does not dominate NP^a. The difference in grammaticalness is apparently keyed to this difference in tree structure.

We will say that a node *A* "commands" another node *B* if (1) neither *A* nor *B* dominates the other; and (2) the *S*-node that most immediately dominates *A* also dominates *B*. The command relation is defined so as to capture the crucial difference between PM3 and PM6. NP^p commands NP^a in PM3, since the first *S*-node above NP^p dominates NP^a. In PM6, on the other hand, the first *S*-node above NP^p does not dominate NP^a; consequently, NP^p does not command NP^a in PM6. We are now in a position to state the major restriction on pronominalization quite succinctly: *NP^a may pronominalize NP^p unless (1) NP^p precedes NP^a; and (2) NP^p commands NP^a.* It is easily verified that this constraint accounts for all of sentences (22)–(48).

The above constraint also works for reflexivization. Normally, reflexivization occurs within a single simple sentence structure, being impossible if NP^p precedes NP^a.

(15)   ***Those men*** outsmarted ***themselves.***

(16)   *****Themselves*** outsmarted ***those men.***

(16) is prevented because (1) NP^p (***themselves***) precedes NP^a (***those men***); and (2) NP^p commands NP^a (since the lowest *S*-node that dominates ***themselves*** also dominates ***those men***). Thus the major constraint that must be imposed on reflexivization follows as a special case from the general restriction that must be imposed on pronominalization.

As things now stand, we have formulated two separate restrictions on pronominalization in English, one to handle conjoined structures and the second to handle all other structures. The restriction adopted for conjoined structures reads as follows: *NP^a may not be used to pronominalize NP^p if NP^a and NP^p are elements* *of separate conjoined structures and NP^p precedes NP^a.* The two restrictions can easily be collapsed, which leaves us with the following as a statement of the major constraint on pronominalization: *NP^a may be used to pronominalize NP^p unless (1) NP^p precedes NP^a; and (2) either (a) NP^p commands NP^a, or (b) NP^a and NP^p are elements of separate conjoined structures.*

To conclude this section, we observe that certain transformations which affect the relative order of *NP*'s in a string must apply before the pronominalization rule if this is to be stated as generally as possible. Let us consider just two, passivization and the preposing of adverbial clauses.

The passive rule must be applicable before the pronominalization rule. Consider the underlying string (49).

(49)   *Algernon killed the mosquito which bit Algernon.*

Our restriction on pronominalization prevents (49) from being transformed to (50) but permits the derivation of (51).

(50)   **He killed the mosquito which bit Algernon.*

(51)   *Algernon killed the mosquito which bit him.*

In the passive, either occurrence of *Algernon* may be pronominalized.

(52)   *The mosquito which bit Algernon was killed by him.*

(53)   *The mosquito which bit him was killed by Algernon.*

If pronominalization preceded passivization, there would be no way to derive (52) without making an *ad hoc* exception to the general constraint on pronominalization that has been formulated. (52) is the passive of (50), but the general constraint does not permit (50). On the other hand, if the passive rule applies first to derive (54) from (49), everything works out all right.

(54)   *The mosquito which bit Algernon was killed by Algernon.*

As formulated, the constraint allows either (52) or (53) to be derived from (54).

Similarly for the preposing of adverbial clauses. The preposing rule would transform (55) to (56).

(55)   *Penelope bit Algernon in the leg while Algernon wasn't looking.*

(56)   *While Algernon wasn't looking, Penelope bit Algernon in the leg.*

If the preposing rule followed pronominalization, (57) could not be derived because of the impossibility of (58).

(57)   *While Algernon wasn't looking, Penelope bit him in the leg.*

(58)   **Penelope bit him in the leg while Algernon wasn't looking.*

On the other hand, both (57) and (59) can be derived from (56).

(59)   *While he wasn't looking, Penelope bit Algernon in the leg.*

Therefore the preposing rule must come before pronominalization.

PRIMACY RELATIONS

Consider sentences (60)–(64).

(60)   *Penelope dislikes Peter and her mother hates him.*

(61) **Peter** hates the woman who rejected **him**.

(62) The woman who rejected **Peter** is hated by **him**.

(63) The woman who rejected **him** is hated by **Peter**.

(64) ***He** hates the woman who rejected **Peter**.

Our constraint on pronominalization correctly predicts that (60)–(63) are grammatical to the exclusion of (64), but there is something more that can be said about these sentences. There is a certain intuitive sense in which (60)–(61) are more natural than (62)–(63), at least for some speakers. The former two instances of pronominalization seem to represent the paradigm or "unmarked" versions of it. This cannot be attributed to meaning, since (61)–(63) are paraphrases. It cannot be attributed to the fact that (62)–(63) are passives, because, of (61), (65), and (66), all of which are active sentences similar in structure, (61) is again the most natural.

(65) The woman who rejected **Peter** hates **him**.

(66) The woman who rejected **him** hates **Peter**.

If we were to divide instances of pronominalization into primary ones and secondary ones on an intuitive basis, (60)–(61) would be primary while (62), (63), (65), and (66) would be secondary. It is more than coincidence that the pronominalization rule formulated by Lees and Klima accounts for (61) but not for (62), (63), (65), or (66).[6]

For the time being, let us restrict our attention to the paraphrases (61)–(64). (61) is grammatical and typical, or unmarked, with respect to pronominalization; (62)–(63) are grammatical but not typical in the same sense; and (64) is ungrammatical. In order to account for these intuitive differences, we will introduce the notion "primacy relation." The relations "commands" and "precedes," both of which are relevant in constraining pronominalization, will be said to fall together as primacy relations. When a node A commands or precedes another node B, A will be said to bear a primacy relation to B. When A both commands and precedes B, A will be said to bear both primacy relations to B.

We may distinguish between two kinds of structural relations that are represented in a P-marker. For one thing, a P-marker represents a set of dominance relations (e.g. S dominates NP; NP dominates N; VP dominates V; S dominates VP). In addition, a P-marker represents a linear ordering of constituents. We have defined a primacy relation in terms of each of these two dimensions of tree structure; the command relation pertains to the former, and the precedes relation pertains to the latter.

The term primacy relation is to be taken seriously. It is suggested that A is in some sense dominant over or superordinate to B when A bears one or both primacy relations to B. In particular, it is suggested that A is less likely than B to be deleted or reduced should A and B dominate identical subtrees. When A bears one or both primacy relations to B, A tends to act as a nucleus while B tends to assume the status of a satellite. It is almost as though A had some power over B which B did not have over A. Although we have approached the notion primacy relation in rather impressionistic terms, this discussion should not be rejected out of hand

---

[6] Lees and Klima, op. cit., p. 23. See footnote 1.

as metaphysical. The notion has been defined quite precisely, and if it is valid (i.e. if it corresponds to some real facet of the psychological structure we call language), it is possible that such intuitively based expressions as "primacy," "have some power over," and "satellite" are not altogether inappropriate.

Let us assume for the moment that it is correct to group commands and precedes together as primacy relations. Let us further assume that the impressionistic discussion of the preceding paragraph has some validity—that A tends to be dominant over B when A bears one or both primacy relations to B, so that, for instance, B is more likely than A to be reduced should they dominate identical subtrees. If we make these assumptions, the intuitive differences among (61)–(64) are immediately explained. (61) displays a typical or unmarked instance of pronominalization; in (61), NP^a bears both primacy relations to NP^p, which makes it very understandable that NP^a should reduce NP^p to satellite status. (62) and (63) are slightly less typical or natural with respect to pronominalization; NP^a bears only one primacy relation to NP^p in these sentences, while NP^p bears the other to NP^a; this balance of power allows pronominalization to take place without the direction of pronominalization being dictated. (64), in which NP^p bears both primacy relations to NP^a, is ungrammatical; a noun phrase that bears both primacy relations to another cannot be reduced by it.

Since this correlation is exactly what one would expect on the basis of the assumptions that were made, we will have explained the intuitive differences noted above if we can justify these assumptions on independent grounds. Two kinds of evidence must now be provided, therefore. First, we must show that there are independent motivations for defining the relations commands and precedes in linguistic metatheory. Second, we must show that there is independent evidence for grouping these two relations together as primacy relations. As part of the demonstration, it should also be shown that A tends in some sense to be dominant over B when A bears one or both primacy relations to B.

Independent grounds for adopting the command relation as a theoretical construct will be presented in the next section. With respect to the relation precedes, we are in a somewhat unusual position. It would be rather pointless to try to show that this relation is useful in describing other grammatical phenomena, since virtually every transformation is written so as to take linear order into account.[7] It is a truism that linear ordering is relevant to grammatical description. Nevertheless, we can make a number of observations that seem pertinent. These observations lend some measure of support to the contention that A tends to be primary in some way, and B secondary, when A precedes B.

Consider sentence (67), which has an immediately underlying structure something like (68).

(67)   *Penelope is intelligent, and Algernon too.*

(68)   *Penelope is intelligent, and Algernon is intelligent too.*

(67) is derived from (68) by deleting *is intelligent* from the second conjunct; this

---

[7]The pronominalization rule is one possible exception. Because NP^a may either precede or follow NP^p, a completely linear representation may not be proper for this rule.

deletion is possible because an identical verb sequence occurs as well in the first conjunct. There is no *a priori* reason to expect the second conjunct to undergo reduction rather than the first conjunct; English could perfectly well allow (69) as grammatical, excluding (67).

(69) **Penelope too, and Algernon is intelligent.*

There are some cases in natural languages where the first of two identical constituents is deleted instead of the second, but these definitely seem to be the exception rather than the rule; the opposite situation seems more natural intuitively and is almost certainly more prevalent. This accords completely with the position that the relation precedes is properly characterized as a primacy relation.

Two further observations come to mind, although it is not absolutely clear that they are relevant. In conjunction, the order of conjoined constituents tends to be correlated with the temporal order or order of importance of the events or things referred to. For instance, compare (70) and (71).

(70) *George put the cat out and locked the door.*

(71) *George locked the door and put the cat out.*

On hearing (71), one might well receive the impression that George threw the cat out the window. For another example, contrast (72) with (73).

(72) *President Johnson and company*

(73) **company and President Johnson*

Another observation which may be pertinent concerns the relative importance of a subject *NP* and a direct object *NP*. The subject is on a par with the predicate as one of the two major constituents of a sentence, whereas the direct object (when there is one) is only one of several constituents of the predicate. Thus it is interesting in the present context to observe that it is much more common in languages for the subject to precede the object in normal word order than for the object to precede the subject.[8] Though they may prove nothing in themselves, these facts are at least compatible with the contention that A tends to assume some degree of primacy over B when A precedes B.

Let us now turn to the evidence for grouping the relations commands and precedes as primacy relations. In the last section, we established the following constraint on pronominalization: *NP^a may be used to pronominalize NP^p unless (1) NP^p precedes NP^a; and (2) either (a) NP^p commands NP^a, or (b) NP^a and NP^p are elements of separate conjoined structures.* Even though the restrictions on pronominalization in conjoined and nonconjoined structures were collapsed in this one somewhat complex statement, it is by no means true that we have reduced them to a single restriction applicable to conjoined and nonconjoined structures alike. In effect, we still have two separate constraints. In nonconjoined structures, the relations commands and precedes are both relevant; NP^p cannot both command and precede NP^a. In conjoined structures, on the other hand, only the latter relation is pertinent; NP^p cannot precede NP^a. But why should there be two separate restrictions, each quite general but neither exhaustive of all types of structures?

---

[8]See Joseph H. Greenberg, ed., *Universals of Language* (Cambridge: M.I.T. Press, 1963), p. 77.

Might it not be possible to find some more abstract principle, applicable to both types of structures, from which the two more specific principles will follow as special cases? It is indeed possible to find such a principle if the relations commands and precedes are grouped together as primacy relations.

The difference between the two restrictions is a simple one; the restriction for nonconjoined structures makes reference to the command relation (NP^p cannot both command and precede NP^a), but the restriction for conjoined structures does not. If the two noun phrases should be in separate conjoined structures, it is sufficient to specify that NP^p not precede NP^a. But there is something about the properties of conjoined structures that would lead us to expect precisely this difference. Consider PM7 and PM8, which represent typical conjoined and nonconjoined structures respectively.

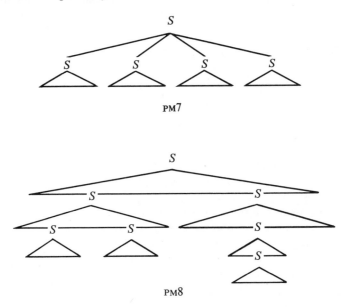

Whether NP^a and NP^p are in separate conjoined structures or not, it is perfectly possible for one to precede the other; in fact, one must precede the other unless one is contained within the other (in which case they cannot be identical and pronominalization is ruled out).

Notice, however, that one node cannot possibly command another if the two are in separate conjoined structures, as in PM7. Relations of dominance are in effect neutralized among conjoined structures and this is the only case where it is simply *irrelevant* to speak of dominance relations in a *P*-marker. The command relation is defined totally in terms of dominance relations, so it too is irrelevant in conjoined structures. For NP^a to command NP^p, it must be the case that the *S*-node which most directly dominates NP^a also dominates NP^p. When NP^a and NP^p are in separate conjoined sentences, this is impossible, since this *S*-node either is conjoined with an *S*-node that dominates NP^p or is itself dominated by an *S*-node conjoined with an *S*-node that dominates NP^p. A situation like that of either PM9 or PM10 must obtain.

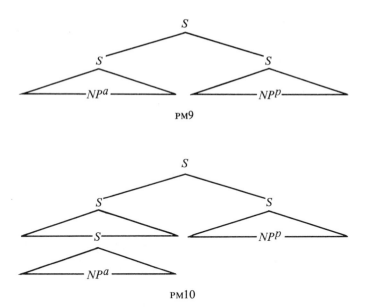

PM9

PM10

Therefore, of the two proposed primacy relations, commands and precedes, only the latter is of any possible relevance in conjoined sentences; only precedes is a relation that can hold between constituents of separate conjoined structures. Herein lies the solution to our problem.

In conjoined structures, where the command relation can have no possible relevance, NP^a can pronominalize NP^p unless NP^p precedes NP^a. In all other structures, where both primacy relations are operative, NP^a can pronominalize NP^p unless NP^p both commands and precedes NP^a. We now see that there is only *one* major restriction on pronominalization, and it may be stated in this way: *NP^a may be used to pronominalize NP^p unless NP^p bears all relevant primacy relations to NP^a.* This one restriction works both for conjoined structures and for other structures (as well as sufficing for reflexivization). Notice, however, that the ability to make this generalization depends crucially on the notion primacy relation. Without this notion as defined, the significant generalization cannot be captured.[9]

Before going on to look for other uses of the command relation, let us return briefly to our distinction between typical, possible but not typical, and impossible cases of pronominalization.

---

[9]In this discussion, we have implicitly assumed that all conjoined structures derive from underlying conjoined sentences and that pronominalization takes place before conjunction reduction. This is by no means a trivial assumption, and it may be false, but it is what allows the new constraint based on considerations of sentence conjoining to carry over automatically to the conjoining of other constituents. But even should it be shown conclusively that this assumption is untenable, the close connection between conjoining—where constituents by definition are arranged linearly instead of hierarchically—and linear ordering in general will almost certainly prove to be the source of the irrelevance of the command relation in conjoined structures. The neutralization of the command relation will have to be explained in somewhat different terms, however.

(60) *Penelope dislikes **Peter** and her mother hates **him**.*

(61) ***Peter** hates the woman who rejected **him**.*

(62) *The woman who rejected **Peter** is hated by **him**.*

(63) *The woman who rejected **him** is hated by **Peter**.*

(64) ****He** hates the woman who rejected **Peter**.*

(61) is typical, (62) and (63) are possible but not typical, and (64) is impossible. If one were asked to categorize (60) on this basis, one would almost certainly classify it as involving a typical instance of pronominalization. But this is just what we would predict. (60) and (61) are alike in that NP^a bears all relevant primacy relations to NP^p in these sentences. (62) and (63) are alike in that NP^a bears only one relevant primacy relation to NP^p, while in (64), NP^p bears all relevant primacy relations to NP^a.

THE CHAIN OF COMMAND

The command relation seems to represent one aspect of tree configuration that is crucial in determining when one noun phrase can be used to pronominalize a second. However, it would be possible to restate the constraint on pronominalization in a more round about way without making reference to this notion. Therefore we would like to find additional motivation for adding it to our kit of theoretical tools for describing languages. In this section we will examine various grammatical phenomena of English whose description is simplified by means of the command relation.

Klima has used the relation "in construction with" to define the scope of negation in English.[10] Given two constituents *A* and *B*, *B* is said to be in construction with *A* if the node *C* that directly dominates *A* also dominates *B*. In PM11, for example, both noun phrases are in construction with *Neg*, since the node *S*, which directly dominates *Neg*, also dominates these two noun phrases.

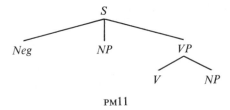

PM11

Similarly, *Neg* is in construction with the subject *NP* of PM11. *Neg* is not in construction with the object *NP*, however, since the node directly dominating the object, *VP*, does not also dominate *Neg*.

The relations commands and in construction with are similar, but they are by no means equivalent given current conceptions of constituent structure. In determining whether *B* is commanded by *A*, one must know if *B* is dominated by *the*

---

[10]Edward S. Klima, "Negation in English," in *SL*, pp. 246–323. The relation is defined on p. 297.

lowest S-node that dominates A. In determining whether *B* is in construction with *A*, on the other hand, one must know if *B* is dominated by *whatever node directly dominates A, whether this is an S-node or not.*

One consequence of this difference is that the relation in construction with cannot be used to state the major constraint on pronominalization,[11] although the command relation can indeed serve this purpose. The following constraint, for instance, would not suffice: *NP^a may be used to pronominalize NP^p unless NP^a both follows and is in construction with NP^p.* This constraint would allow both (74) and (75), though only the former is grammatical.

(74) *I knew **Harvey** when **he** was a little boy.*

(75) **I knew **him** when **Harvey** was a little boy.*

PM12 represents the underlying structure of these sentences.

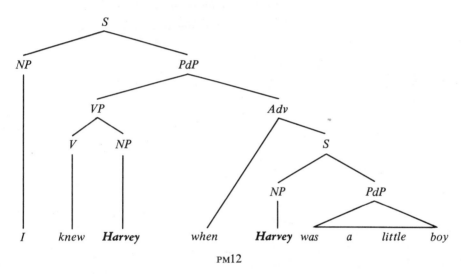

PM12

Since the second occurrence of **Harvey** in PM12 follows the first but is *not* in construction with it, (75) is allowed by this constraint. The first occurrence of **Harvey** both commands and precedes the second, however, so (75) is excluded by the constraint we have adopted.

While the relations commands and in construction with are not fully equivalent, they are equivalent for determining the scope of negation. This being the case, and since the command relation can be used to constrain pronominalization but not the relation in construction with, it is reasonable to adopt the former for both purposes and abandon the latter. There is no point in employing two separate theoretical constructs when only one is required.

If a noun phrase with an indefinite determiner, such as *some*, falls within the

---

[11]This presupposes certain assumptions regarding the internal structure of so-called "simple sentences." We feel that almost nothing of substance is known about this beyond the grossest details (such as what belongs together as a noun phrase). In all essential respects, the constituent structure that we assume in the present discussion will be that adopted by Klima in his paper.

scope of the negative constituent *Neg*, this indefinite determiner is manifested as *any*.

(76) *Peter has some money.*

(77) *Peter doesn't have any money.*

Furthermore, *Neg* may be transported and adjoined to the determiner, which is then manifested as *no*.

(78) *Peter has no money.*

The scope of *Neg* with respect to these two operations can be defined largely (though not entirely) in terms of the notion in construction with. The determiner may be acted upon by *Neg* only if it is in construction with *Neg*. In (79), for instance, the determiner manifested as *some* is not in construction with *Neg*.

(79) *The woman has some money, but Peter still won't marry her.*

The reason is that the *Neg* of (79) is directly dominated by an *S*-node which does not dominate *some*. Hence (79) cannot be transformed to (80).

(80) **The woman has any money, but Peter still won't marry her.*

In PM13, the bold face *NP*'s are all in construction with *Neg*, but no other *NP* is.

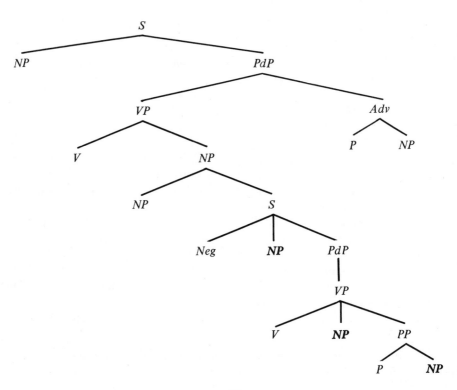

PM13

It is precisely the bold face *NP*'s which *Neg* can affect. (81), for example, has a structure like that of PM13.

(81)   *Some man challenged the claim that **no one** does **anything** for **anyone** for some reason that only he knew.*

From a glance at PM13, it should be apparent that *Neg* commands the same *NP*'s that are in construction with *Neg*. Therefore the notion commands will serve to restrict the scope of negation equally as well as the notion in construction with. They are equivalent in this case because the node directly dominating *Neg* is *S*;[12] *S* is the pivotal node in defining commands, and the directly dominating node is pivotal in the definition of the other relation.

Although it is a necessary condition for *Neg* to operate on *some* that *Neg* command *some*, this is not a sufficient condition. For instance, it must also be stated that *Neg* can reach down into a *that*-clause to affect *some* but not into a relative clause.

(82)   *I didn't realize that she had any money.*

(83)   *I didn't rob the woman who had some money.*

(84)   **I didn't rob the woman who had any money.*

Neg can also reach down into an infinitival complement.

(85)   *I will force you to marry no one.*

This construction brings out an aspect of the command relation which we have not yet touched upon.

Notice that (85) is ambiguous, as Klima points out; it can be paraphrased by either (86) or (87).

(86)   *I will force you not to marry anyone.*

(87)   *It is not the case that I will force you to marry someone.*

Klima very plausibly accounts for this by supposing that *Neg* originates in the embedded sentence when the interpretation of (86) is intended but that it originates in the matrix sentence when the interpretation of (87) is intended. Schematically, the underlying *P*-markers are PM14 and PM15.

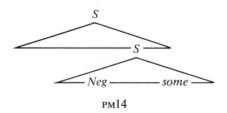

PM14

---

[12]See Klima's article for arguments regarding the position of *Neg* in the underlying tree.

It should be noted that the applicability of the command relation to defining the scope of *Neg* and *Wh* does not depend crucially on the assignment of tree structure to these entities. *Neg* and *Wh* can perfectly well be said to command other elements even if they are represented, say, as syntactic features rather than as distinct nodes. All that is required is a trivial modification of the definition.

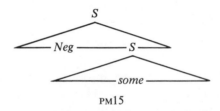

PM15

Since *Neg* commands *some* in both structures, the rule discussed earlier can in both cases adjoin *Neg* to *some* to yield (85), which is thereby ambiguous. Also, two simultaneous occurrences of *Neg* are possible, one in the matrix sentence and one in the embedded sentence (PM16).

(88)   *I won't force you not to marry anyone.*

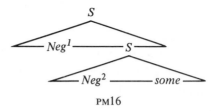

PM16

According to the regular rule of negative placement, *Neg¹* in PM16 could be attached to *some*; an identical transportation takes place with the *Neg* of PM15 in one derivation of (85). However, this transportation cannot be allowed here.

(89)   **I will force you not to marry no one.*

One might try to account for this lack of transportation by placing an *ad hoc* restriction on the negative placement rule to the effect that *Neg* cannot be transported across a string containing another instance of *Neg*. But this restriction will not work because of sentences like (90), derived from PM17.

(90)   *I will force the girl who doesn't want children to marry no one.*

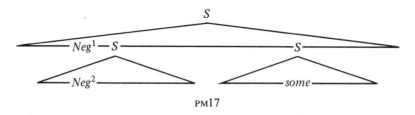

PM17

In the derivation of (90), *Neg²* does not prevent the transportation of *Neg¹*.

The difference between PM16, where *Neg¹* cannot be transported, and PM17, where it can, is that in PM16 *Neg²* commands *some*; *Neg²* does not command *some* in PM17. It seems that an occurrence of *Neg* in some sense "controls" a certain portion of a tree, so that no other *Neg* can encroach on its territory when both command this territory. In PM16, both *Neg¹* and *Neg²* command *some*; *Neg¹* also commands *Neg²*, but *Neg²* does not command *Neg¹*. We will formulate a principle on the basis of these relationships which will prevent (89) but allow (90). Then we will see how this principle fares in other cases. *If (1) two identical nodes A^1 and A^2 both command some other node B; (2) A^1 commands A^2; and (3) A^2 does not command A^1; then any transformational operation involving A and B can apply only with respect to A^2 and B, not A^1 and B.* Thus, if there is a "chain of command" so that A^1 commands A^2, A^2 commands B, and A^2 does not command A^1 but is identical to it, A^2 "controls" B, protecting it from the influence of A^1, so to speak. Such a chain of command exists in PM16 but not in PM17. To have a name for the above principle, let us call it the "principle of control." How general this principle is, and whether it is an absolute constraint on rules or just a tendency, are questions we cannot answer at present.

Klima, noting some syntactic similarities between *Neg* and *Wh*, uses the notion in construction with to delimit the scope of *Wh*.[13] Since *Wh* (like *Neg*) is claimed to be directly dominated by *S*, it should be apparent that the command relation can be substituted for the relation in construction with to the extent that the latter aids in defining the scope of *Wh*. For example, consider the attachment of the interrogative *Wh* to the determiner *some* in forming the question word *what*.[14] The *NP* containing *some* is advanced to initial position as part of this operation. In PM18, *Wh* can be attached only to the bold face occurrence of ***some***.

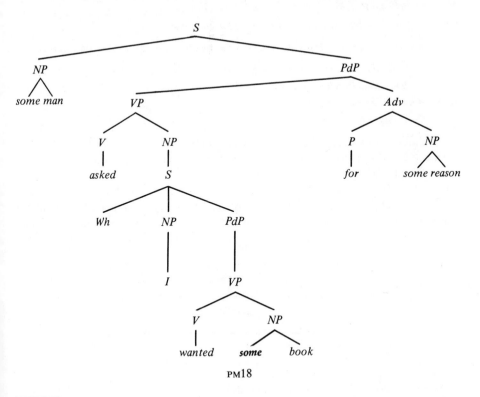

PM18

[13]Klima, op. cit., p. 297.
[14]See Kuroda, op. cit.

The resulting sentence is (91).

(91)   *Some man asked what book I wanted for some reason.*

If *Wh* were attached to any but the bold face instance of **some**, the result would be ungrammatical.

(92)   **What man asked I wanted some book for some reason?*
(93)   **For what reason did some man ask I wanted some book?*

The bold face token of **some** is in construction with *Wh*, and the other tokens of *some* are not. However, *Wh* commands the bold face token but not the others; hence the relation commands can equally well be used in at least partially defining the scope of *Wh*.

Chomsky has noted a constraint on the application of this *Wh* rule that is quite interesting in the present context.[15] He observes that *Wh* cannot reach down into an embedded relative clause (or indirect question) to operate on *some*.

(94)   *Penelope apprehended a man who had assaulted some girl in the park.*
(95)   **the girl who Penelope apprehended a man who had assaulted in the park*
(96)   **Who did Penelope apprehend a man who had assaulted in the park?*
(97)   *Penelope asked who had assaulted some girl in the park.*
(98)   **the girl who Penelope asked who had assaulted in the park*
(99)   **Who did Penelope ask who had assaulted in the park?*

In some cases, however, *Wh* can indeed reach down into an embedded clause.

(100)   *What would Penelope like to find?*
(101)   *the book that Penelope would like to find*
(102)   *Who did she say I saw?*
(103)   *the woman she said I saw*

The difference between these two sets of sentences is that the embedded clause is headed by *Wh* in the former, which are ungrammatical, but not in the latter. This difference is shown in PM19 and PM20.

In PM19, Wh^1 cannot apply to *some*, although it can in PM20. But this is just what is predicted by the principle of control, which was formulated to handle a certain restriction on negative placement. Wh^1 commands Wh^2, but not vice versa,

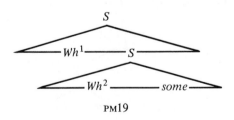

PM19

---

[15]Noam Chomsky, "Current Issues in Linguistic Theory," in *SL*, pp. 50–118. The relevant discussion is on pp. 68–74.

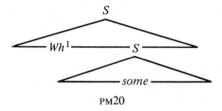

PM20

while both Wh^1 and Wh^2 command *some*. Thus Wh^2 controls *some* and prevents Wh^1 from operating on it.

For a final example of the usefulness of the command relation, let us consider the deletion of the subject of an embedded clause as part of the process of infinitivalization.[16] Subject deletion may occur only if there is another *NP* identical to the subject somewhere in the sentence, but this condition by itself does not suffice.

(104)   *I persuaded Penelope to leave.*

(105)   *I promised Penelope to leave.*

In (104), the subject of *leave* must be *Penelope* in the underlying structure; in (105), *I* must be the deleted subject. Which *NP* can be used to elide the infinitival subject depends on the matrix verb.

However, most *NP*'s are never eligible as antecedents of the deleted infinitival subject. The situation is shown schematically in PM21; the most deeply embedded *S* is the infinitival clause (whose subject is circled), and only the bold face *NP*'s are possible candidates as its antecedent.

Any *NP* dominated by the lowest *S*-node must be excluded as a candidate. We can formulate this by requiring that the infinitival subject not command its ante-

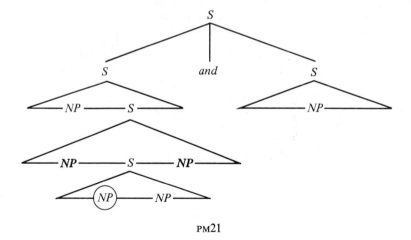

PM21

---

[16]See Peter S. Rosenbaum, *The Grammar of English Predicate Complement Constructions*, (Cambridge: M.I.T. Press, 1967).

cedent.[17] The rightmost *NP* of PM21 must also be excluded; we can accomplish this by requiring that the antecedent command the infinitival subject. This second restriction is acceptable, for both bold face *NP*'s command the subject to be deleted. Still another restriction is needed, however, because the leftmost *NP* of PM21 also commands the infinitival subject but is not eligible to be its antecedent. But this is just what is predicted by the principle of control; by this principle, the bold face *NP*'s both control the infinitival subject, protecting it from the influence of the leftmost *NP*. Therefore no special constraint on the deletion rule is needed for this purpose.[18]

FURTHER PROSPECTS

The constraints on which *NP* can be used to delete the infinitival subject do not have to be stated in terms of the command relation. Another possible statement would be that an *NP* can be used to delete the subject of a clause only if it is contained in the simple sentence structure in which the clause is embedded. In fact, either a constraint of this type or one defined in terms of the command relation would probably serve as a general constraint on embedding that involves identity deletion between the matrix and constituent structures.[19] This raises a much broader question concerning the relation between the theoretical notions

---

[17]It may not be coincidental that the infinitival subject bears all relevant primacy relations to the *NP*'s excluded by this requirement. The infinitival subject could therefore not be pronominalized by any of these *NP*'s either, because of the constraint proposed for pronominalization. Since both deletion and pronominalization are kinds of reduction, this is most suggestive. The constraint on pronominalization may be quite general.

We apparently have to distinguish cases where two nodes mutually command one another from those cases where the relation holds in only one direction. Notice that two nodes command one another mutually if and only if they are in the same simple sentence structure. There appear to be cases where a constituent C^2 can reduce an identical constituent C^1 although C^1 bears both primacy relations to C^2; in each of these cases, though, C^2 also commands C^1 (i.e. the two C's are in the same simple sentence structure). For instance, *each man of those men* reduces to *each of those men*. It may be true that C^2 never reduces C^1 when C^1 bears all relevant primacy relations to C^2 but C^2 bears none to C^1.

[18]Part (3) of the *if*-clause of the principle of control was included with infinitivalization in mind. Without it, each bold face *NP* would exclude the other as a possible candidate to be the antecedent of the infinitival subject.

[19]Consider relative embedding, for example:

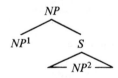

For *S* to be embedded as a relative clause in the *NP* containing it, NP^2 must be deleted (more precisely, reduced to a relative pronoun) by virtue of its identity to NP^1. NP^1 is contained in the simple sentence structure in which the clause is embedded. At the same time, NP^1 commands NP^2 but not vice versa, and any *NP*'s in higher sentence structures will be excluded from consideration by the principle of control.

introduced in this paper on the one hand, and on the other hand an alternative proposal for limiting the scope of transformational operations.

It has been proposed that a distinction be made between "singulary" transformations and "'embedding" rules.[20] Essentially, a singulary rule can apply only within a single simple sentence structure. An embedding rule, however, can take two simple sentence structures into account simultaneously provided that one is nested in the other. An embedding rule can thus reach down into a subordinate clause but can only reach down one echelon of embedding. In this framework, it would be quite easy to impose the restriction on embedding noted above. Let us call this proposal the "restricted domain principle," since it implies that only a restricted portion of a tree structure can be scanned in determining the applicability of a transformation.

We can observe first of all that the restricted domain principle cannot replace the command relation and the principle of control. The principle of control, it will be recalled, prevents the *Neg* of one simple sentence from being attached to *some* in an embedded clause already containing a *Neg*.

(89) **I will force you not to marry no one.*

However, the restricted domain principle cannot be used to state this restriction, for the *Neg* attachment rule can apply within precisely the same domain if the embedded clause happens not to be negative.

(85) *I will force you to marry no one.*

Similarly for the case of *Wh* attachment, which also involves the principle of control. Therefore the need for the theoretical apparatus introduced in this paper cannot be obviated by the restricted domain principle.

Next, we note that the restricted domain principle works in at least one case where constraints based on primacy relations will not (as they are now defined). English has a clause transportation rule[21] that must be limited to two echelons of embedding. This rule derives (107) from (106) by permuting the subject *that*-clause with the following portion of the matrix structure.

(106) **That Peter is a drunk** *bothers Penelope.*

(107) *It bothers Penelope* **that Peter is a drunk**.

If this rule were not restricted in scope to two echelons, the wrong results would obtain in some instances. For example, (108) would erroneously be transformed to (109).

(108) *That Harvey thinks* **that Peter is a drunk** *bothers Penelope.*

(109) **That Harvey thinks (it) bothers Penelope* **that Peter is a drunk**.

In PM22, only S^1 is eligible to be permuted with the *PdP* of the upper sentence, producing (110).

(110) *It bothers Penelope* **that Harvey thinks that Peter is a drunk**.

---

[20]For more detail, see Arnold M. Zwicky and others, *The MITRE Syntactic Analysis Procedure for Transformational Grammars*, MITRE Corporation Information System Language Studies, Number Nine (Bedford, Mass., 1965), pp. 8–10.

[21]This rule is called "extraposition" in Rosenbaum, op. cit.

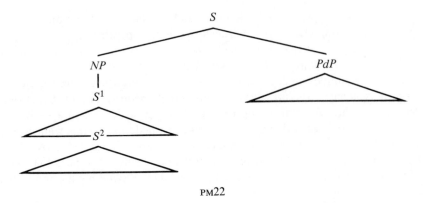

PM22

The principle of control, as now formulated, would not prevent (109), but the restricted domain principle correctly predicts that (109) is ungrammatical.

It would not be difficult to extend the principle of control or to add supplementary principles defined in terms of primacy relations so that the resulting constraints on the application of transformations would prevent (109) while allowing (110). Similarly, one could extend these notions so as to limit most rules in scope to one simple sentence structure, and so on. It would be rather pointless to do so at present, however, since the possibilities have not been thoroughly investigated and no simple principles are known that will work in all cases. For the time being, it is much more interesting to note the extent to which the two approaches to restricting the scope of transformational rules are similar. If one approach is not ultimately reducible to the other, they may both be manifestations of a deeper property of human language.

Their similarity is best observed graphically.

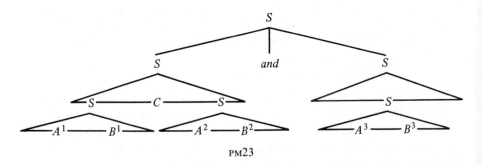

PM23

Consider a transformation involving A and B. According to the restricted domain principle, such a rule could apply to A^1 and B^1, to A^2 and B^2, or to A^3 and B^3; it could not apply, say, to A^1 and B^2. With the command relation, one could impose the same limitation by requiring that A and B command one another; A^1 and B^1 command one another, but A^1 does not command B^2 and B^2 does not command A^1. The similarities between the two approaches are seen even more clearly if we consider a rule involving C and B. As an "embedding" rule, it will be allowed by the restricted domain principle to apply to C and B^1 or to C and B^2, but not to C

and B^3. The same restriction can be imposed by requiring that C command B; C commands B^1 and B^2, but not B^3.

With either approach, then, a special relation is implied between two elements if they are part of the same simple sentence structure, or if they belong to separate simple sentence structures one of which is nested in the other. With either approach one could make the prediction that a rule operating on A^1 and B^2 or on C and B^3 would be quite exceptional.

Notice that the pronominalization rule is an exception with either approach. NP^a and NP^p may be any distance from one another in the tree in terms of echelons of embedding; hence the pronominalization rule violates the restricted domain principle. Likewise, it is an exception to the principle of control.

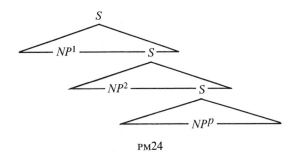

PM24

According to the principle of control, only NP^2 should be eligible to pronominalize NP^p in PM24 (should they be identical), but actually, NP^1 also can. Note too that A^1 could pronominalize B^2 in PM23, and that C could pronominalize B^3.[22]

CONCLUSION

Our original goal was to specify when a definite noun phrase NP^a can be used to pronominalize an identical noun phrase NP^p. The major restrictions on definite NP pronominalization in English are most satisfactorily stated in terms of the relations commands and precedes, which are grouped together as primacy relations: *NP^a may be used to pronominalize NP^p unless NP^p bears all relevant primacy relations to NP^a*. It has been shown that the command relation can be useful in limiting the scope of a variety of transformational operations, particularly when combined with the principle of control, which is defined in terms of the notion commands. Finally, we saw that this approach has much in common with the restricted domain principle for limiting the scope of rule application.

The observations made here are not peculiar to English; this paper, with only

---

[22]It may be significant that the constraints on the pronominalization rule, which is exceptional with either approach, are defined by means of the notion primacy relation; they could not be stated in terms of the restricted domain principle alone. Recall that a linear representation is not fully adequate for the pronominalization rule (see footnote 7). Pronominalization is thus seen to be exceptional with respect to both types of structural relations in a *P*-marker (linear ordering and dominance relations) over which we defined primacy relations. However, both primacy relations are still used to limit the applicability of this rule.

the example sentences changed, would be perfectly applicable to French, point by point. To what extent they are applicable to other languages, related and unrelated, is of course a matter of further empirical study. The definitions and principles that have been formulated here are probably not fully correct in their present form, but they are claimed to represent at least approximations to some aspects of linguistic reality. In particular, it is suggested that a rather abstract view of the relations holding among constituents in a tree structure is relevant in constraining the application of transformational rules.

13

On the Cyclic Nature
of English Pronominalization

JOHN ROBERT ROSS

In this paper, I will attempt to show that certain facts about anaphoric pronouns in English can be easily accounted for if the rule which introduces them is an obligatory, cyclically ordered transformation.[1] These facts are thus not only interesting for their own sake, but also because they provide direct evidence for the correctness of Chomsky's theory of grammar, for it is only within this theory that cyclically ordered rules are countenanced.

I will assume that structures underlying sentences like (1a) must be converted into those that underly (1b) or those that underly (1c) by a transformational rule of PRONOMINALIZATION.

(1)(a) *After John Adams$_i$ woke up, John Adams$_i$ was hungry.*
   (b) *After John Adams$_i$ woke up, he$_i$ was hungry.*
   (c) *After he$_i$ woke up, John Adams$_i$ was hungry.*

This rule replaces some noun phrase (*NP*) in a structure by a definite pronoun of the appropriate gender and number, when the first *NP* is *in the environment of*

Reprinted from *To Honor Roman Jakobson* (The Hague: Mouton & Co., 1967), III, pp. 1669–1682, by permission of the author and Mouton & Co.

This work was supported principally by the U.S. Air Force (Electronic Systems Division) under Contract AF 19(628)-2487; and in part by the Joint Services Electronics Program under Contract DA36-039-AMC-03200(E), the National Science Foundation (Grant GK-835), the National Institutes of Health (Grant 2 PO1 MH-04737-06), and the National Aeronautics and Space Administration (Grant NSG-496).

[1]The notion of the transformational cycle was first presented in Noam Chomsky, *Aspects of the Theory of Syntax* (Cambridge, Mass.: M.I.T. Press, 1965). Readers unfamiliar with the general framework of transformational generative grammar, which is presupposed in the present study, should refer to the above mentioned work by Chomsky and its extensive bibliography.

another *NP* which is identical to the first.[2] It is the purpose of this paper to provide a partial explication for the italicized phrase in the preceding sentence.

Notice that PRONOMINALIZATION must be allowed to work in two directions: it must be able to replace an *NP* to the right of an identical *NP* with a pronoun (as in the conversion of (1a) to (1b)),[3] and it must also be able to replace an *NP* to the left of an identical *NP* with a pronoun (as in the conversion of (1a) to (1c)). I will call the former FORWARD PRONOMINALIZATION and the latter BACKWARD PRONOMINALIZATION. Both forward and backward pronominalization can apply to the (a) versions of examples (2)–(6), as is shown by the (b) and (c) versions.

(2)(a) *That Oscar$_i$ was unpopular didn't disturb Oscar$_i$.*
  (b) *That Oscar$_i$ was unpopular didn't disturb him$_i$.*
  (c) *That he$_i$ was unpopular didn't disturb Oscar$_i$.*

(3)(a) *For your brother$_i$ to refuse to pay taxes would get your brother$_i$ into trouble.*
  (b) *For your brother$_i$ to refuse to pay taxes would get him$_i$ into trouble.*
  (c) *For him$_i$ to refuse to pay taxes would get your brother$_i$ into trouble.*

(4)(a) *Anna's complaining about Peter$_i$ infuriated Peter$_i$.*
  (b) *Anna's complaining about Peter$_i$ infuriated him$_i$.*
  (c) *Anna's complaining about him$_i$ infuriated Peter$_i$.*

(5)(a) *The possibility that Fred$_i$ will be unpopular doesn't bother Fred$_i$.*
  (b) *The possibility that Fred$_i$ will be unpopular doesn't bother him$_i$.*
  (c) *The possibility that he$_i$ will be unpopular doesn't bother Fred$_i$.*

(6)(a) *Whether the mayor$_i$ plans to leave wasn't made clear by the mayor$_i$.*
  (b) *Whether the mayor$_i$ plans to leave wasn't made clear by him$_i$.*
  (c) *Whether he$_i$ plans to leave wasn't made clear by the mayor$_i$.*

However, it is not always the case that PRONOMINALIZATION can work in both directions: in the sentences in (7)–(12), which are transformationally related to those in (1)–(6) by a number of rules which I will not describe in detail here, only forward pronominalization is possible.

(7)(a) *John Adams$_i$ was hungry after John Adams$_i$ woke up.*
  (b) *John Adams$_i$ was hungry after he$_i$ woke up.*
  (c) **He$_i$ was hungry after John Adams$_i$ woke up.*[4]

---

[2]As Chomsky points out, op. cit., pp. 145–146, the notion of identity that is of interest in linguistics includes identity of reference. The second occurrence of *John Adams* in the sentence *John Adams injured John Adams* is understood to have a different referent than the first, while *himself* in *John Adams injured himself* in understood to have the same referent as the subject. Chomsky suggests that certain lexical items be assigned referential features, say integers, and that rules which require identity between lexical items, such as REFLEXIVIZATION and PRONOMINALIZATION, may only apply to *NP* which have been assigned the same integer. Thus two occurrences of the *NP John Adams* will refer to the same individual if they have identical subscripts (as in (1a)), but *John Adams$_i$* and *John Adams$_j$* can never refer to the same individual, for *i* not equal to *j*.

[3]I will use the locution "sentence *A* is converted (transformed, etc.) into sentence *B*" for the more precise, but cumbersome, phrase: "the structure underlying sentence *A* is converted (transformed, etc.) into the one underlying sentence *B*." No theoretical significance should be attached to this abbreviation.

[4]Ungrammatical sentences are prefixed by an asterisk, doubtful ones by a question mark. Note that the string of words in sentence (7c) is only ungrammatical if the pronoun *he* is meant to refer to the same individual as the phrase *John Adams* in the subordinate clause. If *he* refers to someone else (*Washington*, for example) the string of words in (7c) is grammatical. But in the

(8)(a)   *Oscar$_i$ wasn't disturbed that Oscar$_i$ was unpopular.*
  (b)   *Oscar$_i$ wasn't disturbed that he$_i$ was unpopular.*
  (c)   **He$_i$ wasn't disturbed that Oscar$_i$ was unpopular.*
(9)(a)   *It would get your brother$_i$ into trouble for your brother$_i$ to refuse to pay taxes.*
  (b)   *It would get your brother$_i$ into trouble for him$_i$ to refuse to pay taxes.*
  (c)   **It would get him$_i$ into trouble for your brother$_i$ to refuse to pay taxes.*
(10)(a)   *Peter$_i$ was infuriated at Anna's complaining about Peter$_i$.*
  (b)   *Peter$_i$ was infuriated at Anna's complaining about him$_i$.*
  (c)   **He$_i$ was infuriated at Anna's complaining about Peter$_i$.*
(11)(a)   *Fred$_i$ isn't bothered by the possibility that Fred$_i$ will be unpopular.*
  (b)   *Fred$_i$ isn't bothered by the possibility that he$_i$ will be unpopular.*
  (c)   **He$_i$ isn't bothered by the possibility that Fred$_i$ will be unpopular.*
(12)(a)   *The mayor$_i$ didn't make clear whether the mayor$_i$ plans to leave.*
  (b)   *The mayor$_i$ didn't make clear whether he$_i$ plans to leave.*
  (c)   **He$_i$ didn't make clear whether the mayor$_i$ plans to leave.*

The two grammatical sentences in (1) and the one in (7) are derived from exactly the same deep structure—the only difference between them is that in the derivation of the sentences in (1), an optional rule of ADVERB PREPOSING applies to move the *after*-clause to the front of the sentence. The fact that only forward pronominalization is possible in (7), whereas either direction is possible in (1), can be explained by making PRONOMINALIZATION a cyclic rule, ordering it after ADVERB PREPOSING, which may apply or not. If only examples (1)–(12) are considered, it might seem possible to advance an alternative hypothesis: one might argue that PRONOMINALIZATION applies to the deep structure of these sentences, before any other transformational rules have applied, and that it is free to apply either forward or backward. A rule formulated in this way would generate sentences (7c) and (12c), but it might be claimed that the rules of PASSIVE and ADVERB PREPOSING could then be made to apply to such sentences obligatorily to convert them into the acceptable (1b) and (6b), respectively. But, even if we charitably overlook the difficult problem of how the restrictions on these two rules are to be stated (and, incidently, many similar restrictions would be needed for other rules), it is easy to show that this alternative proposal cannot overcome the difficulties posed by sentences like those in (13).

(13)(a)   *Sheila$_i$ answered that question, but Sheila$_i$ still did poorly.*
  (b)   *Sheila$_i$ answered that question, but she$_i$ still did poorly.*
  (c)   **She$_i$ answered that question, but Sheila$_i$ still did poorly.*

If backward pronominalization converts (13a) into (13c), an ungrammatical sentence will result; for *but*-clauses cannot be preposed, as can be seen from the ungrammaticality of (13d),

(13)(d)   **But Sheila$_i$ still did poorly, she$_i$ answered that question.*

and there is no other transformational rule which could apply to (13c) to save it from ungrammaticality.

---

latter case, *he* would have to have a different subscript, say *j*, from the *NP John Adams*, by the convention adopted in footnote 2 above. That is, in such a case, *he* would not be an anaphoric pronoun for some *NP* occurring elsewhere in the same sentence, but would rather be a substitute for some *NP* in an earlier sentence. In this study, I will only be concerned with pronouns which bear an anaphoric relationship to some *NP* occurring in the same sentence.

These facts suffice to reject the proposal that PRONOMINALIZATION should be ordered so as to precede all other transformational rules: it depends on, and thus must operate after, at least the two rules of ADVERB PREPOSING and PASSIVE. Since the latter rule can be shown to necessarily be in the transformational cycle, PRONOMINALIZATION cannot be a precyclic rule.[5] If it cannot apply before the cycle, it must either apply in the cycle or after all cyclic rules have been applied—rules of this last type are called *postcyclic*.[6] Exactly what rules are precyclic, or postcyclic, and why, is not directly relevant to the problem of PRONOMINALIZATION. What is relevant in establishing the claim that this rule is cyclic is the claim made in the present theory of grammar that transformational rules can only be precyclic, cyclic, or postcyclic. I have already shown that PRONOMINALIZATION cannot be precyclic, and facts I will present below will prove that it cannot be postcyclic. The only remaining possibility is that it is cyclic.

Examples (7)–(12) show that PRONOMINALIZATION cannot always be applied backward; example (14) shows that it cannot always be applied forward.

(14)(a) *Realizing that Oscar$_i$ was unpopular didn't disturb Oscar$_i$.*
  (b) **Realizing that Oscar$_i$ was unpopular didn't disturb him$_i$.*
  (c) *Realizing that he$_i$ was unpopular didn't disturb Oscar$_i$.*

Note that (14) differs from (2), in which both forward and backward pronominalization are possible, only in that the former contains the word *realizing* and the latter

(15)

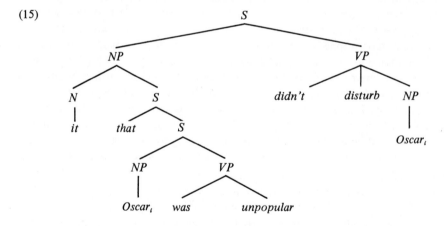

---

[5]In Chapter 1 of his forthcoming book, *Deep and Surface Grammar* (Cambridge, Mass.: M.I.T. Press), George Lakoff defines more precisely the notion of *precyclic rule* and demonstrates that the theory of grammar must be expanded so that such rules are statable in the grammars of particular languages. These rules operate on underlying structures as a whole, and must be able to apply before any cyclic rules have applied. In the same chapter, Lakoff shows that the rule of PASSIVE must be cyclically ordered.

[6]The necessity of constructing the theory of grammar so that postcyclic rules, as well as precyclic and cyclic ones, may be used in writing grammars for particular languages has been realized for some time. An example of a rule which must apply postcyclically is the rule of RELATIVE CLAUSE REDUCTION, which deletes *who is* or *which is*, converting noun phrases containing full relative clauses (*a man who is from Boston*) into noun phrases with postnominal modifiers (*a man from Boston*). The arguments that show this rule to be postcyclic are complex, and I will not present them here.

does not. Nevertheless, as I will demonstrate below, the presence of this single word is traceable back to a radical difference in the deep structures of (2) and (14). (2) is derived from a structure which, for our purposes, can be adequately represented as in (15).[7]

Contrast (15) with (16), which underlies (14):

(16)

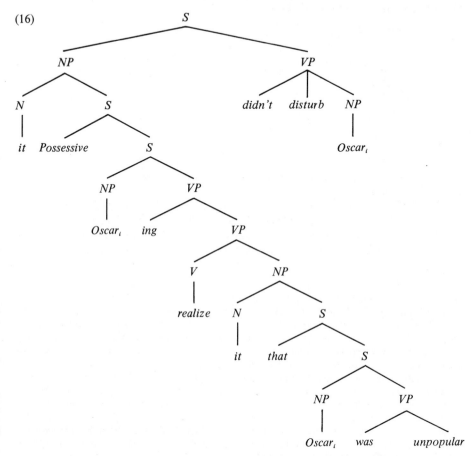

In the course of converting (15) and (16) into (2) and (14), respectively, various transformational rules must apply. These rules have been intensively investigated by Rosenbaum,[8] so I will not state them in any detail here, but merely describe their operation informally. If the optional rule of EXTRAPOSITION were to apply to (15), only forward pronominalization would be possible, and sentence (17) would be produced.

---

[7]In (15), and throughout this paper, I have drastically simplified the constituent structures of the sentences under discussion where more detailed representations would not be relevant to the point at hand. In the case of (15) and (16), for example, I have not given the deepest structure, in which the complementizers *that* and *Possessive–ing* would not appear, but have rather assumed that a transformational rule of COMPLEMENTIZER PLACEMENT has already applied to insert them.

[8]Cf. Peter S. Rosenbaum, *The Grammar of English Predicate Complement Constructions* (Cambridge, Mass.: M.I.T. Press, 1967).

(17) *It didn't disturb Oscar$_i$ that he$_i$ was unpopular.*

If EXTRAPOSITION is not applied, an obligatory rule of IT-DELETION will delete the head noun of the subject *NP* of (15), the abstract pronoun *it*. The only other rule of interest here that remains to be applied is PRONOMINALIZATION, which can apply in either direction to (15). (18) gives a precise statement of the conditions under which PRONOMINALIZATION operates.

(18) PRONOMINALIZATION

$$
\text{SD:} \quad X - \begin{bmatrix} NP \\ -Pro \end{bmatrix} - Y - \begin{bmatrix} NP \\ -Pro \end{bmatrix} - Z \quad \text{(oblig)}
$$

$$
 \quad 1 \qquad 2 \qquad\quad 3 \qquad 4 \qquad\quad 5 \quad ==\Rightarrow
$$

$$
\text{SC:(a)} \quad 1 \qquad 2 \qquad\quad 3 \qquad \begin{bmatrix} 4 \\ +Pro \end{bmatrix} \quad 5 \quad or
$$

$$
\text{(b)} \quad 1 \qquad \begin{bmatrix} 2 \\ +Pro \end{bmatrix} \qquad 3 \qquad 4 \qquad\quad 5
$$

Conditions:
  (i) 2 = 4
  (ii) The structural change shown on line (a) above, FORWARD PRONOMINALIZATION, is subject to no conditions.
  (iii) The structural change shown on line (b) above, BACKWARD PRONOMINALIZATION, is only permissible if the *NP* in term 2 of the structural description (SD) is dominated by (i.e. contained in) a subordinate clause which does not dominate (contain) the *NP* in term 4 of the SD.[9]

----

[9]This formulation of the condition on backward pronominalization was arrived at independently by Paul Postal, by G. H. Matthews and Maurice Gross, and by George Lakoff and me. Also working independently, Ronald Langacker has proposed a nearly equivalent condition (cf. his recent "On Pronominalization and the Chain of Command" [in *MSE*]). Although there are cases where Condition (iii) and Langacker's condition, which he defines in terms of the extremely interesting notion of *command*, produce different results, the two conditions are near enough to being equivalent that I will not discuss their differences here.

It is a difficult and as yet unsolved problem as to whether a universal definition of the notion *subordinate clause* can be found. There are many languages in which subordinate clauses behave differently from coordinate ones (cf., for example, German, where verbs occur at the end of the *VP* in subordinate clauses only), but at present it is not known whether the environments which condition this differential behavior are the same in all languages which exhibit it. For the purposes of this paper I will assume that a specification must be made in the grammar of English as to which clauses are subordinate. These clauses include
(*a*) Clauses starting with *after, before, since, until, although*, etc.—clauses which have traditionally been called adverbial subordinate clauses. That pronominalization can work backwards into such clauses is shown by (1c).
(*b*) Complement clauses with the complementizer *that* (cf. (2c)), with *for-to* (cf. (3c)), and with *Possessive-ing* (cf. (4c)).
(*c*) Complement clauses in apposition to abstract nouns like *fact, idea, theory*, etc. (cf. (5c)).
(*d*) Embedded questions, such as the one in (6c) or the clauses which occur in the object of *wonder* in the following sentences:

$$
I \text{ wonder} \begin{cases} \textit{what he said.} \\ \textit{how he left.} \\ \textit{in what kind of automobile he escaped.} \\ \textit{how to convince Peter.} \\ \textit{etc.} \end{cases}
$$

Restrictive and nonrestrictive relative clauses raise special problems, which I will take up presently.

PRONOMINALIZATION does not, of course, apply on the first cycle in the derivation of either (15) or (16), for in this cycle, the structure being operated on is the one underlying the simple sentence *Oscar was unpopular*, which does not contain two identical noun phrases. In processing (15), the first cycle on which PRONOMINALIZA-TION could be applied is the one on the highest *S*. If forward pronominalization is carried out, sentence (2b) will result. Backward pronominalization is also possible, however, for the clause *that Oscar was unpopular* is a subordinate clause, and if the rule applies in this direction, (2c) results. Comparison of all sentences in examples (1)–(6) with those in examples (7)–(12) will reveal that backward pronominalization is possible in the former group because in these sentences, Condition (iii) on rule (18) is met. Since it is not met in the latter group of examples, only forward pronominalization is possible there.

In processing (16), PRONOMINALIZATION does not apply on the lowest cycle, for the same reasons as above. It is not until the cyclic rules are processing the sentence whose main verb is *realize* that the structural description (SD) of PRONOMINALIZA-TION is satisfied. At this point the input structure to the rule of PRONOMINALIZATION is the one underlying (19).

(19) **Oscar$_i$ realized that Oscar$_i$ was unpopular.*

I have prefixed (19) with an asterisk to indicate that it cannot occur as a grammatical sentence of English if the two occurrences of *Oscar* are taken to refer to the same individual. In other words, PRONOMINALIZATION *must* apply to (19) (and hence, on the cycle in question, to (16) as well).[10] PRONOMINALIZATION can apply forwards to (19) (cf. (20a)), but not backwards (cf. the ungrammaticality of (20b)), because in (19) the conditions under which backward pronominalization could apply are not met: the leftmost identical *NP*, the subject of the entire sentence, is not contained in *any* clause, subordinate or otherwise, which does not contain the second identical *NP*.

(20)(a) *Oscar$_i$ realized that he$_i$ was unpopular.*
   (b) **He$_i$ realized that Oscar$_i$ was unpopular.*

After PRONOMINALIZATION has converted (19) into (20a), the cycle of rules which applies to the sentence whose main verb is *realize* is completed, and the rules reapply to the next higher sentence in (16). When the highest sentence in (16) is reached, before any cyclic rules have applied, the structure being processed is the one underlying (21).

---

[10]By the same token, the (a) versions of sentences (1)–(14) must also be indicated as being ungrammatical—I have left them unstarred only in the interests of expository simplicity.

There are various problems inherent in claiming that PRONOMINALIZATION is always obligatory. J. E. Emonds has called to my attention such sentences as the following:

Willy washed his car and then he polished $\begin{Bmatrix} his\ car. \\ it. \end{Bmatrix}$

in which, for most speakers, PRONOMINALIZATION is optional. I do not at present know under what conditions the rule is optional, but in all cases I have found so far, a coordinate structure was involved. However, for the purposes of the present argument, it is not required that the rule be obligatory under all circumstances, for it is sufficient that it is obligatory in such cases as (19).

(21) **Oscar's$_i$ realizing that he$_i$ was unpopular didn't disturb Oscar$_i$.*

For most speakers, (21) is ungrammatical: the noun phrase *Oscar's* must be deleted, producing (14c). The rule which accomplishes this I will refer to as EQUI NP DELETION —it deletes the subject *NP* of an embedded complement clause which contains the complementizers *Possessive – ing* or *for – to*, subject to the constraint that this *NP* be identical to some *NP* in the matrix sentence. Exactly which *NP* of the matrix sentence the embedded subject must be identical to is a complex and exceedingly interesting problem which has been investigated by Rosenbaum.[11]

After EQUI NP DELETION has applied, no more rules of concern to us here apply. In particular, PRONOMINALIZATION cannot apply, for the subject of the *VP was unpopular* is the pronoun *he*, and the structural description of rule (18) requires that neither *NP* be a pronoun.

Thus it can be seen that (14c) can be derived very simply from (16) if PRONOMINALIZATION is a cyclically ordered obligatory rule, constrained in the way stated in (18).

Sentence (14b), which exhibits forward pronominalization, must now be shown not to be derivable under the formulation of the rule given in (18).

(14)(b) **Realizing that Oscar$_i$ was unpopular didn't disturb him$_i$.*

But this is easy to demonstrate, for the only way (14b) could result would be for the input structure for the last cycle of (16) to be the one underlying (22).

(22) **His$_i$ realizing that Oscar$_i$ was unpopular didn't disturb Oscar$_i$.*

If EQUI NP DELETION were now to delete *his*, the subject of the embedded sentence, under identity with the occurrence of *Oscar* which is the object of the main verb, *disturb*, (23) would result.

(23) **Realizing that Oscar$_i$ was unpopular didn't disturb Oscar$_i$.*

If forward pronominalization were to apply now, (23) would be converted into the ungrammatical (14b).

Notice that this derivation of (14b) depends crucially upon it being possible to have derived (22) as a possible input structure to the highest cycle of rules for (16). But it is easy to see that in order for (22) to be the input to the last cycle, PRONOMINALIZATION must have incorrectly applied backwards on the cycle processing the sentence whose main verb is *realize*. In order to derive (24), the subject *NP* of (22),

(24) **his$_i$ realizing that Oscar$_i$ was unpopular*

it is necessary for PRONOMINALIZATION to apply backward to (19) to produce the ungrammatical (20b), and, as I pointed out earlier, this conversion would violate Condition (iii) on rule (18).

It might be argued that (14b) could be blocked equally well if it were assumed that PRONOMINALIZATION were a postcyclic rule, and some condition were imposed upon forward pronominalization, so that (23) could not be transformed into (14b); for if backward pronominalization is applied to (23), (14c) will result. But what condition could be imposed? That forward pronominalization is impossible if the

---

[11]Cf. Rosenbaum, op. cit., pp. 29–38 n. 8, and also "A Principle Governing Deletion in English Sentential Complementation," IBM Research Paper RC-1519.

leftmost identical *NP* is contained in an object clause of such verbs as *realize* and the rightmost identical *NP* is not contained in it? But this condition is too strong, for it is not in general true that forward pronominalization is blocked "out of" (in the obvious sense) the object clause of verbs like *realize*. Thus a sentence like (25),

(25) **Mary's realizing that Oscar$_i$ was unpopular didn't disturb Oscar$_i$.*

which is derived from a structure exactly like (16), except that *Mary* is the subject of *realize* instead of *Oscar$_i$*, can undergo backward pronominalization (cf. (26a)) *or* forward pronominalization (cf. 26b)).

(26)(a) *Mary's realizing that he$_i$ was unpopular didn't disturb Oscar$_i$.*
  (b) *Mary's realizing that Oscar$_i$ was unpopular didn't distrub him$_i$.*

It can therefore be seen that the only cases where a postcyclic rule of forward pronominalization would have to be blocked "out of" the object clause of verbs like *realize* are cases where the deep structure subject of the verb in question was identical to the *NP* in question in the object clause, a fact which is *explained* if PRONOMINALIZATION and EQUI NP DELETION are cyclic rules, as I have assumed above. (Lakoff, op. cit., has demonstrated that the latter rule must be cyclic.)

Notice also that whether PRONOMINALIZATION is postcyclic or cyclic, Condition (iii) on backward pronominalization will have to be stated anyway, for sentences like the (a) versions of (7)–(13) must still be prevented from being transformed into the corresponding (c) versions, and (19) must not be transformable into (20b). But it is only if PRONOMINALIZATION is formulated as a postcyclic rule that some constraint on forward pronominalization becomes necessary in order for a distinction between (14b) and (14c) to be made. Considerations of simplicity therefore dictate clearly that PRONOMINALIZATION must be formulated as a cyclic rule, not as a postcyclic one.

There is a further point which is closely related to these considerations: compare (27) with the superficially very similar (5), which I repeat here for convenience.[12]

(27)(a) **The knowledge that Fred$_i$ will be unpopular doesn't bother Fred$_i$.*
  (b) **The knowledge that Fred$_i$ will be unpopular doesn't bother him$_i$.*
  (c)   *The knowledge that he$_i$ will be unpopular doesn't bother Fred$_i$.*
  (5)(a) **The possibility that Fred$_i$ will be unpopular doesn't bother Fred$_i$.*
  (b)   *The possibility that Fred$_i$ will be unpopular doesn't bother him$_i$.*
  (c)   *The possibility that he$_i$ will be unpopular doesn't bother Fred$_i$.*

The deep structure of (5), to which either forward or backward pronominalization can apply, is roughly that shown in (28), on the next page.

On the first cycle of rules to apply to (28), when the sentence *Fred$_i$ will be unpopular* is being processed, no rules of relevance to the present discussion apply. On the second cycle, the complementizer *that* is adjoined to the node *S* which dominated the first-processed sentence. PRONOMINALIZATION cannot apply, for the structure up to the second highest occurrence of the node *S* does not contain two identical *NP*. On the third cycle, when the entire sentence is being operated on by the cyclic rules, the verb *bother* selects some abstract complementizer which converts its

---

[12]In this repetition of (5), I have starred (5a), as I indicated was necessary in footnote 10.

(28)

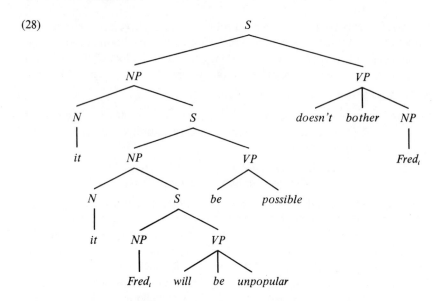

sentential subject into an abstract *NP* which has a substantivized adjective as its head noun: *the possibility that Fred$_i$ will be unpopular.* Many details of this sub-stantivization transformation are as yet unclear, but I am reasonably confident that they can be worked out in such a way that my main claim, that the deep struc-ture of the abstract subject of (5) is approximately that shown under the highest *NP* of (28), will not have to be drastically revised. Following this substantiviza-tion, PRONOMINALIZATION can apply in either direction, for the *that*-clause in apposition to the noun *possibility* is a subordinate clause (cf. footnote 9 above).

Now let us return to (27), where, as was the case in (14), only backward pronom-inalization is possible. It is immediately clear that if the abstract subject of (27), *the knowledge that Fred$_i$ will be unpopular,* is derived from some putatively intransi-tive adjective (say, *known*), on analogy to the derivation of *possibility* from *possible*, the fact that forward pronominalization is excluded for (27) will remain unexplained for if the deep structures of (27) and (5) differed only in that one word, PRO-NOMINALIZATION would affect them identically. Similarly, it is easy to see that the subject of (27) could not derive from a phrase-structure expansion of *NP* like *NP → Det N S*,[13] i.e. from a *NP* like the one shown in (29),

(29)

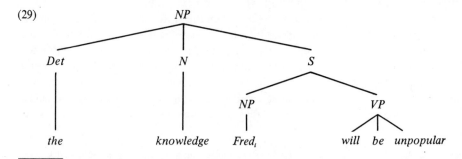

---

[13]Chomsky proposes this rule in his discussion of the base component, op. cit., p. 100.

for there is nothing in the structure of (29) to prevent forward pronominalization from taking place "out of" the *that*-clause in apposition to *knowledge*, and it is not in general the case that such pronominalization must always be blocked with *knowledge,* as (30b) demonstrates.

(30)(a) **Ann's knowledge that Fred$_i$ will be unpopular doesn't bother Fred$_i$.*
   (b) *Ann's knowledge that Fred$_i$ will be unpopular doesn't bother him$_i$.*
   (c) *Ann's knowledge that he$_i$ will be unpopular doesn't bother Fred$_i$.*

I propose that (27) be derived from the deep structure shown in (31), which is different in no essential respects from (16), the deep structure of (14):

(31)

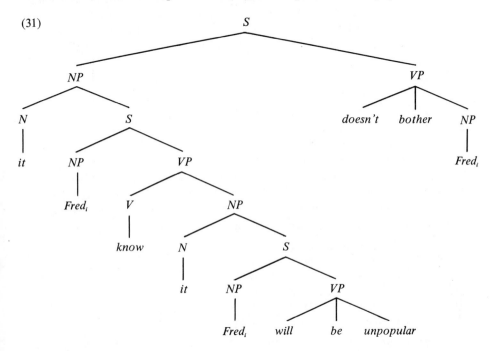

In processing (31), no rules which are of concern to us here apply on the lowest cycle. On the second cycle, after the complementizer *that* has been adjoined to the most deeply embedded *S*, the structural description for PRONOMINALIZATION is met, so the rule must apply. Since backward pronominalization cannot apply (the subject *NP* of *know* is not dominated by a subordinate clause which does not dominate the subject *NP* of *will be popular*), the rule obligatorily converts the latter *NP* into a definite pronoun, producing the sentence *Fred$_i$ knows that he$_i$ will be unpopular.*

On the highest cycle of (31), the verb *bother* specifies that it is possible to adjoin to the second highest sentence the abstract complementizer which triggers the same substantivization transformation which applied in the derivation of (5). After this complementizer has been adjoined, but before the substantivization transformation has applied, EQUI NP DELETION deletes the subject of *know* under identity with the object of *bother*. Then the substantivization rule applies, ending the derivation; PRONOMINALIZATION cannot apply for the same reason it could not apply on the highest cycle of (16).

Thus it can be seen that the derivation of (27) is not parallel to the derivation of the superficially similar (5), but is rather parallel to the derivation of (14), and that the explanation for the impossibility of forward pronominalization in (5) is the same as it is in the case of (14). In both instances it was the assumption that PRONOMINALIZATION is cyclic that made possible an explanation of the facts of extremely similar constructions.

I have postponed until this point the discussion of the interaction between PRONOMINALIZATION and relative clauses because the facts are not so clear-cut as they are in the case of the other types of subordinate clauses listed in footnote 9, and because I suspect there may be dialectal variation in this area. For me, the (c) versions of (32) and (33), where backward pronominalization has applied, differ in acceptability.

(32)(a) *Girls who Sam_i has dated like Sam_i.
    (b) Girls who Sam_i has dated like him_i.
    (c) ?*Girls who he_i has dated like Sam_i.

(33)(a) *Girls who Sam_i has dated say that Sam_i is charming.
    (b) Girls who Sam_i has dated say that he_i is charming.
    (c) Girls who he_i has dated say that Sam_i is charming.

That (32c) is worse, for me, than (33c) seems to be due to the fact that in the latter, the rightmost occurrence of the *NP* Sam_i is contained in a clause which does not contain the leftmost occurrence of this *NP*. The same obtains in the case of non-restrictive relative clauses, as can be seen in (34) and (35).

(34)(a) *Agnes, who Sam_i has dated, likes Sam_i.
    (b) Agnes, who Sam_i has dated, likes him_i.
    (c) *Agnes, who he_i has dated, likes Sam_i.

(35)(a) *Agnes, who Sam_i has dated, says that Sam_i is charming.
    (b) Agnes, who Sam_i has dated, says that he_i is charming.
    (c) ?Agnes, who he_i has dated, says that Sam_i is charming.

For some reason which I cannot explain, (35c) is less acceptable for me than (33c). Nonetheless, in order to capture the clearer differences between (32c) and (33c), and between (34c) and (35c), it seems that the following provision, which was worked out by Edward Klima and me, must be appended to Condition (iii).

(36) If term 2 of the structural description is contained in a restrictive or nonrestrictive relative clause, backward pronominalization is only possible if term 4 is contained in some clause which does not contain and is not contained in this relative clause.

Langacker (op. cit., footnote 9) does not impose condition (36) upon the pronominalization rule, and cites as grammatical several examples which seem to be exactly parallel to (32c) and (34c), which is one of the reasons for my belief that there may be dialect differences in this area.

It does seem to me, however, that some version of (36) must be included in the grammar of all speakers of English, for I know of no speakers who find (37a) and (37b) equally acceptable.

(37)(a) **His$_i$ employers like Sam$_i$.*
  (b) *His$_i$ employers think that Sam$_i$ is charming.*

If the *NP Sam's employers* is derived by means of some rule of AGENTIVE FORMATION from some *NP* containing a relative clause, such as *the ones who employ Sam*, which I believe to be essentially the correct analysis, then condition (36) will differentiate correctly between (37a) and (37b), if the rule of AGENTIVE FORMATION is ordered after PRONOMINALIZATION.

An interesting point arises in connection with the pronominalization of possessive noun phrases. Thus (38a) may be converted into (38b) by the application of forward pronominalization, but backward pronominalization cannot convert it into (38c).

(38)(a) **That Oscar$_i$ was unpopular didn't disturb Oscar's$_i$ mother.*
  (b) *That Oscar$_i$ was unpopular didn't disturb his$_i$ mother.*
  (c) **That he$_i$ was unpopular didn't disturb Oscar's$_i$ mother.*

Comparing (38) with (2), where backward pronominalization is possible (cf. (2c)), we see that the only difference lies in the fact that in (38c) the rightmost occurrence of the *NP Oscar$_i$* is embedded as a possessive modifier of the noun *mother*. It is not the case that possessive noun phrases can never pronominalize other identical noun phrases, as (39b) shows.

(39)(a) **That Oscar's$_i$ mother was unpopular didn't disturb Oscar$_i$.*
  (b) *That Oscar's$_i$ mother was unpopular didn't disturb him$_i$.*
  (c) *That his$_i$ mother was unpopular didn't disturb Oscar$_i$.*

But (39b) is produced by *forward* pronominalization, and the ungrammatical (38c) by *backward* pronominalization. Thus it is evident that in yet another respect, the latter kind of pronominalization is more restricted than the former. A third condition, which I am at present unable to formulate, must be imposed on it which will exclude such sentences as (38c).

In the preceding discussion, I have argued that PRONOMINALIZATION cannot be a precyclic rule, applying before all other transformations; for such a rule would have to be able to operate in both directions, so that both the (b) and (c) versions of examples (1)–(6) would be generated. But if it were allowed to apply backwards, such a rule would generate sentences such as (13c), which could not be saved from ungrammaticality by the operation of later rules, and it would entail imposing many complicated and repetitive conditions, otherwise unnecessary, on such rules as ADVERB PREPOSING, PASSIVE, etc.

I have further argued, on the basis of such examples as (14), that if PRONOMINALIZATION were formulated as a postcyclic rule, complex conditions would have to be imposed on forward pronominalization so that ungrammatical sentences like (14b) would not be produced. Furthermore, even if such conditions were formulated and added to the grammar, Condition (iii) on rule (18) would still have to be stated, so that sentences like (20b) and the (c) versions of (7)–(13) would not be generated.

Only if PRONOMINALIZATION is formulated as a cyclic rule, obligatory in most environments (but cf. footnote 10), can the unnecessary conditions be avoided which would be required if it were considered to be either a precyclic or a postcyclic rule. Furthermore, if it is a cyclic rule, a natural explanation can be found for the otherwise extremely puzzling differential behavior exhibited by superficially identical structures, such as (5) and (27). The naturalness of this explanation therefore provides evidence of the strongest kind for the only theory of language which contains a formal apparatus which allows such rules as (18) to be stated—Chomsky's theory of generative grammar.

14

On So-Called "Pronouns" in English

PAUL M. POSTAL

The following is an informal discussion of certain regularities in the syntactic behavior of forms traditionally called "pronouns" in discussions of English syntax. By informal I mean that, although the analysis suggested involves a number of highly complex grammatical rules and a very special conception of the theory of grammar, no attempt has been made here to formulate or present any of the rules in their correct form. Nor is very much said about the theoretical assumptions these require. My aim is the much weaker one of trying to suggest that a class of facts requires that English grammar be formulated in such a way that it can contain such rules.

Our traditional lore about English grammar[1] recognizes a class of forms often called "pronouns" or "personal pronouns" which include *I, we, you, he, she, it, they*. At the start we may ignore for simplicity the various case forms *us, your, him*, etc., as well as reflexives, although these will become crucial later. Very often it was said that such forms "stand for" or "replace" or "are substitutes for" previously mentioned or understood noun forms. Certain modern students of English such as Robert Allen[2] have noted, essentially correctly, that in many ways such forms actually "replace" whole noun phrases (henceforth *NP*'s) rather than nouns, since they cannot occur with articles, relative phrases, and other elements which can occur in the same *NP* with ordinary nouns. Compare

---

Reprinted from F. Dinneen, ed., the 19th Monograph on Languages and Linguistics (Washington, D.C.: Georgetown University Press, 1966), by permission of Paul M. Postal and the Georgetown University Press.
[1]Cf., for example, O. Jespersen, *A Modern English Grammar* (Copenhagen: Munksgaard, 1949), Part VII, pp. 125–126; G. O. Curme, *A Grammar of the English Language* (Boston: D. C. Heath & Company, 1931), Vol. III, p. 557; R. B. Long, *The Sentence and Its Parts* (Chicago: University of Chicago Press, 1961), pp. 338–356.

[2]In a paper read to the Linguistic Society of America several years ago.

(1)   *The young girl said that she would go.*

where on one reading *she* can be said to "stand for" the whole *NP the young girl* with

(2)   *The large girl can't stand the small one.*

where *one* can only be said to "stand for" the noun *girl*. However, as I argue later, this contrast is a bit misleading since there is reason to assume that the form *one* or its variants is also relevant at one stage to the "replacement" which occurs in sentences like (1).

Early transformational descriptions of English have shown that the vague and unclear traditional notion of "stand for" can, in its *sentence internal*[3] meaning, be precisely formalized by transformational derivation. Thus in a transformational grammar a structure like

(3)   *O'Hara is more intelligent than he seems to be.*

would be derived from a more abstract structure schematically like[4]

(4)   *O'Hara is more intelligent than O'Hara seems to be.*

However, obviously not all pronouns can be so derived, which leads to a differentiation between transformationally introduced pronominal structures and those introduced in the underlying or basic forms, as in

(5)   *He is sick.*

The fact that pronouns have two different origins can then be suggested as the explanation for the ambiguity of reference of the pronoun in sequences like

(6)   *Schwartz claims he is sick.*

There is a great deal right in all this and no one who wishes to discuss English pronouns can afford to ignore the insights and observations which underlie the kinds of descriptions just mentioned. It is the thesis of this paper, however, that these analyses ignore some important facts and that there is concomitantly a good deal

---

[3]I would argue that there is really no other meaning. The idea that a form like *she* in sentences such as *She dances well* is a "replacement" or "substitute" for some other noun, say in "discourse contexts" or the like, seems to me completely without basis. Such an assumption explains nothing for the quite simple reason that there is nothing really to explain. It is quite sufficient to indicate precisely that such forms refer to object-types whose particular referents are assumed by the speaker to be known to the person spoken to.

[4]It is crucial, however, that linguistic theory provide for an indexing of lexical elements, for grammars keep track of whether two or more occurrences of the same lexical item in the deep structure of a single sentence refer to the same entities or not. Thus the underlying structures of *Otis convinced Otis* and *Otis convinced himself* differ only in that the indices of the two items are identical in the latter case but not in the former. When one speaks of identity in a transformational grammar, as we shall informally below, it is necessary to include index identity. It seems natural to take the indices to be simply numbers which are assigned to any lexical item when it is taken from the dictionary and inserted in a deep structure. For further discussion of this question of indexing, cf. N. Chomsky, *Aspects of the Theory of Syntax* (Cambridge, Mass.: The M.I.T. Press, 1965), pp. 145–146; Postal, "A Note on 'Understood Transitively,'" *International Journal of Linguistics*, 32.90–98 (1966).

also wrong in them. Furthermore, what is wrong can be seen to arise from the almost inevitable tendency in grammatical research to assume wrongly that the surface or superficial syntactic forms of sentences provide direct insight into (or are even identical to) their deep syntactic forms.

THE "ARTICLE" CHARACTER
OF SO-CALLED PRONOUNS

In a transformational grammar, each sentence and hence derivatively each part of each sentence has two distinct syntactic structures as part of its overall grammatical description; a highly abstract deep structure relevant for semantic interpretation and a surface structure relevant for phonetic interpretation. These two aspects of syntactic form are in general connected by a long and complex chain of transformational rules which, furthermore, derive a sequence of intermediate forms.[5] In such a grammar it makes no sense to ask such traditional questions as "Is such and such occurrence of form *F* a noun?" It only makes sense to ask such questions *contextually* with respect to a specified structure. That is, one can ask whether such and such occurrence of a form *F* is a noun in the deep structure, a noun in such and such intermediate structure, a noun in the surface structure of the sentence, etc. The answer to some of these questions may be yes, to others no without contradiction. Furthermore and equally importantly, the fact that an element is present in the surface form does not mean it was present in the deep structure and, conversely, absence from the surface form does not necessarily entail absence from the deeper aspect of grammatical structure.

I mention all this only because it is fundamental to my basic claim which is that the so-called pronouns *I*, *our*, *they*, etc., are really *articles*, in fact types of *definite* articles. However, article elements are only introduced as *segments* in intermediate syntactic structures. In the deepest structures they are, I shall suggest, not present segmentally but are represented as syntactic features of nouns, features analogous to *Animate, Human, Countable*, etc.[6] Rather deceptively, the articles which have traditionally been called pronouns are, as a result of certain transformational operations, in many cases assigned a derivative *Noun* status in surface structures.

The evidence for this rather extreme set of assertions is complex, fragmentary, and involved with the analysis of a wide variety of different constructions in English. This greatly limits the possibility of providing a full justification here. I shall however attempt to sketch the reasoning involved and to present those facts which seem most significant. To start, we can easily determine that English *NP*'s, that is, the elements which function as subjects, objects, etc., must be categorized into definite versus indefinite in order for their distributional possibilities to be described properly. In large part, but by no means completely, definite or indefinite status

---

[5]For latest published discussion of this theory in its most recent formulation, cf. Chomsky, *Aspects*.

[6]The introduction of syntactic features into linguistic theory is discussed at length in Chomsky, *Aspects*.

is indicated superficially by a particular article. Thus *the, this, that, these, those* are definite, *a/an, some, Sm,* and *Null*[7] are indefinite. However, proper nouns are definite even though in general they occur without explicit article. There are exceptions, of course, including *The Hague, The Bronx,* as well as fairly productive instances such as names of ships, names of buildings, etc.[8]

Diagnostic environments for definite *NP*'s include special constructions with preposed adjectives illustrated by such sentences as[9]

(7)(a) *Big as the boy was, he couldn't lift it.*
   (b) *Big as Harry was, he couldn't lift it.*
   (c) *Big as that gorilla was, he couldn't lift it.*
   (d) **Big as some giant was, he couldn't lift it.*
   (e) **Big as a dog was, he couldn't lift it.*

Similarly, only definites occur as subjects in constructions like

(8)(a) *Fido is John's.*
   (b) *The house is John's.*
   (c) *That car is John's.*
   (d) **Soup is John's.*

---

[7]*Sm* is the way I shall write here and below the form which occurs in such contexts as *I would like_____applesauce,* a form entirely different from that occurring in contexts like _____ *maniac is outside.* The null form of the indefinite article occurs with mass nouns like *blood, soup, rice,* etc., plural nouns like *cars,* and certain unaccountable abstracts like *truth, happiness,* etc.

[8]It is easy to show by the criteria to be given below that genitive expressions like *Schwartz's nostril, Sam's horse,* etc., are definite. This follows, however, from the fact that such forms are derived from more abstract (but not the most abstract, which involve restrictive relative phrases) structures **the nostril of Schwartz's,* **the horse of Sam's,* etc. Evidence for this is given by the article gap with *the* in the otherwise complete paradigm: *a horse of Sam's, some horse of Sam's, this horse of Sam's, that horse of Sam's, these horses of Sam's, those horses of Sam's* and by the co-occurrence of preposed genitives with superlatives, otherwise restricted to the definite article: *the oldest horse, Sam's oldest horse,* **an oldest horse,* **this oldest horse,* etc.

[9]It might be objected that indefinites may occur in this context counter to our claim because of such forms as *Expensive as butter is, I still prefer it; Strong as gorillas are, they can't outwrestle Superman; Cold as a glacier is, it is still not as cold as outer space;* etc. However, it will be observed that in all of these cases the superficially indefinite *NP*'s must be interpreted *generically.* This very much suggests that one recognizes *Generic* as a syntactic categorization of nouns and insists that [+ *Generic*] nouns are [+ *Definite*]. Later rules may then switch some generic *NP*'s to surface indefinites. As support of this approach, one can note that while definite articles can occur in contexts like (7) with restrictive relatives, this is impossible for these apparent indefinites, a function of the general incompatibility of generic and restrictive: **expensive as butter which I bought yesterday was;* **strong as gorillas who live in Africa are.* The existence of indefinites with adjectives complicates the matter but does not remove the basic point: *rare as good bourbon is; strong as big men are.* That is, if we treat the apparent counterexamples as generics which later turn indefinite, which is in accord with their semantic interpretation, we account for the failure of indefinite + ordinary restrictive to occur here. On the other hand, if one treats the occurring indefinites in the surface forms as instances of deep indefinites, the nonoccurrence of the restrictives with indefinites is inexplicable and *ad hoc* since definites do not exclude ordinary restrictives here: *big as the man who I saw yesterday was.* Such facts seem to me to suggest very strongly that the indefinite examples not be taken as counterexamples to the claim of definiteness in contexts like (7) but only as proof that it is deep structure and not surface structure definiteness which is relevant.

  (e) **Some dog is John's.*
  (f) **A car is John's.*

On the other hand, only indefinites occur in such contexts as

(9)(a) *It was idiocy for Jack to leave.*
  (b) **It was the idiocy for Jack to leave.*
  (c) *It was a scandal that Louis spoke.*
  (d) **It was that scandal that Louis spoke.*

Another diagnostic environment for indefinites is given by constructions with nonlocative, anticipatory *there*:[10]

(10)(a) *There's a book on the table.*
  (b) *There's some object on the table.*
  (c) **There's John on the table.*
  (d) **There's this key on the table.*

But investigation shows that all of the so-called pronouns are thereby definite *NP*'s:

(11)(a) *Big as I am, I couldn't lift it.*
  (b) *Big as they were, they couldn't lift it.*
(12)(a) *It is Billy's.*
  (b) *They are Jack's.*
(13)(a) **It was it for Jack to leave.*
  (b) **It was it that Louis spoke.*
(14)(a) **There's me on the table.*
  (b) **There's you in the house.*

The definite character of *NP* containing so-called pronouns[11] is also shown by various pre-article constructions. Although we cannot go into this in detail, notice

---

[10]In the commentary after the oral presentation it was objected that definite forms can be found in these contexts. The evidence was examples like *there's this guy up here*, etc. But this is a confusion since although these forms exist they are not instances of the construction I was illustrating. Notice, for example, that they answer different questions. Thus if asked *What is there on the table?* one can reply *There's some object on the table* but not *There's this guy on the table.* Moreover, notice that in the so-called counterexamples the *this* is not understood as the definite, demonstrative element, but rather as some kind of *indefinite*. While I do not understand this fact, it certainly shows that such forms do not conflict with any claim of indefiniteness.

[11]Paul Roberts, *English Syntax*, alternate edition (New York, 1964), pp. 14–17, argues, in effect, that the so-called personal pronouns occur with the same phonologically null form of the *indefinite* article that occurs with such indefinite mass and plural *NP*'s as *butter*, *chickens*, etc. However, on page 27 he himself gives part of the evidence showing that this is a mistake. He observes that pronouns occur with pre-article forms *several of*, *many of*, etc., but takes this only to show the contrast between pronouns and proper nouns. But obviously it also shows a contrast between pronouns and those mass and plural *NP*'s which do in fact have the null form of the indefinite article: *several of us*, *many of them*, **many of chickens*. One can only get *many chickens* since the *of* is preserved here only with definites: *many of the chickens*, *many of those artists*, etc. Everything said in the rest of this paper is further argument against the assumption of a *syntactically* indefinite character for pronoun-containing *NP*'s. The *semantically* definite character of such *NP*'s needs no stress although under Roberts' analysis this is an accident, i.e. not a function of the syntactically definite property which yields semantic definiteness in other forms.

that such forms as *which of, some of, all of,* etc., occur only with following definites:[12]

(15)(a) *which of the men*
  (b) *some of the men*
  (c) *all of those cars*
  (d) **which of some men*
  (e) **some of Sm men*
  (f) **all of cars*

But they also occur with following so-called pronouns if these are plural:

(16)(a) *which of you*
  (b) *some of them*
  (c) *all of us*

A similar argument holds for superlative phrases like

(17)(a) *the best of these sheep*
  (b) *the tallest of the men here*
  (c) *the fairest of those maidens*
  (d) **the best of some sheep*
  (e) **the tallest of men here*
  (f) **the fairest of Sm maidens*

which also show the definite character of the pronoun *NP*:

(18)(a) *the best of us*
  (b) *the tallest of you*
  (c) *the fairest of them*

An important problem in constructing a grammar of English is, therefore, the following. Granting that in general the definite or indefinite character of a *NP* is indicated by its article, how is definite status to be assigned formally to *NP*'s based on the so-called pronouns? A possibility is to assume simply that the pronouns are a subclass of nouns which occur in deep structures only with the non-demonstrative definite article *the*, which later drops by a transformational rule. Thus the underlying terminal structure of a sentence like *I went* would be schematically *(the I) went*, where *I* is a noun and *the* its preceding definite article. This would eliminate the other exceptional fact of no article with pronouns at the cost

---

[12]This is really only a fact about surface forms. Such elements do occur with following indefinite plural nouns in deep structures but deletion and reduction take place. Schematically:

which car of Definite cars $\Rightarrow$ *which one of* $\begin{Bmatrix} the \\ these \\ those \end{Bmatrix}$ *cars*

which car of Indefinite cars $\Rightarrow$ *which car*

a certain car of Definite cars $\Rightarrow$ *a certain one of* $\begin{Bmatrix} the \\ these \\ those \end{Bmatrix}$ *cars*

a certain car of indefinite cars $\Rightarrow$ *a certain car*

The assumption that the final noun in such constructions must be an underlying plural although some turn up as surface singulars explains why nouns which have no plurals do not take such forms: **a certain blood.* The assumption of indefinite character is supported by such facts as **There's a certain one of the cars on the rack* but *There's a certain car on the rack.*

of the transformational rule to account for the absence of *the* in the surface structures. The apparent advantages increase if a similar analysis is proposed for proper nouns. Not a bad bargain perhaps, but not an especially good one either.

Moreover, further facts strongly suggest that, while it is right to assume that more abstract NP structures of superficial pronoun-containing *NP*'s involve definite articles, it is wrong to assume either that the articles are *the* or that at the relevant stage the pronouns are nouns. Most important in this regard are the reflexive forms such as those in

(19)(a) *Horace washed himself.*
   (b) *The girl washed herself.*
   (c) *I washed myself.*

As has been argued by Lees and Klima,[13] it is quite clear that reflexive elements must be derived transformationally from underlying *NP*'s which are identical to other preceding *NP*'s, this identity being subject to certain conditions. These have never been fully or exactly stated, but they concern occurrence of the two *NP*'s within the same *simple* sentence structure. This may be ignored here. Thus a sentence like (19a) must be derived from a more abstract, deep structure of the sort schematically indicated: *Horace washed Horace* (subject of course to the remarks of footnote 4). In previous transformational descriptions, reflexive words such as *myself, themselves*, etc., have been treated as compounds of pronouns and a special, transformationally introduced *grammatical* formative *self*. This formative was assumed to be introduced by the very rule which carries out the reflexivization operation as determined by *NP* identity within simple sentence structures.

This analysis of reflexive forms will not do, however. The identity and simple sentence constraints are fundamentally correct and unquestioned here although they involve some mysterious and far from fully solved problems.[14] But the treatment of the element *self* as a grammatical formative is untenable. In fact *self* must be taken to be a noun stem as we see clearly in such phrases as *the expression of self in our society, selfish, selfless*, etc. Compare *piggish, brutish, boyish* and *witless, spineless, timeless*, etc. Notice also the *self/selve* plural alternation parallel to that in such unquestioned noun stems as *wife/wive, life/live*, etc. If, however, the stem *self/selve* in reflexive words is a noun stem, what is the preceding element *my, our, him*, etc.? My answer is that they are, of course, articles, definite articles, in fact genitive-type definite articles. I view the process of reflexivization as a com-

---

[13]R.B. Lees and E.S. Klima, "Rules for English Pronominalization," *Language*, 39. 17–29 (1963) [*MSE*].

[14]One of these is discussed in Postal, "A Note on 'Understood Transitively,' " op. cit. Another derives from the fact that underlying *NP*'s with head nouns which are identical and have identical reference indices cannot differ in any other element. That is, structures of the form *The big boy helped the small boy* cannot be interpreted as contradictory with the instances of boy co-referential. Furthermore, this is apparently not a kind of fact particular to English. It seems then that there is a principle of language which requires identical indices to occur only in nouns which have identical "dominating constituents." This latter term is required because such facts are not restricted only to *NP*'s and nouns. Facts of this general sort are further evidence to me that much of reflexivization and indeed pronominalization generally is really a universal phenomenon.

plex of a number of partially independent operations, some of which are relevant for other grammatical developments such as nonreflexive pronominalization and, most crucially, determination of the surface forms of so-called pronouns. The relevant rules include PRONOMINALIZATION, DEFINITIZATION, REFLEXIVIZATION, GENITIVIZATION, and DEFINITE ARTICLE ATTACHMENT.

However, it will be impossible to understand these grammatical operations if it is not recognized that the terminal elements of deep syntactic structures, i.e. the morphemes, are not unanalyzable atomic symbols. Rather, they are complexes of syntactic, phonological, and semantic features or properties. Phonology and semantics do not concern us here. But the fact that underlying noun stems have a syntactic feature analysis is crucial. The features involved for English must, apparently, include such as *Animate, Human, Masculine, First Person (I), Second Person(II), Third Person (III), Definite, Demonstrative, Proper, Pronoun (Pro), Reflexive, Genitive*, etc. The claim is then that, instead of nouns co-occurring with article morphemes in deep structures as in previous transformational and other treatments, superficial structure article differences are represented at the most abstract level by differences in features of nouns, features like *Definite, Demonstrative*, and, as we see subsequently, also those involving person and gender properties.

The process of PRONOMINALIZATION is, I assume, a rule which specifies a noun stem as [+ *Pro*] if it is identical to some other noun in the same sentence, subject to appropriate and not entirely understood conditions. The rule of REFLEXIVIZATION is one which specifies a noun stem as [+ *Reflexive*] and [+ *Pro*] subject to its identity to another noun stem in the same simple sentence structure (at the point of REFLEXIVIZATION). All nouns start out in the deep structure forms as [–*Reflexive*], i.e. the specification [+ *Reflexive*] is only introduced transformationally.[15] However,

---

[15]If, as seems correct, we take *Reflexive* to be a linguistic universal, i.e. a property characterized within linguistic theory, the constraint on [+ *Reflexive*] introduction is presumably to be extracted from English grammar as a fact about human language as such. And one ultimate argument for the analysis proposed here, under which *self/selve* is a noun stem with the features [+ *Pro*, + *Reflexive*] rather than an *ad hoc* grammatical formative, will be that this contributes greatly toward permitting a universal statement of the reflexivization operation. That is, properties like *Pro* and *Reflexive* are candidates for universal status, but a particular formative of English is not.

Reflexivization can be taken as that subtype of pronominalization relevant to identical *NP*'s within the same simple sentence structure at the point of pronominalization. This latter constraint is necessary because copresence within the same simple sentence is at times a result of previous transformational operations. Hence it is not copresence within the same deep simple sentence structure which is necessarily relevant. For example, in both English and Mohawk the possessor *NP* of a genitive construction reflexivizes by identity to the subject *NP* of a sentence although they start out in different simple sentences. But the processes of genitive formation in both languages insert the possessor *NP* within the same simple sentence as the subject. Thus *Van Gogh cut off his own ear* is the reflexive of *Van Gogh cut off Van Gogh's ear* where the two proper nouns have the same reference index. But the latter involves a deep structure object *NP* containing a relative phrase, i.e. an embedded sentence. Schematically:

(*the ear* [*Van Gogh has Wh some ear*]$_S$)$_{NP}$

Here the *NP Van Gogh* which is subject of *cut off* does not start out as part of the same simple sentence structure as the *NP Van Gogh* which is subject of *has*. Hence at that stage they are not

this is, as we have seen, not true of the feature specification [+ *Pro*] which will be present in some noun bundles in the base, namely, in those underlying such surface *NP*'s as *someone, he, I,* etc., in sentences like

(20)(a) *Someone saw Bill.*
   (b) *He is clever.*
   (c) *I don't believe that.*

Similarly, DEFINITIZATION involves specifying a noun stem as [+ *Definite*] (and generally but not always [–*Demonstrative*] as well) subject to certain conditions including previous transformational specification of [+ *Pro*]. Under these assumptions, the overall processes of reflexivization which occur in sentences like

(21) *A boy hurt himself.*

and pronominalization which occur in sentences like

(22) *A boy said he would help.*

are considered to be quite similar. Both involve specification of the repeated noun as [+*Pro*, + *Definite*, – *Demonstrative*]. The difference is whether or not the specification [+ *Reflexive*] is also assigned.

A crucial assumption is then that there is a relatively late transformational rule in the grammar which adds certain terminal segments, the traditional articles and

---

subject to reflexivization which only comes about because of the results of intervening genitive formation rules. If the relative phrase embedded sentence is not reduced, no reflexivization is possible: **Schwartz loves the horse which himself has.* Exactly analogous facts can be found in Mohawk. Thus we can possibly assume that some rule(s) to mark the head nouns of repeated identical *NP*'s as [+ *Pro*, + *Reflexive* . . .] if they are within the same simple sentence structure at the point of application is a universal. An apparent further universal fact is that all "modifiers" within the *NP* whose head is so marked must be removed, i.e. relative clauses, their reductions, etc. In many languages, of course, and Mohawk is a good example, the reflexive pronouns themselves drop. In Mohawk at least this is not *ad hoc* but a predictable result of the fact that all nonemphatic definite pronouns are elided. This is thus some strong evidence for the claim that reflexivization involves assignment of the feature [+ *Pro*], characteristic of nonreflexive pronouns, as well as [+ *Reflexive*]. There are many grounds for assuming that both reflexivization and pronominalization involve a further feature, which we might call *Derivative*, which distinguishes inherent pronouns from those derived by identity. For example, in English, initial derivative pronoun *NP*'s drop in infinitives and gerunds although nonderivative ones do not. Thus *Bill wants to go* must be interpreted to have *Bill* as subject of both *want* and *go* so that the pronominalized form of the repeated *Bill* has dropped. But in *Bill wants him to go* the subjects of *want* and *go* are not understood as the same. Hence here the pronoun *NP* is not the result of any pronominalization operation but is instead simply the realization of an inherently [+ *Pro*] noun chosen in the base. A possibility would be to assume that all nouns start out [–*Derivative*] and that pronominalization rules assign [+ *Derivative*] thus distinguishing in terms of feature specifications inherent from derivative pronouns.

It should be obvious that all of these suggestions about linguistic universals in regard to pronominalization and reflexivization must be taken as highly tentative and suggestive. We are clearly only on the threshold of understanding what is universal in such processes. But it is certainly not too soon to attempt to characterize this, and one must insist that an important constraint on a correct theory of grammar is that it be able to extract what is universal here from particular linguistic descriptions and state it once and for all within the theory of language.

now also the definite pronouns *I, him, your,* etc., to *NP*'s which previously contained no such segmental elements. The phonological form of the particular article is determined by the features of the head noun stem, these features themselves being partly inherent and determined by the base rules and lexicon which generate deep structures but often partly derivative and determined by previous transformational rules such as PRONOMINALIZATION, REFLEXIVIZATION, and DEFINITIZATION. We might call the kinds of rules of which the article insertion rule is an instance SEGMENTALIZATIONS. These are rules which insert segmental elements into phrase markers on the basis of syntactic feature specifications present at earlier, more abstract stages of derivations. It is a difficult and interesting question exactly how such rules should be characterized. I shall not go into this here.[16]

The kind of derivations I am assuming can be illustrated rather schematically and with many oversimplifications. In Figure 1, I sketch the development of the surface form *A boy said he left* on the analysis where *he* refers to *a boy.* As can be seen, the underlying subject noun of the verb *left* of the embedded sentence is identical to that of the subject noun of the sentence as a whole. This would normally determine an indefinite article for the subject of *left* by virtue of SEGMENTALIZATION. However, the PRONOMINALIZATION and DEFINITIZATION rules turn this noun [+*Pro,* +*Definite,* −*Demonstrative*] *before* SEGMENTALIZATION applies. Therefore SEGMENTALIZATION determines a definite article. Furthermore, since the noun is at this stage [+*Pro,* +*Human,* +*Masculine,* +*III,* −*II,* −*I,* +*Nominative,* −*Genitive*] and since no restrictive relative is present, the relevant article is *he.*[17] I assume here of course that there exist rules which mark nouns with case properties [+*Nominative*], [+*Genitive*], etc., before SEGMENTALIZATION applies. These specifications are predictable from context but we shall not be able to consider their assignment here. ARTICLE ATTACHMENT is the rule designed to account for the fact that *himself, myself,* etc., are single words unlike ordinary

---

[16]It is my feeling, however, that such rules characterize whatever is really common in those features of language which have been referred to as *inflection.* That is, inflectional elements are those segments added by SEGMENTALIZATION provided these segments are added in such a way that they become part of the same *word* as does that element whose features they mark.

[17]Throughout this discussion we make the simplifying assumption that the segment introduced has only phonological properties. But this is clearly incorrect. It seems clear that these introduced segments must also consist of a set of syntactic features. This will, for example, be the basis for explaining the agreements which show up marginally in English in such cases as *these boys, this boy,* but much more fundamentally in languages like Spanish, etc. Furthermore and even more importantly, it is clear that many transformational rules must refer to the syntactic entity "article." But under our approach there is no constituent or node in trees to formalize this reference. Hence this must be done by assigning common syntactic features to all introduced articles. One of the most difficult questions in considering a theory of SEGMENTALIZATION rules is the relationship between the original set of feature specifications (for example, those of a noun) and those of an introduced segment which superficially mark some features of this element (for example, those of an article). It would seem correct to assume that the introduced segment contains a subset of the features of the original segment as well as certain special features to indicate that it is a grammatical not a lexical element and possibly to indicate what kind of lexical element it "derives from."

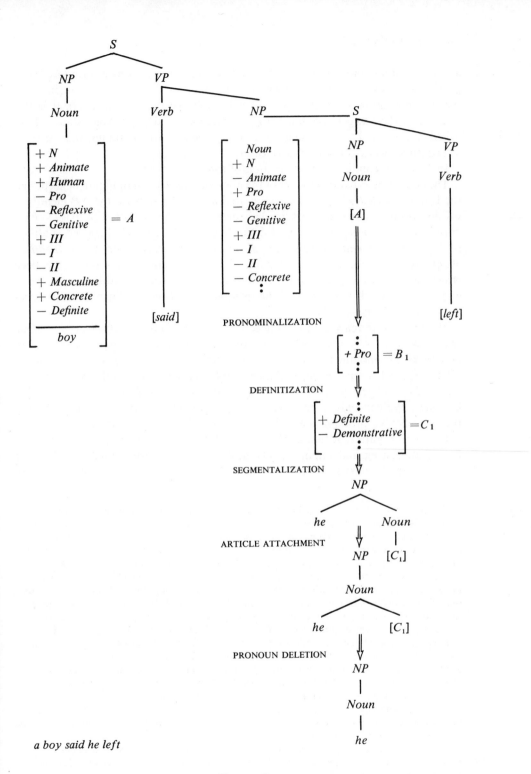

FIGURE 1

article + noun combinations.[18] I assume that this rule works also for nonreflexive pronouns (notice that this is the simplest assumption since it permits statement of the relevant feature context as [+*Pro*] rather than [+*Pro*, +*Reflexive*]). It is this rule which then largely accounts for the "deceptive" derived *Noun* status of so-called pronouns. Later we shall give some evidence for assuming that ARTICLE ATTACHMENT works in nonreflexive cases.

In Figure 2, I indicate the derivation of a reflexive form.

The derivation is parallel to that of the nonreflexive element in Figure 1 except that the feature [+*Reflexive*] is specified as well as [+*Pro*] because the *NP* identity is within a simple sentence structure. This determines the operation of REFLEXIVIZA-TION instead of PRONOMINALIZATION. Furthermore, [+*Reflexive*] triggers addition of the feature [+*Genitive*]. There are, of course, many other origins for [+*Genitive*], all of them transformational. That is, all noun structures start off in the deep structures as [−*Genitive*]. There is, however, an important additional difference and it is this which has disguised the relationship between ordinary so-called pronouns and reflexive words.

Nothing in our analysis thus far accounts for the difference between the terminal two morpheme structure of reflexive words and the single formative character of nonreflexive pronominals. That is, what we have said would suggest that the output *NP* in Figure 1 should be *heone*. This is not the case here nor is the actual phonological form of the pronoun ever present in analogous forms in the standard language. We can only assume, therefore, the existence of a special rule to drop the nonreflexive pronoun stems in such cases. This is the rule called PRONOUN DELETION in Figure 1. Although this seems a bit *ad hoc*, it in fact provides the basis for an interesting and important justification for the posited analysis which we shall give in the next section. I am definitely claiming, however, that were it not

---

[18]There is another rule of article attachment which also works for nouns marked [+ *Pro*]. This involves indefinite forms *some, every, any, no*, etc. It is this rule which accounts for the single word character of *everyone, anywhere, nothing, someone*, etc., in contrast to the two word character of otherwise parallel [−*Pro*] forms *every person, any location, no car, some man*. The same rule also explains the one word character of the question forms *who, what, where, when, how*, etc., as compared with *what person, what car* (**what one, *what thing*), *what place*, etc., since these single word forms are derived from *Wh* + *some* + [+ *Pro*] and their differences are a function of other features of the noun. In other words, the *who* of the interrogative *Who came?* is to the *someone* of *Someone came* as the *what man* of *What man came?* is to the *some man* of *Some man came*. Attachment of article to noun only takes place when the noun is [+ *Pro*]. The same rule may just possibly be the explanation of the partially parallel "relative pronouns." That is, *the boy who saw me* derives from a more abstract form (*the boy* [*Wh some boy saw me*]$_S$)$_{NP}$. The identical noun in the latter may then pronominalize (i.e. turn [+ *Pro*]) which triggers subsequent *Wh* + *some* attachment just as if the feature [+ *Pro*] were inherent as in the interrogative forms. This yields the single word form. However, there are problems here having to do with *which/that* and *who/that* alternations which this account does not explain. The type of pronominalization involved in relatives also involves many difficulties. And there are other problems having to do with question-relative parallels and differences.

It would be natural to attempt to combine the article attachment rules for definites with that for indefinites. But there are important differences. Consider *you big ones; *you (ones) big; someone big; *some big one*. This issue must therefore be considered open.

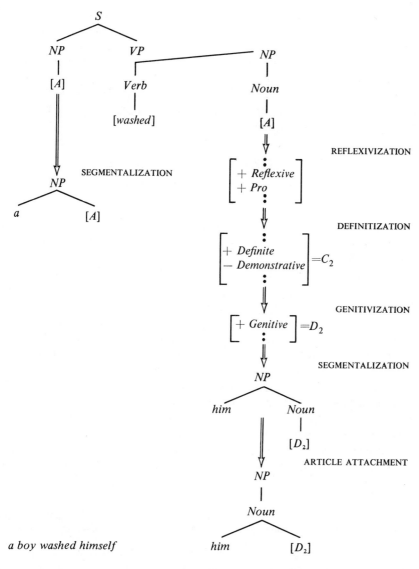

FIGURE 2

for this highly restricted and low level rule our so-called pronouns would in fact have the terminal forms *Ione, *usones, *heone, *itone (or perhaps better *itthing analogous to the indefinite *something). This should make clear why I said earlier that the contrast pointed out by Allen between pronominals like *he, *she, *it*, etc., which replace whole *NP*'s, and pronouns like *one*, which replace individual nouns, is misleading in part. For in fact I claim that the pronoun which would be pronounced *one, *thing*, etc., is also really present in the so-called pronominal cases as well. Further very strong evidence of this will be presented below.

I am assuming, of course, that when transformational rules mark a noun with features like [+*Pro*], [+*Reflexive*], etc., this may trigger subsequent effects not only on article form but also in general determine the phonological form of the noun stem itself. In other words, when a noun is marked [+*Reflexive*] its phonological matrix must be changed from whatever it was originally (for example, *boy*, *lady*, *car*, *goat*, etc.) to *self/selve* depending on [−*Singular*] [+*Singular*].[19] Similarly, specification of a noun as [+*Genitive*] will in regular cases have effects on it leading to the suffix written *'s*.[20]

JUSTIFICATION FOR THE ANALYSIS OF THE SO-CALLED PRONOUNS AS ARTICLES

In the previous sections we have outlined an account of forms like *I, us, their*, etc., whereby they are treated as forms of definite articles. In our terms this means that they are segments added to *NP*'s whose head nouns are [+*Definite*]. The contrasts among the various definite articles are due to other contrasting features of the head noun. The major motivation of this analysis thus far is the parallelism with respect to properties like *Animate, Masculine, I, II, III*, etc., between *he/him* and *himself*, *it* and *itself*, *I/me/my* and *myself*, etc. Once it is recognized that the reflexives consist of something plus a noun stem and that this something differs from the forms of pronouns only in case properties (*Genitive* and *Nominative* values), it is quite natural to assume that pronominalization and reflexivization involve specifying a noun as [+*Pro*, +*Definite*, −*Demonstrative*] and that these along with the inherent features of the noun then determine the form of the article. Hence by parallelism with *himself* we are led to regard *him* as an article whose underlying head noun (which would otherwise show up phonologically as *one*) has been deleted because it was [+*Pro*] either inherently or derivatively by identity. While perhaps not completely implausible, thus far we have certainly given little conclusive ground for accepting such an analysis. Basically it has been shown only

---

[19]Exactly how these shifts of form should be accomplished is not clear. It might be suggested that transformational rules are appropriate here. My own feeling is, however, that this is not correct. Rather I suspect that it should be possible to reuse the dictionary after the transformational rules have been applied so that the dictionary is used both to fill in the lexical items of deep structures and also to specify those aspects of phonological form which are transformationally determined but *ad hoc*, i.e. not a function of general phonological rules. A similar approach should also be used to describe suppletions. How this proposal to reuse the dictionary should be formalized is, of course, a complicated matter which we cannot go into here. Our assumption is, however, that, for example, *self/selve* is the only noun in the dictionary marked [+ *Reflexive*] so that it is the only one which can be correctly selected on the second pass through the dictionary for those positions which have been transformationally marked [+ *Reflexive*]. The dictionary entry for the noun stem *self/selve* (which has no semantic element) thus represents most of what is *ad hoc* to English in ordinary reflexivization.

[20]A difficulty here is that, of course, the phonological suffix is actually added not to the noun but to the final word in the entire *NP* of which the noun marked [+ *Genitive*] is head. Thus: *the boy who is sleeping's dream; the girl I talked to's hairdo;* etc.

that it is possible and that it provides a natural way of handling the definiteness of nonderivative pronouns like *I*, *him*, *you*, and shape parallelisms between these and derivative pronoun forms of the reflexive and nonreflexive varieties. And furthermore the analysis is compatible with the hitherto ignored fact that *self/selve* is a noun stem. More serious evidence in favor of the article analysis is, however, available.

It should be emphasized that the analysis accounts for an otherwise unexplained gap in the *NP* system with respect to the co-occurrence of third person pronouns, definite articles, and restrictive relative phrases. One finds real pronouns actually occurring with the definite article *the* if there is a restrictive relative phrase or one of its reduced variants present in the *NP*:

(23)(a) *I met the one who Lucille divorced.*
   (b) *I met the man who Lucille divorced.*
(24)(a) *I ate the one Schwartz gave me.*
   (b) *I ate the apple Schwartz gave me.*
(25)(a) *I bred the small one.*
   (b) *I bred the small lion.*

but without the restrictives, reduced or not, the pronoun form *one* cannot so occur:

(26)(a) **I met the one.*
   (b) *I met the man.*
(27)(a) **I ate the one.*
   (b) *I ate the apple.*
(28)(a) **I bred the one.*
   (b) *I bred the lion.*

Notice that the analogues with the indefinite article are all right regardless of whether the head noun is [+*Pro*] or not:

(29)(a) *I met someone.*
   (b) *I met some man.*
(30)(a) *I ate something.*
   (b) *I ate some apple.*
(31)(a) *I bred something.*
   (b) *I bred some lion.*

My suggestion is that the gap left by the definite, nondemonstrative form with [+*Pro*] head absences in (26)–(28) is actually filled by the so-called pronoun forms, or, more precisely, by that subset which are third person. That is, the so-called third person pronouns, *it*, *he*, *her*, *them*, etc., are exactly the articles assigned to nouns containing the features [+*Pro*, +*Definite*, −*Demonstrative*, +*III*, −*II*, −*I*] *in the absence of restrictive relative phrases in the relevant NP*. This simultaneously explains the failure of the so-called third person pronouns to occur with restrictive relative phrases or their reductions.[21] Schematically what I am claiming is:

---

[21]Notice that from this point of view the substandard *them guys*, etc., is a perfectly natural sort of minor morphophonemic difference in article shape which one would expect to differentiate different dialects.

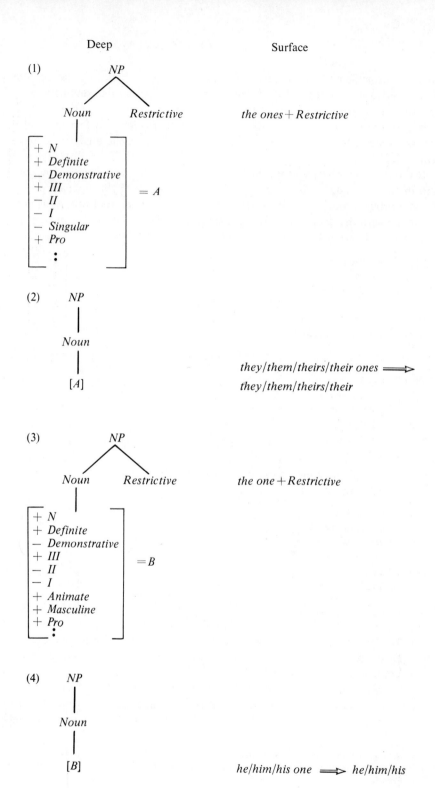

FIGURE 3

An important issue looms of course, an issue which relates to a general failure to discuss the way underlying feature specifications are assigned or how the many restrictions among their possible combinations may be stated. In particular, there is only one form of nondemonstrative definite article, namely, *the*, which occurs with a pronoun that has a restrictive relative (with nonfirst or second persons, see below). But under the present analysis there is a whole contrastive set of nondemonstrative definite articles occurring with the pronouns without restrictives, at least in the singular, namely, *he, she, it,* and their case forms. This means that a set of feature distinctions including those of gender and sex are superficially marked in the definite articles of pronouns without restrictive relatives but not in those of pronouns with restrictives or in those of nouns which are not [+*Pro*] regardless of restrictive occurrence. The first question is whether it is right to assume the underlying distinctions exist even when they yield only the noncontrasting form *the*. In fact, there is good reason to assume that these distinctions are present in the underlying forms in such cases. This follows, for example, from the fact that all relevant types of reflexives are possible:

(32)(a)   *The one who I saw behaved himself.*
  (b)   *The one who I saw behaved herself.*
  (c)   *The one which I saw destroyed itself.*

In order to maintain the generalization that reflexivization is a function of *NP* identity, it is necessary to assume that the underlying pronouns in these cases contrast in features like *Animate, Masculine,* etc. Hence in purely third person cases it is not necessary to restrict contrasting underlying features to pronouns without restrictives. It is rather to be taken as a minor, more or less morphophonemic fact that we do not say things like **he boy, *she girl who I like,* etc., instead of the actual forms with the neutralized *the*.

However, in this discussion of underlying features for pronouns we have ignored the question of features like *I* and *II*. But these involve some of the most important problems and provide some of the most significant evidence for our analysis. One's initial impression is that, under the assumptions which have been made here, it will be necessary to restrict underlying feature specifications [+*I*] and [+*II*] in such a way that they occur only in nouns which are [+*Pro*] and only in nouns which do not have restrictive relatives. This will be necessary to prevent such impossible elements as **I boy, *you person, *you girl who Jack loves,* etc., allowing only abstract *Ione, youone, weones, youones,* which become actual Surface *I, you,* and *we*. However, although there are real restrictions here, the just given statement of them is certainly wrong, or rather too general. For it is fundamental to the present analysis that, in the plural, nonthird person elements can occur with both nonpronouns and/or restrictive relative phrases.

The first forms relevant to this claim are those such as *we men, you guys,* etc., which we take to be cases of [−*Pro*, +*I*. .], [−*Pro*, +*II*. .]. Jespersen, who of course noticed such forms,[22] implied in effect that they were derivatives from appositive relative clauses. In transformational terms this would naturally suggest derivations

---

[22]Jespersen, op. cit., Part II, p. 85.

like, schematically, *we, who are men* ⇒ *we men; you, who are children* ⇒ *you children.* If this solution could be maintained, it would obviate taking *we* and *you* to be articles in such phrases as is insisted here. But in fact this proposal of appositive derivation cannot be right since forms like *we men*, etc., occur in a variety of contexts where appositive relatives may not. Thus, for example, Smith[23] has noted that *NP*'s which are the objects in questions may not have appositive relatives:

(33)(a) **Did you see Bill, who is six feet tall?*
   (b) **Who wrote a novel, which was published by McGraw-Hill?*

And, as she also observed, there are negative contexts which exclude appositive clauses:

(34)(a) **He didn't eat the mango, which I bought for him yesterday.*
   (b) **He didn't write a novel, which was banned as obscene.*

Similarly, other negative contexts exclude appositives:

(35)(a) **No American, who was wise, remained in the country.*
   (b) **None of the cars, which were Chevrolets, were any good.*
   (c) **They never insulted the men, who were democrats*

But the forms like *you guys* occur in all such appositive-excluding environments:

(36)(a) *Did you see us guys?*
   (b) *Who insulted you men?*
   (c) *He didn't like us Americans.*
   (d) *He did not insult you Communists.*
   (e) *None of you guys are any good.*
   (f) *Neither of us professors is quitting.*
   (g) *They never agreed with us planners.*

Furthermore, there are other grounds for doubting the appositive analysis. Notice that the final relative phrase in such prearticle constructions as

(37)   *that one of the men who is sick*

is really associated with the first noun *one*, as shown by the agreement with *sick*. There must therefore be a rule to shift it over the following structure to the end. In nonpronoun *NP*'s this following structure can include article, prenominal modifiers, and postnominal modifiers:

(38)(a) *that one of the tall men who is sick*
   (b) *that one of the men here who is sick*
   (c) *that one of the men who I like who is sick*

Observe, however, that the same relative shift rule must operate in pronoun-containing *NP*'s:

(39)(a) *that one of us who lives here*
   (b) *that one of you guys who betrayed me*
   (c) *that one of you foolish soldiers who deserted his post*

Under the analysis suggested here, where *we, us, you*, etc., are articles, the structure over which the relative must shift in (39) is *exactly the same* as that in (38). But under the appositive analysis the structure would necessarily be radically different, complicating the shift rule, since the derived structure of elements like *we men*,

---

[23]C.S. Smith, "Determiners and Relative Clauses in a Generative Grammar of English," *Language*, 40.48–49 (1964) [Sec. 8] [*MSE*].

you foolish sailors, etc., would have to be rather like

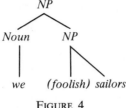

FIGURE 4

Finally, Jespersen to the contrary notwithstanding, the appositive derivation would assign the wrong interpretation since in fact such phrases do not have appositive meanings, at least not always. This is shown clearly by such examples as

(40)(a) *You troops will embark but the other troops will remain*
   (b) *Lets us three men leave first.*

which are certainly not paraphrases of

(41)(a) *You, who are troops, will embark but the other troops will remain.*
   (b) **Lets us, who are three men, leave first; Lets us three, who are men, leave first.*

The fact that (41b) is, in addition, ungrammatical is further evidence of the inadequacy of an appositive derivation for such forms.

It seems clear then that the only conclusion is that such surface *NP*'s as *we men*, etc., must be derived from underlying nouns which are [*–Pro*] and yet contain [*+I*] or [*+II*] specifications. Hence in such sequences we actually find the so-called pronouns *we/us* and *you* as *articles* in *surface structures*. And this is among the strongest evidence for our overall claim that so-called pronouns have essentially the same type of derivation and status as traditionally recognized definite articles.

Having shown that in the plural first and second person forms can occur with ordinary nouns, we can turn to the question of their occurrence with restrictive relatives. And here also we find a contrast with the situation in the singular. For in fact such phrases as

(42)(a) *you men who wish to escape*
   (b) *we Americans who have been struggling here*

seem perfectly natural. And this is even more true when the restrictives are reduced:

(43)(a) *you men here*
   (b) *we honest policemen*
   (c) *you amusing comedians*
   (d) *You diligent Democrats shouldn't put up with lazy ones.*
   (e) *Jones didn't criticize us intelligent workers, only the dumb ones.*

The occurrence of first and second person forms in the plural with restrictive relatives and their reductions leads to a significant justification for the claim that the so-called pronouns are articles and, in particular, for the claim that for standard English a more abstract set of forms *Ione, heone, weones, themones*, etc., underlie the surface elements *I, he, we, them*, etc. We illustrate a relevant derivation for the *we* case (on one analysis. I claim that *we* is in general ambiguous. Cf. below) in Figure 5. Most striking is the fact that the hypothetical pronoun stem *one* actually shows up in surface structures in such forms as

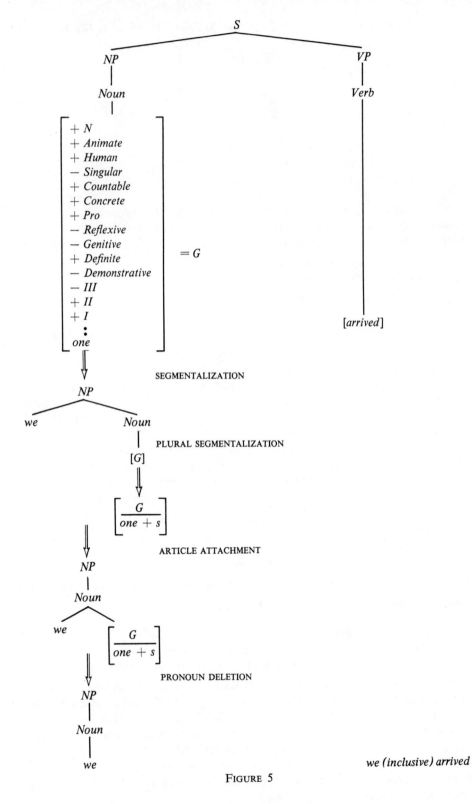

FIGURE 5

(44)(a) *you great ones*
  (b) *us quieter ones*
  (c) *we religious ones*

We take these to have structures exactly analogous to those of *you important men*, *we diligent Democrats*, etc., except that the head noun is [+*Pro*], and analogous to the structure in Figure 5 except for the presence of a restrictive relative. It is the reduction of this relative and the preposing of the remaining adjective which then evidently prevents the attachment of the articles *you, us, we* to the following noun and subsequent deletion of the pronoun stem + plural ending. It may be objected that this analysis is dubious because only the forms with reduced relatives are possible. But in fact, for the present writer at least, unreduced relatives in such cases are possible although with them attachment and deletion occur:

(45)(a) *We who are opposing Fascism disagree with those of you who are not.*
  (b) *You who wish to survive had better shape up.*

This indicates that the rule of ARTICLE ATTACHMENT only takes place when the article is contiguous to the stem. This conclusion is supported further by forms like:

(46)(a) *We here oppose such a move.*
  (b) *You on the East side have no problems.*

where attachment and deletion must be assumed with reduced relatives because they are not preposed.

Jespersen, who noticed examples like (44), had the following to say:

> *Ones* may be used after a personal pronoun in the plural. This is not astonishing when an adj intervenes (as in *you great ones above* . . . or . . . *it is very annoying to us quieter ones*); but it is more difficult to see why *ones* should have been added to a single *we* or *you*. This is found in Scotch dialect . . . , and it is evidently from Scotch that American has taken it. *We'uns* and *you'uns* are especially frequent in the vulgar speech of the Southern states . . . [24]

Jespersen obviously recognizes the problem which such forms as (44) cause for a view which treats *we, you*, etc., as pronouns. His remark that the occurrence of a following noun is not astonishing when an adjective intervenes is defensive. Why is it not astonishing? But even more, the view falls apart completely when faced with the dialect forms *we'uns, us'uns*, etc. The latter provide one of the most crucial justifications for our analysis. For they illustrate a case where the hypothetical forms *weones, youones*, etc., actually are related to pronunciation without the *ad hoc* rule of nonreflexive pronoun stem deletion which must be posited for the standard language.[25] In comparison to Jespersen's puzzlement, the analysis suggested in this paper provides a natural treatment of such forms. For such dialects as contain *us'uns*, etc. my claim would be that the underlying forms and most of the rules are identical to those suggested here for the standard language. But in these lower class systems the rule which drops nonreflexive pronoun stems

---

[24]Jespersen, op. cit., Part II, pp. 261–262.
[25]Notice how they provide justification for the assumption that ARTICLE ATTACHMENT works also for nonreflexive forms.

after attached definite articles is, at least in first and second person cases,[26] restricted to the *singular* and does not work for both singular and plural as in the standard language.[27]

In this analysis of first and second person articles *we, you*, etc., in their occurrences with nonpronouns and restrictives, we have, of course, uncovered differential behavior of the ARTICLE ATTACHMENT RULE. If the noun stem is [+*I*] or [+*II*] the article attaches to a following noun which is [+*Pro*] if nothing intervenes even if there is a following restrictive, reduced or not. But in cases where the noun is both [–*I*] and [–*II*] attachment only occurs when there is no restrictive. Thus one finds (47a, b, and c) and not the analogues to (45):

(47)(a)   *the one who she married*
    (b)   *the one who he married*
    (c)   *the one which I ate*
    (d)   **he who she married*
    (e)   **she who he married*
    (f)   **it which I ate*

I have not indicated how the base rules may be formulated to account for the underlying constraints on combinations of feature specifications in nouns or restrictions between these and external elements such as restrictive relatives. Nor shall I do this here. It should be said, however, that variants of the feature apparatus suggested by Chomsky in *Aspects* seem adequate to do the job, i.e. to specify that in the singular [+*I*] and [+*II*] are incompatible with each other and with [–*Pro*] and restrictive relatives while none of these is true in the plural. Although I cannot go into these matters in detail here, I would like to briefly indicate the kinds of underlying feature bundles which I think must exist and to briefly justify the use of three person features, *I, II,* and *III* which have been implicit in the discussion thus far. In particular, it is important to indicate why we do not simply take first and second persons to be opposite values of one feature.

Given three features of two values there are eight possible combinations. And in the plural in fact six of these occur:

$$
\begin{bmatrix} +III \\ +II \\ +I \end{bmatrix} \quad \begin{bmatrix} +III \\ +II \\ -I \end{bmatrix} \quad \begin{bmatrix} +III \\ -II \\ -I \end{bmatrix} \quad \begin{bmatrix} +III \\ -II \\ +I \end{bmatrix} \quad \begin{bmatrix} -III \\ -II \\ -I \end{bmatrix}^* \quad \begin{bmatrix} -III \\ -II \\ +I \end{bmatrix}^* \quad \begin{bmatrix} -III \\ +II \\ +I \end{bmatrix} \quad \begin{bmatrix} -III \\ +II \\ -I \end{bmatrix}
$$

(a)   (b)   (c)   (d)   (e)   (f)   (g)   (h)

Only the combinations (*e*) and (*f*) are impossible in the plural. (*a*) is, for example, the analysis of the reflexive form in

---

[26] I do not know whether such dialects have forms like *them'uns* where the standard language has *them* but this would hardly be surprising. I presume, however, that they do not have singular *I'un, you'un*. A dialect containing the latter is, however, not at all unthinkable. It would simply be one where the deletion rule has been eliminated entirely for nonthird person forms. The simplest dialect of all would, of course, have no deletion of *one/ones* in any of these cases regardless of person or number.

[27] The assumption here is that minor syntactic differences between closely related dialects are a function of differences in the transformational rules or in the lexicon, not of differences in the set of base rules which determine the general grammatical properties of deep structures.

(48)   *You and I and John can't perjure ourselves.*

(*b*) is the analysis of the reflexive in

(49)   *You and John shouldn't bother yourselves about it.*

(*c*) is of course the analysis of all so-called third person forms. (*g*) is the inclusive *we* and (*d*) is the exclusive *we*. Notice that only the former occurs in the environment after *lets*.

In the singular, on the other hand, only three of the eight possibilities are possible, namely, those in which one of the three features has a plus value and the other two minus values. But since more than four exist in the plural it is clear that two features will not suffice. It should be emphasized that in these analyses I agree very much with Long (op. cit,. p.338) who insists that *we* is not the plural of *I* in the same sense in which *boys* is the plural of *boy*. That is, in our terms none of the three possible combinations of features which yields the article *we* differ from the combination which yields the article *I* only in the value of the feature *Singular*. Features *II* and *III* necessarily have different values as well and the feature *Pro* may also differ since *we* can occur with nonpronouns while *I* cannot.

An important justification for the three feature analysis of person properties is that it provides an important part of the basis for giving a general characterization of the first person-second person interchange in questions and answers. Given feature analyses like those suggested above, the condition is simply that if the values of the features *I* and *II* do not agree in any noun form of the question, the "corresponding" forms in the answer must have the opposite values for each. Thus *did you (singular) eat yet* where the underlying subject noun is [$-I$, $+II$] must be answered *yes, I ate already* where the underlying noun is [$+I$, $-II$]. The question *did you (plural) leave* must be answered *yes, we left* in which the underlying noun is [$+I$, $-II$], i.e. the *we* is understood as exclusive. But *we* can also answer questions which contain *we*: *Do we have ten dollars*; *yes, we do*. This is possible because the question noun has the specification [$+I$, $+II$ . . .], i.e. is inclusive, and does not meet the oppositeness condition requiring a switch in the answer. That *we*-questions may also take *you*-answers follows from the fact that some *we* are [$+I$, $-II$], i.e. exclusive. These facts of question-answer first and second person relations are thus good evidence of the ambiguity of English *we NP*'s. Obviously these question-answer facts discussed here are not really special to English but again involve universal features of language which must ultimately be built into any correct linguistic theory. That this means features like *I*, *II*, *III*, *Pro*, etc. must be universals is simply a further confirmation since this seems clear on many other grounds.

There is one final minor argument in favor of the claim that the traditional personal pronouns are actually forms of definite article. Morphophonemically voicing is essentially predictable in dental, nonstrident continuants, i.e. there is no real [θ]-[ð] contrast in English. In particular, voicing may be predicted in such elements in articles, *the, this, that, these, those*, and in so-called pronouns, *they, them, their, theirs* (not too long ago one could of course have added *thee, thy, thine, thou*). But by assuming that pronouns are articles, these two environments are reduced to one. Analysis of generally so-called adverbial elements also suggests that forms like *then, there, thus* actually have the structure *definite article + certain types of pronoun*[28] so that the same environment covers these as well.

Having mentioned phonology, I can conclude by observing that an analysis like that proposed here for English is to me even more obvious for languages like German and Spanish where, for example, the respective pronoun-definite article similarities between *er-der, sie-die* and *el-el, ella-la* are evidently no accidents. But I leave it for those who know these languages better than I to consider the possibility of such analyses.

---

[28]For some brief discussion, cf. J. Katz and P. M. Postal, *An Integrated Theory of Linguistic Descriptions* (Cambridge, Mass.: The M.I.T. Press, 1964), pp. 127–138.

IV

RELATIVIZATION

Relativization is the process whereby a sentence is embedded as a modifier in a noun phrase. In this way the relative clause becomes the source of productive instances of both pre- and postnominal modifiers. Involving as it does the introduction of relative pronouns, the movement of constituents, and various deletions, relativization provides a rich source of insight into other areas of the structure of English. Thus, each article in this section deals not only with the process of relativization as such but also with how an account of relativization impinges on other aspects of English structure.

Edward S. Klima, in "Relatedness Between Grammatical Systems," raises the questions "Of what nature are the superficial differences in the shape of sentences belonging to different styles [of English]?" and "What is the formal relationship between the individual grammatical systems underlying these different styles?" He discusses not only relativization but also the formation of direct and indirect questions, the problems of case marking in English pronouns, and the ordering of grammatical rules.

Carlota S. Smith, in "Determiners and Relative Clauses in a Generative Grammar of English," shows how, from the adjoined sentence that is the source of the relative clause, various kinds of pre- and postnominal modifiers are formed. She makes the distinction between restrictive relative clauses and appositive (i.e. non-restrictive) relative clauses, sets up classes of determiners on the basis of whether they tolerate one or the other or both kinds of relative clauses, and gives rules for deriving nominal modifiers and appositives.

S.-Y. Kuroda, in "English Relativization and Certain Related Problems," begins by observing the identity in form between the interrogative and relative uses of *what* and *which*. By introducing the two basic determiners *SOME* and *THAT*, and the constituents *Wh* (the interrogative and relative marker) and *Pro*, he develops a system of rules that relates the interrogative and relative uses of *what* and *which*. He also explores the implications of the assumptions made in developing this system for other grammatical processes, such as pronominalization.

Finally, John Robert Ross, in "A Proposed Rule of Tree-Pruning," explores the types of tree structures that result from relativization and subsequent deletion operations. He proposes that there be a convention on derived constituent structure that involves NODE DELETION. He offers evidence from the process of extraposition following relative clause reduction, from verb-particle separation, from comparative formation, and even from Latin grammar.

15

Relatedness Between Grammatical Systems

EDWARD S. KLIMA

1. The problem. As early as the eighteenth century, grammars of the English language included judgments on the grammatical status of historical developments in the syntax of the inflected forms of the interrogative and personal pronouns.[1] At present, the use of *who* for *whom* as the so-called object form of the relative and interrogative pronoun is generally accepted, at least in the United States, as standard colloquial speech. Similarly, the defense of *It is me* against *It is I* has a lengthy history. Finally, constructions like *Him and me are staying*, while not accepted as standard English, have been acknowledged as forming as much a part of a natural and consistent linguistic system (so-called vulgar English) as their socially more acceptable kin. The changing syntax of the pronouns is, of course, basically a historical phenomenon. Because of the normative approach and conservatism of the schools, as well as the strong formative influence of literary tradition, many educated speakers of American English have, as more or less distinct styles of speech, the different syntactic subsystems characterizing these usages.

Reprinted from *Language*, 40.1–20 (1964), by permission of Edward S. Klima and the Linguistic Society of America.

This work was supported in part by the National Science Foundation, and in part by the U.S. Army, the Air Force Office of Scientific Research, and the Office of Naval Research.

[1]Noah Webster, *A Grammatical Institute of the English Language* (Hartford, 1784): "It is very common to hear these phrases 'it was me,' 'it is him.'" Joseph Priestley, *Rudiments of English Grammar* (London, 1798), p. 143: "When the pronoun precedes the verb . . . it is very common, especially in conversation, to use the nominative case . . . as, 'who is this for.'" Priestley also discusses the prevalence of *It is me*. See also Robert Lowth, *A Short Introduction to English Grammar* (London, 1775), pp. 133–136. For a general discussion see Charles C. Fries, *American English Grammar* (New York: Appleton-Century-Crofts, 1940), pp. 88–96, and for references to the literature consult H. L. Mencken, *The American Language* (New York: Alfred A. Knopf, Inc., 1949), p. 447. The current situation among educated speakers in England is represented by Randolph Quirk, "Relative Clauses in Educated Spoken English," *English Studies*, 38 (1957).

Coexisting styles that are basically similar despite the differences they manifest pose the following questions of relevance to structural linguistics. Of what nature are the superficial differences in the shape of sentences belonging to different styles—and, in particular, to what extent are scattered individual differences reducible to a single difference at a higher level of grammatical abstraction? It is clear that numerous differences in style can be described in terms of varying restrictions on the occurrence of a given word or morpheme; thus in one style *them* occurs as a demonstrative complement to nouns where in another style *those* occurs: *Them boys are coming* versus *Those boys are coming*. The present study will show that certain differences reside rather within the constitution of constructions themselves and are most simply analyzed as differences in the formational rules describing such contructions.

There is another pertinent question. What is the formal relationship between the individual grammatical systems underlying these different styles? Whereas the comparison of phonological systems can proceed on the basis of common phonic features, the grammatical (syntactic and morphophonemic) systems of totally different languages have no such real common denominator for comparison. Within different styles of one and the same language, however, comparison of syntactically differing systems is simplified by overall identity of grammatical elements; the words and their combination in constructions are essentially the same. It is hoped that this *control* situation may help to clarify more complicated relationships, like those in historical linguistics between successive stages of one and the same language, or relationships encountered in translating between or comparing related languages.

2. The approach.   In the present study the relationship between systems as well as the nature of their differences will be approached in the following way. The syntactic structure of each system will be considered revealed by the set of rules which most economically generates the sentences of the system.[2] That set of rules will be designated as its grammar (G). The relationship between one style (L_1) and another (L_2) will be thought of in terms of the rules (E_{1-2}) that it is necessary to add as an extension to the grammar (G_1) of L_1 in order to account for the sentences of L_2. A convention will be adopted regarding the place where extension rules may be added to the grammar. They may not be added just anywhere, but must come at the end of certain sets of rules; e.g. extension rules dealing with the case forms of pronouns must come after the set of grammar rules for case in the previous system. By this convention, extension rules are prevented from superseding previous rules. Fundamental structural difference, varying in nature and degree, will be considered to exist between systems L_1 and L_2 when the set of rules G_2 for most economically generating the sentences of L_2 is not equivalent to G_1 plus its extension E_{1-2}.

---

[2]This notion of grammar is developed by Noam Chomsky, *Syntactic Structures* ('s-Gravenhage, 1957). A detailed treatment of specific grammatical problems can be found in Robert B. Lees, *A Grammar of English Nominalizations* (*International Journal of American Linguistics*, 26.3, Part 2, 1960). For a similar notion of simplicity in description, see Morris Halle, "Phonology in Generative Grammar," *Word*, 18.55 (1962) [*SL*].

From the point of view simply of relating coexisting systems, the particular pairing and the direction chosen in extending the grammar of one system to account for the sentences of another are those representing the shortest extension rules, that is, L_1 is compared with L_2, and L_2 with L_3, rather that L_1 with L_3, because E_{1-2} and E_{2-3} are each shorter than a hypothetical E_{1-3}. Similarly, L_1 rather than L_2 is taken as primary in comparing L_1 and L_2 because E_{1-2} is shorter than a hypothetical E_{2-1}.

Although motivated by a purely synchronic principle of simplicity (shortness of rules), the order in which the styles are considered does, in fact, recapitulate comparable aspects in the historical development of the pronouns. This presentation deviates, of course, in an essential way from true historical perspective. It is as if the sequence of pronominal systems, after being abstracted from consecutive stages of the language, were collapsed and each system treated as part of an otherwise identical total system.

3. Representative data. Table 1 shows sentences representative of the four coexisting styles to be related. A blank under any L signifies that the sentence is the same in its final shape as that one on its immediate left. It is assumed that, aside from the differences in final shape presented by the sentences in the table and by the other sentences of the system like them, the rest of the sentences have the same shape.[3]

4. General syntactic considerations. Consider first only L_1, typical of a style that might be referred to as elegant or literary English. Classifying representative sentences into the particular four types A, B, C, D, follows traditional grammatical usage: A represents simple declaratives; B, interrogative structures corresponding to these; C, structures corresponding to interrogatives but contained as constituents of complex declaratives (and related structures) in the form of indirect questions; D, sentences themselves containing structures, so-called relative clauses, closely related to independent sentences. The notions—common to

---

[3]The usage in L_1 is that of general school grammar as described for formal writing by H. W. Fowler and F. G. Fowler, *The King's English* (Oxford, 1922), pp. 60–61. L_2 and L_3 present clearcut divergencies from the former. Styles that are intermediate between those presented here are also possible. At least one such style does in fact exist between L_1 and L_2. In that intermediate style, the interrogative pronoun does not have case marking, except after prepositions, whereas the relative pronoun has case marking under the same conditions as in L_1. A style is also conceivable which contains case-marked pronouns after the verb *be* but maintains the case marking of the relative and interrogative pronouns in object function. Such a system, when formulated, would be more complicated than those presented and would necessitate one set of case-marking rules before *Wh*-attachment (case marking for objects of verbs and prepositions) and another set of case-marking rules after *Wh*-attachment (case marking for pronouns after *be*), such that there would be *Whom could she see?* like *She could see him* but not **Whom was it?* like *It was me*. The usage in L_4 agrees entirely with that of the dialogue in Nelson Algren, *The Man with the Golden Arm* (New York: Doubleday & Company, Inc., 1949) and *The Neon Wilderness* (New York: Doubleday & Company, Inc., 1960). This corpus generally supports observations made for vulgar or substandard English by Mencken in *The American Language* and by Albert H. Marckwardt, *American English* (New York: Oxford University Press, 1958), p. 148. Of particular significance for the present study is the absolute consistency, in the dialogues of Algren, of the usage characterized as L_4, to the complete exclusion of features from other styles.

intuitively based traditional classification—of *correspondence* and *relatedness* between types of structures, are not without analogues, as will be seen, in a rigorous formal description of the language. Formal facts like the recurrence of certain basic grammatical features between representatives of different structural types often accompany such impressions of correspondence and relatedness. For example, the same sorts of subjects and objects (to use traditional terms for major functional units in the syntactic system) occur with the same verbs. Also, the same number agreement holds between subjects and verbs, regardless of the type of structure. But, though the functions of the major elements remain the same, the final shapes of sentences differ according to the type of structure. In particular, the order of the elements differs. In A the subject stands before the finite verb, the finite verb forms the head of a chain of verb forms, interrupted only by certain adverbs, and the object occurs after that verb chain. With respect to the order of such elements, group B is more complicated. Often the particular word order

TABLE 1

	L_1	L_2	L_3	L_4
A(3.01)	*She could see him near me.*			
(3.02)	*He and I left.*			*Him and me left.*
(3.03)	*We two left.*			*Us two left.*
(3.04)	*We all left.*			
(3.05)	*It was I.*		*It was me.*	
B(3.06)	*Could she see him?*			
(3.07)	*Who could see him?*			
(3.08)	*Whom could she see?*	*Who could she see?*		
(3.09)	*With whom did he speak?*			[———]
(3.10)	*Whom did he speak with?*	*Who did he speak with?*		
(3.11)	*Who was it?*			
(3.12)	*Who was the leader?*			
C(3.13)	*He knew whether she could see him, or not.*			[———]
(3.14)	*He knew who it was.*			
(3.15)	*He knew who was the leader.*			
(3.16)	*He knew whom he spoke with.*	*He knew who he spoke with.*		
(3.17)	*He knew with whom he spoke.*			[———]
D(3.18)	*The leader who could see him left.*			
(3.19)	*The leader whom I saw left.*	*The leader who I saw left.*		
(3.20)	*The leader with whom he spoke left.*			[———]
(3.21)	*The leader whom he spoke with left.*	*The leader who he spoke with left.*		

of one sentence as compared with another can be attributed to clear grammatical differences elsewhere in the sentence; for example, inversion in B, as contrasted to the word order in A, coincides with the presence of an interrogative word; normal word order in C despite the interrogative words coincides with subordination. The basic order of elements will be that (or those) from which the ultimate particular word orders, as well as other grammatical features, are most simply specified. Often, while major functional elements like subject and object cannot be specified simply on the basis of their position in the total set of sentences representing all possible structural types, their position in terms of the basic order of elements is significant for their specification. Clearly, in English the relationship between the order of elements and their grammatical function is simpler in A than in B; C and D are more complicated in that they themselves contain instances of A and B within them. In fact, we can refer to the word order of A, with only a few modifications, as basic.

The position of an element is thus relative to the level of syntactic structure. Among grammatical features describable by position at the level characterized by the presence of basic word order is the occurrence of the so-called object form of pronouns in L_1. The occurrence of *him* rather than *he*, *whom* rather than *who*, in the various structures of L_1, follows from a principle of syntactic function that can be stated in a simple way in terms of position in the simple declarative sentence; viz. pronouns following transitive verbs and prepositions occur in their objective form. Thus, in Table 1 (3.01) in L_1 is the ultimate form of a sentence like *She – could – see – he + **Case** – near – I + **Case***. The specification of function at the level of the simple sentence in terms of the occurrence of inflectional forms corresponds to the traditional notion, whereby *him* and *whom* are the forms assumed by the pronouns as *objects* of verbs and prepositions and whereby *whom* in (3.08), (3.09), (3.10), (3.16), (3.19), (3.21) is still considered to be object of a transitive verb or preposition, even though the so-called object is separated from its governor and even precedes it.

5. Direct questions.   Consider first the direct questions in B. The direct question can be thought of essentially as a single sentence, specified by an interrogative marker *Wh* introducing the sentence; for example, (3.06) in L_1 would have the form *Wh – she – could – see – he + **Case***.[4] The interrogative specifier *Wh* can remain unattached or can have attached to it (indicated by +) various elements of the sentence, including instances of the pronoun marked with ***Case***; for example, (3.08) in L_1 is *Wh + he + **Case** – she – could – see*, and (3.07), *Wh + she – could – see – he + **Case***. In this paper I shall avoid the ultimately necessary step of specifying which of two (or more) attached constituents dominates the other; of having to determine, that is, whether the sequence *Wh + he* is a form of the interrogative marker or a form of the pronoun—whether *Wh* dominates, or *he*. The special word order of direct questions can be explained as the attraction of the finite verb form to *Wh* and its attachments: *Wh – she – could – see – he + **Case*** ⇒ *Wh – could – she – see – he + **Case***, and *Wh + he + **Case** – she – could – see* ⇒ *Wh + he + **Case** – could – she – see*. *Wh + she – could – see – he + **Case*** already has the

---

[4] For the symbolism, see Appendix C.

finite verb beside it. In direct questions, unattached *Wh* is not represented phonologically.

6. Indirect questions.   In indirect questions, which are questions embedded as subordinate clauses in other sentences, unattached *Wh* appears as *whether.* Indirect questions reveal another syntactic difference that distinguishes them from corresponding direct questions: *Wh*-attraction, resulting in the characteristic inverted order of direct questions, does not operate in indirect questions, cf. *Whom could he see?* and *I asked him whom he could see.* Indirect questions share this blocking of inversion (*Wh*-attraction) with other subordinate clauses that involve some form of *Wh* in embedding one sentence into another; for example, relative clauses: *The man whom he could speak with left*; certain adverbial clauses: *He left when he could see him, I will leave whether I can speak to him or not*; and also in clauses whose *Wh*-word is sentence-initial: *What he could see pleased him.* Mere sentence-initial position of *Wh* does not suffice to differentiate between inversion and noninversion. Inversion will be appropriately blocked by the insertion of a symbol ***that*** in front of embedded clauses and directly following *Wh* and its attachments.[5] In other words, the attraction of the finite verb form to *Wh* and its attachments does not operate if ***that*** intervenes. Thus the interrogative clause in *He knew whom he could see* would have the form *Wh* + *he* + ***Case*** + ***that*** – *he* – *could* – *see*. The derivation of the sentence would include the embedding of (a) (below) into (b) such that the structure of the former would be that of *it*; after embedding, the sentence would have the form (c).

(6.01)(a) $\begin{bmatrix} Wh - he - could - see - he \Rightarrow Wh - he - could - see - he + \textbf{\textit{Case}} \\ Wh - he - could - see - he + \textbf{\textit{Case}} \Rightarrow Wh + he + \textbf{\textit{Case}} - he - could - see \end{bmatrix} \Rightarrow$

  (b)   *he – knew – it*

  (c)   *he – knew – Wh* + *he* + ***Case*** + ***that*** – *he* – *could* – *see*

(6.02)(a)   *she – could – see – him* $\Big|_{\Rightarrow}$

  (b)   *he – knew – so*

  (c)   *he – knew* – ***that*** – *she – could – see – him*

   The identification of the subordinating mark with the particular form ***that*** is motivated by the following factors: (*a*) Sporadically ***that*** appears with other forms in subordination; for example, *He is better off now that she is gone*; *But that he might do it, I would leave.* (*b*) In relative clauses, ***that*** alternates with the relative pronouns *who*(*m*) and *which* except in certain contexts; for example, *The man whom*

---

[5]The use of ***that*** as marker of subordination has historical justification. In Middle English, all subordinating conjunctions, relative pronouns, and interrogative pronouns (but only in indirect questions, that is, in subordination) were followed optionally by ***that***. *Til it was noon they stoden for to see who that ther com*—Chaucer, *Troilus and Cressyda*, 5.1114; *Oonly the sighte of hire, whom that I serve, . . . wold han suffised right ynough for me*—*Knight's Tale*, 1231; *This is the worchynge of the conclusion to knowe yf that eny planete be directe or retrograde*—*Astrolab*, 330–337. (*The Works of Geoffrey Chaucer*, A. W. Pollard, H. F. Heath, M. H. Liddell, and W. S. McCormick, eds. (London: Macmillan & Co. Ltd., 1913)) See also George O. Curme, *Grammar of the English Language: 3. Syntax* (Boston: D. C. Heath & Company, 1931), p. 218, and Otto Jespersen, *Modern English Grammar*, 3.116 (Copenhagen: Munksgaard, 1928).

she could see left and *The man that she could see left.* (*c*) With certain restrictions, *that* in relative clauses varies with zero just as *that* does in simple declarative clauses; thus we have the alternation *The man that she could see left*; *The man she could see left*, paralleled by *He knew that she could see him*; *He knew she could see him*.

In the direct question, *Wh + he + Case – she – could – see* ultimately yields *Whom could she see?* with inversion, whereas with subordination we have

$$(6.03)$$

$$he - knew \begin{cases} that - she - could - see - he + Case \\ Wh + she + that - could - see - he + Case \\ Wh + he + Case + that - she - could - see \\ Wh + that - she - could - see - he + Case \ (or \ not) \end{cases} \Rightarrow$$

$$he - knew \begin{cases} that - she - could - see - him \\ who - could - see - him \\ whom - she - could - see \\ whether - she - could - see - him \ (or \ not) \end{cases}$$

7. Relative clauses.

The relative clause, which represents a special case of emdedding with subordination, can be described in terms of two sentences that have an identical constituent. Embedding in this case means the subordination of the one sentence to the shared constituent of the other sentence; for example, *The leader whom I saw left* represents the subordination of *I saw the leader* to the identical noun in *The leader left*. The occurrence of the case marker in the relative pronoun can be accounted for most simply by considering the subordination of the sentence after the identical noun has assumed its corresponding pronoun form, that is, after *I – saw – he* is derived from *I – saw – the – leader*. After case marking, the former has the form *I – saw – he + Case*, which, when attached to *Wh*, is embedded with subordination into the nominal of *The leader left*. Marked case for relative pronouns in L_1 is again determined in terms of position with respect to basic word order—roughly, the word order of the simple declarative sentence. The derivation of the sentence would be a fuller form of the following. The final string in the set of derivations (7.01a) is embedded in (b) to yield (c).

$$(7.01)(a) \quad \begin{bmatrix} Wh - I - saw - the - leader \Rightarrow Wh - I - saw - he \\ Wh - I - saw - he \Rightarrow Wh - I - saw - he + Case \\ Wh - I - saw - he + Case \Rightarrow Wh + he + Case - I - saw \end{bmatrix} \Rightarrow$$

(b) *the – leader – left*

(c) *the – leader – Wh + he + Case + that – I – saw – left*

8. Order of rules for subordinate structures.

The structures described by the rules of embedding yielding subordinate clauses fall naturally into three categories: first, simple declarative clauses with *that* (for example, *He knew that she could see him*), second, relative clauses (for example, *The man whom she could see left*), third, interrogative (indirect question) clauses (for example, *She knew whom she could see*). These categories reflect differences in the freedom with which constituents within a subordinate structure may be attached to sentence-initial *Wh*. Sentences like the following indicate that constituents within a declarative clause may be attached to the initial *Wh* of the main clause in questions: *Whom did you think that she could see?* from *Wh – you – Present – think – that – she – Past – can – see – him* by the attachment, in forming questions, of *him* located within the subordinate clause, to *Wh* heading the main clause. Like other interrogative clauses—for example, *He knew whom you thought that she could see*—a nominal in a simple declarative clause may be similarly attached to the *Wh* of a main clause in the formation of a relative clause: *The leader whom you thought that she could see left.* The same freedom of attachment to sentence-initial *Wh* holds for infinitive and gerund complements of the verb, which are not included in the abbreviated grammar that follows but whose description would in no way be incompatible with that grammar (for example, *Whom could you force her to speak with?* and *Whom could you try speaking with?*). Constituents located within relative clauses and interrogative clauses, however, are not attached to a *Wh* before the main clause; i.e. the following are not sentences: **Who could the leader whom spoke with leave?* from the permissible string *Wh – the – leader – whom – he – spoke – with – could – leave*, by the unpermissible attachment, in questions, of a *he* located within the subordinate clause to *Wh* heading the main clause; also **Who could he ask whom spoke with?* from *Wh – he – could – ask – whom – he – spoke – with.*

Such differences in the behavior of declarative clauses, as compared to relative and interrogative clauses, can be accounted for in the formal grammatical description by ordering the transformational rule that describes declarative clauses before the rule for *Wh* attachment, and by ordering the transformational rules describing relative and interrogative clause formation after the *Wh* attachment rule.

Other facts of English necessitate an ordering of the relative-clause rule and the interrogative-clause rule with respect to one another: a constituent within an interrogative clause is not attached to sentence-initial *Wh* to form a relative clause; for example, **The leader whom he asked who could speak with her left* from *The – leader – left* on the one hand and *Wh – he – asked – who – could – speak – with – the – leader* on the other, as an unpermissible source of a relative clause in which the pronominalized form of *the – leader* is attached to *Wh*. Thus, the rule that describes relative clauses (providing for *Wh*-attachment of a pronominalized substantive identical to an antecedent substantive in the main clause and for the embedding of questions with subordination) must precede the rule describing the embedding of questions.

Accordingly, the order of the subordinate-clause rules and the *Wh*-attachment rule for questions would be as follows:

(8.01) i.   Declarative clause embedding
       ii.   *Wh*-attachment for questions
      iii.   Relative clause formation
       iv.   Interrogative clause embedding

9. Prepositional phrases. In the first three styles, at any rate, there are two possible treatments of prepositional phrases, with respect to *Wh*-attachment in questions, interrogative clauses, and relative clauses. The whole prepositional phrase may occur at the front of the sentence (*With whom did he speak?*) or the substantive alone may occur there (*Whom did he speak with?*). The two possibilities can be accounted for in terms of two analyses of a sentence to which *Wh*-attachment is to apply: first, the latter sentence results from the analysis already discussed in §5, whereby a pronoun is taken from its location in a simple sentence (including location after a preposition) and attached to an initial *Wh*;

second, the former sentence requires an extension of *Wh*-attachment to include also the sequence *Prep – Pronoun*, that is, *Wh – he – spoke – with – she* + **Case** $\Rightarrow$ *Wh* + *with – she* + **Case** (+*that*) *he – spoke*. It should be noted that major constituents in general are attachable to *Wh*. The attachment of the various adverbials not treated in this study result in *where, when, why, how*. The attachability of prepositional phrases to *Wh* is then just another aspect of this general grammatical feature. As with the other instances of *Wh*-attachment, the whole constituent is attached to the right of *Wh*, thus necessitating an additional rule for correctly locating the preposition to the left of *Wh* and its attachment (preposition placement rule); that is, *Wh* + *with – she* + **Case** (+*that*) *he – spoke* $\Rightarrow$ *with – Wh* + *she* + **Case** (+*that*) *he – spoke*.

The necessity of an additional operation to resolve the sequence *Wh* + *Prep – Pronoun* resulting from *Wh*-attachment is not, however, an indication of arbitrariness in the formulation of *Wh*-attachment, for the sequence serves also to prevent the reduction, in relative clauses, of *with whom* to *with that on a par with the permissible reduction of *whom*, when not preceded by a preposition, to *that*; for example, *The man whom I spoke with left*; *The man that I spoke with left*; *The man with whom I spoke left*; but not **The man with that I spoke left*. Thus after the rule for *Wh*-attachment and relative-clause formation but before the rule for preposition placement, there is a rule applicable to relative clauses but not to interrogative clauses (consult footnote 5 for further differences): *Wh* + *he* (+**Case**) + *that* $\Rightarrow$ *that*. The sequence *Wh* + *prep – Pronoun* (+**Case**) + *that* is thus correctly excluded from this rule and the absence of the reduction of *who(m)* to *that* after prepositions is incorporated in the grammar rules in a natural way.

10. Coordinate conjunction.   Conjoined forms like (3.02) *He and I left* can be considered the result of the replacement of a plural subject by any number of other compatible subjects. From the sentence *He – left* and the sentence *I – left* the subjects conjoin by means of *and* and replace the plural subject of *We – each – left* to yield *He – and – I – each – left*. In L_1, the marked or unmarked (as to **Case**) quality of the pronouns is carried over into conjunction. The reason for resorting to a third sentence with a plural substantive in conjoining two substantives, rather than simply combining them, is that, in the product of the conjoining operation, elements occur that are not proper to the unconjoined source sentences and that cannot, like *and*, readily be attributed to the conjoining operation itself. Such, for example, are constituents like *both* and *each*, as well as the plural ending of the verb with conjoined subjects that are singular in number. (*He and John are both here* like *They are both here* but not *He is both here). In the present analysis, the grammatical number of nominal constituents will be treated as a separate constituent (*leader* will be represented as *leader – Sg* and *leaders* as *leader – Pl*). Conjoined substantives, each along with its own individual number constituent, will be analyzed as transformationally replacing a nominal constituent (to wit, a pronoun) that occurs before the plural number constituent *Pl* (that is, *Pronoun – Pl* ends up as *John – Sg – and – the – leader – Sg – Pl*). The original *Pl* marker is left intact. Thus additional transformational phenomena dependent on the presence of plural number in a nominal constituent can be accounted for without the presence of a plural substantive; among such phenomena is the number agreement of the finite verb with the subject.

11. The grammar of the first style.   In the grammar comprising the rules for generating the sentences of L_1, the constituent structure level, abbreviated to the special demands of the present study, has the following general appearance. The rules provided here are to be considered a segment of a total grammar. It is assumed that other facts of the language can be accounted for by the mere addition of new rules or, at any rate, without any basic changes in the rules proposed in this study.

(11.01) $S \rightarrow (Wh)$ *Subject – Predicate*

(11.02)   *Predicate* $\rightarrow$ *Tense* $(V^m) \begin{Bmatrix} V^s \\ Verb\ (Nominal) \end{Bmatrix} (Prep - Location)$

(11.03)(a)   *Subject – Tense* $(V^m)\ V^s \rightarrow it - Sg - Tense\ (V^m)\ V^s$
       (b)   *Subject* $\rightarrow$ *Nominal*

(11.04)   *Verb – Nominal* $\rightarrow \begin{Bmatrix} V^t \\ V^p - Prep \end{Bmatrix}$ *Nominal*

(11.05)   *Verb* $\rightarrow \begin{Bmatrix} V^c - Complement \\ V^i \end{Bmatrix}$

(11.06) $V^s \rightarrow be$

(11.07) $V^t \rightarrow \begin{Bmatrix} hit \\ ask \\ see \\ know \end{Bmatrix}$

(11.08) $V^p \rightarrow speak$

(11.09) $V^c \rightarrow \begin{Bmatrix} believe \\ think \\ know \end{Bmatrix}$

(11.10) $V^i \rightarrow leave$

(11.11) $V^m \rightarrow can$

(11.12)   *Tense* $\rightarrow \begin{Bmatrix} Past \\ Present \end{Bmatrix}$

(11.13)   *Complement* $\rightarrow so$

(11.14)   *Prep – Location* $\rightarrow near - Location$

(11.15)   *speak – Prep* $\rightarrow speak - with$

(11.16)   *Location* $\rightarrow \begin{Bmatrix} there \\ Nominal \end{Bmatrix}$

(11.17)   *Nominal* $\rightarrow \begin{Bmatrix} Pronoun - Number\ (Modifier) \\ \begin{Bmatrix} John \\ the\ leader \end{Bmatrix} Number \end{Bmatrix}$

(11.18)   *Number* $\rightarrow \begin{Bmatrix} Sg \\ Pl \end{Bmatrix}$

(11.19)(a)   *Pronoun – Sg* $\rightarrow \begin{Bmatrix} someone \\ something \end{Bmatrix} Sg$

       (b)   *Pronoun* $\rightarrow \begin{Bmatrix} I \\ he \\ she \\ it \end{Bmatrix}$

(11.20) $I - Pl - Modifier \rightarrow I - Pl - two$

The transformational rules, in their appropriate order, that account for the grammatical features associated with case, are the following:

(11.21)   I.   *Case marking:* $\begin{Bmatrix} V^t \\ Prep \end{Bmatrix}$ *Pronoun* $\Rightarrow$ $\begin{Bmatrix} V^t \\ Prep \end{Bmatrix}$ *Pronoun* + **Case**

II.   *Wh*-attachment and embedding (in which (a²) optionally becomes (a³) to form interrogative word questions): (a), (b), and (c) are embedded in (d), (f), and (e) as indicated, to yield (d¹), (e¹), and (f¹); (a¹) becomes (a³) in connection with relative clause formation (e), the *Nominal* of (a¹) representing a pronominalized appropriate case-marked constituent otherwise identical to the nominal of (e). The order of the rule is that given in §8.

$$\begin{Bmatrix} (a^1) & Wh - X \begin{Bmatrix} Prep - Nominal \\ Nominal \end{Bmatrix} Y \\ (a^2) & Wh - X \begin{Bmatrix} Prep - Pronoun + \textbf{Case} \\ Pronoun\ (+\ \textbf{Case}) \end{Bmatrix} Number - Y \end{Bmatrix} \Rightarrow$$

$$(a^3) \quad Wh + \begin{Bmatrix} Prep - Pronoun + \textbf{Case} \\ Pronoun\ (+\ \textbf{Case}) \end{Bmatrix} Number - X - Y$$

$$S^1 \begin{Bmatrix} (a) & \text{(the result (a}^3) \text{ of } Wh\text{-attachment on (a}^1) \text{ or (a}^2)) \\ (b) & Wh\text{-}Subject - Predicate \\ (c) & Subject - Predicate \end{Bmatrix}$$

$$S^2 \begin{Bmatrix} (d) & \text{(embedding (c)} \ldots think - so \\ (e) & \text{(embedding (a}^1) \text{ via (a}^3) \ldots Nominal \\ (f) & \text{(embedding (a}^3), \text{ (b)} \ldots know - it \end{Bmatrix} \Rightarrow$$

$$S^3 \begin{Bmatrix} (d^1) & \ldots think - \textbf{that} - Subject - Predicate \\ (e^1) & \ldots Nominal - Wh + \begin{Bmatrix} Prep \ldots \\ Pron \ldots \end{Bmatrix} Number + \textbf{that} - X - Y \\ (f^1) & \ldots know - Wh + \begin{Bmatrix} Prep \ldots \\ Pron \ldots \end{Bmatrix} Number + \textbf{that} - X - Y \end{Bmatrix}$$

What precedes is a general characterization of the main rules involved in the formation of question and subordinate clauses. The rules are grouped according to the nature of the transformational operations involved, not according to their actual order of application.[6]

---

[6]This follows the analysis suggested by Chomsky, *Syntactic Structures*, p. 69, [*MSE* pp. 59–60]. Elsewhere (pp. 69 and 112) he loosens the formulation, attaching *Wh* to the more general constituent *noun phrase*. (See also Lees, *A Grammar of English Nominalizations*, p. 36). Harris treats the attachments of *Wh* as pro-morphemes, whose full forms appear in the corresponding assertion; see Zellig Harris, "Co-occurrence and Transformation," *Language*, 33.3 (1957) [*SL*]. While for the purposes of the present study I allow *Wh* questions to be based on the personal pronouns, as a more precise analysis I would propose deriving questions (but not relative clauses) from sentences in which the pronoun to be attached to *Wh* is one of the indefinites: *someone, anyone, somebody, something*, etc. In this way, certain features of questions, direct and indirect, containing interrogative words (though not of relative clauses) would be accounted for; e.g. *Who else left?* like *Someone else left; Whom did he see of importance* like *He saw someone of importance.* If we consider **Case** applicable also to the indefinites (**Case** has no phonological form with *someone*, just as it has none with *it*), the rest of the analysis need not be changed essentially. Similarly, the relative *which*, derived from *Wh* + *it* (+ **Case**)–*Number*, will have a natural basis of differentiation from the interrogative *what*, which, according to the improved analysis, is derived from *Wh* + *something* (+ **Case**)–*Sg*.

III.   Conjoining: S^1: $X - Nominal - Y$
S^2: $X - Nominal - Y$
S^3: $X - Pronoun \ (+ \textbf{\textit{Case}}) \ Pl - Y$

$\Rightarrow X - Nominal - \textbf{\textit{and}} - Nominal - Pl - Y$

where the constituents represented by a given cover symbol (X or Y) are the same in all three sentences, except for the constituents of S^3 mentioned in §10, and where *Nominal* includes *Number* and may include **Case.**

IV.   Preposition placement: $Wh + Prep - Pronoun \Rightarrow$
$Prep - Wh + Pronoun$

V.   *Wh*-attraction:
$Wh \ (+ \ Pronoun + \textbf{\textit{Case}} - Number) \ Subject - Tense \ (V^m) \ Verb \Rightarrow$
$Wh \ (+ \ Pronoun + \textbf{\textit{Case}} - Number) \ Tense \ (V^m) \ Subject - Verb$

Other rules carry into sentences the string emerging from the phrase-structure level, along with operators accumulated in the transformational level:

(11.22)   *Tense*-attachment: $Tense - \bar{V} \Rightarrow \bar{V} + Tense$

(11.23) do – support: $- Tense \Rightarrow do + Tense$

(11.24) $Wh + Pronoun - Number \ (+ \textbf{\textit{that}}) \Rightarrow who$
$Wh + Pronoun + \textbf{\textit{Case}} - Number \ (+ \textbf{\textit{that}}) \Rightarrow whom$
$Wh + \textbf{\textit{that}} \Rightarrow whether$

(11.25) $Wh - X \Rightarrow X$

(11.26) $I + \textbf{\textit{Case}} - Sg \Rightarrow me$
$he + \textbf{\textit{Case}} - Sg \Rightarrow him$
$I - Pl \Rightarrow we$
etc.

(11.27) $do + Past \Rightarrow did$
$can + Past \Rightarrow could$
$speak + Past \Rightarrow spoke$
etc.

Similar rules would attach *Pl* as *s* to an immediately preceding noun and ultimately remove all other number markers. Thus the dangling *Pl* resulting from the rule of conjoining at (11.21, III) is removed with the same operation that removes the empty *Sg* (singular) after nouns in English, and to this extent is no more arbitrary; that is, *leader – Pl ⇒ leader + s*, and then the rule $X - Number \Rightarrow X$.

12. The second style as an extension.   Consider now L_2, one variety of standard, colloquial English. To account for the sentences of L_2 proceeding from the grammar of L_1, a rule (E_{1-2}) must be added to the latter that reduces clause-initial *whom* to *who*. The case form, however, is retained in L_2 when *whom* is preceded by a preposition, as in (3.09) (*With whom* . . .) versus (3.10) (*Who . . . with*). The extension E_{1-2} occurs after *Wh*-attachment but before preposition placement, thus leaving . . . *with whom* . . . So $G_1 + E_{1-2}$ (the G_1-based grammar of L_2) has the following difference in appearance:

(12.01) $L_1 + E_{1-2}$:   . . .

III.   *Wh*-attachment
E_{1-2}. $Wh + Pronoun + \textbf{\textit{Case}} - Number \Rightarrow Wh + Pronoun -$
$Number$

IV. *Preposition* placement

　. . .

13. The grammar of the second style.   Though the extended set of rules above, given G_1, accounts for the sentences of L_2, the very same sentences (from the point of view of L_2 independently) are most economically described by a grammar (G_2) differing from that of L_1 by the order of transformational rules. In G_2, the rule of case marking depends on the position of the elements of the sentences as they occur after *Wh*-attachment. The difference in order of rules reflects the fact that while in L_1 case marking is dependent on function (namely on whether or not the element is a grammatical object), in L_2 **Case** is a concomitant of position, reckoned only after certain rearrangements of the basic order of elements. In L_2 **Case** is not associated with functional elements, if, at a particular point in the sequence of ordered transformational rules, those elements happen not to be situated after (that is, to the right of) the factors motivating **Case**-attachment. Other things being equal, the grammar G_2 consists of the same phrase-structure rules as G_1, but the order of the transformation rules is as follows:

(13.01) G_2: I.　*Wh*-attachment
　　　　　　II.　Case marking
　　　　　III.　Conjoining
　　　　　IV.　*Preposition* placement
　　　　　　V.　*Wh*-attraction

14. The third style as an extension. L_3 differs from L_2 in containing a further extension of the positional determination of **Case** to cover also the predicative use of the personal pronouns, that is, when they follow V. Position here as elsewhere is reckoned after *Wh*-attachment. Accordingly, (3.05) *It was me* is case-marked in L_3, but (3.11) *Who was it?* and (3.14) *. . . who it was . . .* are not marked. Extension E_{2-3} has the following effect on G_2.

(14.01) $G_2 + E_{2-3}$: I.　*Wh*-attachment

　　　　　　　　　　II.　Case-marking: $\begin{Bmatrix} V^t \\ Prep \end{Bmatrix}$ *Pronoun – Number* $\Rightarrow$

　　　　　　　　　　　　　$\begin{Bmatrix} V^t \\ Prep \end{Bmatrix}$ *Pronoun +* **Case** *– Number*

　　　　　　E_{2-3}. V^s *– Pronoun – Number* $\Rightarrow$
　　　　　　　　　V^s *– Pronoun +* **Case** *– Number*
　　　　　III.　*Conjoining*

　. . .

15. The grammar of the third style.   In G_3, the difference attributable to E_{2-3} is represented by the extension of case marking to all pronouns following verbal form $\bar{V}$, such that **Case** becomes entirely a positional feature without functional reference. The phrase structure of G_3 remains the same, as does the ordering of transformational rules. In terms of the class of units $\bar{V}$, the generalization is expressed simply as

(15.01) G_3: . . .
　　　　　II.　Case marking:
　　　　　　　$\begin{Bmatrix} Prep \\ \bar{V} \end{Bmatrix}$ *Pronoun – Number* $\Rightarrow$ $\begin{Bmatrix} Prep \\ \bar{V} \end{Bmatrix}$ *Pronoun +* **Case** *– Number*

　　　　　　. . .

The ordering of *Wh*-attraction after case marking accounts for the fact that in the final form assumed by sentences, the unmarked form also occurs regularly after a $\bar{V}$, for example, *Has he left?*; *Who is he?* When case marking applies to these sentences, however, they have the form *Wh – he – has – left* and *Wh + pronoun – he – is*.

16. The fourth style as an extension.   If we examine the sentences of L_4 from the point of view of G_3, the L_4 sentences manifest a further extension of case marking to all pronominal forms before *Tense*, except for interrogative-relative *who* and unconjoined pronouns directly adjacent to *Tense*:

(16.01) $G_3 + E_{3-4}$:   I. *Wh*-attachment
             II. Case marking
         III. Conjoining

$$E_{3-4}. \quad \textit{Pronoun} - \textit{Number} \begin{Bmatrix} \textbf{\textit{and}} \\ \textit{Pl} \\ \textit{Numeral} \end{Bmatrix} \Rightarrow$$

$$\textit{Pronoun} + \textbf{\textit{Case}} - \textit{Number} \begin{Bmatrix} \textbf{\textit{and}} \\ \textit{Pl} \\ \textit{Numeral} \end{Bmatrix}$$

             IV. *Wh*-attraction

In L_4 and to some extent even in L_3, when we go beyond the limited number of constructions treated *explicitly* in this study, the contexts in which **Case** is added, with respect to previous grammars, are more diversified than would appear from (16.01) (explicitly because I would claim that the inclusion of those constructions is, in all other instances, only a matter of detail). Not included are absolute constructions (*Must of been almost a month 'n me thinking, hoping, that Doc was all in the past. . .*[7]) and various types of ellipses (*Who's the ugliest guy in the jail? . . .Me* and *Who's to take care of him if not me?*[8]). Given these and various other individual extensions, a shorter description is ultimately achieved by the addition of the following two rules as E_{3-4}:

(16.02) $G_3 + E_{3-4}$:   I. *Wh*-attachment
             II. Case marking
         E'_{3-4}.   Extension of case marking to all *Pronouns* not attached to *Wh* (i.e. not preceded by +):
                – Pronoun – Number ⇒ *Pronoun – **Case** – Number*
         III. Conjoining (E'_{3-4} and conjoining may occur in either order)
         E''_{3-4}.   *Pronoun + **Case** – Number Tense* ⇒ *Pronoun – Number – Tense*

                . . .

In the structure resulting from conjoining, the constituent *Pl*, which represents the number of the constituent replaced by the conjoined nominals, leaves a string to which E''_{3-4} (16.02) does not apply, and to which case marking in G_4 will not apply. In the derivation of (3.02) in L_4, for example, at the point of the second

---

[7]Algren, *The Neon Wilderness*, p. 153.
[8]Algren, *The Man with the Golden Arm*, pp. 14 and 84.

extension to $G_3 + E_{3-4}$, the string has the shape *him – Sg – and – me – Sg – Pl – Tense – leave*.

The situation in (16.01) invites comparison with the single rule treated as E_{2-3} (see (13.01)), to which are similar the many differences in case-marking contexts lumped together in E_{3-4}. When added separately in some arbitrary order and in such a way that each individual extension results in a separate L with its own G, no one of the differences between L_3 and L_4 entails more than a simple extension of context, just as is the case in E_{2-3}. At some point, however, in the series of individual E's and resultant G's between L_3 and L_4, one (or certain) of the G's will reveal a major structural difference compared to the preceding G's; and further individual differences leading to L_4 are in terms of this structurally different G. In other words, what is treated here as L_4 should perhaps more realistically be regarded, say, as L_6 in a hypothetical series L_3, L_4, L_5, L_6, each with its own grammar (G_3, G_4, G_5, G_6). The special form of the two-rule E_{3-4} at (16.01) would then result from trying to describe directly in terms of L_3 all the differences between L_3 and the hypothetical L_6—differences preceding and following at least one G (in the series G_3 through G_6) that manifests a fundamental structural difference, say G_5.

The interrogative conjunction *whether* appears not to occur in L_4 in sentences like (3.13); it seems to be replaced here entirely by *if*. Similarly, L_4 has no sentences containing a preposed preposition with a relative-interrogative like . . . *with whom he spoke* ((3.09), (3.17), (3.19)). Additional extension rules will be required to eliminate such constructions. Extension rules of this type, however, are different in nature from those already proposed; I shall go no further into the problem in this paper.

17. *The grammar of the fourth style.* Grammar G_4 differs from $G_3 + E_{3-4}$ in its rules at both the transformational and the phrase-structure level. The base forms of the personal pronouns emerging from phrase structure are those previously resulting from combination with the case markers. The order of the transformational rules is different; case marking now occurs later in the grammar even than conjoining and is limited in application, as regards the personal pronouns, to position immediately before the finite verb. The ultimate positional nature of case marking in L_4 thus does not observe even the very weakly functional principle of similarity involved in conjoining. If sentences like (3.09) (*With whom did he speak?*) and (3.19) (. . . *with whom he spoke* . . .) are admitted in L_4, the marking of the relative-interrogative form remains essentially the same as in G_3. In that case, while the marked forms of the personal pronouns yield *I, he, they*, etc., that of the interrogative-relative yields *whom*.

It would lead to greater homogeneity of style and would certainly be more consistent with the usage in the sample corpus not to admit as part of L_4 the sequence of preposition plus *whom* in . . . *with whom he spoke* . . . as in (3.09) and (3.19). Then in G_4, *Wh*-attachment will analyze the string *Wh – he – spoke – with – Pronoun* only as *Wh – . . . Pronoun* and not also as *Wh – . . . Prep – Pronoun*, as in the other grammars. From this point of view consider constructions like *John, according to whom we were at fault, would not condone such action*, as well as related ones not discussed here like *The concert during which he slept was a great success*; that is, constructions of L_1, etc., which do not permit the separation of the preposition from its object in relative clauses. If such inseparable prepositional constructions are not considered a part of L_4 either, *Wh*-attachment is simplified and preposition placement is omitted from the grammar, as are operations involved in realizing the form *whom*. Rules that are unnecessary when L_4 is considered in this way are bracketed below.

In L_4, as in the other systems, case marking applies before the inverted order characteristic of direct questions. This accounts for the presence, in certain sentences, of *I, he, they*, etc., after the finite verb. Seeming exceptions to the rules of case marking in G_4 like (3.04) in S_4 (*We all left*), or *They each left* versus *Us two left* are best explained on the basis of the special structural position of words like *each* and *all* in these sentences—namely, that though grammatically restricted by the nature of the nominal, these forms are constituents rather within the predicate of the sentence, as is seen in the expanded form *They have all left* varying with *They all have left*.

The structure of G_4 shows the following differences from the preceding styles:

(17.01)   *Pronoun* $\rightarrow \begin{Bmatrix} me \\ him \\ her \end{Bmatrix}$

(17.02)   (Same as (11.24) in G_1):
           Wh + Pronoun – Number (+ ***that***) $\Rightarrow$ *who*
           [*Wh* + *Pronoun* ***Case*** – *Number* (+ ***that***) $\Rightarrow$ *whom*]

(17.03)   *me* + ***Case*** – *Sg* $\Rightarrow$ *I*
           him + ***Case*** – *Sg* $\Rightarrow$ *he*

The transformations accounting for the introduction of ***Case*** in G_4 and for the ultimate word order of the sentences now have the following form and order.

(17.04)   I.   *Wh*-attachment
           II.   Conjoining
           III. [Preposition placement with case marking:
                 Wh + *Prep* – *Pronoun* – *Number* $\Rightarrow$ *Prep* – *Wh* + *Pronoun* + ***Case*** – *Number*]
           IV.   Case marking: – *Pronoun* – *Number* – *Tense* $\Rightarrow$ – *Pronoun* + ***Case*** – *Number* – *Tense* (the sequence – *Pronoun* . . . differentiated from + *Pronoun* . . . , that is, the rules do not apply to *Wh* + *Pronoun*). See the paragraph after (16.02) for the absence of case marking with conjoined subjects.
           V.   *Wh*-attraction

18. Summary.   The preceding study has examined in sequence four systems. A given system and the one following it in the sequence are compared to see how the differences between them, in terms of the sentences that each contains, are reflected in their individual grammars. An operation common to the four systems —the attachment, motivated by position, of a marker (***Case***) to a certain class of words (*Pronouns*)—is found to manifest a progressively weaker relationship to function. Table 2 summarizes the phrase structure differences and the differences in the ordering of the main transformations involved.

TABLE 2

	L$_1$	L$_2$	L$_3$	L$_4$
	Pronoun → *I, he, she, it*			*Pronoun* → *me, him, her, it*
I	Case marking	*Wh*-attachment	*Wh*-attachment	*Wh*-attachment
II	*Wh*-attachment	Case marking	Extended case marking	Conjoining
III	Conjoining	Conjoining	Conjoining	[Preposition placement]
IV	Preposition placement	Preposition placement	Preposition placement	Case marking
V	*Wh*-attraction	*Wh*-attraction	*Wh*-attraction	*Wh*-attraction

APPENDIX A
ON PRIORITY IN COMPARING STYLES

At the end of §2, I claim that the adopted direction and pairing of systems offers the shortest extensional rules. To verify that claim, compare the length of E$_{1-2}$ (12.01) with that of the additional case-marking rules that would be necessary, after case marking in G$_2$, to account for the sentences of G$_1$:

$$G_2 + E_{2-1}: \quad \text{I.} \quad \textit{Wh}\text{-attachment}$$
$$\text{II.} \quad \text{Case marking}$$

E_{2-1}. *Wh* + *Pronoun – Number – Subject – Tense* (V^m)

$$\begin{Bmatrix} Verb \\ Verb - Prep \end{Bmatrix} \Rightarrow Wh + Pronoun + \textbf{\textit{Case}} - Number - Subject -$$

$$Tense \ (V^m) \begin{Bmatrix} Verb \\ Verb - Prep \end{Bmatrix}$$

III. Conjoining

. . .

The extreme length of E$_{2-1}$ is necessary in order to correctly mark the interrogative-relative for case in preclausal position, where the following conditions at least must be met: (*a*) the *Subject* must follow the *Pronoun*, that is, the *Pronoun* is not itself *Subject* and therefore is not case-marked; (*b*) the constituent *Verb* must occur, that is, the main verb is not *be*; (*c*) there must be a preposition without object. The progressive tense forms necessitate further specification in order to pass from L$_2$ to L$_1$, since otherwise *Wh* + *Pronoun – Number – Subject – Tense – is* would be ambiguous: it might represent . . . *is – hitting* or it might represent the copula *be*. Even lengthier specifications would be necessary when relative clauses like the following are considered: L$_2$ *The man who they claim John hit* compared with L$_1$ *The man whom they claim John hit*. (See also Appendix B.)

E$_{2-3}$ (14.01) is an exception to the proposed principle of economy in selecting the primary system in extension rules, since E$_{2-3}$ is of the same length as extension rules that proceed rather from G_3 to G_2. The lack of superiority of one analysis over the other can be attributed to the trivial nature of the differences between G_2 and G_3. The inconsistency would be resolved by passing directly from L_1 to L_3, that is, in combining in one extension the effect of E_{1-2} and E_{2-3}. While I have observed some differentiation in usage consistent with separate treatment of the two phenomena, there is probably not sufficient reason to speak of a distinct style. On the other hand, there is historical justification for this separation.[9]

APPENDIX B
MULTIPLE EMBEDDING

The accumulation and duplication of declarative, interrogative, and relative clauses and their multiple overlapping, with one another and with elements of simple interrogative structures, present only an apparent contradiction to the ordered set of rules describing *Wh*-attraction and embedding, discussed in §8 and characterized generally at (11.21) II: Rule i Declarative clause embedding; Rule ii *Wh*-attachment for questions; Rule iii Relative-clause formation; Rule iv Interrogative-clause embedding. A sentence like the following is an example; its complexity is dictated by the need to illustrate the various possibilities of multiple embedding.

(B1)   *Who said that I asked what John thinks that the people whom you like who enjoy the game which you enjoy talk about ?*

Complex sentences like this, whose description is intimately connected with the order of the grammar rules discussed in §8, are accounted for if their derivation is considered in the following way. Sentences—in the form they have at some stage in their derivation prior to the four operations above, describing *Wh*-attachment and embedding—are arranged in chains. Each chain consists of a finite number of sentences. Each of the rules, in the order given above, runs up the particular chain of sentences and is applied where appropriate. With transformations operating with two sentences (that is, with binary transformations), like the various types of embedding, the result of a given transformation becomes a new lower member, which, paired with the next sentence in the chain, is subject to the same binary transformation; for example, by Rule iii below (for relative-clause formation), (de) as lower member, paired with (c), results in (cde); (cde), in turn, becomes the new lower member which, paired with (b), results in (bcde). The description of (B1) would include the following chain of sentences to which the formal transformation rules apply. In the chain, *someone* and *something* in (d) and (g) replace the personal pronouns in the derivation of interrogative word questions in accordance with footnote 6; the repeated nouns in (a), (b), and (c) resulting in relative pronouns are assumed to have undergone pronominalization and, subsequently, the case marking appropriate to the style in question, which in (B1) is that of L_1.

(B2)(a)   *Wh – you – enjoy – the – game* ⇒ *Wh – you – enjoy – it* + **Case**
   (b)   *Wh – you – like – the – people* ⇒ *Wh – you – like – they* + **Case**
   (c)   *Wh – the – people – enjoy – the – game* ⇒ *Wh – the – people – enjoy – it* + **Case**
   (d)   *the – people – talk – about – something*
   (e)   *Wh – John – thinks – so*

[9]Karl Brunner, *Die englische Sprache*, 2.104 (Halle, 1950–1951).

(f)   *I – asked – it*

(g)   *Wh – someone – said – so*

As the four ordered rules run up the chain from (g) to (a), they apply to the sentences in the following way. Sentences or pairs of sentences unaffected by the rule in question are bracketed.

(B3) Rule i: [a], [b], [c].

  (d – e).   *Wh – John – thinks – that – the – people – talk – about – something*

  (f – g).   *Wh – someone – said – that – I – asked – it*

Rule ii: [a], [b], [c].

  (de).   *[Wh + something]$_{what}$ John – thinks – that – the – people – talk – about*

  (fg).   *[Wh + someone]$_{who}$ said – that – I – asked – it*

Rule iii: (a – bcde).   *what – John – thinks – that – the – people – whom – you – like – who – enjoy – the – game*
  [Wh + it + Case – that]$_{which}$
  you – like – talk – about

  (b – cde).   *what – John – thinks – that – the – people*
  [Wh + they + Case – that]$_{whom}$
  you – like – who – enjoy – the – game – talk – about

  (c – de).   *what – John – thinks – that – the – people*
  [Wh + they – that]$_{who}$ enjoy – the – game – talk – about

  [fg].

Rule iv: (abcd – fg).   *Who – said – that – I – asked – what – John – thinks – that – the – people – whom – you – like – who – enjoy – the – game – which – you – like – talk – about*

The same chain will result in several different sentences. Because of the optional quality of Rule ii, for example, the chain of sentences at (B2) may result also in *[Wh – ⇒ Ø] did someone say that I asked whether [Wh + that ⇒ whether] John thinks that the people whom you like who enjoy the game which you enjoy talk about?* Moreover, it may happen that a particular chain composed of the same sentences as in (B2) but in another order will never result in a single sentence but rather in several sentences—for example, if sentence (a) in (B2) comes after (g). In the latter case, the chain will yield *[Wh – ⇒ Ø] did – you – enjoy – the – game?* and, among other possibilities, *Who said that I asked what John thinks that the people whom you like who enjoy the game talk about?* Given the order in which the rules apply, the former sentence is never capable of having the next sentence up the chain—that is, (g)—embedded in it.

APPENDIX C
SYMBOLISM

→ describes phrase structure rules; $x → y$ reads "x is written as y."

A hyphen indicates simple concatenation.

+ indicates connection.

$x – z → y – z$ is a phrase structure rule restricted by context: "x is rewritten y in the context z."

( ) indicate the optional presence of a constituent and imply simple concatenation: $x(y)$ reads "x alone or the sequence $x - y$."

Braces indicate a selection of one and imply simple concatenation.

$\Rightarrow$ describes transformational rules; $[x - y]_z \Rightarrow [y - w - x]_a$ reads "The structure represented by any sequence $x - y$ that is a z is convertible into the sequence $y - w - x$, which is itself an a."

Symbols of transformational origin are written in boldface italic: *that, and, Case.* This practice is mnemonic only.

$[x - y]_z$ is an extrasystemic mnemonic device which reads "$x - y$, which ultimately is represented by z."

A right angle at the lower right indicates a transformation whose source includes two or three sentences; the result appears below or to the right of the angle.

Transformations within brackets, without subscripts, indicate that the sentences have already undergone those transformations; brackets without subscripts are also used extrasystemically for various expository purposes.

The symbols, whether letters (V^i or Sg) or words (*Verb*), represent formally motivated structural elements in the analysis of sentences. No symbol is postulated if it does not account for a grammatical difference, that is, if it does not result in some difference in the shape of sentences generated by the grammar. (This is in keeping with the notion of simplicity presented in §2.)

A line above a symbol indicates that it is an extrasystemic abbreviating device; for example, $\bar{V}$ is the list of all verb forms to which *Tense* is attached.

Roman numerals indicate the relative order of transformational rules.

Successive minuscules indicate indifference as to order.

Arabic numerals order phrase-structure and morphophonemic rules, but the abbreviated version presented here is crude and only approximate.

X and Y are cover symbols for whatever (including nothing at all) occurs in a given position.

16

Determiners and Relative Clauses in a Generative Grammar of English

CARLOTA S. SMITH

1. Introduction. This paper will discuss some ramifications of the rules for producing noun modifiers in English. Most noun modifiers can be accounted for in a generative grammar by three transformational rules.[1] The first of these adjoins a sentence to a noun as a relative clause, and the other two form postnominal and prenominal modifiers by the operations of deletion and order change respectively. These three transformations will be referred to as embedding rules.[2] They are applied once, in order, to a given sentence, and adjoin that sentence to a noun phrase as modifier. Not every noun phrase can accept a relative clause, however; for the embedding rules to work properly the grammar must include certain constraints on their application. The determiner of the noun phrase is the decisive element in the acceptance of relative clauses.

Traditionally, grammarians have recognized two kinds of determiners: *the*, usually called the definite determiner, and *a*, usually called the indefinite determiner. It is now common to regard other elements as determiners, or as parts of determiners: mass nouns (such as *sincerity* and *butter*) and proper names are said to have determiners that are phonetically zero. Further, it is convenient to regard *all*, *any*, and the like as part of the determiner (these items are frequently

---

Reprinted from *Language*, 40.37–52 (1964), by permission of Carlota S. Smith and the Linguistic Society of America.

This work was supported in part by the National Science Foundation.

[1] The generative grammar that is the frame of reference for this paper is that developed primarily by Noam Chomsky; see his *Syntactic Structures* ('s-Gravenhage, 1957) and later papers. I would like to thank Chomsky, Lila Gleitman, and Hugh Matthews for helpful discussions of this paper.

[2] For a detailed discussion of the embedding rules see C. Smith, "A Class of Complex Modifiers in English," *Language*, 37.342–65 (1961).

called predeterminers). And finally, prenominal genitives such as *his* and *John's* are shown to behave as determiners by transformational criteria. Speakers make distinctions of definiteness and indefiniteness for all noun phrases, not just those with the determiners *the* or *a*. For instance, *John* is said by many speakers to be more definite than *the man*, which is in turn more definite than *any man*; *my book* is more definite than *the book*. When the class of determiners is extended to include other items besides *the* and *a*, the traditional categories of definite and indefinite do not cover all the new cases. At least three categories are mentioned in the preceding sentence.

The traditional categories of determiners are inadequate not only in speakers' intuition but also in a generative grammar. Certain transformations, e.g. the embedding rules, require that at least three classes of determiners be set up. The classes of determiners formed in respect to the embedding rules differ semantically in that the members of one class are more (or less) definite than the members of another. *The, any*, and *John*, for instance, belong to different classes. Speakers' intuition about the definiteness of determiners, then, corresponds to the classification necessary for the embedding rules.

2. Phrase structure rules for determiners.   There are two kinds of relative clause: restrictive, with *Wh* directly following the noun, and appositive, with *Wh* separated from the noun by comma or comma intonation. They will be referred to as *R* and *A* relatives respectively. Consider now a group of sentences where both kinds of relatives occur, and not all of which are grammatical.

A Rel (1)   *John, who knows the way, has offered to guide us.*
R Rel (2)   **John who is from the South hates cold weather.*
A Rel (3)   *They pointed to a dog, who was looking at him hopefully.*
R Rel (4)   *They pointed to a dog who was looking at him hopefully.*
A Rel (5)   **Any book, which is about linguistics, is interesting.*
A Rel (6)   *The book, which is about linguistics, is interesting.*
R Rel (7)   *Any book which is about linguistics is interesting.*
R Rel (8)   *He lives in a skyscraper that is twenty stories high.*
R Rel (9)   *The man who fixed the radio left this note.*

The examples show that not all noun phrases accept both kinds of relative clause. Grammaticalness depends on the determiner of the containing noun phrase[3] and the kind of relative that occurs with it. Sentence (5) is ungrammatical; but (6), identical except for the determiner, is grammatical; and sentence (7), like (5) except that the relative clause is restrictive, is grammatical also.

There are, then, selectional restrictions between determiners and relative clauses. When the restrictions are stated, three classes of determiners emerge: those accepting only *A* relatives, those accepting both *A* and *R* relatives, and those accepting only *R* relatives. These classes correspond to an intuitive classification of determiners as to definiteness; definiteness is associated with *A* relative clauses, indefiniteness with *R* relative clauses. The three classes are named *Unique, Specified*,

---

[3]"Containing" sentences dominate "contained" sentences: in *The ball that he bought is blue* the containing sentence is *The ball is blue*, the contained is *He bought the ball*.

and *Unspecified*, to indicate that they are distinct from the traditional definite and indefinite determiners: with *R* relatives, *Unspecified* determiners occur: *any, all*, etc.; with *R* and *A* relatives, *Specified*: *a, the*, $\emptyset$; with *A* relatives only, *Unique*: $\emptyset$ (proper names). The traditional distinction occurs in the rules that produce determiners, since it is needed at other points in the grammar.

Determiners are developed by expansion rules at the phrase-structure level of the grammar. An additional element, a relative marker, will be produced as part of the determiner. Determiners will have *R* and/or *A* relative markers when they can accept *R* and/or *A* relative clauses. The relative transformation will be applicable only to noun phrases that have the appropriate relative markers, and will adjoin sentences as relative clauses to the markers. Phrase structure rules to produce determiners with the appropriate relative markers follow; only those determiners immediately relevant to the embedding rules are included here.

Noun phrase	$\rightarrow$ *Determiner* + *Substantive*
	Proper Name + (*A*)
Determiner	$\rightarrow$ *Specified* + (R) + (A)
	Unspecified + (R)
Proper name	$\rightarrow \emptyset$
Specified	$\rightarrow$ (*Predeterminer*) + $\begin{array}{l}\textit{Definite}\\\textit{Indefinite}\end{array}$
Unspecified	$\rightarrow \begin{array}{l}a\\\textit{Predeterminer}_1\end{array}$
Definite	$\rightarrow$ *the* (+ *Intensifier*$_1$ if no *A* and no *Predeterminer*)
Indefinite	$\rightarrow$ *a* (+ *Intensifier*$_2$ if no *A* and no *Predeterminer*)
Predeterminer$_1$	$\rightarrow$ *each, every, some, all, any*, etc.
Intensifier$_1$	$\rightarrow$ *very* etc.
Intensifier$_2$	$\rightarrow$ *mere, utter, perfect, real*, etc.

The optional expansion to *Intensifier* needs some explanation. *Intensifier* is the name given here to a small class of modifiers, e.g. *mere, utter*. These words are so different from adjectives as to require separate treatment, and can be effectively developed as part of the determiner.

Intensifiers differ from adjectives in that they do not occur in the kernel structure *Noun Phrase is Adjective*; they do not behave as noun constituents under transformations; they do not occur with *R* relative clauses in a noun phrase. The last two facts point to their status as determiners. There are selectional restrictions between intensifiers and determiners, although they are relatively weak; compare

(10) *A mere child stood before him.*

(11) **The mere child stood before him.*

(12) *The very thought amazed her.*

(13) **A very thought amazed her.*

Finally, note that predeterminers and intensifiers are mutually exclusive:

*three of the mere children
*some utter fools

Therefore the phrase structure rules provide that certain determiners are optionally expanded to include either predeterminers and *R* markers or intensifiers. Two classes of intensifiers are set up: 1 occurs with the definite determiner, 2 with the indefinite determiner.[4]

3. The relative clause transformation.

One sentence may be embedded to another as a relative clause if the two sentences share a noun phrase, as Harris and many others have pointed out. A noun phrase will be said to be "shared" for two sentences if the substantive of the noun phrase and the relative markers of the noun phrase are identical in both sentences. Note that in this interpretation shared noun phrases need not be identical, since the specified category of determiners has more than one member. (The section below on genitives will give some reasons for this.)

The relative transformation has no direction: if two sentences share a noun phrase, either may be embedded to the other as a relative clause.

The relative transformation adjoins a sentence to a marker as a relative clause. Markers are produced after determiners in the phrase structure rules, yet relative clauses occur after nouns. Before a clause is adjoined to a noun phrase it is convenient to move the markers to postnominal position; to allow for this change, the relative transformation is written in two parts. The first part of T relative (the relative transformation) is applied to the shared noun phrase in the containing sentence, and affects only the relative marker(s). It shifts the marker(s) beyond the noun and changes the structure of the noun phrase, moving the markers from the "determiner" to the "noun phrase" node of the descriptive tree.

The second part of the relative transformation adjoins relative clauses to the appropriate markers.

The R relative rule adjoins a relative clause to the left of an R marker. Notice that it leaves the R marker, thus allowing for further adjunctions. If T relative is applied to a noun phrase already containing a relative clause, only the adjunction part of the transformation applies. A morphophonemic rule will provide that in the final representation of the sentence the R marker is phonetically zero.

The A relative rule replaces an A marker with a relative clause enclosed by commas or comma intonation. Only one A relative clause may be embedded to a noun phrase.

SKETCH OF RELATIVE TRANSFORMATION[5]

I. Order change

Structure: $X + Determiner + Marker + Noun + Y$
$$1 \qquad 2 \qquad\quad 3 \qquad\quad 4 \qquad 5$$

where *Marker* is R and/or A

---

[4]An exception must be made for intensifiers occurring with nouns like *fact, theory, idea*. Intensifiers usually occurring only with *a* may occur with *the* before such nouns. These nouns are exceptional on other grounds also: the transformation adjoining a sentence to a noun with *that* applies only to them. Note that this transformation does not apply when the noun has an R relative clause, nor when its article is indefinite.

The mere fact that he went surprised me. (*Intensifier, that + S*)

*A mere fact that he went surprised me. (same)

*The mere fact that he unearthed surprised him. (*Intensifier, R relative*)

[5]The transformation must be stated in greater detail, according to the structure of the contained sentence and the role played in it by the shared noun phrase. Cf. Edward S. Klima, "Relatedness Between Grammatical Systems," *Language*, 40.1–20 (1964) [*MSE*]. For simplicity, since these points are not relevant here, I assume that the shared noun phrase is the subject of the contained sentence.

Change: 1 2 4 3 5

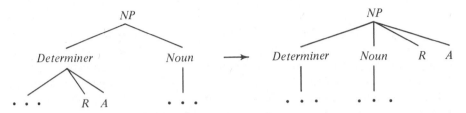

II. *R* relative adjunction

   Structure: S_1: *X Y Z (R) (A) W*
                 1 2 3 4   5 6
             S_2: *X Y (R) (A) Z W*
                 7 8 9 10 11 12

   Conditions: (i) 4 is not null
              (ii) $3 + 4 + 5 = 9 + 10 + 11$
              (iii) $2 \ldots 5$ is *NP*

   Change: 1 2 3 *Wh* 12 4 5 6

   A-relative adjunction

   Structure: same as above

   Conditions: (i) 5 is not null
              (ii) $3 + 4 + 5 = 9 + 10 + 11$
              (iii) $2 \ldots 5$ is *NP*

   Change: 1 2 3 4, *Wh* 12, 6

4. The deletion transformation. The deletion transformation optionally deletes *Wh* from certain relative clauses. When applied to *R* relatives it produces post-nominal modifiers and intermediate structures from which prenominal modifiers are formed. When applied to *A* relatives it produces truncated *A* relatives; that is, the comma separating the clause from its noun remains.

Deletion of *Wh* (or *Wh is*) from *R* relative clauses produces the following post-nominal modifiers:

Prepositional phrase:

(14)   *He married a girl (who is) from Texas.*

Sentence:

(15)   *I know a man (whom) George knows.*

(16)   *He saw a man (who was) walking in the park.*[6]

Adjective + complement:

(17)   *He climbed a mountain (that is) higher than Everest.*

Adjective and intermediate form:

(18)   *I heard something (that was) odd.*

(19)   *I have a hat (that is) green.* (T-order change must be applied.)

To provide for the production of only grammatical sentences, certain restrictions must be made on the transformation. Not all relative clauses accept deletion.

For noun phrases with *Specified* determiners indefiniteness is associated with postnominal position and definiteness with prenominal position. If a noun has

---

[6]This sentence has more than one reading; see §5.

a definite determiner its adjectival modifiers either precede or are adjoined to it with the relative *Wh*. Since adjectival complements only follow a noun, adjectives with complements cannot be directly adjoined to a noun phrase with a definite determiner.[7] An *R* relative clause of the form *Wh is Adjective + Complement* is available for the deletion transformation only if the determiner in the containing noun phrase is not definite. Here the grammar calls for distinction betweeen *a* and *the* as definite and indefinite determiners (they are both of the *Specified* category).

The deletion transformation does not apply when an *R* relative clause has the form *Wh is Noun Phrase* or *Wh Verb X*. These structures must be excluded to avoid ungrammatical sentences like these:

(20) **I know a man a chemist.*

(21) **I know a man knows George.*

Wh is may be deleted from certain *A* relative clauses, e.g. those of the form *Wh is Noun Phrase* and *Wh is Adjective + Complement*. These are just the forms that are not available for deletion in *R* relative clauses.

(22) John, *(who was)* a good salesman, charmed them immediately.

(23) The girl, *(who was)* bored, yawned delicately.

The deletion rule correctly allows that more than one *R* relative clause may directly follow a noun. As I have noted above, an R relative clause may be embedded to a noun phrase already having an *R* relative clause, and to a noun phrase having prenominal or postnominal modifiers that have been produced by the embedding rules.

Two *R* relatives:

(24) *John met a man[1] who was from New York[2] who had never been to the top of the Empire State Building.*

R relative and postnominal modifier:

(25) *John met a man[1] from New York[2] who had never been to the top of the Empire State Building.*

R relative and prenominal modifier:

(26) *I caught a[1] white rabbit[2] that had escaped from its cage.*

Certain combinations are excluded: prepositional phrases and adjectives with complements directly follow the noun, and no deleted relative (without *Wh*) follows *V + ing + P N*. *Wh is* may be deleted from relatives of the form *Noun Phrase is Adjective* only if the clause directly follows the noun, since the order-change rule is obligatory for lone adjectives (see next section).

Sketch of deletion transformation

Structure: (i)   *W Determiner R Noun X Wh is Y Z*

$$\underbrace{}_{1} \quad \underbrace{}_{2} \quad \underbrace{R\ Noun\ X}_{3} \quad \underbrace{Wh\ is}_{4} \quad \underbrace{}_{5} \underbrace{}_{6}$$

Conditions:

(a) if X is not null, $\begin{Bmatrix} Y \\ X \end{Bmatrix}$ is not $V + ing + Q$

---

[7]Adjectival complements are phrases or clauses dependent on a preceding adjective (*blue in the face, taller than George*, etc.). For a detailed discussion see the paper mentioned in footnote 2.

(b) if Y is not $V + ing + Q$, X is null

(ii) $W \; \underbrace{Indef \; Det}_{} \; X \; \underbrace{Noun}_{} \; \underbrace{Wh \; is}_{} \; \underbrace{Adj + Comp}_{} \; Y$

      1   2   3   4   5   6

Condition:

if $Adj + Comp$ is comparative, *Noun* in *Comp* is not indefinite

(iii) $W \; Determiner \; \underbrace{X \; Noun}_{} \; Y \; Wh \; NP \; Z \; R$

      1   2   3   4   5   6

(iv) $W \; Determiner \; \underbrace{X \; Noun}_{} \; Y, \; \underbrace{Wh \; is}_{} \; \left\{ \begin{array}{l} NP \\ Adj \; (+ \; Comp) \end{array} \right\}, \; Z$

      1   2   3   4   5   6

Change: delete 4

5. The order-change transformation.

5. *The order-change transformation.* The third embedding rule moves adjectives from postnominal to prenominal position, and must be applied to any lone adjective following any noun unless that noun is indefinite. It is optional for postnominal adjectives with complements. (By postnominal I understand elements directly following the noun—that is, without the relative *Wh*.) Thus the order-change transformation applies to a relative clause only if the transformation has been applied to it.

No special provision is made for the occurrence of $V + ing$ and $V + ed$ in postnominal position, although sentences having these forms after the noun do occur. The verbal forms in postnominal position do not come from relative clauses and therefore are produced by other transformational rules than the ones discussed here. Consider, for instance, the following sentences:

(27)   *John saw the man running.*

(28)   *John saw the letter opened.*

If *running* and *opened* were the result of deletion of *Wh* from a relative, it should be possible to embed an *R* relative clause to the preceding noun. However, the embedding of *R* relatives to the object nouns of (27) and (28) produces ungrammatical results:

(29)   **John saw the man running who wore a black homburg.*

(30)   **John saw the letter opened which was from Mary.*

The sources for (28) and (29) are not sentences with relative clauses, then, but rather the following:

Source for (28):   *John saw the man while he (John) was running.*
                         John saw that the man was running.
Source for (29):   *John saw the letter being opened.*

I have given the order-change rule in some detail elsewhere (footnote 2); here I will merely sketch it.

SKETCH OF ORDER-CHANGE TRANSFORMATION

Obligatory
   Structure: $X \; Determiner \; \underbrace{Y \; Noun}_{} \; Adjective \; Z \; W$

                1   2   3   4   5 6

       Conditions:

         (a) 4 and 5 are not constituents

(b) *Noun* in 3 is not indefinite

Change: 1 2 4 3 5 6

Optional

Structure: *X Determiner Y Noun Adjective Comp Z*

     1 2 3 4 5 6

Change: 1 2 4 3 5 6

The optional rule specifies that in certain cases 4 precedes the determiner rather than the noun. Further optional rules are applicable under certain conditions to the complements of adjectives.

The remaining sections of the paper give some additional rules and restrictions that show the scope of embedding rules to extend beyond the noun modifiers previously discussed. The additions will not change the rules but rather relate them to genitives, predicate sentences, and the negation and question transformations. The correct production of these constructions will be shown to depend in part on the embedding rules.

6. Possessive genitive constructions.   Among the determiners mentioned at the beginning of the paper, but not developed in the phrase structure rules, are prenominal genitives like *John's* and *his*. This section presents a transformational derivation for prenominal genitives that relates them to other possessive genitive (henceforth genitive) constructions and to other sentences of the language in an economical and natural manner. All genitive constructions will be derived from a basic genitive transformation and certain variations on the embedding rules. The constructions to be accounted for are these:

(31)   *The hat is John's.*

(32)   **A hat is John's.*

(33)   *... the hat which is John's ...*

(34)   *... a hat which is John's ...*

(35)   *... a hat of John's ...*

(36)   *... the hat of John's ...*[8]

(37)   *... John's hat ...*

From a source sentence a possessive genitive transformation will produce simple genitive sentences like (31). This transformation will be introduced in the sequence of transformational rules so that it precedes the embedding rules; the other genitive constructions will result from the operation of the embedding rules (with certain variants). When the embedding rules have been applied successively to a sentence formed by the genitive transformation, all genitive constructions will have been formed.

The genitive transformation will produce sentences like (31) from source sentences with *have*. It will operate in roughly the following manner:

T-genitive

Structure: *Noun phrase have Determiner Substantive*

     1   2   3   4

Change: *The 4 is 1's*

---

[8]Some speakers find this construction unacceptable. For them the rule that produces (37) from (36) is obligatory (see below).

The source of (31) according to this derivation is thus (38):

(38)   *John has a hat* →

(31)   *The hat is John's.*

Note that the transformation specifies that the definite determiner *the* occur in the subject noun phrase of a genitive sentence. Sentences identical except that they have the indefinite determiner in this position are ungrammatical (for instance, (32) above). It is not exceptional for a transformation to specify that the definite determiner occur in the resultant sentence. Other transformations that do so are nominalizations (*the shooting of hunters; *a shooting of hunters*) and the adjunction of a sentence to a noun (*the fact that he did it; *a fact that he did it*). These are cases previously mentioned in the grammar.

The relative transformation, applied to a sentence resulting from T-genitive and a sentence with which it shares a noun phrase, will produce genitive relative clauses. Sentence (31) yields either (33) or (34), the relative transformation operating as outlined in §3.

S_1: . . . *the hat* . . .
S_2: *The hat is John's.*   → *S*: . . . *the hat which is John's* . . .

S_1: . . . *a hat* . . .
S_2: *The hat is John's.*   → *S*: . . . *a hat which is John's* . . .

Note that in the second example the containing sentence has the indefinite determiner *a*. Although genitive sentences obligatorily have *the* as the determiner in the subject noun phrase, they occur as relatives in noun phrases with either *a* or *the*. The formation of both relatives is allowed by the relative transformation, since it is applicable to sentences with shared noun phrases. (Noun phrases are said to be shared if they have identical substantives and identical relative markers; *a* and *the*, both of the *Specified* category, both have optional *R* and *A* relative markers.)

Postnominal genitives ((35) and (36) above) will be formed by a variant of the deletion transformation, applied to genitive relative clauses. The direct postnominal modifiers previously considered are formed by deletion of *Wh* or *Wh is* from a relative clause. For the postnominal genitive, however, *Wh is* must be replaced by *of*. An obligatory rule applicable only to genitives will introduce this constant if the deletion rule has been applied. The rule will have roughly this form:

T-deletion II (obligatory after deletion transformation)
   Structure: *X Determiner Y Noun Genitive Z*
                     1   2   3   4
   Change: 1 2 *of* 3 4

Applied to (33), the deletion transformation and the obligatory addition will thus correctly form the postnominal genitive (36) (and similarly for (34) and (35)):

   S: . . . *the hat which is John's* . . . → *S*: . . . *the hat of John's*

An extension of the third embedding rule, order change, will form genitive determiners from postnominal genitives. As a prenominal the genitive has two unique characteristics: it behaves as a determiner, and does not allow further embedding of *R* relative clauses. Within the framework of the embedding rules both of these characteristics are easily provided for. An addition to the order change transformation, applicable only to genitives, will replace the determiner of a noun phrase by a genitive. It will also delete both the *R* marker and the constant *of*. Note that although *R* relatives do not occur in noun phrases with a prenominal genitive, prenominal genitives occur with *A* relatives and with nouns that have prenominal modifiers. The latter are formed by earlier applications of the embedding rules to the *R* marker that is deleted by the genitive order-change transformation. Thus (38) and (39) are grammatical, but (40) is not.

(38) ... *the man's old car* ...

(39) ... *the man's car, which he bought last year* ...

(40) * ... *the man's car that he bought last year* ...

The second genitive transformation will have the following form.

T-Genitive order change
  Structure: *X Determiner Y Noun of Genitive R (A) Z*
                 1   2   3   4   5   6 7 8
  Change: 1 5 3 7 8

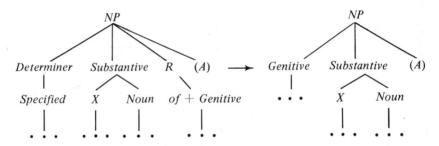

This transformation will correctly produce sentence (37) from (36):

   S: ... *the hat of John's* ... → S: ... *John's hat* ...

This account of the possessive genitive construction is based directly on the phrase structure and embedding rules set up previously. The rules allow the embedding of genitives to a shared but not necessarily identical noun phrase, and the simple blocking of *R* relatives after prenominal modifiers and a prenominal genitive have been formed. Both of these are crucial steps in the production of genitives.

7. Predicate sentences.   I come now to a rule that makes fine distinctions with respect to relative clauses and determiners. The sentences to which the rule applies are not usually rejected out-of-hand by native speakers, but it is generally said that they are somewhat odd. One might say that the sentences are only marginally ungrammatical, or, alternatively, that the rule distinguishing them is a marginal rule. As might be expected, marginal rules have a limited domain and few ramifications.

The sentences to be discussed below have *is* as their main verb. They will be referred to as predicate sentences, and sentences with other verbs will be referred to as common sentences. Predicate sentences differ from common sentences in many respects; their differences are so fundamental that they are distinguished in both phrase structure and obligatory transformational rules of the grammar. In applying the embedding rules to predicate sentences I have found that they must be distinguished from common sentences in this area as well as others previously noticed.[9] The embedding rules, then, contribute to a characterization of predicate sentences.

Consider the following sentences, all of which have specified determiner *the* in the object noun phrase. (41)–(43) are said to be odd or incomplete by speakers, but the same sentences with *R* relatives embedded to the object (44)–(46) are no longer said to be odd.

(41) *John is the linguist.*

(42) *The janitor is the philosopher.*

(43) *My sister is the doctor.*

(44) *John is the linguist who spoke at the meeting.*

(45) *The janitor is the philosopher with whom I discuss Kant.*

(46) *My sister is the doctor who cured Allan.*

It seems, then, that predicate sentences must contain *R* relative clauses if they have certain *Specified* determiners in the object position. If the object noun phrase has *the*, it is obligatory that a relative clause be embedded to it. Constraints on the subject or object noun phrases of particular verbs are not unusual in a grammar; for instance, a certain class of verbs requires plural subjects. Note that this constraint distinguishes predicate sentences from common sentences with respect to the embedding rules: it is not necessary to distinguish either subject or object position for the latter, and T-relative is always optional for them.

It has often been noticed that predicate sentences with the sequence of determiners *a Noun is the Noun* are unacceptable, while any sequence of determiners may occur in common sentences. Sentence (47) is unacceptable in this way:

(47) **A janitor is the philosopher.*

The proposed addition excludes this sentence in its present form: it must have an *R* relative clause with the predicate noun phrase.

The subject and predicate noun phrases of a predicate sentence have different constraints with respect to relative clauses; according to the preceding discussion, they may be said to differ in definiteness. The predicate noun phrase stands alone only when it has the indefinite determiner; moreover, *A* relatives (which are associated with definiteness) are not embedded if it has the indefinite determiner, as the following sentences show.

(48) **He is an anthropologist, who studies Indian tribes.*

(49) **He is an anthropologist, whom I met at a party last week.*

Additions must thus be made to the embedding rules, specifying that (*a*) the *R* relative transformation be obligatory for sentences with a certain structure, and

---

[9]Some rules that differentiate between *is* and common verbs are given in *Syntactic Structures* and by R. B. Lees, *The Grammar of English Nominalizations* (*International Journal of American Linguistics,* 26:3 Part 2, 1960).

that the sentence embedded be a common sentence; and (*b*) the *A* relative transformation must be blocked for sentences with a certain structure. Common
sentences with *Specified* determiners may contain *R* or *A* relative clauses, but
certain predicate sentences obligatorily contain *R* relatives and others exclude *A*
relatives. To produce these sentences the grammar must have relatively fine
distinctions among determiners (within the *Specified* category) and must distinguish subject and predicate positions. In terms of the interpretation I have
given, subject and predicate noun phrases in predicate sentences must be at certain
degrees of definiteness, while common sentences impose no such restriction. One
may conclude that *is* is less definite than a common verb, or that common verbs
contribute a certain element of definiteness to their subjects and objects.

8. Negation and questions.   This section will show that negation and questions
are, to a certain extent, associated with indefiniteness in English.

Between certain transformations there is a mutual block: if one is applied the
other is not, and vice versa. Such a relationship holds between negation and
the A relative transformation. If the object of a verb has an *A* relative clause the
sentence is not negated; and if the subject has undergone negation, *A* relative
clauses are not embedded to object or adverbial-object noun phrases. For instance,

(50) **He didn't eat the mango, which I bought for him yesterday.*

(51) **He didn't eat the mango, which was overripe.*

(52) **He didn't write a novel, which was published by McGraw-Hill.*

(53) **He did not use the air mattress, which belongs to the Halls.*

This restriction applies only to objects and certain adverbials. Thus the following
negated sentences, whose subjects have *A* relative clauses, are grammatical.

(54)   *The American contestant, who broke training, did not win the race.*

(55)   *The novel, which was published by McGraw-Hill, was not successful.*

The restriction is related to the fact that sentences are negated in English in
the predicate. The only way to negate an entire sentence is to use an impersonal
construction, for example *It is not the case that* + *Sentence*. The scope of a negative includes the entire predicate of a sentence, but *A* relative clauses are beyond
the scope of the main verb, which is the keystone of the predicate. Thus in the
predicate of a sentence the *A* relative and negation transformations are mutually
exclusive.

The block on *A* relative clauses includes other negatives, such as *rarely* and
never. (The relationship between various negative constructions has been pointed
out by Jespersen, and most recently by Edward S. Klima.[10])

(56) **No antique dealer, who had any sense, wanted to buy the table.*

(57) **John rarely spades his plot, which he planted last spring.*

(58) **We never go to the opera house, which is in Boston.*

Certain question transformations and the *A* relative are also mutually exclusive.
The question transformations involved are those whose scope extends to the

---

[10][See Edward S. Klima, "Negation in English," in *SL*.]

entire predicate of a sentence. In (59) and (60) the verb is questioned and the object has an *A* relative clause; in (61) and (62) the subject is questioned and the object has an *A* relative clause.

(59) **Did he paint a mural, which hangs in the Hotel Prado?*

(60) **Did John, who is a journalist, write a novel?*

(61) **Who ate the mango, which Eleanor bought yesterday?*

(62) **Who wrote a novel, which was published by McGraw-Hill?*

The scope of the question transformation extends to an entire sentence if its subject is questioned. If the object is questioned, however, the subject may have an *A* relative clause: *Did the accident, which was quite serious, upset them?*

Mutually exclusive transformations are handled simply in a generative grammar, since its rules are ordered. The later transformation will not apply if the earlier option has been taken. Since questioned and negated sentences allow fewer transformations than those with relative clauses, the rules will be ordered so that T-relative precedes the question and negation transformations. The *A* transformation removes the *A* relative marker; the necessary restrictions can easily be made by the statement that negation and question transformations do not apply to a given string unless an *A* marker occurs in the appropriate noun phrase.

Throughout this discussion I have associated *A* relative clauses (or the possibility of embedding them) with definiteness, and *R* relative clauses (similarly) with indefiniteness. The mutually exclusive transformational relationships associate questions and negation with *R* relatives, that is, with indefiniteness. They also give further support to the general interpretation. *A* relative clauses are outside the scope of transformations that affect a whole sentence, and therefore they are in a sense independent of the noun phrases to which they are embedded. The semantic intuition about *A* relative clauses is that they are maximally definite; the restrictions shown above give a formal version of this intuition.

NOTE ON THE GENERIC DETERMINER "THE"

The following discussion is concerned with sentences that are said to be generic, or to have a generic determiner; the two formulations are usually used almost interchangeably: a sentence that has a generic determiner is a generic sentence. The determiner in question is *the* with singular affix. To set the stage I give as examples two sentences said by many speakers of English to be generic.

(1)   *The cat is a mammal.*

(2)   *The country doctor is highly respected in the American small town.*

In the first sentence, *the* is generic; in the second, both occurrences of *the* are generic.[11]

Some traditional grammarians (Jespersen, Kruisinga, and Curme among them)

---

[11]A generic noun is usually taken to be a noun that is grammatically a count noun but semantically a mass noun. Thus in the first example *the cat* refers to a class of cats rather than a particular cat.

give special mention to sentences like these, saying that here the determiner *the* has a general sense, whereas it usually has a particular sense. In other words, in certain cases they give a special interpretation of *the*. Recently some formal treatments of English determiners have suggested a category of generic determiners, presumably to account for such sentences. Both Lees and Sørensen,[12] for instance, think that special grammatical rules are necessary to account for generic sentences. It seems, however, that this step is superfluous: generic sentences are produced by a grammar of English without any special provision for them. Generics may be considered the name given to a particular interpretation of the definite article; an inquiry about them asks what circumstances allow this interpretation and what circumstances preclude it. The analysis offered here agrees with that of traditional grammarians; it is concerned especially with drawing the line between grammar and its interpretation.

The assumption that generic determiners must be accounted for separately in a grammar rests on a prior assumption that generic determiners, or sentences that contain generic determiners, have certain properties such that they must be differentiated grammatically from other sentences. But this is a misapprehension, apparently; generic sentences do not in fact differ from others.

In the first section of this paper certain determiners were shown to have restrictions with respect to relative clauses, and were classified according to their acceptance of relative clauses. If generic determiners were unlike others, one might expect them to need a special classification; but none is needed. *The* in generic sentences behaves exactly as provided for in the *Specified* category; both particular and generic *the* accept both restrictive and appositive relative clauses. In terms of the distinctions previously found necessary for determiners, then, generics do not form a separate class.

Generic determiners are sometimes said to be unlike others in that they are incompatible with certain tenses. Sørensen, for instance, states that the perfect tenses and generic determiners are mutually exclusive, or incompatible. But the sense in which he uses "incompatible" is an unusual one. He says not that sentences with generic determiners and main verb in a perfect tense are ungrammatical, but that they are not generic. Sørensen's test is as follows: he takes sentences accepted as generic (whose verbs are not in a perfect tense); he changes the tense to perfect, and then finds that the sentences are "no longer" acceptable as generic. This sense of incompatibility is quite special. Usually elements are said to be incompatible when their combination results in sentences that are odd or ungrammatical, for instance,

(3) *He will go home yesterday.*

In Sørensen's examples a change in tense does not produce odd sentences but sentences which are not usually interpreted in the particular manner under consideration; that is, they are not usually taken to be generic sentences:

(4) *The early bird catches the worm.*

(5) *The early bird caught the worm.*[13]

---

[12]See R. B. Lees, "On the Constituent Structure of English Noun Phrases," *IBM Research*, 1961 [*American Speech*, 36.160–168 (1961)]; H. G. Sørensen, *Word Classes in Modern English* (Copenhagen: Gad, 1958).

[13]The possibilities of this example seem to depend on extralinguistic knowledge; if *bird* were changed to *dinosaur*, for instance—*The dinosaur caught the worm*—the sentence might be acceptable as generic in a book about the habits of dinosaurs.

According to Sørensen's view the second version of the proverb is not interpreted as generic because it has a perfect tense. The proposed restriction on generics and tenses does not hold, however, if lexical items are chosen with reasonable care. Among the examples of generic sentences that follow several have perfect tenses. The changes Sørensen notes in sometimes generic sentences are changes from one interpretation to another, not from a grammatical sentence to an ungrammatical one.

The statement was made earlier that the grammar will produce all generic sentences without any special provision for them. The grounds for the statement are partly that all generic determiners can be interpreted as either generic or particular, depending on the context; they are in a certain sense ambiguous. This sentence, for instance, can be interpreted as generic: *The cat is a hunter;* but if the context is a discussion of a particular cat the sentence will be interpreted as referring to that particular cat, and *the* as definite rather than generic. If there are no properties which characterize generic sentences uniquely, and if all instances of the generic determiner can be taken as instances of the definite determiner, the rules for producing sentences with definite determiners will also produce generics. Consider now a group of sentences which have been said by speakers to be interpretable as either generic or particular. Sentences with different structures are included in the group.

(6) *The potato, which was the principal foodstuff in Peru, was unknown in Mexico.*

(7) *London has no place for the cafe.*

(8) *The radio has not yet extinguished reading.*

(9) *The airplane is superseding the railroad.*

(10) *The early bird will catch the worm.*

(11) *The corporation was a force to be reckoned with in medieval society.*

(12) *The automobile had been replaced by the friendly robot.*

(13) *The Lord Mayor's Show brought out the suburbanite in full force.*

(14) *The rogue belongs to no class.*

(15) *The beaver will take a singular place among the animals who have molded the face of the earth.*

(16) *The dinosaur was killing off the smaller animals.*

(17) *English huntsmen regard the fox as an animal to be envied.*

If the foregoing is correct, an account of generic sentences will give rules of interpretation rather than rules of syntax. It is appropriate to look for rules, since presumably generic sentences are understood in a consistent way. Two general interpretations of *the* are usually distinguished. A noun if previously mentioned is taken as particular, and its determiner is the definite or anaphoric *the*; a noun if taken as a class noun or as typical class member is generic, and its determiner is the generic *the*. "Previous mention," on which the anaphoric use of *the* depends, is a loose term that covers a variety of grammatical and contextual cases. The model case is a pair of sentences in which the definite article in the second sentence is said to be dependent on the previous sentence: *I saw a man. The man was scowling.* It has been persuasively argued by Beverly Robbins[14] that the definite article is

---

[14]"The Transformational Status of the Definite Article in English," *Transformation and Discourse Analysis Projects*, No. 38 (University of Pennsylvania, 1961). Mrs. Robbins discusses the definite article in great detail, giving many examples of both anaphoric and generic *the*.

anaphoric in noun phrases with relative clauses, with the relative clause constituting previous mention. In certain kinds of prose, especially in fiction, *the* may be used for a particular noun and the sentences following it may be equivalent in effect to previous mention. *The* is also used with uniques—*the sun* is a favorite example—where previous mention consists of the extra-linguistic knowledge that there only is one. This is only a sketchy beginning of a catalog of anaphoric *the*, but it is enough to indicate the wide range of cases subsumed under this term.

Generally, the generic determiner can be characterized in contradistinction to the definite determiner: generic determiners are simply those that are not anaphoric. Since anaphoric *the* cannot always be established syntactically, an interpretative rule based on the grammar must classify many occurrences of *the* as ambiguous—that is, it must allow either a generic or an anaphoric interpretation. An interpretative rule can apparently do no more than exclude (as definitely not generic) instances where the grammar points to an anaphoric interpretation of *the*. In such cases *the* cannot be interpreted as generic (the second sentence below), even though in other contexts the same sentence may be interpretable as generic.

(18) *Harry has a dog. The dog is vigilant.*

If the scope of "anaphoric" is taken to include knowledge that is beyond the range of the grammar (for instance, knowledge of uniques), many other occurrences of *the* will be interpreted as clearly not generic. Roughly, a narrow rule for the interpretation of the definite article might be this: if there is grammatical previous mention, the determiner *the* must be interpreted as anaphoric; if not, *the* may be interpreted as either generic or anaphoric.

Sentences taken as generic do not have a characteristic structure, as the preceding examples show. Moreover, there are some constructions by which many sentences not taken as generic may become available for generic interpretation. Sentence adverbials of certain types frequently allow generic interpretation. Thus the following sentence is usually not taken as generic; but when it has adjoined to it one of the sentence adverbials listed below it, it is usually taken as generic.

(19) *The cocker spaniel hunted for food.*

(20) *In olden times,*

(21) *Before house pets became fashionable,*

(22) *When not fed at home,*

(23) *During . . . ,*

In fact it seems that almost any sentence can be made a possible generic sentence by the addition of one of these sentence adverbials (with the proper lexical choice). This is, incidentally, another argument against setting up a separate generic determiner in the grammar. Adverbials like those above—*during the middle ages, before 1066, under the reign of Elizabeth*—may be said to "frame" a sentence, and sentences so framed may be taken as generic.

Framing adverbials allow generic interpretation of sentences which apparently have grammatically anaphoric determiners. In the following example the second sentence has a framing adverbial and an ambiguous *the*; the determiner can be interpreted either as anaphoric or as generic.

(24) *A shepherd approached. In earlier times, the shepherd wore picturesque costume.*

In the light of this example and others like it, the interpretive rule suggested must be modified to allow a generic reading of *the* in sentences with framing adverbials and contexts with grammatical previous mention. The modification might read: (*a*) The determiner *the* may be interpreted as either anaphoric or generic if there is no grammatical previous mention, or if the sentence in question has a framing adverbial; (*b*) If there is grammatical previous mention and the sentence in question has no framing adverbial, the determiner *the* must be interpreted as anaphoric.[15]

These are no more than sketches of rules. No precise account of "grammatical previous mention" has been given; it is frequently (as here) taken to mean the occurrence of two noun phrases with identical substantives, the first having the determiner *a* and the second the determiner *the*. But, as mentioned earlier, various subtle factors may establish previous mention that is difficult if not impossible to trace syntactically. An even more serious objection to the interpretive rules suggested is that sentences that may be generic are rarely taken as ambiguous; contexts wider than a sentence usually establish their interpretation. In a dramatic setting, a sentence such as *He played the fool* might be clearly anaphoric, referring to a certain part in a certain play; while in another situation *the fool* might be taken as generic. In the light of all this, the sketchy rules here given do not explicate very much. They do give some content, perhaps, to the notions of an interpretation allowed by the grammar and an interpretation not allowed by the grammar. They also underline the necessity for distinguishing between grammar and interpretation of grammar in the analysis of sentences.

---

[15]A careful study would add to such an interpretive rule as this. For instance, *the* in object position is not taken as generic if the subject noun phrase is a proper name.

17

English Relativization
and Certain Related Problems

S.-Y. KURODA

1. It seems rather a remarkable fact that the words that are used as interrogative pronouns are also used as relative pronouns. Thus, the form

(1) *which lay on the table*

may be an interrogative clause as in

(2) *Which lay on the table, the bread or the cake, was the issue.*

and a relative clause as in

(3) *The material which lay on the table was the tissue.*

The pronoun *what*, too, possesses the relative use as well as the interrogative. The two uses of *what* are contrasted in the examples given in Lees (1960):

(4) *What lay on the table was the issue.*
(5) *What lay on the table was the tissue.*

What used as in (5) is called an independent relative pronoun, since it apparently lacks an antecedent.[1]

Reprinted from *Language*, 44.244–266 (1968), by permission of S.-Y. Kuroda and the Linguistic Society of America.

Most of this work was carried out at the Research Laboratory of Electronics, M.I.T., and was supported in part by Joint Services Electronics Programs, the National Science Foundation, the National Institute of Health, the National Aeronautics and Space Administration, and the U.S. Air Force.

[1]The human, place, and time *Wh*-words *who*, *where*, and *when* are also used either as interrogatives or as relatives. However, unlike the nonhuman case, these *Wh*-words as relatives may be used either with an antecedent or independently, except for *who*, whose independent relative use is archaic; see §4 below. We say simply *nonhuman* to mean *nonhuman, nonplace, nontime*.

How deep is the significance of this fact? On the one hand, one could assume that it is a mere accident; the interrogative *which* and the relative *which*, or the interrogative *what* and the relative *what*, are generatively unrelated words which happen to have the same phonetic shape, like *bank* (of a river) and *bank* (where one saves money). On the other hand, one might be able to assign certain common semantic characteristics to these two kinds of pronouns; their morphological identity would then be a natural consequence of their semantic identity.

The current transformational analysis of relativization in English seems to fall between these two extremes. Indeed, it postulates the same marker *Wh* for relativization and for interrogation. The basic[2] form of (3) would be given as[3]

(6) *the material (Wh the material lay on the table) was the tissue*

But no serious attempt seems to have been made to relate semantically this occurrence of the marker *Wh* to its use as the interrogative marker. Rather, the marker has been regarded as simply representing certain common formal characteristics involved in relativization and interrogation.

However, the common formal characteristics which are currently supposed to be captured by postulating the same marker *Wh* for these two different constructions seem to be restricted to the area of syntax in the narrow sense, and no care has been taken to account for common *morphological* characteristics involved in them. To be more specific, both in relativization and interrogation the *Wh*-word is to be preposed, and postulating the identical marker *Wh* for both of these constructions, one transformation will suffice to take care of the preposing in both cases; the marker *Wh* can be regarded as representing this common syntactic characteristic of preposing the *Wh*-word. On the other hand, current transformational analysis of English makes no claims concerning the morphological identity of the interrogative and relative pronouns. Indeed, not much has been said about the derivation of the phonetic form of the relative pronoun *which* other than that a later morphophonemic rule derives it from the marker and certain syntactic feature specifications for the noun following the marker; a rule essentially equivalent to

(7) *that which → what*

seems to have been considered as a rule to derive the independent relative pronoun *what*. Neither relates in any deeper sense the derivation of these relative pronouns to that of the homonymous interrogative pronouns.

Suppose the forms *whech* and *whet* are used as relative pronouns in place of *which* and *what*, but not as interrogative pronouns. Following the current analysis this hypothetical English is to be regarded as having the same structure as real English up to the minor difference of one or two different phonological feature specifications in certain morphophonemic rules. After all, the morphological iden-

---

[2]By a basic form we mean the underlying form, with irrelevant details omitted. This basic form is only as deep as we need to assume it to be for our present concern. It is a heuristic, rather than a strictly technical, term.

[3]More exactly this is the form which current transformational analysis would assume to be the basic form of (3). According to our analysis the determiner before *material* inside the parentheses would be assumed to be indefinite, as will be given in (142) below.

tity of the relative and interrogative pronouns must simply be regarded as accidental within the current analysis.

Of course there is no reason *a priori* why the morphological identity we are talking about should not be accidental. Indeed, it is obviously too strong a restriction for a grammar that two words with the same phonetic form must be accounted for from an identical source on a sufficiently deep level, unless their assumed identity obviously contradicts their semantic distinctness, as in the case of the two homonymous nouns *bank*. For example, it is improbable that one could successfully account for all the different uses of the word *to* from one identical source in some reasonable sense. On the other hand, there is *a priori* no reason, either, why the morphological identity in question should be accidental. The problem is one to be settled by linguistic investigation, and perhaps the only way to settle the problem is to try to work out an analysis of relativization which accounts for the morphological identity of the relative and interrogative pronouns and see whether the analysis is compatible with, or, more favorably, adds any insight to, the broader description of English grammar.[4]

Thus, we first set up a problem which is rather formal or mechanical in character: to construct an analysis of relativization which explains in some reasonable sense the morphological identity of the relative and interrogative pronouns, restricting our consideration to data directly related to the problem. We shall proceed in a purely mechanical way without much regard to the linguistic significance of the discussion until we arrive at a desired analysis. Then we shall examine the linguistic significance and implications of the conclusions drawn and the assumptions made in arriving at this analysis in order to establish the formally attained results as linguistically significant.

However, our present study remains informalized and merely suggestive in certain respects. In fact, our problem will be seen to be closely related to the description of the entire determiner system and also to the general treatment of pronominalization. But treatment of these problems with any degree of exhaustiveness is well beyond the scope of this paper. Yet, it is hoped that our conclusions will be sufficiently clear in their essential points so that they can easily be incorporated into a more extended and exhaustive study of English syntax.

2.   We are to deal with four entities, *what* and *which*, both as interrogatives and as relatives. Of these four, the interrogative *what* seems to have been most extensively discussed so far in the transformational study of English syntax. It has been proposed that the interrogative pronoun *what* is derived from the underlying representation *Wh + something*:[5]

(8)   *Wh + something → what*

We will take this as an established analysis of the interrogative pronoun *what* without any further justification and will base our argument on this assumption. More exactly, however, the indefinite pronoun *something* must further be analyzed into the determiner *SOME* and the noun *Pro*:

---

[4]In this paper we shall leave open the problem of whether or not the *Wh*-interrogative and *Wh*-relative words are related not just formally but even substantially or semantically.

[5]See Chomsky (1964), pp. 38ff.; Katz and Postal (1964), p. 93; and Klima (1964a), n. 6.

(9)   *SOME Pro* → *something*

SOME will be called the *indefinite determiner*. By *SOME* is not meant exactly the word *some; some* is certainly to be considered to alternate with *any* in certain contexts. *SOME* is assumed to underlie both of them. We are not concerned with this alternation in this paper, however; in the following examples *SOME* may be realized either as *some* or as *any* without any further explanation. *Pro* is a special noun, *pronoun*. To be more exact, *Pro* must be considered to be a syntactic feature, and combined with other syntactic features such as humanness, masculineness, singularness, etc., and with an appropriate determiner, it would also give rise to such words as *someone, he, it,* etc., which are usually called indefinite and personal pronouns. But since in the main body of this paper we shall deal exclusively with nonhuman singular nouns, for the sake of brevity those other features will not be mentioned explicitly and *Pro* is treated as if it were a noun.

The underlying representation *Wh + something* of the interrogative pronoun is now given more exactly as

(10)   *Wh + SOME Pro*

Each occurrence of this form in a sentence is as a whole dominated by the node *noun phrase* and the form *Wh + SOME* is dominated by the node *determiner*. The plus sign here and elsewhere in what follows is an informal device to indicate that the form connected by it occupies the position of determiner. Now, given the analysis (10), the phonetic form *what* is not assumed to be derived from (10) by the application of (9) and (8). Rather, we introduce the rules

(11)   *Wh + SOME* → *what*
(12)   *Pro* → ∅   (after *what*)

This is because (11) will also account for the interrogative adjective *what* as in

(13)   *what book*

whose underlying form would be

(14)   *Wh + SOME book*

Let us now turn to the relative pronoun *what* and try to account for it by means of (11). Take (5) as an example of a sentence with an independent relative clause. The matrix verb phrase and the constituent verb phrase in (5) are clearly

(15)   *was the tissue*

and

(16)   *lay on the table*

respectively. The subjects of these sentences with which relativization connects them into one must be co-referential and identical. Let us denote this noun by X. We follow the already established assumption that the relative clause is preceded by the marker *Wh*; as remarked earlier this serves to account for the preposing of the *Wh*-words in interrogation and relativization uniformly. The basic form of (5) must then take the form

(17)   *Det X (Wh + Det X lay on the table) was the tissue*

Here, *Det* represents a determiner to be determined further. If the *Det* that follows

Wh is taken as *SOME* and *X* is taken as *Pro*, (11) and (12) will yield the form *what*. Whatever the *Det* at the beginning of (17) might be, one more additional rule:

(18)   *Det Pro* → ∅   (before *Wh* + *SOME Pro*)

would suffice to derive (5) from:

(19)   *Det Pro* (*Wh* + *SOME Pro lay on the table*) *was the tissue*

The assumption that the *pivotal* noun of the *relative-complex*[6] sentence (5) is *Pro* is certainly semantically permissible, or even mandatory. Owing to the deletion rule, (18), the initial *Det* in (19) cannot be specified any further just by observing sentence (5).

Thus, at this point, let us turn our attention to the sentence

(20)   *That which lay on the table was the tissue.*

which has been related to (5) by certain traditional grammarians and transformationalists as well. In transformational terms (5) has been supposed to be derived from (20) by rule (7).[7] Let us try to determine the basic form of (20). In this form the antecedent of the relative clause can easily be identified as *that*, which is usually called a demonstrative pronoun. As a noun phrase *that* must be analyzed into a determiner and a noun. The noun involved in *that* is taken as *Pro*. The determiner involved in it will be defined as the definite determiner and denoted by *THAT*. Then, the basic form of (20) would appear as

(21)   *THAT Pro* (*Wh* + *Det Pro lay on the table*) *was the tissue*

where the *Det* after *Wh* is a determiner yet to be determined. Comparing (20) and (21) and recalling that *what* is derived from *Wh* adjoined to a determiner, *SOME*, one would conclude that *which* is derived from *Wh* adjoined to this determiner, *Det*. Since we have so far introduced only two determiners, to take the remaining one, *THAT*, as the *Det* in question would be the simplest solution; we introduce the rule

(22)   *Wh* + *THAT* → *which*

and generalize (12):

(23)   *Pro* → ∅   (after *what* and *which*).

(21) is now replaced by

(24)   *THAT Pro* (*Wh* + *THAT Pro lay on the table*) *was the tissue*

Now, compare (19) and (24). *Wh* is followed by *SOME* in (19) and *THAT* in (24). Thus if (5) and (20) should derive from one basic source, either (19) or (24) is not the basic form; either a rule to convert the *SOME* in (19) to *THAT* or a rule

---

[6]We call a sentence relative-complex if it contains a relative clause. More exactly, when we say a sentence is relative-complex, our attention is specially turned to a particular relative clause attached to a noun phrase of the main clause of the sentence. By the pivotal noun of such a sentence we mean the noun which appears both in the matrix and constituent sentences by means of which they are conjoined into one relative complex sentence; that is, the pivotal noun appears in general as the so-called antecedent in the matrix sentence, and is replaced, in an informal sense, by the relative pronoun *which* in the constituent sentence.

[7]In that case there is of course no need to set up an underlying form like (19).

to convert the *THAT* in (24) following *Wh* to *SOME* would be necessary. Conversely, such a rule would be sufficient to relate those two sentences, provided that the *Det* in (19) is taken as *THAT*, which would not raise any serious problems.

There is no *a priori* reason why two synonymous sentences like (5) and (20) must be derived from one basic source. However, a rule that converts *SOME* in the context of (19) into *THAT* is required in the grammar for an independently motivated reason to which we shall return later. The rule takes the form

(25) N_1 *X Det* $N_2 \rightarrow N_1$ *X THAT* N_2
         if $N_1 = N_2$

Thus, one can assume without making the entire grammar more complex that (5) and (20) share the identical basic form, which is

(26)   *THAT Pro (Wh + SOME Pro lay on the table) was the tissue*

This conclusion is reinforced by the fact that all four possible combinations of the two determiners *SOME* and *THAT* must be assumed to appear in the matrix and constituent sentences of relativization of different types, and indeed the three combinations other than the one found in (26) must be assigned to sentences different either from (5) or from (20).

Let us first consider the following sentence:

(27)   *Something which surprised Mary pleased John.*

This can be derived from

(28)   *SOME Pro (Wh + THAT Pro surprised Mary) pleased John*

directly by (9), (22), and (23). No other form would seem more plausible than (28) as the basic form of (27).

But there is another sentence:

(29)   *Anything which surprised Mary pleased John.*

Under the assumption that *any* is a variant of *SOME*, (29) would also appear to have the basic form (28). But obviously (27) and (29) are not synonymous and cannot be derived from one identical source. Indeed, (29), but not (27), can be paraphrased by

(30)   *Whatever surprised Mary pleased John.*

Note that here again we encounter the form *what*. If we take

(31)   *SOME Pro (Wh + SOME Pro surprised Mary) pleased John*

as the basic form, rule (25) together with (22) and (23), will lead (31) to (29) in the one instance, and in the other rule (18) together with (11) and (12) will lead (31) to (30), provided that the morph *ever* is appropriately inserted in (30).[8] Thus,

---

[8]Actually one may find examples in which *ever* is not inserted after *what*, though rarely after pronominal *what* but more frequently after a determiner *what*. Thus, the example in Curme (1931), p. 213,

(A)   *His mother gives him what he asks for.*

would be paraphrased by

(B)   *His mother gives him whatever he asks for.*

rather than by

by introducing the basic form (31), not only do we assign different basic forms to the nonsynonymous sentences (27) and (29), but we also account for the synonymy of sentences (29) and (30).

Finally, let us consider the sentence

(32)   *That, which surprised Mary, pleased John.*

Here, the so-called demonstrative pronoun *that* is assumed to refer to some definite object or incident given in the discourse context, and the relative clause is assumed to be nonrestrictive. Note that here the sequence of words *that which* cannot be substituted for by *what* as is the case with *that which* in (20). Assuming that the basic form of (32) is

(33)   *THAT Pro (Wh + THAT Pro surprised Mary) pleased John*

this fact can automatically be accounted for without referring to any marker of nonrestrictive relativization which one might assume in the basic form of (32).

3.   In the rest of the paper, we shall examine within a broader scope of English syntax the linguistic significance of the assumption made in the preceding section on a rather restricted formal basis.

We introduced two basic determiners *SOME* and *THAT*. The indefinite determiner *SOME* was defined as the determiner in *something* and appears as *some* or *any*. The definite determiner *THAT* was defined as the determiner in the pronoun *that*. The *some-any* alternation has been dealt with elsewhere in the literature of transformational studies,[9] and, as the basic form of this alternation, *SOME* may be familiar. However, some more clarification may be in order concerning the nature of *THAT*.

The word *that* is usually called a demonstrative pronoun, or a demonstrative

---

(C)   *His mother gives him that which he asks for.*

Then, though (A) is superficially similar to (5),

(D)   *His mother gives him SOME Pro (Wh SOME Pro he asks for)*

would be taken as the basic form of (A). Further, the sentence by G. Eliot cited in Jespersen (1927),

(E)   *I shall take what measures I think proper.*

would be paraphrased by

(F)   *I shall take whatever measures I think proper.*

Though here we are not dealing with the determiner use of the word *whatever*, the pair (E) and (F) obviously illustrates the same point as the pair (A) and (B) does.

As we shall mention later, the human *Wh*-word *who* may also be used as an independent relative pronoun, though this use has now become archaic. Opposite to the case with *what*, in most cases the independent relative *who* is indefinite in meaning and "much more infrequently is it a definite person that is indicated" (Poutsma, 1916, p. 987). Thus, for example, *who* in

(G)   *Whom the Gods love die young.*

(H)   *Who steals my purse steals trash.*

would be substituted for by *whoever*, and it is rather difficult to find examples of the independent relative *who* which is not replaceable by whoever; for such an example, see (52), which is cited in Poutsma (1916).

[9]Klima (1964a).

adjective when it is followed by a noun. As a demonstrative pronoun *that* is used in opposition to another demonstrative pronoun, *this*. However, the word *that* may also be used sometimes in a neutral way with respect to the *this-that* opposition. In this use *that* is much like *it*, as a pronoun, and *the*, as a determiner. Actually, historically *that* is said to have been originally a pronoun neutral with respect to demonstrativeness, like French *ce*, which characteristic has been handed down in the form of the definite article, *the*.[10] Yet this characteristic is still retained to some degree also in the form *that*. In certain particular contexts this neutral character of *that* is more conspicuously perceivable. Thus, for example, the word *it* cannot receive an extra-stress and it must be substituted for by *that* in the context under an extra-stress; we do not have

(34) **I know ít.*

and

(35) **Ít I know.*

but we can say, without any implication of contrast with *this*,

(36) *I know thát.*

and

(37) *Thát I know.*

Further, as is well known, *it* cannot be modified by a prepositional phrase; we cannot say,

(38) **Let his fate and it of his poor wife be remembered.*

Instead, we say,

(39) *Let his fate and that of his poor wife be remembered.*

Here again *that* is obviously neutral, not contrasted with anything that might be referred to by *this*. Thus, one can assume that *it* and certain occurrences of the so-called demonstrative pronoun *that* (i.e. nondemonstrative uses of *that*) are different phonetic realizations of one syntactic entity, which can be assumed to be *THAT Pro*.

The demonstrative use of *that* is irrelevant to our present study. It would be quite natural to suppose, however, that the demonstrative *that* differs from the neutral *that* only in one or two syntactic feature specifications. One may assume that the personal pronouns, among which is included *it*, and the demonstrative pronouns are all assigned determiners with the feature specification *Definiteness*, which specification would also be assigned to the definite article. Then, our *THAT* may be ambiguously but systematically understood both as this feature specification and as the particular determiner with this feature specification which is the least specified for the other features. Correspondingly, *SOME* may also be understood as the feature specification *Indefiniteness* assigned to certain determiners, including the indefinite article, *a*. But these assumptions are not particularly important for the purpose of our present study.

---

[10]*NED.*

4. We assumed that the word *which* is derived from the underlying representation *Wh + THAT*. The procedure to get this assumption was rather mechanical; the two determiners *SOME* and *THAT* are distributed between the two *Wh*-words *what* and *which*. The basic form *Wh + SOME* for the interrogative pronoun *what* has long since been substantiated in transformational studies, as we noted above. It has also been proposed by Katz and Postal (1964) that the interrogative *which* be regarded as definite. Indeed, as they noted, the difference between the contrasting pairs of *Wh*-questions like

(40)   *What lay on the table?*

and

(41)   *Which lay on the table?*

appears to be that between questioning a definitely marked domain versus questioning an indefinitely marked domain. Note further that *which*-questions generally expect answers with definite nouns, while *what*-questions do not. These remarks would substantiate semantically the analysis that *which* is derived from *Wh + THAT*.

However, some of the arguments given in Katz and Postal (1964) concerning the definite-indefinite distinction in *Wh*-words seem to be open to question. They claim that "single-word question forms" are indefinite, and the correlation of single-wordness and indefiniteness is referred to as a syntactic support of the definite-indefinite distinction of *Wh*-forms. Thus, according to them not only *what*, but also *who*, *where*, and *when* are indefinite as opposed to *which one*, *which place*, and *which time*, which are definite. These "single-word" forms would be derived from forms something like *Wh + SOME Pro [+Human]*, *Wh + SOME Pro [+Place]*, and *Wh + SOME Pro [+Time]*. We agree that these underlying indefinite pronoun forms yield *who*, *where*, and *when*. However, the converse does not seem to hold; these underlying forms are not sole sources of the "single-word" forms *who*, *where*, and *when*. In orther words, unlike the nonhuman case where the definite-indefinite contrast is clearly maintained by *which* and *what*, the *Wh*-words *who*, *where*, and *when* appear to be ambiguous, either derived from the above underlying indefinite pronoun forms or from the underlying definite pronoun forms, *Wh + THAT Pro [+Human]*, *Wh + THAT Pro [+Place]*, and *Wh + THAT Pro [+Time]*. To see this, let us first consider the following:

(42)   *You may read* Syntactic Structures *or* La Nausée.

This statement can be followed by the question

(43)   *Which do you prefer to read?*

but not by

(44)   *What do you prefer to read?*

However, the statement

(45)   *You may see Chomsky or Sartre.*

can be followed by

(46) *Who do you prefer to see?*

although it can also be followed by

(47) *Which one do you prefer to see?*

and the latter may be preferred under certain circumstances, because *which one* is unambiguously definite. Similarly,

(48) *You may see him in Boston or in Paris.*

and

(49) *You may see him on Saturday or on Sunday.*

can be followed by:

(50) *Where do you prefer to see him?*

and

(51) *When do you prefer to see him?*

Actually, the fact that *who, where, when,* but not *what,* are ambiguously definite and indefinite is important to note in connection with our present study. Indeed, unlike the nonhuman case where as a relative pronoun *which* is always used with an antecedent and *what* is exclusively used as an independent relative pronoun, *where* and *when,* and also *who,* though only in the archaic use, can be used as independent relatives as well as with an antecedent. This can be accounted for precisely by the fact that *who, where,* and *when,* but not *what,* are ambiguously definite and indefinite. Thus the sentences with independent relative clauses

(52) *Who was the thane lives yet, but under heavy judgment bears that life.*

(53) *But you do as you like with me—you always did, from when first you began to walk.*

(54) *She walked away to where Mr. Cross was speaking to George.*

are assumed to have the following basic forms which parallel (26):

(55) *THAT Pro [+ Human] (Wh + SOME Pro [+ Human] was the thane) lives yet, but under heavy judgment bears that life*

(56) *But you do as you like with me—you always did, from THAT Pro [+Time] (at Wh + SOME Pro [+Time] first you began to walk)*

(57) *She walked away to THAT Pro [+Place] (at Wh + SOME Pro [+Place] Mr. Cross was speaking to George)*

Rule (18) applied to (55)–(57) will eliminate *THAT Pro [+Human]*, *THAT Pro [+Time]*, and *THAT Pro [+Place]*, respectively. Since *Wh + SOME Pro [+Human]*, *Wh + SOME Pro [+Time]*, and *Wh + SOME Pro [+Place]* yield *who, when,* and *where,* we get (52)–(54) from (55)–(57). If rule (18) is not applied to (55)–(57), rule (25) will convert *SOME* in (55)–(57) to *THAT*. Since *Wh + THAT Pro [+Human]*, *Wh + THAT Pro [+Time]*, and *Wh + THAT Pro [+Place]* also underlie *who, when,* and *where,* we get

(58) *The one who was the thane lives yet, but under heavy judgment bears that life.*

(59) *But you do as you like with me—you always did, from the time when first you began to walk.*

(60)   *She walked away to the place where Mr. Cross was speaking to George.*

These forms paraphrase (52)–(54) as (20) paraphrases (5).[11]

   Though not particularly essential, one more remark will be added concerning our analysis of *which*. One may raise an objection to our analysis, because while one can say,

(61)   *Which of those dresses does Mary like?*

and

(62)   *Which one of those dresses does Mary like?*

one cannot say

(63)   **Mary likes that of those dresses.*

and

(64)   **Mary likes that one of those dresses.*

However, one can certainly say

(65)   *Of those dresses Mary likes that one.*

Note further that (61) and (62) can be paraphrased by

(66)   *Of those dresses which does Mary like?*

and

(67)   *Of those dresses which one does Mary like?*

The following pairs of sentences may further be added for observation:

---

   [11]To get (53) and (59) from (56), and (54) and (60) from (57), the preposition *at* before the *Wh* marker must be deleted. The use of *where* and *when* which may generally be regarded as adverbial may be better illustrated by such examples as

   He will remain where he is now.
   Mary saw him when he entered the room.

The derivation of these forms parallels that of (53) and (54) up to an additional deletion of the preposition *at* in the matrix sentence as well. The basic form of these sentences would be

   He will remain at THAT Pro [+ Place] (at Wh + SOME Pro [+ Place] he is now)
   Mary saw him at THAT Pro [+ Time] (at Wh + SOME Pro [+ Time] he entered the room)

Examples (53) and (54), which are taken from Poutsma (1916), are used so as not to be involved more than is necessary in the problem of the deletion of the preposition *at*.

   Incidentally, if the independent relative *what* were to be accounted for by rule (7), the independent relative *who*, *where*, and *when* would likewise be accounted for by the rules like

   the one who → *who*
   the place where → *where*
   the time when → *when*

These rules would be considered natural, since they only involve deletion of a pronominal, and hence in a sense redundant, element. But, then, one would have to expect the rule

   that which → *which*

in place of (7). The fact is, however, that the word *which* is never used as an independent relative pronoun. On the other hand, according to our interpretation of the independent relatives, the fact that we have the *unnatural*-looking *distributional* law (7) alongside the *natural*-looking *distributional* laws above is simply due to the independently ascertained fact that *what* is indefinite while *who*, *where*, and *when* are ambiguous.

(68)   *Mary likes the reddest of those dresses.*

(69)   *Of those dresses Mary likes the reddest.*

and

(70)   *Mary likes some of those dresses.*

(71)   *Of those dresses Mary likes some.*

Perhaps each of the pairs of sentences is derived from one common basic form which would be like the following:

(72)   *Mary likes the (of those dresses) reddest dress*

(73)   *Mary likes some (of those dresses) dresses*

Presumably non-co-referential generalized pronominalization[12] applies to the second occurrence of *dress* in each of these basic forms and converts it to *Pro*, which is eventually phonetically realized as *one* or deleted. An appropriate order change after pronominalization will yield (68) and (69) from (72), and (70) and (71) from (73), respectively. The basic form of (65) is now assumed to be

(74)   *Mary likes that (of those dresses) dress*

and the corresponding *Wh*-basic form

(75)   *Mary likes Wh + that (of those dresses) dress*

can be taken as the common basic form of (61), (62), (66), and (67). Thus, the lack of (63) and (64) is understood to be of a rather superficial nature, caused by certain restrictions imposed on the order change transformations that derive forms like (68) and (69) from (72). Finally, note that we do not have

(76)   **What of those dresses does Mary like?*

But neither do we have

(77)   **Mary likes some of those dresses.*

with *some* taken as singular.

5.   Let us now discuss transformation (25). We shall call it DEFINITIZATION. There are two issues involved here. One is to justify the transformation in the particular formalism given in (25) on grounds independent of those given earlier, i.e. to explain the morphological identity of the *Wh*-words. The other issue is to clarify the relation between our DEFINITIZATION and so-called pronominalization. Let us begin with the former.

The essential significance of transformation (25) is that the indefinite determiner *SOME* is replaced by the definite *THAT* if the noun it modifies is preceded by another occurrence of the same noun.[13] The introduction of such a transformation is meaningless unless it is shown that the indefinite determiner is found in certain basic forms, but appears as the definite determiner on the surface. Before trying to justify the particular formalism given in (25), however, let us first make our problem more general and try to see whether there are any basic forms which contain an indefinite noun phrase, not necessarily of the form *SOME N*, that appears on the

---

[12]See §5.

[13]More exactly, another occurrence of the same noun with the same reference.

surface as definite, not necessarily of the form *THAT N*. To answer affirmatively to this question, observe the following pair of sentences:

(78)   *Mary saw a salesman smile when he entered the room.*

(79)   *When a salesman entered the room, Mary saw him smile.*

Adverbial clauses may in general be preposed, and apparently (79) is the result of such preposing form (78). However, the mechanical preposing of the *when*-clause in (78) will result in

(80)   *When he entered the room, Mary saw a salesman smile.*

which is not synonymous with (78) and may not be related to it by the preposing transformation. To keep the preposing transformation general so that it applies not only to the general case where the main clause and the adverbial clause do not contain an identical co-referential noun as illustrated by the pair

(81)   *Mary saw a salesman smile when John entered the room.*

(82)   *When John entered the room, Mary saw a salesman smile.*

but also to the special case where the two clauses contain co-referential occurrences of an identical noun, as in (78) and (79), the common basic form of (78) and (79) must be assumed to be

(83)   *Mary saw a salesman smile when a salesman entered the room.*

with two occurrences of the indefinite noun, *a salesman*. Then (78) will be derived from (83) by the process of pronominalization, replacing the *a salesman* inside the adverbial clause by the pronoun *he*, while (79) will be derived from (83) by first applying the preposing transformation and then the process of pronominalization, replacing the *a salesman* inside the main clause by the pronoun *him*.[14]

   With examples (78) and (79) it has been established that indefinite noun phrases may underlie occurrences on the surface of the personal pronouns, a particular type of definite noun phrase. But to derive (78) and (79) from (83) a transformation with the particular formalism (25) may not be needed; an indefinite noun phrase like *a salesman* may well be replaced directly by the pronoun *he*. To justify (25), we have yet to see, more specifically, that indefinite determiners may underlie certain surface occurrences of the definite determiner *THAT*.

---

[14]However, there are some further complications involved in the process of pronominalization when one takes into consideration that case in which a definite noun is to be pronominalized. Thus, consider the sentences obtained by replacing *a salesman* in (78) and (79) by a definite noun *John:*

(A)   *Mary saw John smile when he entered the room.*

(B)   *When John entered the room Mary saw him smile.*

These sentences would be derived from the basic form

(C)   *Mary saw John smile when John entered the room.*

in the same way as (78) and (79) are derived from (83). However, in addition to (A) and (B) one can also say,

(D)   *When he entered the room Mary saw John smile.*

Thus, one would have to assume that the process of pronominalization may proceed right to left if the noun to be pronominalized is definite.

To see this easily, one may refer to the following pair of sentences similar to (78) and (79) which would probably be at least semi-grammatical:

(84) *Mary saw a salesman smile when that salesman entered the room.*

(85) *When a salesman entered the room, Mary saw that salesman smile.*

But *that salesman* in these forms would have to be substituted for by the pronoun *he*.[15] To make our argument more convincing, then, it would be better to cite the following examples:

(86) *John must have figured out some manner in which he would disappear before he actually disappeared in that manner.*

(87) *Before he actually disappeared in any manner John must have figured out that manner in which he would do it (= would disappear).*

As in the case of (78) and (79), (86) and (87) must share the common basic form which contains two occurrences of the indefinite noun phrase *SOME manner:*

(88) *John must have figured out SOME manner in which John would disappear before John actually disappeared in SOME manner*

If DEFINITIZATION (25) is applied to (88), (86) will be derived; if the transformation that preposes adverbial clauses and then DEFINITIZATION are applied to (88), we will get (87). Note in this case *that manner* in (86) cannot be substituted for by the pronoun *it*; we cannot have

(89) **John must have figured out some manner in which he would disappear before he actually disappeared in it.*

This completes the justification of the introduction of DEFINITIZATION (25).

We shall now discuss the relation between our DEFINITIZATION and so-called pronominalization. This part would not be needed any longer for the purpose of justifying *definitization* and in this sense would be somewhat outside the main theme of this paper. But the following argument is added for the sake of completeness and for the sake of its own interest.

Once DEFINITIZATION (25) is established, it is claimed that the grammatical process which has hitherto been understood under the name of pronominalization is divided into two transformations, one DEFINITIZATION and the other, we shall call PRONOMINALIZATION. PRONOMINALIZATION will be given as:

(90) $N_1 \, X \, N_2 \rightarrow N_1 \, X \, N_2 \, [+ \, Pro]$
      if $N_1 = N_2$

In both DEFINITIZATION (25) and PRONOMINALIZATION (90) we have the condition $N_1 = N_2$. The process of pronominalization has generally been understood to take place under the condition of co-referentiality. However, under our assumption that PRONOMINALIZATION follows DEFINITIZATION, PRONOMINALIZATION can be relieved of the co-referentiality condition. For example, in the process of obtaining (78) from (83), the second occurrence of *a salesman* in (83) will first be replaced by *THAT salesman* under the co-referentiality condition by means of DEFINITIZATION, and then the latter will be changed into *THAT salesman* $[+Pro]$ simply under the

---

[15]According to one informant, (79) is not acceptable, but (85) is. If this is the case (85) as well as (86) can be used as a convincing example of the application of DEFINITIZATION.

identity condition of nouns. The phonetic form of the pronoun *he* will be derived later by a morphophonemic rule something like[16]

$$(91) \quad THAT \begin{bmatrix} + \textit{Human} \\ + \textit{Singular} \\ + \textit{Masculine} \\ + \textit{Pro} \end{bmatrix} \rightarrow he.$$

Thus the same expressions $N_1 = N_2$ in (25) and (90) are assumed to have different meanings. To avoid confusion we rewrite DEFINITIZATION (25) informally as follows:

(92) $N_1 \ X \ Det \ N_2 \rightarrow N_1 \ X \ THAT \ N_2$
    if $N_1 = N_2$ (co-referential)

If the so-called process of pronominalization were to be captured independently of DEFINITIZATION the pronominalization transformation would also have to refer to co-referentiality. This fact itself would not perhaps be rated a disadvantage by any proposed simplicity criterion for grammars, and would not be sufficient to justify our assumption that so-called pronominalization is divided into two steps. However, it would be more important to note that PRONOMINALIZATION relieved of the co-referentiality condition can be understood as a more general process than just a subpart of so-called pronominalization. Indeed, PRONOMINALIZATION can be assumed to be involved also in non-co-referential anaphora in such sentences as

(93) *John prefers hard pencils to soft ones.*
(94) *John prefers sour milk to fresh.*

Here, *soft ones* in (93) and *fresh* in (94) would be derived from *soft pencils* and *fresh milk* via *soft Pro* and *fresh Pro* respectively, the latter being the results of PRONOMINALIZATION applied to the former. The fact that this process of nonco-referential anaphora and the so-called (co-referential) pronominalization share certain syntactic characteristics may be cited in favor of the assumption that these two processes involve an identical transformation, PRONOMINALIZATION. In fact, in certain contexts a co-referential noun phrase cannot be replaced by a personal pronoun and by and large in the same contexts a nonco-referential repeated noun cannot be replaced by the indefinite pronoun *one(s)* or be deleted. Take, for example, the following sentence:

(95) *That was the manner of disappearing John described to Mary and he actually disappeared in that manner.*
(96) *That was the day John told Mary he would disappear and he actually disappeared on that day.*

In these sentences *that manner* and *that day* cannot be replaced by the definite pronoun *it*; we do not have

(97) *That was the manner of disappearing John described to Mary and he actually disappeared in it.*

---

[16]A slightly more detailed exposition of pronominalization in terms of syntactic features and the significance of such a treatment of pronominalization, in particular concerning the distinction between the independent and anaphoric uses of pronouns, may be found in Kuroda (1965).

(98) **That was the day John told Mary he would disappear and he actually disappeared on it.*

It appears that noun phrases in a manner adverbial and a time adverbial prepositional phrase may be definitized but not replaced by personal pronouns. Similarly such nouns cannot be replaced by indefinite pronouns. Thus, one says,

(99) *That was the manner of disappearing John described to Mary but he actually disappeared in some other manner.*

(100) *That was the day John told Mary he would disappear but he actually disappeared on some other day.*

but not

(101) **That was the manner of disappearing John described to Mary but he actually disappeared in some other one.*

(102) **That was the day John told Mary he would disappear but he actually disappeared on some other one.*

We can assume that the impossibility of (97), (98), (101), and (102) is due to a restriction imposed on one transformation, PRONOMINALIZATION, whatever the exact specification of that restriction would have to be.

6. We have seen that all of the four possible combinations of the definite and indefinite determiners *THAT* and *SOME* may appear in the matrix and constituent sentences of relativization, as illustrated by the basic forms (26), (28), (31), and (33). These basic forms account for the forms of the relative pronouns appearing in their phonetic realizations and also for their possible alternant phonetic realizations. The rules which relate these basic forms to their phonetic realizations have been examined and justified in a broader perspective. Essentially our syntactic argument is now complete.

In this section we shall examine these basic forms, or, more specifically, the way the determiners appear in them, from a different viewpoint. We shall investigate the possible semantic or substantial significance of the distribution of the determiners between the matrix and constituent sentences of each of these types of basic forms. Indeed, we shall see that the observed distribution is not arbitrary in a certain semantic sense.

To see this, let us first take up (26) and examine each of the component sentences separately. The marker *Wh* appearing in (26) is introduced for the sake of relativization; disregarding this marker, we have the constituent sentence

(103) *SOME Pro lay on the table*

As a speech form this basic form would appear as

(104) *Something lay on the table.*

The matrix sentence of (26) is

(105) *THAT Pro was the tissue*

This sentence would appear as

(106) *That (or it) was the tissue.*

But note that

(107)   *Something lay on the table. It was the tissue.*

would be a discourse which paraphrases (5) and (20).

To be sure to advocate the basic form (26) for (5) and (20) solely on the basis of the semantic argument that discourse (107) paraphrases (5) and (20) would not be convincing. But the basic form (26) for (5) and (20) has already been established on purely syntactic grounds, and under these circumstances it is very remarkable that (107) paraphrases (5) and (20), since there is no reason *a priori* to expect that the basic form of a complex sentence is composed of simple sentences, an appropriate arrangement of which would represent an acceptable discourse paraphrase of that sentence.

However, the way in which basic forms like (26) and discourses like (107) are related is not in general quite as simple as might be suspected from the above observation. In particular, it must be made clear that we do not assume that discourses like (107) are the basic forms of complex sentences like (5) and (20). In the technical sense of generative syntax we do not relate sentences (5) and (20) to discourse (107). The point we are interested in is solely the fact that the way the two determiners are assigned to the two co-referential occurrences of the pivotal noun in the two component sentences of relativization is paralleled by the way they are assigned to the two co-referential occurrences of the same noun in the corresponding two component sentences of a certain discourse paraphrase of the relative-complex sentence.

Indeed, as a matter of fact, there would be no room in the present theoretical scheme of generative syntax of sentences to say that certain sentences are derived from certain discourses. But aside from this general constraint it is impossible simply from the nature of our specific problem to claim that basic forms like (26) are exactly derived from discourses like (107). To see this, it is necessary to observe relative-complex sentences like (5) which, however, contains two co-referential occurrences, in the matrix and constituent sentences, of a noun which is not the pivotal noun of relativization. Take, for instance, the sentence

(108)   *Some policeman recorded what Mary explained to him.*

Besides the pivotal noun of relativization, *Pro*, the noun *policeman* appears twice in (108) co-referentially, the latter occurrence of it being pronominalized as *him*. We know that different determiners are assigned to the two co-referential occurrences of the pivotal noun phrase *Pro* in the basic form of (108), *THAT* to the one in the matrix sentence, and *SOME* to the one in the constituent sentence. Concerning another noun which occurs twice in (108) co-referentially, i.e. *policeman*, we shall now contend that both of its occurrences are assigned the indefinite determiner, *SOME*, in the base form. To see this, consider the passive counterpart of (108):

(109)   *What Mary explained to some policeman was recorded by him.*

Comparing (108) and (109) we are led to assume that their basic form is[17]

---

[17]According to the current transformational analysis, the corresponding active and passive sentences are assigned different base forms. See Chomsky (1965). Yet, our argument holds under the assumption, which seems reasonable, that these base forms can differ only in the presence and absence of the passive marker *by*.

(110)   *SOME policeman recorded that Pro (Mary explained Wh + SOME Pro to SOME policeman)*

Now, as discourse (107) paraphrases (5), the discourse

(111)   *Mary explained something to some policeman. He recorded it.*

paraphrases (108). But the phonetic realizations of the constituent sentence and the matrix sentence of (110) are, disregarding the marker *Wh*, as follows:

(112)   *Mary explained something to some policeman.*

(113)   *Some policeman recorded it.*

Thus, we cannot say that discourse paraphrase (111) is the basic form of (108).

    This observation puts in relief a syntactic characteristic of the pivotal nouns found in (5) and (108). We observed earlier that if an adverbial clause contains a co-referential occurrence of a noun which also occurs in the main clause, both occurrences of the noun are assigned an identical determiner. We have just observed that co-referential occurrences of a noun in the matrix and constituent sentences of relativization are also assigned an identical determiner in the basic form, unless the noun is pivotal in relativization. Thus, it appears in general that if a complex sentence contains two co-referential occurrences of a noun, one in the main clause and the other in the subordinate clause, both of these occurrences are assigned an identical determiner. But the pivotal noun in relativization is exceptional to this general statement. Perhaps this exceptional character of the pivotal noun in relativization with respect to the identity of determiners in co-referentiality is precisely a reflex of its syntactic characteristic that co-referentiality of two occurrences of it is syntactically required when two component sentences are combined into a relative-complex sentence by relativization. The other general case of co-referential occurrences of a noun in the main and subordinate clauses is syntactically accidental, due to particular lexical choices which happen to be made in the two clauses. The pivotal noun in relativization plays in a sense the role of a conjunction in addition to its usual nominal function. Different determiners are assigned to the co-referential occurrences of the pivotal noun as if to express this conjunctional role of the pivotal noun. Indeed, the way different determiners are assigned to the occurrences of the pivotal nouns in the matrix and constituent sentences in (26) and (110) reflects the way the component sentences are to be ordered in their discourse paraphrases (107) and (111), and consequently the way the component propositions are to be understood to be conjoined in the complex proposition represented by the complex sentences (5) and (108).

    We shall now turn to another type of relative-complex sentence illustrated by the basic form (28) of (27) in which different determiners are assigned to the pivotal noun in the matrix and constituent sentences, in this case *SOME* in the matrix sentence and *THAT* in the constituent sentence. We shall see again that the way the determiners are assigned to the component sentences reflects the way the component propositions are to be conjoined in the complex proposition represented by the relative-complex sentence (27) in the sense specified above. Indeed, the basic forms of the matrix and constituent sentences of (27) are, disregarding the marker *Wh*,

(114)   *SOME Pro pleased John*

(115)   *THAT Pro surprised Mary*

These basic forms would yield the speech forms

(116)   *Something pleased John.*

(117)   *It surprised Mary.*

Note that

(118)   *Something pleased John. It surprised Mary.*

would be taken as a discourse paraphrasing (27).

   However, one may object to this observation by pointing out that the discourse of the reversed order of the components

(119)   *Something surprised Mary. It pleased John.*

may also be considered to paraphrase (27). Then it would be completely arbitrary to associate (27) with one of the two paraphrases in order to keep the parallelism in the assignment of determiners. However, let us note the following two points. First, as discourse (118) pairs with (119), the relative-complex sentence (27) pairs with

(120)   *Something which pleased John surprised Mary.*

The basic forms of the matrix and constituent sentences of (120) are

(121)   *SOME Pro surprised Mary*

(122)   *THAT Pro pleased John*

Thus, (120) is to (119) what (27) is to (118). Second, certain types of predicates exclude one of the paired discourses and also one of the corresponding paired relative-complex sentences. In fact, an indefinite noun with a specific referent is in general not allowed as subject of a copulative predicate, and hence in particular one would not say,

(123)   **Something was big and black. It startled Mary.*

On the other hand the discourse to be paired with this form in the above sense

(124)   *Something startled Mary. It was big and black.*

is all right, since here the subject of the copulative predicate is definite. Correspondingly, one would not say,

(125)   **Something which startled Mary was big and black.*

while

(126)   *Something which was big and black startled Mary.*

or

(127)   *Something big and black startled Mary.*

is acceptable. From these two observations, if each relative-complex sentence of the type (27) is associated with a discourse paraphrase which shows the parallel assignment of determiners to the noun used as the pivot in relativization, relative-complex sentences of this type can be systematically associated with discourses of the type (118) which paraphrase them.

The type of relative-complex sentences exemplified by (32) have the definite determiner assigned to both occurrences of the pivotal noun. They can be paraphrased by discourses which contain two definite occurrences of the noun in question. (32) can be paraphrased by

(128)   *That pleased John. It surprised Mary.*

Again in this case the discourse of the reversed order

(129)   *That surprised Mary. It pleased John.*

may also be considered to paraphrase (32), and the relative-complex sentence

(130)   *That, which pleased John, surprised Mary.*

would be paired with (32). In this case, however, whichever of these two discourses one assumes to be associated with (32), and the other with (130), one can say that the relative-complex sentences are associated with discourse paraphrases which exhibit a parallel distribution of determiners, since anyway only the definite determiner is involved both in the relative-complex sentences and their discourse paraphrases. Owing to the fact the noun in question, i.e. the noun that appears as the pivot of relativization in (32) and (130), appears as definite from the beginning of discourse (128), its component sentences are symmetrically related, and their particular sequential order is meaningless. Thus, in the first place, (128) and (129) are virtually equivalent, while (118) and (119) are not, and second, the fact that the pivotal noun is assigned the same definite determiner both in the matrix and constituent sentences in (32) reflects this symmetric character of the conjoining of the two component propositions expressed by (32).

The remaining, fourth type of relativization represented by (29) with the basic form (31) assigns the indefinite determiner *SOME* to the pivotal noun both in the matrix and constituent sentences in the basic form. The basic forms of the matrix and constituent sentences of (29) are

(131)   *SOME Pro pleased John*

and

(132)   *SOME Pro surprised Mary*

respectively. These basic forms would appear on the surface as

(133)   *Something pleased John.*

and

(134)   *Something surprised Mary.*

Mere arrangement of these sentences or their variants with *anything* in place of *something* cannot paraphrase (29) as a discourse. In the three types of relativization so far treated the matrix and constituent sentences are independent of each other as logical propositions, and it is a merely syntactic motive that combined them into one sentence; from the purely logical point of view one could in those cases dispense with the syntactic device of generating complex sentences and could always use appropriate sequences of simple sentences in their place. In the present case, however, the two propositions represented by (134) and (133), for example, are related in (29) by the premise-conclusion relationship, and the need for the formation of a complex sentence is rooted essentially in the logical nature of the proposition to be expressed by (29). This need is fulfilled in (29) by the syntactic device of relativization. However, relativization is not the unique device for this purpose; nor is it the primary one, either. Indeed, relativization can be used to combine a premise and a conclusion only if they happen to contain the same noun, as *Pro* in (133) and (134). A more general way to combine a premise and a conclusion is conjoining them by means of the conjunction *if*. Thus, (29) can be paraphrased by

(135)   *Anything pleased John if it surprised Mary.*

The basic form of (135) would be assumed to be

(136)   *SOME Pro pleased John if SOME Pro surprised Mary*

for the same reason as we assumed (83), for example, to be the basic form of (78); in fact the *if*-clause in (136) may be preposed to yield the speech form

(137)   *If anything surprised Mary, it pleased John.*

In the preceding three cases we have noted that the distribution of determiners in the matrix and constituent sentences of a relative-complex sentence preserves the information the determiners would give in an appropriate discourse paraphrase of the sentences, i.e. whether or not the noun appearing as the pivotal noun in the relative-complex sentence is conceived of as definite at the beginning of the discourse, and if not which component sentence precedes the other so that the noun appears as indefinite in the former but as definite in the latter; the combination of determiners serves as a sufficient indicator of the way in which two component propositions are conjoined into one in the relative-complex sentence. In the present case, the relative-complex sentence (29) cannot merely be decomposed into two simple sentences; the proposition expressed by (29) is inherently complex. Though the pivotal noun in (29) functions syntactically in a way similar to the preceding cases in conjoining the two component sentences, the way that the two occurrences of the pivotal noun are related to each other with respect to the definite-indefinite relationship does not express the semantic nature of the conjoining. Thus, the *semantic* role in the conjoining of the two components into one proposition (29) played by the two occurrences of the pivotal noun is, in this case, essentially not more than the two occurrences of the same noun in sentences like (83) or the two occurrences of the same noun, *Pro*, in (136) which paraphrases (29). Then, one would conclude, the fact that the basic form (31) contains two occurrences of *SOME Pro* is semantically compatible with our earlier observation that in general two occurrences of the same noun—one in the main clause and the other in the subordinate clause—take the same determiner; thus, the distribution of determiners in the matrix and constituent sentences seems also to reflect the semantic nature of the pivotal noun in the formation of the type of relative-complex sentences represented by (29).[18]

---

[18]Since sentences like (29) and (30) are paraphrased by sentences like (135) and (137), the derivation of the former from the latter may easily be proposed. However, no convincing evidence other than those which are direct consequences from their synonymity (and hence actually not real ones) seems to have been presented so far. The fact established here, i.e. in the first place the pivotal noun appears indefinite both in the matrix and constituent sentences of the basic

Thus, in each of the four cases, the distribution of the determiners in the matrix and constituent sentences can be said to reflect the semantic nature of the conjoining of two component propositions syntactically realized by relativization transformation.

7. Our present study ends at this point. As has been seen, however, we have dealt only with those relative-complex sentences in which the pivotal noun is *Pro*. This is a serious restriction if the present study is aimed at an analysis of English relativization in general. A further remark or two would therefore be required on this shortcoming of the present study.

It is recalled that our preceding discussion is divided into two parts, one syntactic and the other semantic. But we do not rely on the latter in establishing the basic forms of relative-complex sentences and the rules that relate those basic forms to their speech forms. The semantic discussion has been added to show that a certain semantic or substantial significance can be assigned to the results obtained by syntactic or formal means. It is easily noticed that the development of our syntactic argument hinges on the existence of the particular rule (18). But for this rule, the indefinite determiner in the constituent sentences of the basic forms (26) and (31) would not be uncovered by any formal means. Now the rule (18) can only be partially generalized in the general case of relativization. In fact, corresponding to (30), one may have sentences like

(138)   *Whatever present surprised Mary pleased John.*

which is paraphrased by

(139)   *Any present which surprised Mary pleased John.*

However, one cannot have

(140)   **What material lay on the table was the tissue.*

which would correspond to (5) as a paraphrase of (3). Thus, one would have the same formal grounds as in the case of (30) to assume that the basic form of (138) and (139) is

(141)   *SOME present (Wh SOME present surprised Mary) pleased John*

while, unlike the case of (20), no immediate formal justification can be given for assuming that the basic form of (3) is

(142)   *THAT material (Wh SOME material lay on the table) was the tissue*

At this point one would have to have recourse to semantics in some way. The meanings of (20) and (141) would be assumed to differ just in that the word *material* is more specified semantically than *Pro*. The difference between the basic forms of (20) and (3) would have to be just what corresponds to this semantic difference. This would lead us to assume that (142) is the basic form of (3). Note that

---

form of a relative-complex sentence of this type, and secondly the same noun appears also indefinite both in the main and subordinate clauses of the basic form of the *if*-sentence that paraphrases the relative-complex sentence, is not a direct consequence of the synonymity of these sentences. Yet, this would not be sufficient evidence to draw a conclusion that relative-complex sentences of the type in question must be syntactically related to *if*-sentences.

this assumption is not simply semantically motivated; it is based on the syntactic argument made on (20) and a theoretical principle which one may call the principle of consistency between syntax and semantics. The observance of this principle is more important in this case; assignment of particular determiners in the basic forms of relative-complex sentences is not only formally justified inasmuch as they explain syntactic properties of those sentences in which *Pro* is the pivot, but it is also claimed that it has a substantial semantic significance, reflecting the semantic nature of the conjoining that is syntactically realized by relativization, and this semantic nature is not due to any semantic particularity of the special noun *Pro*.

However, not all of the syntactic properties involved in relativization seem to present themselves in relative-complex sentences with *Pro* as their pivot, at least in an obvious way, and the method of reduction of the general case to the special case with *Pro* by means of the principle of consistency may not work for all instances of sentences with relative clauses. For instance,

(143)   *The red object which lay on the table was the tissue.*

is grammatical, *red* being either restrictive or nonrestrictive; that is, there may or may not have been more than one object which lay on the table, but at most one of them was red. Assume that *red* is read restrictively. In the examples treated above with *Pro* as the pivotal noun, if the pivotal noun is definite in the matrix sentence, it is indefinite in the constituent sentence of restrictive relativization. Then one might wish to have

(144)   *SOME object was red*

as the basic form of the relative clause which eventually appears as a prenominal adjective *red* in (143). But (144) would be impossible since, as remarked earlier, an indefinite noun with a specific referent is not generally allowed to be the subject of a copulative predicate. Note, however, that an indefinite noun phrase with a so-called pre-article construction may be the subject of such a sentence, as in

(145)   *One of the objects which lay on the table was red.*

Indeed, (143) may be paraphrased by

(146)   *Some objects lay on the table. One of them was red. It was the tissue.*

Then, one may consider something like

(147)   *THAT object (Wh + SOME of THOSE objects (Wh + SOME objects lay on the table) was red) was the tissue*

as a possible candidate for being the basic form of (143). But remaining within the scope of the present study one cannot give any syntactic basis for this assumption or any other possible alternatives.[19]

Thus the task of generalizing our present study as a syntactic investigation must be done, if ever possible, in a broader perspective of English syntax.[20]

---

[19]An alternative to (147) which one may easily come upon would be

THAT object (Wh + SOME object (Wh + THAT object was red) lay on the table) was the tissue

[20]The claim that a noun modified by a relative clause may take different determiners in the

REFERENCES

Annear, Sandra S. (1965), "English and Mandarin Chinese: Definite and Indefinite Determiners and Modifying Clause Structures." *Project on Linguistic Analysis Report*, 11, Ohio State University.

Chomsky, Noam (1964), *Current Issues in Linguistic Theory. Janua Linguarum*, 38. The Hague: Mouton & Co.

—— (1965), *Aspects of the Theory of Syntax*. Cambridge, Mass.: M.I.T. Press.

Curme, George Oliver (1931), *A Grammar of English: Syntax*. Boston: D. C. Heath & Company.

Jespersen, Otto (1927), *A Modern English Grammar*, Part III. London/Copenhagen: George Allen & Unwin/Ejnar Munksgaard.

Katz, Jerrold J., and Paul M. Postal (1964), *An Integrated Theory of Linguistic Descriptions*. Research Monographs, No. 26. Cambridge, Mass.: M.I.T. Press.

Klima, Edward S. (1964a), "Relatedness Between Grammatical Systems." *Language*, 40.1–20; in *MSE*.

—— (1964b), "Negation in English," in *SL*.

Kuroda, S.-Y. (1965a), *Generative Grammatical Studies in the Japanese Language*. Ph.D. dissertation, M.I.T.

—— (1965b), "A Note on English Relativization." Mimeographed.

Langacker, Ronald W. (1966), *A Transformational Syntax of French*. Ph.D. dissertation, University of Illinois.

Lees, Robert B. (1960), *The Grammar of English Nominalizations*. Supplement to *International Journal of American Linguistics*, 26.3 (July 1960), Part II.

Murray, James A. H., Henry Bradley, W. A. Craigie, C. T. Onions, eds. (1933), *The Oxford English Dictionary*. Oxford: The Clarendon Press.

Poutsma, Hendrik (1916), *A Grammar of Late Modern English*. Groningen: P. Houdrhoff.

---

matrix and constituent sentences was made independently by Annear (1965) and Kuroda (1965a), (1965b). Annear argued, on semantic grounds, for setting up basic forms of relative construction similar to those given above. Langacker (1966) arrived by syntactic arguments at the conclusion that indefinite determiners underlie French relative pronouns.

18

A Proposed Rule of Tree-Pruning

JOHN ROBERT ROSS

It is the purpose of this paper to point out an inadequacy in the derived tree structures which are assigned to sentences by the present theory of transformational generative grammar, and to suggest a way of remedying this inadequacy. Four syntactic problems whose solution seems to depend on and support the proposed way of remedying the inadequacy will be discussed.

The inadequacy can be clearly seen in the structures which the present theory assigns to noun phrases like *his yellow cat.*

(1)

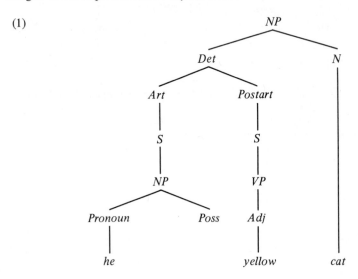

Reprinted from *Mathematical Linguistics and Automatic Translation,* Harvard Computation Laboratory, Report No. NSF-17, 1966, pp. IV-1 to IV-18, by permission of John Robert Ross and the President and Fellows of Harvard College. A version of this paper was presented at the Winter Meeting of the Linguistic Society of America, Chicago, Illinois, December 30, 1965.

What should be noted about (1) is that it makes the assertion that the possessive pronoun *his* and the adjective *yellow* are both sentences, for both are dominated in (1) by the node *S*. The reason for this is that both are derived from relative clauses by rules which are fairly well understood, though their details are anything but clear. That is, the noun phrase *his yellow cat* will be derived from an underlying *NP* with two relative clauses: *the cat which he has which is yellow*. But it certainly seems counterintuitive to claim that the whole string *his yellow cat caterwauls incessantly* is a sentence and also that the words *his* and *yellow* are sentences. Therefore, in order to avoid this intuitively incorrect result, I propose that the following metarule, or convention, be added to the theory of grammar.

(2)   Delete any embedded node *S* which does not branch (i.e. which directly dominates only *NP* or *VP*).

I am indebted to George Lakoff for pointing out to me that this rule must be restricted only to embedded sentences—without such a restriction, rule (2) would delete the node *S* in imperative sentences like *come here*, for when the subject noun phrase *you* is deleted, the *S* dominates only a *VP*.

This rule must not be thought of as applying in sequence with other rules of grammar, i.e. as occupying a fixed place in the rule-ordering. Rather it should be thought of as a condition upon well-formedness of trees, which may operate at many points in a derivation of a sentence: whenever some configuration of rules produces a node *S* which does not branch, rule (2) operates and deletes that node. It is clear that this rule will operate correctly in the case of (1) above and will delete the node *S* above *his* and *yellow*. Let us now examine four other cases where there seem to be even more compelling reasons to delete upper structure in trees.

It is clear that the sentences in (3) must be related, as must the sentences in (4).

(3)(a)   *A student who had been drinking heavily came in.*
  (b)   *A student came in who had been drinking heavily.*
(4)(a)   *A proof that this problem is unsolvable will be given.*
  (b)   *A proof will be given that this problem is unsolvable.*

I suggest that sentences (3a) and (4a) are closer to their underlying forms than (3b) and (4b), and propose that the latter sentences be derived from the former by a rule which, following Rosenbaum, I will call EXTRAPOSITION.[1]

(5)   EXTRAPOSITION:

$X [[Indef]_{Det} N - S]_{NP} - Y$

1	2	3	$\Rightarrow$	(optional)
1	0	3	2	

This rule which, like all rules discussed here, is given in a highly oversimplified form, merely moves a sentence which is embedded in a *NP* and which follows a noun with an indefinite determiner to the end of the sentence which contains the *NP*.

---

[1]Cf. P. S. Rosenbaum, *The Grammar of English Predicate Complement Constructions* (Cambridge, Mass.: M.I.T. Press, 1967).

It has been suggested by Carlota Smith (cf. her paper "A Class of Complex Modifiers in English," *Language*, 37: 342–365, 1961) that postnominal noun modifiers be derived from relative clauses by an optional rule which deletes *who* or *which* followed by *is* or *was*. Thus the noun phrases *a jug from India* and *someone heavy* would be derived from *a jug which is from India* and *someone who is heavy* respectively. But note the behavior of the reduced relative clauses *from India* and *heavy* with respect to the rule of EXTRAPOSITION:

(6)(a)   *A jug which was from India got broken.*
  (b)   *A jug got broken which was from India.*
  (c)   *A jug from India got broken.*
  (d)   **A jug got broken from India.*

(7)(a)   *Someone who was heavy must have slept in this bed.*
  (b)   *Someone must have slept in this bed who was heavy.*
  (c)   *Someone heavy must have slept in this bed.*
  (d)   **Someone must have slept in this bed heavy.*

The full-relative clauses in (6a) and (7a) will extrapose (cf. (6b) and (7b)), but the reduced relative clauses in (6c) and (7c) will not. But the ungrammaticality of (6d) and (7d) is easily accounted for if rule (5), EXTRAPOSITION, is ordered so that it follows Carlota Smith's rule of RELATIVE CLAUSE REDUCTION.

(8)   RULE ORDERING:

RELATIVE CLAUSE REDUCTION: $\begin{Bmatrix} who \\ which \end{Bmatrix} \begin{Bmatrix} is \\ was \end{Bmatrix} \rightarrow \emptyset$ (optional)

EXTRAPOSITION (optional)

As (9) illustrates, when a relative clause is reduced by the deletion of *who is* or *which is*, the node which dominates the clause ceases to branch, and will thus be deleted by rule (2).

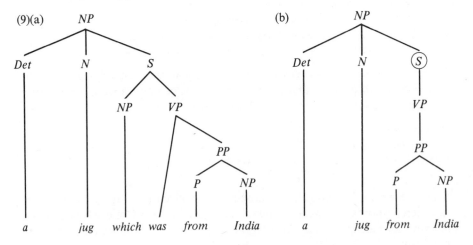

After the circled node *S* has been deleted in tree (9b) by rule (2), the tree will not meet the structural index of rule (5), EXTRAPOSITION, which, it will be recalled, only applies to sentences, so the reduced relative clause *from India* will not be affected by the rule. The same holds true in the case of *heavy*. So here is a case where it is not merely counterintuitive to assert that *heavy* and *from India* are sentences—if this assertion is made, the rule of extraposition will produce the wrong results.[2]

The next problem I will take up has to do with verb particles (e.g. the word *up* in *look up*). There is a rule in English, PARTICLE SEPARATION, which moves a particle to the right of an object *NP*, providing that this *NP* is not "complex."

(10) PARTICLE SEPARATION:

$$X \; V - Prt - NP - Y \quad \text{(obligatory if 3 is a pronoun)}$$
$$\underbrace{1} \quad 2 \quad 3 \quad 4 \Rightarrow \text{(blocks if 3 is "complex")}$$
$$1 \quad 0 \quad 3 \; 2 \; 4 \quad \text{(optional otherwise)}$$

Rule (10) permutes a particle and a following *NP*.[3] This rule is obligatory if the object *NP* is a pronoun (*look him up*, not **look up him*), and it blocks in case the *NP* is "complex"—for instance, **look the girl who I went out with up* is impossible.

But the notion of complexity has long resisted any adequate formulation. In his paper, "On the Notion 'Rule of Grammar' " (reprinted in *SL*), Noam Chomsky points out that complexity cannot be equated with length, for (11a) is more acceptable than (11b), although the former is longer than the latter:

(11)(a)   *He called almost all the seven men from Boston up.*
　(b)   **He called the man you met up.*

I propose the following definition: A *complex NP* is one which dominates a sentence. Using this definition in conjunction with rule (2), NODE DELETION, it is possible to explain why (11b) above is worse than (11a), and also why (12b) and (13b) below are worse than (12a) and (13a), respectively.

(12)(a)   *He dreamed a really tough problem up.*
　(b)   **He dreamed a problem which was really tough up.*   (Complex *NP*)
(13)(a)   *I sent the jug from India out.*
　(b)   **I sent the jug which was from India out.*   (Complex *NP*)

When *which was* is deleted in (12b) and (13b), the sentence which dominates the relative clauses *which was really tough* and *which was from India* will cease to branch, as in the example involving extraposition. Rule (2) will delete these sentences, and the noun phrases *a really tough problem* and *a jug from India* will no longer be complex, thus allowing particles to be moved around them.

---

[2]I am grateful to my colleague, D. Terence Langendoen, for pointing out to me in conversation a solution which does not involve node deletion. The facts contained in (6) and (7) could be accounted for easily by assuming an order which is the reverse of that shown in (8). If RELATIVE CLAUSE REDUCTION is specified so that it will apply only when the relative clause immediately follows the noun it modifies, then it is clear that this rule could never apply if EXTRAPOSITION had previously applied. Thus the arguments I have proposed depend critically on an ordering of the rules in which RELATIVE CLAUSE REDUCTION precedes EXTRAPOSITION. At present, however, I know of no conclusive evidence which would require this ordering or the reverse ordering. Langendoen argues for the reverse ordering in his paper "Prosthetic *It* in English," Project on Linguistic Analysis, Report No. 13 (Ohio State University, 1966).

[3]For a detailed treatment of various problems concerning the grammar of particles, cf. Bruce Fraser, *An Examination of Verb-Particle Constructions in English*, Ph.D. dissertation, M.I.T., 1965.

It is, however, evident, that the definition of complexity which I have given above is not a necessary condition for the nonseparability of verb particles. In sentence (14a), even though the object *NP* does not dominate the node *S*, separation is not possible (cf. the ungrammaticality of (14b)):

(14)(a) *He shot down a man from a village on a mountain in a country in Europe.*
   (b) **He shot a man from a village on a mountain in a country in Europe down.*

Apparently there is some complicated interaction between length and complexity, as I have defined it, which determines when a particle can be moved around an object *NP*, but there are many things which I do not understand about this problem. But I do not claim to have provided a complete solution to the problem of "complexity"; rather I claim that the notion I defined will be a factor in the eventual solution, and that some rule of node deletion is necessary to account for the difference in acceptability between (12a) and (12b), or between (13a) and (13b).

The third case where it seems that convention for node deletion is necessary arises in connection with a problem in Latin word order. In Latin verse, it is possible to permute a pre- or postnominal modifier with the other major constituents of the clause which contains the nominal. Thus sentences like (15b) can be derived from a more basic (15a):

(15)(a) *Homō bonus amat fēminam pulchram.* ⎫ 'The good man loves the beautiful
   (b) *Pulchram homō amat fēminam bonus.* ⎭ woman.'

An actual example from Horace (*Carmina* (Odes) I, 5) was kindly provided to me by Robin Lakoff.

(16)

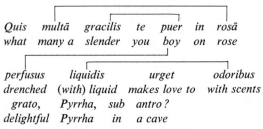

Quis   multā   gracilis   te   puer   in   rosā
what   many a   slender   you   boy   on   rose

perfusus   liquidis   urget   odoribus
drenched   (with) liquid   makes love to   with scents
grato,   Pyrrha,   sub   antro?
delightful   Pyrrha   in   a cave

'What slender boy, drenched with perfumes,
Is making love to you, Pyrrha,
On a heap of roses, in a delightful cave?'

Discontinuous constituents like *multā . . . rosā*, *liquidis . . . odoribus*, *grato . . . antro*, etc., are derived from constructions with contiguous constituents by a rule roughly of the form of (17):

(17) FREE WORD ORDER:

$$X - \left\{ \begin{Bmatrix} NP \\ VP \\ N \\ V \\ Adj \\ Adv \end{Bmatrix} \begin{Bmatrix} NP \\ VP \\ N \\ V \\ Adj \\ Adv \end{Bmatrix} \right\} - Y \quad \text{(condition: } S_i > 2 \text{ if and only if } S_i > 3)$$

1   2   3   4 ⇒ (optional)
1   3   2   4

Rule (17) scrambles major constituents, *subject to the restriction that they be in the same clause.* But notice that in (18), the underlying structure for (15b), the adjectives *bonus* and *pulchra* are not in the same clause as the words *homō, amat,* and *fēminam*. This explains why there are no sentences like (18b): rule (17) will not permute the adjectives out of the relative clauses which contain them.

(18)(a) Approximate underlying structure for (15b):

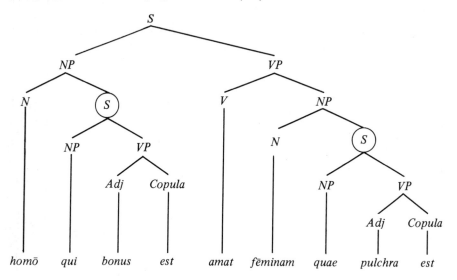

(b) **Pulchra homō qui est amat bonus fēminam quae est.*

Assuming that adnominal adjectives in Latin are derived from relative clauses containing predicate adjectives (*qui ... est* will be deleted by a rule which corresponds to Carlota Smith's rule of relative clause reduction in English (cf. (8) above)), we can see that the rule of node deletion must be operative in Latin as well as in English. For as soon as the sentences circled in (18a) have undergone deletion of *qui ... est* and *quae ... est,* they will cease to branch and thus will be deleted by (2). This will in effect put *bonus* and *pulchra* in the same clause as *homō, amat,* and *fēminam,* and will thus allow rule (17) to permute them with one another to derive sentence (15b).

Note that the adjective *pulchra* is marked as an accusative only if *quae ... est* has been deleted; i.e. there are no relative clauses like **quae pulchram est.* It would seem that the cyclical case-marking transformation should be stated in such a way that it will mark every markable element in a *NP except elements dominated by an S contained in the NP being marked.* So when the circled node *S* in (18) is deleted after *quae ... est* has been deleted, the status of *pulchra* changes in two ways. First, as noted above, it becomes eligible for permutation with the other major elements of the highest *S* in (18), and second, the rule of case marking will apply to it, yielding *pulchram.* But there is a problem with this analysis which I do not at present see how to solve. If the words *qui ... est* are deleted in the sentence *videō hominem qui deō similis est* 'I see a man who is like a god,' the adjective *similis* 'like' will be converted to an accusative (i.e. *similem*) by the case marking rule, just as *pulchra* became *pulchram*, but the noun *deō* 'god' (dative case) will not change its marking to become *deum* (accusative case). In other words, the claim that every markable element in a *NP* is marked except those in contained sentences is too weak—it would allow *deō* to become *deum*. The following condition is still not correct, but I know of no way to extend it insightfully to cover all cases:

Condition on case-marking rules:

> Case is marked on every markable element in a *NP* except elements dominated by a *S* or by a *NP* which is contained in the *NP* being marked.

The final case I wish to discuss is more complex than the other three, but for this reason it is probably also the most interesting. It has to do with the fact that while sentence (19) can occur with or without the final *is*, the noun phrase *that man* can only be relativized (i.e. moved to the front of the sentence) if this *is* has been deleted (cf. (20)).

(19)(a)   *John is taller than that man (is).*

(20)(a)   *He is a man who John is taller than.*
   (b)   **He is a man who John is taller than is.*

In order to explain the ungrammaticality of (20b), it will be necessary for me to give a brief sketch of what I believe to be the underlying structure for comparative constructions. Notice first that words like *any* and *ever* may occur in *than*-clauses:

(21)   *He solves problems faster than any of my friends ever could.*

But these words occur characteristically in negative sentences (and in questions and *if*-clauses), and are excluded in affirmative sentences:

(22)(a)   **Any of my friends could ever solve those problems.*
   (b)   *Could any of my friends ever solve those problems?*
   (c)   *At no time could any of my friends ever solve those problems.*
   (d)   *If any of my friends ever solve those problems, I'll buy you a drink.*

Notice furthermore that negative elements cannot occur in *than*-clauses:

(23)(a)   **He is taller than nobody here.*
   (b)   **Bill ran faster than I couldn't.*

These two facts strongly suggest that a negative element is present in the structure which underlies the *than*-clause. This element causes *some* to be converted to *any*, *sometime* to be converted to *ever*, and various other changes which are contingent on the presence of a negative element. After all these changes have been made, the negative element is deleted. Given all this evidence, which seems to indicate that comparative constructions have negative sentences in their derivational history, quite a plausible deep structure can be set up which will underlie both (19) and (24):

(19)   *John is taller than that man (is)*

(24)   *John is tall to an extent to which that man is not (tall).*

(25) Approximate underlying structure for (19):

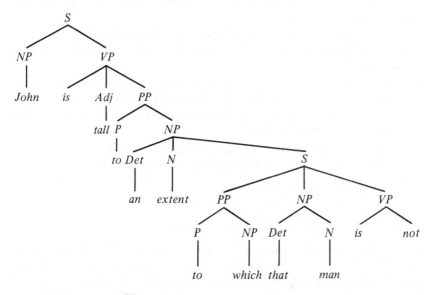

To simplify presentation, I have given in (25) a structure to which several transformations have already applied; for instance, the rule which optionally deletes *tall* in the relative clause has applied. Rule (26), COMPARATIVE INTRODUCTION, will apply to (25) and convert it to (27):

(26) COMPARATIVE INTRODUCTION:

$$X - \begin{Bmatrix} Adj \\ Adv \end{Bmatrix} - \underbrace{to\ an\ extent\ to} - which - Y - not - Z$$

1	2	3	4	5	6	7	⇒ (optional)
1	2 + er	0	than	5	0	7	

(27)

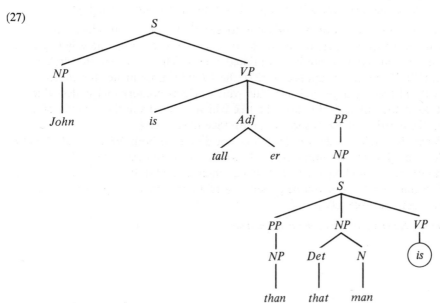

This rule adjoins *-er* to the compared adjective or adverb, substitutes *than* for the relative pronoun *which*, and deletes *to an extent to* and *not*. Tree (27) is the result of applying (26) to (25).

The fact that the *NP that man* in (27) cannot be relativized (recall the ungrammaticality of (20b)) now follows from a general restriction on relative clause formation in English:

(28)   A *NP* which is the subject of an embedded *S* (that is, a *NP* which is directly dominated by a node *S* other than the topmost node *S*) may not be relativized (i.e. moved to the front of the sentence) unless it is the first constituent of the sentence of which it is the subject.

Restriction (28) explains why the noun phrase *the girl* is relativizable in (29a) (cf. (29b)), but not in (29c) (note the ungrammaticality of (29d)).

(29)(a)   *I thought the girl was hungry.*
   (b)   *She is the girl who I thought was hungry.*
   (c)   *I thought that the girl was hungry.*
   (d)   **She is the girl who I thought that was hungry.*

In (29c), the noun phrase *the girl* cannot be relativized because the embedded sentence of which it is the subject (*that the girl was hungry*) does not start with the subject *NP* but rather with the clause introducer *that*. In (29a), it is possible to relativize the girl, because in this sentence an optional rule has applied and deleted the clause introducer *that*.

It should be evident that restriction (28), which is needed in the grammar to explain the ungrammaticality of (29d), will also explain why the noun phrase *that man* is not relativizable in (27): in the embedded sentence of which it is the subject, *that man* is preceded by the word *than*.

In order to explain why the noun phrase *that man* becomes relativizable if the circled *is* in (27) is deleted, it is necessary to reformulate rule (2), NODE DELETION.

(2′)   NODE DELETION:
   An embedded node *S* is deleted unless it dominates both *NP* and *VP*.

A moment's reflection is sufficient to see that (2′) will produce the correct results in the three cases discussed so far. Let us now examine the way (2′) works in the case at hand. There is an optional rule which may delete the circled node *is* in (27). If this rule is applied to (27), the *VP* which dominates the circled *is* will be deleted too, by a general metarule which deletes nonterminal nodes which do not dominate any lexical items. The tree which results from the deletion of *is* and then the deletion of *VP* is shown in (30). (See next page.)

Since the circled node *S* in (30) does not dominate both *NP* and *VP*, it will be deleted by (2′). The resulting tree is shown in (31). (See next page.)

Since there is no longer any embedded sentence in (31), it is clear that restriction (28) cannot apply, so it will be possible to relativize the noun phrase *that man* to form sentences like (20a).

(20)(a)   *He is a man who John is taller than.*

(30)

(31)

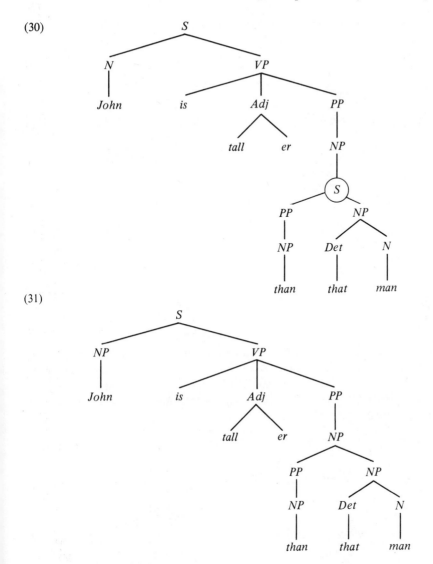

Actually, in order to account for sentences like those in (32), it is necessary to make one final revision in the principle (2′).

(32)(a) *To report the incident was wise of John.*
  (b) *It was wise of John to report the incident.*

Both of the sentences in (32) are derived from an underlying structure roughly like that shown in (33) by a rule which deletes the subject *NP* of the embedded sentence, subject to the condition that it be identical to the *NP* in the prepositional phrase, and in the case of (32b), the rule of EXTRAPOSITION.

The rule which deletes the subject *NP* of the embedded sentence converts (33) into (34).

(33)

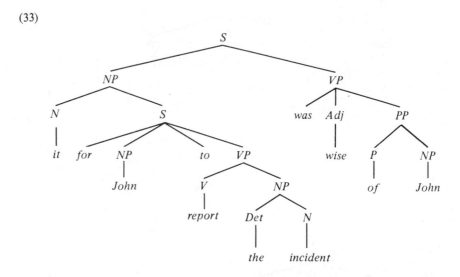

Notice that the circled node *S* in (34) does not dominate both *NP* and *VP* and would therefore be deleted by condition (2'). But this would produce the wrong results, for if the phrase *to report the incident* ceases to be dominated by the node *S*, EXTRAPOSITION will not be able to apply to it and we will not be able to derive (32b). This indicates that a revision of (2') is necessary.

(34)

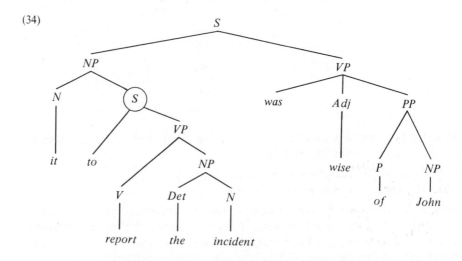

The revision is easy to make after inspecting Table 1. In the left column of Table 1 are the cases where node deletion occurs, and in the right are the cases where node deletion does not occur.

Tᴀʙᴇ 1

Deletion occurs		*Deletion does not occur*	

Condition (2″) will give the results summarized in Table 1:

(2″)   Nᴏᴅᴇ ᴅᴇᴄᴇᴛᴉᴏɴ:

An embedded node *S* is deleted unless it immediately dominates *VP* and some other constituent.

In summary, I have tried to show, on the basis of four examples, that a rule such as (2), (2′), or (2″) is necessary to prune unwanted upper nodes from derived trees. It seems most likely to me that such pruning rules will be universal conventions, rather than particular rules of English or Latin, but more data might disprove this conjecture. My main goal has been to call attention to some evidence which suggests that there is a need for rules of this kind.

V

OTHER ASPECTS
OF ENGLISH SYNTAX

The articles in this section do not group themselves about any one unifying theme. Some deal with areas in which little work has been done so far; others, with recent proposals. They may profitably be considered as starting points for further discussion and investigation.

First, R. B. Lees, in "Grammatical Analysis of the English Comparative Construction," presents a treatment within the earlier framework of transformational grammar. A comparative sentence has two independent sentences as its source. Elements from the constituent sentence are embedded in the main sentence as an adverbial modifier to an adjective or to an adverb. Lees shows that ambiguous comparatives have different sources, but stylistic variants, on the other hand, have a single source to which various optional transformations have been applied.

Peter S. Rosenbaum, in "Phrase Structure Principles of English Complex Sentence Formation," discusses the two processes of *noun phrase complementation* and *verb phrase complementation*. He presents arguments for including in the phrase structure rules of English certain rules for expansions of both noun phrase and verb phrase that include the recurrence of *S*, sentence. This reintroduction of *S* is the basis for much of the recursive power of a generative grammar.

In "Attachment Transformations," S.-Y. Kuroda discusses several problems in the development of transformational grammatical theory. By an "attachment" transformation is meant one which incorporates specific single constituents dominated by *S* into some other constituent within the same sentence. Unlike other transformations, attachment transformations may affect meaning—not, however, change meaning, but rather refine it. In this paper Kuroda also examines the role of transformations as filters; that is, transformations let through only those sentences that have proper deep structures.

John Robert Ross, in "Adjectives As Noun Phrases," presents syntactic arguments for considering adjectives—and adjective phrases—to be dominated by *NP* in their deep structure. In support of this claim, Ross cites several transformational processes that work alike for both adjectives and noun phrases: replacement by pro-forms, formation of nonrestrictive relative clauses, pseudo-cleft constructions, equative forms, topicalization, and question formation.

Finally, Charles J. Fillmore, in "Toward a Modern Theory of Case," presents his very interesting thesis that *every* noun phrase is required to begin with a preposition. Each such *Preposition – Noun Phrase* combination is then dominated by some category label, such as agentive, objective, locative, and so forth. Fillmore further suggests that in the deep structure of English prepositions behave like "cases." He thus provides the formal machinery for expressing the often repeated observation that where other languages use cases to express certain functional relations inside sentences English uses prepositions.

19

Grammatical Analysis
of the English Comparative Construction

R. B. LEES

No standard handbook of English grammar fails to describe for the reader the difference between those adjectives which are "compared" by means of the -*er* and -*est* suffixes on the one hand, and those polysyllabic adjectives, or adjectivals, which require the use of a preceding *more* and *most*. Examples will always be given of sentences containing the *as-much-as* and the *more-than* constructions. And compendious works, such as those of Jespersen and Poutsma, will also provide numerous examples of other more or less related constructions in *as* and *than*.[1]

But there is also a number of previously unmentioned restrictions and peculiarities characterizing these, or some of these, constructions which demand explanation. In some cases a handbook will offer a historical "explanation" of a particular structure, should one be available, but since all of these constructions may be productively derived *ad libitum* it is reasonable to demand of the grammarian that he explain *how* an unschooled speaker of English manages to do this.[2] To my knowledge, the only satisfying way to accomplish this is to formulate a more or less complex, ordered set of grammatical rules which correctly enumerates

---

Reprinted from *Word*, 17.171–185 (1961), by permission of R. B. Lees and the Linguistic Circle of New York, Inc.

[1]See, for example, Otto Jespersen, *A Modern English Grammar*, Part VII (London: George Allen & Unwin Ltd., 1954 and 1958), Chaps. X and XI: Comparison; G. O. Curme, *Syntax* (Boston: D.C. Heath and Co., 1931), pp. 498–508, and for various similar constructions, pp. 294–308.

[2]That is, one can reasonably demand two kinds of linguistic explanations: (*a*) how a speaker is able correctly to construct an unlimited number of new comparative expressions, and (*b*) how the language in which he constructs them evolved into its present state. Clearly, the historical explanation (*b*) presupposes the descriptive explanation (*a*), for to specify how the rules of a language have changed through time one must first be able to specify the rules.

all and only the well-formed sentences containing these constructions and which fulfills certain strict but reasonable requirements of grammatical analysis. For example, the rules offered must fit in well with an adequate total grammar of English sentences; the way in which each expression is derived by means of the rules must automatically yield an exact specification of its grammatical structure; and these rules must be completely explicit, mechanically applicable, and free of dependence upon intuition or special art.[3]

The most obvious constraints on the free generation of comparative constructions are, of course, precisely those least likely to be pointed out, for they appear naturally to fall under common-sense semantic considerations. Yet, upon closer examination, we can see that many regularities in these conditions are easily explained on purely grammatical grounds. (Let me remark parenthetically that it is quite reasonable to welcome success in explaining any apparently semantic regularity on the basis of grammar as a concrete result of linguistic science, for it is precisely the semantic features of sentences which are in such bad need of elucidation and the grammatical features which can so easily be studied independently.)[4]

We shall begin with a rather commonplace observation, but one the explanation of which already requires us to formulate a set of rules for deriving comparative constructions from simpler sentences. Notice the following facts:

(1)   *The boy is amazed.*

(2)   *The man is amazed.*

but not

(3)   **The table is amazed.*

and, correspondingly, also not

(4)   **The boy is more amazed than the table.*

although

(5)   *The boy is more amazed than the man.*

Or, similarly, we have the following triplet:

(6)   *The meeting is adjourned soon.*

(7)   **John is adjourned soon.*

(8)   **The meeting is adjourned sooner than John.*

Note, incidentally, that there is nothing inherently wrong with the particular sequence of words chosen in (8), for we have

(9)   *The meeting is adjourned sooner than John expected.*

It is just that we know intuitively that if the sequence in question (i.e. (8)) is to be a sentence, then it must have a grammatical structure very similar to that of another type, exemplified by the equally impossible

---

[3]The descriptive explanation consists then simply in imputing the formulated rule to the speaker, or to his knowledge of the language.

[4]See R. B. Lees, "The Grammatical Basis of Some Semantic Notions," *Eleventh Annual Round Table Conference,* Georgetown University, 1960 [Washington, D.C., 1962].

(10) *The meeting is adjourned sooner than John is adjourned.*

and it is the latter part of *this* sequence which has caused the difficulty.

If we could account for the fact that the pseudo-sentence

(11) *John is adjourned.*

is ungrammatical, then we could account in the same way for the impossibility of (10) and therefore also perhaps of (8). Of course, to do so would further require us to connect the two in some formal way. But this is exactly what a transformational generative grammar of English enables us to do.[5]

Now it has already been pointed out in many other places that if we are to formulate a reasonably simple grammar for English, then we shall wish to employ exactly the same apparatus to effect these two connected restrictions simultaneously, and that this is alone sufficient to motivate our formulating the grammar in such a way that the longer sentence-type (10) be derived *from* the shorter (11), perhaps together with some other underlying source-expression.[6] Before attempting such a formulation, however, let us observe some other peculiarities.

Notice next that there are certain sentences which can be understood in two different ways, i.e. which are structurally ambiguous:

(12) *I speak Spanish as well as French.*

that is

(13) *I speak Spanish as fluently as I speak French.*

or

(14) *I speak Spanish in addition to French.*

Taking a truly hard-headed position, we may have to recognize still a third interpretation:

(15) *I speak Spanish as well as (Mr.) French does.*

Whatever derivation we decide to use to explain comparative sentences, we shall want it also to cast light on why the sentence in question (12) is ambiguous, in fact even triply ambiguous.

Again, it has already been noted that a grammatical description in which some sentence-types are derived from others can easily serve to explicate ambiguities; we require that on independent grounds it be expedient to formulate the rules so as to provide at least two different ways in which one particular sequence of morphemes can be derived.[7] In this particular case, we aim at rules of generating comparatives which should yield the given sentence (12); but we also require that

---

[5]For the latest summary of the arguments for a transformational extension of the usual constituent-structure expansion-rule model of grammars, see N. A. Chomsky, "On the Notion 'Rule of Grammar,' " in *PAM* [*SL*].

[6]Ibid., also see R. B. Lees, *The Grammar of English Nominalizations*, Bloomington: Indiana University Research Center in Anthropology, Folklore, and Linguistics, Publication Number 12, July 1960 (*International Journal of American Linguistics*, 26:3, Part II), especially pp. xviii–xix.

[7]See N. A. Chomsky, "Three Models for the Description of Language," *Transactions on Information Theory*, Institute of Radio Engineers, IT-2 (1956), p. 118 [*RMP*, pp. 113–114].

some other rules yield that very sequence. In particular, we shall wish the sentence when construed like (13) or like (15) to be some kind of comparative, but when construed like (14) to be a sort of conjunction.

Ambiguities are cases in which one sentence has two different grammatical structures. But there are also cases in which two different sentences which appear to have the same structure on the surface must be assigned contrasting underlying syntactic constituent-structure.[8] For example,

(16)   *He comes as frequently as John.*

(17)   *He comes as frequently as every day.*

are intuitively quite different, although their morpheme sequences are similar. And there are also forbidden examples, such as

(18)   **He comes as frequently as six feet.*

(19)   **He jumps as far as every day.*

Here we might say that there are certain classes of adverbials, that the constituent inside of the comparative construction is an adverbial, that the final constituent is also an adverbial, and finally that these two adverbials are constrained to choice from the same class.

A minor question impinging upon matters of good style is often mentioned in handbooks, namely the choice of subjective or objective form for pronouns in final position after comparative expression, as in

(20)   *I know him better than she.*

(21)   *I know him better than her.*

It is also pointed out that these latter two cases can be in contrast, parallel to

(22)   *I know him better than she does.*

(23)   *I know him better than I do her.*[9]

Thus, if the first two sentences (20) and (21) are derived *from* the latter two we shall be able to explain the contrast, but we shall then have to formulate exactly how the reductions are to take place. For example, we cannot say simply that the final verb may be first replaced by the pro-verb *do* and then may be deleted entirely, else we should permit

(24)   *I know him better than they say she does* →

(25)   **I know him better than they say she.*

Another constraint which must be built into the rules we seek to formulate is on the appearance of the negative particle. Notice that the first constituent of the comparative construction is freely affirmative or negative, but that the second constituent cannot be negative:

(26)   *I know him better than she does.*

(27)   *I don't know him better than she does.*

---

[8] As in the cases discussed in N. A. Chomsky, *Syntactic Structures*, ('s-Gravenhage: Mouton & Co., 1957), pp. 73–75, 81–83 [*MSE*, pp. 63–65 and 68–69], 89–90; or in R. B. Lees, "A Multiply Ambiguous Adjectival Construction in English," *Language*, 36.207–221 (1960).

[9] As in Curme, op. cit., p. 303.

(28) **I know him better than she doesn't.*

Notice furthermore that this constraint is true also for the so-called "negative verbs," for we also have no

(29) **I know him better than they denied she does.*[10]

While we are considering this constraint on the appearance of negative in the comparative construction it is also appropriate to note another peculiarity. Like negative sentences, questions, subjunctive expressions, and others, the comparative construction may be called "affective," following E. S. Klima.[11] These so-called affectives may contain *ever* and also *any* for *some*, as well as other special expressions:

(30) *I haven't ever seen any.*

(31) *I have seen some.*

(32) **I have ever seen any.*

Similarly, with comparatives:

(33) *It is as good as I have ever seen.*

(34) *It is as good as any I have seen.*

(35) *It's as good as ever.*

Furthermore, there is a special negative pre-modifier for the comparative:

(36) *I'm not taller than he.*

(37) *I'm no taller than he.*

(38) **He is no tall.*

Before formulating the actual rules for enumerating such expressions it is essential that we decide, at least tentatively, what kind of constituent-structure the comparative constructions are going to be said to have. We have already presented evidence in favor of the view that

(39) *He is as tall as she.*

is to be derived from

(40) *He is as tall as she is (tall).*

But the same derivation is not available for the minimal

(41) *He is as tall as that.*

It would seem reasonable to regard the material which follows the second *as* in (39) through (41) as a kind of adverbial, parallel to the *that* of

(42) *He is that tall.*

from which we might also later derive the as yet unanalyzed

(43) *How tall is he?*

---

[10]The "negativity" of certain verbs was first pointed out to me by Professor Edward S. Klima of the Massachusetts Institute of Technology in a paper read before the Seminar on Transformational Grammar at University of Pennsylvania, 1959. [Cf. Edward S. Klima, "Negation in English," in *SL*.]

[11]A study of his so-called "affective" expressions is now in preparation. [Cf. Klima, op. cit.]

(44)   *That's how tall he is.*

though perhaps not the anomalous

(45)   *That's all the taller he is*

Notice parenthetically, however, that it is not exactly parallel to the pre-adjectival modifier in

(46)   *He's **six feet** tall.*

since such a "quantifier" may occur only before one of a special group of quantifiable adjectives such as *tall, wide, deep, old*, etc., but there is no such pre-adjectival modifier possible before other adjectives, as in

(47)   *He's that warm.*

(48)   *It's that new.*

Now, the *that* of (41) would seem to be a *pro*-adverbial standing for any of the indefinitely long expressions which can follow *as* in such a sentence. The *that* of (42), on the other hand, appears to be a kind of pre-adverbial or pre-adjectival adverbial modifier which, though differing from *very, quite, rather*, etc., will be very useful now in deriving questions and comparatives in the following way: by operating upon the *that* as adverbial with the so-called *Wh*-transformation we obtain

(49)   *How tall he is . . .*

Or, had the sentence already been questioned, we would have derived

(50)   *Is he that tall? →*

(43)   *How tall is he?*

And secondly, considering the *as . . . as* and the *more . . . than* expressions to be (comparative) operators like the *Wh*, and permitting them to replace the *that*, even though discontinuously, we obtain

(42)   *He is that tall → He is as tall as . . .*
         or → He is more tall than . . .

Of course, later morphophonemic rules which ensure the proper phonemic shape for comparative adjectives will also include rules to convert such expressions with monosyllabic adjectives as *more tall* into the appropriate inflected form *taller*.

Thus, we have indicated an analysis of comparatives, except for special conditions and constraints which must be imposed, though it is not yet completely clear what the form of the other underlying sentence must be. To begin with, we might suppose that the latter has the simplest possible form, as in

(42)   *He is that tall.*⎫
(51)   ⎬ *→ He is as tall as I am.*
(52)   *I am tall.*   ⎭

and we suppose further that subsequent rules permit certain reductions of the transform to yield

(53)   *He is as tall as I.*

and even certain stylistic developments to yield the colloquial

(54) *He is as tall as me.*

But if we are to have the most uniform rules, and if we are at the same time to account for such examples as

(55) *He is as tall as I am wide.*

then we must suppose that the transform contains the entire constituent-sentence (as I call the second source-sentence in a generalized grammatical transformation rule).[12] This produces awkward expressions which must be reduced, but the conditions for these reductions may be easy to formulate. Note, incidentally, that we do not shy away from introducing further complications of this kind since they affect only the obligatory rules of the grammar, permitting greater simplifications in the optional component.[13] The desired reduction need only delete the adjective whenever it is identical to the preceding adjective, and the derivation would now be

(42) *He is that tall.*⎫

(56)   ⎬ $\rightarrow$ *He is as tall as I am tall* $\overset{ob}{\rightarrow}$

(51) *I am tall.*⎭

(52)   *He is as tall as I am* $\overset{op}{\rightarrow}$

(53)   *He is as tall as I* $\overset{op}{\rightarrow}$

(41)   *He is as tall as that.*

Let me remark also why we choose to include the *that*-constituent in the matrix-sentence (or first source-sentence of the transformation rule).[14] It seems that the constituent-structure of transforms may most easily be derived from that of the source-sentences by a uniform process of substitution: linguistic theory need say only that the constituent-structure of a component of a transform is simply that of the underlying constituent which it has replaced.[15] In our case, the constituent-structure of the component *as tall as I am* is Adjective, since it replaced the adjectival constituent *that tall* in the matrix-sentence; second, the constituent-structure of *as . . . as I am*, which happens to be phonemically discontinuous, is *Attributive Adverbial*, since it replaced the adverbial *that* in the matrix-sentence. We have now only to say how the latter adverbial had obtained this constituent-structure.

But this is easy . . . we need only permit the morpheme *that* to be generated along with *very, quite, rather*, etc., in the constituent-structure component of the grammar by means of ordinary expansion-rules together with its following adjectival. For example, in the copula-type sentence of the form

$Nom + Aux + be + Pred$

we permit the predicate *Pred* component to be expanded by a rule as

$$Pred \rightarrow \left\{ \begin{array}{c} Nom \\ Loc \\ (Adv_a) + Adj \end{array} \right\}$$

---

[12]See Lees, *Nominalizations*, p. 55.

[13]Ibid., p. 32.

[14]Ibid., p. 55.

[15]Ibid., p. 50, n. 24; also Chomsky, "Rule of Grammar," Sec. 3.

where *Nom* is a nominal, *Loc* is a "locative" place-adverbial, and $Adv_a + Adj$ is an adjective modified by a preceding attributive adverbial, one of which is the morpheme *that*.[16] This constituent-structure Adv_a is then transmitted through the later transformation to the substituent *as . . . as I am tall*, or *more . . . than I am tall*, which replaces the *that*.

From the meaning of the transform-sentence we might wonder whether the adjectival from the second, or constituent-, sentence does not also contain a similar attributive adverbial. One reason this might be desirable is that it would help us to specify more rigorously what can be the form of the second source-sentence, for clearly we cannot have any arbitrary sentence whatever in that position, as in

(42)   *He is that tall.*

(57) $\rightarrow$ **He is as tall as I was a new arrival.*

(58)   *I was a new arrival.*

although it is remotely possible that we shall wish to include as grammatical

(42)   *He is that tall.*

(59) $\rightarrow$ *He is as tall as I was new an arrival.*

(60)   *I was that new an arrival.*

We shall gain more information on this question by looking now at other kinds of examples of the comparative construction.

We note that comparatives may also be constructed with adverbial expressions, as in

(61)   *He walks as slowly as I do.*

Again, in these adverbial versions we are led to formulate the transformation so as to yield the full second source-sentence with subsequent obligatory and optional reductions, for we might also have such examples as

(62)   *He sings as badly as she plays well.*

which we can presume to be derived from

(63)   *He sings that badly.*

(64)   *She plays well.*

Note also, incidentally, that there is no necessity to reduce the second verb when the two underlying subjects are different:

(65)   *He sings as badly as she sings* $\overset{op}{\rightarrow}$

(66)   *He sings as badly as she does* $\overset{op}{\rightarrow}$

(67)   *He sings as badly as she.*

In addition to these examples produced by a process which turns on adverbial expressions in exactly the same way as did the adjectival examples presented before, there are also others of the form

(68)   *The attacks come as frequently as once a day.*

---

[16]This is then a slight extension, or improvement, of the constituent-structure expansion-rules given in Lees, ibid., p. 13.

which of course cannot be construed in the same way as

(69)   *The attacks come as frequently as the retreats.*

Here the discontinuous *as ... as once a day* component appears to be parallel in function to the former *as ... as I am*; that is, it appears to be an adverbial modifier of *frequently*, as though derived from an expression *that frequently*, parallel to *that tall*. Accordingly, we may derive

(70)   *The attacks come that frequently.*
(71)   *The attacks come once a day.* $\Big\} \rightarrow$

(72)   *The attacks come as frequently as the attacks come once a day* $\overset{ob}{\rightarrow}$
(68)   *The attacks come as frequently as once a day.*

And again, the reason we choose to include in the transform for further reduction the obligatorily deleted subject and verb is that there are other examples in which, when the subject and verb do *not* repeat those of the preceding source-sentence component, the latter are *not* elided:

(73)   *The attacks come as frequently as the retreats came rarely.*

From these examples it would seem that the transformational rule in question can be said to apply just in case the two source-sentences contain each an appropriate adverbial. But in the first set of derivations we formulated for the adjectival case there was no adverbial constituent in the second source-sentence (52). Perhaps it is then correct to require that there be one, in the following way:

(42)   *He is that tall.*
(74) $\Big\} \rightarrow$ *He is as tall as I am that tall* $\overset{ob}{\rightarrow}$
(75)   *I am that tall.*

(56)   *He is as tall as I am tall* $\overset{ob}{\rightarrow}$
(52)   *He is as tall as I am.*

Before summarizing in formal rules these constraints on the comparative construction, let us first examine in greater detail the particularities of the subsequent reduction-transformation rules which will be required. First of all, the attributive adverbial *that* which appears in the latter part of the transform must be deleted in all cases, for we have no

(76)   **He is taller than I am that wide.*

Second, when the adjectival constituent in the second part exactly repeats that of the underlying matrix-sentence, then it too is deleted:

(77)   *He is taller than I am wide.*
(78)   *He is taller than I am.*
(79)   *He is taller than I.*
(80)   **He is taller than I am tall*

Third, whenever the second verb exactly repeats the first, then it too may be deleted, but only optionally:

(81)   *He eats faster than I eat.*
(82)   *He eats faster than I.*

(83)   *He can eat faster than I can eat.*

(84)   *He can eat faster than I can.*

(85)   *He is eating faster than I am eating.*

(86)   *He is eating faster than I am.*

From these examples we also see that the preceding auxiliary can remain *in toto*; we are therefore led to regard the first case (82) as a secondary reduction from:

(87)   *He eats faster than I do.*

for the pro-verb *do* can then be taken as the normal carrier of the tense morpheme for the case where there is no other member of the auxiliary component present, as in negative and in questions.[17]

We must then go on to specify the conditions under which various members of the *Aux* can be deleted and also when the entire verb phrase is reduced to zero. First, we note that any number of *Aux* members may be retained by deletion in order from the right-hand side:

(88)   *He would have been talking louder than I would have been talking.*

(89)   *He would have been talking louder than I would have been.*

(90)   *He would have been talking louder than I would have.*

(91)   *He would have been talking louder than I would.*

(92)   *He would have been talking louder than I.*

Second, we must note that the last reduction to zero verb phrase is not always permitted, for we have

(93)   *He says that she talks more loudly than they say she does.*

(94)   *He says that she talks more loudly than they do.*

(95)   *He says that she talks more loudly than they.*

(96)   **He says that she talks more loudly than they say she.*

That is to say, the final verb phrase, reduced to a phrase in *do, have, be,* or a modal such as *can,* is not reducible to zero if it is within a subordinate clause of the constituent-sentence; only the verb phrase of the main clause of the underlying constituent-sentence may be completely deleted.

We are now finally ready to formulate a set of rules to generate such constructions.[18]

GT:

$$\left.\begin{array}{l} X + that + A + Y \\ Z + B + W \end{array}\right\} \rightarrow X + \left\{\begin{array}{l} as + A + Y + as \\ more + A + Y + than \end{array}\right\} Z + B + W$$

where (1) $A = Adj$ and $B = that + Adj$

or (2) $A = Man_x$, and $B = Man_x$

and where Man_x is a particular subclass of manner adverbials of the form

$Man = (Adv_a) Adj + ly$ or its equivalent, where Adv_a is an attributive adverbial and where $Z + B + W$ is not negative

---

[17]Lees, ibid., pp. 35–36; Rule (T41*), p. 49; and references to Chomsky therein.

[18]The conventions for writing grammatical rules are those of Lees, ibid.

Reductions:

T1:

$$X \begin{bmatrix} as + Adj + Y + as \\ more + Adj + Y + than \end{bmatrix} Z + that + Adj + W \rightarrow$$

$$X \begin{bmatrix} as + Adj + Y + as \\ more + Adj + Y + than \end{bmatrix} Z + Adj + W$$

T2:

$$X \begin{bmatrix} as + Adj_1 + Y + as \\ more + Adj_1 + Y + than \end{bmatrix} Z + Adj_2 + W \rightarrow$$

$$X \begin{bmatrix} as + Adj_1 + Y + as \\ more + Adj_1 + Y + than \end{bmatrix} Z + W$$

where $Adj_1 = Adj_2$

T3 (optional):

$$X + Vb_1 \begin{bmatrix} as + Adj + Y + as \\ more + Adj + Y + than \end{bmatrix} Z \left(\begin{bmatrix} Ing \\ En \end{bmatrix} \right) Vb_2 + W \rightarrow$$

$$X + Vb_1 \begin{bmatrix} as + Adj + Y + as \\ more + Adj + Y + than \end{bmatrix} Z + W$$

where $Vb_1 = Vb_2$

T4 (optional):

$$X \begin{bmatrix} have + En \\ M \end{bmatrix} be + Y \begin{bmatrix} as + Adj + Z + as \\ more + Adj + Z + than \end{bmatrix} W \begin{bmatrix} have + En \\ M \end{bmatrix} be + U \rightarrow$$

$$X \begin{bmatrix} have + En \\ M \end{bmatrix} be + Y \begin{bmatrix} as + Adj + Z + as \\ more + Adj + Z + than \end{bmatrix} W \begin{bmatrix} have \\ M \end{bmatrix} + U$$

T5 (optional):

$$X + M + have \, (Y) \begin{bmatrix} as + Adj + Z + as \\ more + Adj + Z + than \end{bmatrix} W + M + have + U \rightarrow$$

$$X + M + have \, (Y) \begin{bmatrix} as + Adj + Z + as \\ more + Adj + Z + than \end{bmatrix} W + M + U$$

T6 (optional):

$$X + Tns \begin{bmatrix} M_1 \\ Aux_{b_1} \end{bmatrix} Y \begin{bmatrix} as + Adj + Z + as \\ more + Adj + Z + than \end{bmatrix} Nom \, (Prev) \, Tns \begin{bmatrix} M_2 \\ Aux_{b_2} \end{bmatrix} Y + W \rightarrow$$

$$X + Tns \begin{bmatrix} M_1 \\ Aux_{b_1} \end{bmatrix} Y \begin{bmatrix} as + Adj + Z + as \\ more + Adj + Z + than \end{bmatrix} Nom + W$$

where Y is in the main clause of the constituent-sentence

In conclusion I should like to take note of several other features of the so-called comparative constructions. Notice to begin with the following triple ambiguity:

(97) *He had known more attractive women than Annie.*[19]

which can be construed either as

(98) *He had known women more attractive than Annie.*

(99) *He had known more attractive women than Annie had known.*

(100) *He had known attractive women other than Annie.*

Clearly (99) is an ordinary comparative construction such as we have just analyzed.

---

[19]The example is taken from Jespersen, op. cit., p. 397.

When (97) is construed like (100) it appears to contain a colloquial stylistic variant of the word *other*, as in

(101)   *He had known more attractive women than just Annie.*

But (98) can be construed only as a normal post-nominal modifier construction from the relative-clause sentence

(102)   *He had known women who were more attractive than Annie.*[20]

What then is the original triply ambiguous sentence (97) when construed in this latter way?

When the nominal in question is singular, we have

(103)   *He had known more attractive a woman than Annie.*

(104)   *He had known a woman more attractive than Annie.*

the latter being again a reduction from

(105)   *He had known a woman who was more attractive than Annie.*

Thus we seem to have a special inversion of comparative post-nominal modifiers:

> *a book that good → a book better than that → a better book than that*
> *books that good → books better than that → better books than that*

Taking the "equative" form of the comparative construction, we have

> *a book that good → a book as good as that → as good a book as that*
> *books that good → books as good as that → as good books as that*

Thus, we see that this inversion operates in a slightly different manner in the two comparatives; the so-called "comparative-degree" adjective follows the indefinite article, but the equative *as* + *Adj* precedes it.

There is also a special effect on the so-called *it*-inversion, that is, stylistic variations of the form

(106)   *That he goes is good →*

(107)   *It is good that he goes.*[21]

When the *Adj* is comparativized first, then one can have two different orders:

(108)   *That he goes is better than that →*

(109)   *It is better than that he goes.*

(110)   *That he goes is better than that I go →*

(111)   *It is better that he goes than that I go.*

Finally, I must comment briefly on the overall significance of the comparative transformations. The comparative rule serves to expand the attributive adverbial into an infinite class of expressions in the same way that nominalizations do the nouns,[22] the complement transformations the verbs,[23] the relative-clause and post-nominal modifier rules the adjectives, and various subordinate-clause constructions

[20]Lees, op. cit., pp. 85–94.
[21]Lees, ibid., p. 94.
[22]Ibid., Chap. III.
[23]Ibid., p. 9, and references to Chomsky therein.

in *if, when, although, whether, since*, etc., do the nonattributive adverbial.[24] This fact is what characterizes the major syntactic categories of the language, and is, in my view, a far more fundamental feature of major categories than is the fact that these usually also contain a large but finite lexicon of single-word members, as in the cases of noun and verb.[25] These transformations extend the finite multiplicity of certain grammatical categories to that of at least one denumerably infinite subset of sentences.

---

[24]I.e. rules which would expand, say, *then* in *He came then* to *when I left*, a transform of *I left*, yielding *He came when I left*, etc.

[25]Lees, "The Grammatical Basis," pp. 9–10 and nn. 19–21.

20

Phrase Structure Principles
of English Complex Sentence Formation

PETER S. ROSENBAUM

The purpose of this study is to show that the theory of English syntax contains at least two phrase structure rules (cf. Chomsky, 1956, 1961) which introduce sentences. The first of these exemplifies the principle of NOUN PHRASE COMPLEMENTATION by which a sentence is introduced under the immediate domination of a noun phrase (*NP*). The second is VERB PHRASE COMPLEMENTATION, involving the introduction of a sentence under the immediate domination of a verb phrase (*VP*). These rules, couched in a workable phrase structure context, will be postulated at the outset. (For a more complete phrase structure component incorporating the principles of noun phrase and verb phrase complementation, cf. Rosenbaum and Lochak, 1966.) It will then be shown (i) that these rules follow as a consequence of syntactic theory previously formulated and independently justified and (ii) that the incorporation of these rules into the grammar of English leads to a compelling account of a wide range of English complex sentence phenomena.

I

1.1. The phrase structure rules.

I. $S \rightarrow NP\ Aux\ VP$

II. $VP \rightarrow V \left(\left\{ \begin{matrix} NP \\ PP \end{matrix} \right\} \right) \left(\left\{ \begin{matrix} PP \\ S \end{matrix} \right\} \right)$

Reprinted from the *Journal of Linguistics*, 3.103–118 (1967), by permission of Peter S. Rosenbaum and the Cambridge University Press. At the author's request, certain changes have been made in the references.

The research reported in this paper was sponsored in part by the Air Force Cambridge Research Laboratories, Office of Aerospace Research, under Contract AF 19(628)-5127. The author wishes to express his gratitude to Paul Postal, Noam Chomsky, John Ross, and George Lakoff.

III. *PP → Prep NP*
IV. *NP → (Det) N (S)*

1.2.1. NOUN PHRASE COMPLEMENTATION. The principle of noun phrase complementation explains the linguistic phenomena exemplified in the following sentences.

(1)(a) *Everybody recognizes the fact that modern airplanes are fast.*
  (b) *The fact that modern airplanes are fast is recognized by everybody.*

In the above sentences it is observed that the determiner *the*, the noun *fact*, and the sentence *That modern airplanes are fast* function as an irreducible syntactic unit with respect to the process of passivization. Since the process of passivization involves the transposition of noun phrases (cf. Chomsky, 1957, Chaps. 5, 7), noun phrase complementation, through the assumption that the sentence *That modern airplanes are fast* is dominated by a noun phrase, explains the syntactic units observed.

1.2.2. VERB PHRASE COMPLEMENTATION. Consider the pseudo-cleft construction in English; in particular, sentences such as

(2)(a) *She prefers truth.*
  (b) *What she prefers is truth.*

This correspondence suggests that a rule exists in English by which noun phrases are "pseudo-clefted." Indirect support for this view is supplied by the principle of noun phrase complementation since English contains pseudo-cleft constructions corresponding to sentences (1a and b), namely,

(3)(a) *What everybody recognizes is the fact that modern airplanes are fast.*
  (b) *What is recognized by everybody is the fact that modern airplanes are fast.*

Consider now a sentence like the following:

(4) *She prefers to talk with us.*

This sentence shows a typical instance of noun phrase complementation, one in which the head noun of the noun phrase complement construction and the initial noun phrase of the complement sentence itself have been deleted (cf. Rosenbaum, 1965, 1967, 1968). Note that this sentence participates in the pseudo-cleft construction (5).

(5) *What she prefers is to talk with us.*

But now consider the following sentence:

(6) *She condescended to talk with us.*

This sentence is analogous to (4); but the rule of pseudo-cleft formation cannot be employed to form sentence (7).

(7) **What she condescended was to talk with us.*

Clearly, either the proposed pseudo-cleft analysis is incorrect, despite the very considerable support one can find for it (cf. Ross, 1967), or there is some specific condition in English grammar that explains why the pseudo-cleft rule can be used to form (5) but not (7).

Such an explanation is provided by the principle of verb phrase complementation. (The possibility that sentences such as (6) may be derivative of noun phrase complement structure is developed in Lakoff, 1965). This principle provides an underlying structure for sentence (6) in which the complement sentence *to talk with us* (actually *she talk with us*: cf. §2.5) is dominated immediately by a verb phrase, as in the *P*-marker (8).

(8)

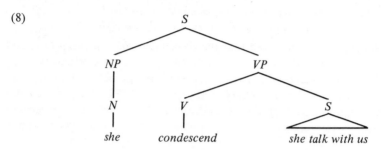

Since the complement sentence *talk with us* is not analyzable as a noun phrase (NP), the pseudo-cleft process must fail, thereby explaining the ungrammaticality of sentence (7). In sentence (4), the same complement sentence is analyzable as a *NP*, as illustrated in the *P*-marker (9).

(9)

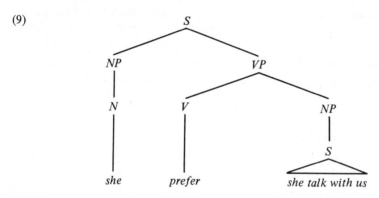

The pseudo-cleft process, applicable to noun phrases, predictably generates sentence (5).

The mere assertion that sentence (6) has a verb phrase complement analysis does not validate the principle of verb phrase complementation for it is conceivable that the nonapplication of the pseudo-cleft process to sentence (6) is governed by some other law. What gives the principle of verb phrase complementation greater plausibility is the natural explanation which it offers for important syntactic phenomena other than pseudo-cleft formations. Consider, for example, the passive construction in English with respect to such pairs as

(10)(a) *Nine out of ten people prefer to drink beer.*
  (b) *To drink beer is preferred by nine out of ten people.*
(11)(a) *Nine out of ten people condescend to drink beer.*
  (b) **To drink beer is condescended by nine out of ten people.*

In the event that the principle of verb phrase complementation does not hold, so that it is not this principle which explains the ungrammaticality of sentence (7), then the ungrammaticality of sentence (11b) has no explanation. Its ungrammaticality must be viewed as an *ad hoc* lexical restriction which the verb *condescend* imposes on the passive transformation. The verb *condescend* must be listed, in other words, in such a way as to indicate the nonapplicability of passivization. If the principle holds, on the other hand, then the ungrammaticality of sentence (11b) is no longer *ad hoc*; this ungrammaticality is predictable. Since the process of passivization involves the permutation of *NP*'s and since the complement sentence *to drink beer* in (11b) is not analyzable as an *NP* (rather, it has roughly the structure given in *P*-marker (8)), this sentence is prevented from undergoing passivization. In other words, the principle of verb phrase complementation not only explains the nonapplication of the pseudo-cleft process to a number of complex sentences; it furthermore explains the nonapplication of the process of passivization to these same sentences.

II

2.1. Testable consequences. A derivation based upon a set of phrase structure rules predicts, in effect, the structure and properties of a set of English sentences. In the following section, we shall be concerned with validating the claims implicit in the derivations of complex sentences allowed by the phrase structure rules postulated in 1.1.

2.2. Basic derivations. A cursory examination of the proposed phrase structure rules reveals a large generative capacity even if the depth of embedding of the symbol *S* is restricted. With the artificial restriction that an *S* which dominates an *S* may not itself be dominated by an *S*, most interesting and revealing derivations can be constructed. These derivations include four instances of noun phrase complementation, namely, SUBJECT COMPLEMENTATION, OBJECT COMPLEMENTATION, INTRANSITIVE OBLIQUE COMPLEMENTATION, and TRANSITIVE OBLIQUE COMPLEMENTATION, and two instances of verb phrase complementation, TRANSITIVE VERB PHRASE COMPLEMENTATION and INTRANSITIVE VERB PHRASE COMPLEMENTATION.

2.2.1. SUBJECT COMPLEMENTATION. The term SUBJECT COMPLEMENTATION refers to derivations generated through the application of PSR I (reproduced for convenience in (12)) and PSR IV (13).

(12) *S → NP Aux VP*

(13) *NP → Det N S*

The application of this sequence of rules may be graphically represented either by a *P*-marker, e.g. (14), or, equivalently, by a labelled bracketing, e.g. (15).

(14)

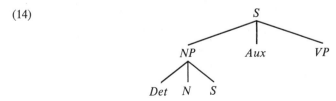

(15)   [[*Det N S*]$_{NP}$ *Aux VP*]$_S$

Complex sentences in English corresponding to this derivation are easily found, e.g. sentence (16) which has the labelled bracketing (17):

(16)   *The fact that she sleeps proves nothing.*

(17)   [[[*the*]$_{Det}$[*fact*]$_N$[*that she sleeps*]$_S$]$_{NP}$[*proves nothing*]$_{VP}$]$_S$

Support for the claim that sentence (16) is an instance of noun phrase complementation comes from two observations. First, the string *the fact that she sleeps* acts as a single syntactic unit under passivization, which yields sentence (18).

(18)   *Nothing is proved by the fact that she sleeps.*

Second, sentence (16) has a corresponding pseudo-cleft formation (19):

(19)   *What will prove nothing is the fact that she sleeps.*

2.2.2. OBJECT COMPLEMENTATION.   Object complementation refers to the derivation in which PSR IV (the subrule shown in (13)) applies to the output of the subrule of PSR II given in (20).

(20)   *VP → V NP*

In conjunction with PSR I, the derivation given in the *P*-marker (21) and the labelled bracketing (22) is generated.

(21)

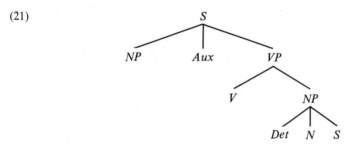

(22)   [*NP Aux* [*V* [*Det N S*]$_{NP}$]$_{VP}$]$_S$

Perhaps the most common noun phrase complement construction in English, the derivation (21) is supported by countless observations of which sentence (23) is an instance:

(23)   *We support the view that time is money.*

(24)   [[*we*]$_{NP}$[[*support*]$_V$[[*the*]$_{Det}$[*view*]$_N$[*that time is money*]$_S$]$_{NP}$]$_{VP}$]$_S$

Notice, once again, that sentence (23) undergoes passivization and has a corresponding pseudo-cleft formation:

(25)   *The view that time is money is supported by us.*

(26)   *What we support is the view that time is money.*

2.2.3. INTRANSITIVE OBLIQUE COMPLEMENTATION.   This type of noun phrase complementation involves the subrules of 1.1. given in (27).

(27)(a)   *S → NP Aux VP*
   (b)   *VP → V PP*
   (c)   *PP → Prep NP*
   (d)   *NP → Det N S*

The derivation based upon these subrules is summarized in the *P*-marker (28) and the labelled bracketing (29). (It is assumed here that the subrule (27d) applies to the *NP* generated by the subrule (27c). But sentences exist, it should be noted, where (27d) may apply as well to the *NP* generated by (27a), e.g. *Our chance to go to the circus depends on your arriving here on time.*)

(28)

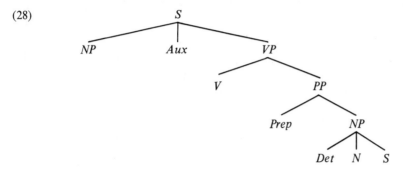

(29)   [*NP Aux* [*V* [*Prep* [*Det N S*]ₙₚ]ₚₚ]ᵥₚ]ₛ

A typical English sentence corresponding to this derivation is

(30)   *Everyone thinks about the idea that misery loves company.*

Again, observe the passive (31) and pseudo-cleft (32) versions of (30):

(31)   *The idea that misery loves company is thought about by everyone.*

(32)   *What everyone thinks about is the idea that misery loves company.*

Sentence (30) can be assigned the structure given in (33).

(33)   [[*everyone*]ₙₚ[[*thinks*]ᵥ[[*about*]ₚᵣₑₚ[[*the*]ₐₑₜ[*idea*]ₙ[*that misery loves*
        company]ₛ]ₙₚ]ₚₚ]ᵥₚ]ₛ

2.2.4. TRANSITIVE OBLIQUE COMPLEMENTATION.   This type of noun phrase complementation involves the subrules of 1.1. given in (34).

(34)(a)   *S → NP Aux VP*
   (b)   *VP → V NP PP*
   (c)   *PP → Prep NP*
   (d)   *NP → Det N S*

With rule (34d) applying to the output of rule (34c), the set of rules will generate the derivation given in the *P*-marker (35) and the labelled bracketing (36).

(35)

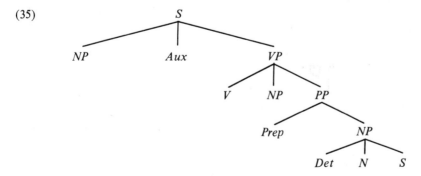

(36)   [*NP Aux* [*V NP* [*Prep* [*Det N S*]$_{NP}$]$_{PP}$]$_{VP}$]$_S$

Justifying this derivation is sentence (37).

(37)   *I will convince you of the fact that she drinks beer.*

The noun phrase complement construction cannot undergo passivization in (37), but the analysis is supported nonetheless by the existence of a pseudo-cleft counterpart:

(38)   *What I will convince you of is the fact that she drinks beer.*

2.2.5.   INTRANSITIVE VERB PHRASE COMPLEMENTATION.   The fundamental difference between noun phrase complementation and verb phrase complementation is that the latter involves the recursion of sentences under the immediate domination of verb phrases rather than under the immediate domination of noun phrases. The term INTRANSITIVE VERB PHRASE COMPLEMENTATION refers to derivations in which a verb phrase is expanded into a verb and a sentence by the subrule of PSR II given in (39).

(39)   *VP → V S*

In conjunction with PSR I, the subrule (39) provides for the derivation represented by the *P*-marker (40) and the labelled bracketing (41).

(40)

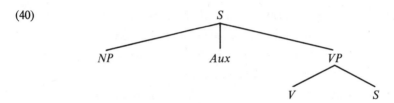

(41)   [*NP Aux* [*V S*]$_{VP}$]$_S$

Sentences exemplifying the phenomenon of intransitive verb phrase complementation are given in (42).

(42)(a)   *Bill tended to think big.*
  (b)   *We endeavored not to antagonize him.*
  (c)   *The teacher condescended to talk with Bill's mother.*

Notice that none of the sentences in (42) has a corresponding pseudo-cleft formation, i.e. all of the sentences in (43) are ungrammatical.

(43)(a)   **What Bill tended was to think big.*
  (b)   **What we endeavored was not to antagonize him.*
  (c)   **What the teacher condescended was to talk with Bill's mother.*

These data suggest, then, that a sentence like (42a) can be assigned the structure given in (44).

(44)   [[*Bill*]$_{NP}$[[*tended*]$_V$[*to think big*]$_S$]$_{VP}$]$_S$

2.2.6.   TRANSITIVE VERB PHRASE COMPLEMENTATION.   This type of verb phrase complementation involves the subrule of PSR II given in (45) which, in conjunction with PSR I, yields the derivation summarized by the *P*-marker (46) and the labelled bracketing (47).

(45) $VP \rightarrow V\ NP\ S$

(46)

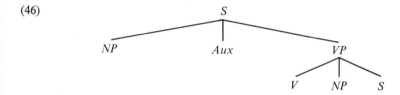

(47) $[NP\ Aux\ [V\ NP\ S]_{VP}]_S$

Exemplifying the above derivation are sentences like the following:

(48)(a)   *Nothing tempts Bill to be interviewed by the company.*
  (b)   *Nothing tempts the company to interview Bill.*

    There are two reasons for the assertion that sentences (48) are instances of transitive verb phrase complementation. First, the two sentences differ in meaning, a fact which, in the present analysis can be explained quite naturally on the assumption that the two sentences differ in their underlying structure. In terms of the principle of transitive verb phrase complementation, the underlying structures of the two sentences differ in that the noun phrase *Bill* (48a) is dominated immediately by the verb phrase in the main sentence; the string *to be interviewed by the company* is a complement sentence dominated immediately also by the verb phrase. For (48b), the noun phrase dominated immediately by the verb phrase is *the company*; the string *to interview Bill* is a sentence dominated by the verb phrase. The partially derived verb phrase structure of the two sentences are given in (49).

(49)(a)

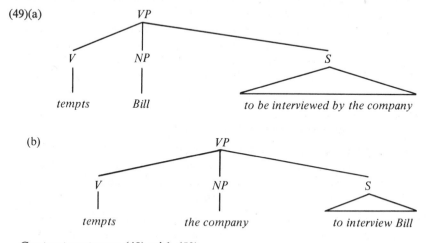

(b)

    Contrast sentences (48) with (50).

(50)(a)   *We want Bill to be interviewed by the company.*
  (b)   *We want the company to interview Bill.*

The synonymy of the two sentences above is explained by the fact that their underlying structures are identical (with the possible exception of the semantically uninterpreted passive marker in the underlying phrase marker for (50a); cf.

Katz and Postal, 1964: Chap. 3), having an underlying verb phrase structure of the following form:

(51)

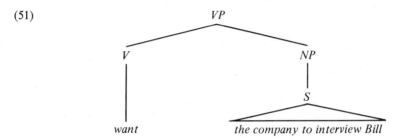

Sentence (50a) differs from sentence (50b) only in that the complement sentence in the former has undergone the process of passivization.

The second reason for viewing sentences (48) as instances of transitive verb phrase complementation has to do with the idiosyncratic selectional restrictions on verbs (cf. Chomsky, 1965, Chap. 2). Contrast the sentences (52) with the sentences (53):

(52)(a) *We dared the doctor to examine John.*
  (b) *We dared John to be examined by the doctor.*
(53)(a) *We dared the geologist to examine the rock.*
  (b) **We dared the rock to be examined by the geologist.*

The difficulty with sentence (53b) is that the verb *dare* may not have an object which is nonhuman. The principle of transitive verb phrase complementation allows us to state this restriction since it provides an analysis for sentence (53b) in which *the rock* is a noun phrase dominated immediately by *VP* (in a structure similar to (49)). If the string *the rock to be examined by the geologist* had been assigned a noun phrase (object) complement analysis, as it is in sentences (54), then we should not have been able to explain the ungrammaticality of (53b). This is so because verbal selection is not sensitive to the initial noun phrase of a complement sentence.

(54)(a) *We want the geologist to examine the rock.*
  (b) *We want the rock to be examined by the geologist.*

Since the principle of transitive verb phrase complementation so naturally permits an explanation of the ungrammaticality of sentence (53b), as well as the non-synonymy of sentences (48), we are led to the conclusion that sentences (48) are instances of transitive verb phrase complementation.

2.3. Complex derivations.   The phrase structure rules in 1.1 provide for the infinite recursion of sentences under the domination either of noun phrases or verb phrases. For example, consider the recursion of object complement constructions as generated by the sequence of subrules given in (55).

(55)   *S → NP Aux VP*
     VP → V NP
     NP → Det N S

The recursive application of these subrules will produce derivations of considerable complexity. Consider, for example, the derivation (56).

(56)

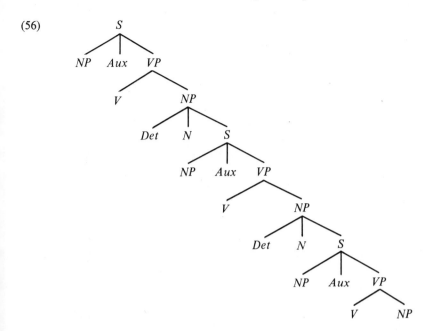

The existence of sentences in English corresponding to such complex derivations as (56) can be established with no difficulty. Consider, for example, the following:

(57) *We recognize the fact that she mentioned the claim that this sentence is complex.*

The following evidence supports other complex derivations.

(58) SUBJECT COMPLEMENTATION: *The fact that the fact that she wants to go home appals me appals me.*

(59) INTRANSITIVE OBLIQUE COMPLEMENTATION: *Everybody worried about the possibility that she talked about the fact that I want to go home.*

(60) TRANSITIVE OBLIQUE COMPLEMENTATION: *I will convince you of the fact that I reminded Bill of the possibility that Mary uses Brylcream regularly.*

(61) INTRANSITIVE VERB PHRASE COMPLEMENTATION: *She often tends to endeavor to get rid of her peculiar habits.*

(62) TRANSITIVE VERB PHRASE COMPLEMENTATION: *We tempted him to defy Mary to use moustache wax on her pigtail.*

These examples are seen to justify the recursive character of the general principles of noun phrase and verb phrase complementation.

2.4. Lexical subcategorization for noun phrases. The correctness of PSR IV depends in part upon whether English contains nouns which correspond to the subcategories (63) predicted by this rule.

(63)(a) $[Det\ N]_{NP}$
  (b) $[N]_{NP}$
  (c) $[Det\ N\ S]_{NP}$
  (d) $[N\ S]_{NP}$

Nouns possessing the subcategorization of (63a, b, c) abound in English, e.g. *teapot, John,* and *fact,* respectively.

(64)(a) $[[the]_{Det}[teapot]_N]_{NP}$ *fell on the floor*
   (b) $[[John]_N]_{NP}$ *slept late*
   (c) $[[the]_{Det}[fact]_N[that\ John\ slept\ late]_S]_{NP}$ *worries me*

In its explanation of the distributions above (64), PSR IV predicts the existence
of some phenomenon in English corresponding to the subcategorization (63d).
But the existence of such a correspondence is not immediately obvious and, consequently, the general validity of PSR IV is thrown into doubt. This difficulty is
further compounded by the fact that noun phrase complement constructions seem
to exist which are not characterizable at all by PSR IV, thereby seeming to render
PSR IV incomplete as well as inconsistent with linguistic reality.

Consider such sentences as

(65)   *John discovered that she drinks beer.*

The grammaticality of the corresponding passive sentence (66a) and the pseudo-
cleft (66b) is evidence that the string *that she drinks beer* is a noun phrase complement sentence.

(66)(a) *That she drinks beer was discovered by John.*
   (b) *What John discovered was that she drinks beer.*

The difficulty for PSR IV arises in the fact that the noun phrase complement construction in (65) apparently contains no head noun and consists solely of a complement sentence, as in the *P*-marker (67).

(67)

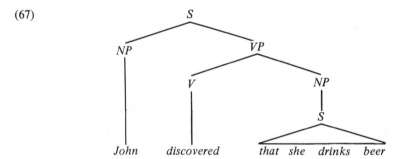

It is clear immediately that PSR IV is incapable of generating the noun phrase
complement construction in (67) since the expansion of *NP* into at least *N* is
obligatory.

Both problems, (i) that the subcategorization (63d) is nonproductive and (ii)
that PSR IV fails to generate a derivation corresponding to (67), can be resolved
on the assumption that the missing noun in (63d) and in sentence (65) is the pronoun *it*. If this hypothesis is true, then the subcategorizational gap represented by
(63d) is filled and, furthermore, PSR IV is now seen to be capable of generating the
structure underlying sentence (65). Moreover, this hypothesis offers a coherent
explanation for the existence of the pronoun *it* in sentences like the following:

(68)   *I dislike (it) for you to worry about me.*
(69)   *I wouldn't guarantee it that this is true.*

A testable consequence of this analysis is the prediction that there exists in
English some syntactic process by which the pronoun *it* is deleted before a com-

plement sentence. If such a process does not exist, the proposed analysis leaves us without an explanation of the "headless" noun phrase complement construction in sentence (65). It is unnecessary to look far for evidence that English does, in fact, make use of a pronoun deletion process before sentence complements. Consider the following pair of sentences:

(70)(a) *The assertion that she drinks beer was made by Tim.*
   (b) *The assertion was made by Tim that she drinks beer.*

This pair of sentences suggests that English employs the syntactic process of EXTRAPOSITION (cf. Rosenbaum, 1965), a term coined to refer to the process by which a complement sentence of a noun phrase complement construction is permuted to the end of the sentence.

Now consider the corresponding pair:

(71)(a) *That she drinks beer is known by Tim.*
   (b) *It is known by Tim that she drinks beer.*

It is natural to explain the relatedness of (71a) and (71b) in terms of the process of extraposition. But observe that such an explanation presupposes either a process which introduces the pronoun *it* (for an explanation of (71b)) or a process which deletes the pronoun *it* (for the explanation of (71a)) just in case this pronoun immediately precedes a complement sentence. Since the latter alternative conforms to the logical requirements of the hypothesis concerning PSR IV proposed above, the hypothesis that PSR IV introduces a pronoun *it* in the distribution (63d) is strongly confirmed. (Perhaps even more compelling evidence supporting this analysis is the fact that no transformational introduction of the pronoun *it* can be devised which preserves a reasonable semblance of generality.)

2.5. The structure of complement sentences. Since the expansion of *S* into *NP Aux VP* is obligatory, PSR I predicts that embedded sentences necessarily have an underlying subject noun phrase. This may seem a trivial prediction in the light of sentences like

(72) *I think that John left early.*

where a subject noun phrase, i.e. *John,* not only exists, but where, furthermore, this noun phrase cannot be deleted under any conditions. But consider now sentences like

(73) *I would prefer to play the piano.*

The string *to play the piano* is, of course, a noun phrase complement and it is intuitively clear that the implicit subject of this embedded sentence is *I.* Aside from this linguistic intuition,[1] there are other perhaps more objective data which bear on the theoretical claim that embedded sentences invariably have subject noun

---

[1]Intuition can be a dubious guide in the matter of determining exactly what the subject of the underlying embedded sentence is. Chomsky (personal communication) points to such sentences as *John helped Bill solve the problem or John helped write the book.* On the reading that "John neither solved the problem nor wrote the book, but helped to do both" the selection of *John* as the subject of the underlying sentence seems inconsistent. So, similarly, would be the selection of *Bill* or *someone* since neither solved a problem or wrote a book, but collaborated with John to do these things.

phrases in the underlying structure even though these noun phrases may be deleted by some transformational process applying to a derived *P*-marker.

Consider the following data:

(74)(a)   *I would prefer for you to play the piano.*
  (b)   **I would prefer for me to play the piano.*
  (c)   *I would prefer to play the piano.*

(75)(a)   *We dislike (it) for you to be so coy.*
  (b)   **We dislike (it) for us to be so coy.*
  (c)   *We dislike to be so coy.*

(74) and (75) show that a sentence containing an object complement construction is ungrammatical if (i) the subject of the complement sentence is identical to the subject of the main sentence *and* (ii) the former is actually present in the string, as in (74b) and (75b). The question is whether the sentences (74c) and (75c), where the subject of the complement sentence is missing, fill the gap posed by the (b) sentences or whether the grammaticality of (74c) and (75c) is totally unrelated to the ungrammaticality of the (b) sentences.

Consider, in the light of this question, the following sentences involving the reflexive construction in the complement sentences (for the formal details of this analysis of reflexivization, cf. Lees and Klima, 1963):

(76)(a)   *I would prefer for you to shoot yourself.*
  (b)   **I would prefer for me to shoot myself.*
  (c)   **I would prefer to shoot yourself.*
  (d)   *I would prefer to shoot myself.*

Reflexivization in sentence (76a) is clearly dependent upon the fact that the object of the complement sentence is identical to its subject, i.e. both subject and object noun phrases are *you*. Observe that reflexivization does not take place where subject and object are not identical.

(77)(a)   **I would prefer for you to shoot himself.*
  (b)   *I would prefer for you to shoot him.*

The fact that the noun phrase *you* is not deletable as the subject of the embedded sentence is illustrated by the ungrammaticality of sentence (76c). If the reflexivization of (76d) is to be explained by the same laws which explain the reflexivization of (76a)—thereby providing the greatest possible generalization—it follows that the process of reflexivization depends upon the existence of a subject noun phrase in the complement sentence, in particular *me*, prior to the application of the reflexivization transformation. It must be assumed, in other words, that the phrase structure did, in the case of (76d), generate a subject noun phrase *me* (76b) in the complement sentence. This conclusion is completely consistent with PSR I.

III

This paper is an attempt to demonstrate that the theory of English syntax includes two principles of phrase structure. These are (i) the principle of noun phrase complementation and (ii) the principle of verb phrase complementation, captured in PSR I and PSR II respectively. A number of reasons have been adduced for believing these principles to be correct in their essentials.

First, these two principles provide for an extremely general formulation of the processes of passivization and pseudo-cleft formation.

Second, the principles provide for the derivation of syntactic structures which correspond closely to many English complex sentence phenomena.

Third, the principle of noun phrase complementation leads to a convincing explanation of the lexical gap encountered when a noun phrase is expanded as *N S*.[2]

Fourth, the principles predict the existence of certain transformational processes. The principle of noun phrase complementation leads to a formulation of the process of EXTRAPOSITION and the process of PRONOUN DELETION, both of which formulations are confirmed in English syntax. Both principles suggest the existence of a process deleting the subject noun phrase of complement sentences.

There is a great deal which the principles of noun phrase and verb phrase complementation do not tell us about the structure and properties of complex sentences. The explanation of many such properties can be seen to reside in intricacies of the transformational processes applying to complex sentence structures. But the principles nonetheless offer an explanation of a wide range of syntactic phenomena and should be accorded, at least for the present, a measure of credibility.

REFERENCES

Chomsky, Noam (1956), "Three Models for the Description of Language," *I.R.E. Transactions on Information Theory*, Vol. IT-2; in *RMP*.

——— (1957), *Syntactic Structures*. The Hague: Mouton & Co.

——— (1961), "On the Notion 'Rule of Grammar,'" in *PAM*; *SL*.

——— (1965), *Aspects of the Theory of Syntax*. Cambridge, Mass.: M.I.T. Press.

Katz, J. J., and Paul M. Postal (1964), *An Integrated Theory of Linguistic Descriptions*. Research Monograph No. 26. Cambridge, Mass.: M.I.T. Press.

Lakoff, George (1965), *On the Nature of Syntactic Irregularity* (Ph.D. dissertation, Indiana University), *Mathematical Linguistics and Automatic Translation*. Harvard Computation Laboratory, Report No. NSF-16, Cambridge, Mass.

Lees, R. B., and Edward S. Klima (1963), "Rules for English pronominalization." *Language*, 39. 17–28 [*MSE*].

Rosenbaum, Peter S. (1965), *The Grammar of English Predicate Complement Constructions*. M.I.T. Cambridge, Mass.: M.I.T. Press, 1967.

---

[2]In the most recent formulation of the phrase structure principles under discussion (cf. Rosenbaum, 1967), the distinction reflected in the distributions *Det N S* and *N S* is rendered by the syntactic feature [± *Pronoun*]. The head noun of the complement construction will be assigned the feature [+ *Pronoun*] or [-*Pronoun*] along with the contextual feature [+____*S*] which indicates that the head noun takes a complement. Thus the lexical gap under discussion remains but is reflected in terms of the feature [± *Pronoun*] rather than in terms of a determiner constituent *Det*.

—— (1966), "A Principle Governing Deletion in English Sentential Complementation." IBM Research Report RC 1519, Yorktown Heights, N. Y. In P. S. Rosenbaum and R. A. Jacobs, eds., *Readings in English Transformational Grammar* (Waltham, Mass.: Blaisdell Publishing Company, to appear).

—— (1967), "English Grammar II," *Specification and Utilization of a Transformational Grammar*. Final Report, Contract No. AF 19(628)–5127, Yorktown Heights, New York.

—— and R. A. Jacobs (1968), *English Transformational Grammar*, Chap. 28. Waltham, Mass.: Blaisdell Publishing Company.

Rosenbaum, Peter S., and D. Lochak (1966), "The IBM Core Grammar of English," *Specification and Utilization of a Transformational Grammar*. Scientific Report No. 1, Contract AF 19(628)–5127. In W. Weksel and T. G. Bever, eds., *Structure and Psychology of Language* (New York: Holt, Rinehart & Winston, Inc., to appear).

Ross, J. R. (1967), *Constraints on Variables in Syntax*. Ph.D. dissertation, M.I.T., in preparation.

21

Attachment Transformations

S.-Y. KURODA

I

By way of introduction let us summarize briefly how the so-called *Wh*-questions have been dealt with in transformational studies of English. In brief, three stages of development can be distinguished.

Chomsky in his pioneer work (1957) gives the following transformations for *Wh*-questions:

(1) T_{w_1}:
　　Structural analysis: $X - NP - Y$ (X or Y may be null)
　　Structural change: $X_1 - X_2 - X_3 \rightarrow X_2 - X_1 - X_3$

(2) T_{w_2}:
　　Structural analysis: $NP - X$
　　Structural change: $X_1 - X_2 \rightarrow Wh - X_1 - X_2$
　　where $Wh - Animate\ Noun \rightarrow who$
　　　　　 $Wh - Inanimate\ Noun \rightarrow what$

A noun phrase constituent to be questioned is brought to the sentence initial position by T_{w_1} and has the marker *Wh* adjoined by T_{w_2}. For our present problem the particular mechanism by which the questioned constituent is brought into initial position is not essential, and we will not be concerned with it any more.

Later the following formulation was suggested by Klima.[1] To generate an interrogative sentence the marker *Wh* is introduced in the phrase structure in

---

In the author's Ph.D. dissertation, *Generative Grammatical Studies in the Japanese Language*, M.I.T., 1965, a particular type of transformation, called attachment transformation, is used for the description of Japanese syntax. But the currently accepted framework of transformational grammars does not permit such transformations, and in Chapter 1 of his dissertation the author attempted to justify the introduction of such transformations. The following is a revised version of this chapter.

[1]See Klima (1964), especially n. 6.

sentence-initial position, and it is adjoined optionally to an indefinite pronoun inside the sentence to yield a *Wh*-question. If *Wh* is not adjoined to a pronoun it is supposed to give rise to a *yes-no* question. Thus the transformation responsible for *Wh*-questions would take the form

(3)   *Wh X some – Pro → X Wh – some – Pro*
  where *Wh – some – Pro → who* if *Pro* is *Animate*
  Wh – some – Pro → what if *Pro* is *Inanimate*

Finally the most recent formulation is found in Katz and Postal (1964). The marker *Wh* is assumed to be generated in the phrase structure precisely within the noun phrase constituent that is to be questioned, and no attachment transformation like (2) or (3) is introduced.

The crucial point of this development of the treatment of *Wh*-questions is this. In the earlier position of Chomsky, an affirmative sentence, its *yes-no* question, and any of its *Wh*-questions obtained by replacing one of the noun phrases by a *Wh*-word, all presumably have the same underlying form. In Klima's formulation, *yes*-no questions containing one or more indefinite pronouns and *Wh*-questions obtained by replacing any of these by a *Wh*-word have the same underlying form; for example,

(4)   *Did someone buy something?*
(5)   *Who bought something?*
(6)   *What did someone buy?*

are all supposed to be derived from

(7)   *Wh someone bought something*

by nonapplication and appropriate applications of (3), respectively. The fact that nonsynonymous sentences are derived from one and the same base form by a transformation is precisely what Katz and Postal objected to in this treatment. Their analysis assumed different base forms for the different questions (4)–(6).

With our brief account of the last position, one may get an impression that no transformation is required altogether in treating *Wh*-questions. But as will be seen later some transformational device is needed to discard ill-formed strings; the difference is whether to use a transformation to generate just well-formed strings or to use another as a filtering device to discard ill-formed strings.

In what follows it will be seen that transformation (3) is considered as an example of an attachment transformation in our sense,[2] and it is claimed that such a rule should be allowed as a syntactic rule to deal with *Wh*-questions. This obviously conflicts with the principle, proposed in Katz and Postal (1964), that transformations do not affect meaning, or its refined reformulation by Chomsky (1965) that the semantic interpretation of the sentence is given by its (generalized) base form. But this does not necessarily imply that, so to speak, the spirit of the principle is abandoned altogether. In the first place, attachment transformations are permitted as rules in syntax, because their semantic effect can be justified by their particular formal characteristics. It is not maintained that just any kind of meaning-changing

---

[2]See Sec. 5.

transformation, such as negation,[3] imperative, or nominalization transformations can be freely introduced in the way they were once used in transformational studies. Second, it will be seen that our justification for attachment transformations is itself based on the assumption that, except possibly for the semantic effect of attachment transformations, a meaning of a sentence is determined by its base phrase marker. Furthermore, it will be noted that the semantic effect of an attachment transformation is simply a refinement of the meaning; after the attachment transformation is applied the meaning of the base form will simply be more specified than before.

But it might appear that whatever justification is given for attachment transformations, introduction of extra conditions on the principle that meaning is determined by the phrase structure base forms immediately implies a fatal loosening of the theory. However, this is not so. We loosen the conditions on transformations, but, as will be seen, we tighten the conditions on base forms.

II

Consider the pairs of sentences below. Each pair is regarded as representing a discourse.

(8)(a) *The storm destroyed his house.*
   (b) *The flood even devastated his farm.*[4]

---

[3]It has been said that the negative sentence is in general ambiguous in many ways. For example, *John did not disappear yesterday with the time machine* may be read either to imply that John did not disappear at all, that John disappeared yesterday but not with the time machine, or that John disappeared with the time machine but not yesterday. Thus, roughly, it appears that *not* may be taken as negating various constituents of the sentence as well as the sentence itself. Then, one may conclude that negation is also to be explained by means of attachment transformations. Note that this does not mean that the kind of negation transformation that was assumed in the earliest framework of transformational grammar is to be restored; according to that framework, the negative marker was introduced into the positive sentence by means of a transformation.

[4]According to one informant, the discourse (8 a–b) is well-formed, but combining the two sentences into one by means of *and* results in an unnatural form:

The storm destroyed his house and the flood even devastated his farm.

Another informant accepted (8 a–b) only after some hesitation. Thus it is expected that some readers may disagree as to the acceptability of this discourse. However, grammaticality encompasses more than just "good" speech, and with this in mind perhaps even doubtful readers can judge the discourse as well-formed. The author, as a non-native speaker of English, cannot dispute the judgment of a native speaker about the grammaticality of English forms. Those who cannot at all accept (8 a–b) as a discourse are simply asked to follow our discussion with the assumption that it is acceptable. The importance of the argument that follows lies in certain of its general theoretical aspects and not in its syntactic interpretation of a particular English construction. Even if (8 a–b) is not acceptable, it is believed that the English word *even* can still be treated along the lines sketched below with some modification. The essential point of this example is that two sentences which, unlike examples (9) and (10), do not contrast with each other with respect to certain constituents may be connected by means of *even*. Semantically this can be expected in a context in which the incident expressed by the second sentence is less plausible than that expressed by the first. Thus, in our example, to help to understand the intended point of our discussion, one may imagine a place which is less expected to be afflicted by floods than by storms.

(9)(a) *The storm destroyed his house.*
   (b) *It* (= the storm) *even devastated his farm.*
(10)(a) *The storm destroyed his house.*
    (b) *It* (= the storm) *destroyed his farm even.*
(11)(a) *The storm destroyed his house.*
    (b) *The flood also devastated his farm.*
(12)(a) *The storm destroyed his house.*
    (b) *It* (= the storm) *also devastated his farm.*
(13)(a) *The storm destroyed his house.*
    (b) *It* (= the storm) *destroyed his farm also.*

In each of the above pairs two sentences, or parts of sentences, are put in contrast. More precisely, whole sentences are put in contrast in (8) and (11), predicates in (9) and (12), and objects in (10) and (13). From this we may assume that the words *even* and *also* modify the whole sentence in (8b) and (11b), the predicate in (9b) and (12b), and the object in (10b) and (13b). That is, it may be assumed that the words *even* and *also* are directly dominated by the node *S* in (8b) and (11b), by the node *VP* in (9b) and (12b), and by the node *NP* in (10b) and (13b). Thus the phrase structure of these sentences may, with some simplification of irrelevant details, be represented as in (14.1–6).

It is important to note that the position of *even* or *also* before the verb in the surface representation is ambiguous with respect to the deep representation, either modifying the whole sentence as in (8b) and (11b) or the predicate as in (9b) and (12b). The position of *even* and *also* in the surface representations (8b) and (11b) is the result of a late transformation.

(14.1)

(14.2)

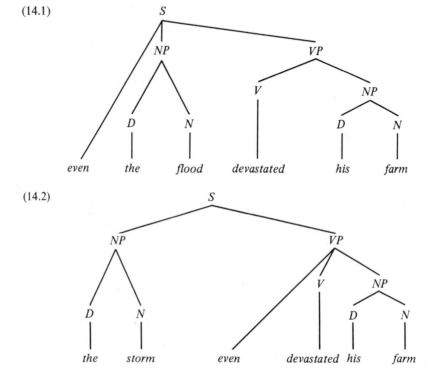

(14.3)

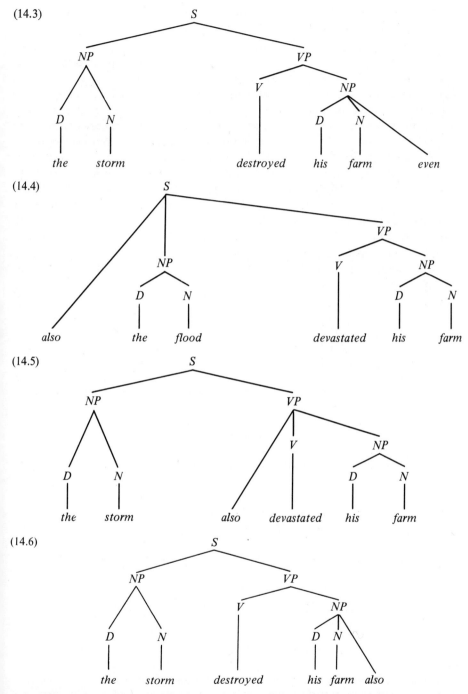

(14.4)

(14.5)

(14.6)

Although these phrase structure representations of sentences (8)–(13) appear to be reasonable, there are further considerations involved in a generative analysis of *even* and *also*. It has been stated that the predicates of (9b) and (12b) are contrasted with those of (9a) and (12a), and the objects of (10b) and (13b) with those of (10a) and (13a). It might further be said that this is reflected in the positioning of *even* and *also* in the representations of these sentences; i.e. if *even* or *also* is directly dominated by *VP*, the contrast is made with respect to the predicate, and if dominated by the object *NP*, the contrast is made with respect to the object. It is maintained here, however, that the fact that the predicates are contrasted in (9b) and (12b) and the objects in (10b) and (13b) is essentially independent of the fact that the second member of each pair contains the word *even* or *also*, and *a fortiori*, independent of the position of this word in the basic representation. The contrast is more strongly specified in (9) and (12) than in (8) and (11), and still more strongly specified in (10) and (13), simply because the pairing of sentences is, so to speak, more structured in (9) and (12), and even more so in (10) and (13), than in (8) and (11). All this leads us to recognize that the necessary and sufficient information for the semantic and phonological interpretations of sentences (9b), (10b), (12b) and (13b) as members of discourse pairs (9), (10), (12), and (13), is simply that the word *even* or *also* is contained in the sentences. In other words, given the above assumptions, there seems to be nothing to prevent us from taking the basic representations[5] of (9b), (10b), (12b), and (13b) to be of the same form as that of (8b) and (11b):

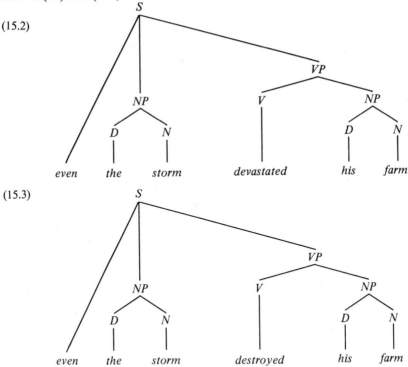

—————————
[5]We shall use the term *basic representation* (or *basic form*) as a loose substitute for the exact term *base form* when we represent a base form in a conveniently simplified way with omission of details which are not relevant to current discussions. For example, in our present examples the node *Aux* is completely suppressed and in this respect the basic representations given here are far from the true base forms intended to be represented by them.

(15.5)

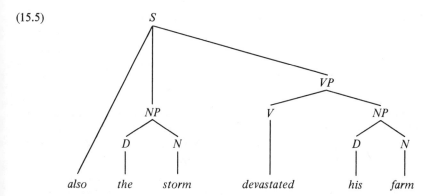

(15.6)

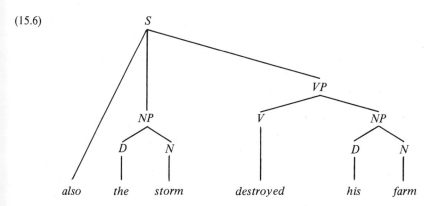

Then (14.2), (14.3), (14.5), and (14.6) will be considered as derived representations of (9b), (10b), (12b), and (13b) respectively. The following transformation is introduced:[6]

$$(16) \quad X_1 \begin{Bmatrix} VP_1 \\ NP_1 \end{Bmatrix} Y_1 \# \# \begin{Bmatrix} even \\ also \end{Bmatrix} X_2 \begin{Bmatrix} VP_2 \\ NP_2 \end{Bmatrix} Y_2 \quad \rightarrow$$

$$X_1 \begin{Bmatrix} VP_1 \\ NP_1 \end{Bmatrix} Y_1 \# \# X_2 \begin{Bmatrix} even \\ also \end{Bmatrix} + \begin{Bmatrix} VP_2 \\ NP_2 \end{Bmatrix} Y_2$$

where $X_1 = X_2$, $Y_1 = Y_2$

This transformation will generate discourse forms (8)–(13).

If it were supposed that sentences containing *even* or *also* always appear as part of a pair as in (8)–(13), transformation (16) would be sufficient to account for such sentences. This would mean, however, that we would have to regard as ungrammatical any simple sentences containing *even* or *also*, unless they were explicitly paired as in (8)–(13). This seems a too severe and counterintuitive limitation on the notion of grammaticality. It must be assumed, then, that some mechanism is

---

[6]The following convention will be established for the plus sign used in connection with an adjunction transformation: when an element *E* is adjoined to a certain constituent, for example, *NP*, from the left (or from the right), *E + NP* (or *NP + E*) indicates that *E* becomes the left-most (or right-most) constituent directly dominated by *NP*.

needed to generate forms like (8b)–(13b) in isolation. Two different formulations will be introduced.

The first, which we shall call the *unspecified compounding approach*, makes use of the same transformational formalism as in (16) but allows the first component of compounding $X_1 \begin{Bmatrix} VP_1 \\ NP_1 \end{Bmatrix} Y_1$ to be deleted. Since the content of the first component is to be considered semantically unspecified, it is natural to assume that it is also syntactically unspecified when deleted; that is, more formally, what is deleted is a string of (terminal) syntactic symbols, e.g. $Det - N - V - Det - N$, but not a string of words, e.g. *John saw Bill*. Accordingly, it is to be assumed either that the deletion transformation (hence also transformation (16)) takes place before the lexical rule is applied or that the lexical rule can leave unspecified those syntactic symbols to which transformations (in particular, transformation (16) and the deletion transformation in question) will apply.

The second approach, which we shall call the *attachment approach*, will introduce the following optional transformation:

(17) $\begin{Bmatrix} even \\ also \end{Bmatrix} X \begin{Bmatrix} VP \\ NP \end{Bmatrix} Y \rightarrow X \begin{Bmatrix} even \\ also \end{Bmatrix} + \begin{Bmatrix} VP \\ NP \end{Bmatrix} Y$

Trees of the form (14.2) or (14.3) and (14.5) or (14.6) will be derived from trees of the form (14.1) and (14.4), respectively, by this transformation.

The difference between these two approaches is not limited to the transformational formalism; they also involve different rules to assign the phrase structure to independent sentences containing *even* or *also*. In the attachment approach the following phrase structure rule is introduced:

(18) $S \rightarrow \begin{Bmatrix} even \\ also \end{Bmatrix} NP\ VP$

In the unspecified compounding approach, on the other hand, the string $\begin{Bmatrix} even \\ also \end{Bmatrix}$ $NP\ VP$ is well-formed only if it is the second member of the compounding, and hence the role of (18) is taken by the rule[7]

(19) $S \rightarrow \begin{Bmatrix} even \\ also \end{Bmatrix} NP\ VP$ in env. S _____

If a simple sentence is defined as having only one occurrence of S in its basic form, sentences like (8b)–(13b) (in isolation) are simple sentences in the attachment approach but not in the unspecified compounding approach.

---

[7]This is not the only phrase structure rule for sentences containing *even* or *also* in the unspecified compounding approach. For example, one might have the rule

$Sen \rightarrow S \left(\begin{Bmatrix} even \\ also \end{Bmatrix} \right) NP\ VP$

This fact does not change the main point of our discussion. Incidentally, so long as it is considered that generative grammar must concern itself with explicitly paired discourses like (8)–(13), rule (19) is also needed in the attachment approach to generate the form $S \begin{Bmatrix} even \\ also \end{Bmatrix} S$ but not

$*\begin{Bmatrix} even \\ also \end{Bmatrix} S\ S.$

III

There is still another approach which may be considered standard in the recent framework of transformational theory. Transformations are now viewed not only as devices to yield surface representations from basic representations but also as devices to filter out ill-formed base forms. In accordance with this line of thinking, the following explanation may be given for sentences like (8b)–(13b).

(14.1)–(14.6) will now be taken as the basic representations of (8b)–(13b). The words *even* and *also* are expanded under the nodes *S*, *VP*, and *NP* by the phrase-structure rules, which are something like

(20) $S \rightarrow \left(\left\{ \begin{array}{c} even \\ also \end{array} \right\} \right) NP \; VP$

(21) $VP \rightarrow \left(\left\{ \begin{array}{c} even \\ also \end{array} \right\} \right) V \; NP$

(22) $NP \rightarrow \left(\left\{ \begin{array}{c} even \\ also \end{array} \right\} \right) D \; N$

It is, however, supposed that *even* (or *also*) directly dominated by *S* is mutually exclusive with *even* (or *also*) directly dominated by *VP* or *NP*. Thus forms like the following are assumed to be ill-formed:

(23) **The flood even even devastated his farm.*

(where the first *even* is assumed to modify the whole sentence and the second the predicate), and:

(24) **The flood even destroyed even his farm.*

However, as context-free rules, (20)–(22) will produce these unacceptable forms, and a transformation must therefore be introduced to filter them out.[8]

It could be maintained that the attachment approach complicates the overall theoretical scheme of generative grammars because it introduces transformations like (17), which presumably change meaning, and that the filtering approach does not add a new notion because the concept of filtering is needed in grammars anyway. However, the following may be worth noting in this regard.

If unacceptable forms like (23) and (24) are formed and then filtered out, the filtering procedure has to take place within the realm of simple sentence formation. But conceptually (as well as formally, as will be pointed out later) there is a difference between the filtering of ill-formed complex sentences and ill-formed simple sentences. Indeed, one of the fundamental properties of grammars is that the symbol *S* is the sole recursive element in the phrase structure rules, and hence every sentence is reducible to a certain combination of simple sentences. Filtering in connection with sentence embedding (i.e. complex sentence formation) can be regarded as related to this particular recursive property of language. Vaguely but highly suggestively, the filtering out of ill-formed complex forms (i.e. generalized base

---

[8]Technically speaking, it is certainly possible to formulate a set of phrase-structure rules that will generate only grammatical forms. It seems obvious, however, that the restriction on *even* and *also* is transformational, and that an attempt to account for it within the phrase structure would simply miss this linguistically significant fact.

forms) may be regarded in a sense as a process which selects, out of all possible free sequences of sentences (that can be considered discourses in the most extended sense), those that can be combined into one sentence. Furthermore, the ill-formedness arising from an inappropriate combination of sentences may still, in some sense, be differentiated from the total "chaos" of meaning that exists in cases like (23) and (24). Indeed, at least insofar as a generalized base form can be paraphrased by a sequence of simple sentences (let us call this discourse paraphrase), its discourse paraphrase can have a meaning (although the meaning may be anomalous) even if it is ill-formed as a complex sentence. For example, assume that

(25)   *A man whom John knows is standing there.*

may be paraphrased by

(26)   *A man is standing there.*
(27)   *John knows that man.*

If someone says

(28)   *A man is standing there.*
(29)   *John knows that boy.*

it will strike the hearer as strange, but this strangeness is somewhat like the strangeness of, say,

(30)   *This round table is square.*

Sentence (30) may be put in the discourse form

(31)   *This table is round.*
(32)   *It is square.*

In the sense that (31)–(32) has a meaning, (28)–(29) may also be considered to have a meaning, and so may the generalized base form

(33)   *a man # John knows that boy # is standing there*

Let us compare the anomalous discourses (28)–(29) and (31)–(32). If language did not possess the syntactic device of relativization, complex sentences like (25) and (30) with relative clauses would not occur, and the ideas expressed by such sentences would instead be expressed by the compounding of simple sentences like (26)–(27) and (31)–(32). If that were the case, any significant difference between the anomaly of (28)–(29) and that of (31)–(32) might not be detected. Given the relativization transformation, however, the anomaly of (28)–(29) will be detected syntactically and filtered out, while apparently there is no transformation *fine* enough to distinguish anomalous ideas such as expressed in (30).

   Let us now look at this more formally. Since not many syntactic descriptions with an explicit formulation of the filtering process are available as yet, it is difficult to make definite statements. Still, it seems reasonable to suppose that the filtering out of unacceptable forms in sentence embedding is an automatic result of some general procedures in accordance with particular types of transformations. Take, for instance, the case of the relative clause transformation as discussed in Chomsky (1965). The phrase

(34)   *the man # the man persuaded John to be examined by a specialist #*

is well-formed and will be actualized as

(35)   *the man who persuaded John to be examined by a specialist*

But the form

(36)   *the man # the boy persuaded John to be examined by a specialist #*

is ill-formed and will be filtered out. The relative clause transformation involves a deletion, and, according to Chomsky, (36) is blocked because of the general condition that only recoverable deletion is permitted. Thus the filtering out of form (36) results automatically from the particular form of the relative clause transformation and from a general principle, i.e. the identity condition on deletion, and it is not the case that a special filtering procedure must be formulated as a rule of English grammar. It does not seem accidental that filtering in connection with the relative clause transformation is taken care of in a completely general way; relative clause formation is a very general grammatical device which probably exists in every language.[9] It is not immediately clear whether filtering can work in such a general way with transformations that are less general than relativization. At any rate it still seems reasonable to say that filtering is more or less connected with the *positive* role of transformations in deriving surface forms from well-formed base forms. With regard to filtering within the realm of simple sentence formation, e.g. the filtering out of forms like (23) and (24), the situation seems different. Here it appears that we must introduce special filtering transformations which have no positive role at all in deriving the surface forms of sentences.

Thus, it can be seen that conceptually as well as formally the filtering out of ill-formed *simple* sentences is quite different from the filtering out of ill-formed *complex* sentences. Consequently, the fact that the notion of filtering is necessary in connection with complex-sentence formation does not automatically guarantee that it can be used in simple-sentence formation.[10]

---

[9]Recently, E. Bach (1965) made an interesting remark on this point.

[10]Insofar as it is considered to filter out ill-formed *complex* sentences, the filtering function of the transformational component has always been implicit in transformational theory in the selection of permissible transformational markers (cf. Chomsky (1965)). *Explicit* recognition of the filtering function is quite important, however, in that it allows the structural conditions, formerly fully stated in each transformation, to be captured in more general terms and to be reduced, in the most favorable cases, to universal properties of the particular elementary transformations involved (cf. the above discussion of relativization taken from Chomsky (1965)). Thus, making the filtering function explicit can serve to simplify the grammar of a language considerably without essentially changing its theoretical basis. On the other hand, the implications involved in introducing transformations that serve only to filter out certain ill-formed simple sentences cannot be understood merely as a clarification of the earlier theory.

It may be appropriate to add here the following remark lest more implication than we intend be drawn from our objection to filtering simple ill-formed sentences. There are different types of ungrammaticalness involved in human language. The kind of ungrammaticalness which is treated above may suggestively be called syntactic ungrammaticalness as opposed to morphological ungrammaticalness, as illustrated by the following examples. As has often been remarked, of the two English nouns, *invasion* and *aggression*, which have similar meanings, the one is related to a verb, *invade*, while the other lacks the corresponding verb **aggress*. If it were the case that

IV

Let us now turn our attention to interrogative sentences. There are, currently, two different views about the markers involved in such sentences. One view assumes two markers, *Q* and *Wh*, while the other assumes only *Wh*. We shall subscribe to the latter view here, but the essential point of our discussion would not be affected should two markers be set up instead of one.

It is quite clear that *Wh*-words require some kind of transformational treatment in the formation of simple sentences. A *Wh*-word can occur in a simple sentence only if that sentence is not a *yes-no* question. Stated more formally, a node labeled *NP* may dominate *what*, for example, only if the marker *Wh* does not appear at the head of the sentence. This contextual restriction is similar to that observed for *even* and *also*.[11] If there is recourse to a filtering device, *NP* will first be freely expanded to *what*, and then a filtering transformation will apply to filter out sentences with occurrences of *Wh* both at their head and internally.

Unlike *even* and *also*, *Wh*-words have been much discussed in transformational studies of English. Except for the recent work by Katz and Postal (1964), the positioning of *Wh* in certain noun phrases is dealt with by a singulary transformation.[12] Our intention here is to present a (metagrammatical) justification for the use of a singulary transformation to describe *Wh*-questions.

---

aggress could be used as a verb, one would quite reasonably expect that syntactically it would behave much like *invade*. In particular, whatever relationship holds between *invade* and *invasion* would hold between *aggress* and *aggression*. To deal with this situation in our description one might introduce the morpheme *aggress* in the dictionary with nearly the same syntactic specifications as *invade*, but with an additional proviso that this morpheme may be phonologically realized only if it is followed by the nominalization morpheme *-ion* or by the actor morpheme *-or* in the surface structure. Then the form

(A)   *The Normans aggressed against England.*

must be taken to be well-formed, so far as its basic form is concerned, just as

(B)   *The Normans invaded England.*

is well-formed. But (A) is not a grammatical sentence, since it violates the morphological condition imposed on the morpheme *aggress*. Or one may say that the basic form corresponding to (A) is filtered out because the occurrence of the morpheme *aggress* in it cannot be phonologically realized. We do not mean to exclude such phonologically unrealizable but syntactically well-formed basic forms. Note that the basic form corresponding to (A) can be assumed to be semantically interpreted just in the same way as the basic form corresponding to (B) is.

This conditional phonetic unrealizability is presumably only one aspect of a more general grammatical phenomenon that one may understand by the name of *surface constraint*, which will be discussed in David Perlmutter's Ph.D. dissertation, M.I.T., in preparation.

[11]It should be noted that *Wh*-words can appear more than once in a sentence:

Who bought what?

while *also* or *even* cannot:

*Even John even bought books.
*Also John also bought books.

We shall return to this point later. In the meantime, to simplify our discussion, we shall restrict ourselves to sentences with at most one *Wh*-word.

[12]Chomsky (1957), Lees (1962), Klima (1964). For a comparison of the treatment in these works, see in particular Klima (1964), n. 6, and Katz and Postal (1964), Chap. 4, n. 10.

Let us consider the following *Wh*-question:

(46)   *Who bought books?*

This is in some sense related to compound sentences each of whose components is a *yes-no* question like

(47)   *Did John buy books?*

Let us suppose that we are given a particular discourse context in which three persons, *John, Bill,* and *Tom,* are referred to. Put into this context, (46) is paraphrased by the disjunctive sentence

(48)   *Did John buy books, or did Bill buy books, or did Tom buy books?*

Then (48) may be transformed into

(49)   *Did John, Bill, or Tom buy books?*[13]

For any set of n human nouns $N_1, N_2 \ldots N_n$, we can possibly conceive of a discourse context in which (46) is equivalent to

(50)   *did N_1 buy books, or did N_2 buy books . . . or did N_n buy books*

or to its transform

(51)   *did $N_1, N_2 \ldots$ or N_n buy books*

Similarly, for any set of n nouns $N_1, N_2 \ldots N_n$ insofar as their syntactic feature specifications are compatible with the context

(52)   *John bought _____.*

we can conceive of a discourse context in which

(53)   *What did John buy?*

is equivalent to

(54)   *did John buy N'_1, or did John buy $N'_2 \ldots$ or did John buy N'_n*

or to its transform:

(55)   *did John buy $N'_1, N'_2 \ldots$ or N'_n*

It is probably too much to claim the converse of the above statements in the strict sense, that is, to claim that whenever (46) or (53) is uttered we can paraphrase it in that particular context by forms like (50) or (54) with an appropriate choice of nouns $N_1 \ldots$ (*or $N'_1 \ldots$*). When one asks a question like (46) or (53), he may not have a *definite* idea of the possible candidates for the answer. Still, to some extent it can be said that such a question can be approximated by certain disjunctive questions of the type (50) or (54). The fact that one can always surprise a questioner by giving a totally unexpected answer may be indirect evidence that the questioner presupposes the range of possible answers to some extent.

---

[13]The surface forms (48) and (49) are, except for intonation, homophonous with the *yes-no* question of the disjunctive affirmative sentences

John bought books or Bill bought books or Tom bought books.

or

John, Bill, or Tom bought books.

(48) and (49) should not be confused with this *yes-no* question.

In this sense interrogative sentence (46) (or (53)) stands in a special relation, with respect to paraphrasability, to the set of disjunctive questions like (50) (or (54)).

It should be clear, however, that it is not meant either that (46) or (53) is paraphrased by anything that might be considered as an infinite disjunction or that an infinite disjunction is the base form of (46) or (53). Indeed such an infinite entity cannot be allowed to be generated as a sentence by the finite devices of grammar, and cannot exist at all and therefore cannot paraphrase or underlie any speech form. In grammar, both syntactically and semantically, those interrogative sentences ought to be explained directly and independently from disjunction.[14]

But it is another story to give some motivation for a particular form of the rules related to the generation of *Wh*-questions by referring to the generative process of disjunctive sentences. In fact, if *Wh*-questions and disjunctive *yes-no* questions are semantically closely related, it would not be surprising if some parallelism is noticed between their generative processes. Conversely speaking, when a rule to generate *Wh*-questions is proposed, if the generative process of *Wh*-questions by means of that rule can be justified with reference to the process of generation of disjunctive *yes-no* questions, it would motivate the introduction of that proposed rule in the grammar.

The basic representation of the interrogative sentence (47) is taken to be

(56)   *Wh John bought books*

The disjunctive questions (50) and (54) will have the basic forms

(57)   *Wh N_1 bought books, or Wh N_2 bought books . . . or Wh N_n bought books*
(58)   *Wh John bought N_1' or Wh John bought N_2' . . . or Wh John bought N_n'*

These forms will be transformed into

(59)   *Wh $(N_1, N_2 . . . or N_n)$ bought books*
(60)   *Wh John bought $(N_1', N_2' . . . or N_n')$*

which are intermediate forms of (51) and (55). On the other hand, the following explanation of (46) and (53) has been proposed. The basic forms are

(61)   *Wh someone bought books*
(62)   *Wh John bought something*

Then *Wh* is adjoined to *someone* and *something*; respectively, to give

(63)   *Wh + someone bought books*
(64)   *John bought Wh + something*

---

[14]Harris (1964) derives the *Wh* from the disjunction of all nouns in an appropriate subcategory of nouns. For example, he had

(A)   *I wonder whether N_1 or N_2 or . . . or $N_n V_i \Omega_i \rightarrow$*
(B)   *I wonder who $V_i \Omega_i$*

where $N_1, N_2 . . . N_n$ are all the nouns in the subcategory of human nouns (p. 49). Although one may detect some similarity in orientation, our position is different from his. Our basic form for
(B)   would be
(C)   *I wonder Wh someone $V_i \Omega_i$*

and no disjunction, either finite or infinite, is involved in its derivation.

from which (46) and (53) will be derived. But note now the formal similarity between the schemata (59) and (60) and the basic forms (61) and (62). Indeed, in place of the schemata $(N_1, N_2 \ldots or\ N_n)$ and $(N_1', N_2' \ldots N_n')$ in (59) and (60) there appear *someone* and *something* in (61) and (62), respectively. But the semantic relationship of the disjunctive question (51) (or (55)) and the *Wh*-question (46) (or (53)) can be said to be precisely paralleled by that of (59) and (61) (or (60) and (62)) (or more specifically that of the schema $(N_1, N_2 \ldots or\ N_n)$ and *someone* (or the schema $(N_1', N_2' \ldots or\ N_n')$ and *something*)). This would justify our supposing that (61) and (62) underlie (46) and (53) respectively. But (59) (or (60)) further contains the information that it is derived by compounding with respect to a particular constituent, the subject (or object). This is paralleled by the adjunction of *Wh* to the corresponding constituent *someone* (or *something*). To make an analogy between the compounding with respect to a particular constituent and the adjunction of *Wh* to that constituent is not at all arbitrary, in view of the fact that the sentence adverbials such as *even* and *also* are adjoined to a particular constituent, in case sentences are compounded with respect to that constituent, as seen from examples (8)–(13). Thus the following rule is justified:[15]

$$(65) \quad Wh\ X\ some\ \begin{Bmatrix} one \\ thing \end{Bmatrix}\ Y \rightarrow X\ Wh + some\ \begin{Bmatrix} one \\ thing \end{Bmatrix}\ Y$$

Let us now put together the observations made here and in the preceding section. On the one hand, the discussion in Section 3 indicates that transformations related to complex-sentence formation can be regarded in a natural way as filters which separate certain anomalous meanings from other meanings (which can be anomalous like (30), however). But the application of filtering in simple-sentence formation is not compatible with this natural interpretation of transformations as filters. Indeed, with regard to interrogative sentences, it would be necessary somehow to filter out forms like

(66)   *Wh who saw Bill?*

which, like (24) and (25), seem to represent complete semantic chaos.[16] On the other hand, it was shown in this section that an approach which is essentially

---

[15]This rule will be reformulated below to take care of sentences with more than one *Wh*-word, as in footnote 11.

[16]It might be thought that (66) could be considered the basic form of the echo question

(A)   *Did who see Bill?* (Echo question)

which could be a response to, for example,

(B)   *Did John see Bill?*

However, one can also think of an echo question as a reaction to an affirmative sentence:

(C)   *John saw Bill.*
(D)   *Who saw Bill?* (Echo question)

Question (D) is different from both (A) and the *Wh*-question

(E)   *Who saw Bill?* (*Wh*-question)

This seems to indicate the difficulty involved in dealing with echo questions solely with the marker *Wh* and taking (66) to be the basic form for (A). At present, however, we are not proposing any particular method for treating echo questions.

faithful to the original formulation of transformational theory can also be given a very natural (metagrammatical) interpretation. Thus this attachment approach would seem to be better justified than the filter approach.

Finally, to explain sentences such as

(67)   *Who bought what?*

we assume here that *Wh* can be attached more than once. Thus rule (65) is revised as follows:

(68) $Wh \ X \ some \begin{Bmatrix} one \\ thing \end{Bmatrix} Y \rightarrow Wh \ X \ Wh + some \begin{Bmatrix} one \\ thing \end{Bmatrix} Y$

This formulation states that if *X* or *Y* contains *some*, *Wh* is still available for attachment to it by the same rule. To remove the sentence-initial *Wh*, one more rule is needed:[17]

(69) $Wh \ X \rightarrow X$ if *X* contains *Wh*

In appropriate contexts (67) may be paraphrased by

(70)   *Did John buy books or did John buy magazines or did Bill buy books or did Bill buy magazines?*

This sentence can obviously be generalized by a schema containing an arbitrary number of human nouns and an arbitrary number of nonhuman nouns.

V

Note the formal similarity between rule (17) and rule (65). Once (65) or (68) is introduced into the grammar as a rule, there seems to be no formal reason for not introducing (17) as well. But one must ask whether (17) has some substantial justification of its own. Furthermore, in this case we must take the unspecified compounding approach as well as the filtering approach into consideration in our justification of rule (17) and the attachment approach it embodies.

If we examine closely what it is that the unspecified approach seems to express, it turns out that rule (17) has the same kind of justification as rule (65). Consider first the sentence

(71)   *Even John bought books.*

It is assumed that this sentence implies the existence of some other sentence(s) with which it is put in contrast. According to the unspecified compounding approach, this other form would be represented by an unspecified sentence, *NP bought books*. The precise meaning of "unspecified" here is not immediately clear. However, one may certainly say that *someone (something)* in rule (65) represents in some sense an unspecified noun (actually the unspecified noun phrase *NP* has also been used in the formulation of the *Wh*-question transformation), and may recall the role of *someone (something)* in the discussion justifying rule (65). Then, one may note that in appropriate contexts what seems to be meant by

---

[17]Apparently this deletion rule may have to be combined with the familiar rule for the deletion of *Wh* in *yes-no* questions. We will not be concerned with this problem here.

(72) *NP bought books and even John bought books*

is paraphrased by

(73) *Bill bought books and even John bought books.*

It was mentioned previously that in the basic representations, *even* is assumed to be attached to the whole sentence. Thus, the basic form for (73) is

(74) *Bill bought books and even (John)$_{NP}$ (bought books)$_{VP}$*

Since (72) is assumed to appear as (71), it follows that (71) is assumed to be synonymous with (74) in appropriate contexts. As before, the number of nouns need not be two, and appropriate contexts may be conceived of in which (71) is synonymous with

(75) *N_1 bought books, N_2 bought books ... N_{n-1} bought books, and even (John)$_{NP}$ (bought books)$_{VP}$*

where N_1, N_2 ... N_{n-1} are n-1 arbitrary human nouns. Consequently, just as (46) stands in a special relation to schema (50) with respect to paraphrasability, so does (71) with schema (75). Now the transformation which is similar to (16) but extended to n terms will transform (75) into

(76) *N_1 bought books, N_2 bought books ... N_{n-1} bought books, and (even John)$_{NP}$ bought books*

Furthermore, as schema (51) was derived from schema (50), the following schema may be derived from (75):

(77) *(N_1, N_2 ... N_{n-1} and even John)$_{NP}$ bought books*

In the case of the *Wh*-question, the subschema N_1, N_2 ... N_{n-1}, *or N_n* was replaced by *someone*. But in the present case there is no need for the intervention of neutral forms such as *someone*, since the form *even John* is sufficient to represent the subschema N_1, N_2 ... N_{n-1}, *and even John*. The operation of the adjunction of *even* represents, as does the operation of the adjunction of *Wh*, the structuring in the unspecified compounding. The same argument holds for the word *also*. Thus, if (65) is admitted as a syntactic rule, (17) can be admitted on the same grounds. Under this interpretation, (17) is as informative as (or more informative than) (16) used with the first component unspecified and appears formally simpler.[18]

Rules like (17) and (65) will be called attachment transformations. Formally and substantially they are characterized as follows. Formally they have one of the following forms:

---

[18]The relation between rules (16) and (17) may need a further comment. Rule (17) was introduced to generate independent sentences with *even* or *also*. Rule (16) is still needed, as long as discourses like (8)–(13) are assumed to be within the range of generative grammars. More generally, for each $n > 1$, a version of rule (16) extended to n terms is to be assumed, as well as a shortening rule to derive forms like (77) from forms like (76). Just how such a *schema of rules* should be incorporated into the grammar is as yet not clear. At any rate, rule (17) should not be confused with a schema of rules: any rule, or combination of rules, of the schema of rules like (16) and the shortening rules cannot generate sentences like (71). The relation between rule (17) and this schema of rules parallels the relation between rule (65) and the schema of rules that derives forms like (51) or (55) from forms like (50) or (54); each rule of the schema is needed to generate a sentence like (49), but none can generate (46).

(78)   Left-sided noniterative:
$$M X C Y \to X M + C Y$$

(79)   Left-sided iterative:
$$M X C Y \to M X M + C Y$$

(80)   Right-sided noniterative:
$$X C Y M \to X C + M Y$$

(81)   Right-sided iterative:
$$X C Y M \to X C + M Y M$$

Here C denotes certain constituents or morphemes to be specified in each rule. An iterative attachment is generally to be accompanied by a deletion transformation of the form

(82) $M X M + C Y \to X M + C Y$

or

(83) $X C + M Y M \to X C + M Y$

Substantially an attachment transformation is assumed to be given a metagrammatical interpretation similar to that given to (17) and (65). It stands in a special relation, with respect to paraphrasability, to a particular schema of sentence compounding. The attachment transformation itself will not establish within the grammar a paraphrase relationship of the sentences to be generated by it with certain definite compound sentences, or, needless to say, with any infinite compound sentence, which does not exist. But each realization of the schema can be assumed to paraphrase a sentence generated by the attachment if given an appropriate context. The operation of the adjunction of M to C reflects a particular structuring in the corresponding sentence compounding which puts the constituent C into relief. The attachment transformation and the corresponding schema of sentence compounding are independent in their effect as generative rules; a sentence generated by the attachment transformation is generated precisely by that transformation and the rules of sentence compounding have nothing to do with its generation. But it would be assumed that the very existence of the attachment rule in the grammar is closely related, or, rather, totally dependent on, the existence of the corresponding schema of sentence compounding.

The form of the sentence compounding corresponding to an attachment transformation is not necessarily a disjunction or conjunction of sentences of the same structure. The word *only* may be compared with a compounding of a positive sentence and a set of negative sentences such as

(84)   *John bought a book but Bill did not buy a book, Tom did not buy a book . . .*

Concerning the formalism given in (78)–(81) the following remark must be added. First, those rules are not meant to be solely and always directly responsible for the actual appearance of the syntactic element M in actual speech forms. Those rules may have to be supplemented by other low-level rules which determine the actual phonological shape and position of M and/or its possible phonological effect on other constituents, especially on the constituent C, to which M is attached by a rule of the form (78)–(81). Thus, for example, in the case of *Wh*-attachment (65), it must be supplemented by a morphophonemic rule which has the effect of converting *Wh* + *someone* and *Wh* + *something* into *who* and *what*, respectively; to generate the speech form (10b) the attachment transformation (17) must be supplemented by a rule which converts *even his farm* into *his farm even*. Such rules can be compared with the rule, for example, which inverts the subject and the first auxiliary in the *yes-no* question, i.e. in the sentence with the *Wh* marker left unattached to any constituent, or with the rule which moves *even* to the preverbal position in the sentence with *even* unattached to any constituent, thus yielding, for example, (8a) from (14.1).

Secondly, then, one would immediately note some arbitrariness in the formalism given by (78)–(81). Indeed, one might formulate the *even*-attachment rule, for example, so that it attaches *even* to the right of *C*:

(85)   *even X C Y* → *X C* + *even Y*

Appropriate low-level transformations would be introduced to yield the correct surface realization of *even* in each speech form. For that matter, no justification was given either for the occurrence of *even* in sentence-initial position in the basic form, rather than, say, in sentence-final position. In the case of *Wh*-attachment (65), we simply followed the formalism already familiar in the study of English syntax, but there one can give certain justification for the sentence-initial position of the *Wh* marker.[19] Yet the attachment of *Wh* to the left of *someone* or *something* seems to remain arbitrary.[20] This apparent arbitrariness of the position to be assigned to the marker *M* before and after the attachment transformation takes place would suggest that the formalism given in (78)–(81) has a serious defect from the formal point of view. This arbitrariness could be removed if one renders neutral with respect to the left-right relation the positional relationship of *M* to the entire sentence and to the particular constituent *C* before and after the application of the attachment transformation. This cannot be attained so long as one deals with transformations formalized in terms of strings of syntactic formatives and/or their categories (i.e. terminal symbols and nonterminal symbols in the sense of the phrase structure). But the desired neutralization can be attained if one allows *M* to be interpreted as a syntactic feature, or better yet, as a feature specification assigned to an appropriate constituent. Thus, in the basic form *M* would be assumed to be a feature specification assigned to the node *Sentence*, which may be reassigned to a smaller constituent by means of the attachment transformation. Actually, Chomsky has recently proposed to generalize the syntactic feature theory in order to allow higher nodes to be assigned syntactic features.[21] The theoretical scheme of this proposal, then, would provide a basis for formulating attachment transformations, so that they are free from the apparent arbitrariness involved in the formulation given in (78)–(81).

---

[19]See, for example, arguments given in Katz and Postal (1964), pp. 87ff.

[20]Rule (65) must be generalized in such a way that *Wh* may be attached to the determiner *some*, whether it is followed by a noun or a pronoun. For the convenience of the exposition we simplified the situation and talked only about *Wh*-questions in which the *Wh*-words appear as pronouns. When the rule is so generalized, *Wh*, after attachment, appears to the left of the noun to be modified by it; yet the question remains essentially the same: whether or not one can justify the attachment of *Wh* to the left of the determiner *some*.

[21]Lectures, 1966.

In this work, however, we do not have recourse to extended syntactic features in our formulation of attachment transformations. For one thing, reformulation of attachment transformations in terms of syntactic features would be straight-forward, once the general theoretical scheme of the extended feature theory is accepted. More important, however, would be the problem of what the general criteria are by which one is allowed to regard some syntactic entity as a syntactic feature. Taking the word *even* as an example, there is no essential problem in reformulating the transformation that attaches *even* as a syntactic feature, once one has decided to introduce a syntactic feature corresponding to the word *even*. The moot point lies rather in how one decides to regard *even* as a feature. It is not a familiar kind of feature like HUMANNESS, which subcategorizes a category of syntactic formatives. If one considers *even* as a feature, the attachment transforma-tion of *even* can be formulated without recourse to an arbitrary linear ordering. However, it is not obvious that the elimination of linear ordering is a sufficient criterion for considering *even* as a syntactic feature. Strictly applied, this argu-ment might force one to have recourse to syntactic features whenever one does not have real motivation for the ordering of constituents in the base structure.[22] Furthermore, though it is true that the formulations given in (78)–(81) contain the possibility of giving rise to arbitrariness in general, yet in each particular case the arbitrariness will not necessarily present itself to its full extent. In fact, as noted above, there is some evidence for considering the *Wh* marker to be a pre-sentential adverbial, in which case the sentence-initial position of *Wh* would be justified.[23] At the present stage of our investigation it would seem advisable not to resort too hastily to the device of using syntactic features in formulating attachment transfor-mations, thus obscuring the general problem of how syntactic features are to be characterized. Instead we should try to find out to what extent formulations such as (78)–(81) lead to formal arbitrariness. By doing so we may be in a better posi-tion to find out which formal caracteristics of syntactic entities may be interpreted as syntactic features in connection with attachment transformations.[24]

---

[22]Assume that there is a language in which a manner adverbial may be put either before or after the main verb. Then, one would be forced to assume that either manner adverbials are features of verbs, or verbs are features of manner adverbials, in order to get rid of the arbitrariness of their mutual order in strings of formatives which necessarily arises if one assumes both manner adverbials and verbs are syntactic formatives.

[23]In most examples of attachment transformations in Japanese it would not be considered arbitrary to attach particles to the right of appropriate constituents, since they generally have a surface actualization as postpositions.

[24]It would be interesting, in connection with our discussion of attachment transformations, to refer to the often cited remark that the schema of context-free grammar is sufficient for artificial computer languages. We have already remarked that transformations are used to filter out ill-formed base forms, and it is proposed that their use as filters be restricted to complex-sentence formation. As a consequence of this restriction attachment transformations are introduced into grammars. Another aspect of transformations which bears on meaning would be the selective lexical rule that inserts lexical entries into abstract base forms. All other effects of transformations are morphophonemic in the broad sense that they determine phonetic forms of sentences but are semantically irrelevant. Now, filtering and selective transformations would not be necessary in computer languages, probably because use of computer languages always assumes pre-editing by human programmers. As for attachment transformations, there is no need to make computers

REFERENCES

Bach, E. (1965), "On Some Recurrent Types of Transformations." Report of the Six-teenth Annual Round Table Meeting on Linguistics and Language Studies, Georgetown University.

Chomsky, Noam (1957), *Syntactic Structures*. The Hague: Mouton & Co.

―――― (1965), *Aspects of the Theory of Syntax*. Cambridge, Mass.: M.I.T. Press.

Harris, Zellig S. (1964), "The Elementary Transformations." Prepublication copy, University of Pennsylvania Transformations and Discourse Analysis Papers, No. 54.

Katz, J. J., and Paul M. Postal (1964), *An Integrated Theory of Linguistic Descriptions*. Research Monograph No. 26. Cambridge, Mass.: M.I.T. Press.

Klima, Edward S. (1964), "Relatedness Between Grammatical Systems." *Language*, 40.1–20; in *MSE*.

Lees, R. B. (1960), *The Grammar of English Nominalizations*. Supplement to *International Journal of American Linguistics*, 26:3 (July 1960), Part II.

---

understand such words as *also* and *even*, on the one hand, and on the other hand computers cannot understand such words as *what* and *only* directly. In a situation where someone would use a *Wh*-question in interhuman communication, when dealing with a machine he has to specify explicitly the range of objects about which the question is asked and he must put the question in disjunctive form over this range. With a human being the questioner can leave this range linguistically indefinite by using a *Wh*-question. The same holds for *only*. This ability to be imprecise and thus to attain economy in communication seems to be a characteristic which distinguishes interhuman communication from artificial communication, and it is precisely in this situation that attachment transformations intervene in human languages.

22

Adjectives As Noun Phrases

JOHN ROBERT ROSS

Recent research into the nature of underlying syntactic structure by Paul Postal and by George Lakoff has indicated that the parts of speech which have traditionally been called *verbs* and *adjectives* should really be looked upon as two subcategories of one major lexical category, *predicate*. Some of the facts that lead to this conclusion are given in (1).

(1)(a) There are transitive verbs such as *bring, trust to, depend on,* etc., and intransitive verbs such as *sleep, billow, elapse,* etc.; similarly, there are transitive adjectives such as *fond of, wild about, mad at,* etc., and intransitive adjectives such as *dead, red, absurd,* etc.

  (b) Some verbs such as *know, hope, read,* etc., require animate subjects (*The wrestler hoped for a quick victory,* but not **The driveway hoped for a quick victory*), while other verbs such as *elapse, entail, subtend,* etc., exclude animate subjects (*Two weeks elapsed,* but not **My Latin teacher elapsed*). Similarly, some adjectives such as *despondent, aware, contrite,* etc., require animate subjects (*The wrestler was despondent,* but not **The driveway was despondent*), while others such as *valid, moot, gibbous,* etc., exclude animate subjects (*Your argument is valid,* but not **Your nephew is valid*).

  (c) Some verbs such as *jump, kick, build,* etc., can occur in imperative sentences, while others such as *resemble, inherit, doubt,* etc., cannot (*Jump over it,* but not **Resemble Jonathan*). Similarly, some adjectives such as *polite, honest, reasonable,* etc., can occur in imperatives, while others such as *swarthy, fat, pregnant,* etc., cannot (*Be polite,* but not **Be swarthy*).

This paper was presented at the Winter Meeting of the Linguistic Society of America, which was held in New York on December 28, 1966. This work was supported in part by the Joint Services Electronics Program under Contract DA 36-039-AMC-03200(E); in part by the National Science Foundation (Grant GP-2495), the National Institutes of Health (Grant MH-04737-05), the National Aeronautics and Space Administration (Grant NsG-496), and the U.S. Air Force (ESD Contract AF 19(628)-2487).

I am indebted to Morris Halle, to Paul and Carol Kiparsky, and to George Lakoff, for many helpful criticisms and suggestions.

These facts, and there are many others like them, constitute part of the evidence for the correctness of the claim that adjectives and verbs are members of the same lexical category, a claim which I will not further justify in this paper, but will assume is correct. It should be obvious, however, that to accept this claim is not to maintain that verbs and adjectives behave identically in all respects, but only that their deep similarities outweigh their superficial differences in syntactic behavior.

There are many American Indian languages, such as Mohawk and Hidatsa, and African languages, such as Gã, a language of Ghana, which do not exhibit the main syntactic feature which differentiates adjectives and verbs in English, i.e. the fact that the former are always preceded in simple sentences by the copula *be*. In such languages, sentences like (2) are expressed by a word-for-word equivalent of (3).

(2) *Henry is hungry.*
(3) **Henry hungries.*

The question I wish to discuss is the following: in languages exhibiting the copula, what is the deep structure of sentences like (2), which contain predicate adjectives? And what is the status of the copula *be* in these languages? Is it merely an empty morpheme, which has been inserted by a transformational rule to "carry" tense and person inflections? Or is it instead present in the deep structure of (2)?

I wish to argue for this latter possibility, and to claim that the deep structure of (2) is roughly that shown in (4) (I use the feature specification [+V] to designate the lexical category of *predicate*): note that (4) *contains* as an embedded sentence the structure which would underlie (3):

(4)

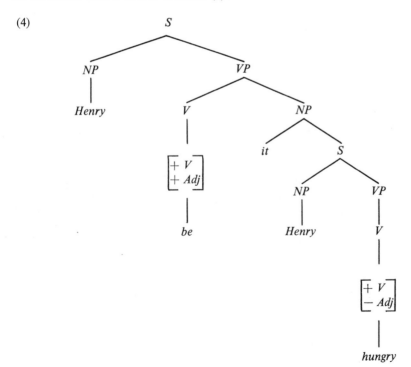

I am claiming, therefore, that the underlying structure of (2) is in all significant respects exactly parallel to (6), which is the underlying structure of (5).

(5) *Alice tried to cough.*

(6)

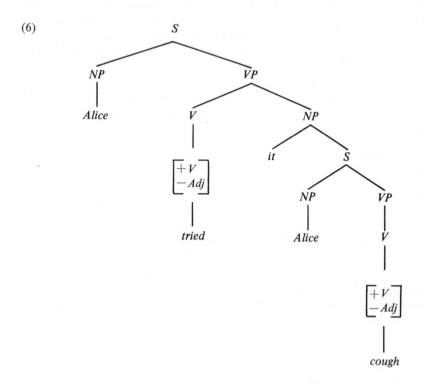

Furthermore, the derivation of (5) from (6) parallels exactly the derivation of (2) from (4). The verb *try*, which takes an abstract noun phrase as its object, is lexically marked in such a way that the rule of EQUI–NP DELETION, which deletes the subject of an embedded sentence if it is identical to some *NP* in the matrix sentence, must always apply to it—there are no sentences like (7).

(7) **Alice tried for Bill to cough.*

If the verb *be* is entered in the lexicon with the same kind of marking as *try* has, the embedded subject, *Henry*, in (4) will always be deleted by the rule of EQUI–NP DELETION. Then rule (8), IT-DELETION, which applies in deriving (5) from (6), will also apply in deriving (2) from (4).

(8) IT-DELETION:
$$X - [it - S]_{NP} - Y$$
1   2 3   4 $\Rightarrow$ (obligatory)
1   0 3   4

Various automatic conventions of tree-pruning[1] will delete several nonterminal

---

[1]For a description of a convention which prunes the node *S* under certain conditions, see my

nodes in (4): the node *NP* which dominates the object of *be*, the embedded node *S*, and possibly also the node *VP* which exhaustively dominates *hungry*, leaving a derived tree roughly of the form of (9), which I will assume to be approximately the correct derived structure for sentence (2).

(9)

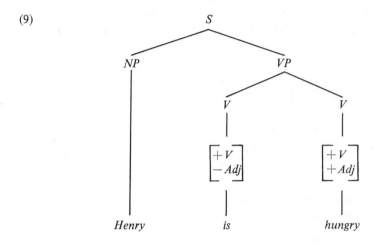

Thus far I have shown that if (4) is assumed to be the deep structure of (2), and if *be* is entered in the lexicon with the same markings as *try*, rules which are necessary in any event in the grammar of English and conventions of tree-pruning can be used to convert (4) into (9), the approximately correct derived structure of (2). But I have not yet given any evidence which motivates assuming as abstract a deep structure as (4) for sentence (2). In other words, while it may well be *feasible* to derive (2) from (4), and while such a derivation may not engender any complication in the grammar, I have not yet shown that such a derivation is *necessary*. The rest of the paper is devoted to this end.

There are two claims implicit in (4) which require motivation: (i) the claim that *be* is a true *verb* (i.e. that it is marked $\begin{bmatrix} +V \\ -Adj \end{bmatrix}$ in the lexicon, and that this verb is present in the deep structure, and not merely some transformationally introduced morpheme whose only function is to carry tense and person inflections, or some totally different phrase structure category, *Copula*, which is not related at all to lexical verbs and adjectives; and (ii) the claim that this verb *be* takes an abstract *NP* as its object in the deep structure, and is thus deep structurally similar to such lexical items as *try*, *know*, *believe*, *want*, etc. Claims (i) and (ii) above are relatively independent: even if the second claim is correct, the first might be wrong. Even if I can show that the morpheme *be* must be followed by an abstract *NP*, it might still be argued that it should be dominated by the phrase structure node *Copula* instead of the feature bundle $\begin{bmatrix} +V \\ -Adj \end{bmatrix}$, or that it is not present in the deep structure. There are arguments which support the stronger claim, (i), but they are

"A Proposed Rule of Tree-Pruning," in *Mathematical Linguistics and Automatic Translation*, Harvard Computation Laboratory, Report No. NSF-17, 1966; in *MSE*.

detailed and beyond the scope of this paper, so I will concentrate only on claim (ii).[2] I will present below six arguments which support the postulation of (4) as the deep structure of (2).

1. In many languages, pro-forms which replace adjectives are morphologically identical to pro-forms which replace abstract noun phrases. Thus in German, just as (10a) may be converted into (10b), so (11a) may be converted into (11b).

(10)(a) *Peter hat gewusst, dass es regnen würde, aber Anna hat nicht gewusst, dass es regnen würde.*
      'Peter knew that it would rain, but Anna didn't know that it would rain.'

  (b) *Peter hat gewusst, dass es regnen würde, aber Anna hat es nicht gewusst.*
      'Peter knew that it would rain, but Anna didn't know it.'

(11)(a) *Peter ist klug, aber die Frauen sind nicht klug.*
      'Peter is smart, but the women aren't smart.'

  (b) *Peter ist klug, aber die Frauen sind es nicht.*
      *'Peter is smart, but the women aren't it.'[3]

The same facts obtain for French: just as (12a) may be converted into (12b), so (13a) may be converted into (13b).

(12)(a) *Pierre savait qu'il allait pleuvoir, mais Anne ne savait pas qu'il allait pleuvoir.*
      'Peter knew that it was going to rain, but Ann didn't know that it was going to rain.'

  (b) *Pierre savait qu'il allait pleuvoir, mais Anne ne le savait pas.*
      'Peter knew that it was going to rain, but Ann didn't know it.'

(13)(a) *Pierre est intelligent, mais les femmes ne sont pas intelligentes.*
      'Peter is intelligent, but the women aren't intelligent.'

  (b) *Pierre est intelligent, mais les femmes ne le sont pas.*
      *'Peter is intelligent, but the women aren't it.'

If the rule which converts (10a) into (10b) and (12a) into (12b) is formulated as in (14),

(14) SENTENCE DELETION:

$$X - S - Y - \left[\left[\begin{array}{c} + N \\ + Pro \\ + Abstract \end{array} \right] - S \right]_{NP} - Z$$

$$\begin{array}{ccccccc} 1 & 2 & 3 & 4 & 5 & 6 \Rightarrow \text{(optional)} \\ 1 & 2 & 3 & 4 & 0 & 6 \end{array}$$

Condition: $2 = 5$

then this same rule will also operate to derive (11b) and (13b) from (11a) and (13a) respectively, if a deep structure similar to (4) is assumed to underlie sentences (11) and (13).

The English glosses of (10a) and (10b) show that rule (14) operates in the

---

[2]Some of the arguments which support claim (i) are presented in my dissertation, *Universal Constraints on Variables in Syntactic Rules*, M.I.T., in preparation.

[3]At present I have no explanation for the fact that the English gloss of (11b) is ungrammatical.

grammar of English, but for some mysterious reason, the pronoun *it* cannot function as a pro-adjective except after the verb *look*, and after certain nonfinite forms of the verb *be*.

(15)(a)   *Harry is smart, although he doesn't look it.*
  (b)   *People want me to be polite, but being it is often difficult.*[4]

There are other less restricted pro-adjectives in English which are morphologically identical to pronouns—in (16), the pronoun *that* clearly substitutes for the adjective *beautiful*.

(16)   *They said that Sheila was beautiful, and that she is.*

Thus the facts of sentences (10)–(13) and (15)–(16) support the analysis in (4), for if no *NP* follows the verb *be*, both the rule of SENTENCE DELETION and the rule which introduces the pronoun *that* will have to be made more complicated.

2.   Consider next nonrestrictive relative clauses, such as the embedded clause in (17).

(17)   *This table, which was made in Ireland, is very strong.*

There is good evidence which indicates that such clauses are derived from conjoined sentences by a rule which adjoins one of the conjoined sentences to some *NP* in the other.[5] Thus the structure underlying (18a) is first converted to the one underlying (18b) and finally to the one underlying (17).

(18)(a)   *This table is very strong and this table was made in Ireland.*
  (b)   *This table, and it was made in Ireland, is very strong.*

The fact that the rules which form nonrestrictive relative clauses only embed conjoined sentences onto *noun phrases* thus indicates that at the stage of the derivation of (19) at which the nonrestrictive clause *which she was* is adjoined to the adjective *beautiful*, that adjective must be dominated by the node *NP*.

(19)   *That Sheila was beautiful, which she was, was not realized until later.*

The clause *which she was* in (19) should not be confused with sentential relative clauses, such as the embedded clauses in (20).

(20)   *Sheila was beautiful,* $\begin{cases} \textit{which was too bad.} \\ \textit{which Tom refused to admit.} \end{cases}$

Sentential relative clauses, like *which was to bad*, can be inserted after *beautiful* in (19) in place of the clause *which she was*, and grammatical sentences will result. In fact, it is always the case that sentential relatives, like those in (20) can replace nonrestrictive relative clauses which have been adjoined to adjectives, but the converse is not true, as (21) shows.

(21)   *That it had rained,* $\begin{cases} \textit{which was too bad,} \\ \textit{which Tom refused to admit,} \\ \textit{*which she was,} \end{cases}$ *was not known.*

---

[4]I am grateful to Dwight Bolinger for calling my attention to this example.
[5]Cf. George Lakoff, *Deep and Surface Grammar* (M.I.T. Press, to appear), Chap. 1.

The ungrammaticality of (21), if the clause *which she was* is present, clearly shows that this clause is different from the two sentential relatives, and that this clause can in fact only be adjoined to *adjectives*, as I claimed above. But since the clause *which she was* is clearly a nonrestrictive, and since the rules which form nonrestrictive clauses are most simply formulated if these clauses are only adjoined to *noun phrases*, the existence of such sentences as (19) and general considerations of simplicity provide strong evidence for the correctness of the claim that (4) is the correct deep structure of (2).

3.   A detailed description of the grammar of pseudo-cleft sentences, i.e. sentences such as those in (22),

(22)   *What fell down was the table.*
What I didn't know was that the earth is flat.
What I hate is having to write papers.
The one who killed Caesar was Brutus.
Where I want to sleep is under the bed.
The reason that I got up was because I was hungry.

would reveal that such sentences are most simply accounted for if the constituents which follow the verb *be* are analyzed as noun phrases.[6] This means, for example, that in (22) the phrases *the table, that the earth is flat, having to write papers, Brutus, under the desk,* and *because I was hungry* are all to be analyzed, not too surprisingly, as being noun phrases. And since there exist such sentences as (23),

(23)   *What Marcus has never been is courageous.*

by the same criterion, the adjective *courageous* must be dominated by the node *NP* at some point in the derivation of (23), unless the rule which forms pseudo-cleft sentences is to be made more complex in some way. But if (4) is in fact the correct analysis of predicate adjectives, it is not necessary to complicate the statement of the pseudo-cleft rule in any way in order for (23) to be generated.

4.   Consider equative sentences, which contain colons, like sentence (24).

(24)   *I've had enough: either the cat goes or I go.*

When equative sentences only differ by one *NP*, the rule given in (25). EQUATIVE DELETION, optionally deletes the repeated part of the sentence which follows the colon.

(25)   EQUATIVE DELETION:
$$X - NP - Y - :   X - NP - Y$$
$$1 \quad 2 \quad 3 \quad 4 \quad 5 \quad 6 \quad 7 \Rightarrow \text{(optional)}$$
$$1 \quad 2 \quad 3 \quad 4 \quad 0 \quad 6 \quad 0$$

This rule optionally transforms the (a) versions of sentences (26)–(28) to their (b) versions.

(26)(a)   *Rodney built [what I wanted him to build]$_{NP}$: he built [a golden igloo]$_{NP}$.*
      (b)   *Rodney built [what I wanted him to build]$_{NP}$: [a golden igloo]$_{NP}$.*

---

[6]To demonstrate this here would go beyond the scope of this paper—many arguments supporting this claim are given in my dissertation, op. cit., footnote 2.

(27)(a) *He knows [something he won't admit]$_{NP}$: he knows [that the war is futile]$_{NP}$.*

(b) *He knows [something he won't admit]$_{NP}$: [that the war is futile]$_{NP}$.*

(28)(a) *Billy slept [where I would never sleep]$_{NP}$: he slept [under the desk]$_{NP}$.*

(b) *Billy slept [where I would never sleep]$_{NP}$: [under the desk]$_{NP}$.*

In fact, the phrases which can appear after the verb *be* in pseudo-cleft sentences are the same as the phrases which can follow the colon in sentences like (26)–(28). This includes adjectives, as might be expected:

(29)(a) *Tom is [what his brother never will be]$_{NP}$: Tom is [totally fearless]$_{NP}$.*

(b) *Tom is [what his brother will never be]$_{NP}$: [totally fearless]$_{NP}$.*

The fact that (29b) is grammatical indicates that the phrase *totally fearless* must be dominated by *NP* in (29a) so that EQUATIVE DELETION can apply to convert (29a) into (29b). Once again, this fact supports the analysis I proposed at the beginning of this paper.

5. In German, there is a rule of TOPICALIZATION which optionally moves to the front of a sentence some *NP* contained in that sentence. This rule, stated roughly in (30),

(30) TOPICALIZATION:

$X - NP - Y$

1   2   3   ⇒ (optional)

2 1   0   3

converts the structures underlying the (a) versions of (31)–(33) into the structures underlying the corresponding (b) versions.

(31)(a) *Wir haben [Bohnen]$_{NP}$ gegessen.*

(b) *[Bohnen]$_{NP}$ haben wir gegessen.*
'We ate beans.'

(32)(a) *Ich wollte [unter dem Schreibtisch]$_{NP}$ schlafen.*

(b) *[Unter dem Schreibtisch]$_{NP}$ wollte ich schlafen.*
'I wanted to sleep under the desk.'

(33)(a) *Er hat die Bohnen [genüsslich]$_{NP}$ gegessen.*

(b) *[Genüsslich]$_{NP}$ hat er die Bohnen gegessen.*
'He ate the beans with great enjoyment.'

Again, to go deeply enough into the details of German syntax to justify sufficiently the formulation of the rule of TOPICALIZATION that I have given in (30) would take me beyond the scope of this paper, but if it is assumed to be correct, then the fact that adjective phrases too, like *stolz auf dich*, can be topicalized (cf. (34b))

(34)(a) *Dein Vater muss [stolz auf dich]$_{NP}$ sein.*

(b) *[Stolz auf dich]$_{NP}$ muss dein Vater sein.*
'Your father must be proud of you.'

provides further evidence for the correctness of the analysis of predicate adjectives implicit in (4).

6. Finally, let us examine the QUESTION FORMATION rule in English: (35) contains an approximate statement of this rule.

(35) QUESTION FORMATION:

$Q - X - NP - Y$
1   2   3   4 $\Rightarrow$ (obligatory)
1 3 2   0   4
Condition: 3 dominates *Wh + some*

This rule must be restricted as follows: if the *NP* in term 3 of (35) starts a larger *NP*, the smaller *NP* cannot be moved, and the transformation must instead move the larger *NP* to the front of the sentence. Thus when rule (35) applies to (36a), this restriction will prevent the generation of the ungrammatical (36b), while allowing the grammatical (36c) to be generated.

(36)(a) *Q   you are reading* [[*Wh + somebody's*]$_{NP}$ *book*]$_{NP}$
   (b) **Whose are you reading book?*
   (c) *Whose book are you reading?*

Now notice that an exactly similar situation obtains when a preposed adverb of degree is questioned from in front of an adjective. It seems likely that the question word *how* should be analyzed as deriving from the noun phrase *to what extent*. If this is correct, and if (4) is the correct underlying structure for (2), then the facts of (37) are explained without any further conditions having to be stated on the rule of QUESTION FORMATION.

(37)(a) *Q   John is* [[*to Wh + some extent*]$_{NP}$ *old*]$_{NP}$
   (b) **How is John old?*[7]
   (c) *How old is John?*

If a *NP* underlies the word *how* in (37c), and if the phrase *how old* is also a *NP*, then the ungrammaticality of (37b) (in the intended sense) is accounted for by the same restriction which is necessary in any event to exclude (36b). But *how old* can only be dominated by *NP* if the analysis of predicate adjectives implicit in (4) is assumed. Hence the parallelism of (36) and (37) also supports the analysis I have proposed.

In the first part of this paper, I argued that if (4) were assumed to be the deep structure of (2), *Henry is hungry*, no additional apparatus would have to be added to the grammar of English to convert (4) into (9), the approximately correct surface structure of (2): the derivation would parallel exactly the derivation of such sentences as (5), *Alice tried to cough*. In the second half of the paper I presented six arguments from widely varying areas of syntax which seem to me to necessitate the analysis which the first part of the paper showed to be feasible.

---

[7] I have starred (37b), not because it is ungrammatical in all senses (for it is a perfectly acceptable variant of *In what respect is John old?*), but rather because it is clearly not related to (37c).

23

Toward a Modern Theory of Case

CHARLES J. FILLMORE

I

In Chapter 2 of his book *Aspects of the Theory of Syntax*,[1] Chomsky points out the essentially *relational* nature of such grammatical concepts as subject (of a sentence) and object (of a verb, or of a predicate phrase) as opposed to the *categorial* nature of such notions as verb or noun phrase. The important distinction is there drawn between grammatical relations or grammatical functions, on the one hand, and grammatical categories on the other hand.

The distinction can be captured in formal grammars, according to Chomsky, by introducing category symbols as constituent labels in the phrase structure rules of the base component, and by defining the grammatical relations as in fact relations among category symbols within the underlying phrase-markers provided by the base. Thus sentence, noun phrase and verb phrase, for example, are provided as category symbols by the base, while the notion subject is defined as a relation between a noun phrase and an immediately dominating sentence, the term object as a relation between a noun phrase and an immediately dominating verb phrase.

My purpose in this essay is to question the deep-structure validity of the notions subject and object, and also to raise doubts about the adequacy of Chomsky's

Reprinted with slight revision from Project on Linguistic Analysis Report No. 13 (Columbus, Ohio: The Ohio State University Research Foundation, August 1966), pp. 1–24, by permission of Charles J. Fillmore and the Project on Linguistic Analysis.

This paper is a longer version of a paper entitled "A Proposal Concerning English Prepositions," in F. Dinneen, ed., *19th Monograph on Languages and Linguistics* (Washington, D.C.: Georgetown University Press, 1966). The Georgetown version was less complete in several respects since it was required to have a twenty minute reading time.

[1]Noam Chomsky, *Aspects of the Theory of Syntax* (Cambridge, Mass.: M.I.T. Press, 1965), especially pp. 63–74.

proposals for formally reconstructing the distinction between grammatical categories and grammatical functions. My inquiry will lead to a proposal which renders unnecessary the distinction in English grammar between noun phrase and preposition phrase, and to the suggestion that something very much like grammatical *case* plays a role in the groundwork of grammars that is much less superficial than is usually recognized.

I begin my argument by asking, concerning such expressions as *in the room, toward the moon, on the next day, in a careless way, with a sharp knife,* and *by my brother,* how it is possible in grammars of the type illustrated in *Aspects* to reveal both the categorial information that all of these expressions are preposition phrases and the functional information that they are adverbials of location, direction, time, manner, instrument, and agent respectively. Instead of having a category label *Time,* it ought to be possible—if Chomsky's proposal is adequate —to recognize that a preposition phrase whose head is a Time noun has the syntactic function *Time Adverbial* within the constituent which immediately contains it.

It seems impossible to provide both types of information in a natural way for the reason that there may be several adverbial expressions in a simple sentence, there are ordering restrictions among these, and if they all start out with the same category, Preposition Phrase, there is no known device by which the further expansion of this category can be constrained according to the permitted order of adverbial types in a single sentence.

Most of the sample phrase structure rules for English that I have seen recently have introduced categorially such terms as *Manner, Frequency, Extent, Location, Direction,* etc. In these grammars, for the constituents mentioned, either the strictly categorial information is lost, or else it is rescued by having nonbranching rules which rewrite each of these adverbial-type categories as *Preposition Phrase.* In any case the formal distinction between relations and categories is lost, and the constraints on the further expansion of these preposition phrases that depend on the types of adverbials they manifest need to be provided, as suggested above, in ways that have not yet been made clear.[2]

Other grammars that I have seen contain rules allowing more than one preposition phrase in the expansion of a single category. In the abbreviated form of these

---

[2]The problem on such restricted expansion has not been ignored. Chomsky has proposed (ibid., p. 215) that "there is some reason to suspect that it might be appropriate to intersperse certain local transformations among the rewriting rules of the base. Thus adverbial phrases consisting of *Preposition-Determiner-Noun* are in general restricted as to the choice of these elements, and these restrictions could be stated by local transformations to the effect that *Preposition* and *Noun* can be rewritten in certain restricted ways when dominated by such category symbols as *Place Adverbial* and *Time Adverbial.* In fact, one might consider a new extension of the theory of context-free grammar, permitting rules that restrict rewriting by local transformations (i.e., in terms of the dominating category symbol), alongside of the fairly widely studied extension of context-free grammar to context-sensitive grammars that permit rules that restrict rewriting in terms of contiguous symbols." The proposal given below amounts to incorporating Chomsky's suggestions in the form of a convention on the rules which assign complex symbols to prepositions and nouns.

rules, each of these preposition phrases is independently optional. Difficulties in establishing the constraints on expanding these categories just in case more than one was chosen remain as before, and two new technical difficulties arise. If there are two independently optional preposition phrases in the expansion of *Verb Phrase*, then we get the same result by skipping the first and choosing the second as we do by choosing the first and skipping the second. The first technical difficulty, then, is that different choices in the base do not correspond to differences in the structure of sentences.[3] The second is that now the syntactic relation *preposition-phrase-under-verb-phrase* is not unique in a verb phrase just in case more than one preposition phrase has been chosen.

The obvious alternative within the present conception of grammar is to introduce new structure in such a way that whenever a sentence contains more than one preposition phrase, they are all under immediate domination of categories of different types. If the number of distinct types of preposition phrases is large, this solution differs from providing separate category labels for each adverbial only by greatly increasing the constituent-structure complexity of sentences.

With these difficulties understood, I should next like to ask whether two of the grammatical functions which Chomsky accepts—namely subject and object—are in fact linguistically significant notions on the deep structure level. The deep structure relevance of syntactic functions is with respect to the projection rules of the semantic theory. The semantic component recognizes semantic features associated with lexical elements in a string and projects from them the meaning of the string in ways appropriate to the syntactic relations which hold among these elements. It is my opinion that the traditional subject and object are not to be found among the syntactic functions to which semantic rules must be sensitive.

Consider uses of the verb *open*. It seems to me that in sentences (1) and (2)

(1) *The door will open.*

(2) *The janitor will open the door.*

there is a semantically relevant relation between *the door* and *open* that is the same in the two sentences, in spite of the fact that *the door* is the subject of the so-called intransitive verb and the object of the so-called transitive verb. It seems to me, too, that in sentences (3) and (4)

(3) *The janitor will open the door with this key.*

(4) *This key will open the door.*

the common semantically relevant relation is that between *this key* and *open* in both of the sentences, in spite of the fact that *this key* superficially is the subject of one of the sentences, the object of a preposition in the other.

In naming the functions of the nominals in these sentences, that of *the janitor* we might call *Agentive*; and that of *this key*, *Instrumental*. The remaining function to find a name for is that of the subject of an intransitive verb and the object of

---

[3]This problem vanishes if parentheses in phrase structure rules are understood as having purely abbreviatory functions.

a transitive verb: a term we might use for this function is *Objective*.[4] None of these functions, as we have seen, can be identified with either subject or object.

If we allow ourselves to use these terms *Objective*, *Instrumental*, and *Agentive*, we might describe the syntax of the verb *open* as follows: it requires an Objective, and tolerates an Instrumental and/or an Agentive. If only the Objective occurs, the Objective noun is automatically the subject. If an Instrumental also occurs, either the Objective or the Instrumental noun may be the subject, as seen in sentences (5) and (6).

(5)   *This key will open the door.*

(6)   *The door will open with this key.*

If an Agentive occurs, an Instrumental noun cannot be the subject, but, if it occurs, it must appear in a preposition phrase after the Objective, as in (7).

(7)   *The janitor will open the door with this key.*

The Objective noun can be made subject even if the sentence contains Instrumental and Agentive elements, just in case the verb is capable of assuming its passive form. The Instrumental and Agentive expressions, in this case, contain their appropriate prepositions, as in (8) and (9).

(8)   *The door will be opened with this key.*

(9)   *The door will be opened by the janitor.*

In the case of two syntactic functions—Instrumental and Agentive—the noun phrase is preceded by a preposition just in case it has not been made the subject of the sentence. When we add to our consideration the many cases where object nouns are also marked by prepositions as in such sentences as (10) and (11)

(10)   *She objects to me.*

(11)   *She depends on me.*

and when, further, we see that even in cases like *open*, the Objective has a preposition associated with it in certain nominalizations, as in (12)

(12)   *The opening of the door by the janitor with this key*

we see that an analysis of syntactic functions in English requires a general account of the role of prepositions in our language.

The verb *open*, fortunately, is not unique in governing syntactic relations that are not identifiable with subjects and objects. Other verbs that behave in similar ways are *advance, bend, bounce, break, burn up, burst, circulate, close, connect, continue, crumple, dash, decrease, develop, drop, end, enter (contest), expand, hang, hide, hurt, improve, increase, jerk, keep away, keep out, move, pour, repeat, retreat, rotate, run, rush, shake, shift, shine, shrink, sink, slide, spill, spread, stand, start,*

---

[4]The term *Objective* should not be confused with the surface syntactic relation *object* nor with the surface case *accusative*. It would be possible to borrow the term *nominative* from the grammatical tradition of studies of the so-called "ergative" languages (e.g. the northern Caucasian languages), but it is my belief that the choice of this term may well have been responsible for the common assumption that the "ergative" languages are languages in which transitive sentences are obligatorily passive.

starve, stir, stretch, turn, twist, wake up, wind, withdraw. My interpretation of these words is that they have a certain amount of freedom with respect to the syntactic environments into which they can be inserted—a freedom which I assume can be stated very simply. The alternative is to regard these verbs as having each two or three meanings corresponding to their intransitive use or their capability of taking subjects whose relation to the verb can be construed instrumentally in one meaning, agentively in another.[5]

II

I recognize, therefore, various categorially introduced noun phrase types—suggestive, it seems to me, of the traditional notion of "cases"—each, in English, beginning with a preposition. The syntactic relationship of each of these types to the main verb of the sentence is defined with reference to the category under which it is introduced, having no direct connection with whatever eventual status it may have as subject or object. The following assumptions are meant to develop the scheme I have in mind by means of a series of specific assumptions.

2.1. The first of these assumptions is that the major constituents of a sentence (*S*) are Modality (*Mod*), Auxiliary (*Aux*), and Proposition (*Prop*). The first phrase structure rule is (13).

(13) $S \rightarrow Mod - Aux - Prop$

I use *Proposition* rather than *Predicate* because it includes what will end up to be the subject of the sentence. Notice that the Auxiliary is in immediate constituent relationship with the entire Proposition, not a subconstituent of the Proposition. I assume this structure assignment to be semantically justified.

2.2. The constituent Modality contains interrogative and negative elements, sentence adverbials, time adverbials, and various other adverbial elements that are understood as modalities on the sentence as a whole rather than subconstituents of the constituent containing the main verb. I have no strong convictions that these various elements actually comprise a single constituent, but for the time being we may assume that they do. For the purpose of the present discussion I shall also assume that this modality element is optional, and that it is not involved in any of the observations that I shall be dealing with here.[6]

---

[5]Edward S. Klima has pointed out to me that the instrumental versus agentive role of the possible subjects of *open* has syntactic as well as semantic importance, as can be seen in the unacceptability of the conjunction seen in (i):

(i) *The janitor and the key will open the door.*

Two agentive subjects may be conjoined, two instrumental subjects may be conjoined, but not one of each.

[6]For various reasons, I am convinced that instead of treating *Negative* as an optional subconstituent of the optional constituent Modality, it is better to introduce, as an obligatory subconstituent of the obligatory constituent Modality, a disjunction of the elements *Negative* and *Affirmative*. This choice appears to be necessary because of various semantic rules whose effect is to reverse the negativity value of a sentence—changing affirmatives to negatives and negatives to affirmatives.

In the rest of the present discussion, however, I shall omit mention of the Modality constituent, acting as if the first rule rewrites *Sentence* as *Auxiliary + Proposition*.

2.3. The category Proposition includes the verb and all those nominal elements which are relevant to the subclassification of verbs. The rules for rewriting Proposition take it into an obligatory verb followed by the somewhat independently optional elements Objective (*Obj*), Dative (*Dat*), Locative (*Loc*), Comitative (*Com*), Instrumental (*Ins*), and Agentive (*Ag*).[7]

Roughly speaking, all adverbial elements capable of becoming subjects or objects are introduced in the expansion of Proposition; all others—Time, Benefactive, Frequentative, etc.—are modality elements. The concepts involved are presumed to be among the substantive universals specified by the grammatical theory.

2.4. All of the nonverb constituents of propositions are Noun Phrase (*NP*). The relevant rule takes each of the terms I have mentioned and rewrites it as noun phrase:

$$(14) \quad \begin{Bmatrix} Obj \\ Dat \\ Loc \\ \ldots \end{Bmatrix} \to NP$$

The syntactic functions appropriate to noun phrases, in other words, are identified categorially. The elements which dominate *NP* are distinct from what we might wish to call the true grammatical categories in that their further expansion is

---

[7]The variety of expansions of the proposition displays the range of kernel sentence types in the language. Some possible expansions of *Prop* are these (linked parentheses indicate that at least one of two adjacent terms must be chosen):

> *Prop* → *V Obj* (*Dat* ◊ *Ag*)
> *Prop* → *V Obj Loc* (*Dat* ◊ *Ag*)
> *Prop* → *V Obj* (*Ins* ◊ *Ag*)
> *Prop* → *V Obj Com*
> *Prop* → *V S* (*Dat* (*Ag*))
> *Prop* → *V S Obj* (*Ag*)

Sentences illustrating various choices in the expansion of *Prop* are given below:

(i)	*John has a car.*	$V^{\frown}Obj^{\frown}Dat$
(ii)	*I gave John a car.*	$V^{\frown}Obj^{\frown}Dat^{\frown}Ag$
(iii)	*I bought a car.*	$V^{\frown}Obj^{\frown}Ag$
(iv)	*A coat is in the closet.*	$V^{\frown}Obj^{\frown}Loc$
(v)	*John has a coat in the closet.*	$V^{\frown}Obj^{\frown}Loc^{\frown}Dat$
(vi)	*John put a coat in the closet.*	$V^{\frown}Obj^{\frown}Loc^{\frown}Ag$
(vii)	*The door opened.*	$V^{\frown}Obj$
(viii)	*The key opened the door.*	$V^{\frown}Obj^{\frown}Ins$
(ix)	*The janitor opened the door.*	$V^{\frown}Obj^{\frown}Ag$
(x)	*The janitor opened the door with the key.*	$V^{\frown}Obj^{\frown}Ins^{\frown}Ag$
(xi)	*John is with his brother.*	$V^{\frown}Obj^{\frown}Com$
(xii)	*John turned out to be a liar.*	$V^{\frown}S$
(xiii)	*John thinks that he is too old.*	$V^{\frown}S^{\frown}Dat$
(xiv)	*I persuaded John that he was too old.*	$V^{\frown}S^{\frown}Dat^{\frown}Ag$
(xv)	*I forced John to go.*	$V^{\frown}S^{\frown}Obj^{\frown}Ag$

unary and many-to-one. What this suggests is that the form of grammars which I am proposing is at bottom one in which the underlying structures of sentences are representable as rooted trees with labeled nodes and labeled branches. This could be equivalent to a phrase structure grammar in which, beginning from *S*, all even-numbered branchings are unary.

Borrowing from Tesnière[8] I shall use the term *actant* for these elements within propositions which unarily dominate noun phrases.

2.5. Another important assumption is that every noun phrase begins with a preposition.

(15) $NP \rightarrow P\,(Det)\,(S)\,N$

Thus we see that the distinction between noun phrase and preposition phrase is no longer necessary. This is all to the good, of course, since *preposition phrase* has always been a terminological nuisance. We would really like all constituents labeled *X-Phrase* to be constituents having *X*'s as their heads.

2.6. The lexical categories Preposition (*P*) and Noun (*N*) take by convention the name of the actant dominating their noun phrase as one of the features making up the complex symbols associated with each of these categories. For Agentives, for example, the convention will fill in the feature [+ *Agentive*] as shown in (16).

(16)

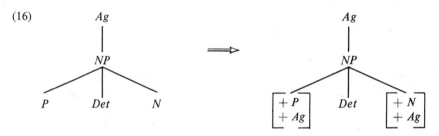

2.7. The selectional restrictions associated with lexical categories serving given syntactic functions will be provided by appropriate subcategorization. We may wish to guarantee, for instance, that agent nouns are animate, a decision expressed by rule (17).

(17) $\begin{bmatrix} + N \\ + Ag \end{bmatrix} \rightarrow [+\ Anim]$

The feature [+ *Animate*] may be required for Benefactives and, under certain environmental conditions, for Datives as well.

2.8. Some prepositions may be filled in by optional choices from the lexicon. In Locative phrases, though in some cases the preposition may be automatically determined, generally the choice is optional: *over, under, in, on, beside*, etc. These are the prepositions that bring with them semantic information.

---

[8]Lucien Tesnière, *Eléments de syntaxe structurale* (Klincksieck, Paris, 1959), especially pp. 105–115.

2.9.   Other prepositions are determined by inherent syntactic features of specific governing verbs. Thus *blame* requires the Objective preposition to be *for*, the Dative preposition to be *on*.

2.10.   The remaining prepositions are filled in by rules which make use of information about the actants. Thus, the Objective preposition is *of* if it is the only actant in the proposition or if the proposition contains an Instrumental or an Agentive; otherwise it is *with*. The Instrumental preposition is *with* just in case the Agentive co-occurs; otherwise it is *by*. The Agentive preposition is *by*.

2.11.   The subject of a sentence is selected, in accordance with certain rules, from among the propositional actants. A transformation places the noun phrase selected to serve as subject to the left of the auxiliary. In Objective-Agentive sentences, unless the auxiliary contains the passive marker, the Agentive becomes the subject, as in (18).[9]

(18)

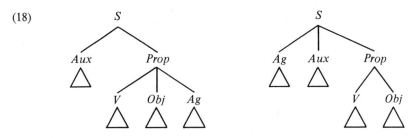

Notice that the proposition that has had one of its actants moved to the subject position is what is traditionally called the predicate.

2.12.   All prepositions are deleted in subject position. (19) shows that after the Objective *of the dog* becomes the subject of the verb *die*, it loses its preposition.

(19)

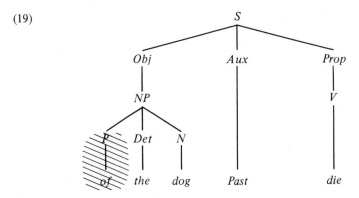

2.13.   A later rule—a rule to which many verbs and certain actants are exceptions —deletes prepositions after verbs:

---

[9]The triangles represent the subtrees dominated by the categories under which they are drawn.

(20)

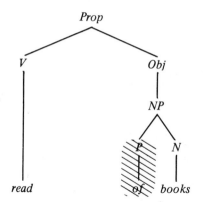

2.14. Various grammatical processes affect the conditions under which the preposition-deletion rule operates. In nominalizations the Objective preposition stays, as in *the death of the dog* or *the reading of books*.

2.15. In some contexts, the choice of subject offers certain options. We have seen already that in (21)

(21) *will open of the door with this key*

either the Objective or the Instrumental can be made subject, giving us either (22) or (23).

(22) *The door will open with this key.*

(23) *This key will open the door.*

In the sentence whose underlying form is (24)

(24) *Pres swarm with bees in the garden*

either the Objective *with bees* or the Locative *in the garden* may be made subject, losing its preposition in the process. Notice the sentences

(25) *Bees swarm in the garden.*

where initial *with* has been lost, and

(26) *The garden swarms with bees.*

where initial *in* has been lost.

2.16. When Objective and Dative or Objective and Locative are left behind after a subject has been chosen, they may be permuted—subject to certain constraints involving the identification of pronouns. Examples where preposition deletion does not take place are (27) and (28).

(27) *Talk about this to Dr. Smith.*

(28) *Talk to Dr. Smith about this.*

Examples with loss of the postverbal preposition are (29)

(29) *Blame the accident on John.*

where *for* was deleted, and (30)

(30) *Blame John for the accident.*

where *on* was deleted. James Heringer of Ohio State University and J. Bruce Fraser of the MITRE Corporation have given me many more examples like this one.[10]

2.17.   In some cases the transformation which provides the subject of a sentence must be thought of as *copying* the selected actant in front of the auxiliary. In Objective-Locative sentences in which the verb is *be*, one subject-selection possibility is the Objective. Thus from (31)

(31)   *Pres be with some books on the shelf*

with some books can be made subject giving us, after the *with* drops out, (32).

(32)   *Some books are on the shelf.*

Alternatively, however, the Locative actant may be *copied* in the subject position, giving us (33).

(33)   *on the shelf are with some books on the shelf*

If the left copy of the Locative actant is replaced by its pro-form, we end up with (34).

(34)   *There are some books on the shelf.*[11]

---

[10]Fraser speaks of these verbs as having alternate meanings. *Spray*, according to Fraser, has one meaning in (i)

(i)   *Spray the wall with paint.*

another in (ii).

(ii)   *Spray paint on the wall.*

I would say merely that the nonagentive actants associated with *spray* are, in these sentences, *with paint* and *on the wall*. They may occur in either order, but whichever one comes first loses its preposition. Other examples from Fraser are (iii) to (x):

(iii)   *Stuff cotton into the sack.*
(iv)   *Stuff the sack with cotton.*
(v)   *Plant the garden with roses.*
(vi)   *Plant roses in the garden.*
(vii) *Stack the table with dishes.*
(viii) *Stack dishes onto the table.*
(ix)   *Make a chair out of wood.*
(x)   *Make wood into a chair.*

[11]I would expect that the expletive *it* can be handled in an analogous way. Nominalized sentences are copied in the subject position, giving us something like (i).

(i)   *that he is a liar is true that he is a liar*

Now, either the right copy can be deleted or the left copy can be replaced by *it*, resulting in (ii) or (iii) respectively.

(ii)   *That he is a liar is true.*
(iii) *It is true that he is a liar.*

It is likely that the *copying* method of providing subjects should be generalized to all cases, with, simply, the right copy getting deleted in a majority of cases. Where the expected deletion of the right copy is not effected, we get such somewhat deviant sentences as (iv) and (v), borrowed from Jespersen,

(iv)   *He is a great scoundrel, that husband of hers.*
(v)   *It is perfectly wonderful the way in which he remembers things.*

2.18.   The verb *have* is here interpreted as a variant of the verb *be* in front of the Objective after a noun phrase. Whenever a Locative or a Comitative is made the subject of a proposition whose verb is *be*, this is done by subject copying. Unless, as in the existential sentences, the left copy is changed to *there*, the nominal part of the right copy will be pronominalized. (Possibly what this means is that the repeated noun gets deleted and the features that at this stage have been assigned to the determiner serve now to select a pronoun.)

The Locative copying can be seen in (35):

(35)

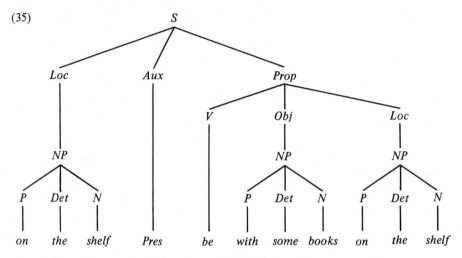

From (35) we get, at a certain stage, something like (36).

(36) **on the shelf is with some books on the shelf*

The sentence-initial preposition is deleted, the repeated phrase *the shelf* is replaced by *it*, *with* is deleted, and *be*, after noun phrase and before an Objective, gets changed to *have*.[12] The resulting sentence is (37)

(37)   *The shelf has some books on it.*

which, thus, I regard as a simplex.

Analogous phenomena are observed in Objective-Comitative sentences. There too we find *have* only when the Objective is not the subject. In sentence (38)

(38)   *The children are with Mary.*

---

because where the right copy didn't get deleted, the left copy got pronominalized. This seems, too, to be a way of handling cases where a preposition gets left behind in passive sentences. The deletion of the right copy is sometimes only partial, leaving the preposition behind, as in

(vi)   *Mary can be depended on.*

[12]In my present view of the design of a grammar I hold that the lexicon may be divided into two sections, a major-category lexicon which inserts semantically relevant lexical items into underlying phrase-markers, and a minor-category lexicon which inserts "function words" into surface phrase-markers. If *be* and *have* are regarded as words in the minor-category lexicon, it will not be necessary to speak, as I have here, of "changing *be* to *have*." The structural conditions for inserting *be* and *have* will simply be different.

the Objective is the subject, *be* remains unchanged, and the Comitative preposition stays. If the Comitative is made subject, it is done so by copying, the right copy eventually undergoing pronominalization. Here *be* is followed by an Objective, so it becomes *have*, and in the Objective case the preposition is deleted. Whereas before we had (38) with *are*, we now have (39) with *has*.

(39)   *Mary has the children with her.*

In Objective-Dative sentences, at least for those cases where the Dative noun is animate, the Dative becomes subject by transposition rather than by copying. (Alternatively we can say that in this case the right copy is always deleted).

With Objective-Dative sentences it appears that the choice of subject is determined by the verb. The verb *belong*, for example, requires the Objective to be subject, as in (40)

(40)   *The typewriter belongs to Terry.*

while the verb *be* requires the Dative as subject, as in (41).

(41)   *Terry has the typewriter.*

2.19.   Verbs in the lexicon will be classified according to the propositional environments into which they may be inserted. Using brute force methods for the time being I allow options in the statement of these environments. Thus a verb like *wake up* would have the feature (42)

(42) $[+ \underline{\hphantom{xxxx}} Obj\ (Inst)(Ag)]$

while a verb like *kill* would have the feature (43)

(43) $[+ \underline{\hphantom{xxxx}} Obj\ (Inst \lozenge Ag)]$

where the linked parentheses indicate that at least one of two adjacent terms must be chosen.

For *wake up* we have sentences like (44) with Objective only; (45) with Angentive; (46) with Instrumental; and (47) with both Agentive and Instrumental in addition to the Objective.

(44)   *I woke up.*

(45)   *My daughter woke me up.*

(46)   *An explosion woke me up.*

(47)   *My daughter woke me up with an explosion.*

For *kill*, on the other hand, we have (48)–(50) but not (51).

(48)   *Fire killed the rats.*

(49)   *Mother killed the rats.*

(50)   *Mother killed the rats with fire.*

(51)   **The rats killed.*

2.20.   Notions of synonymy can now be separated from notions of syntactic distribution. The verbs *kill* and *die*, for instance, may be given the same semantic characterizations. The relation between the verb and the Objective is the same for both words, the difference between the verbs being of a syntactic nature, in that *kill* requires a co-occurring Agent or Instrument, *die* does not allow an Agent to be directly expressed as part of the same proposition. In this respect, the essential difference between the proposals presented in this paper and those of

Lakoff[13] appears to be that Lakoff seeks for "synonymous" words identity of semantic reading and what he calls the *lexical base*, but not identity in *lexical extension*; I seek only identity of semantic reading. In other words, I do not expect to find in formal grammars support for the distributional definition of meaning.

III

I believe that certain advantages derive from incorporating into a transformational grammar the proposals that have just been sketched, in addition to the possibly unimportant one that sentences do not turn out to need quite so much branching structure as they do in grammars that need to recognize syntactic relations in terms of immediate-domination relation between categories.

3.1.   One of the specific advantages of my interpretation of *have* is in the simplification this analysis allows to the relative clause reduction rule.

I have said that the Objective preposition in sentences with Datives, Locatives, or Comitatives but without Instrumentals and Agentives is *with*. The preposition appears in this form in a sentence like (26), but it disappears after *be* under those conditions which ordinarily change *be* to *have*, as in (52).

(52)   *The garden has bees in it.*

In older versions of the grammar of English, one relative clause reduction rule was needed for relative-clause-plus-*be*, changing (53) into (54)

(53)   *the boy who is in the next room*

(54)   *the boy in the next room*

and another rule was needed for relative-pronoun-plus-*have*, changing (55) into (56)

(55)   *the boy who has the red hat*

(56)   *the boy with the red hat*

The first of these rules deleted the identified element, the second replaced the identified element by *with*.

If it is true, however, that *have*, abstractly, is *be* before Objectives, then a single rule will now cover both of these cases. From (53) we get (54) and from (57) we get (56).

(57)   *the boy who is with the red hat*

We need to require only that the relative-clause reduction rule precede the rules for creating *have* and deleting *with* after *be*.[14]

3.2.   Notions like that of the "understood agent" can be clarified within this scheme. There is a distinction, in other words, between not choosing an Agent on the one hand, and choosing an Agent and subsequently deleting it on the other hand. The distinction is revealed in the choice of preposition.

---

[13]See George Lakoff, *On the Nature of Syntactic Irregularity* (Ph.D. dissertation, Indiana University), *Mathematical Linguistics and Automatic Translation*, Harvard Computation Laboratory, Report No. NSF-16, 1965.

[14]But see footnote 12.

The verb *kill*, I have said, must take either Instrumental or Agentive and may take both. The Instrumental preposition is *by* if there is no Agentive present, otherwise it is *with*. The Agentive—as in the case of passive sentences—may be a dummy.

Suppose that we construct passive sentences with *kill* where the Objective is *the rats* and the Instrumental is *fire*. In one case we will omit an Agentive, in the other case the Agentive will be chosen but it will be a dummy. Where the Agentive is present in the deep structure, the Instrumental preposition is *with*; where there is no Agentive, the Instrumental preposition is *by*. Since the Agentive is a dummy, it gets deleted.

The resulting sentences are (58) and (59).

(58)   *The rats were killed by fire.*

(59)   *The rats were killed with fire.*

If my analysis is correct, there is an "understood agent" in the sentence with *with*.

Incidentally, the earlier examples with *open* were a little misleading. I implied that in a sentence like (60)

(60)   *The door was opened with this key.*

the underlying representation of the sentence contained only the actants Objective and Instrumental. If the above observations on *with* and *by* are true, however, the sentence should actually be understood as having an implied human agent, and it should be distinct in this respect from a sentence like (61); and I believe it is.

(61)   *The door was opened by the wind.*

3.3.   More general advantages associated with these proposals relate to the interpretation of historical changes and cross-language differences in lexical structure.

3.3.1.   Certain historical changes in language may turn out to be purely syntactic, and, in fact, may pertain exclusively to the status of particular lexical items as exceptions to given transformations, in the sense of Lakoff. Thus the English verb *like* did not change in its meaning or in its selection for Objective-Dative sentences, but only in its status as an exception to the rule that fronted actants are neutralized to the so-called nominative form.

3.3.2.   Lexical differences across languages may not be as great as we might otherwise have thought. It would ordinarily be said that English *kill* and Japanese *korosu* have different "meanings" because the Japanese verb requires an animate subject while English allows us to say that *fire killed him*, *a falling stone killed him*, and the like. Once we see that even in English both *kill* and *die* have the same underlying semantic representation, the difference between the two situations appears to be rather superficial. Both languages have words with the same meaning which can co-occur with Objective and Instrumental. English has two such verbs, one of which allows the Instrumental phrase to become the subject. The difference is no deeper than that.

4.   There are, as the reader may have guessed, a great many extremely serious problems which continue to be completely mysterious. Does this system provide the constituent structure needed for coordinate conjunction? How are predicate-adjective or predicate-noun sentences to be dealt with in this scheme? Do manner adverbials belong inside the proposition or are they part of the modality? How is the relation sometimes found between manner adverbials and the "subject" of the sentence to be expressed in this system? What about the generalizations on noun phrase interchange? Many of these problems, fortunately, are no *less* serious in subject-object grammars.

I could summarize my remarks by saying that I regard each simple sentence in a language as made up of a verb and a collection of nouns in various "cases" in the deep structure sense. In the surface structure, case distinctions are sometimes preserved, sometimes not—depending on the language, depending on the noun, or depending on idiosyncratic properties of certain governing words. Belief in the superficiality of grammatical case rises from consideration of the "nominative," which really constitutes a case neutralization that affects noun phrases that have been made the subject of a sentence, and of the "genitive," which represents another kind of neutralization of case distinctions, one which occurs in noun phrase modifiers derived from sentences, as illustrated by the reduction to the so-called "genitive" of both Agentive and Objective in such expressions as *the shooting of the hunters.*

VI

APPLICATIONS
AND IMPLICATIONS

The articles in this section explore some implications of the transformational analysis of English syntax for other areas of language study. First, S. Jay Keyser's "The Linguistic Basis of English Prosody" illustrates the way in which a system of metrics—the English iambic pentameter line—selects, from all the possible sentences of English, just those sentences that are "metrical"—that is, just those syllable sequences that meet the requirements of the iambic pentameter line. This article beautifully illustrates application of modern linguistic theory to literary problems.

Elizabeth Closs, in "Diachronic Syntax and Generative Grammar," first presents discussions of the analysis of the English verb phrase during various stages in the development of English from Old English to the present. She then examines various hypotheses about the nature of linguistic-grammatical change.

Three of the contributions deal with the child's acquisition of language. Although each article treats a different range of phenomena, a number of common findings emerge. First, it is apparent that the child is not merely imitating adult utterances but is creating his own new utterances. Second, he seems to be doing this on the basis of a set of grammatical rules—structural regularities—that he constructs for himself from his experience of English. His grammar is not just a simplified version of the adult's grammar; indeed, there are structural regularities in the speech of children that may reflect a system rather different from that of the adult. Finally, as the child's grammar becomes more complex, it approaches that of the adult in complexity and form.

Paula Menyuk's "Alternation of Rules in Children's Grammar" discusses this greater complexity as a function of increase in age and delineates the child's system of rules as it approximates more and more that of the mature adult. Jeffrey S. Gruber, in "Topicalization in Child Language," discusses one construction type, the so-called topic-comment construction, as it appears in the speech of one child at one stage in the language-learning process. Here he shows how a *consistent* explanation of the regularities in the speech of this child necessitates positing a structure for certain sentences that is different from that of the adult's corresponding sentences, even where the superficial form of the sentences might suggest the adult analysis. He then draws some tentative conclusions about what might be innate and what might be learned in child language. Edward S. Klima and Ursula Bellugi-Klima, in "Syntactic Regularities in the Speech of Children," describe the development of children's speech through three periods of increasing complexity. As the grammar becomes more complex, the relationship of semantic structures to surface structures becomes more indirect, resulting in a greater range of possible sentence types.

Finally, Peter S. Rosenbaum's "On the Role of Linguistics in the Teaching of English" summarizes the distinction between the transformational grammatical study of English and the structuralist approach. Rosenbaum discusses the relevance of linguistics to the teaching of English and illustrates how transformational grammar might clarify assumptions that underlie "correct writing."

24

The Linguistic Basis of English Prosody

S. JAY KEYSER

The business of prosody, according to Robert Bridges (1966, p. 91) is the characterization of the rules which specify the treatment of syllables in verse, whether they are to be considered as long or short, accented or unaccented, elidible or not. What is especially appealing about Bridges' view of prosody is that it emphasizes a distinction of overriding importance in the study of prosody; namely, the distinction between the abstract metrical pattern of a line and the rules which determine when that abstract pattern is suitably filled by an arrangement of linguistic material.

The abstract metrical patterns of English poetry have generally been considered to be composed of various types of feet which in certain combinations make up a larger unit called the line or verse. For example, the iambic pentameter line, consisting of five iambic feet, each foot containing two positions, which we distinguish by the symbols W (= weak) and S (= strong), may be represented as follows:

(1)

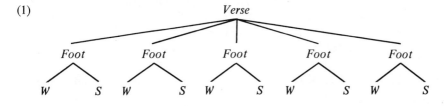

This paper was first delivered at the Linguistic Society of America meeting held in December 1966. It is based upon Morris Halle and S. Jay Keyser (1966). The theory of prosody represented as the revised theory below is a modification of the view expressed in Halle and Keyser. The theory so modified was shown by Halle to account for Russian verse in a paper delivered before the Slavic section of the Modern Language Association in December 1966. The present paper attempts to show that the modified version is sufficient to account for the mainstream of English metrical verse from Chaucer through to the present. Indeed, with a few relatively minor adjustments, English and Russian metrical verse are the result of the same metrical principles.

The trochaic pentameter line may be presented as

(2)

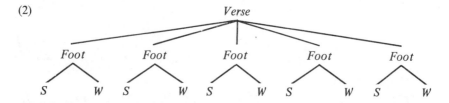

The anapestic dimeter line as

(3)

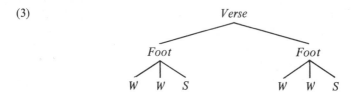

and so on.[1]

Given abstract metrical patterns such as those in (1), (2), and (3), Bridges supposes that the prosodical rules tell us when these patterns have been successfully filled by a given line. It is the first task of the prosodist to provide a precise characterization of these rules.

Consider this first line of a sonnet by Keats:

(4)   *Much have I travelled in the realms of gold*

beside the title of the sonnet from which it comes:

(5)   *On First Looking Into Chapman's Homer*

If one believes there is a difference between these two lines, expressed in one way by noting that the title could not appear as a line in the sonnet, then one view of the character of the rules which determine when linguistic material fulfills an abstract metrical pattern (in this instance (1), the iambic pentameter pattern) is immediately excluded. Thus dominant among some scholars is the supposition that a poet need not accept the stress pattern of words as given by the rules of his language, but may engage in "legitimate shifting of the accent for the sake of the meter." The chief exponent of this view is the Dutch scholar Ten Brink (1901, §279). According to him, it is permissible to shift the stress in words so that (5) becomes, in a metrical context

(6)   *On First Looking Into Chapman's Homer*

The difficulty with this view is that it fails to make the right distinction between a metrical and an unmetrical line. According to it, any line with sufficient number of syllables is metrical. But anyone familiar with English poetry knows that meter

---

[1]For a convenient survey of the various types of line in English poetry, see Alden (1902).

arranges linguistic stresses as well as syllables and that the arrangements never require linguistic stresses be violated.

Let us consider a different view of the rules which determine when a given linguistic construction fulfills an abstract metrical pattern. Many scholars hold that a poet is not free to change the stress patterns as given by the rules of his language. Rather he must take those patterns as given and select from among them those which fulfill the abstract metrical pattern. The main concern of these prosodists, the author among them, has been with describing the rules which determine this selection.

We begin with the following set of rules:

(7)   The Strict Iambic Pentameter Theory:
   Rule i.   The iambic pentameter line consists of five feet to which may be appended one or two extra-metrical syllables.
   Rule ii.   The iambic foot consists of two positions, a weak position followed by a strong one.
   Rule iii. Each strong position is occupied by a syllable with strong stress.
   Rule iv.   Each weak position is occupied by a syllable less strongly stressed.

Rule i and Rule ii of (7) specify the abstract metrical pattern in (1) above.[2] Rule iii and Rule iv, on the other hand, specify when a given line is a bona fide realization of (1). In particular, they claim that within each foot each weak position must always contain a syllable with less linguistic stress than the syllable in each strong position. Let us consider how (7) deals with the following lines:

(8)   Shakespeare's 73rd Sonnet—opening quatrain:
   That time of year thou mayst in me behold
   When yellow leaves, or none, or few do hang
   Upon those boughs which shake against the cold
   Bare, ruined choirs where late the sweet birds sang.

According to (7), the first three lines in (8) are metrical. Each line has ten and only ten syllables and each even syllable contains greater stress than each preceding odd syllable. The lines may be successfully divided into five feet. The fourth line, however, is not metrical. Thus whereas it, too, contains ten syllables, it is not the case that each even syllable contains greater stress than each preceding odd syllable. Hence *Bare, ru-* does not constitute a proper foot since the first syllable contains the same level of stress as the second syllable. This is in violation of Rule iv. We are forced to suppose, therefore, that the fourth line of (8) is unmetrical, at least when scanned according to (7). However, even a cursory examination of English poetry in the iambic tradition reveals that such lines, far from being exceptional, are quite common. Indeed, in the poetry of some poets, such as John Donne, they predominate.

Consider, for example, the following lines:

(9)(a)   *Silent upon a peak in Darien*   (Keats, "On First Looking into Chapman's Homer")

---

[2]Extrametrical syllables are common in poets such as Chaucer, for whom these syllables are always unstressed. The treatment of these syllables in other poets is an empirical question. Since the burden of the argument to follow does not depend on the treatment of these syllables, we shall ignore them from here on.

(b) (i) *Rocks, caves, lakes, fens, bogs, dens and shades of death*   (Milton, *Paradise Lost*, II.621)

(ii) *As ook, firr(e), birch, asp(e), alder, holm, popler*

(iii) *Wylugh, elm, plane, assh, box, chasteyn, lynde, laurer*   (Chaucer, "Knight's Tale," 2921–2922)

(iv) *Day, night, houre, tide, time, worke, and play*   (Shakespeare, *Romeo and Juliet*, III.v. 178)

(c) (i) *Yet dearly I love you and would be loved fain*   (Donne, "Holy Sonnet XIV")

(ii) *Divorce me, untie or break that knot again*   (Donne, "Holy Sonnet XIV")

(iii) *Flies strike the miraculous water of the iced*   (Robert Lowell, "As a Plane Tree by the Water")

(iv) *And Agamemnon dead. Being so caught up*   (Yeats, "Leda and the Swan")

(d) *Twenty bookes clad in blak or reed*   (Chaucer, *Canterbury Tales*, "Prologue," 294)

(e) (i) *Follow your saint, follow with accents sweet*   (Campion, "Follow Your Saint")

(ii) *Wondring upon the word: quaking for drede*   (Chaucer, "Clerk's Tale," 358)

(iii) *For one restraint, Lords of the word besides*   (Milton, *Paradise Lost*, I.32)

(iv) *And now 'tis passed. What next? See the long train*   (Thoreau, "I'm Thankful That My Life Doth Not Deceive")

(v) *Appeare in person here in Court. Silence*   (Shakespeare, *Winter's Tale*, III.i.10)

Each one of these lines represents a common departure from the iambic pattern and realization rules of (7). Thus (9a) contains a foot with a strongly stressed syllable preceding a weaker stressed one, namely *Silent*, in violation of Rule iii and Rule iv. It also contains a foot with both syllables without stress, namely *-ien* in *Darien*, and this in violation of Rule iii and Rule iv as well.

The lines in (9b. i–iv) are composed of a series of nouns in coordinate construction. In all of them the even syllables contain strong stressed syllables; however, the odd syllables do as well, thereby violating Rule iv.

The lines in (9c. i–iv) represent a different kind of violation. Whereas the preceding lines all contain ten syllables which could be divided into five, albeit irregular, feet, these lines contain more than ten syllables. They are in violation of Rule ii which requires that every foot contain no more than two syllables.

On the other hand (9d) contains nine syllables. It has too few syllables and is also in violation of Rule ii which requires that every foot contain no less than two syllables.

Finally, consider the lines in (9e. i–v). All of these lines contain a violation of Rule iii and Rule iv since they all exhibit a foot with the strong and weaker stressed syllables in the wrong positions. These violations are set apart from the above since they also involve a preceding major syntactic break, indicated by a comma, semicolon, colon, or period. For example, in (9e. ii) *quaking* constitutes a fourth foot with a strong stress in an odd position and a weaker stress in the even position. Notice, however, that a major syntactic break which is often actualized as a pause precedes *quaking* in the line. (The relevance of this will become clear later.)

All of the variant lines listed in (9) have long been noted by English prosodists. In the face of them no prosodist can seriously adhere to the theory outlined in (7).

And no prosodist ever has. Indeed, in the face of the lines in (9) there is only one alternative open to the prosodist; namely, to modify (7). The reason for doing so is this: while (7) does account for a large number of lines, the number of lines which it does not account for is still too large to ignore or to relegate to an unmetrical status. It is not that prosodists are unwilling to suppose that poets like Chaucer, Donne, and Shakespeare could write an unmetrical line, but rather their recognition that whatever else might constitute an unmetrical line, the fourth line in (8) and all of those in (9) may not reasonably be included among them. In other words, prosodists have opted to modify (7) because of an intuitive judgment that the similarities between the fourth line in (8) and the preceding three are far greater than the dissimilarities. (The same holds true of (9) and the first three lines of (8) as well.)

The theory of iambic pentameter which has generally been adopted by prosodists consists of (7), the strict iambic pentameter theory, to which is appended a list of so-called "allowable deviations"—"allowable" because the lines they are intended to characterize are too numerous to be considered unmetrical, and "deviations" because they depart from (7) above:[3]

(10)   Allowable Deviations:
      i.   Inverted first foot
      ii.   Heavy foot or spondee
      iii. Extra slack syllable internal to the line and elided
      iv.   Dropping of the first slack syllable
      v.   Internal trochaic (or other) substitution

It was mentioned above that a reasonable goal of any theory of prosody is to provide a way of telling a metrical from an unmetrical line. The modified theory makes this distinction as follows: a line is unmetrical if it does not adhere to the strict iambic pentameter theory or if it is not accounted for by one of the "allowable deviations" appended to the strict theory.

While the modified theory accounts for all of the lines in (8) and in (9)—and therefore the vast majority of lines which, under any reasonable theory, ought to be accounted for—it fails in certain important respects. For one thing, it fails to explain why these particular deviations should be "allowable" and no others. Why, for example, do we not find on the list in (10) provision for lines which drop the second, third, or fourth slack syllable and not just the first? Or why do we not find iambic lines which exhibit five inversions instead of just one or two and these only in highly specific positions.

For another thing, appending a list of "allowable deviations" to the strict iambic pentameter theory fails to explain certain systematic asymmetries between various meters in English. Thus Otto Jespersen (1900; Gross, p. 126) observed that whereas an iambic line could tolerate a trochee in the first two syllables, a trochaic line could not tolerate an iamb in the first two syllables. He cites the following couplet from Longfellow:

(11)   *Tell me not in mournful numbers*
                Life is but an empty dream

---

[3]Baum (1961), Wimsatt and Beardsley (1959) and Alden (1902) are just a few who adhere to the "allowable deviation" modification of the strict theory.

and notes that the second line may not be replaced by

(12)   *A life's but an empty dream*

which begins with an iamb.[4]

By the same token Jespersen might have noticed that while the iambic line permits an optional dropping of the first slack syllable, the trochaic line permits the addition of an initial slack syllable. Thus the following trochaic couplet from Keats' *Fancy* is relevant:

(13)   *All the buds and bells of May*
                            From dewy sward or thorny spray

This relationship between the iambic and trochaic lines would remain unexplored under a theory of prosody which simply accounted for each deviation as another entry on a list.

Jespersen (1900; Gross, p. 117) also notes that major syntactic breaks—what he refers to as pauses—appear to play an important role in the metrical behavior of a line. And if we return to the list of allowable deviations, we find that internal trochaic substitution is almost invariably accompanied by a preceding major syntactic break. Indeed, this break is indicated orthographically by a comma, semicolon, colon, or period more often than not. This strongly suggests that internal trochaic substitution (9e. i–v) and heavy feet or spondees (9b. i–iv) are the result of the same metrical principle, rather than unrelated entries on a list.

At this point, then, let us consider yet a third theory which attempts to account for the same metrical data as that accounted for by the modified theory, namely all of the lines in (8) and (9), but in terms of a set of prosodical rules which endeavor to explain why we have to do with just these kinds of lines and no others:

(14)   Revised Iambic Pentameter Theory:

    Rule 1.   The *iambic pentameter line* consists of ten positions plus one or two extra-metrical syllables. The odd numbered positions are weak; the even numbered strong.

    Rule 2.   A position is normally constituted by a single syllable, but under certain conditions two adjacent syllables may constitute a single position (*synalepha*), or a position may remain unactualized (*catalexis*).

        Synalepha: assignment of two vowels, when separated by no more than a single sonorant consonant, to a single position.

        Catalexis: occupation of the initial position by zero phonetic material.

    Rule 3.   *Stress maxima* may occupy only strong positions.

        Stress maximum: a syllable carrying more stress than either of the two syllables adjacent to it in the same syntactic constituent within a line of verse.

---

[4]Indeed, the possibility of a systematic explanation of this phenomenon is hinted at by W. K. Wimsatt (cf. Sebeok, 1960, p. 206): "it is not at all clear to me why the trochaic substitution in the first foot is so acceptable in the iambic line. I'm never able to make up my mind whether it is because it just happened, as Mr. Ransom, I think, suggests, sort of got established, or whether there is some peculiar reason."

Rule 1 specifies the abstract metrical pattern as follows:

(15)

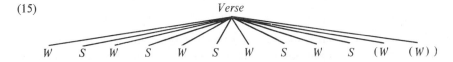

$$W \quad S \quad W \quad S \quad W \quad S \quad W \quad S \quad W \quad S \quad (W \quad (W))$$

The major difference between (15) and (1) is that the latter makes use of an intermediate level, namely the level of the foot. It may be that further study will require a modification of (14) to introduce this level. The foot will play no role in what follows, however.

Rule 2 and Rule 3, then, specify when a given line is a bona fide realization of (15). They provide for a particular way of scanning a line to determine whether it is suitable for inclusion in a poem whose metrical pattern corresponds to (15). The procedure for scanning a line is as follows: in each line we first establish position occupancy. This is done by numbering the different syllables in the line from left to right.[5] If the number is ten, a one-to-one occupancy of positions by syllables is assumed, in accordance with Rule 2. If the number is one less than ten, a check is made to determine if a one-to-one syllable to position assignment can be made by assuming an unactualized initial position, again in accordance with Rule 2. If the number of syllables is more than ten, a check is made to determine if two adjacent syllables may be assigned to a single position in accordance with Rule 2. It is possible for other alternatives to be determined by Rule 2. Thus a line may be both catalectic (headless) and still require two adjacent syllables be assigned a single position internally.[6]

After having established syllable to position assignments, one then locates stress maxima in the line in accordance with the definition in (14). This involves location, not only of the main linguistically given stresses in words, but a comparison of the linguistically given stress with that of the surrounding syllables. In those cases where a major syntactic break intervenes between two syllables, neither syllable may, in accordance with the definition, constitute a stress maximum. Note also that a main stress in the first position of an iambic line will never count as a stress maximum since it is not surrounded on both sides by syllables of lesser stress. A main stress on the last syllable of an iambic line will not count as a stress maximum unless an extrametrical syllable has been appended (but see footnote 8). In much rhyming verse, the possibility of a final syllable not bearing main stress is masked by the additional constraint that only stress-bearing syllables may rhyme. This is true, for example, of Chaucer. Browning, on the other hand, does

---

[5]It is important to keep in mind that in so counting we exclude extrametrical syllables.

[6]A second condition which has to do with the assignment to a single position of sequences of monosyllabic words and/or single syllables, one of which is unstressed, is omitted from this discussion. It is this condition which allows for dissyllabic positions composed of such sequences as *of a*, *to the*, etc. A full discussion of this condition and the way it operates in Chaucer will be found in Halle and Keyser (1966).

not impose this constraint on rhymes.[7] Moreover, in blank verse the tenth syllable is often unoccupied by a main stress as the following line shows:

(16)   *No light, but rather darkness visible*   (Milton, *Paradise Lost*, I.63)[8]

We have established stress maxima and position occupancy. It only remains to choose that particular assignment of syllables to positions which insures that stress maxima will occur in strong positions in accordance with Rule 3. All lines for which such a choice is possible are metrical lines; all lines for which such a choice is impossible are unmetrical lines.

At this point, then, let us return to the lines in (8) and (9). The first line in (8) contains ten syllables and four stress maxima, the largest number of stress maxima an iambic pentameter line can tolerate. Indicating a stress maximum by the symbol we may scan the line as follows:

(17)   *That time of year thou mayst in me behold*

Lines such as this one exhibit the most common actualization of the abstract iambic pentameter pattern. Each position contains a single syllable and each strong position contains a stress maximum. The fourth line in (17), however, exhibits a departure from this pattern. While each position contains a single syllable, not every strong position is occupied by a stress maximum. Thus while there is a strong linguistic stress on *Bare* and on *ru-* neither constitutes a stress maximum since the surrounding syllables are not in the same syntactic constituent. Using the numeral 1 to indicate strong linguistic stress, we may scan the fourth line in (8) as follows:

(18)   *Bare, ruined choirs where late the sweet birds sang*

Notice, however, that lines such as (18) are a natural consequence of the revised theory since, according to Rule 3 of that theory, strong positions *may* be occupied by a stress maximum. It does not assert that every strong position *must* be so oc-

---

[7]Consider, for example, the closing couplet from Browning's "My Last Duchess":

Taming a sea-horse, thought a rarity,
Which Claus of Innsbruck cast in bronze for me !

Here there is no linguistic stress on the *-y* of *rarity* and yet it rhymes with the stressed *me*. Such rhymes are permissible though not common. In Chaucer they are nonexistent due to a stricture against unstressed syllables rhyming.

[8]Bridges (1921, p. 39) observes, "Tyrwhitt is quoted as saying that one of the indispensable conditions of English blank verse was that the last syllable should be strongly accented. The truth seems to be that its metrical position in a manner exonerates it from requiring any accent.— Whether the 'last foot' may be inverted is another question.—A weak syllable can very well hold its own in this tenth place, and the last essential accent of the verse may be that of the 'fourth foot.' The analogy with the dipody of the classical iambic, and with the four-minim bar of the old alla breve time in music is evident." Note that the occurrence of an extrametrical syllable will turn a main stress in the last position of an iambic verse and in the first position of a trochaic verse into a stress maximum. This suggests that stress maxima, in these positions are not crucial to the meter. It may be that evidence will come to light which requires that the last accent of an iambic line be given a special metrical status and, presumably, the initial stress of a trochaic line. For the present we follow Bridges (see above) and suppose that main stress in these positions is not essential to the meter.

cupied. To put it differently, Rule 3 asserts only that if there are stress maxima in a line, they must fall within a strong position. From the point of view of (14), both (17) and (18) are metrical lines, and there is no necessity for recourse to an "allowable deviation" list.[9]

Before considering the lines in (9), let us consider the phrase *sweet birds* in (18). Notice that *sweet* has not been marked as a stress maximum. The reason for this is that commentators on British stress (cf. Jones, 1960, §959) have observed that the level of stress between an adjective and a following noun is the same.[10] If this is so, then *sweet* may not constitute a stress maximum since it does not contain greater stress than the surrounding syllables. The same is true of *birds*. In other words, *Adjective + Noun* sequences in British English apparently are treated metrically as if there were a major syntactic break between the adjective and the noun. This view is substantiated by the fact that one finds the adjective of an *Adjective + Noun* construction occurring in *W* as well as *S* positions in a verse. Consider, for example, the lines

(19)(a) *The Miller(e) was a stout carl for the nones* (Chaucer, *Canterbury Tales*, "Prologue," 545)

(b) *The course of true love never did run smooth* (Shakespeare, *A Midsummer Night's Dream*, I.i. 134)

Without the assumption of level stress in *Adjective + Noun* constructions, these lines would be unmetrical. In the first line *carl*, with greater linguistic stress than *stout* and *for* would constitute a stress maximum, but one which occurs in a weak (the seventh) position. In the second line, *love* would have greater stress than *true* and the first syllable of *never*. It, too, would contain a stress maximum in a weak (the fifth) position. There are, however, a great many lines like those in (19), not only in Chaucer and Shakespeare, but in poets throughout the history of English.

---

[9]The rules in (14) contain several options. Rule 2 allows, first, for a one-to-one occupancy of syllables to positions, then under certain conditions for dissyllabic or empty positions. Similarly, Rule 3 allows for all strong positions to be occupied by a stress maximum but does not require that every position be so occupied. We shall assume that the earliest alternative in Rule 2 and that actualization of Rule 3 in which every strong position is occupied by a stress maximum is the most neutral realization of the iambic line. All lines which require a later alternative of Rule 2 or fewer than four stress maxima or some combination of both, we shall suppose to represent a more complex realization of the pattern. It will become clear that some poets show a tendency toward the more complex realizations, giving the appearance of avoiding wherever possible the most neutral actualization (cf. Appendix). In general we replace the notion of "tension," which has played so dominant a role in recent metrical discussions, with the notion of more or less complex actualizations of a line. The primary reason for this is that the notion of "tension" tends to blur the distinction between an unmetrical and a metrical line. The notion of complex actualizations maintains this distinction.

[10]In American English the adjective of an *Adjective + Noun* combination is subordinated in stress. Thus with 1 = *primary stress* and 2 = *secondary stress*, we stress *old man* as *óld mán* (2 over old, 1 over man). This constitutes an important difference between British and American stress patterns. On the other hand, stress in compound nouns is the same in both dialects of English; thus *bláckbird* (1 over black, 2 over bird) (British and American) beside *bláck bírd* (1 over black, 1 over bird) (British) and *blàck bírd* (2 over black, 1 over bird) (American).

(For other examples see Jespersen, 1900; Gross, p. 116). Level stress and the use of the stress maximum provides a ready explanation for such lines.[11]

Let us now turn to the lines in (9), the main body of data which has led to the list in (10). Immediately we find that lines (9b. i–iv) exhibit the same metrical principle which gave rise to (18) above. Thus a series of nouns in coordinate construction may occur in an iambic line precisely because they are separated from one another by a major syntactic break and are excluded from stress maximum status. To illustrate we may scan (9b. i) as follows:

(20)   *Rocks, caves, lakes, fens, bogs, dens and shades of death*

In this line there is a one to one assignment of syllables to positions. Moreover, the stress maximum, in this case the only one, on *shades*, occupies the strong position. Rule 2 and Rule 3 admit this line as a possible actualization of the abstract metrical pattern in (15). We again find a list such as (10) unnecessary.[12]

Notice, also, that all of the lines in (9e. i–v) exhibit major syntactic breaks between adjacent strong stresses which are thereby eliminated from stress maximum status. Thus, we may scan (9e. v) as

(21)   *Appeare in person here in Court. Silence*

Hence lines (17) though (21) are all treated as metrical lines in accordance with the theory in (14). So, too, is (9d) which may be scanned as

(22)   *Twenty bookes clad in blak or reed*

In order to achieve this scansion, however, we must suppose that the first position is occupied by an unactualized syllable in accordance with the third alternative of Rule 2. By doing so, the remaining syllables may be assigned in a one-to-one fashion to weak and strong positions so that only strong positions contain the stress maxima. In other words, (22) is an instance of the so-called headless line.

---

[11]It is always possible to appeal to a special explanation, such as emphatic stress to avoid difficulties like (19). Thus one might argue that Chaucer is intending the reader to give special emphasis to *stout* and hence the line is regular. Recourse to emphatic stress, however, is expensive. For one thing, any word can receive emphatic stress and, with it as a metrical tool, one can make almost any line metrical. Indeed, recourse to emphatic stress is merely a less radical version of Ten Brink's "legitimate shifting of the stress for the sake of the meter" principle. We assume, most conservatively, that the linguistic givens of a language which the poet may not violate refer to language under normal stress assignment unless there is very strong contextual grounds for assuming otherwise.

[12]Wimsatt (Sebeok, 1960, p. 201) comments on (20): "I maintain that when we have 'Rocks, caves, lakes, fens, bogs, dens, and shades of death' and 'Immutable, immortal, infinite,' both of those lines are iambic pentameter, and if they are not both iambic pentameter, the contrast of their length, their speed, their weight, and all that sort of thing, loses a great deal of its interest. If we find them in a prose composition, there is nothing remarkable about it. It is just the fact that it is very agile—it is very, very gifted in a virtuoso way." Wimsatt's intuition that both lines are iambic is formally captured by the realization Rule 2 and Rule 3 of (14) which admit both lines. We have already seen how (20) is scanned. With it we may compare the scansion of *Immutable, immortal, infinite*. In this line there is a one to one assignment of syllables to positions as in (20). However, only the first and third strong positions are actualized by a stress maximum. A major syntactic break prevents the fourth strong position from being so realized and, as in (5) above, the line ends in an unstressed syllable.

Notice, that the assumption of an unactualized first position does not permit a stress maximum to be assigned to *twent-* since this syllable is still not surrounded by syllables of lesser stress within the same constitutent in the verse.

This brings us to (9a), the line with the so-called inverted first foot. We scan it as follows:

(23)   *Silent upon a peak in Darien*

The first syllable, *Sil-* is not a stress maximum because, like *twent-* in (22) it is not surrounded on *both* sides by a syllable with lesser stress. Notice, however, that given a theory of prosody which utilizes a stress maximum, one would expect to find, in the first position, syllables bearing all manner of linguistic stress, precisely because a stress maximum may never appear in that position. And this, of course, is precisely what one does find in the iambic line. Again we have an instance of a so-called "allowable deviation" which, from the point of view of a theory using a stress maximum is a natural consequence. A list such as (10) is again obviated.

But now let us consider the asymmetry noted earlier between an iambic and a trochaic line. The former allows inversion; the latter does not. Now we can understand why. A theory using the stress maximum allows inversion in iambic lines since such inversion does not place a stress maximum in a weak position. Inversion in the beginning of a trochaic line, however, will place a stress maximum in a weak position and thereby violate the meter. This is precisely what happened in (12) above. The asymmetry, then, is explainable in terms of a theory which makes use of the stress maximum. In terms of a modified theory the asymmetry is purely accidental (cf. footnote 4).

Let us turn, finally, to the lines in (9c. i–iv). If (9d) contains too few syllables, these lines contain too many. It is necessary, therefore, to resort to one of the still unused alternatives provided by Rule 2 of (14); namely, synalepha. Consider, first, (9c. i). Locating first the stress maxima, it appears as

(24)   *Yet dearly I love you and would be loved fain*

Notice, however, that unlike (17)–(21) and (23), we may not assume a one to one syllable to position assignment; (24) has too many syllables. We must now determine if any of the syllable sequences in (24) can be treated, metrically speaking, as a single position. Two of them can. By virtue of the alternative contained in Rule 2 whereby a sequence of two vowels separated by no more than a single sonorant consonant may be assigned to a single position, we may designate *-ly I* and *you and* as dissyllabic positions. Indeed, by doing so, we produce a syllable to position assignment which places stress maxima in strong positions and thereby renders (24) metrical. By underlining dissyllabic positions and assuming all not-underlined syllables as belonging to a single position, we complete the scansion of (24) as follows:

(24′)   *Yet dearly I love you and would be loved fain*

The scansion of (9c.3) is of some interest since, for it to be metrical, we must suppose that the word *miraculous* occupies just two positions. This is provided for by Rule 2 and the line is scanned

(25)   *Flies strike the miraculous water of the iced*

Thus (14) and the modified theory consisting of (7) and (10) account for precisely the same set of data. The latter, however, masks the fact that spondaic and trochaic substitutions in a line are dependent upon preceding major syntactic breaks, a relationship which can be captured in a theory using the stress maximum. Further, given the stress maximum, we expect to find stressed and unstressed syllables in the initial positions of iambic lines and this, of course, is what we do find. We see, also, that the asymmetry between the trochaic and iambic line is now explicable. Initial inversion is avoided in a trochaic (though not in an iambic) line since it gives rise to a stress maximum in a weak position; that is, to a violation.

If one's goal is simply to describe in some fashion the class of lines which are considered metrical in the iambic tradition, then either the revised or the modified theory will do the job. If, however, one would like to go further and understand why those particular lines are metrical and no others, one must seek an alternative to the modified theory. The revised theory is such an alternative.

Let us consider one final line. It is the first line of a sonnet by John Keats which begins[13]

(26)   *How many bards gild the lapses of time!*
   A few of them have ever been the food
  Of my delighted fancy,—I could brood
  Over their beauties, earthly, or sublime:
  And often, when I sit me down to rhyme,
   These will in throngs before my mind intrude:
   But no confusion, no disturbance rude
  Do they occasion; 'tis a pleasing chime.

Reviewing this sonnet in the *Examiner*, Leigh Hunt criticized the first line for its metrical irregularity, saying that "by no contrivance of any sort can we prevent this from jumping out of the heroic measure into mere rhythmicality." Bridges, however, apparently regarded the line as acceptable, viewing "the inversion of the third and fourth stresses as very musical and suitable to the exclamatory form of the sentence" (cf. de Sélincourt, 1905, p. 397) The modified theory would also regard the line as metrical, one exhibiting trochaic substitutiton in the third and fourth feet, a deviation which is permissible since it appears on the list in (10). To understand how the revised theory treats the line we must first locate stress maxima. These are

(27)   *How many bards gíld the lápses of time*

Next, syllable to position occupancy must be established. The line, counting from left to right, has ten syllables. Therefore, we assume a one-to-one assignment in accordance with Rule 2. The final scansion, then, is

(27′)

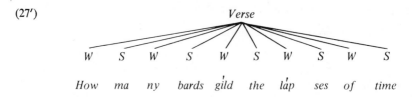

---

[13]I am indebted to my colleague Allen Grossman for bringing this line to my attention.

The revised theory labels the line unmetrical because it places stress maxima in weak positions in violation of Rule 3. But now observe what the line is about. It speaks of *lapses of time* in a poem which goes on to praise a few great bards because they occasion no rude disturbance as opposed to lesser poets who, by contrast, do. Apparently Keats is praising the metrical facility of great poets and condemning that of lesser ones who exhibit *lapses of time;* that is, inferior meters. The first line, then, is a caricature of what it is about. It contains, in a double sense, a criticism of bad poets, and Keats' metrical pun demands that the line be unmetrical.

That the interpretation of (27′) is correct is suggested by the closing sestet:

(28)
> *So the unnumber'd sounds that evening store:*
> *The songs of birds—the whisp'ring of the leaves—*
> *The voice of waters—the great bell that heaves*
> *With solemn sound,—and thousand others more,*
> *That distance of recognizance bereaves,*
> *Make pleasing music, and not wild uproar.*

The alignment of the *few* and their *pleasing chime* with the *pleasing music* of the *unnumber'd sounds* of nature now suggests the proper equation. Great poets achieve naturalness even though constrained by meter; lesser poets are unable to. They can only *gild* their inferior command of metrical principles; literally, masking poor facility with "specious luster."

The metrical wit exhibited in the opening line of this sonnet depends on accent and sense.[14] As we have seen, the line must be deemed unmetrical; otherwise it loses its point. The revised theory provides the proper metrical interpretation. The modified theory does not. The line, then, is the exception that proves the rule.

APPENDIX

In this appendix, two poems are scanned in full in terms of (14). The first poem is chosen because it represents the work of a poet whose lines constantly depart from the most neutral actualization of the line but which, nonetheless, adhere quite explicitly to metricality as defined by (14). The poem is "Holy Sonnet XIV," by John Donne and is scanned as follows:

> *Batter my heart, three-personed God, for you*
> *As yet but knock, breathe, shine, and seek to mend;*
> *That I may rise and stand, o'erthrow me and bend*
> *Your force to break, blow, burn and make me new.*
> *I, like an usurped town to another due,*

---

[14]A somewhat less convincing example is contained in the last line of (28) in which the phrase *and not wild uproar* appears. Its linguistic stresses are heavily clustered; thus, *and not wild uproar.* However, none qualifies as a stress maximum. Thus the phrase constitutes a complex actualization of the second half of the verse as contrasted with the neutral actualization of the first half. In some sense the neutral to complex movement of the meter mirrors the sense of the line.

> Labour to admit you, but O, to no end!
>
> Reason, your viceroy in mee, mee should defend,
>
> But is captived, and proves weak or untrue
>
> Yet dearly I love you and would be loved fain
>
> But am betrothed unto your enemy.
>
> Divorce me, untie, or break that knot again,
>
> Take me to you, imprison me, for I
>
> Except you enthrall me, never shall be free,
>
> Nor ever chaste except you ravish me.

Notice that only the last line represents the neutral actualization of the iambic pattern (see footnote 9). All others are more complex actualizations of the pattern. Indeed, Donne's tendency to choose actualizations of the abstract pattern which depart from the most neutral actualization is characteristic of his metrical style.

The second poem scanned, "After Long Silence," by William Butler Yeats, is chosen because it offers an opportunity for comparison with a scansion based upon a version of the modified theory which appears in Cleanth Brooks and Robert Penn Warren (1942, pp. 224–232).[15] In terms of (14) it is scanned as follows:

> Speech after long silence; it is right,
>
> All other lovers being estranged or dead,
>
> Unfriendly lamplight hid under its shade,
>
> The curtains drawn upon unfriendly night,
>
> That we descant and yet again descant
>
> Upon the supreme theme of Art and Song:
>
> Bodily decreptitude is wisdom; young
>
> We loved each other and were ignorant.

Like the Donne poem, the first line represents an actualization of the iambic pattern without a single strong position occupied by a stress maximum; this because of level stress in British English between an adjective and the following noun and because of the major syntactic break intervening between *silence* and *it*. The line is also headless. In the third line the first syllable of *lamplight* constitutes a stress maximum, bearing greater linguistic stress than the surrounding syllables. The same holds true of *hid* which also qualifies as a stress maximum. In the sixth line we again find an *Adjective + Noun* and, as in the first line, level stress prevents either from being a stress maximum. The poem, then, is accountable in terms of the same theory which accounts for Donne. Indeed, it is seen to exhibit precisely the same array of metrical effects, only less often and in less concentrated doses.

In the Brooks and Warren scansion, the first line appears as

> Speech | af ter long | si lence; | it | is right

---

[15]This interpretation is itself the subject of an article by Ronald Sutherland (1958), which the reader may also find useful for purposes of comparison.

What is unsatisfactory about this scansion is that, in an iambic pentameter poem, we find in one line (cf. Gross, 1966, p. 181) an anapest, a trochee, two monosyllabic feet and one iamb. Such an analysis is virtually claiming the poem begins in prose. In terms of (14) the line contains an unactualized first position but with an otherwise one-to-one syllable to position assignment. Its departure from the most neutral actualization of the line is simply due to the poet's manipulation of the major syntactic breaks in the line. It is scanned as follows:

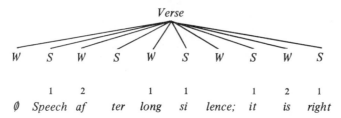

There is an abundance of heavy stresses, but none surrounded by lesser/stresses within the same constituent. It is this which gives the line its complex structure. The prosodist's intuition that this line is of a piece with all the others in the poem is formally captured by Rule 2 and Rule 3 of (14) which admit all of them as bona fide actualizations of the iambic pentameter pattern.[16]

REFERENCES

Alden, Raymond (1902), "The Foot and the Verse," *English Verse*. New York: Henry Holt and Company. Reprinted in Gross.

Baum, Paull, F. (1961), *Chaucer's Verse*. Durham, N. C.: Duke University Press.

Bridges, Robert (1921), *Milton's Prosody*. Oxford: Clarendon Press. Reprinted 1965.

———— (1966), "A Letter to a Musician on English Prosody," *Collected Essays, Papers, &c, of Robert Bridges*. Oxford: The Clarendon Press. Reprinted in Gross.

Brooks, Cleanth, and Robert Penn Warren (June, 1942), *Understanding Poetry*. New York: Henry Holt and Co.

de Sélincourt, E. (1905), *Poems of John Keats*. London: Methuen & Co., Ltd.

Gross, Harvey, ed., (1966), *The Structure of Verse: Modern Essays on Prosody*. New York: Fawcett World Library.

Halle, Morris, and S. Jay Keyser (1966), "Chaucer and the Study of Prosody." *College English*, 28:3, pp. 187–219.

Jespersen, Otto (1900), "Notes on Meter," *The Selected Writings of Otto Jespersen*. London: George Allen & Unwin, Ltd, 1962. Reprinted in Gross.

Jones, Daniel (1960), *Outline of English Phonetics*, 9th ed. Cambridge.

Sebeok, Thomas A., ed. (1960), *Style in Language*. Cambridge, Mass.: M.I.T. Press.

---

[16]A. Grossman has suggested that the headless opening line which begins *Speech after long silence* is a metrical pun in which *silence* is underscored by the unactualized (i.e. silent) first position. If so, this line, like the opening line of the Keats' sonnet, constitutes an interesting example of the semantic use of meter.

Sutherland, Ronald (1958), "Structural Linguistics and English Prosody." *College English*, 20:1. Reprinted in Gross.

Ten Brink, B. (1901), *The Language and Meter of Chaucer*, 2nd ed., rev. by F. Kluge, trans. by B. Smith. London.

Wimsatt, W. K., Jr., and Monroe C. Beardsley (1959), "The Concept of Meter: An Exercise in Abstraction." *Publications of the Modern Language Association*, 74.585–598. Reprinted in Gross.

25

Diachronic Syntax
and Generative Grammar

ELIZABETH CLOSS

1. The problem. The objectives of diachronic linguistics have always been to reconstruct the particular steps by which a language changes, and also to hypothesize about processes of language change in general. Recent discussion of the latter problem has frequently involved five closely related proposals.[1] First, language changes by means of a series of individual innovations. These innovations consist primarily in the addition of single rules to the grammar of the adult speaker. Second, these innovations usually occur at some point of break in a grammar; for example, "before the first morphophonemic rule involving immediate constituent structure of the utterance . . . before the phonological rules that eliminate boundary markers from the representation."[2] Third, these innovations are passed on to the next generation when the child imitates the adult. A child may internalize the adult's grammar; or, more probably, he will simplify it. This is because children have an ability, not shared by most adults, to construct by induction from the utterances to which they have been exposed, the simplest grammar capable of generating sentences. The simplification will give rise to a discontinuity in transmission from generation to generation. In the interests of preserving intelligibility, this discontinuity will be minimal. Fourth, whenever the discontinuity results in

Reprinted from *Language*, 41.402–415. (1965), by permission of Elizabeth Closs and the Linguistic Society of America.

I am deeply indebted to Morris Halle and Edward S. Klima for valuable criticism of an earlier draft of this paper. My thanks are also due to Sheldon Sacks, James Sledd, and Robert P. Stockwell for many helpful suggestions.

[1]For these proposals and their corollary, see especially Morris Halle, "Phonology in Generative Grammar," *Word*, 18.64–68 (1962), and the revised version in *SL*, pp. 344–349.

[2]*Word*, 18.66, n. 12; *SL*, p. 346, n. 13.

radical changes such as restructuring, a mutation occurs. Finally, these mutations, which affect the overall simplicity of the grammar, are rare.

The significance of the intelligibility criterion is summarized by Halle as follows:

> Linguistic change is normally subject to the constraint that it must not result in the destruction of mutual intelligibility between the innovators—i.e. the carriers of the change—and the rest of the speech community. . . . This restriction clearly affects the content of the rules to be added . . . the number of rules to be added must also be restricted, for very serious effects on intelligibility can result from the simultaneous addition of even two or three otherwise innocuous rules.
>
> It may be somewhat less obvious that the requirement to preserve intelligibility also restricts the place in the order where rules may be added. All other things being equal, a rule will affect intelligibility less if it is added at a lower point in the order than if it is added higher up.[3]

A corollary of these various proposals is that the simplest rules in a synchronic grammar will mirror the relative chronology of those additions which do not affect the overall simplicity of the grammar. In other words, synchronic grammars reflect *innovations*. They do not, however, reflect *mutations*.

These arguments have been presented mainly in connexion with phonological change. Ramification in all other areas of the grammar has been taken for granted, but has not been investigated in detail. Klima hints at the validity of the general claim that a synchronic syntax reflects historical change when he remarks in his article, "Relatedness Between Grammatical Systems,"

> Although motivated by a purely synchronic principle of simplicity (shortness of rules), the order in which the styles are considered does, in fact, recapitulate comparable aspects in the historical development of the pronouns.[4]

No systematic attempt has, however, been made to investigate the five hypotheses cited above in the light of syntactic change. It is the purpose of this paper to make such an attempt, and to draw some minimal conclusions which any theory of language change must include.

2. Representative data.   The investigation will be based on the history of the verbal auxiliary *Aux* in English. The relationship between one period of the language and another will be presented in terms of the relationships between transformational generative[5] grammars of ninth-century Old English, mid-fifteenth-

---

[3] *Word*, 18.66; *SL*, p. 346.

[4] Edward S. Klima, "Relatedness Between Grammatical Systems," *Language*, 40.1–20 (1964) [*MSE*].

[5] The notion of grammar is developed by Noam Chomsky, *Syntactic Structures* ('s-Gravenhage, 1957).

Questions have frequently been raised concerning the feasibility of using this notion of grammar in historical analysis, in particular concerning the appeal to intuition. A linguist theorizing about a living language ideally has as a control his own native intuition and that of the speakers around him, or at worst the native intuition of speakers of a language foreign to him. Against such intuition he can test, among other things, degrees of grammaticality and types of ambiguity. With dead languages, however, the linguist can rely only on the limited data available to him, and at best on a secondary "native intuition" which can arise only after several years of close associa-

century Middle English, late-sixteenth-century Early Modern English,[6] and Modern English. By *Aux* I mean the tense marker, modals, the perfect and progressive helping verbs, and a few other helping verbs which will be specified in the course of this paper.

Attempts will be made to reconstruct the intermediate steps that account for the *Aux* structures and so to account for the types of innovations that can reasonably be assumed to underlie the observed mutations.

3. Modern English. Consider first Modern English *Aux* constructions as a type of control, since they are well known and have been accounted for in grammars that fulfill the strongest requirements of transformational generative theory.[7]

The set of optional Modern English auxiliary verbs is established according to the following criteria: position relative to other verbs, especially in passives, negatives, emphatics, interrogatives; use in tag questions and other reduced sentences; occurrence with *n't*; and possiblity of occurrence under weak stress. These verbs include (1) the subset of modals *M* (*can, may, must, shall, will*), which all require a following verb in its base form, as in *I will go, I will have gone* where *go* and *have* are base forms; (2) the nonmodal operators: *have* requiring a past participle marker *PP*, and *be* requiring a present participle marker *PrP*. Any one or more of these subsets of auxiliary verbs may occur optionally, but only in the order described: *M – have – PP – be – PrP*.

In addition to these optional formatives, every verbal construction obligatorily carries one tense marker *T*, whether the helping verbs are present or not. *T* always

---

tion with the language. He can find very few, if any, syntactically minimal pairs from which to set up paradigms of grammatical versus ungrammatical sentences. Deviation and ambiguity are even more elusive. If we take in its strongest terms the requirement placed on linguistic theory that it should characterize and predict all and only the sentences of the language and also account for the native speaker's competence in producing and understanding utterances of the language, we might ultimately conclude that a grammar can be written only by a native speaker, not a foreigner, and that grammars of dead languages cannot be written at all. The degree of accuracy will naturally vary according to the degree of acquaintance with the language. But this does not mean that all investigation of language not native to the linguist must *de facto* be abandoned, any more than any theory of history, whether cultural or geological, must be rejected because we cannot recapture all and only the characteristics of previous eras. We may quite legitimately put forward a theory of a dead language, in terms of a grammar which fulfills the requirements of descriptive adequacy and explanatory power. This theory will be based on all observable data, and also on unobservable data when necessary, i.e. when the logical consequences of the model would not match the observable data without this hypothesis. As in analysis of a living language, that model will be the simplest which will characterize the sentences of the corpus, and so the infinite set of unobserved sentences which pattern with them. Within such a framework, deviance as well as grammaticality can tentatively be made explicit.

[6]For fuller versions of these grammars, see Closs, *Syllabus for English 110, History of English*, pp. 11–16, 24–29, 34–37 (mimeographed, University of California, Berkeley, 1964); *Deep and Surface Structure in Old English* (in preparation).

[7]See especially Chomsky, "A Transformational Approach to Syntax," in Archibald A. Hill, ed., *Third Texas Conference on Problems of Linguistic Analysis in English* (Austin, 1962), pp. 131–132, 144–147 [*SL*]; Klima, "Negation in English," *SL*, pp. 251–253 et passim; Robert B. Lees, *A Grammar of English Nominalizations* (Bloomington, 1960), pp. 19–20 et passim. For a discussion of the criteria by which the set of auxiliary verbs is set up, see James Sledd, *A Short Introduction to English Grammar* (Chicago, 1959), pp. 106–109.

occurs with the first member of the construction: *He would have come, *He will has come, *He will have comes*. For this reason, *T* is generated to precede the helping verbs and *MV* and every *Aux* is said to contain at least *T*. The formants can all be generated by the following rules. Only those elements relevant to *Aux* constructions are included here.

3.1 $S \rightarrow NP - VP$

3.2 $VP \rightarrow Aux - MV$

3.3 $MV \rightarrow \begin{Bmatrix} V_t - NP \\ V_i \\ \vdots \end{Bmatrix}$

3.4 $Aux \rightarrow T\,(M)\,(have - PP)\,(be - PrP)$

3.5 $M \rightarrow$ can, may, must, shall, will

A low-level affix switch rule assigns *T* to its correct position after the verbal base immediately following it.

Verbal constructions with *do* can all be accounted for by blocking the minimal auxiliary formant *T* from the main verb base in negatives, emphatics, interrogatives, tag questions, and imperatives, as in

(1)   *He does not go.*

(2)   *He does go.*

(3)   *Does he go?*

(4)   *What does she see?*

(5)   *She went home, did she?*

(6)   *Do be good.*

In other words, *do* is automatically and obligatorily generated as a dummy carrier wherever *T* is blocked from a main verb base *MV*.

4. Old English.   The shape of the optional part of *Aux* was considerably different at other stages of the language, and this one factor to a very large extent accounts for the differences in structure of active statements, and also of passives, negatives, and interrogatives.

As at all other periods, *T* was obligatory in Old English. There is a subset of the optional helping verbs which functions very largely like the subset of modern modals, and whose members are actually their cognates: *cunn-, mag-, mot-, scul-, will-*, all requiring an infinitive marker *Inf*. These may be exemplified by

(7)   *Or.*214.5: *Þær hie hit georne ongitan cuþen*[8]
      'When they could readily understand it'

(8)   *Or.*100.19: *Ic mæg eac on urum agnum tidum gelic anginn þæm gesecgan*
      'I can also tell of a beginning similar to that in our own times'

(9)   *Or.*30.33: *For ðon þe hio hyre firenluste fulgan ne moste*
      'Because she could not satisfy her desires'

---

[8]Quotations for Old English are derived from Henry Sweet, ed., *King Alfred's Orosius*, EETS 79 (London, 1883), abbreviated *Or.*; and from Henry Sweet, ed., *King Alfred's West-Saxon Version of Gregory's Pastoral Care*, EETS 45, 50 (London, 1871), abbreviated *CP*. References are to page and line numbers.

(10) *Or.218.20: Ic sceal eac niede þara monegena gewinna geswigian þe on eastlondum gewurdon*
'I shall also by necessity be silent about those many battles that took place in the East'

(11) *Or.140.30: Þa he & þa consulas hie attellan ne mehton*
'When he and the consuls could not count them'

In addition there is the cognate of the Modern English perfect helping verb, *habban* 'to have,' which requires *PP*, provided that *MV* is transitive (V_t):

(12) *Or.172.18: Ac him hæfdon Pene þone weg forseten*
'But the Carthaginians had blocked his way'

Occasionally *MV* may be one of a small set of intransitives (V_i), largely a set of verbs of movement, here classified as $V_{i_{move}}$, as in

(13) *Or.196.22: Þa Scipio hæfde gefaren*
'When Scipio had gone'

The perfect auxiliary of intransitives is regularly, however, formed by the verb *wesan* 'to be' – *PP*, as in

(14) *Or.4.17: Hu Orosius sæde þæt he wære cumen*
'How Orosium said that he had come'

(15) *Or.236.19: Þider hi þa mid firde gefaren wæron*
'To the place where they had then marched with the army'

There are also three progressive auxiliary verbs requiring *PrP* (realized in Old English as *-ende*). They are *wesan* 'to be', *beon* 'to be', and *weorðan* 'to become', here classified as the subset *BE*. Examples of each of these progressives are

(16) *Or.236.29: & him æfterfylgende wæs*
'And was following him'

(17) *Or.12.35: Þæt seo ea bið flowende ofer eal Ægypta land*
'So that this river floods all the land of Egypt'

(18) *CP.405.25: Ðin eagan weorðað gesionde ðinne bebiodend*
'Your eyes shall see your master'

Progressive but apparently not perfect auxiliary verbs may occur with *M*. In (19), for example, we find *M* and progressive. Sentences like (20) with *M* and progressive would be possible, but not (21) with *M* and perfect auxiliary, nor (22) with *M – Perfect – Progressive*:

(19) *Or.110.10: Nu ic wille eac þæs maran Alexandres gemunende beon*
'Now I shall also consider Alexander the Great'

(20) *Ic sceal feohtende beon*
'I shall be fighting'

(21) **Ic sceal gefuhten habban*
'I shall have fought'

(22) **Ic sceal feohtende gebeon habban*
'I shall have been fighting'

A further restriction is placed on the nonmodal operators: they do not occur in passive formations. Although we find (23) with the passive auxiliary formant (*BE* requiring *PP*) in the environment of *M*, (24) and (25) with passive formants

in the environment of perfect and progressive auxiliary verbs respectively are
ungrammatical:

(23)   *Or.*128.5: *Þa Darius geseah þæt he oferwunnen beon wolde*
      'When Darius saw that he would be conquered'

(24)   **Þæt he oferwunnen geworden hæfde*
      'That he had been overcome'

(25)   **Þæt he oferwunnen wesende wæs*
      'That he was being overcome'

The examples above demonstrate that the word order is very different from that
in Modern English. At the end of the ninth century of the following patterns are
favored, but are by no means exclusive:[9]

(*a*) In coordinate *and* clauses and in subordinate clauses, especially temporal
clauses with time adverbs, the finite verb (*MV* carrying *T*) often occurs at the
end. If there are helping verbs, *MV* will usually be followed by the nonmodal
operators and *M*. The last helping verb will carry *T*. For coordinates see (16), for
subordinates (7), (9), (11), (15), (23).[10]

(*b*) In independent clauses,[11] the finite verb occurs nonfinally except in simple
intransitive sentences. If a helping verb is present, *MV* will usually be preceded
by *M* or a nonmodal operator, as in (8), (10), (12), (18). When there are two helping
verbs, *M* will usually precede *MV*, and the perfect or progressive will follow, as
in (19).

Most linguists consider that the order *Subject (SU) – Object (O) – Main Verb
(MV) + Auxiliary (Aux)* which is typical of coordinate and dependent clauses is
a "reversal" of the normal order *SU – Aux – MV – O*. In terms of simplicity of
description and explanatory power, however, it is by far the simplest to set up
the Old English verb phrase in the order *SU (O) MV + Aux*. This will automatically account for most coordinate and subordinate clauses. A rule will then specify
that in independent clauses the last helping verb is moved to position before *MV*;
in this way just one rule will account for the fact that if there is one helping verb,
it precedes *MV*, but if there are two, only *M* precedes *MV*. Other orders will be
accounted for by a stylistic variant rule. Independent motivation for such an

---

[9]Recent detailed discussion of word-order problems include S. O. Andrew, *Syntax and Style
in Old English* (Cambridge, 1940); Paul Bacquet, *La structure de la phrase verbale à l'époque
Alfrédienne* (Paris, 1962); C. R. Barrett, *Studies in the Word-Order of Aelfric's Catholic Homilies
and Lives of the Saints* (Cambridge, 1953); Charles R. Carlton, *Syntax of the Old English Charters*,
unpublished Ph.D. dissertation, Michigan, 1958, pp. 170–256; David P. Harris, "The Development of Word-Order Patterns in Twelfth-Century English," in Albert H. Marckwardt, ed., *Studies
in Languages and Linguistics in Honor of Charles C. Fries* (University of Michigan, 1964), pp.
187–198; Bruce Mitchell, "Syntax and Word-Order in 'The Peterborough Chronicle' 1122–
1154," *Neuphilologische Mitteilungen*, 65.113–144 (1964).

[10](13), (14), (17) are examples of deviation from this rule.

[11]"Independent clauses" here include "demonstrative clauses" introduced by demonstrative
adverbs *þa* 'then', *þonne* 'then', *þær* 'there' in which the finite verb or one helping verb usually
precedes the subject (cf. Andrew, *Syntax and Style in Old English*, p. 3). Both independent clauses
with demonstrative adverbs and those without share the main features of verb order under discussion.

analysis is provided by negative constructions formed with *ne*. If the verb is finite, *ne* precedes *MV*:

(26) *Or.*19.10: *He cwæð þæt nan man ne bude be norðan him*
      'He said that no man lived north of him'

If there is a helping verb in type (*a*) sentences, *ne* precedes the last helping verb, as in (9) (11); in type (*b*) sentences it precedes whichever helping verb precedes *MV*. The negative of (19) would therefore be

(27) *Nu ic nille eac þæs maran Alexandres gemunende beon*
      'Now I shall also not consider Alexander the Great'

Furthermore, this analysis obviates the necessity of an affix switch rule, a rule which has no independent motivation, especially as *T* never has to be blocked from *MV* in Old English to generate a dummy carrier.

The *Aux* will therefore be optimally generated by[12]

4.1 $S \to NP - VP$

4.2 $VP \to MV + Aux$

4.3 $MV \to \begin{Bmatrix} NP - V_t \\ V_i \\ \vdots \end{Bmatrix}$

4.4 $V_i \to \begin{Bmatrix} V_{i_{move}} \\ V_{i_x} \end{Bmatrix}$

4.5 $Aux \to \left(\begin{Bmatrix} PP - habb, \text{ in env. } V_t\underline{\quad}, V_{i_{move}}\underline{\quad} \\ PP - wes, \text{ in env. } V_i\underline{\quad} \\ (PrP - Be)\,(Inf - M) \end{Bmatrix} \right) T$

4.6 $M \to cunn, mag, mot, scul, will$

4.7 $BE \to beo, wes, weorþ$

5. Middle English. By the thirteenth century, the normal word order is similar to that in Modern English. That is, we find *Aux – MV (O)* favored in both independent and dependent clauses. The simplicity criterion therefore requires that this order be generated as basic for Middle English. Such analysis furthermore provides just the kind of information we need to account for the fundamental differences in verb-phrase order between Old and Middle English. Although there is not the independent motivation that *do* provides in Modern English for setting up the members of *Aux* in the order *T (M)* . . . , since no dummy carrier is generable in Middle English, this analysis is simplest, as all other orders can then be derived easily from the basic form. Other constructions can also be neatly accounted for. The negative, for example, is formed during the earlier part of the Middle English period by *ne* preceding *T – First Base* as in (28); or by *nat* following *T – First Base* as in (29); or by both *ne* and *nat* as in (30). By the fifteenth century, negatives are more generally formed by *not* ~ *nat* after *T – First Base*, as in (31), (32):

---

[12]The rules are particularly interesting in that they are basically similar to those suggested by Emmon Bach for German, "The Order of Elements in a Transformational Grammar of German,' *Language*, 38.263–269 (1962).

V_{i_x} in Rule 4.4 stands for the class of all V_i that are not $V_{i_{move}}$. It includes verbs homonymous with the members of $V_{i_{move}}$.

(28) Ch.*Mel*.2266: *He ne foond neuere womman good*[13]
     'He never found a good woman'

(29) Ch.*Mel*.2170: *It aperteneth nat to a wys man*
     'It is not suitable for a wise man'

(30) Ch.*Mel*.2220: *Yet ne wolde he nat answere sodeynly*
     'Yet he did not want to answer immediately'

(31) *PL*.III.104.22 (1456): *And yff the maters went not to my maister entent*
     'And if the matters did not go according to what my master had planned'

(32) *PL*.III.87.1 (1456): *And of suche as I will not write*
     'And of such things as I will not write about'

As far as the shape of *Aux* is concerned, there has been considerable increase in the complexity of membership, but there is already greater environmental generalization for the perfect participle constructions. The modals are the cognates of the Old English forms and need not concern us here. As in Old English, Early Middle English modals require *Inf*, but owing to a regular late-fourteenth- and early-fifteenth-century rule, this marker is lost and is usually not overtly marked by the mid-fifteenth century. The perfect auxiliary has undergone partial reversal of context restriction: *have – PP* is used for both transitives and intransitives:

(33) *PL*.III.103.24 (1456): *Which Fenn hath promised (V_t) to doo*
     'Which Fenn has promised to do'

(34) *PL*.IV.17.10: *Wherfore the people was greved be cauce they had labored (V_i) so often*
     'For this reason the people were grieved because they had labored so often'

(35) Ch.*Mel*.3000: *For ye han entred (V_i) in to myn hous by violence*
     'For ye have entered my house by violence'

A subset of V_i may also occur with *be – PP*; its members, interestingly enough, are mainly the cognates of exactly those same verbs of movement which in Old English were the only ones that could occur with *habb – PP*:

(36) *PL*.IV.68.13: *But I undrestande ther is comen an other writte to the undrescheryff*
     'But I understand that another writ has come to the undersheriff'

(37) Ch.*Mel*.2160: *And by wyndowes ben entred*
     'And have entered through the windows'

There is only one progressive formant: the verb *be* requiring *PrP*. More significant for the history of *Aux* is that the progressive occasionally appears after the perfect helping verb, instead of being mutually exclusive with it. When this is the case, only *have – PP*, not *be – PP*, precedes the progressive formant. Examples of this complex construction occur mainly in poetry, as in Chaucer's *Knight's Tale*:

---

[13]Quotations for Middle English are taken from Hans Kurath, Sherman Kuhn, John Reidy, eds., *Middle English Dictionary* (Ann Arbor, 1954–); James Gairdner, ed., *The Paston Letters 1422–1509* (London, 1904), abbreviated *PL*., with references to volume, page, and line numbers; and Geoffrey Chaucer, *The Text of the Canterbury Tales*, John M. Manly and Edith Rickert, eds. (Chicago, 1940).

(38) Ch.*Kt.T.*929: *We haue been waytynge al this fortenyght*
'We have been waiting all this fortnight'

(39) **We been been waytynge al this fortenyght*

Of special interest is the additional use from Early Middle English times of *do* and *gin* as auxiliaries, both requiring *Inf* at their first introduction.[14] Both were originally used only as main verbs; throughout the period homonymous verbs *do* 'to cause to' and *gin* 'to begin to' persist as main verbs taking infinitive complement nominalizations; another homonymous verb *do* was a member from Old English times of a small class of substitutive verbs. The auxiliary verbs in question originated in poetry; *do* spread to prose by the late fourteenth century, cf.

(40)   *Appeal Usk in Bk.Lond.E.26/101* (1384): *So they diden pursuwe thynges a-yeins the Franchise of london for euer*
'So they pursued matters opposing the franchise of London for ever'

Gin, however, never became established in prose. Only *do* is generated as a formant in the mid-fifteenth-century grammar; a complete version of this grammar would generate *gin* as a deviant member of *Aux*, restricted to poetry. A grammar of Middle English prior to c.1380 would, however, specify restriction to poetry of both *do – Inf* and *gin – Inf* (*Inf* is still marked at this time).[15]

Among examples of auxiliary *do* in the *Paston Letters* are

(41)   *PL.III.2.26* (1454): *As for the prist that dede areste me*
'As for the priest who arrested me'

(42)   *PL.IV.149.37* (1465): *More plainly than I may do wryte at thys tyme*
'More plainly than I may write at this time'

(43)   *PL.IV.143.14* (1465): *Yf they wold do pay such dewts*
'If they would pay such debts'

From (42), (43), and several other passages, it is clear that *do* may occur after *M* and *have – PP*. There is independent motivation for analysing *do* as a second position nonmodal operator mutually exclusive with *be – PrP*: both, for example, fail to occur in passive formation.

The grammar must therefore specify at least the following phrase-markers:

5.1 $S \rightarrow NP - VP$

5.2 $VP \rightarrow Aux - MV$

5.3 $MV \rightarrow \begin{Bmatrix} V_t - NP \\ V_i \\ \vdots \end{Bmatrix}$

---

[14]Clear loss of identity as *MV* is indicated by the occasional interchange in different MSS of *gin–Inf* and *do–Inf*; cf. *Cursor Mundi*, Göt. 2009 (c. 1400): *A neu liuelad gan he bigin* 'He began a new kind of life', with MS variants *con*, *cun* (reduced forms of *gan*) and also *dud*. A summary and bibliography of studies on *do* and *gin* is provided in Tauno F. Mustanoja, *A Middle English Syntax, I: Parts of Speech* (Helsinki, 1960), pp. 600–615.

[15]On some of the problems in accounting for specifically poetic deviance, cf. Samuel R. Levin, "Poetry and Grammaticalness," in Horace Lunt, ed., *Proceedings of the Ninth International Congress of Linguists* ('s-Gravenhage, 1964), pp. 308–315.

5.4 $V_i \rightarrow \begin{Bmatrix} V_{i_{move}} \\ V_{i_x} \end{Bmatrix}$

5.5 $Aux \rightarrow T\,(M)\left(\left\{\begin{matrix} (have-PP)\left(\begin{Bmatrix} be-PrP \\ do \end{Bmatrix}\right) \\ be-PP, \text{ in env. } \underline{\hspace{1cm}} \ V_{i_{move}} \end{matrix}\right\}\right)$

5.6 $M \rightarrow$ conn, mow, moot, shal, wol

6. Early Modern English.

6. Early Modern English.   By the late sixteenth century we find further changes. The chief of these are further development of *have – PP* in the environment of V_i; the spread of *do* as an auxiliary verb; and the appearance of the progressive it passive constructions.

As in Middle English, *do* is not a dummy carrier, but a regular optional member of *Aux*; *do* constructions occur side by side with finite verb constructions in un-emphatic assertion, negative, and interrogative sentence types. In one particular, however, the behavior of *do* differs from that of its cognate in Middle English: it invariably occurs without other helping verbs:

(44)   *N.I.191.21–25: Alledging many examples . . . how studie dooth effeminate a man*[16]
'Alleging there were many examples . . . of how study makes a man effeminate'

(45)   **Alledging many examples how study may do effeminate a man.*

(46)   *N.I.158.17: Thereby I grew to consider how many base men . . . enjoyed content at will*
'From this I came to consider how many base men . . . . enjoyed contentment at will'

(47)   *N.I.185.16: I do not doubt (Doctor Diuell) but you were present*
'I do not doubt (Dr. Devil) that you were present'

(48)   *N.I.208.12: That loue not to goe in greasie dublets*
'That do not like to walk about in greasy doublets'

(49)   *N.II.314.1: Why did I enter into anie mention of my owne misusage?*
'Why did I make any mention of the way I myself was misused?'

(50)   *N.II.302.5: Why iest I in such a necessarie perswasiue discourse?*
'Why do I jest in such a necessary persuasive discourse?'

A few Early Modern Northern manuscripts still show use of *do* after other operators, both in prose and in poetry:

(51)   *Reg.Manor Scawby Lincolnsh. (1597): That the Carrgraues shall doe execute theire office truely*
'That the Cargraves shall execute their duties properly'

(52)   *Scot.poems 16th C.II.189 (1578): And many other false abusion The Paip hes done invent*
'And the Pope has invented many other false abuses'

Since *do* as a second-position nonmodal operator is restricted to Northern dialects, we may assume that by the sixteenth century in England at least *do* had become

---

[16]Data for Early Modern English are derived from the *Oxford English Dictionary;* and Ronald B. McKerrow, ed., *The Works of Thomas Nashe* (Oxford, 1958), abbreviated *N.*, with references to volume, line, and page numbers.

an independent helping verb, mutually exclusive with modals, perfect and progressive auxiliaries; it is still incompatible with the passive formant.

In the light of the considerations given above, *Aux* may be set up for Early Modern English by the following rules:

6.1 $S \rightarrow NP - VP$

6.2 $VP \rightarrow Aux - MV$

6.3 $MV \rightarrow \begin{Bmatrix} V_t - NP \\ V_i \\ \vdots \end{Bmatrix}$

6.4 $V_i \rightarrow \begin{Bmatrix} V_{i_{move}} \\ V_{i_x} \end{Bmatrix}$

6.5 $Aux \rightarrow T\left(\left\{ \begin{matrix} (M)\left(\begin{Bmatrix} (have - PP)\ (be - PrP \\ be - PP,\ \text{in env.}\ \underline{\quad}\ V_{i_{move}} \end{Bmatrix} \right) \\ do \end{matrix} \right\} \right)$

6.6 $M \rightarrow$ *can, may, must, shall, will*

Of particular interest is the sporadic appearance of the progressive in passive formations. Unlike passive constructions with other members of *Aux*, these passives are not formed with *be – PP*. We find patterns of the kind *The man is seeing by X*, not *The man is being seen by X*.[17]

(53) Deloney, *Gentle Craft* 132.45:[18] *While meat was bringing in*
       'While food was being brought in'

The final stages in the development to Modern English consist in the loss of *be – PP* in the environment of most intransitive verbs, the restriction of *do* during the eighteenth and nineteenth centuries to certain explicitly determined environments, and the requirement of *be – PP* in passive constructions, whatever the membership of *Aux*. At the present stage of the language, *Aux* provides the least choices, but is also maximally generalized.

7. Types of change.   These then are the major mutations in the history of *Aux*. Comparison of the different grammars reveals several types of change, all of which have far-reaching effects on sentence structure. The changes may be summarized as follows:

(*a*) reversal of order
(*b*) loss of class-context restriction
(*c*) realignments of existing structures, without radical system change, as when the Old English maximal *Aux* was extended to *T (M)* and two successive optional nonmodal operators
(*d*) addition or loss of formants, as when *do* was added, and later when *be – PP* (*Perfect Auxiliary Verb*) was lost

---

[17]The latter is a modern construction which did not come into general use until the nineteenth century. The first clear instance of a pasisve of this type cited by Fernand Mossé, *Histoire de la forme périphrastique être + participe présent, II: Moyen-anglais et anglais moderne* (Paris, 1938), paragraph 263, is from a letter by Robert Southey: *A fellow whose uppermost upper grinder is being torn out by a mutton-fisted barber*. For detailed discussion of the history of the passive progressive, see Mossé, op. cit., paragraphs 231–281.

[18]Thomas Deloney, *Works*, Francis O. Mann, ed. (Oxford, 1912).

(*e*) and finally, closely related with this, really radical changes of system membership, e.g. when *do*, which was a member of the lexical system, gave rise to an operator in the syntactic system; or later when *do*, which was an optional member of *Aux*, became an obligatory, predictable element, generable as a formative in the transformational component.

8. Innovations accounting for changes.   It remains to be seen how these changes came about and how they may be considered a paradigm of language change in general.

The minimal change that must be postulated to account for reversal of word order is the growing tendency to favor *SU – Aux – MV (O)* order in all clauses. This tendency, which is amply attested by twelfth-century data, must have developed in two stages: first, preponderance of constructions with a finite verb or one helping verb preceding *O*, as in (19); and second, attraction of a second optional member of *Aux*, if present, to pre-*O* position. The word "tendency" is used advisedly. All through Old English, both *Aux – MV* and *MV + Aux* patterns existed. What must be accounted for is the fact that the optimal grammar for Old English specifies *MV + Aux* and a rule allowing for certain stylistic switches of auxiliary verbs, but no affix-switch rule. The optimal grammar for Middle English, on the other hand, specifies *Aux – MV*, a rule allowing for certain stylistic switches of auxiliary verbs, and an affix-switch rule. Any synchronic Old English grammar will mirror the two orders for auxiliary verbs. For Middle English we need a new grammar. In other words, the mutations can only be reflected by a different set of rules.[19]

The same is true of changes in context restriction of the perfect auxiliary. As OE *habb – PP* came to predominate, it took over the function of *BE – PP*. We might postulate that since those intransitive verbs that were most frequently used (verbs of movement) could occur with both *habb – PP* and *BE – PP*, $V_{i_{move}}$ became a model for other intransitive verbs which, although more numerous, were less frequently used. It is also noteworthy that Middle English was a time when word formation by changes of class membership or extension to new class

---

[19]A synchronic grammar cannot account for these changes, except so far as it treats different dialects, or different reflexes of different changes. When Klima ["Relatedness Between Grammatical Systems," in *MSE*] says the order in which he describes the rules for pronouns in different dialects reflects the historic order of change, he is actually referring to the order of mutations, not innovations. Each set of rules for each dialect requires different ordering of basically the same rules. Each set has its own unique relationship to the rest in the structure of the language, and cannot be collapsed under the same grammar except as a discrete subset of the grammar. It has been suggested that grammars should provide rules accounting for synchronic relatedness between grammatical systems, such that different systems may be regarded as modifications or extensions of a given basic system. This is essentially what Klima's grammar does for pronouns. In addition, it has been suggested that grammars should provide rules accounting for diachronic relatedness between grammatical systems, also such that the different systems may be regarded as modifications or extensions of a given basic system. Such grammars would reveal with great clarity the similarities and differences between stages of the language, and would provide in simpler, i.e. more compact, form the same information that separate grammars of different stages of the language provide. They cannot, however, specify actual change or provide historical perspective. A grammar of the actual changes would be a kind of algebra accounting in the simplest way possible for all relevant changes, in their chronological order.

membership was becoming particularly common; in particular, many new transitives were being formed from intransitives.[20] This meant that class-context restriction was no longer clear, and that ambiguity between the perfect auxiliary formant *be – PP* and the homonymous passive formant could arise.[21]

A further innovation was the extension of the mutually exclusive set of perfect and progressive auxiliaries to two compatible nonmodal operators. Throughout the history of English up to the nineteenth century, and still today in the case of most sentences in which the main verb is the copula *be*, the structure "base *be* followed by base *be*" has been ungrammatical or at least deviant. Although Modern English sentences of the type *The students are being attacked* are grammatical, *The students are being hungry* is ungrammatical. Strong pressure against such structures must account for the lack of passive progressives with the passive formant in Early Modern English. It also seems to account for the lack of progressives following perfect auxiliaries of the type *be – PP* in Middle English. Unless we are to assume that perfects followed by progressive helping verbs were possible only in transitive verb constructions, we are led to conclude that the two nonmodal operators became compatible *after* both intransitives and transitives could take *have – PP* as the perfect auxiliary. Once the two became compatible, a mutation arose.

Although I have attempted so far to cover only those changes that took place within the *Aux* rule alone, I have had to mention far-reaching repercussions on the whole system. Change in word order requires, for simplicity of description and explanatory power, the introduction of an affix-switch rule. Behavior of progressive auxiliaries raises the question of the co-occurrence of two *be* bases. Other changes in the *Aux* further demonstrate clear cases of overall system changes. *Do*, which was a main verb requiring infinitive nominalizations, came to be reinterpreted as an auxiliary, presumably because it was followed by an unmarked infinitive. Perhaps pressure of continued association with the main verb *do* (which, as a main verb, could be preceded by auxiliary verbs) countered the tendency to use *do* in modal position; instead it came to fill the same slot as the progressive. This slot was in itself somewhat variable since it was an innovation. The very character of this third position may account for the fact that *do* came to be used more and more as an independent unit which could not tolerate other auxiliary verbs in its enviroment. Its failure to pattern with other members of *Aux* then further favored the eventual mutation, by Modern English, to nonmembership in the regular *Aux* construction, and to restriction to certain predictable environments.

9. Theory of language change.   Given a knowledge of mutations, such as those in the development of *Aux*, and of the innovations that account for those mutations, can we say that the five proposals for a theory of language change outlined at the beginning of this paper account for syntactic change?

The proposition that language changes by means of a series of individual in-

---

[20]See F. Th. Visser, *An Historical Syntax of the English Language* (Leiden, 1963), pp. 93–138.

[21]Visser, ibid., p. 131, suggests that this ambiguity was one of the factors leading to the transitivization of intransitives.

novations seems to be fully supported by the history of the *Aux*, in which we can see each step develop individually. The second proposal is that the innovations usually occur at the end of some natural division of the grammar. This must give us pause. Within the syntactic component there are three main points of break: the point where the phrase structure ends and the lexicon begins; the point where the lexicon ends and the transformational subcomponent begins; and finally the point where the syntactic component ends and the morphophonemic begins.[22] Of the changes discussed, the only one that enters at such a break is the affix-switch rule, and this is the result of a mutation, not an innovation giving rise to a mutation; besides, it is largely motivated by simplicity of description rather than by actual language data when it is introduced for Middle English. Changes in context restriction of the perfect and progressive verbs occur within the high-level *Aux* rule, and do not enter at the end of the phrase structure. *Do* extends lexical membership of the category of infinitive complement taking transitives to nonlexical membership of this same high-level *Aux* rule; again, it is not possible to hypothesize that it entered as a low-level phrase structure subcategory and was then reinterpreted as part of the *Aux*. The third proposal, that innovations are passed on to generation after generation, and the fourth, that mutations occur when the new generation reinterprets a grammar so as to effect radical changes such as restructuring, seem to be well borne out by syntactic evidence. The viability of the fifth proposal, however, that mutations are rare, is doubtful as far as syntactic change is concerned. The *Aux*, which is such a small part of the grammar, demonstrates at least six types of mutation. The four different types of pronominal usage which Klima discusses support in a totally unrelated area the observation that mutation in syntax is not rare, although it seems to be relatively infrequent in phonological change.

In view of the factors discussed above it appears that any theory of language change must include the proposals that language changes by means of the addition of single innovations to an adult's grammar, by transmission of these innovations to new generations, and by the reinterpretation of grammars such that mutations occur. Restriction of innovations to points of break seems not to be viable as a generalization for language change, nor does the statement that mutations are rare. Both these proposals must be limited to the area of phonological change.

---

[22]Further subdivisions may or may not be made according to the particular model of grammar adopted. Grammars like Lees's *The Grammar of English Nominalizations* [*IJAL* 26:3 (1960), Part 2] allow for certain groupings in the phrase structure according to sets of subcategorizations; Charles Fillmore's study "The Position of Embedding Transformations in a Grammar," *Word*, 19.208–231 (1963), specifies groupings for two-string versus one-string transformations. In the latest models, however, such as Chomsky's blocking grammar and Klima's nonblocking grammar (cf. Klima, "Current Developments in Generative Grammar," *Kybernetika* [1.184–197 (Prague, 1965)]), the phrase structure component is minimal and cannot be subject to groupings. Context restrictions and subcategorizations are largely specified in a lexicon in which the only significant groupings are the overall categories *N, V, Adj*, etc.; only in the filter transformations do we find areas in which the concept "point of break" is significant for syntax.

26

Alternation of Rules
in Children's Grammar

PAULA MENYUK

In the study of children's grammar, attempts are made to describe the process of acquisition and the process of development of grammar, and to describe them in such a way that possible explanations for their occurrence become evident. There have been many descriptive studies which have used labeling procedures to describe language data. These studies have been concerned with both the phonological and syntactic components of grammar. For example, there have been very careful studies of phonological occurrences in language development which have been termed phoneme types (Irwin, 1952). There have also been very careful studies of syntactic occurrences in language development which have been termed complexity of sentence structure (Templin, 1957). These studies have found that phoneme frequency and phoneme type increase with age, as do mean sentence length and complexity of sentence structure. It has essentially been found that output and complexity (defined in terms of the number of phoneme types and proportion of compound-complex sentences a child uses) increase with age. In addition to the fact that the process of increasing complexity occurs, it has also been noted

Reprinted from the *Journal of Verbal Learning and Verbal Behavior*, 3.480–488 (1964), by permission of Paula Menyuk and Academic Press, Inc.

This investigation was supported in part by the U.S. Army Signal Corps, the Air Force Office of Scientific Research, and the Office of Naval Research; in part by the National Science Foundation (Grant G-16526), the National Institutes of Health (Grant MH-04737-03), and the National Aeronautics and Space Administration (Grant NsG-496). Additional support was received through Fellowship MPD-8768-C3 from the National Institute of Mental Health, Public Health Service. A part of this paper was presented at the biennial meeting of the Society of Research in Child Development, April 1963. Grateful acknowledgement is given to the children and teachers of the Young Israel and Beacon Nursery Schools and the Edith C. Baker School in Brookline, Massachusetts.

that the child at a very early age uses all the basic types of sentence structures that an adult uses (McCarthy, 1930; Templin, 1957). At the same time, at both the phonological level (McCurry and Irwin, 1953) and the syntactic level of performance (Templin, 1957) the child produces structures which are more or less gross approximations to completely well-formed structures, and these approximations still occur long after the child has begun to use all the basic syntactic structures he will ever use. It seems, then, that three things occur in the development of grammatical ability: the child increases the number of varying types of structures that he uses, he increases the frequency of usage of these varying types of structures, and he gradually eliminates his approximations to completely well-formed structures.

It was noted in a previous study (Menyuk, 1963) that the frequency of occurrence and number of these approximations gradually decrease as an increasingly mature population is observed. However, a closer examination of the data showed that there were significant differences in the particular forms of approximation used at various age levels. In this study a generative model of grammar was used to describe these approximations to completely well-formed structures and to observe trends in their usage as related to age. The purpose of this study is to present an adequate description of the process of increasing complexity and, also, a possible explanation for the occurrence of these approximations in the process.

With a generative model of grammar, it is hypothesized that the perceiver or child has incorporated both the generative rules of the grammar and a heuristic component that samples an input sentence, and by a series of successive approximations determines which rules were used to generate this sentence (Halle and Stevens, 1962; Matthews, 1961; Miller and Chomsky, 1963). Furthermore, taking into account the limitations of the nervous system for memorizing all instances of sentences heard and storing them for later use, it is hypothesized that instead of memorizing every sentence he has been exposed to and imitating these sentences, the child uses a set of rules to generate not only the sentences he has heard, but also other possible examples. In addition, his linguistic behavior is systematically extended without formal instruction. If that is the case, older children should produce fewer approximations to complete sets of rules, and they should produce structures which are closer approximations to completely well-formed structures than younger children. As an increasingly mature population is observed and more complex stuctures are used by more children, there should be periods during which the numbers of children using approximations to these more complex structures should rise. Finally, there should be some evidence that the sentences produced are not strict imitations of those heard in the language environment of the children.

METHOD

The generative model of grammar used in this study to describe the rules for formulating the sentences produced is viewed as having a tri-partite structure (Chomsky, 1957). The first level is phrase structure, where kernel or simple-active-declarative sentences are fomulated from rules for stringing together parts of speech. The second level is transformations, where more complex sentence types are generated by rules for addition and/or deletion, permutation, and substitution within or among kernel sentences. The rules which operate on one kernel sentence are termed simple transformations. Rules which operate on two or more kernels are termed general transformations. The third level is morphology, where inflectional rules, dependent on the previous sequences, are applied.

The 159 children in this study ranged in age from 2 years, 10 months to 7 years, 1 month. They were homogeneous in socioeconomic status and IQ. Over 78% of all the children's parents were in the occupational categories of professional, and semi-professional and managerial. The remainder were in the occupational category of clerical, skilled trades, and retail business. Thus, parental occupations for all the children fall within the upper 24% range of a middle class population (The Minnesota Scale for Paternal Occupation, 1950). There were no significant differences in the mean IQ's of the nursery school group (133.4, $SD = 17.36$), the kindergarten group (126.63, $SD = 16.75$), and the first grade group (132.0, $SD = 13.4$) as measured by the Full Range Picture Vocabulary Test (Ammons and Ammons, 1958).

Language was elicited and tape recorded in various stimulus situations: (1) responses to the projective test, *The Blacky Pictures* (Blum, 1950), (2) conversation with an adult (the experimenter) generated by some of the questions suggested in the test manual, and additional questions introduced by the experimenter, and (3) conversation with peers generated by role playing in a family setting. The 8 children in the population under 3 years of age were each observed for the first half of a school day ($1\frac{1}{2}$ hours) and then, on another day, for the second half of the school day, making a total of 3 hours of observation. During this time they were engaged in a variety of activities in which monologues, conversation with an adult (the teacher), and conversation with peers occurred. A written transcription was made of each child's language production.

The language sample produced by each child was analyzed by means of the generative model previously described, that is, the rules for generating each sentence, both those which produced completely well-formed structures and those which did not, were postulated. The latter rules were termed rules restricted to a children's grammar.

For a quantitative analysis of the usage of rules which produced not completely well-formed structures, the age range was divided into 4-month periods. To observe trends in usage for each alternate restricted form throughout the age range, the number of children within each period who were using each of the syntactic structures which were sometimes replaced by a not completely well-formed structure was calculated. Then the number of children within each period who used the various alternate restricted forms was calculated. The percentage of children in each period who simultaneously used each structure and who also used some alternation of this structure was also computed. This proportionate rather than absolute calculation was preferable since no child in this age group used *only* the alternate restricted form, instead, the child used either the completely well-formed structure or the structure and some alternate restricted form or did not use the structure at all. This was also done to avoid exaggeration of the percentages of children using not completely well-formed structures (particularly those used with transformations) at the older age levels. For example, from 2 years, 10 months to 3 years,

2 months, only 25% of the children use the reflexive transformation. By 4 years, 10 months, 80% of the children use this transformation, and from 6 years, 6 months on to the end of the age range, 100% of the children use this transformation. Therefore the percentage of children not using the rule that in third person *Pronoun + Possessive + Reflexive* becomes *Pronoun + Object + Reflexive* (*myself*, *yourself* but *himself* not *hisself*) was calculated in terms of the number of children using the reflexive transformation within each age period.

The various restricted forms were then classified according to the level of grammar at which they occurred (phrase structure, transformations, or morphology). They were further classified in terms of the rules postulated for their generation (rules with omissions, substitutions, or redundancies at the phrase structure and morphology levels, and partial rules in simple or general transformations at the transformation level). The age periods in which peak usage of these classes of alternate restricted forms occurred and the peak percentages of children using these classes in these peak periods were averaged. This was done in order to observe which classes of forms predominantly occurred at different times throughout the age range.

RESULTS

Three facts should be kept in mind about the use of the restricted forms. A few of these rules can be found in the grammar of some adults, although it seems unlikely that they are in the grammar of the parents of these children. They have been reported in other dialects than that found here, and primarily in dialects of populations of low socioeconomic status. The sentences produced from these rules were deviations from completely well-formed sentences but were not outside a set of possible sentences. For example, a child might generate the sentence *I know what is that* from these rules but not the nonsentence *That is what know I* or any such departure. Finally, these restricted rules occur infrequently in the total language sample.

As was stated before, the use of alternate rules occurs at all three levels of the grammar. At the phrase structure level verbs, nouns, articles, prepositions, and particles are sometimes omitted or used redundantly. Also, substitutions of verbs, articles, and prepositions take place. At the transformation level, having optionally chosen a transformation, the children sometimes do not observe all the obligatory combinational rules used in their correct order or the contextual constraints needed to derive this transformation. At the morphology level of the grammar, again, omission of rules, redundancies in rules, and substitutions take place. These occur with verbs, nouns, adverbs, pronouns, and possessive forms. The following are examples of such rules.

Examples at the phrase structure level. An example of the use of alternate restricted rules at this level of the grammar is the use of verbs. Sometimes sentences are formed without the verb; sometimes verbs are selected in certain contexts where the properties of the verb are generalized to include the properties of different verbs; and sometimes the properties of a verb are added to the complete properties of a verb phrase.

Verbs are omitted:
  Sentence becomes *Noun Phrase + Verb Phrase*
  Verb Phrase becomes *be + Predicate* or
  Verb Phrase becomes *Predicate*
  Example: *This is mine.*
         This green.
Verbs are substituted:
  Verb becomes *Verb Transitive* or *Verb Intransitive*
  Verb Transitive becomes *Verb T₁*, *Verb T₂*, etc., or
  Verb Transitive becomes *Verb T*$_{1,2}$, etc.
  Example: *He tries to take the knife away.*
         He tries to take the knife from falling.
Verbs are used redundantly:
  Verb Phrase becomes *Modal + Verb*
  Modal becomes *can, may, will*, etc., or
  Verb Phrase becomes *Modal + Modal + Verb*
  Modal becomes *will + may*, etc.
  Example: *He'll do that.*
         He'll might get in jail.

Other examples of alternate restricted forms occurring at the phrase structure level are

Noun Phrase omission:
  Look at.
Noun phrase redundancy:
  I want it the paint.
Preposition omission:
  He'll have to go the doctors.
Preposition substitution:
  He took me at the circus.
Preposition redundancy:
  Take it off from there.
Article omission:
  Daddy has new office.
Article substitution:
  I want a milk please.
Article redundancy:
  I like the Donny.
Particle omission:
  Put the hat.
Particle redundancy:
  The barber cut off his hair off.

Examples at the transformation level. Omission of obligatory rules takes place in simple and general transformations. As an example, with simple transformations, at the beginning of the age range when verb phrase is being expanded from just main verb to *be + Present Participle + Verb*, and the contraction transformation is applied, as it always is except in emphatic sentences, the children sometimes omit the contracted form. By the contraction transformation the verb phrase becomes *be + Contraction + Present Participle + Verb*.

Omission of contraction:
  be + Contraction becomes *'m, 're, 's* or
  Be + Contraction becomes ∅
  Example: *I'm going.*
          I' going.

Later in the age range when verb phrase is further expanded to *have + Perfect Participle + be + Present Participle + Verb* and the contraction transformation is applied, the same result occurs and the children produce, for example, both *I've been thinking about that* and *I' been thinking about that.*

An example with general transformations is the omission of tense agreement in conjunction. The most commonly used general transformaton is conjunction where Sentence 2 is added to Sentence 1. Sometimes the children use this transformation omitting the obligatory rule that verb tense in Sentence 2 must agree with verb tense in Sentence 1.

  Noun Phrase + Verb Phrase + Tense and Noun Phrase + Verb Phrase + Tense of Sentence 1 or
  Noun Phrase + Verb Phrase + Tense and Noun Phrase + Verb Phrase + Tense
  Example: *He cut him and he made him cry.*
          They mixed colors and they pour buckets.

In addition to the omission of obligatory rules at the transformation level there are examples of generalization of rules, that is, rules which result in completely well-formed structures in some contexts are used in contexts where they do not produce these same results. In these instances a further necessary differentiation is not made. One example with simple transformations is the use of a double negative form. This seems to be a result of the generalization of the rule that *no + Noun Phrase* equals negation and may stem from the fact that there are instances in which *no + Noun Phrase* is a rule which results in a completely well-formed structure but *any + Noun Phrase* does not, or both are permissible. The following are examples:

Declarative:
  You can put no more water in it but not *You can put any more water in it.*
Imperative:
  Put no more water in it but not *Put any more water in it.*
Question:
  Can you put no more water in it?
  Can you put any more water in it?

It is only in the negative transformation, *You can't put no more water in it,* that *no + Noun* does not result in a completely well-formed structure.

An example with general transformations is the generation of sentences with a relative clause. In the formulation of the *Wh*-question the following ordering of rules is postulated. The sentence becomes *That is X + Wh.* By permutation, *Wh + X that is* results. By the question transformation *Wh + X is that* results, and by morphological rules the sentence *What is that?* is derived. In the relative clause transformation some of the children attach the relative question to Sentence 1 and produce *I know what is that.* This is done without observing the ordering necessary in this transformation; that is, Sentence 2 should be attached to Sentence 1 in the form *Wh + X that is* and not after the question transformation. This alternate restricted form also seems to stem from a generalization since in certain instances *Sentence 1 + Wh-question* results in completely well formed structures. The following are some examples:

> *I know which is mine* but not *I know which do they like.*
> *I know who's going* but not *I know who is he.*
> *I know what's bad* but not *I know what will we play.*

Other examples of alternate restricted forms occurring with simple and general transformation are

Inversion restrictions:
Subject-object:
> *Crayons I want.*

Verb number:
> *Here's two clouds.*

No question:
> *Who he is kissing?*

There substitution:
> *It was snow yesterday.*

No separation:
> *Take off it.*

Reflexive third:
> *They're hurting theirselves.*

Pronoun restriction:
> *My mother washes and he cleans.*

Adjective restriction:
> *Do you like this papers.*

Examples at morphology level. An example of the use of alternate restricted forms at this level of the grammar is the use of plural markings for nouns. Sometimes pluralization is not marked; sometimes pluralization is marked in an incomplete manner; and sometimes pluralization is marked incorrectly and redundantly.

Plural markers are omitted:
> *Noun Plural* becomes *Noun + S* or *Noun + $\emptyset$*
> Example: *I go lots of places.*
> *She has lots of necklace.*

Plural markers are substituted:
> *Noun plural* becomes *Noun + S* or *Noun Singular + S*
> Example: *Put the knives there.*
> *Those are wolfs.*

Plural markers are used redundantly:
> *Noun Singular* becomes *Noun* or *Noun + S*
> Example: *Give me the dough.*
> *Give me some soaps.*
> *Noun Plural* becomes *Noun + S* or *Noun + S + S*
> Example: *He has big feet.*
> *Where are the peoples.*

Other examples of alternate restricted forms occurring at the morphology level are

Verb form omission:
> *She like that.*

Verb form substitution:
 He growed up fast.
Verb form redundancy:
 She splashted herself.
Adverb form omission:
 You play nice.
Adverb form redundancy:
 You have to draw straightly.
Pronoun subject substitution:
 Me like that.
 Him is a bad boy.
Possessive form omission:
 That's mes.
Possessive form substitution:
 That's mys.
Possessive form redundancy:
 That's mines.

From the quantitative analysis of the data the following results were obtained. In general the use of alternate rules gradually declines as one observes an increasingly mature population. There are singificant differences in the percentage of children using these forms in the first 4-month age period and in the last age period. Table 1 shows the percentages of children using all types of omissions, substitutions, and redundancies at both the phrase structure and morphology levels of the grammar and all types of nonobservation of rules in simple and general transformations from 2 years, 10 months to 3 years, 2 months and from 6 years, 10 months to 7 years, 1 month.

The decline in the use of alternate rules is not asymptotic in nature but, rather,

TABLE 1

PERCENTAGE OF CHILDREN USING RESTRICTED FORMS AT
BEGINNING AND END OF AGE RANGE

	Age	
Restricted forms	3 years/ 2 months	7 years/ 1 month
Phrase structure		
Omissions	38	12[a]
Substitutions	42	9[a]
Redundancies	22	23
Transformations		
Simple	43	16[a]
General	38	12[a]
Morphology		
Omissions	53	29[a]
Substitutions	35	4[a]
Redundancies	25	7[a]

[a]Significantly different at 0.01 level.

fluctuating. The specific alternate rules which are used by a sizeable number of the children in any given age period change as an increasingly mature population is observed, and increasingly complex structures are used by more of the children. As examples at the transformation level, Figure 1 shows the fluctuation in the percent of children omitting the contracted forms of *be* and *have* in verb phrase formation (a simple transformation) and omitting the obligatory tense restriction in all types of conjunction (a general transformation) throughout the age range. It should be noted that there is a rise in the percentage omitting contracted forms at the 4 years, 2 months level, and this coincides with a rise in the number of children who are adding the auxiliary *have* to verb phrase formation.

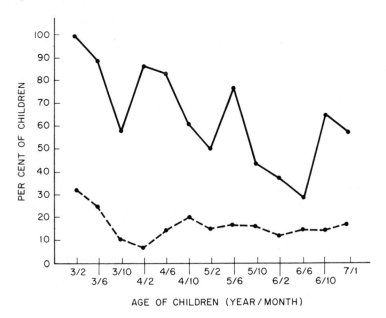

FIGURE 1. Usage of the restricted forms *omission of contraction* (———) and *no tense restriction* (– – –) given at 4-month periods as examples of the fluctuation of usage of all restricted forms throughout the age range.

There are rises in omission of tense restriction in conjunction when the percentage of children using conjunctions other than *and* (*because, so, if*) also rises from 31% at the beginning of the age range to 54% at 4 years, 2 months; 65% at 5 years, 10 months; and 82% at 7 years, 1 month.

Table 2 gives the total percentages of children using all types of alternate rules at each of the three levels of the grammar at 4-month age periods. The fluctuation in usage noted for specific alternate rules is reflected in the rises and declines in usage found throughout the age range, although, as stated before, the general trend is downward.

TABLE 2

PERCENTAGE OF CHILDREN USING RESTRICTED FORMS
AT THE THREE LEVELS OF GRAMMAR GIVEN AT
FOUR-MONTH AGE LEVELS

Age (Years/months)	Restricted forms		
	Phrase structure	Transformations	Morphology
3/2	34	27	38
3/6	24	20	30
3/10	27	20	28
4/2	21	15	23
4/6	29	25	37
4/10	15	22	20
5/2	26	16	13
5/6	17	14	22
5/10	8	13	12
6/2	18	8	19
6/6	11	4	10
6/10	17	11	14
7/1	16	9	13

When the age periods for peak use of classes of alternate rules at the three levels of the grammar are averaged, and then the peak percentages of children using these forms, the following results are obtained. At the phrase structure level the type of restricted form which peaks earliest and highest is omission. Then comes substitution, and finally redundancy. At the transformation level nonobservation of obligatory rules with simple transformations peaks earliest and highest. The peak

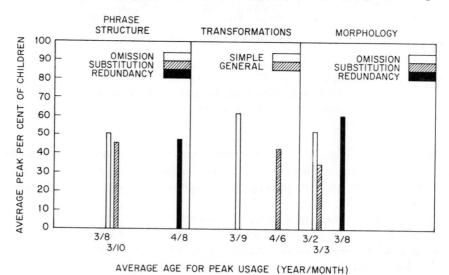

FIGURE 2. Average ages for peak usage of classes of restricted forms at the three levels of grammar.

for use of alternate restricted forms with general transformations occurs later when, in fact, more of the children use some of these transformations. At the morphology level again omissions peak earliest, then substitutions and later redundancies. The peaks for omissions and substitutions occur very early in the age range and are very close together. At this level, the peak for redundancies occurs comparatively early and is the highest. These results are shown in Figure 2.

DISCUSSION

The children's usage of grammar did become increasingly complex over the age range observed. This complexity was not related simply to increasing sentence length or proportion of usage of what has been termed compound or complex sentences or, in the terms of a generative model of grammar, general transformations. These changes are extensions of behavior without additional rules in the grammar. To conjoin two sentences needs the same application of rules as conjoining three or four. To delete and substitute as in relative clauses needs the same application of rules whether it is done once in ten minutes or three times. This increasing complexity is also dependent on the child's ability to proceed from the application of the most general rule to the application of increasingly differentiating rules, in a certain order, to produce a particular syntactic structure. It should be noted that throughout the age range the children use increasingly elaborate structures, and, therefore, the requirements for generating these structures are increased. In accordance with the model of grammar used for description, all instances of the use of restricted forms represent the use of an elementary rule with or without some of the additional steps required; that is, rules for addition, deletion, permutation, and substitution are applied but without observation of ordering in some instances, and in other instances, without using the combination of these elementaries required to produce the completed form of these structures.

Three developmental trends emerge from this analysis of the use of alternate restricted forms. First, usage of these forms declines as the population observed matures. Second, there are fluctuations or rises in the percentages of children using particular alternate restricted forms and these fluctuations coincide with rises in the percentages of children using particular structures which were more elaborate than others at certain age levels. Third, varying degrees of generalization take place throughout the age range from greatest generalization to increasing differentiation to complete differentiation and, possibly, new organization. This behavior reflects the hypothesis of the model of grammar used for description (to determine by a series of successive approximations the rules used to generate a structure) since what occurs throughout the age range are less and less gross approximations to the completely well-formed structure. For example, at the phrase structure and morphology levels of the grammar, omission represents the greatest generalization, then substitution and redundancy before complete differentiation. At the transformation level of the grammar there occurs generalization of rules which are applicable in the partial formation of structures or are applicable in certain contexts but in other contexts do not result in completely well-formed structures.

One aspect of the new organization of rules required for the generation of completely well-formed structures is differentiation between nonterminal and terminal rules. For example the children must determine that use of a modal such as *can*, *may*, or *will* + *Verb* is a terminal rule and that two modals are mutually exclusive in the same context. We say *He might get into jail* or *He will get into jail* but not *He'll might get into jail*. They must determine that the question transformation is a terminal rule in certain contexts and cannot be substituted within a sentence to produce new structures. We say *What is that?* but not *I know what is that*. The children must determine that certain tense and plural markers are also terminal. We say *pushed* and *people* but not *pushted* and *peoples*.

In summary, the data indicate that younger children's usage of grammar is simpler than older children's or adults' usage of grammar because more of the younger children use an incomplete set of rules to produce a syntactic structure, because more of the older children use the alternate restricted forms associated with the generation of more complex structures, and because increasing levels of differentiation are found going toward complete differentiation as older children are observed. The word usage is stressed because, although in some instances a child seemed to apply only the elementary rule or an incomplete set in the formulation of a syntactic structure, in other instances he applied the complete set of ordered rules to formulate this same structure.

In addition, the data obtained in this study indicate that language acquisition and development are not just dependent on imitation. Some intervening operations seem necessary for the child to be able to organize the data he hears in terms of the grammar of his language and to reproduce them in these same terms. If language production is merely an imitative function, then children should be producing sentences first with omissions, because of the limitations of memory, and then complete sentences. One might assume that the other types of restricted forms produced by children are a result of imitation of peers. In that case, one would expect a random production of these forms. The results of this study indicate that the process is neither random nor one of remembering to put in more of the missing parts of sentences as the child matures.

The restricted forms produced in a particular order beyond omission, such as substitution, redundancy, incorrect ordering, and nonobservation of contextual constraints and their gradual elimination, reflect the child's improving ability to generate particular structures from increasingly more differentiated sets of rules as he matures rather than just imitation of sentences heard.

SUMMARY

This paper analyzes the use of alternate restricted rules (rules which produce not completely well-formed structures) found in children's grammar in an attempt to present an adequate description of increasing complexity in grammar as children mature.

Language samples were obtained from 159 children ranging in age from 2 years, 10 months to 7 years, 1 month. Each child's language sample was analyzed by means of a generative model of grammar.

The data indicate that increasing complexity is not simply related to the acquisition and increased usage of more complex sentence types. Increasing complexity is also dependent on children's improved ability to proceed from the application of the most general rule in the formulation of a syntactic structure to the increasingly differentiating rules, and then to the complete ordered set needed for a particular structure. As the structures used become more complex, the completed ordered sets of rules needed for their generation become more complex.

The data also indicate that language acquisition and development cannot be explained as merely an imitative process since there are systematic levels of hehavior in language production which cannot be accounted for by imitation of a model.

REFERENCES

Ammons, R. B., and H. S. Ammons (1958), *Full Range Picture Vocabulary Test*. Missoula: Psychological Test Specialists.

Blum, G. S. (1950), *The Blacky Pictures*. New York: Psychol. Corp.

Chomsky, N. (1957), *Syntactic Structures*. 's-Gravenhage, The Netherlands: Mouton & Co.

Halle, M., and K. Stevens (1962), "Speech Recognition: A Model and a Program for Research," *I.R.E. Transactions on Information Theory*, IT-8.

Irwin, O. C. (1952), "Some Factors Related to the Speech Development of the Young Child." *Journal of Speech and Hearing Disorders*, 17.269–279.

Matthews, G. H. (1961), "Analysis by Synthesis of Sentences of Natural Languages," *National Physical Laboratory, Symposium No. 13*, London, pp. 531–543.

McCarthy, D. (1930), *Language Development of the Preschool Child*. Minneapolis: University of Minnesota Press.

McCurry, W. H., and O. C. Irwin (1953), A Study of Word Approximations in the Spontaneous Speech of Infants." *Journal of Speech and Hearing Disorders*, 18.133–139.

Menyuk, P. (1963), "Syntactic Rules Used by Children from Preschool Through First Grade." *Journal of Child Development*, pp. 533–546.

Miller, G. A., and N. Chomsky, "Finitary Models of Language Users," in *HMP*.

Templin, M. C. (1957), *Certain Language Skills in Children*. Minneapolis: University of Minnesota Press.

The Minnesota Scale for Paternal Occupation (1950). Institute of Child Welfare, University of Minnesota.

27

Topicalization in Child Language

JEFFREY S. GRUBER

I. SURVEY

In this paper we will analyse certain aspects of the syntax of one child who was acquiring English.[1] We will try to show that this child did not at one stage manifest the subject-predicate construction for his sentences in the way that adult English speakers do. Even though nouns *appeared* to be used as the subjects of subject-predicate constructions, further analysis of the data disclosed that these nouns act as the topics of topic-comment constructions. Such topic-comment constructions appear at times in adult English speech. For instance, in the sentence *Salt, I taste it in this food*; *salt* is the topic, and *I taste it in this food* is the comment. This sentence would have the tree structure shown in Figure 1.

In this figure an ordinary English sentence, showing a subject-predicate construction, is dominated by *S'*. This *S'*, which in turn is immediately dominated by *S*, is the comment. The *NP* immediately dominated by *S* is the topic. On the other hand, the *NP* and *VP* immediately dominated by *S'* are the subject and predicate of the comment, respectively. In the comment, the *NP* with the same referent as the topic is represented by the pronoun *it*.

Reprinted from *Foundations of Language*, 3.37–65 (1967), by permission of Jeffrey S. Gruber and *Foundations of Language*.

This work was supported in part by the Joint Services Electronics Program under Contract DA36-039-AMC-03200(E); and in part by the National Science Foundation (Grant GK-835), the National Institutes of Health (Grant 2PO1MH-04737-06), the National Aeronautics and Space Administration (Grant NsG-496), and the U.S. Air Force (ESD Contract AF19(628)-2487), and also NIH (Grant 2-T01 HD 00111-01).

I am indebted to M. Bullowa and W. Browne for having helped me with the manuscript, and to N. Chomsky and E. Klima for their comments and criticisms contributing to the theoretical considerations in this paper. I am especially grateful to M. Halle, whose patient perusal and discussion of this paper with me much improved its content.

[1] Material for this study comes from the longitudinal data collected by M. Bullowa, M.D., under NIH Grant MH 04300–01–04, "Development from Vocal to Verbal Behavior in Children."

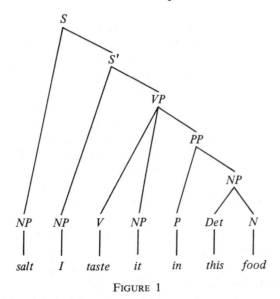

FIGURE 1

We shall say that the topic *NP*, dominated by *S*, is co-generated with the comment *S'*, also dominated by *S*. Saying that *NP* and *S'* are co-generated merely indicates that they are dominated by the same *S* in the surface structure. We say nothing as yet about the way in which this co-generation is to be effected. *S'* will be the symbol used to indicate a comment clause when it is necessary to distinguish the node dominating such a clause from the node dominating the sentence as a whole.

While such constructions as these seem somewhat accessory to the adult grammar of English, they were essential to the child's grammar at the stage under study. Moreover, this type of construction was absent in our data for the speech of the child's exclusively English speaking parents. The child could thus have had no model for these constructions, and they must therefore represent independent creations of his own (based perhaps on creative interpretations of adult speech).[2]

Topic-comment constructions exist as an essential part of the adult grammar in many languages, such as Chinese and Japanese. In these languages, a topic noun phrase, in addition to being part of the syntactic construction outlined previously, has a specific semantic interpretation, further differentiating it from the subject noun phrase.[3] We have found no evidence that the child's constructions

---

[2]It has been suggested that the child in the process of acquiring his mother tongue utilizes an innate knowledge of the structure of language (N. Chomsky, "The Logical Basis of Linguistic Theory," *Proceedings of the Ninth International Congress of Linguists, Cambridge, Mass., 1962.* (The Hague: Mouton & Co., 1964) [*SL*]; E. Lenneberg, "A Biological Perspective of Language," in E. Lenneberg, ed., *New Directions in the Study of Language* (Cambridge, Mass.: M.I.T. Press, 1964)). The existence of such innate knowledge implies the existence of language universals. All human languages must be similar to each other in the sense that each is a particular development of that sort of linguistic system for which the child is predisposed. We here seek to discover language universals by studying language acquisition.

[3]S.-Y. Kuroda, "Generative Grammatical Studies in the Japanese Language," Ph. D. dissertation, M.I.T, June 1965.

possess any special interpretation when compared with the subject-predicate construction, although it is possible that they do. We relate the topic-comment constructions of the child to those noted in Chinese and Japanese, nonetheless, because the syntactic form of both of these constructions is very similar, and because they both appear to play essential parts in their respective grammars.

The precise formalization[4] of these topic-comment constructions will be discussed below. Because of their ultimate similarity to the subject-predicate construction in English, we will suggest that the subject-predicate is merely a special case of the topic-comment construction. If this is the case, i.e. if the topic-comment construction is a logically more fundamental construction than the subject-predicate construction, so that the former underlies the latter, this would provide a possible explanation for the child's independent creation of it. The spontaneous creation of the topic-comment construction could then be attributable to the innate capabilities of the child, to his innate "knowledge" of language.

This child, Mackie,[5] produced sentences which suggested a topic-comment interpretation when a little over two years of age, at least between 790 and 881 days, the period studied. The major evidence appeared in the differences between Mackie's treatment of pronouns and of nouns when used as apparent subject of the sentence.

In this paper we will tentatively employ the term *subject* to refer to the noun or pronoun immediately preceding the verb in Mackie's sentences, either in the surface structure or on an underlying level. In general, such terms from traditional grammar as noun, pronoun, verb, etc., will be used to refer to syntactic categories as one would use them in describing adult English. How far these usages should be regarded as adequate or significant definitions for the grammar which Mackie has internalized will become apparent by the end of this paper.

One of the most noticeable characteristics of Mackie's speech at this stage is that most of his sentences have either a pronominal subject or no subject expressed at all. A noun appears as subject only rarely. Nouns as objects of verbs or of prepositions are frequent, however. Of 297 instances of nouns used by Mackie, only 11 times was a noun used in the preverbal position that we call subject position in English. In 61 cases the noun seemed to be used as the object of a verb

---

[4]The formal tools used will be those that have been developed through work in the field of generative grammar (N. Chomsky, *Aspects of the Theory of Syntax* (Cambridge, Mass.: M.I.T. Press, 1965)). A generative grammar is an attempt to formalize precisely the infinite set of sentences grammatical in a given language, specifying explicitly what is left to intuition in traditional grammars.

[5]Mackie was recorded for a half-hour weekly, from birth until approximately 30 months of age. The recording was resumed at 34 months of age. The recorded observations consist primarily of interactions between the child subject and those in his environment with minimal interaction between the observers and the subject family. Two tracks of magnetic tape at 7½ ips and 16 mm. black and white two-frame-per-second film are taken at each observation. One tape track records the subject's vocalizations and environmental sounds; the other records description of ongoing behavior and interaction whispered into a shielded microphone and a patterned timing signal. (M. Bullowa, L. G. Jones, and T. G. Bever, "The Development from Vocal to Verbal Behavior in Children," in U. Bellugi and R. Brown, eds., *The Acquisition of Language, Monographs of the Society for Research in Child Development*, Serial No. 92, 1964, Vol. 29, No. 1, pp. 101–107).

or a preposition, and the remaining 225 cases consisted of nouns used in isolated noun phrases, in the position following the copula, or in an ambiguous usage. While the noun often appeared following the copula, as in *That's a truck*, the subject of the copula was always a pronoun.

The parents, too, seldom used nouns as subjects during the recorded observations. This fact would seem to suggest that the same explanation is possible for the disuse of nouns by the child as by his parents: namely, that given the concrete referential situations about which they are most likely to speak, pronouns are merely more convenient to use than nouns. However, as we shall see below, there is good reason to reject this as an explanation for the child's speech. A more satisfactory interpretation of the evidence is that the child, in his grammar, generates a "subject" noun in a quite different way from a "subject" pronoun. Hence our evidence has significance for the internalized grammar of the child, not just for his behavior in a given situation.

II. TOPICALIZATION IN SENTENCES WITH INTERROGATIVE PRONOUNS

Consider first how Mackie forms questions with interrogative pronouns (e.g. *where, what, why*, etc.) preposed to the sentence. During this period we find the following such questions (this is an exhaustive list):[6]

(1)(a) *What do wheel?*
   (b) *What does the truck?*
   (c) *Where went the wheel?*
   (d) *Where's the a a truck?*
   (e) *Where's the wheel?*
   (f) *Where's the man?*
   (g) *What is this?*
   (h) *Who's that?*
   (i) *Why it go?*
   (j) *Where it is?* (4×)

We see that such questions with an apparent noun subject have the normal order of subject followed by main verb inverted, as in examples (1a–f). (We will regard sentences (1g) and (1h) in the same way, allowing *this* and *that* to be considered like nouns.) However, when a pronoun such as *it* was subject, there was no apparent inversion, as in examples (1i–j).

In the English grammar of adults, sentences with an interrogative pronoun preposed have inversion of the auxiliary verb and the subject. This is acounted for by the following transformational rule, in which $Q + NP$ represents an interrogative pronoun, NP the subject noun phrase, *Aux* the auxiliary verb, and X the rest of the sentence:

---

[6]Transcription of the child's utterances were made to approximate morphemes of adult English as closely as possible. When, for example, *where's* is transcribed, we do not necessarily imply that this is indeed a contraction in Mackie's language derived from *where is*, but only that Mackie's utterance seemed to come close to this English word in sound. If an utterance is repeated more than once in the corpus, the number of times is indicated by a numeral followed by a "×".

Tr-1: $Q + NP \quad NP \quad Aux \quad X$
        $\quad\quad\ 1 \quad\quad\ \ 2 \quad\quad 3 \quad\quad 4 \rightarrow 1\ 3\ 2\ 4$

Mackie's sentences in (1), therefore, deviate from those of his parents in two ways.

First of all, in an adult English grammar, the inversion transformation Tr-1 applies without regard to whether the subject *NP* is a noun or a pronoun. *NP* may refer to either. Hence an adult grammar yields inversions in both utterances *What is it?* and *Where is John?* For the child, however, we do not obtain *Where is it?* but rather (1j) *Where it is?* The inversion transformation would apply only in the case that the subject of the underlying sentence is a noun, for we do obtain *Where's the man?* and similar sentences (1d–h).

Secondly, for the grammar of an adult English speaker, the inversion transformation never applies to main verbs. We do not obtain such a sentence as *Where went the wheel?* in adult English. But in the child's speech, we find just this sentence and others similar to it, sentences (1a–c). The child's transformation therefore would have to apply to main verbs if and only if the verb has a noun subject. This would give us (1a–c), but not sentences of the type *Why go it?* with a pronoun subject. Instead we obtain *Why it go?* (1i), without inversion. Finally, for the adult, inversion *always* applies to the copula of interrogative sentences, e.g. *Where is it?* and *Where is the man?* But for the child this transformation would have to be restricted to the copula *be* when *be* has a noun subject.

A transformational rule with the above specifications is possible. Its form would be that of Tr-2:

Tr-2: $Q + NP \quad (Det +) N \quad V \quad X$
        $\quad\quad\ 1 \quad\quad\quad 2 \quad\quad\ \ 3 \quad 4 \rightarrow 1\ 3\ 2\ 4$

Such a transformation, used by child, would have no model in the questions presented to him by the adult. The environments of its application would be broader for the types of verb to which it applies and more restricted for the types of subject. It is difficult to imagine how such a highly specific transformational rule Tr-2 could have been arrived at by the child, who would have been presented with evidence for a transformational rule of quite different specifications, Tr-1.

However, we might attempt to account for the child's application of the inversion transformation to all verbs, including main verbs, as a type of over-generalization. It is true that the auxiliary verb is not yet manifested in the child's grammar. Consequently, he would not be expected to make the distinction between main verbs and auxiliary verbs. It might be reasonable therefore to suggest that the child's inversions shown in (1a–f) are manifestations of an inversion transformation which, applying indiscriminately to all verbs, is a rough precursor of the adult transformational inversion which applies only to auxiliary verbs.

But if we assume that the child at the period under discussion has internalized an inversion transformation such as Tr-2, especially if it is a precursor of the adult transformation, then we would expect it to remain in some form as a part of his grammar at subsequent stages of development. However, this is not the case. A sampling eight months later showed no inversion whatever for such questions as above. Questions with interrogative pronouns and apparent noun subjects at the later period have the form seen in the following examples:

(2)(a) *Where this guy goes?*
(b) *What that guy do?*

It would only increase the mystery to say that the child could have learned to use an inversion transformation at one time and ceased to use it at a later time.

Postulating a transformational inversion for the child in questions with interrogative pronouns is unsatisfactory on still further grounds. Klima and Bellugi[7] have observed a stage in the development of child language (presumably after the period under discussion) at which there is inversion in questions answerable by *yes* or *no* and also pre-position of interrogative pronouns, but at this stage there appears to be a performance limitation barring the two transformations from applying together.

Inversions for questions answerable by *yes* or *no* are accounted for in adult grammar by a transformational rule similar to Tr-1. Instead of there being an interrogative pronoun $Q + NP$ as the necessary condition for such a transformation, there is only the underlying question marker Q, which is generated at the beginning of the sentence and later deleted.[8] Hence, for the adult, an inversion transformation applied for all instances of Q (either Q itself or $Q + NP$). We replace rule Tr-1 by the modified form Tr-3.

Tr-3: $Q\,(+ NP)$ *NP*   *Aux*   *X*
$1 \qquad\ \ 2 \quad\ \ 3 \qquad 4 \rightarrow 1\,3\,2\,4$

This will yield in the adult grammar sentences such as *Is the toy a truck?* in which Q exists alone at the beginning of the underlying sentence, as well as sentences such as *Where is the truck?* in which $Q + NP$ is at the beginning.

An interrogative pronoun is generated at the beginning of a sentence by a pre-position transformation that removes a noun phrase from its ordinary position in a sentence and unites it to the question marker at the beginning of the sentence (forming $Q + NP$). This transformation is as follows:

Tr-4: Q *X*   *NP*   *Y*
$1 \quad 2 \quad\ 3 \quad\ 4 \rightarrow 1 + 3\,2\,\emptyset\,4$

For example, from an underlying tree structure such as Figure 2, we obtain by applying only Tr-4 the tree structure shown in Figure 3. Subsequent application of Tr-3 in the adult grammar yields the surface tree of adult English shown in Figure 4.

At the stage which Klima and Bellugi report, the child has apparently internalized Tr-3 and Tr-4. One obtains, using only Tr-3, sentences of the type *Is the toy a truck?* Also, one obtains, using only Tr-4, *What the toy is?* But one does not obtain sentences such as in Figure 4, *What is the toy?* in which both Tr-3 and Tr-4 must apply to the same tree.

The period we are discussing, however, is different from that just presented, since both apparent inversion, Tr-3, and pre-position of interrogative pronouns,

---

[7]E. S. Klima and U. Bellugi, "Syntactic Regularities in the Speech of Children," in J. Lyons and R. J. Wales, eds., *Psycholinguistic Papers: The Proceedings of the 1966 Edinburgh Conference* (Edinburgh University Press, 1966), pp. 183–208 [revised version in *MSE*].

[8]J. Katz and P. Postal, *An Integrated Theory of Linguistic Descriptions*, Research Monograph No. 26 (Cambridge, Mass.: M.I.T. Press, 1964), pp. 79–116.

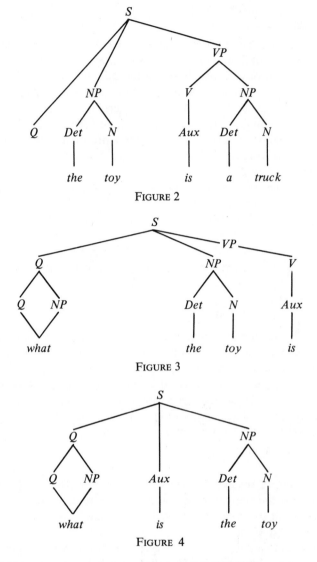

FIGURE 2

FIGURE 3

FIGURE 4

Tr-4, sometimes occur together in our period. Also there does not seem to be true inversion, Tr-3, applying alone in the case of *yes-no* questions. We only have apparent inversion in the appearance of *do* or *does* before the subject.

(3)(a) *Does it work?*
  (b) *Do I make this way?*

No other auxiliary appeared before the subject to yield such sentences as *Is it a dog?, Is he running?,* or *Has he a book?* In addition, we have no examples of the auxiliary *do* appearing after an interrogative pronoun during the period studied.

In cases when *does* or *do* does not appear, the question marker is manifested only by a rising intonation in the child's speech, and not by any sort of inversion, as may occur in adult speech. For example, each of the following utterances was distinguished as a question by a rising intonation:

(4)(a)   *You fight?*
   (b)   *See it?*
   (c)   *You fix it?*
   (d)   *Me show you?*
   (e)   *Go round?*
   (f)   *That go?*
   (g)   *That broke?*
   (h)   *That truck?*
   (i)   *That's a train?*
   (j)   *It's wagon?*

It would be unwarranted to postulate an inversion, Tr-3, operating only in such cases as (3a) and (3b). Moreover, before inversion appears with other auxiliaries or in other instances of *yes-no* questions, or before other auxiliaries appear at all, it would be best to consider this *do(es)*, not as an auxiliary, but as a question marker. In other words, *do(es)* is itself an optional phonological materialization of the question marker *Q* assumed always to underlie *yes-no* questions, but which is never so manifested in adult English. We can then avoid requiring inversion to occur. Against this is the apparent agreement that seems to exist between *do(es)* and the subject, *does* occurring with the third person singular and *do* with all other pronouns. There were no examples with *do(es)* with noun subjects. This agreement, however, does not imply that the word which agrees with the subject is necessarily a verb. In Mackie's speech, verbs cannot be so characterized, since there is no consistent agreement between the verb and its subject. Although it is possible that *do(es)* is a verb here, we will assume it is not a verb, and that there is no inversion.

At the stage under discussion then, inversion Tr-3 does not occur alone as a transformation. Consequently it would be a complication to assume that inversion occurs only when pre-position of an interrogative pronoun, Tr-4, also occurs. Moreover, such a situation would not fit in consistently with the subsequent stage which Klima and Bellugi report, at which inversion Tr-3 occurs in addition to pre-position Tr-4 but at which these two transformations still cannot occur together.

If we do not account for the peculiar inversion of word order by an inversion transformation, to what then do we attribute the phenomenon we have been discussing?

We propose that the appearance of a noun as the subject of a sentence such as *Where went the wheel?* is due to the co-generation of a clause generated without an overtly manifested subject, together with a noun phrase. That is, we will generate the comment clause and the topic noun phrase of a topic-comment construction. Just how the co-generation of such a noun phrase is to be formulated will be discussed in Section VI. It has been indicated, however, that most of Mackie's sentences at this time have subjects manifested only by pronouns or not manifested at all. Both *Where it went?* and *Where went?* occur, the latter having no subject expressed. These would have tree structures derived from the underlying tree structures (Figures 5 and 6) respectively:

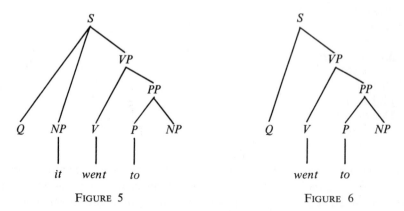

FIGURE 5   FIGURE 6

The pre-position transformation Tr-4 may effect the pre-posing of prepositional phrases, *PP* (as well as noun phrases, *NP*), after which a preposition such as *to* may no longer appear in the output. Hence, after application of Tr-4, we obtain the derived trees of Figures 7 and 8.

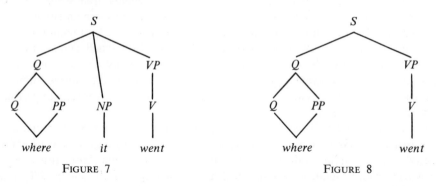

FIGURE 7   FIGURE 8

Generating the clause of Figure 8, *Where went?*, with a noun phrase such as *the wheel* following it, we obtain *Where went the wheel?* which would then have the tree structure given in Figure 9, according to our hypothesis.

The obvious selectional restrictions between the co-generated noun phrase, e.g. *the wheel*, and the verb, e.g. *went*, will be treated in Section VII.

Questions of the form

(5)   *The wheel where went?*

formed by generating the two elements mentioned above in the opposite order did not occur, however, although we might expect such a question to occur. Its nonoccurrence could be attributed to a limitation on the number of noun phrases generated at the same side of the comment clause. In such interrogative sentences as those above there is already an interrogative pronoun attached to the beginning of the sentence by Tr-4, which may eliminate the possibility of another noun phrase being attached there. We shall mention this problem again in Section VI.

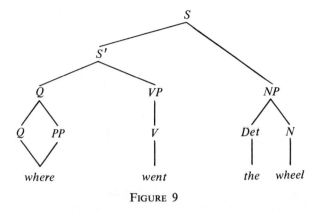

FIGURE 9

The nonoccurrence of *Where the wheel went?* at this stage will be accounted for by allowing only pronouns as subjects (alternating with no subject expressed at all). Such sentences are exemplified by the trees of Figures 5 and 6. Otherwise such a sentence could be generated merely by moving *where* in *The wheel went where?* to the head of the sentence as in adult grammar. On the other hand, the occurrence of *Where it went?* is readily accounted for in the child's grammar. But since the categorization of *it* (or *he, I,* or *she,* for example) will be such as not to allow it to be used as topic, i.e. generated at the beginning or end of *S',* we can explain the nonoccurrence of *Where went it?*.

Thus the phenomenon described above can be explained by assuming that the child utilizes at this stage some notion of topicalization, whereby he can state the topic before or after the sentence, in much the same way as is found in languages such as Chinese and Japanese. Topicalization, we recapitulate, means that some major constituent of a sentence, such as a noun phrase, which is identical with (or has the same referent as) a constituent in the given sentence, may be generated before or after this sentence. In the given sentence, then, this noun phrase is represented by a pronoun or by nothing at all. The co-generated constituent is called the topic, and the given sentence is called the comment.

III. TOPICALIZATION WITH NOUNS IN SENTENCES WITHOUT INTERROGATIVES

If this is the correct interpretation of the apparent inversion presented, we should expect to find evidence of topicalization in the child's declarative sentences. Topic-comment constructions indeed seem to appear overtly in the sentences

(6)(a) *It broken, wheels.*
   (b) *Car, it broken.*

In these constructions the topic is after the comment clause and before *it* respectively. The subjects are manifested by pronouns in the comment clauses. The topic has the same referent as the subject pronoun. Sentences (6a) and (6b) have tree structures as in Figures 10 and 11 respectively.

The topic noun phrase may in other instances have the same referent as the object of the verb. And further still, it may relate to some noun phrase by a relation

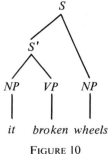

FIGURE 10

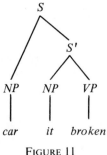

FIGURE 11

of possession rather than by identity of reference. In (7a–c), we have the topic referring to the object. In (7b–c), we have the topic related to the noun in the comment clause as possessor to the thing possessed.

(7)(a) *Those other, put them?*
   (b) *Car, he take the wheel.*
   (c) *He take the wheels, fire engine.*

For sentences (7b–c), approximate paraphrases in adult English would be *As for the car, he took its wheel,* and *As for the fire engine, he took its wheels.*

For (7c), interpretations other than topicalization are possible. For example, paraphrasing it as *He took the wheel off the fire engine,* we would consider the omission of the preposition *off* as a factor in its generation; with the paraphrase *He took the wheels of the fire engine,* we would have a genitive construction. But the word order in the child's grammar for a genitive construction is *fire engine wheels,* omitting *'s.* Also, positive evidence leads us to believe (7c) is a topic-comment construction. Sentences (7b) and (7c) both occurred during the same period of communication and interation between Mackie and his father, the falling intonation characteristic of declarative sentences is manifested independently in both *He take the wheels* and *fire engine,* and there is a short but distinct pause between the two parts.

We should also expect there to be declarative topic-comment constructions in which the subject of the comment clause, rather than being manifested by a pronoun, is not manifested at all. Indeed, these would be just those rare cases of a noun apparently used as the subject of a declarative sentence. Thus, with ∅ representing the absent subject, we have from an underlying

(8)(a) *Girl, ∅ go away*

which has the tree structure as given in Figure 12, the resulting sentence

(8b) *Girl go away.*

(8b) would have the tree structure of Figure 13 if this were an ordinary subject predicate construction. Compare Figures 12 and 13.

Figure 12 is entirely parallel to Figure 11 above, differing in whether or not the subject is generated. This sentence, which actually occurred, would have as paraphrase something like *As for the girl, she went away.* On the same day the utterance

(9a) *Go way wheels.*

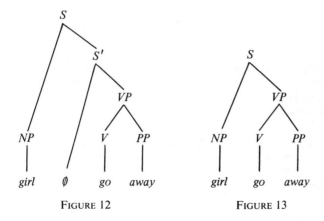

FIGURE 12   FIGURE 13

was observed, which we may take to be of the same structure, coming from

(9b) ∅ *go way, wheels*

where the topic appears after the comment clause. (9b) would have the tree structure of Figure 14.

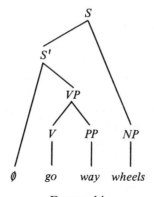

FIGURE 14

This figure is entirely parallel to Figure 10, except that the subject is again not manifest. Similarly we have both of the following:

(10)(a) *Choo choo over there.*
  (b) *Over there train.*

in which we have comment clauses with absent subjects, and with topics before and after the comment clauses respectively.

That the position of the topic before or after the comment clause is perfectly arbitrary is demonstrated by the occurrence of the four sentences of (8), (9), and (10) on the same day.

Are all occurrences of nouns apparently used as subjects really topics at this stage? If they are not subjects, one would have no reason to expect any greater number of occurrences of the noun before the comment or predicate than after it. Indeed there is very nearly an equal distribution. The following sentences, together with those of (8–10), exhaust the cases of possible topicalization, where nouns are generated as topics to declarative comment clauses with subjects absent.

(11)　　Topic After the Comment:　　　(12)　　Topic Before the Comment:
　(a)　*All broken wheel.*　　　　　　　　(a)　*Dump truck all fixed.*
　(b)　*Break pumpkin.*　　　　　　　　　(b)　*Other wheel broke.*
　(c)　*In there wheels.*　　　　　　　　　(c)　*Truck broke.*
　(d)　*In there baby.*　　　　　　　　　　(d)　*Wheel in there.*
　(e)　*There's the man.*　　　　　　　　　(e)　*Pony in there.*
　(f)　*There's the truck.*　　　　　　　　(f)　*Motor in the car.*
　(g)　*There's the wheel.*　　　　　　　　(g)　*Fire truck there.*
　(h)　*Go truck.*　　　　　　　　　　　　(h)　*Mama goes.*
　(i)　*Go in there train.*　　　　　　　　(i)　*Wheels move.*
　　　　　　　　　　　　　　　　　　　　　(j)　*The wheel fall on.*

In some of the sentences above there is a short but significant pause indicating the juncture between the sentence and the topic. This is clearly the case in (10b), *Over there train*, as well as in (12g), *Fire truck there*, and (11h), *Go truck*. A clear juncture is not always discernible, however, although the mere potentiality of a juncture could indicate a topic-comment construction.

It was difficult to discern whether (12f) was really *Motor in the car* or *Motor in there, car*. In the case of the latter, we would have *car* as topic following the sentence, relating to *motor* or *there*.

A number of the sentences of (11) and (12) may have analyses alternative to topicalization. The sentences beginning with *there's the* (11e–g) may have an analysis for the child distinct from the one given above, since these are acceptable constructions in adult grammar and persist in later stages after other instances of topicalization have disappeared. (The same applies to the interrogative sentences beginning with *where's the*, previously mentioned, examples (1d–f).) These sentences may, for example, have the same analysis as for the adult, being caused by an inversion transformation applying to sentences of the type *The wheel is there*. It is doubtful that the child derives them in this way, however, since this requires the generation of nouns in subject position. Alternatively, the sentences may be generated in a fashion completely parallel to nominal or copular sentences of the type *That's a wheel*. Then *there* would be the same type of introductory pronoun as *that* above.

The sentence *There the wheel in there*, and others like it, occur in the child's speech, and are not cases of topicalization since no noun phrase occurs either at the beginning or at the end of the sentences. If *in there* can be omitted from this construction, then we would have a sentence such as (11e–g). However, it is also possible that some of the sentences of (12), such as *Wheel in there* with apparent topic before the comment clause, have a similar origin; that is, the sentence *There wheel in there*, with *there* omitted. Consequently some of the sentences of (11), and some of those of (12), may in fact be formed by means other than topicalization.

It is true that in adult English discourse topicalization as here described sometimes occurs. For example, in the course of conversation it is natural to say such a sentence as *The house we saw yesterday, the Smiths have decided to buy it*. However, in the speech of Mackie's parents such a construction is apparently a rare occurrence, if it occurs at all. There were, in fact, during the period studied, no clear cases of such topicalization in their recorded discourse, a good deal of which has been collected along with Mackie's productions. The sentences which most nearly approximated it in our sample were either affirmations of Mackie's naming some object or they were ellipses of a common type. For example, when Mackie pointed out an object, saying *the boy*, his father affirmed this, saying *Boy. See the boy up there?* In another instance, Mackie's mother asked him *What is it? A pumpkin?*, which question is an ellipsis of *What is it? Is it a pumpkin?* Mackie's adoption of the topic-comment construction as an essential part of his grammar therefore cannot be attributed to imitation of his parents' speech. It seems to have been an independent innovation.

IV. TOPICALIZATION WITH PRONOUNS

There is no evidence to suggest that Mackie used pronouns such as *he, she, it, I*, as topics. Whereas there were instances of verbs followed by noun subjects, there were no instances of verbs followed by the above pronoun subjects. As was seen in Section II, the same situation obtained in interrogative sentences in which nouns but not pronouns appeared after the verb. With declarative sentences also, it is unlikely that there is an inversion transformation re-ordering subject and verb; in such a case, the transformation would hold only if the subject were a noun. Now, however, we can understand the distinction in the uses of nouns and the above pronouns in terms of topicalization, by saying that nouns may be used as topics, while such pronouns may not be.

While it appears that the pronouns above cannot ever be used as topics, this is not the case for pronouns such as *me, him, them*, those commonly used as objects. Thus there is a distinction between Mackie's use of so-called case-marked and unmarked pronouns.[9] Mackie was found to use both marked (*me, him, them*) and unmarked pronouns (*I, he, it*) as apparent subjects of copular sentences. Thus to express *He is a dog*, Mackie might say *He dog*, or *He's dog*, or *He's a dog*, as well as *He is a dog*. Or he might use the so-called marked form, as in *Him dog*. However, in all circumstances where Mackie used the marked form, the copula was absent. During this period, Mackie was found to say the following copular sentences beginning with a marked pronoun. This list is exhaustive:

(13)(a) *Him bear.*
   (b) *Him bad dog.*
   (c) *Them eyes.*
   (d) *Me no bear.*

But there were no examples of sentences of the form *Him's a bad dog* or *Him is a bad dog*.

We shall interpret the sentences of (13) as manifesting the topic-comment construction. If we say that the case-marked pronouns apparently used here as sub-

---

[9]E. Klima, "Relatedness Between Grammatical Systems," *Language*, 40.1–20 (1964) [*MSE*].

jects are really topics, then to avoid generating *Him's a bear* we need only avoid generating the copula in sentences in which the subject is not manifested. This must be done in any case, since there are no such sentences as *Is a bear*. If the subject pronoun is absent, so is the copula; hence the absence of the copula in *Him bear* could be attributed to the absence of the subject pronoun, in which case the pronoun *him* would be the topic.

To be more explicit, *He's a bear* would have the ordinary tree structure of adult English, namely as in Figure 15. On the other hand *Him's a bear* does not occur. That is the tree structure of Figure 16, with *him* the topic does not occur. Figure 16 does not occur since its postulated subtree, namely Figure 17, does not occur.

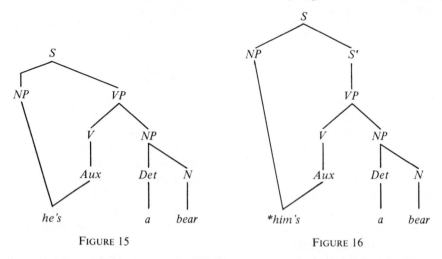

FIGURE 15   FIGURE 16

What does occur is the isolated noun phrase, *Bear*, which, if we treat it as a variant of *He's a bear* with the subject and copula absent, will have the tree structure of Figure 18. If Figure 18 is a subtree of a topic-comment construction in which *him* is the topic, we would have sentence (13a), whose tree is given in Figure 19.

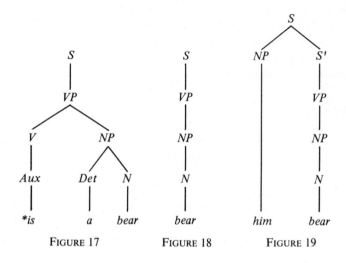

FIGURE 17   FIGURE 18   FIGURE 19

The case-marked pronouns also appear as the subjects of noncopular sentences. In the subject position we have either marked or unmarked pronouns:

(14) Unmarked:
    (a) *I wanna.*
    (b) *He take the wheel, fire engine.*
    (c) *I show you?*
    (d) *I write.*
    (e) *I see the tree.*
    (f) *He bites anyone.*

(15) Marked:
    (a) *Me wanna truck.*
    (b) *Me take the wheel.*
    (c) *Me show you?*
    (d) *Me draw.*
    (e) *Him go right back.*
    (f) *No him no bite.*

That the cases of marked pronouns as subjects are instances of topicalization is supported by the contrast in intonation pattern between such instances as (14c) and (15c). In (14c), as expected for questions, there is a continuous rise starting from the first morpheme *I*. However, in (15c), there is a fall in pitch on the first morpheme *me* followed by the expected interrogative rise for the rest of the sentence. In other words, for (15c), *me* has the intonation of a declarative sentence, and stands separated from the rest of the sentence. Such a break seems to be impossible if the subject position is occupied by an unmarked pronoun, which cannot be a topic. However, the declarative intonation on the topic is not obligatory, since later repetitions of *Me show you?* have a continuous rise.

There were two occurrences of case-marked pronouns used as topic after the comment clause. One of these was a sequence of copula-type sentences like those given in (13):

(16) Car them them car.

If we consider the string composed of the first two morphemes as a unit, then it appears that we have a sequence of comment followed by topic. Actually, however, except for the fact that nouns proper are more commonly used as the object of the copula than are case-marked pronouns, we have no reason to say which of these morphemes is topic and which is comment.

The other instance of a pronoun appearing as topic after the comment was the utterance:

(17) *Catch me.*

This sentence did not have the meaning which normal English word order would suggest. The meaning apparently was *I can catch it*. This can be seen from the behavioral context in which (17) appeared. Mackie and his father were playing at tossing things to each other. After Mackie said the above, his father responded with *Can you catch the pumpkin?*. Then Mackie repeated what he himself had just said, with the topic preceding the sentence this time. He said *Me caught it*, followed by *Me catch it*. The sort of ambiguous construction we have in sentence

(17), is just what one would expect in the case of topicalization with a transitive verb.

We must seek to explain the distributional differences between case-marked and unmarked pronouns. It appears from the foregoing that the case-marked pronouns have the same distribution as nouns do while the unmarked pronouns are restricted to preverbal or precopular position. The former can be used as topics, while the latter cannot.

Suppose that the case-marked pronouns are categorized in the child's grammar precisely like nouns while the unmarked pronouns are not so categorized. There is further evidence to support this view. In the following utterance the marked pronoun *him* appears to be used as the noun head of a noun phrase.

(18)   *He's a bad him.*

Moreover while both case-marked and unmarked pronouns appear in subject position, in other positions, such as in isolation, or as the objects of verbs or of prepositions, only the case-marked pronouns appear. This distribution has been observed by others (Klima, personal communication).

Such a distribution can also be very simply interpreted if we assume that the unmarked pronouns cannot be treated like nouns (or noun phrases), while the marked ones must be so treated. Then, for example, *him* is allowed in apparent subject position, as the topic noun phrase, while it is not possible to get *he* as the object noun phrase. We will say that in isolation, as topics, or as the objects of verbs or prepositions, we have only noun phrases. Conversely, as subjects we only have the unmarked pronouns. All noun phrases and case-marked pronouns which appear to be subjects are identified as topics. The noun phrase itself does not occupy subject position.

We will later face the question why the case-marked pronoun is categorized as a noun while the unmarked pronoun does not come to be categorized in this way by the child.

V. FORMALIZATION OF SENTENCE TYPES

Let us now consider the formal generation of these strings. The copular sentence could be derived by the rules

R-1: $S \rightarrow (Pro)\ NP$
R-2:   *Pro* → he, she, they, I, we, you, it, this, that
R-3:   *NP* → (*Det*) *N, him, me, them, you, this, that*, etc.

The constituent *Pro* is optional, since the subject is often absent. We shall not discuss the nature of *Det*, the determiner, which is of independent interest. Note that we are treating case-marked pronouns as instances of the noun phrase, *NP*. Perhaps to treat them as instances of the noun would be more precise (cf. (18)). The essential thing is that these case-marked pronouns be classified with noun phrases, which are free in their occurrence, as opposed to the unmarked pronouns, *Pro*, which are much more restricted and are not included among possible elements of the noun phrase. The elements dominated by *Pro* are just those which occupy subject position quite generally, and serve no other purpose.

The copula (*'s, is, 'm*, etc.) could be inserted by a transformational rule. It never occurs except when *Pro* is present, and its form is determined by the form of *Pro*. Thus, for example, *'s* is used for *he* and *it*. Such a transformational rule would be:

$$\text{R-4 (optional):} \quad \#\# \quad \underset{1}{Pro} \quad \underset{2}{NP} \quad \#\# \quad \rightarrow 1 + \begin{Bmatrix} 's \\ 'm \\ 'r \\ is \end{Bmatrix} 2$$

There is no evidence to suggest the copula is independent of the pronoun. By inserting the copula by a transformation we are essentially treating the sequence of *Pro* followed by the copula as an optional spelling of *Pro*. That is, *he's* is another form of *he*, *I'm* is another form of *I*, etc. In fact, the spelling of *Pro* as *Pro* + *Copula* is possible even when followed by a verb phrase, *VP*, as in ordinary non-copular sentences. These would be utterances of the form *I'm go* and *He's put* which are observable in our data and reported by others.[10] Such utterances have been thought of as instances of the child's rendition of the progressive aspect. That is, the child says the above instead of *I'm going* or *He's putting*, leaving off the *ing* ending of the progressive from the verb. However, an alternate interpretation, proposed here, is that the child says the above instead of *I go* and *He put*.

Instead of having both the rewriting rule for *Pro* (R-2) and the transformational insertion of the copular elements with environmental restrictions (R-4), we can combine the two in a new rule for rewriting *Pro*, in which the elements rewritten have optional spellings. This would be

$$\text{R-5:} \quad Pro \rightarrow \begin{Bmatrix} that \\ this \\ he \\ it \\ she \end{Bmatrix} \left(+ \begin{Bmatrix} 's \\ is \end{Bmatrix} \right), \quad \begin{Bmatrix} they \\ we \\ you \end{Bmatrix} (+ \; 're), \; \mathrm{I} \; (+ \; 'm)$$

There will be no copula when we have a case-marked pronoun in place of *Pro*, since the presence of a copula, being an optional spelling of *Pro*, depends on the presence of *Pro*. We are treating case-marked pronouns not as elements of *Pro*, but as nouns. How the case-marked pronouns (and the nouns) can be generated in subject position will be treated when the mechanics of topicalization is discussed below (Section VI).

To account also for the ordinary noncopular sentences we extend R-1 into

$$\text{R-6:} \quad S \rightarrow (Pro) \begin{Bmatrix} NP \\ VP \end{Bmatrix}$$

followed by the expansion of *VP* into its many forms, one of which is

$$\text{R-7:} \quad VP \rightarrow V \; NP$$

in which *NP*, as has been said, will include, for example, *him* but not *he*.

VI. FORMALIZATION OF TOPICALIZATION

We can formalize the generation of topic-comment expressions in several ways. One way is to say that a topic-comment expression consists of the juxtaposition

---

[10]E. Klima, personal communication; also R. H. Weir, *Language in the Crib*, Janua Linguarum, Series Major, 25 (The Hague: Mouton & Co., 1962).

of two types of sentence: the free noun phrase, as generated by choosing *NP* in R-6 without *Pro*, and a sentence of any type generated by R-6. In other words, topicalization can be treated as some sort of conjunction between two underlying sentences. The relation of identity or possession called for between the topic and some element in the comment clause, has already been described.

Alternatively, we can generate topic-comment expressions by specifying a rule whose right side elements consist of a noun phrase (*NP*) and a sentence (*S′*) of any type generated by R-6; the topic and the comment respectively. These right side elements must be order-free with respect to one another. This would be a rule such as

R-8: $S \rightarrow NP\ S'$

The order has to be free since both orders occur.

A third possibility is to have a rule establishing order of the form

R-9: $S \rightarrow S'\ NP$

followed by an optional transformation preposing the *NP*:

R-10: $S'\ NP$
$\quad\quad 1\quad 2 \rightarrow 2\ 1$

A fourth possible hypothesis for the mechanism of topicalization is that some noun phrase of the sentence is extraposed either before or after the sentence. According to this hypothesis nouns would have to be generated in subject position and would then be extraposable. We might still maintain that the unmarked pronouns are not categorized as nouns by the child, while marked pronouns are, since only nouns, including marked pronouns, would be extraposable.

The first formulation (juxtaposition of two sentence types) has the advantage over all the others of accounting for certain intonation patterns sometimes occurring in topic-comment constructions: at times the topic is uttered with a declarative intonation independent of the rest of the sentence. For example, the topic may have a declarative intonation while the comment clause has an interrogative intonation. Furthermore, identifying the topic with an isolated noun phrase is supported by the fact that it is just those pronouns which cannot occur in isolation (*he, she, it, I*, etc.), which also do not occur as topics. We cannot explain the disuse of these pronouns as topics by saying that they have alternate forms when used as topic, since *it*, unlike *he*, has no alternate form.

The second formulation is unsatisfactory in that a rule such as R-8, with free order, is a type of rule never before used in phrase structure grammars. Phrase structure rules which establish order among the right side elements have always been found necessary, since a particular order has always been assumed to be basic. There is, however, no certainty in this assumption.

In the third and fourth formulations, one could account for the absence of *The wheel where went*, by limiting the application of the relevant preposing transformations to one application of either of them. To get this sentence, first *where* and then *the wheel* would have to have been moved to the head of the sentence, two preposings. In the third formulation, one could restrict rule R-10, a rule similar to Tr-4, from applying when Tr-4 does, so that only *Where went the wheel?* would be obtained, provided preposing the interrogative pronoun Tr-4 were obligatory.

The fourth formulation, however, would allow the utterance *Where the wheel went?*, sentences of which type have not been found in the corpus investigated. We would have the added specification that extraposition to the end of the sentence is obligatory for the subject when an interrogative pronoun is preposed.

The first three formulations postulate an underlying form to characterize the topic-comment construction, whereas the fourth characterizes topicalization as a process. Formulating topicalization as a process of extraposition would automatically establish the identity relation between the topic and some noun phrase within the comment clause. However, it would not account for the suspected instances of topicalization in which the relation between the topic and the noun phrase within the comment clause is one of possession rather than of identity.

Taking the process of extraposition as our formulation of topicalization means that in some instances noun phrases must be generated as subjects so that they could then be extraposed. But this would amount to abandoning the idea, which we have labored to demonstrate, that noun phrase subjects are really not generated in *S* by the child. Nouns would be generated as subjects on a par with nouns generated anywhere else. We are postulating, however, that at this early stage of development of language, the sentence structure and the processes of its generation are simpler than those of the adult. Saying that subject position is restricted to morphemes categorized as *Pro* implies a simplicity of structure which will be discussed below; and postulating that topicalization is really the co-generation of a noun phrase and a sentence seems to be simpler and more basic than postulating extraposition.

Extraposition in the child's grammar would make the process of generation of sentences more complex than in adult grammar, since subject noun phrases would have to be generated before extraposition occurred. Consequently the child would have an additional rule in his grammar, extraposition, compared to the rules which the adult has as an intrinsic part of his grammar. If topicalization were extraposition, one would expect Mackie's present stage to be preceded by a period in which subjects were generated, this being followed by the addition of topicalization by extraposition as a new rule to the grammar. However, the preceding stage is probably one in which neither subjects nor topics are generated, judging from other reports (see below).

Our main reason in the formalization of topicalization for favoring an underlying form over a process is that it is then possible, as we shall see, to understand why case-marked pronouns are considered nouns, and unmarked pronouns are not; in addition, by this means light can be shed on the very essence of the subject-predicate construction itself, and its origin.

VII. SUBJECTLESS SENTENCES

Thus far we have surmised that the child, at the stage of development under discussion, generates sentences in which only an unmarked pronoun, not a noun phrase, can serve as subject (Rule R-6). But is the element *Pro* to be considered a subject in the same sense as the term would be used in describing adult English?

Since the term subject is universally defined for adult grammars as the noun phrase immediately dominated by an *S* node, usually the highest node of the sentence, and since the element *Pro* is emphatically not a noun phrase, the element *Pro* cannot be a subject with the same definition as for adult English.

There are, however, further considerations which lead to the conclusion that it would be unwise to consider *Pro* even as a rough precursor to the adult subject. Note that if we combine the topic noun phrase, *NP*, with the comment clause, *S'*, we have the sequence *NP S'*. Expanding *S*, here *S'*, by R-6, we have the sequence *NP Pro VP*. Thus if the whole sequence is thought of as being dominated by *S*, then we could characterize this eventual stage of development by the rule $S \to NP$ *Pro VP*. Since *Pro* may be absent, this rule is sometimes identical to $S \to NP\ VP$. It is this rule, with a *NP* in subject position, which the child will ultimately have to arrive at. But if topicalization and Rule R-6 together reduce to the rule $S \to NP$ *VP*, we cannot regard *Pro* as the precursor of the subject *NP*, since the topic is. Hence the node labelled *Pro* should not be considered a rudimentary subject at all, but rather some sort of introductory word to verbs. It is more or less a verbal article, or perhaps on a par with an inflectional affix of a verb.

It is reasonable to reformulate Mackie's grammar in accordance with the above. Let us emphasize the fact that *Pro* is not the subject by removing it from the right side of R-6 and specifying it as a feature of the verb. Then instead of R-6 we would have simply

R-6′: $S \to VP$

After R-7 has applied we could expand *V* into a set of features by R-11:

$$\text{R-11:}\quad V \to \begin{bmatrix} Pro \\ \left\{ \begin{matrix} V' \\ Cop \end{matrix} \right\} \end{bmatrix}$$

The notation signifies that every verb is specified for a value of the feature [*Pro*] plus either [*V'*] or [*Cop*]. The features implied in [*Pro*], [*V'*], and [*Cop*] would then be optionally manifested before the verb, constituting the same variety of spellings as for *Pro* generated by R-5. The feature [*Cop*] (for the copula) has a zero manifestation. It means that a copula is implied, and not some other type of verb, [*V'*] which is generally manifested.

In this way we treat the elements of *Pro* as features of the verb, not as a noun phrase. To maintain that *Pro* is not a subject noun phrase, we must favor for our formulation co-generation of an underlying *NP* outside of *S* over extraposition of some *NP* in *S* (e.g. the subject). Note, however, that although the element *Pro* is not a noun phrase, it must have referential qualities, since the co-generated topic noun phrase must be identical to it in reference.

Figure 12, in accordance with our new formulation, would become the tree structure of Figure 20. If we had chosen to spell out the appropriate features of [*Pro*] we would obtain the sentence of Figure 21.

Note that now all our topic-comment sentences are structurally similar to subject-predicate sentences, even when a pronoun appears as subject, since the pronoun is now a part of the verb phrase.

Given that *Pro* is not a subject noun phrase, we can now understand why

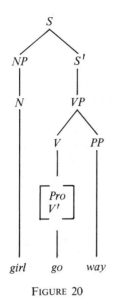

FIGURE 20

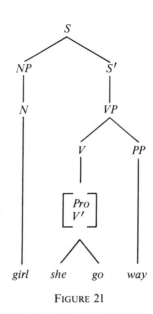

FIGURE 21

the case marked pronouns are treated as nouns, while the unmarked pronouns are not. That a pronoun such as *him* is treated as a noun phrase is quite a reasonable generalization for the child to have made. For *he*, however, the child does not make this generalization. *He*, the unmarked pronoun, is presented to the child only in the subject position. Since by R-6' the child does not generate noun phrases in the subject position, he will not recognize *he* as a noun phrase. Rather he will assume *he* (or its optional spelling *he's*) to be a preverbal introductory particle or an inflection of the verb.

Thus, we surmise that the child constructs, instead of subject-predicate relations, what could be called predicate sentences as characterized by R-6'. A predicate sentence would be one that describes a situation without specifying any element of that situation as the thing which the sentence is about. It would be a subjectless or topicless sentence. (Consider, for example, the English sentence *There's a man in the room*, as a possible predicate sentence.)

The existence of subjectless sentences at some stage in the acquisition of language has further implications. Let us touch upon the relationship between the child's use of pronouns and their usage in some adult dialect of English. It is true that in some adult dialects the marked pronoun can appear in subject position in certain contexts. For example, in some subdialects of English the marked pronoun will appear as subject if not immediately preceding the verb. In such a dialect one would have *They read books* with the unmarked pronoun; but one would also have *Them two read books*, with the marked pronoun, when the marked pronoun is separated from the verb by some morpheme, such as the numeral *two*. Moreover, there is the tendency in modern English dialects to use the marked pronoun in isolation, rather than the unmarked form. In answer to the question *Who's there?*, one would reply *me*, rather than *I*, even though the full form of the answer is *I am here*, and not *Me am here* or *Me is here*. In other words, there is a drift in

English speaking communities toward a grammar in which the pronoun, once used only as object, has come to be used in additional contexts. This same drift has been manifested in French to an even greater degree than in English. In French, for example, sentences paralleling examples (13) are now acceptable adult forms.

One might propose to explain the child's use of pronouns by saying that in learning English he has been exposed to a dialect such as those above and apprehended the distinction in the usage of pronouns employed in it. To some degree this may be true. However, in the dialect of Mackie's parents there did not seem to be any instances of case-marked pronouns used in subject position. In addition, the distinction employed in adult grammars is in general more subtle than that manifested by the child: for example, *them* may be used as subject, but only if it does not immediately precede the verb. But more importantly, we are led to refrain from resting on this conclusion by looking at the situation in another way: on the basis of the manner in which the child acquires language we can explain precisely the historical drift described in the previous paragraph.

We propose that for a child learning English, the form of the pronoun which is used for the object of the verb or of the preposition is the form which he first recognizes as a noun phrase. Until much later he does not recognize the form used for the subject, *Pro*, as any more than an introductory particle or a verbal inflection, since he does not recognize the subject or unmarked form as a noun phrase. To the extent that the child's first hypotheses regarding his mother tongue persist uncorrected into adulthood, the marked pronoun will be the form used with the same generality with which the noun phrase is used; and to the same extent, the unmarked pronoun will be the form restricted to positions immediately preceding the verb. In other words, the marked, or more highly specialized, pronoun in the adult grammar will become the unmarked one, or more highly generalized one in the child's grammar and vice versa.

This explanation is consonant with the hypothesis that linguistic changes occur by means of innovations occurring during the child's acquisition of language.

One would expect that such an historical drift in the use of pronouns would be universal among languages at certain stages. The form of the pronoun used as the subject becomes more and more restricted in this usage, more and more bound to the verb as an inflection; while the form used in the verb phrase becomes used in wider and wider circumstances. The speculated universality of this sort of drift rests on the universality of the child's failure to generate noun phrase subjects in his early grammars.

VIII. SIGNIFICANCE OF TOPICALIZATION

Let us compare the topic-comment construction with the *Pivot + Open-class* construction discussed by Braine[11] and others. According to Braine, the child's first two-word utterances are constructed by the concatenation of an element of a small, closed class of words, called the pivot class, with an element of the open

---

[11]M. Braine, "The Ontogeny of English Phrase Structure: The First Phase," *Language*, 39.1–13 (1963).

class, usually a noun. It often happens that a pivot-class word appears before an open-class word, a noun, as for examples in *All-gone shoe*. Here, just as in the case of Mackie's speech, the order is the reverse of what would be possible for an adult, who would say *The shoe is all-gone*. We might seek to explain the position of apparent subjects after the predicate in (11) by analysing these sentences as *Pivot + Open-class* constructions.

However, the situation must be different for Mackie, whose stage of language development is beyond the two word sentence stage referred to by Braine. Note that while Braine says that his *Pivot + Open-class* construction may deviate from the order expected on the basis of adult grammar, it also appears that a given element of the pivot class has a fixed position, either before or after the open-class word. This is not true, for example, for *go way* and *over there* in our material, both of which appear both before and after a noun (8b, 9a, and 10a–b). Hence Braine's phenomenon, which is of earlier appearance, is different from the phenomenon here presented.

In his review of current results[12] and speculations on the development of language, D. McNeill[13] specifies, among others, two rules which are present in the early grammars of children, presumably at a stage prior to the stage at which we are describing Mackie. (Mackie's speech prior to this period has not yet been investigated.) These rules are, as specified by McNeill,

McN R-1: $S \rightarrow (P) + NP$

$NP \rightarrow \begin{Bmatrix} (P) + N \\ N + N \end{Bmatrix}$

McN R-2: $S \rightarrow Pred\text{-}P$

$Pred\text{-}P \rightarrow (V) + NP$

$NP \rightarrow \begin{Bmatrix} (P) + N \\ N + N \end{Bmatrix}$

Here we have the usual symbols, except that *P* stands for a pivot-class word. *Pred-P* stands for *Predicate Phrase*, and *V* stands for a main verb, such as *go*, *put*, etc. *P* is a word like *that* or *he*, used in rule McN R-1 to yield sentences like *That a man* and *He dog* and hence is like our *Pro*. The expansion of *NP* is the same for both rules. Note then that we can reformulate McN R-1 and McN R-2. Except for the expansion of *NP*, they together generate the same strings as the following set of rules:

[12]M. Braine, loc. cit.; R. Brown, "The Acquisition of Language," *Disorders of Communication*, 42 (1964); R. Brown and C. Fraser, "The Acquisition of Syntax," in C. N. Cofer and B. S. Musgrave, eds., *Verbal Behavior and Learning* (New York: McGraw Hill, 1963); R. Brown and C. Fraser, "The Acquisition of Syntax," in U. Bellugi and R. Brown, eds., *The Acquisition of Language, Monographs of the Society for Research in Child Development*, Serial No. 92, 1964, Vol. 29, No. 1, pp. 79–92; R. Brown and U. Bellugi, "Three Processes in the Child's Acquisition of Syntax," *Harvard Educational Review*, 34.133–151 (1964); S. Ervin, "Imitation and Structural Change in Children's Language," in E. Lenneberg, ed., *New Directions in the Study of Language* (Cambridge, Mass.: M.I.T. Press, 1964).

[13]D. McNeill, "Developmental Psycholinguistics," mimeographed, Harvard Center for Cognitive Studies, to appear in the *Handbook of Social Psychology*. [Cf. D. McNeill, "Developmental Psycholinguistics," in F. Smith and G. A. Miller, eds., *The Genesis of Language: A Psycholinguistic Approach* (Cambridge, Mass.: M.I.T. Press, 1966), p. 40ff.]

McN R-3: $S \rightarrow VP$
McN R-4: $VP \rightarrow (V) NP$
McN R-5: $V \rightarrow \begin{Bmatrix} V \\ P \end{Bmatrix}$

McNeill observes that the child's sentences do not consist of a subject NP followed by a predicate VP. These are subjectless sentences. The pronominal elements in the class designated by P, while perhaps confusable with subjects, as our *Pro* is, are more like introductory words or affixes. These comprise a small closed class of morphemes, as opposed to the large open classes, such as N and V. At this stage there seems to be an association between the pivot class, P, and the verb, V.

McN R-3 is identical to our R-6', and McN R-4 is similar to R-7. McN R-5 can be interpreted as generating verbal features, as does our R-11. The only difference is in the ultimate manifestation of these features. For McN R-5 either the verbal features (V) or the features of *Pro* (here P), but not both, can be manifested. For Mackie's speech for rule R-11 either the verbal features or those of *Pro* or both may be manifested, the features of *Pro* being spelled out to the left of V.

We contend that at Mackie's stage of development the elements dominated by P in McNeill's notation (namely, those we have dominated by *Pro* in our notation) are still categorized in the same way as pivot-class words. They are not to be regarded as noun phrase subjects. Rather they are a part of the verb.

Thus the child's first grammars generate subjectless sentences. A similar phenomenon seems to occur in Japanese. In a recent talk[14] D. McNeill pointed out that a Japanese child learning his mother tongue very seldom used the phrase postposition *wa*[3]. This particle is used to indicate a topicalized noun phrase, the topic of the sentence. The noun phrase followed by *wa* is placed at the beginning as the topic. What McNeill has observed may be an example of the very same fact observed with Mackie. At some stage of development Japanese children learning Japanese produce topicless predicates just as English-learning children produce subjectless predicates.

If at an early stage the child produces sentences composed of nouns in isolation, or produces subjectless sentences, how then does the subject-predicate construction ultimately arise as the child reaches adult competence? McNeill recognizes his two rules given above as the two halves of sentence structure which need to be combined together to yield the form of adult sentences. He speculates that the combining of these rules is precisely what happens.

This sort of development is just what we have found. The co-generation of a noun phrase with a predicate sentence characterizes topicalization here described. It would seem then that the topic-comment relation is the precursor of the subject-predicate relation.

---

[14]D. McNeill "Some Universals of Language Acquisition," Harvard Center for Cognitive Studies Colloquium, Cambridge, Mass., January 20, 1966. [Cf. D. McNeill, "The Creation of Language by Children," in J. Lyons and R. J. Wales, eds., *Psycholinguistic Papers: The Proceedings of the 1966 Edinburgh Conference* (Edinburgh University Press, 1966), p. 104ff.]

The case of the Japanese children described above seems to suggest that the notions of "subject" and "topic" may be essentially the same thing. The relations of *subject-predicate* and *topic-comment* may refer to the same underlying psychological reality. In fact, the similarity of these notions to the more general relation of *figure-ground*, which is perhaps more immediately relevant to other psychological phenomena, has been suggested (M. Bullowa, personal communication).

Topic-comment constructions seem to evolve into subject-predicate constructions, the notion of subject being a special case of the notion of topic. The peculiar feature of the subject, perhaps, is that the subject is the obligatory, most deeply embedded topic of the sentence in a language which is so structured as to have it. Languages with topicalization such as Japanese, may topicalize several times in one sentence. English has one and only one topic, namely the subject, unless the passive sentence represents topicalization of some other noun phrase in addition.

The stage of development of Mackie's grammatical skills discussed in this paper seems to be a transitional one. It is the stage presumably after he would generate the *Pivot + Open-class* constructions that Braine shows, and after the period when subjectless predicates alone are generated. But it is before the period when he constructs English sentences in accordance with the subject-predicate relation. The topic-comment construction characterizes this intermediate stage.

It is due to the independence of topicalization from normal English structure that sentences were produced sufficiently strange in appearance to spark an investigation of their nature; but it is due also to this very independence or universality of topicalization that it is reasonably successful as a means of communication between the child and his parents. The parents can interpret the child's utterances in terms of the subject-predicate constructions which adult speakers generate. The child can interpret the parents' subject-predicate constructions in terms of his own topic-comment constructions, of which the subject-predicate construction is a special case.

We speculate that a child learning a language for the first time first produces sentences without subjects. Then he uses the innately known topic-comment construction to compose richer sentences. Later, if he is learning English, he comes to give this construction its special characteristics, ultimately arriving at the subject-predicate construction.

28

Syntactic Regularities
in the Speech of Children

EDWARD S. KLIMA and URSULA BELLUGI-KLIMA

What we have set as our goal is the grammatical capacity of children—a part of their general linguistic competence. The question of course is how to arrive at this competence. The utterances produced—which might seem to be a direct access to competence—cannot give the total answer. There is really no way to determine which of the child's utterances are grammatically nondeviant in terms of his own grammar. And even if the grammatically nondeviant utterances could be reliably determined, they could only give hints as to the total grammatical capacity of the child, which includes not only what has been produced (or understood) but also what could be produced (or understood). The situation is the same as that involved in describing our own adult grammar if we limited ourselves to what had been uttered over some short period of time and faithfully gave equal weight to everything uttered, no matter how it actually came out. What is actually done, in analyzing the adult language, is to select. Sentences are selected which are felt intuitively to be most free of deviances, and then one goes beyond the mere corpus to develop a more structured theory that excludes sentences which are wrong g ammatically (i.e. which present clear deviances) and that explains the status of the other cases. The range of difficulties that face the analyst in describing the language of children

Reprinted with revision from J. Lyons and R. J. Wales, eds., *Psycholinguistics Papers* (Edinburgh University Press, 1966), pp. 183–208, copyright © 1966 by Edinburgh University Press, by permission of Edward S. Klima and Ursula Bellugi-Klima and the Edinburgh University Press.

This work was supported in part by The Joint Services Electronics Project under contract BA 36-039-AMC-03200 (E), in part by The National Science Foundation Grant GP-2495, The National Institute of Health Grant MH 0473-05, The National Aeronautics and Space Administration Grant NSG-496, The U.S. Air Force ESD contract AF 19 (628-2487), and Public Health Service Research Grant MH7088-04 from the National Institute of Health.

on the basis of their utterances should be illuminated by examining a sketch of grammatical structure in adult English.

Approaching the grammar of child language from the other direction answers certain of the problems—that is, from the point of view of the child's ability to understand sentences. Sentences the child understands describe the scope of his grammar more accurately than those he produces, just as with the adult. But if the child's "understanding" of adult sentences is examined, there is some evidence to suggest that the child comprehends sentences according to his existing grammar. Where comprehension involves syntactic characteristics not present in the child's utterances it seems that this does not represent a relatively rich grammar coupled with a much poorer production device, but rather a limited grammar coupled with a liberal perceptual device that sifts out or bypasses unfamiliar material. As an example, with children whose speech did not contain passives, we tested comprehension of the passive construction, using pairs of pictures. One picture showed a cat being chased by a dog, and another a dog being chased by a cat. When the children were asked to show *The cat is being chased by the dog*, a number of them pointed to the picture of the cat chasing the dog.[1] This suggests that these children may have been processing the passive sentences as if they were active sentences, i.e. in terms of usual *Subject–Verb–Object* relations, sifting out the unknown material, specifically the passive auxiliary and the agentive preposition. We plan to use as much information on comprehension of syntax as possible in investigating the grammar of children.

A striking characteristic of the language acquisition situation is the fact that the particular linguistic ability that develops in the individual child as he gradually masters his native language is grossly underdetermined by the utterances he hears. Not only does he understand, produce, and recognize as perfectly normal countless sentences he has never heard, but he will recognize as deviant in some way or other countless utterances that he has heard produced during his linguistically formative years. The child will recognize as deviant all the various slips of the tongue, false starts, interrupted completions, and noises that are present in our everyday utterances. Given the external characteristics of language acquisition, the psycholinguist asks: How do any two children—to say nothing of those of a whole speech community—arrive at anywhere near the same language? How does a particular language—each time it is acquired by a child—keep from changing radically? Since language does not change radically in this situation, there must surely be some general principles at work, and it is the principles underlying language acquisition which we want eventuallly to illuminate.

But first, prior questions must be investigated. If one looks closely at the development of speech in children who have heard totally independent language environments during the early period of language acquisition, it may well be that each will follow an independent path in his grammatical growth and syntactic patterns. And if the limitations on what the child produces have little relationship to his grammatical capacity, one would not expect that a study of children's speech would

---

[1]Colin Fraser, Ursula Bellugi, and Roger Brown, "Control of Grammar in Imitation, Comprehension, and Production," *Journal of Verbal Learning and Verbal Behavior*, 22, (1963).

reveal regularities in the order of appearance of structures across children. We propose to investigate the development of negative and interrogative structures in the speech of three children in order to examine some of these aspects of language development.

THE LANGUAGE ACQUISITION PROJECT

We have as data for this research a developmental study of three children whom we have called Adam, Eve, and Sarah in previous reports with Roger Brown and his associates. Tape recordings of mother-child interchanges were made regularly in the children's homes. Each child was followed by a different investigator. The families were totally unacquainted and independent of one another, and each child heard a different set of sentences as "input." The children were begining to string words together in structured utterances when we began the study. One child was 18 months old, another 26 months, and the third was 27 months old; however, all three were at approximately the same stage of language development.

For each child, then, there are two to four sessions of the speech of the mother and child per month as data. These sessions were tape recorded and later transcribed together with a written record made at the time of the recording which includes some aspects of the situation which relate to the meaning of the interchange. In order to describe stages in development we picked two end points in terms of mean utterance length. The first period is from the first month of study for each child—i.e. the mean utterance length is about 1.75 morphemes; the last is from the month in which the mean utterance lengths approach 3.5 morphemes for each of the three children; and the second period is between the two (see Figure 1).

Each period represents several thousand child utterances. From the total speech we isolated the negative statements and the questions for analysis, and have suggested outlines for a study of the development of these systems in the children's speech. We have used the children's utterances and evidence about the childen's understanding of these constructions in the language of others, in attempting to consider the children's developing grammatical capacities.

I

NEGATION IN ENGLISH

To begin, let us touch on some of the linguistic facts about the terminal state toward which the children are progressing, that is, the syntax of English negatives and interrogatives. We shall consider *Neg* as a formant which combines with parts of the sentence to constitute negation in the sentence. Among the realizations of *Neg* are the negative particle *not* and its contracted form *n't* (e.g. *It isn't true*), and a small set of negative words including the negative pronouns *nobody* and *nothing* (*Nobody came*), the negative determiner *no* (e.g. *No students passed*), the negative adverbs *never* and *nowhere*. Although there are many complexities in the total picture of negation in adult English that do not occur at all in the early pe-

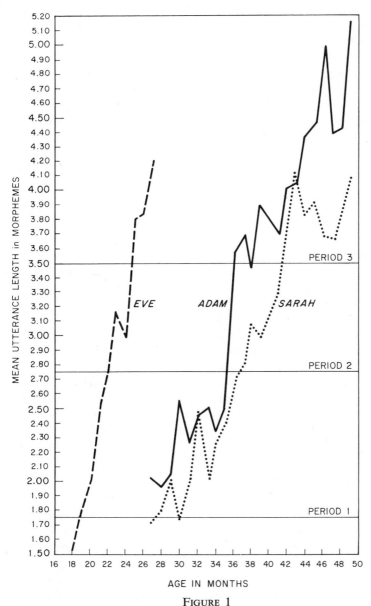

FIGURE 1

riods, the basic facts about negation in simple sentences are all relevant—in particular the form and position of the negative formant.

Negation and auxiliary verbs.   The negative particle *not* appears most simply in conjunction with the auxiliary verbs (*Aux*) in English and is generally contracted with them in speech. Consider first the modal auxiliaries (*M*) (*will, can, may, must, could, would, shall, should*, etc.) and notice that the negative particle is located after the first auxiliary verb of the sentence if there is one. Compare these sets of affirmative and negative sentences:

The man will finish today.	*The man won't finish today.*
The baby can sit up.	*The baby can't sit up.*
He will have been doing it.	*He won't have been doing it.*

In sentences in which *be* comes first in the verb phrase (whether as progressive (*be–PrP*) or passive (*be–PP*) auxiliary) or as main verb, the negative particle follows *be*, as it does *have* when the latter is auxiliary for the perfect (*have–PP*) and occurs first in the verb phrase and also, restrictedly, when *have* is the main verb:

They are coming here.	*They aren't coming here.*
Her face is red.	*Her face isn't red.*
I have done it.	*I haven't done it.*
I have time for that.	*I haven't any time for that.*

In each case, the contraction of the negative element with the auxiliary is optional. One can say either *They cannot go* or *They can't go*, although the latter seems more frequent in informal speech.

The negative element is not attached to other main verbs, nor does it stand in place of an auxiliary; thus we do not say **I wantn't it* or **I not want it*, but rather *I don't want it.*[2] The auxiliary verb *do* occurs in negative sentences with the particle *not* where the affirmative version of a sentence does not have an auxiliary verb, and not only carries the negative particle but also the tense marker (*T*). *He made it* is the affirmative sentence corresponding to *He didn't make it*. Thus auxiliary *do* is left unspoken in affirmative declaratives and imperatives—except under special conditions as in *Do be quiet* and *He did so leave*.

Negative imperative. We analyze negative imperatives as having auxiliary *do* followed by the negative formant, then optionally *you* (or an indefinite *anybody*), then the imperative modal auxiliary (*Imp*) (which in certain circumstances is realized as *will* or *can*), and finally the main verb:

> *Don't be late, will you!*
> *Don't you do that again.*
> *Don't anybody move.*

Negation and indefiniteness. Special cases aside, sentences of standard English permit only one negative formant per main verb. The presence of such a negative formant provides an appropriate condition for the occurrence of one or more indefinites (*Indef*) (*any, anybody, anything, anywhere, ever*) as subject, objects, or other complement to the main verb in the same environments in which indeterminates (*Indet*) (*some, somebody, something, somewhere, once*) occur in the corresponding affirmative declaratives and imperatives. Compare the following sets:

*You have **some** milk.*	*You haven't **any** milk.*
*Give me **some** more.*	*Don't give me **any** more.*
*I want **something**.*	*I don't want **anything**.*
***Somebody** left **something**.*	***Nobody** left **anything**.*

We shall describe this negative coloring as the conversion of indeterminates into indefinites in the context of a negative formant. However, no indefinites may precede the form representing the final realization of the negative formant, whether

---

[2]An asterisk preceding an utterance means that this is not a grammatical sentence of English.

this form is the negative particle *not*/*n't* or a negative word (e.g. *nobody*). Thus *Nobody left anything* is grammatical but not **Anybody left nothing*. Note particularly in this respect the special form of active-passive pairs:

Nobody saw anything new.
Nothing new was seen by anybody.

and not **Anything new was seen by nobody* which would be predicted by the identity, otherwise holding, between object of the active and subject of the passive, on the one hand, and subject of the active and agent of the passive, on the other. We capture this fact by assuming that the negative formant combines with an indefinite (or the first of several indefinites) which is then realized as a negative word (*any* as *no*, *anybody* as *nobody*, etc.), obligatorily if the indefinite precedes the main verb and all its auxiliaries; otherwise, optionally. Compare the single possiblility *Nobody saw him* with the alternates of its corresponding passive *He wasn't seen by anyone* and *He was seen by nobody*.

Negation not included in this study.   The sections described above cover the problems which arise in relation to negatives in the children's speech as far as we have considered it in this study. Symptomatic of sentence negation in adult English is the possible occurrence of an *either*-clause (*I didn't like it and he didn't either*); the negative appositive tag (*I don't like dogs, not even little ones*); and the question tag without *not* (*He's not going is he?*). None of those occur in the children's speech in these early stages. Affixal negation does not occur either (*unfortunately, impossible, unmade*), nor do inherently negative words like *doubt, reluctant*.

This discussion comprises part of what we mean by the negative system and the auxiliary system in adult English; that is, the occurrences and nonoccurrences involving those parts of the grammar. We will try to capture the nature of these systems by a set of rules something like those on the following pages, although undoubtedly as more is learned about grammatical systems in general and about English in particular, the form of these rules will be different. We feel that in their present state they do at least capture the spirit of this part of the grammar in a way that is compatible with other aspects of the grammar of English. One can think of the rules as giving some verifiable substance to our claim that these occurrences and nonoccurrences fit together in some systematic way.

RULES FOR NEGATION IN ADULT ENGLISH

The verb phrase with its auxiliaries has at one level in its derivation the following possible forms:

$$[T-do]_{Aux_1} (Neg) \left[\begin{Bmatrix} Imp \\ M \end{Bmatrix} (have-PP)(be-PrP)(be-PP) \right]_{Aux_2} \left[\begin{Bmatrix} V \\ be \\ have \end{Bmatrix} (NP)... \right]_{VP}$$

or after contraction of *not* to *n't*:

$$[T-do\ (Neg)]_{Aux_1}]$$
etc.

This represents the underlying structure after certain transformations (the details of which are not important in this study) have already operated; for example, the positioning of the negative formant, the occurrence of the passive auxiliary.

Transformations:

I. Replacement of *do*:

$$T - do - (Neg) - \begin{Bmatrix} M \\ have \\ be \end{Bmatrix} \Rightarrow T - \begin{Bmatrix} M \\ have \\ be \end{Bmatrix} - (Neg) - \emptyset$$

II. Negative Coloring:
1. $X^1 - Indet - X^2 - Neg - X^3 \Rightarrow X^1 - Indef - X^2 - Neg - X^3$
2. $X^1 - Neg - X^2 - Indet - X^3 \Rightarrow X^1 - Neg - X^2 - Indef - X^3$
(if *Neg* is treated as occurring initially in the underlying string, then a simpler formulation is possible.)

III. Formation of Negative Words
1. Obligatory
$X^1 - Indef - X^2 - Neg - X^3 \Rightarrow X^1 - Neg + Indef - X^2 - \emptyset - X^3$
2. Optional
$X^1 - Neg - X^2 - Indef - X^3 \Rightarrow X^1 - \emptyset - X^2 - Neg + Indef - X^3$

IV. *Do* Deletion:
$T - do - V \Rightarrow T - \emptyset - V$
or, expanded to include imperatives as approximately:

$$T - do - (Imp) \begin{Bmatrix} V \\ be \\ have \end{Bmatrix} \Rightarrow T - \emptyset - (Imp) \begin{Bmatrix} V \\ be \\ have \end{Bmatrix}$$

NEGATION IN CHILDREN'S SPEECH

What it is that the child learns in becoming a mature speaker of the language is, of course, the whole system which we have tried to capture by the rules above, and certainly not those particular tentative rules. It should be understood that when we write rules for the child grammar it is just a rough attempt to give substance to our feeling about, and general observations demonstrating, the regularity in the syntax of children's speech.

We have intentionally allowed ourselves much freedom in the formulation of these rules. Even within this freedom we feel that at the very earliest stages perhaps we fitted the language unjustifiably to what we assume to be the underlying structure of adult language. These rules reflect but certainly do not describe completely the utterances produced by the child. Whenever possible we took into consideration comprehension of utterances; but comprehension, like speech, only reflects grammatical capacity. Our aim in both cases is to find basic regularities.

One of the ultimate objectives in describing such regularities is to discover—given the child's own linguistic abilities as they have developed at some particular stage and given the utterances that he hears—what system or possible systems the child will ascribe to the language. We are interested in the basis for particular constructions; notably those that characterize the language of all three children.

Not very much is known about how people understand a particular sentence or what goes into producing one; but something is known about the systematicity of adult language. It has seemed to us that the language of children has its own systematicity, and that the sentences of children are not just an imperfect copy of those of an adult.

Are there hazards in considering the grammar of a child's language from the point of view of his speech? Of course there are many. One possibility is that the limitations on what is produced have nothing at all to do with the grammar but have to do with factors of memory, immediate requirements of explicitness, and the like. However, if this were the case, one would not expect the order of appearance of certain structures, and in particular certain systematic "mistakes," to be regular across children. We want to emphasize here that we are not dealing with the expression of semantic concepts on the part of the child, or of basic grammatical notions like subject function and transitivity; rather we are concerned with the way he handles lower-level syntactic phenomena like position, permutability, and the like.

Period 1.   The sentences we want to describe from Period 1 are taken from the protocols of all three children:

> *More . . . no.*
> *No singing song.*
> *No the sun shining.*
> *No money.*
> *No sit there.*
> *No play that.*
> *No fall!*
> *No heavy.*
> *No want stand head.*
> *No Mom sharpen it.*
> *No Fraser drink all tea.*

Unless otherwise noted, the sentences included in this study represent large numbers of like utterances in the children's speech, and are not to be considered isolated examples but rather reflections of recurrent structures occurring in the children's spontaneous speech. Notice that there are no negatives within the utterances, nor are there auxiliary verbs. The element which signals negation is *no* or *not*, and this element either precedes or follows the rest of the utterance.

Let us refer to the elements *Mom sharpen it, more, the sun shining,* in the above sentences as the *Nucleus.* Notice incidentally that there seems to be limited structure to the nucleus. The sentences consist largely of nouns and verbs without indication of tense or number. Inflections, prepositions, articles, adjectives, adverbs, and auxiliary verbs rarely occur.

The negation system at Period 1 can be considered as follows:

(1) $\left[\left\{ {no \atop not} \right\} - Nucleus \right]$ or $[Nucleus - no]$

At this stage, there is no clear evidence that the child even understands the negative embedded in the auxiliary of adult speech, without at least some reinforcement. During this early period, the mothers often reinforce their negative statements as in *No, you can't have that*, to insure the children's comprehension of the negative impact of the sentence. What is interesting in the speech of the child at this stage is that he employs extremely limited means for negative sentences in his own speech, and the same system is repeated in all three subjects. In subsequent periods there may indeed be an initial sentence adverb *no*, but this initial element is not a sufficient or even necessary part of sentence negation.

The rule for negation that we have given serves many negative functions in the child's speech at Period 1.

Adult: *Get in your high chair with your bib, and I'll give you your cheese.*
Child: *No bibby.*
Adult: *Oh, you don't want your bibby?*

Adult: *Well, is the sun shining?*
Child: *No the sun shining.*
Adult: *Oh, the sun's not shining?*

(An adult leans over to talk to the child. Child looks up and puts up a hand in warning.)
Child: *No fall!*

Period 2.   Some of the sentences we want to describe, again from all three children, are as follows:

I can't catch you.
I can't see you.
We can't talk.
You can't dance.
I don't sit on Cromer coffee.
I don't want it.
I don't like him.
I don't know his name.
No . . . Rusty hat.
Book say no.
Touch the snow no.

Don't leave me.
Don't wait for me . . . come in.
Don't wake me up . . . again.

That not "O," that blue.
That no fish school.
That no Mommy.
There no squirrels.

He no bite you.
I no want envelope.
I no taste them.

A characteristic of child language is the residue of elements of previous systems, and the sentences produced might well be described as a coexistence of the rules at Period 1, and a new system. Let us begin with a basic structure something like

(2)   *S → NP – (Neg) – VP*

where the formant *Neg* has as possible lexical representatives *can't, don't, not,* and occasionally *no.*

The auxiliary verbs can be thought of as occurring in the speech of the children only when accompanied by a *Neg*, since it is a fact that the auxiliary verbs do not occur in questions or declarative utterances at this stage. They occur only in negative sentences, and in these limited forms. This first rule can be related to the shape of sentences by the following rules:

(3) $Neg \rightarrow \begin{Bmatrix} no \\ not \\ V^{neg} \end{Bmatrix}$

(4) $V^{neg} \rightarrow \begin{Bmatrix} can't \\ don't \end{Bmatrix}$

where the particular selection of the negative is determined by the Main Verb with *don't* and *can't* restricted to occurrence before instances of nonprogressive main verbs.

Two auxiliary verbs appear in the negative form, *don't* and *can't*. These are considered as lexical representations of V^{neg} since there are no occurrences of *I can do it, Can I have it?, He shouldn't have it, They aren't going*, etc., but only instances of the sort described above. The negative element is also found within the sentence, but not connected to an auxiliary verb, as in *He no bite you*.

There are a number of sentences with *no* or *not* followed by a predicate. There is a limited class of subjects in this set. The negative imperative has appeared in the speech of all three children, in the form *Don't leave me*. In the previous period the imperative form was presumably *No fall*. There is at this period an affirmative imperative as well, as in *Come here* and *Do it*. There are hardly any sentences with indefinite determiners or pronouns, but there are by now personal and impersonal pronouns, possessive pronouns, articles, and adjectives.

It is clear that the child understands the negative embedded in the auxiliary of the sentence by this period. For example:

Mother: *Oh, we don't have any bread.*
Child: *We have buy some.*

Mother: *He doesn't have a ball.*
Child: *Why not he have ball?*

There is also evidence that the child uses negatives to contradict a previous proposition either expressed or implied, as in

Mother: *Did you play in the snow?*
Child: *No, play sunshine.*

Mother: *You told me to sit on it.*
Child: *No, you sit **there**.*

Period 3.   A sample of the sentences to be described, again from all three children:

Paul can't have one.
I can't see it.
This can't stick.
We can't make another broom.

I didn't did it.
Because I don't want somebody to wake me up.

I don't want cover on it.
I don't . . . have some . . . too much.
You don't want some supper.
You didn't caught me.
You didn't eat supper with us.
I didn't see something.
Paul didn't laugh.
I didn't caught it.

I gave him some so he won't cry.
'Cause he won't talk.
Donna won't let go.

No, I don't have a book.
No, it isn't.
That was not me.
I am not a doctor.

This not ice cream.
This no good.
They not hot.
Paul not tired.
It's not cold.

I not crying.
That not turning.
He not taking the walls down.

Don't put the two wings on.
Don't kick my box.
Don't touch the fish.

I not hurt him.
I not see you anymore.
Ask me if I not made mistake.

In the speech of the children, the modal auxiliaries *do* and *be* now appear in declarative sentences and questions, as well as in negative sentences; so we can now begin with a basic structure like

(5) $S \rightarrow NP - Aux - VP$

and suggest some such rules as follow:

(6) $Aux \rightarrow T - V^{aux} - (Neg)$

(7) $V^{aux} \rightarrow \begin{Bmatrix} do \\ can \\ be \\ will \end{Bmatrix}$

where *be* is restricted to predicate and progressive and is optional, *can* and *do* are restricted to nonprogressive main verbs.

Transformations:

  I. Optional *be* Deletion:
     $NP - be \rightarrow NP - \emptyset$

 II. *Do* Deletion:
     $do - V \rightarrow V$

In the speech of the children at this period the negative auxiliary verbs are now no longer limited to *don't* and *can't*, and the auxiliary verbs now appear in declarative sentences and questions, so that the auxiliary verbs can be considered as separate from the negative element of the sentence.

Indeterminates now start appearing in the children's speech, in affirmative utterances as *I want some supper* or *I see something*. The children's negative sentences have the form *I don't want some supper* and *I didn't see something*. The negative versions are clearly not imitations of adult sentences, and indicate that the complex relationship of negative and indefinite has not yet been established. Examples of indefinite coloring are rare, and do not appear with any regularity until subsequent stages.

RULES FOR NEGATION IN CHILDREN'S SPEECH

Period 1:

(1) $\left[\left\{ {no \atop not} \right\} - Nucleus \right]_S$ or $[Nucleus - no]_S$

Period 2:

(2) $S \rightarrow NP - (Neg) - VP$

(3) $Neg \rightarrow \left\{ {no \atop not \atop V^{neg}} \right\}$

(4) $V^{neg} \rightarrow \left\{ {can't \atop don't} \right\}$

where the particular selection of the negative is determined by the main verb with *don't* and *can't* restricted to occurrence before instances of nonprogressive main verbs.

Period 3:

(5) $S \rightarrow NP - Aux - VP$

(6) $Aux \rightarrow T - V^{aux} - (Neg)$

(7) $V^{aux} \rightarrow \left\{ {do \atop can \atop be \atop will} \right\}$

where *be* is restricted to predicate and progressive, *can* and *do* to nonprogressive main verbs.

Transformations:

I. Optional *be* Deletion
$NP - be \Rightarrow NP - \emptyset$

II. *Do* Deletion
$do - V \Rightarrow V$

II

INTERROGATIVES IN ENGLISH

For questions in adult English, we represent the interrogative nature of the sentence by the formant Q, with which may be associated (*a*) interrogative words (represented here by *Wh* + *Indet* in various functions, ultimately realized as *what*, *who, which, where, how, why*); or (*b*) the sentence as whole in the form of a *yes/no* question represented here by *Wh* preceding the major parts of the sentence, i.e. *Q–Wh–NP–Aux–VP*. In direct *yes/no* questions, *Wh* has no lexical realization, whereas in the corresponding indirect questions it is realized as *whether*. Compare *Will John leave?* with *They wonder **whether** John will leave*. In adult English, either the whole sentence may be questioned (a *yes/no* question) or one or more parts may be questioned (an interrogative word question).

If *Q* and either an interrogative word (*Wh* + *Indet*) or the *Wh* of *yes/no* questions precede the *entire* subject noun phrase of the sentence, then that noun phrase and the first auxiliary verb are inverted. If the interrogative word is part of the subject, then there is no inversion. Thus *What will that person make?* and *Will that person make something?* but no inversion in *Which person will make something?* Auxiliary *do* is unspoken, unless some element (e.g. the subject because of inversion) intervenes between *do* and the main verb. (Recall that in negation, the negative particle also had the effect of preserving the otherwise unspoken auxiliary *do*.)

RULES FOR QUESTIONS IN ADULT ENGLISH

$S \rightarrow Q - Wh - NP - Aux - VP$

$VP \rightarrow$ (as on [*MSE* bottom p. 453])

$NP \rightarrow \begin{Bmatrix} \cdots \\ Wh + Indet \text{ (provided that } Q \text{, but not } Q - Wh \text{, introduces } S) \end{Bmatrix}$

Transformations:

I.   Replacement of *do*:

$$T - do - (Neg) - \begin{Bmatrix} M \\ have \\ be \end{Bmatrix} \Rightarrow T - \begin{Bmatrix} M \\ have \\ be \end{Bmatrix} - (Neg) - \emptyset$$

II. Interrogative Preposing (optional):

$Q - X^1 - Wh + Indet - X^2 \Rightarrow Q - Wh + Indet - X^1 - X^2$

III. Interrogative Inversion:

$Q - Wh (+ Indet) - NP - Aux_1 - X \Rightarrow Q - Wh (+ Indet) - Aux_1 - NP - X$

IV. *Do* Deletion:

$T - do - V \Rightarrow T - \emptyset - V$

QUESTIONS IN CHILDREN'S SPEECH

Period 1.   The questions to consider, from all three childen, are

> *Fraser water?*
> *Mommy eggnog?*
> *See hole?*
> *I ride train?*
> *Have some?*
> *Sit chair?*
> *No ear?*
> *Ball go?*

Who that?
Why?
What(s) that?
What doing?
What cowboy doing?

Where Ann pencil?
Where Mama boot?
Where kitty?
Where milk go?
Where horse go?

Again, one can consider the elements *Fraser water, Mommy eggnog, Ann pencil, milk go*, in the above questions as the nucleus. As with the negative, in Period 1 there is very limited structure to the nucleus, which consists primarily of nouns and verbs without indication of tense and number.

The questions without an interrogative word can be thought of as $Q^{yes/no}-$ *nucleus*, where the *yes/no* marker is expressed as rising intonation. There are no other identifying characteristics of *yes/no* questions in adult English, since there are no auxiliaries, and there is no form of subject-verb inversion. From the contexts of mother-child interchange, it seems that these rising intonation sentences are frequently responded to by the adult as if they were *yes/no* questions. The formulation suggested is

(8) $S \rightarrow Q^{yes/no} - Nucleus$

The *Wh*-questions can be described as a list which includes only a few routines that vary little across the three children. The most common questions are some version of *What's that?* and *Where NP (go)?* and *What NP doing?* It is not at all clear that the *What* in *What cowboy doing?* has any relationship to a grammatical object of the verb *do* (that is, that it is a special case of *Q*-nucleus where the particular interrogative occurs as the object of *do*). What might be said, with reservation, is that, indeed, there is a relationship in the child's speech between sentences like *go NP* and *where NP go* but that the special interrogative form is bound to the particular word *go* and does not at all have the generality of the adult structure. Paraphrases of the above questions for the child might be *I want to know the name of that thing; I want to know what you call that action;* and *I want to know the location of that (previously present) object.* One might tentatively suggest a formulation as follows:

(9) $S \rightarrow Q^{what} - NP - (doing)$
(10) $S \rightarrow Q^{where} - NP - (go)$

Let us take as an example the interrogative word questions in which the object of a verb is the missing constituent and has been replaced by a preposed *what*. If one looks at the set of these questions, which the mother asks the child in the course of the samples of speech, one finds that at Period 1 the child generally does not respond or responds inappropriately, as in

Mother: *What, did you hit?*
Child: *Hit.*

Mother: *What did you do?*
Child: *Head.*

At this period, then, the children are producing questions that only superficially resemble those questions in which the object of a verb has been questioned and preposed, and they do not understand this construction when they hear it.

Period 2. Some of the questions to consider are

See my doggie?
That black too?
Mom pinch finger?
You want eat?
I have it?

Where my mitten?
Where baby Sarah rattle?
Where me sleep?

What book name?
What me think?
What the dollie have?
What soldier marching?

Why you smiling?
Why you waking me up?

Why not he eat?
Why not me sleeping?
Why not . . . me can't dance?
Why not me drink it?
You can't fix it?
This can't write a flower?

There is some development in the superficial structure of the sentences since Period 1. Notably, pronouns have developed, articles and modifiers are more often present, some inflections (present progressive and plurals) occur, and the verb phrase may include a prepositional phrase or preverb. There are no modal auxiliaries in affirmative sentences, and only two negative modal forms (*don't* and *can't*). There are few indeterminates or indefinites.

There seems to be a gradual development of rules and not necessarily the wholesale replacement of one total system by another. Constituent questioning is developing. Although the interrogative word *what* appears in sentences which have a missing object, there are nonetheless occurrences of that interrogative without those conditions. It is perhaps premature to associate this word in each case with a specific deleted constituent of the sentence. But certainly there is already some association of what will be referred to as zero interrogative constituent and the interrogative introducers *what, where,* and *why.* That is, in Period 2 Q^{what} (perhaps also Q^{where}) has begun in its function of requesting the information that would be supplied by a specific syntactic constituent of the sentence (the object of a verb) and the questioned constituent is left blank. We suggest that the child's question *What the dollie have?* may well have some such structure as

$$Q^{what} - [the\ dollie]_{NP} \; [\; [have]_V \; [\phi]_{NP}]_{VP}$$

and that already there is a general relationship between introductory *what* and the occurrence, without an expressed object noun phrase, of any verb like *have*. In Period 2, there is still no inversion of subject and verb in *yes/no* questions.

By this period there are appropriate answers to most questions. The responses reflect that the child understands that the object of a verb or preposition is being questioned:

> Mother: *What d'you need?*
> Child: *Need some chocolate.*

> Mother: *Who are you peeking at?*
> Child: *Peeking at Ursula.*

> Mother: *What d'you hear?*
> Child: *Hear a duck.*

We suggest for Period 2:

$$(11) \quad S \rightarrow \begin{Bmatrix} Q^{yes/no} \\ Q^{what} \\ Q^{where} \\ Q^{why} \end{Bmatrix} Nucleus$$

$$(12) \quad Nucleus \rightarrow NP - V - (NP)$$

$$(13) \quad NP \rightarrow \begin{Bmatrix} \ldots \\ \emptyset \text{ if the sentence is introduced by } Q^{what} \end{Bmatrix}$$

Period 3. The questions to consider are

> *Does the kitty stand up?*
> *Does lions walk?*
> *Is Mommy talking to Robin's grandmother?*
> *Did I saw that in my book?*
> *Oh, did I caught it?*
> *Are you going to make it with me?*
> *Will you help me?*
> *Can I have a piece of paper?*
> *Where small trailer he should pull?*
> *Where the other Joe will drive?*
> *Where I should put it when I make it up?*
> *Where's his other eye?*
> *Where my spoon goed?*
> *What I did yesterday?*
> *What he can ride in?*
> *What you had?*
> *What did you doed?*
> *Sue, what you have in you mouth?*
> *Why the Christmas tree going?*
> *Why he don't know how to pretend?*
> *Why kitty can't stand up?*
> *Why Paul caught it?*
> *Which way they should go?*
> *How he can be a doctor?*
> *How they can't talk?*

How that opened?
Can't it be a bigger truck?
Can't you work this thing?

Between the previous period and this one many parts of the children's grammar have undergone developments. There is now a class of verbal forms that inverts with the subject in certain interrogatives (*yes/no* questions) and may take the negative particle with it. One particular verb, *do*, occurs only in its function as a helping-verb in inverted questions and negatives, seldom in interrogative word questions. At this point, the system that has been developed bears striking similarities to the adult pattern. Notice, however, that the auxiliary verbs are not inverted with the subject noun phrase in interrogative word questions. There are other aspects that set the child's system apart from the adult language; namely, the child does not produce the full set of sequences of the adult auxiliary system. In the adult system, the possible sequences are $(M)(have–PP)(be–PrP)$; that is, any combination of these, but always in that order, where tense appears always on the first, or if none of these are present, then with the main verb. The children, at this stage, do not produce any combinations of auxiliaries.

Considerable development is found in the children's grammar by this period. In addition to the noun and verb inflections appearing in the previous period, one finds possessive markers, third person singular present indicative, and the regular past indicator. The sentences are no longer limited to simple English sentences. There is considerable development in complexity, and we find relative clauses and other clauses for the first time: *You have two things that turn around; I told you I know how to put the train together; I gon' get my chopper for chopping down cows and trees; Let's go upstairs and take it from him because it's mine.*

Let us begin with the same basic structure as for negatives at Period 3:

(14) $S \rightarrow (Q(Wh)) - NP - Aux - VP$

(15) $Aux \rightarrow T - V^{aux} - (Neg)$

(16) $V^{aux} \rightarrow \begin{Bmatrix} can \\ do \\ will \\ be \end{Bmatrix}$

(17) $NP \rightarrow \begin{Bmatrix} Wh + Indet \\ \ldots \end{Bmatrix}$

Transformations:

  I.   Interrogative Word Preposing:
      $Q - X^1 - Wh + Indet - X^2 \Rightarrow Q - Wh + Indet - X^1 - X^2$

  II. Interrogative Inversion (characterizing only *yes/no* questions):
      $Q - Wh - NP - Aux - X \Rightarrow Q - Wh - Aux - NP - X$

  III. *Do* Deletion:
      $do - V \Rightarrow V$

In *yes/no* questions, we have noted that the children invert the auxiliary component with the subject noun phrase appropriately. Affirmative sentences generally have an auxiliary. In interrogative word questions, however, the auxiliary is generally not inverted. The auxiliary form of *be* is optional at this stage, and the auxiliary *do* is not present in the final shape of most of the interrogative word questions.

RULES FOR QUESTIONS IN CHILDREN'S SPEECH

Period 1:

  (8) $S \rightarrow Q^{yes/no} - Nucleus$

  (9) $S \rightarrow Q^{what} - NP - (doing)$

 (10) $S \rightarrow Q^{where} - NP - (go)$

Period 2:

 (11) $S \rightarrow \begin{Bmatrix} Q^{yes/no} \\ Q^{what} \\ Q^{where} \\ Q^{why} \end{Bmatrix} Nucleus$

 (12) $Nucleus \rightarrow NP - V - (NP)$

 (13) $NP \rightarrow \begin{Bmatrix} \cdots \\ \emptyset \text{ if the sentence is introduced by } Q^{what} \end{Bmatrix}$

Period 3:

 (14) $S \rightarrow (Q\ (Wh)) - NP - Aux - VP$

     For further details see the description of *Period* 3 on [*MSE* p. 464].
Transformations (as on [*MSE* p. 464]):

  I. Interrogative Word Preposing

 II. Interrogative Inversion (characterizing only *yes/no* questions)

III. *Do* Deletion

SUMMARY

    The speech of the three children consists primarily of a small set of words strung together at the earliest period we have investigated in two and three word sentences. Among the early systematic aspects of child speech in its step-by-step approximation to the adult system are the following: in the early period the negatives and an ever-growing class of interrogative introducers occur first in the sentence, as sentence modifiers in the basic framework. The association of the interrogative word with other constituents of the sentence is very limited at first, restricted at the beginning to a complement of one or two particular verbs (e.g. *go* in *where NP go*). Only later does the association apply to whole categories, such that the preposing of *Wh* + prefixed elements can be spoken of with any generality. The auxiliary verb emerges first (anticipated perhaps by the optional occcurrence of the copula *be*) always associated with negatives (as *can't, don't*). Not until afterwards do the modal auxiliary verbs and *do* appear inverted with the subject, and then only in the *yes/no* questions (i.e. the question not introduced by an interrogative word). At the same time, the modal auxiliary verbs, but not *do*, finally emerge independent of interrogatives and negatives. Not until the next period does the inversion of auxiliary verbs extend to questions introduced by an interrogative word. Negation is embedded in the auxiliary verbs by this third period, but the complex relation of negative and indefinite is not established yet. We have attempted to capture the regularities which we found in the speech of the three childen in the rules which we have suggested for negatives and interrogatives.

SYMBOLS

S	Sentence	*T*	Tense marker
Neg	Negative formant	*Wh*	Interrogative word
Q	Interrogative formant	*have – PP*	Perfect
X	Variable	*be – PrP*	Progressive
Det	Determiner	*be – PP*	Passive
Aux	Auxiliary verb	*M*	Modal auxiliary verbs
Imp	Imperative modal auxiliary	$+$	Incorporated with
		( )	Symbol enclosed is optional
MV	Main verb	[ ]$_{subscript}$	Node dominating enclosed constituent
NP	Noun phrase		
VP	Verb phrase	{ }	Choose one of list
Indet	Indeterminate	$\emptyset$	Null
Indef	Indefinite		

29

On the Role of Linguistics in the Teaching of English

PETER S. ROSENBAUM

The growing enthusiasm on the part of many teachers of English for giving careful attention to linguistic matters is noteworthy for several reasons. It speaks well for the teacher since it suggests the birth of a scholarly concern for developments in the field of language study and a professional attitude toward linguistic insights which have potential educational value. Furthermore, this enthusiasm vindicates the many linguists who have held that linguistic science could be of importance in the teaching of English. But discussions of the relevance of linguistics to the teaching of English have been in progress for a considerable time now, and even the most cursory glance at the literature indicates a disappointing lack of progress. Few familiar with this debate and its meager results will disagree that one of the problems has been a continuing inability to answer satisfactorily the obviously central question, namely, "which linguistic description?"

The last thirty years has seen the development of a variety of descriptions of the structure of English. Among the more frequently mentioned proposals are the conceptions of Fries; the immediate constituent approach of Bloch, Wells, and

Reprinted from the *Harvard Educational Review*, 35.332–348 (1965), by permission of Peter S. Rosenbaum and the *Harvard Educational Review*.

This work was written while the author was a member of the Research Laboratory of Electronics at M.I.T. and was supported in part by the Joint Services Electronics Program under Contract DA 36–039–AMC-03200 (E); in part by the National Science Foundation (Grant GP-2495), the National Institutes of Health (Grant MH–04737–05), the National Aeronautics and Space Administration (Grant NsG-496), and the U.S. Air Force (ESD Contract AF 19 (628)–2487). The author wishes to express his gratitude to Professors Noam Chomsky and Paul Postal of M.I.T. and to Professor Israel Scheffler of Harvard University who read earlier versions of this article and provided much helpful criticism.

Hockett; the phonological syntax of Trager and Smith, and Hill; Harris' morpheme to utterance procedures; and the two distinct transformational notions of Harris on the one hand and Chomsky on the other. The question of which, if any, of these linguistic descriptions might justifiably be employed in the classroom is, of course, many-sided. But one of the more frequently alluded to criteria is entirely linguistic in nature and is bound up in a general concern for the validity or correctness of linguistic descriptions.[1] The historical emphasis on validity or correctness seems entirely appropriate even though it does no homage to the popular preoccupation with behavioral goals and outcomes as the basis for the evaluation of curricula. The issue is not whether the information contained in a given linguistic description can be taught and learned successfully, for surely there is no description which is so difficult that it cannot be taught and learned in some form,[2] but precisely one of the status of the information itself. One might hope to diminish the centrality of the content, thereby making it unnecessary, perhaps, to choose among the various linguistic descriptions, by demonstrating the utility of one or the other description in the teaching of literate skills, e.g. composition. But this hope should not be taken too seriously since the most recent account of empirical research in this area indicates the inconclusiveness of all such demonstrations:

> Reviews of educational research, however, have continually emphasized that instruction in grammar has little effect upon the written language skills of pupils. The interpretation and curricular applications of this general conclusion have ranged from the view that grammar and usage should not be taught in isolation from written composition to the position that formal grammar merits little or no place in the language arts curriculum.[3]

Thus, the validity of proposed linguistic descriptions remains the most pertinent consideration.

The major approaches to syntactic description can be collapsed under two rubrics. The first, which is known popularly as the *structural-descriptive* approach to linguistic analysis includes the work of Fries, Bloch, Wells, Hockett, Trager,

---

[1]See for instance, Sumner Ives, "Linguistics in the Classroom," *College English*, 17.165–172; Donald J. Lloyd, "The Uses of Structure and the Structure of Usage," *The English Record*, 6.41–46, and "A Linguistic Approach to English Composition," *Language Learning*, 3.109–116; James Sledd, "Coordination (Faulty) and Subordination (Upside-Down)," *College Composition and Communication*, 7.181–187; Robert J. Geist, "Structural Grammar and the Sixth Grade," *American Speech*, 31. 5–12; Archibald A. Hill, "Prescriptivism and Linguistics in English Teaching," *College English*, 15.395–399; Robert C. Pooley, "New Approaches to Grammar," in J. A. Rycenga and J. Schwartz, eds., *Perspectives on Language* (New York, 1963); Henry Lee Smith, Jr., "The Teacher and the World of Language," *College English*, 20.172–178; Owen Thomas, "Generative Grammar: Toward Unification and Simplification," *The English Journal*, 51.94–99; and Charles C. Fries, "Advances in Linguistics," *College English*, 25.30–37. [All of these, except the article by Pooley, have been reprinted in *RAEL* 1958 or 1964.]

[2]This is a special case of J. S. Bruner's hypothesis that "any subject can be taught effectively in some intellectually honest form to any child at any stage of development" as proposed in his *The Process of Education* (Cambridge, 1961), p. 33.

[3]H. C. Meckel, "Research on Teaching Composition and Literature," in N.L. Gage, ed., *Handbook of Research on Teaching* (Chicago, 1963), p. 974.

Smith, Hill, and others.[4] The second, the *transformational* version of generative grammar, is represented, for example, by the work of Chomsky, Halle, Lees, Klima, Matthews, and Postal.[5] If the question of the validity of linguistic descriptions is to be spoken to in any serious way, it is necessary to consider two aspects of evaluation. The first pertains to the evaluation of a particular description within a given theoretical framework. For instance, which of two transformational descriptions of the relative clause structure in English is better? The second aspect of evaluation deals with the comparison of various forms of linguistic description. Is it possible, for example, to compare the structural approach to linguistic inquiry with the transformational approach in any meaningful way? In view of the well-documented interest in the validity of linguistic descriptions on the part of those involved in the educational implementation of these descriptions, it may be fruitful to examine the major approaches to linguistic inquiry in terms of evaluation in somewhat greater detail.

Underlying the structural view of language is a set of assumptions about the goals of behavioral studies and scientific inquiry which limit the range of relevant phenomena to a corpus of observed utterances. This limitation suggests a curious contradiction since, quite invariably, representatives of the structural tradition speak of language as a set of behavioral patterns common to members of a given community involving a set of verbal interchanges between two or more people.[6] There is no non-arbitrary upper bound on the number of acceptable utterances which could comprise the speech behavior of a given community. Thus the linguists of the structural school seem, at least implicitly, to be thinking of language as a potentially infinite set of utterances. But this position is completely contradicted by the properties of a structural linguistic description. All structural analysis is ultimately based upon observable data, i.e. data recorded by simple listening or by various instruments such as oscillographs, sound-spectrographs, and so on.[7] If this methodological requirement is taken literally, then the result of a structural analysis, the linguistic description of a language, is actually a description of only

---

[4]Charles C. Fries, *The Structure of English* (New York, 1952); Bernard Bloch, "Studies in Colloquial Japanese," in *RIL;* Rulon Wells, "Immediate Constituents," in *RIL;* Charles Hockett, "Two Models of Grammatical Description," in *RIL;* Zellig S. Harris, "From Morpheme to Utterance," in *RIL,* and *Methods in Structural Linguistics* (Chicago, 1951); W. Nelson Francis, *The Structure of American English* (New York, 1958); Archibald A. Hill, *Introduction to Linguistic Structures* (New York, 1958); and George L. Trager and Henry Lee Smith, Jr., *An Outline of English Structure* (Norman, Oklahoma, 1951).

[5]Noam Chomsky, *Syntactic Structures* (The Hague, 1957); Chomsky, "On the Notion 'Rule of Grammar,' " in *PAM [SL],* and *Aspects of the Theory of Syntax,* (Cambridge, 1965); Morris Halle, "On the Role of Simplicity in Linguistic Descriptions," in *PAM,* 89–94; Halle, "On the Bases of Phonology" and "Phonology in Generative Grammar," in *SL;* Robert B. Lees, *The Grammar of English Nominalizations, International Journal of American Linguistics,* 20.3 (July 1960), Part II, and "A Multiply Ambiguous Adjectival Construction in English," *Language,* 36.207–221 (1960); Jerrold J. Katz and Paul M. Postal, *An Integrated Theory of Linguistic Descriptions* (Cambridge, 1964); Edward S. Klima, "Negation in English," in *SL.*

[6]W. Nelson Francis, "Revolution in Grammar," *Quarterly Journal of Speech,* 40:299–312, especially Sec. 2 [*RAEL* 1964].

[7]Francis, *The Structure of American English,* pp. 15–16.

a finite corpus of events. There is clearly an equivocation on the term "language" here which leads to two equally damaging conclusions. If an arbitrary natural language is taken to consist of an infinite set of sentences, then the results of a structural investigation do not constitute a description of language at all, but of something else. On the other hand, should a language be construed as nothing more than the corpus stored in a set of tape recordings, then the task of saying anything of scientific interest about the psychological and linguistic properties of the endless repertoire of sentences which not only define the language of a speech community but which are the personal property of every normal member of this community belongs to a branch of science other than linguistics.

The extreme preoccupation with observable data in linguistic analysis probably stems from Leonard Bloomfield's particular version of scientific inquiry, a version which most structural linguists have accepted at face value. In Bloomfield's view, science dealt exclusively with accessible events and the task of scientists was the induction of general laws from these events.[8] Thus, the central object of investigation in a linguistic science as conceived by Bloomfield was necessarily actual speech. For Bloomfield, the only information of scientific interest was that provided by physical phonetics and the context in which phonetic data were observed.[9] This view is implicit in all structural work and one never finds a popularization of structural linguistics which does not give prominence to assertions about the centrality of speech.[10] For our purposes, the effects of Bloomfield's views on the goals of linguistic inquiry are more important than the causes. By restricting the domain of linguistic investigation to phonetic and contextual data. Bloomfield excluded a vast range of perhaps even more accessible data as linguistically and scientifically useless; this data being the extraordinarily rich body of knowledge which a human speaker has about his language. We will return to this neglected aspect of linguistic information later.

The goal of linguistic science, to determine inductively the laws governing the behavior of observable linguistic data, was unfortunately one step removed from the problem immediately confronting those linguists who were anxious to adopt the Bloomfieldian point of view. The induction of general laws from a body of data presupposes a prior classification of this data. For structural linguistic inquiry, this meant that a requirement for further research was the precise specification of the relevant facts. It was necessary to decide on the linguistic importance of the various aspects of the continuous flow of sound coming from the recording device or from the speaker directly. Thus, in a certain sense, the task before the structural linguist was "pre-scientific": to provide materials upon which a science of language could operate productively. Central to the search for the facts of language was also a concern for the general efficiency with which these facts could be stated.[11]

---

[8]Leonard Bloomfield, *Linguistic Aspects of Science* (Chicago, 1955).

[9]Bloomfield, op. cit., p. 21, and *Language* (New York, 1933), especially Chap. 2.

[10]For instance, George P. Faust, "Terms in Phonemics," *College Composition and Communication*, 5.30 (February 1954) [*RAEL* 1958 and 1964].

[11]For discussion see Charles Hockett, "A System of Descriptive Phonology," in *RIL*, p. 101, or Archibald A. Hill, *Introduction to Linguistic Structures*, especially Chap. 4, Sec. 1, on the classification of sounds.

The overall problem, therefore, consisted in providing a methodology which would yield the facts of language in terms of a consistent and optimally efficient classificational scheme.

The structural methodology for discovering the facts of language is now quite well known. In its most general formulation, the method involves a set of putative discovery procedures which are supposed to isolate automatically a set of linguistic units in a hierarchical arrangement and to present an inventory of the speech data which are found to represent these units. Quoting from what is probably the most widely known structural analysis of English,

> The presentation of the structure of a language should begin, in theory, with a complete statement of the pertinent linguistic data. This should be followed by an account of the observed phonetic behavior, and then should come the analysis of the phonetic behavior into the phonemic structure, completing the phonology. The next step is to present the recurring entities— composed of one or more phonemes—that constitute the morpheme list, and go on to their analysis into the morphemic structure. In that process the division into morphology and syntax is made. After the syntax, one may go on from the microlinguistic (linguistics proper—phonology and morphemics) to metalinguistic analyses.[12]

Structural linguists have been more successful in proposing and employing discovery procedures which fairly effectively produce an analysis and classification of sound sequences than they have in determining the measure or measures to be used in evaluating the adequacy of these classifications in terms of efficiency. An important issue is involved in the failure of the structural linguists to come to grips with the problem of evaluation. The question of which measure of efficiency will most appropriately evaluate alternative structural descriptions has no obvious answer. How do we know what the right measure is? Is efficiency to be defined in terms of the number of discrete symbols or entities in a description? Is it going to have anything to do with the type of symbols which the description utilizes? These questions cannot be answered without proposing a set of conditions which the measure of efficiency must meet. Suppose I am working for a grocer and he tells me to unpack a crate of oranges and to construct the most efficient display of oranges in the front window. Unless the grocer tells me the conditions that the optimally efficient arrangement must meet, my task is an impossible one. Similarly, unless a set of conditions on the measure of efficiency for linguistic descriptions is established, there is no reason to choose one measure of efficiency over another. Such conditions cannot be an aspect of the subject matter in a science of language, as conceived by Bloomfield, since they would constitute a level of abstraction which has no observable basis whatever. If, on the other hand, such conditions are taken to be theoretical constructs, laws governing the form that a linguistic description may take, then the whole business becomes circular since such laws can be inferred only from a classified set of data in the first place. Since there is no non-arbitrary measure of efficiency which can be employed in the evaluation of alternative struc-

---

[12]Trager and Smith, op. cit., p. 8.

tural descriptions of a set of observed data, it is impossible to compare and rank these descriptions.

Furthermore, the taxonomic framework provides no basis for choosing between structural and nonstructural descriptions. The fundamental problem here is that a structural linguistic description is a taxonomic classification. No such classification, whether it be of books in the library, fish in the sea, or sounds of speech, can be right or wrong, valid or invalid, true or false. Such a classification is inevitably nothing more than an arrangement of the data which makes no claims whatever about the nature of the data. A linguistic theory which is capable of evaluating the form of a linguistic description must presuppose an explicit statement of the facts which any adequate description must represent and characterize. Given such a statement it is not only possible to develop a theory which will decide on the adequacy of linguistic descriptions in terms of their ability to characterize the facts; it is absolutely necessary to develop such a theory. Without it, there is no possibility of determining the success of any type of linguistic description claiming to account for these facts.

The most readily accessible body of facts about language is the information which is available to any speaker concerning his native language. There are several aspects of a speaker's linguistic competence on which considerable consensus is found in the literature.[13] A speaker can understand sentences which he has never heard before. Similarly, he can produce new sentences on the appropriate occasion. Second, a speaker knows implicitly that certain sentences in his language are ambiguous while others are not. Still other sentences are synonymous. Third, he is capable of detecting differences in the relations which words have to one another in sentences even though these relations are not explicitly specified in the phonetic representations of sentences. Many other similar abilities could be cited.

Bloomfield and his followers have rejected such linguistic data with the assertion that introspective evidence involves a spurious mentalism which fails on the grounds of nonobjectivity.[14] On this view, one's intuitions about language exist only in the private domain, in one's mind, and are thus not fit materials for a science of language. Essentially, the argument is that the mind is inaccessible to scientific investigation because the attributes of the mind, such as linguistic intuition, are not subject to objective study. Intuitions are not physical events which can be monitored and recorded. Thus the study of linguistic data dealing with the speaker's knowledge of his language necessarily belongs to some field other than linguistic science. This view has been severely criticized in the recent linguistic and philosophical literature[15] and little new can be added to the discussion. If it is the case that any significant linguistic theory must provide evaluation criteria

---

[13]The various linguistic abilities possessed by native speakers of a language are discussed in much of the transformational literature. In the educational literature, see Lees, "Transformation Grammars and the Fries Framework," in *RAEL* 1964, pp. 137–146, and Paul M. Postal, "Underlying and Superficial Linguistic Structures," *Harvard Educational Review*, 34.246–266 [*MSE*].

[14]See, in particular, Bloomfield, *Linguistic Aspects of Science*, pp. 12–13, and Archibald A. Hill, "Linguistics Since Bloomfield," *Quarterly Journal of Speech*, 41.253–260.

[15]The most extensive remarks on this subject are found in Jerrold J. Katz, "Mentalism in Linguistics," *Language*, 40.124–137 [*RPL*].

for linguistic description, then the consistency of the introspective data brought forth in support of such a theory is clearly a major consideration. The consistency of introspective evidence is not, however, nonempirical, i.e. incapable of being verified. Suppose one asks, for instance, how to test the judgment that the implicit subject of the complement verb *leave* in the sentence "*The boy promised his mother to leave the party early* is the same as the explicit subject of the whole sentence, *the boy*, and that the implicit subject of the same verb in the sentence *The boy told his mother to leave the party early* is the same as the object of the verb *tell*, i.e. *his mother*. This is not only an empirical question, but one with an obvious answer. This supposedly nonobjective fact will be attested to by every normal native speaker of English who understands the question. Objectivity, therefore, is not a property which a theory of the speaker's linguistic knowledge necessarily lacks and it is probably pointless to devote further consideration to such objections.

Adopting the view that an adequate linguistic description must account for the speaker's linguistic capacities, we can think of a linguistic theory as being, at least in part, a set of constraints on the form of any description which can attain this end. The constraints specify, in other words, the way in which the goals of the linguistic inquiry can be attained. The linguistic theory acquires, therefore, the capacity to evaluate possible linguistic descriptions in terms of their ability to characterize the speaker's knowledge of his language. Such a theory is said to explain the speaker's knowledge because the form of the linguistic description which most adequately accounts for the facts is a logical consequence of the constraints comprising the linguistic theory.[16]

In this view of linguistic inquiry, the object of research is two-fold: first, to determine precisely the constraints, or laws if you will, which govern the form of the constructs employed in the linguistic descriptions which best characterize the varied instances of human linguistic ability; second, to determine the particular instances of the descriptive constructs within an arbitrary language. The latter constitutes the actual construction of a linguistic description. Recent work on the transformational version of generative linguistics represents the first modern attempt to develop a linguistic theory and a descriptive apparatus which have as a goal the explanation of the speaker's linguistic knowledge. The literature contains a substantial amount of material on both aspects of linguistic inquiry and no reiteration is called for here.[17] The virtue of a transformation approach to linguistic research from the standpoint of the issue of validity is that if a particular version of linguistic description fails to satisfy the constraints imposed by the linguistic theory, then it can be said with justification that the description is wrong. Similarly, if the constraints on the form of the linguistic description do not result in a set of descriptive constructs which satisfactorily account for the facts, then this version of the theory is wrong. Measures for determining the validity of a particular descrip-

---

[16]See Chomsky, "Three Models for the Description of Language," *I.R.E. Transactions on Information Theory*, Vol. IT–2, (1956) [*RMP*], and "Explanatory Models in Linguistics," in E. Nagel, P. Suppes, and A. Tarski, eds., *Logic, Methodology, and Philosophy of Science* (Stanford, 1962), pp. 528–550. An exceptionally lucid presentation of the more important issues relating to explanation in science is found in Israel Scheffler, *The Anatomy of Inquiry* (New York, 1963).

[17]See the transformational literature referred to earlier.

tion of a given language as well as a general form of linguistic description are consequently provided.

The discussion of evaluation procedures for contemporary versions of linguistic research provides one fruitful avenue for confronting the issue of the validity of linguistic descriptions. The basic result of this discussion is the finding that the structural approach to linguistic inquiry fails to provide a principled basis for choosing among particular linguistic descriptions and forms of linguistic description. (The fact that taxonomic linguistic descriptions can be evaluated in terms of internal consistency is irrelevant since any linguistic description can be judged in this way.) It would not seem unreasonable, therefore, to exclude structural linguistics from further consideration and to pass over to the deeper and ultimately more important question concerning the pedagogical implementation of a verifiable linguistic theory and description of the structure of English. It is natural to inquire, at this point, into the purely linguistic bases for a program designed to incorporate the valid results of linguistic research into the curriculum. Such an inquiry may prove of little value, however, since certain considerations deriving from what is already known about the nature of the constructs employed in a transformational description of language indicate that the constructs themselves do not and cannot automatically provide any new educational insights. Rather, the ultimate value of valid linguistic descriptions in the teaching of English seems to depend entirely on the ingenuity and imagination of linguists, teachers, and educators competent in both areas.

A transformational grammar characterizing linguistic competence is a finite specification of the infinite set of pairs of phonetic signals and semantic interpretations comprising the sentences in a natural language. This specification is abstract in the sense that it is not detectable on the basis of the physical data alone. It must be inferred from the knowledge which people have about sentences in their language. The specification is, in effect, an abstract representation of this knowledge offered in terms of hypothetical syntactic structures upon which semantic interpretations and phonological realizations are defined. The necessity of positing such abstract sentence structures and the form that these structures must have is a topic to which much attention has been devoted.[18] The formal apparatus employed in the explanation of the speaker's ability to deal with the infinite set of sentences in his language consists of a set of ordered rules which recursively enumerate the sentences of this language. The structures underlying sentences, often represented by tree diagrams, are not objects of substance having material existence in the real world; rather they merely constitute a record of the application of a particular set of rules.

The rules in a transformational grammar are quite different from the rules countenanced by prescriptive linguistic descriptions and from the instructions

---

[18]For discussion of the formal aspects of transformational grammars see Chomsky, "Three Models for the Description of Language" [*RMP*], also "On the Notion 'Rule of Grammar'" [*PAM; SL*], and "Formal Properties of Grammars," in *HMP;* Chomsky and George Miller, "Finitary Models of Language Users," and "Introduction to the Formal Analysis of Natural Language," in *HMP*.

for sentence building found in so many textbooks. The rules postulated in the syntactic component of a transformational grammar are either those which specify a set of abstract underlying structures, upon which a semantic interpretation for the sentence is based, or those which derive *superficial*, alternatively *surface*, structures, which receive a phonetic interpretation, as a function of the underlying structure.[19] These claims about the nature of the rules employed in an adequate description of syntax suggest that recent educational popularizations of transformational grammar have grossly misunderstood the results of transformational research. To quote from one textbook published very recently,

> This chapter is a study of *transformational* grammar. *Transform* means
> "to change;" thus, you will see how basic sentences are changed, or transformed,
> to produce other sentences that are interesting and varied.[20]

Ongoing work in transformational grammar shows that it is incorrect to think of two sentences as being related by a transformational rule or set of rules which somehow convert one sentence into another. Rather, when various considerations force the conclusion that two or more sentences are syntactically related, this relation is reflected in those aspects of underlying structure which both sentences share. Thus the burden of representing a common source for two or more sentences falls not on the transformational rules of the grammar which generate surface structures, but on the rules which generate underlying structures.[21]

The abstract constructs offered in a transformational description are designed solely for purposes of description and explanation. Neither the transformational theory nor the transformational description of the syntax of English contains any implicit pedagogical recommendation. From neither does it follow that a transformational description of English should be taught in the classroom. From neither does it follow that instruction in transformational grammar will improve performance in the literate skills. With respect to the latter assertion, consider an analogy from physical education, in particular the pedagogy of the forward pass. Any instance of the physical event identified as a forward pass has certain mechanical properties which are characterized by the Newtonian theory of mechanics. The descriptive apparatus of this theory, consisting of such constructs as mass, acceleration, velocity, time, distance, and so forth, is a consequence of the theoretical constraints imposed upon a description seeking to account for the mechanics of physical events. To teach a potential quarterback the mechanics of the forward pass is to teach him how this type of event works. It is not to teach him how to make it work. The Newtonian theory itself gives us no reason to believe that instruction in the mechanics of the forward pass will affect the quarterback's becoming a good passer one way or the other. Similarly, to study and practice the constructs of a transformational grammar may result in an understanding

---

[19]See Chomsky, *Aspects of the Theory of Syntax*, and Postal, "Underlying and Superficial Linguistic Structures" [*MSE*].

[20]Mellie John and Paulene M. Yates, *Building Better English*, 4th ed. (New York, 1965), p. 463.

[21]Several illustrations of common underlying structure for related sentences are given in Peter S. Rosenbaum, *The Grammar of English Predicate Complement Constructions*, [Cambridge, Mass.: M.I.T. Press, 1967], passim.

of how the student's language works, but not necessarily in an understanding of how to make it work.

But the mere fact that the answers to various educational problems do not spring forth full blown from the linguistic research on transformational grammars does not imply that the results of this research will fail to provide a new and valuable dimension in which to consider traditional problems in the teaching of English. This fact simply asserts that a linguistic description does not enumerate educational benefits. It remains not with the linguistic theory or description, but with the informed educator, whether he is a teacher, linguist, or specialist informed in both areas, to determine the applicability of valid linguistic results to the teaching of English. It may prove informative to devote the remaining pages to a brief illustration of some of the ways in which a transformational approach to language study can make significant contributions to the field of English teaching. The purpose of the following discussion is not to provide a complete manual of applications, but merely to indicate the wide range of educational situations in which the results of transformational research might be utilized. The three cases to be presented concern (*a*) the content of the English curriculum in general, (*b*) the evaluation of certain traditional criteria employed in the evaluation of composition, and (*c*) a possible explanation for the continuing lack of correlation between instruction in grammar and improved performance in the literate skills.

The desirability of including a description of the structure of English in the English curriculum, whether this description be traditional, structural, or transformational, is ultimately a matter of judgment; it is a matter of belief. But the decision is no easier to make for all that it precludes the frustrations often accompanying empirical evaluations. On the contrary, the resolution of this issue demands recourse to a set of principled reasons which provide support for the opinion that there is virtue in instruction in linguistic descriptions. The establishment of such a set of reasons, not to mention their subsequent assessment, is a matter of great complexity. This assertion assumes some importance in view of the fact that the single generally accepted reason for teaching linguistic descriptions turns out to be no reason at all. Reference is being made here to the contention that so called "normative values" in the use of language should be taught and are best taught by means of a suitable linguistic description. Since the object of such instruction is a prescribed performance of spoken and written English, normative considerations do not defend instruction in linguistic descriptions on the grounds of any value which inheres in the subject matter independent of behavioral goals. Rather, they provide a reason for using linguistic descriptions pedagogically in order to achieve certain performance effects in the use of language. There may indeed be merit in achieving these effects, but it is of importance to recall that a belief in the power of instruction in grammar to accomplish this task flies in the face of overwhelming empirical evidence that there is no connection between instruction in linguistic descriptions and the performance of literate skills.

It is a particularly curious fact that normative considerations have often been construed as a reason for ranking traditional grammar over both structural and transformational grammars. The basis of this argument resides in the assumption that normative values are maintained in a traditional grammar while they are neglected totally in other forms of linguistic description. This argument becomes vacuous when we observe that normative values pertain not to a linguistic description, but to a particular language, in this case a special dialect of English, described by a linguistic description. Any form of description which takes as its subject matter this special dialect of English can be said to be normative. Thus, normative considerations not only fail to offer a good reason for incorporating an arbitrary linguistic description into the English curriculum, they also fail to provide a reason for introducing a specific linguistic description into the curriculum.

Implicit in the goals of a transformational theory of language and the grammars which follow from this theory are several new considerations. A transformational grammar is a system which reveals and expresses the regularities which underlie a given natural language as completely as possible. In providing the most general account of linguistic structure, the transformational approach to linguistic inquiry yields new insights into human intellectual capacity, namely, those innate properties of the human mind which allow for the acquisition and use of language. In pursuing this capacity through the linguistic mechanisms which underlie competence in language, the student is involving himself in a study which has had intrinsic intellectual appeal for centuries, the study of those abilities which make human beings human. The fact that linguists working on syntax have, as yet, treated only the broad outlines of an adequate grammar suggests that this study is a living field, one whose issues provide significance both for studying the results thus far attained and for following the stated aims further. There seems good justification, therefore, for the inclusion of the results of the transformational approach to linguistic inquiry in the English curriculum. The educational implementation of a transformational description of the structure of English not only introduces the student to the live tradition of scholarship in language study, but, perhaps even more important, to the results of the one form of inquiry which has begun to achieve some success in providing an explicit account of one aspect of an extremely complex human competence. It would seem fitting to support the educational implementation of any linguistic description which can justifiably claim success in this area. In any case, it is a nontrivial virtue of the transformational approach to language study that it provides a rationale with which it is at least possible to disagree. This in itself is an event of some importance in the history of classroom applications of linguistic descriptions.

The second illustration is concerned with the fact that the design of curricula for the teaching of composition is conditioned by a variety of factors which take the form of accepted canons for good writing. These canons invariably include such items as clarity (meaning nonambiguity), grammaticality, logical structure, and so forth. On one level of analysis, these constraints, as well as many others, are entirely reasonable since they set necessary conditions for successful written communication. This fact, however, does not imply that these canons may not, in certain ways, be contradictory. For instance, might it not be the case that to satisfy the condition of clarity it would be necessary to break a rule of grammar, and conversely? A conclusive exploration of this possiblity will necessarily depend upon the use of a theoretical framework for language analysis in which considerations of both clarity and gramaticality play a role.

Exploiting a transformational analysis of English, one can prove that the canons for good writing are quite often in conflict. In a typical example, the rule of clarity is incompatible with the grammatical rule disallowing the infamous "split infinitive" construction. It can be shown, furthermore, that emphasis on the former must actually reinforce the use of the latter. By way of illustration, consider the following ambiguous sentence:

(1)   *Joshua commanded the children to shout forcefully.*

This sentence is at least two ways ambiguous. The adverb *forcefully* could modify either the main verb *command* or the verb in the complement sentence *shout*. In other words, either the "command" could have been forceful or the "shout" could have been "forceful." Seeking to conform to the canon of clarity, a student writer must convert this sentence into some nonambiguous form. One mechanism of disambiguation which English allows is the application of an extremely general transformational rule which places an adverb, originating at the end of a verb phrase (i.e. that constituent containing the verb and, optionally, a verbal object), immediately before the verb. For instance,

(2)   *John swept the floor vigorously.*
(3)   *John vigorously swept the floor.*

In this fashion, sentence (1) can be disambiguated to specify the interpretation of the sentence in which the adverb *forcefully* modifies the main verb *commanded*, as in sentence (4).

(4)   *Joshua forcefully commanded the children to shout.*

The adverb placement transformation has the peculiar property that it usually can apply only if a verb is, in fact, the first element in the verb phrase. Thus in infinitival verb phrases like *to shout* the adverb placement transformation cannot apply since the *to* and not the verb *shout* is the first element.[22] If the adverb placement transformation is forced to apply, that is, if the rule is broken, then split infinitive constructions necessarily result, as in sentence (5).

(5)   *Joshua commanded the children to forcefully shout.*

The student writer is caught, therefore, on both horns of the dilemma. If he wishes to disambiguate sentence (1) in such a way as to specify the interpretation of this sentence in which the adverb *forcefully* modifies the complement verb *shout*, he must break the adverb placement rule thereby producing a split infinitive construction. If, on the other hand, the preservation of grammaticality is the student's primary concern, then sentence (1) must remain ambiguous.

This logical bind is not the fault of the teacher, who is concerned with compositional excellence defined at least in part in terms of clarity. Nor is it the fault of the student, who is simply incapable of meeting this demand without restructuring his language. Nonetheless, the logical dilemma exists and it becomes clear that, short of ruling all infinitival constructions out of English, a poor compromise, either the canon of clarity must be weakened or the split infinitive must be accepted into the domain of fully grammatical constructions.

---

[22] A defense of this analysis is provided in Rosenbaum, ibid.

This demonstration is presented as evidence that the problem of the split infinitive is not the normative-moral dilemma that it has been conceived to be for such a long time.[23] Similar evidence could be presented for a variety of cases. The transformational perspective provides a tool for examining the consequences of whatever decision is made or, for that matter, of making no decision at all. Deliberation without reasons leads nowhere. The history of the split infinitive is a case in point. It is true, to be sure, that a transformational grammar will not provide the principles for assessing the reasons which bear on the issue of the split infinitive and similar constructions. But this approach to the study of language will provide the raw material for the exercise of judgment; it will provide coherent reasons, and this can only be viewed as a major contribution to the solution of a traditionally muddy set of problems.

The third illustration deals with the outlines of a possible explanation for the continuing failure to find successful classroom techniques for changing linguistic performance in speech and composition. The general premise of this explanation is that certain aspects of this problem are the consequence of gravely underestimating the complexity of dialect differences and the problems involved in altering dialects on the syntactic level. It does not take a linguist to determine that there is considerable dialect variation in the United States on the phonological level and on the lexical level, that is, the levels of sound and meaning. But only very recently has it been shown that dialect differences on the syntactic level are far more systematic than has heretofore been recognized.[24] It will prove informative to explore this finding in slightly greater detail.

It is difficult to find a textbook on grammar which does not point out the alternation of the word *for* in the following sentences.

(6)(a) *Mary would hate for the boys to arrive early.*
　(b) *Mary would hate the boys to arrive early.*

Similarly, such textbooks usually describe the alternation of *'s* in the following sentences.

(7)(a) *Does your mother dislike your brother's coming home late?*
　(b) *Does your mother dislike your brother coming home late?*

Simply looking at the linear sequence of words in these pairs of sentences, one finds little reason to suspect that the deletion of *for* in (6b) has anything whatever to do with the deletion of *'s* in (7b). The *for*, for instance, precedes the subject of the complement sentence, *the boys*; the *'s* on the other hand, follows the subject of the complement sentence, *your brother*.

Considerations brought to bear in the development of a general theory of complement structures, of which (6) and (7) are instances, indicate that the initial impression, based solely upon examination of the linear sequence of words, is incorrect.[25] In the most general description of such complement constructions

---

[23]For an interesting discussion and sufficiently complete bibliography, see R. C. Pooley, *Teaching English Usage* (New York, 1946), especially pp. 100–106.

[24]Rosenbaum, "A Transformational Approach to a Syntactic Dialectology," a paper delivered to the December 1964 meeting of the Linguistic Society of America in New York City.

[25]Rosenbaum, *The Grammar of English Predicate Complement Constructions*, p. 114.

both the *for* and the *'s* are shown to share exactly the same position in the under-lying structure of these sentences. Furthermore, both the *for* and the *'s* are option-ally deleted by exactly the same transformational rule. In other words, (6a) is provably related to (6b) in precisely the same way as (7a) is related to (7b), that is, by the transformational rule which deletes *for* in (6) and *'s* in (7).

Implicit in this description is the claim that judgments about these pairs of sentences made by native speakers of English will conform to the linguistic des-cription. In other words, the grammar predicts that the speaker of the dialect of English in which sentence (6a) is preferred over sentence (6b) will also prefer sen-tence (7a) over sentence (7b). If the deletion of both *for* and *'s* is correctly charac-terized in terms of a single rule, then the speaker who does not allow the deletion of *for* also will not allow the deletion of *'s*. On the other hand, the speaker whose grammar contains this single rule will delete both *for* and *'s*. Preliminary empirical investigations, which are being reported elsewhere in much greater detail,[26] seem to confirm this prediction.

If it is true, as the above considerations suggest, that superficially diverse linguis-tic forms are psychologically related, then the task of affecting changes in the linguistic system of a speaker becomes immeasurably more complex. Consider, for instance, the plight of the teacher of composition who is anxious to preserve the grammatical dictum common to many textbooks that the *'s* as in (7a), should not be deleted. It will not be sufficient merely to reinforce the gerundive construc-tions with the *'s*, for every performance of sentences like (6b) to which the student attends may reinforce exactly the opposite usage from that which the teacher desires to elicit. Three other factors make this problem even more complex. First, it may well be that the teacher will consider the syntactically related linguistic forms to be fully grammatical, in which case the probability of producing contradictory behaviors is quite high. In other words, *for* may be deleted in every infinitival complement construction which the teacher utters. Second, it is folly to assume that the linguistic environment outside of the classroom could be appropriately controlled to any significant degree. Finally, and perhaps most problematical, it is not impossible that other rules in the speaker's grammar which are requisite to the production and comprehension of sentences whose grammaticality is beyond question will reinforce the rule which deletes *for* and *'s*.[27] In this eventuality, the only way out is an absurdity; to eliminate the reinforcing transformations by somehow ruling the grammatical sentences requiring these rules out of English.

The intent of the third illustration is to argue that the failure of current teaching techniques based on instruction in grammar to implement significant changes in linguistic performance is predictable from the fact that the tasks which these tech-niques must perform are virtually unknown. To effect a permanent change in linguistic behavior is to effect a change in grammar, the set of rules underlying linguistic competence, with all that such a change might entail. Certain require-

---

[26]Thomas G. Bever and Peter S. Rosenbaum, "The Psychological Verification of Linguistic Rules" (to appear).

[27]A case having just these properties is described in Rosenbaum, *The Grammar of English Predicate Complement Constructions*, pp. 58–67.

ments on alterations of this sort were mentioned above, but those were merely suggestive. It would be wildly presumptuous to speculate on the possibility of improving teaching techniques at the present time. The issue of an improved pedagogy can be addressed seriously only at such time as an explicit account of the linguistic rules which characterize linguistic behavior becomes available. Perhaps our vision of the ultimate task as one of changing linguistic behavior will prove completely misguided. Economy, if nothing else, dictates that it is better to find out what the problem is before trying to solve it. To the extent that transformational grammar continues to provide insights of increasing depth into the structures underlying linguistic ability, it would seem only good sense to exploit this form of inquiry to its fullest capacity.

If the preceding arguments are sound, then not only can the transformational approach to linguistic inquiry claim priority in further discussion of the role of linguistics in the teaching of English, but the structurally oriented suggestions for the teaching of English which have actually found use in certain classrooms must be reconsidered. This conclusion should be taken as positive evidence that a new stage in the development of linguistic science is upon us and that the educator may begin to profit from giving his attention to the results of the ongoing linguistic debate. It has taken American linguistics some time to devise theories which can offer valid results for educational purposes, but the time has come. It is now up to all of those persons who are in any way concerned with the teaching of English to respond to this provocative and important new challenge.